Social Psychology
Principles and Themes of Interpersonal Behavior

The Dorsey Series in Psychology

Advisory Editors
Wendell E. Jeffrey
University of California, Los Angeles

Salvatore R. Maddi
The University of Chicago

Social Psychology

Principles and Themes
of Interpersonal Behavior

William D. Crano

Lawrence A. Messé

both of
Michigan State University

1982
DORSEY PRESS
Homewood, Illinois   60430

ISBN 0-256-02403-0
Library of Congress Catalog Card No. 81–70949
Printed in the United States of America

1 2 3 4 5 6 7 8 9 0 H 9 8 7 6 5 4 3 2

To our children—
Jenny and Sam,
and Nick, Dan, and Steve,
whose patience and affection never wavered

Preface

When social psychology was in its infancy—which, in fact, was not many years ago—it seemed almost mandatory for introductory texts to begin with a demonstration of the field's intellectual ties with the great minds of the past. In books of this era, such unlikely bedfellows as Hammurabi, Spinoza, Ibn Khaldun, and Aristotle often found themselves occupying the same sentence. The attempt at association with the giants of intellectual history no doubt was motivated in part by the hope that linking social psychology with past luminaries would cause some of their light to reflect on a discipline whose legitimacy was far from established. Thankfully, this phase of self-consciousness was short-lived, and the number of ancient referents in our introductory textbooks diminished as the value of the field became self-evident.

Later writers had a different problem: they had to provide a reasonable definition of what was by now a burgeoning enterprise. In these books, definitions of social psychology characteristically took one of two forms. In one type of text, the emphasis was placed on brevity—"social psychology is the scientific study of people's behaviors, their institutions, and the mutual interplay between them"—at the expense of completeness and utility. The one positive thing that could be said of efforts of this type was that they did not waste much time before getting to the heart of the matter. An alternative route was taken by those who aimed for completeness, often at the expense of readers' interest and patience. We shall not attempt to synopsize efforts of this type, as it is easy to predict one's own reaction to a 40-page definition of a field whose interest value was far from established in the mind of the reader. In any event, since the realm of social psychology is so broad, the definitional approach was almost certain to prove inadequate to the task at hand.

An alternative introductory strategy that recently has gained popularity in social psychology might properly be dubbed the storybook approach. In this form, a principle or set of principles is illustrated through the use of an interesting example. A number of fine textbooks in social psychology have made use of this mode of presentation with some success, and we have adopted a modified version of this tack ourselves in this book. In the present instance, however, the story format is used in the service of a more important instructional tactic, which we have called the thematic approach. In this approach, we concentrate on the presentation of the psychological themes that underlie the many phenomena that historically have been studied in isolation. This approach is our attempt to integrate ideas that traditionally have been viewed as unrelated. In doing this, we provide a framework through which the extensive and diverse subject matter of social psychology can be meaningfully summarized.

Through the combination of our thematic approach and the use of examples, we illustrate the connection between social psychological concepts and the events that affect people's lives. It is our belief that this presentation style will facilitate the reader's understanding of the phenomena that are examined in this book.

THE PLAN OF THIS BOOK

The 13 chapters of this textbook are divided into three sections. In Section 1 (Chapters 1–3), we present in detail the basic integrative constructs—which we have termed *core concepts* and *integrative themes*. These integrative constructs serve as a framework for reviewing the substantive topic areas of social psychology, which are discussed in the nine subsequent chapters of the book. Thus, the major terms that are introduced in the first three chapters are utilized repeatedly in the material that follows. We have capitalized these integrative concepts throughout the book to call the reader's attention to the pervasiveness of these basic social psychological processes for a host of apparently different human behaviors.

Section 2 (Chapters 4–8) presents the major theories and research findings relevant to social cognitions—beliefs about people, ideas, and things—and the consequences that these cognitions have for interpersonal behavior. In Section 3 (Chapters 9–13), we examine more directly the important facets of interpersonal behavior, which can range from the formation of friendships to working together in groups. Finally, in an Epilogue, we provide one final example to support our position that a small number of fundamental processes underlie the diverse forms of human social activity.

THE PREPARATION OF THIS BOOK

In most collaborative efforts of this type, the major responsibility for the various chapters is divided among the individual authors. We decided to adopt a somewhat different approach: through the use of a computer with word processing software, we were able to write this book as a true collaboration. In producing this book, we both sat before the computer and wrote virtually every word of it together. As a consequence, we share equally any credit that is due as well as any blame for whatever shortcomings there are in this book. While we do not recommend this type of "togetherness" for everyone, we found our collaboration to be both fun and intellectually stimulating. Each of us learned a lot about social psychology from the other, both through exchanging information about substantive issues and through our participant observation of an extended and intense social interaction. We are living proof of the social psychological principle (discussed in Chapters 2, 11, and 12) that extended opportunities to interact often result in an increase of mutual regard and affection between the interactants.

Of course, no book of this type is ever really a work of only two people. We received considerable assistance in our efforts from our friends and colleagues in the field and from our wives.

Of the many individuals who have reviewed this work, we are particularly grateful to Marilynn Brewer (University of California, Santa Barbara), and Carol Werner (University of Utah), who read and commented in detail on every chapter of the text as it progressed through its many metamorphoses. Salvatore Maddi (University of Chicago), the Consulting Psychology Editor for Dorsey Press, also provided us with a great deal of continuing guidance and support, for which we are very thankful.

In addition, we are very appreciative of the helpful efforts of Donald Elman (Kent State University), Tom Jackson (Fort Hays State University), Charles Petranek (Indiana State University—Evansville), Glenn Reeder (Illinois State University), and Bernard Spilka (University of Denver), whose comments at various stages of the book's development proved invaluable.

Finally, we wish to express our deeply felt gratitude to Suellen and Susan, our wives, for the help that they individually provided us in the organizational and editorial tasks that were essential in completing this book. Without their love, patience, and tolerance over the 2½ years that this book was in progress, our task would have been much more difficult.

William D. Crano
Lawrence A. Messa

Contents

Social Psychology
Principles and Themes of Interpersonal Behavior

1

STEPHEN L. FELDMAN/PHOTO RESEARCHERS, INC.

Core Concepts and Integrative Themes

This is a book about social psychology. More than any other field of inquiry, social psychology concerns itself with the study of fundamental human endeavors. The unique mission of social psychology is to understand how and why people behave as they do when they are with others, and the effects that such social experiences have on the way they will later think, feel, and subsequently act. Given the scope of such a mission, it should not be surprising that in many ways, the discipline is a hybrid—its concerns include phenomena that are central to all of the social sciences. As such, social psychology shares common interests with anthropology, economics, political science, psychology, and sociology, and its breadth has produced a wealth of diverse information. While students of social psychology usually find this material interesting and stimulating, they often view this state of affluence as a mixed blessing, since the immense amount of information that the field has amassed often proves difficult to master.

It is our belief that students can better appreciate social psychology when some organization is imposed on the diverse materials that constitute its domain. In this book, we have provided one such organizational framework, which we present in the three chapters of Section 1. This framework employs two types of integrative constructs—*core concepts* and *themes*.

Core concepts. In our view, two general but overriding concepts lie at the core of all social behavior: the *Social Context* in which an action occurs and the *Personal Structure* of the person who performs or perceives the action. The Social Context is comprised of the features in the environment, both in the physical setting and in other people, that affect the ways in which a person behaves. Personal Structure, on the other hand, consists of the features within the individual that influence his or her thoughts and actions. Viewing social psychology from the perspective of these two core concepts emphasizes that at least on an abstract level, there are common elements to all human social behavior.

Integrative Themes. At a less abstract level, a set of processes or *themes* underlie the phenomena social psychologists generally have studied in isolation of one another. Such apparently diverse human activities as getting acquainted with another person, changing one's mind, working with others to solve a problem, beating up someone, are all affected by a rather small number of basic psychological processes. In Chapters 2 and 3, we define five themes we believe play a crucial role in the expression of most social behaviors. One theme is concerned with people's attempts to control the behaviors of others. A second theme focuses on the development and consequences of emotional attachments between people. A third theme involves the impact of uncertainty on human activity. The processes by which people decide among alternative actions constitutes yet another theme. The fifth theme is concerned with people's attempts to maintain consistency among their beliefs and actions, and between themselves and others.

In the remainder of the book, we use the five themes and two core concepts as tools to integrate the diverse subject matter of our field. Taken together, they provide a framework that can help to organize what, for many, might otherwise be a bewildering assortment of facts and speculations about social behavior.

The Core Concepts of Social Context and Personal Structure

The focus of this chapter is a detailed analysis of the core concepts of *Social Context* and *Personal Structure*. First, a brief introduction to these constructs will be presented. Then, to demonstrate how social behavior can be analyzed profitably within this framework, a frightening and dramatic incident will be described (one that actually occurred some years ago in the life of one of the authors), followed by a discussion of the events that transpired in terms of the core concepts. In doing so, we hope to motivate the reader to begin thinking as a professional social psychologist would and to analyze social behavior in terms of the core concepts presented. The diversity of the concerns discussed—although they are derived from a single episode—provides graphic evidence of the wide range of phenomena that social psychologists consider interesting. After a discussion of the social psychological aspects of this incident, we will discuss more formally the two core concepts that help to organize the field of social psychology. Before proceeding any further, we present a brief sketch of the concepts that play an important role in our discussion.

Roughly speaking, the social field consists of all of the potential determinants of a social act in any given setting. While it is a useful summarizing term, the social field is so inclusive a conceptualization that it is not helpful in classifying or analyzing complex social behavior. The determinants that comprise the social field, however, can be broken down into two major categories—Social Context and Personal Structure.

Social Context refers to the physical and interpersonal environment in which a social behavior occurs. Such apparently diverse features of the Social Context—the number of people present, their appearance and behavior, the temperature, and the physical surroundings—all have significant roles in de-

ERIKA STONE/PETER ARNOLD, INC.

The context in which events transpire can make it difficult for observers to determine what is happening.

termining a person's actions. It is not surprising, then, that the variables that comprise the Social Context long have been central concerns of social psychology.

In addition to the Social Context, another set of factors that operate to determine social behavior are the personal characteristics that individuals bring with them to any given social encounter. Differences exist among people with regard to their beliefs, feelings, concerns, and motivations; and these differences, along with other important personal variables such as intelligence, sex, race, age, and religion, can affect a person's actions. These important behavioral determinants are subsumed under the core concept of Personal Structure. Of all the elements that comprise the Personal Structure, *beliefs* are perhaps the most important to social psychology. Beliefs consist of the set of facts, opinions, impressions, and socially defined rules of conduct held by each individual that can operate as guides to that person's behavior.

These central constructs will be discussed in much greater detail later in this chapter. For the moment, however, this brief summary should enable the reader to perceive and organize some of the more important factors that influenced the actions which occurred in the following story. As noted, the core concepts play a major role in our attempt to organize and to understand social behavior. Therefore, it would be helpful for the reader to keep these constructs in mind when reading the following narrative.

A NIGHT IN A COURTYARD

Late one evening, toward the end of the summer of 1963, the following event took place in the life of one of the authors. At the time, he and his wife, both in their early 20s, had been married for little over a year, and they were living in Evanston, Illinois in a large, four-story apartment building that was constructed in the shape of an inverted *U*. For those unfamiliar with this area of the country, Evanston is an affluent, somewhat conservative suburban community just north of Chicago, that hugs the western shore of Lake Michigan.[1]

At about 12:30 A.M. on that fateful night, the couple's nightly routine was interrupted by an unusual sound that apparently came from the courtyard below. In one sense, any sound that occurred at this time of night would have been unusual, since most of the tenants in the building were much older than the couple (a conservative average estimate of their ages would be approximately 65 years), and these tenants typically turned in at about 8:30 P.M. But this particular noise was also unusual in a different sense, since it was the sound of a high-pitched voice that began as a loud laugh and ended about 20 seconds later as a piercing scream.

Being a social psychologist in training at the time, and a nosy person in general (perhaps the two attributes are related), the husband immediately stopped what he had been doing and rushed to the window to see what was happening; a short time later his wife joined him at the window. The physical layout of the building made for very difficult observation of the exterior at night. It had eight entrances, equally spaced along the inside of the *U;* each entrance was partially illuminated after dark by pairs of quaint, old-fashioned, and rather ineffective, lighting fixtures. Thus, at night, the courtyard, its shrubbery, and its walkways made up a patchwork of strange shapes, dim lights, and dark shadows—a setting reminiscent of such masters of suspense as Alfred Hitchcock and Roman Polanski. In this real-life instance, the low level of illumination literally clouded the vision of the husband and wife, who were now anxiously attempting to pinpoint the location of the strange noise.

They could make out the outline of two people standing in the entrance-way across the courtyard and somewhat to the left of their apartment. There was sufficient light to see that one of the people was definitely a female and that the person with her probably was a man. This latter judgment

---

[1] At this time, Evanston's major claim to fame was that it contained within its boundaries both the main campus of Northwestern University and the national headquarters of the Women's Christian Temperance Union (WCTU). Consistent with this second fact, the Evanston of this era had ordinances that prohibited the sale, possession, and consumption of alcoholic beverages within its borders. Of course, this state of affairs generated a brisk business for the multitude of liquor stores, bars, etc., that literally surrounded Evanston to the south (Chicago) and to the west (Skokie). Skokie's liquor regulations were much less restrictive than those of Evanston, perhaps because its keepers of the public trust, correctly surmising that the town was landlocked, were less concerned about the possibility of an inebriated constituent falling into the lake.

was less positive because of the positioning of the pair in the entranceway. Also, both people—the female for certain—appeared to be at least as young as the couple observing them.

The husband and wife stood in the window and watched the pair in the entrance below engage in a repetitive sequence of behaviors. (The specific actions of the pair were hard to see at best, and sometimes were totally unobservable when they moved completely into the shadows.) At all times, the woman's left arm or hand was connected in some way with the right hand of the other person; it appeared either that they were holding hands (remember, this was 1963) or that he (?) was holding her wrist. When their bodies moved closer together, the woman would begin to 'laugh' loudly. As the two figures melted into one, the observers no longer could make out any specific actions; however, they could see a general increase in the tempo of the pair's activity, after which they heard the 'laugh' turn into a 'scream.' After about 20 seconds, the two bodies would abruptly break apart, and a short silent period would follow. Then the sequence of behaviors would be repeated, including the laughing and screaming.

The couple at the window watched this curious scenerio unfold, all the while discussing what apparently was happening and what they should do. Was the other actor a male? Probably. Definitely. Probably. Were they holding hands, or was he holding onto her? The observers could not tell. Were they embracing? Was he trying to rape her? Was she in trouble? Why was she laughing? Why was she screaming? Why was she laughing and screaming? They could not decide.

What should they do? Assume the best and ignore the pair, shut their windows, and go back to what they had been doing? No one else in the building seemed to be concerned about, or even aware of, what was happening in the courtyard, since, during the time the couple stood at the window, the rest of the windows in the building—at least all those that they could see—remained dark.

Should the husband go down for a closer look? If so, what should he do if the female was really being hurt or held against her will? Should he try to stop the man himself? (The reader should understand that the author was, and is, a master of the time-honored techniques of self-defense popularized by Woody Allen, variously called crying, begging, and cowardly grovelling.) Should he call the police? Now? Should he try to get a closer look before deciding whether to call the police? What if nothing were wrong? How embarrassing that would be for all concerned if the police were called and nothing had been wrong! But, what if the man were really hurting her? Should he and his wife get involved?

After what seemed to be an extended period of observation and emotional discussion which probably lasted only a few minutes, the husband called the police. Fortunately, nothing was seriously wrong. As the police later explained to the relieved but embarrassed couple, the female was a college-aged woman from out of town who was visiting her grandmother, a tenant in the building. She had gone out on a date—probably somewhere in Chicago or Skokie—and both she and her escort had consumed more hard spirits than they should have. Apparently, the couple was merely saying an extended good-night. Due to her somewhat hazy grasp on things, however, the young woman was quite ambivalent about the manner in which her date was trying to express his appreciation for having had the pleasure of her company that evening. Her date, on the other hand, was not at all ambivalent. As both were somewhat intoxicated, their extended exchange had been carried out in a loud volume, and thus their actions called themselves to the attention of the author and his wife.

SOCIAL PSYCHOLOGICAL ANALYSIS

Many different aspects of this story would interest social psychologists who were attempting to pinpoint the factors that affected the thoughts and behaviors of the actors. While not all of the aspects of this event would be monitored by all social psychologists (some would focus on a single actor, variable, or event to the exclusion of everything else), we shall present an extended social psychological analysis of the episode. We will start the analysis by focusing on the actual and potential actions of the observers. Later, we will devote some discussion to the behaviors of the noisy young couple and those of the police.

The Observers

To begin with, many social psychologists would be quite interested in understanding the reasons why the observers went to the window in the first place. It is clear from the story that this was not the typical behavior of the inhabitants of the apartment complex. How did the observers differ from these other people? We know from the description of the episode that they were younger and also that the male observer was (and is) characteristically nosy. Why should these characteristics have made a difference? Perhaps because they were younger, the author and his wife went to bed at a later time than the other residents. Thus, there may be nothing psychologically significant about the fact that the couple went to the window while no one else stirred, because they were still awake and were aware of the disturbance outside, while the others, being asleep, could not have known of the possible trouble taking place.

On the other hand, it is quite conceivable that there were many other people in the apartment complex who heard the young woman's cries but who failed to respond to her apparent distress. Why? Perhaps being an old person in an urban area hardens one to the needs of others. Perhaps old people in big cities learn to "mind their own business" (indeed, maybe this is how one becomes an old person). On the other hand, their nonresponse could have been a function of the erroneous idea that other people had already acted, or perhaps it was a result of their extreme uncertainty about the appropriate action to take. Was their inaction a function of fear or callousness, uncertainty or faulty judgment, or simply a result of their being asleep? It would be worthwhile to uncover the answer to this question, for in doing so much could be learned about contemporary American society, at least as it is lived or perceived by older inhabitants of large metropolitan centers.

Focusing more closely on the actions of the observers themselves provides data that might be used by other social psychologists in their analyses of this event. For example, many would be interested to know why the young couple observing this particular pattern of visual and auditory stimuli were so undecided about their most appropriate course of action. Why did they not call the police immediately or simply forget the whole affair and go back to what they had been doing before being interrupted?

We might approach an answer to this question by studying the responses of individuals when they are confronted with a confusing series of stimuli. Almost by definition, an *emergency* is a situation with which people have had little prior experience; if a person knows how to respond to an emergency situation, much of the anxiety is removed from the event, and the psychological nature of the emergency is drastically altered. An example of this kind of experienced response is provided by the actions of the police. They too were confronted with the same pattern of behaviors that so unnerved our observers; yet, it would be safe to say that they had no doubt about the best way to handle this situation. Why? Possibly because their behaviors in such circumstances were well practiced; and even if they had not been—if this were the first call of the evening by two rookies—it was made clear to them during their police training days that certain situations called for certain behaviors. To the police, the appropriate course of action was obvious; their role in this drama was written long before the curtain opened.

Another aspect of the description of the episode that might prove intriguing to psychologists concerns the emphasis that was placed on the action of the male witness (that is, the author). Notice that almost all of the possible responses to the potential emergency are couched in terms of the man's reaction. Should *he* go down for a closer look? Should *he* intervene if the woman were being harmed? Should *he* call the police? Should *he* get involved in this? Why was such attention paid to the actions of the man? Well, obviously the story was written by two males, one of whom was an actor in this event, and his perspective is the one most likely to be presented. But is that all there is to it? We do not think so.

It is clear to most of us that even today, when sex-linked constraints on people's behaviors are lessening to some extent, a male is the more likely candidate to intervene in a potential emergency situation of this sort. Despite the author's distaste for any physical encounter that might cause him pain, it was clear to him, to his wife, and we would bet, to the reader, too, that it was more appropriate for the man to stick his nose into this problem. Why? Because most of us have learned from our earliest childhood days that in situations involving possible violence or criminal actions, it is the man's job to act in some way—to intervene directly, to report the incident to the proper authorities, and so on. Society has defined the situation this way, and most of us probably accept this definition as correct on the basis of little direct experience.

For some social psychologists, the person whom society identifies as the appropriate actor might, in itself, be unimportant. But they might be very interested in studying those situations in which there is no clear allocation of responsibility to one actor or another, or to structure interactions in such a way that people's perceptions of the individual responsible for acting are in conflict. Under such conditions, we learn much of the various tactics of influence that people employ in subtle but powerful ways.

In one sense, almost all of the field's literature concerning interpersonal conflict is based on situations of this type. We think this tactic is quite appropriate, as much of the conflict that we witness in everyday life occurs as a function of conflicting perceptions regarding the definition of a situation by two or more participants. For example, if I see the responsibility for a certain action (say, taking out the garbage or washing the dishes) to be yours, but you define it the other way around, we are soon going to approach each other in a less than friendly manner. Social psychologists find such interactions very intriguing and structure many of their experimental scenerios with these kinds of dynamics in mind. The reactions of people placed in these situations

BURK UZZLE/MAGNUM PHOTOS, INC.

Wouldn't you try to help this crying child?

of conflicting behavioral expectations have told us a lot about the ways that individuals approach and resolve difficult interpersonal situations.

Of course, socially derived expectations concerning the degree to which a specific action is appropriate can operate at more than one level of specificity. For example, we might question why the observers to the potential rape had *any* feelings of responsibility concerning the young woman who had earlier interrupted their customary late-night routine. Obviously, they did not know the woman, and it was quite possible that she would not have wished them to intervene even if they were acquainted.

To begin to understand the witnesses' feelings of discomfort and uncertainty, we need only reflect on the child-rearing practices that all of us have undergone. We are taught to believe that kindness is a virtue, and we thus learn to help others—especially if there are little or no costs involved. Small-scale kindnesses of this type are relatively common occurrences in everyday life. For example, anyone who has ever been in a large supermarket or department store has probably been confronted with the sight of young, crying children who have somehow become separated from their parents. There is almost no question about the appropriate response in this situation, and unlike the behaviors exhibited in the example, neither the sex of the child nor of the potential helper plays a major role in the determination of the response—most adults, either male or female, would attempt to help the child in some way. Indeed, the appropriate behavior is so clear in this situation that a person who failed to respond properly would be viewed as very callous.

When faced with the possibility of a less-than-civil response to a well-intentioned act, however, a number of additional concerns become important. Consider the difficulties with which our observing couple had to deal. First of all, it was not clear that anything bad was happening to the young woman. For example, suppose that she actually were enjoying herself (she seemed to be laughing). If this were the case, then intervention very likely would have had some negative consequences for all parties. At the very least, an unwanted intervention would have resulted in the acute embarrassment of the observers and the interrupted couple. Even if the situation had been accurately identified as an assault, factors still remain that operate against intervention. For example, if the young woman were in desperate need of help, the author's intervention would have entailed the risk of physical confrontation with her assailant and the possibility of a severe beating. Here, we have a clear instance of a conflict between a group of well-learned responses: the altruistic reaction, which calls for our assisting those in need of help (especially if their actions did not cause the problem); and the self-interested reaction, the tendency to avoid unpleasant and/or dangerous encounters.

There can exist tremendous differences among people in the extent to which altruistic response tendencies are learned or internalized, and these individual differences are both predictable and amenable to modification by outside forces. For example, some people never help anyone, under any circumstances, whereas others are constantly ready to act, no matter what the needy cause. Social psychologists have studied this issue, and have developed a number of approaches that allow us to identify characteristically altruistic and characteristically nonaltruistic persons. Quite often, external circumstances override the general behavioral rule that the individual has learned, and these circumstances generate responses that appear contrary to the actor's usual behavioral inclinations. For example, suppose that our author had been the black belt karate champion of Chicago and, in addition, just loved to use his skills on unsuspecting adversaries. Given this circumstance, it seems very likely that he would not have been quite so reluctant to physically intervene in the potential emergency. But suppose that earlier in the evening, this same individual had broken both of his hands in an unsuccessful attempt to crack a concrete block. In this situation, it is very likely that he would curtail his tendency to intervene. An external circumstance—two broken hands—would have moderated the expression of his more typical action. While the situational factors that cause actors to behave in ways that seemingly are inconsistent with their Personal Structure are usually more subtle than that furnished in our example (broken hands), such factors do occur with some frequency and present serious obstacles to those social psychologists interested in Personal Structure. These inconsistencies, however, are also one reason why many find the study of the Personal Structure so challenging and rewarding.

The Dating Couple

Let us now leave our formerly vascillating observers and turn our attention to the actions of the couple being observed. What was it about their behavior that the social psychologist might find interesting or worthy of study? First of all, as we learned from the police report, the young couple had just returned from a date. Obviously, those social psychologists interested in attraction and the factors that affect a person's impressions of others would be interested in a number of different segments of this interaction. For example, had the young couple ever dated before? If so, were the kinds of behavior that so puzzled the naive observers typical of their usual good-night routine? If their behaviors were not typical, what was so special about this particular encounter that elicited these actions? Suppose, on the other hand, that the young couple had never dated before. If such were the case (and in fact it was), why was the woman's escort so attracted to her? Or was he? Were his behaviors merely the replaying of a well-rehearsed behavioral "script" that he enacted on all of his first dates? If so, what factors affected the establishment of such a curious set of behaviors and of the beliefs or opinions about the appropriate actions of men and women on dates that gave rise to or reinforced such actions? If the young man's behaviors were not at all characteristic of him, then what specific features of the young woman or of the setting influenced him to act in this manner? What would cause such a strong response? Why was he so attracted to his date? Was she beautiful? Did she remind him of a long-lost flame? Was the moon particularly beautiful that night?

Was the music on the car radio unusually romantic? Was it her perfume? Once the answers to these questions were learned, the psychologist would be in a much better position to understand the young man's actions.

It would be a mistake to neglect the actions of the other actor in this menage, the somewhat recalcitrant young woman. The same items of information concerning the young man's behavior are also of interest in analyzing the actions of the young woman. Why was she alternately laughing and screaming? Did all young women of the mid-1960s act in this manner at the completion of a date? Was she speaking to him in a language that was totally understood by both, one that would have been interpreted correctly by almost any other young person at the time? Did she always scream at the end of an evening out? Was she really ambivalent about her date's actions? If so, why? What was it about him that caused her response? Why were they both embarrassed when interrupted by the police?

Valid answers to all or any of these queries would provide some important clues as to why the young man and woman behaved as they did. These answers would be particularly relevant to social psychologists to the extent that they provided information about the more general processes that influence typical behaviors in such circumstances. This is so because social psychologists are more interested in uncovering general principles of behavior than they are in understanding the actions of any specific person. While the behaviors of the observed couple are intriguing, they are but a single example of a multitude of interesting activities that can occur in the context of dating and courtship. It is through the examination of the responses of many people that we are able to derive general principles of interpersonal relations.

The Police

Finally, as social psychologists, we might want to study the actions of the police in this matter. We have noted already that, unlike our very uncomfortable witnesses, the police apparently had no reluctance whatever about breaking in on the rather private encounter of the young people. Why not? At a very obvious level of analysis, the police were armed, and the dating couple probably was not. Thus, the police probably had little fear that they would come out second-best in a physical encounter. Also, they were trained and paid to do just this sort of thing. Their actions were appropriate for the role that they had learned and the responsibilities that they had assumed as members of the city's police department. Had they refused to intervene, for whatever reason, we would have been very surprised. Why? Because they would have failed to perform a whole series of functions, specified by society, that they had earlier agreed to perform.

Also of interest are the policemen's actions after breaking into the extended goodnight. Recall that they made a special point to come to the observing couple's apartment to explain the situation. Why did they feel obliged to do this? Obviously, the observers would have remained anxious and agitated had the police not informed them of what had happened, and they were relieved to learn that the young woman had not been in serious trouble. Yet, the police were under no formal obligation to discuss the case with the people who called them. Were they obeying the explicit policy of the Evanston police department, or did they act out of courtesy, aware that the observers would have remained upset had they not been informed of the outcome of this unnerving encounter? We suspect the latter.

CORE CONCEPTS: DEFINITIONS AND APPLICATIONS

We are now in a position to present a more formal social psychological analysis of the major factors that appear to have moderated the behaviors of the actors in the story. As noted earlier, we believe that the variables of central importance in social psychology can be summarized under two major headings—Social Context and Personal Structure.

Social Context

It is something more than a truism that human actions do not take place in a vacuum. All behaviors occur in some *physical context,* and most of what we do takes place in the presence of others—that is, in an *interpersonal context.* Moreover, a considerable portion of the behaviors that humans perform while alone are based on past encounters with other people. *Taken together, the physical and interpersonal environment within which human activity occurs is the Social Context.*

When investigating the Social Context, the social psychologist attempts to uncover the environmental and interpersonal forces that affect the behaviors observed. Obviously, the Social Context is composed of a tremendous number of variables that can potentially affect behavior; therefore, some organizational framework is clearly indicated. The following are brief descriptions of what we consider to be the major contours of the Social Context.

Physical Environment. Although physicists might quibble with the imprecision of our statement, by *physical environment* we mean the collection of nonhuman qualities and elements that comprise the field in which the social behavior of interest occurs. Of course, physical structures such as buildings, chairs, tables, their component properties, and their arrangement in space are parts of this physical environment. Other aspects of this environment are qualities such as temperature, humidity, illumination level, time, and so on. A large number of these physical environmental factors played a role in the behavior of the individuals depicted in the story presented earlier.

To begin with, the occurrence took place at night. It seems likely that this fact alone had a major impact on the events that transpired. For example, traditionally in our culture, dusk signals a relative shift from outdoor to indoor activity. The decrease in pedestrian and auto traffic is just one aspect of this general pattern. This factor might very well have led the young couple in the courtyard to assume that they were totally alone. Thus, the physical environment, or at least this aspect of it, may have had a major impact on their behaviors.

Similarly, the physical arrangement of the apartment building also played a role in the drama. The configuration of the courtyard contributed to the couple's sense of privacy at the same time that it amplified the sounds (giggles, grunts, and shrieks) that they emitted. Moreover, the dim lighting and surrounding shrubbery created a very ambiguous situation for the observers, who as a consequence were extremely puzzled about the nature of the activity that they were witnessing. While a few hundred people lived in the relatively limited area occupied by the apartment building, the walls between apartments effectively isolated the tenants from one another and virtually eliminated any easy communication among them. For this reason, the telephone, another aspect of the physical environment, became the sole link between the two witnesses and others who might help them solve their dilemma (in this case, the police).

Interpersonal Environment. The *interpersonal environment* consists of the people in a situation. Of necessity, the analysis of this component of the Social Context is explored from the vantage point of a specific actor. The interpersonal variables that affect one actor can have very different consequences—including no effect at all—on another individual involved in the same situation.

Consider, for example, the actions of the young woman in the courtyard. To her date, her behavior might well have been interpreted as lighthearted invitations to further exploratory play. From the point of view of the couple who witnessed this encounter from a different physical and psychological vantage point, the young woman's behavior was ultimately interpreted in a very different light. The vantage point of the police was quite different from that of the young man or the witnesses; the cues that they had observed were not sources of indecision but rather a stimulus for a series of well-practiced behaviors.

To understand the behavior of the actors in this context, it is critical to understand their particular interpretations of the cues that others had presented. To talk of an objective social reality is to deny the fact that each of us views this reality from a different vantage point, and this different perspective, of necessity, mediates social behavior. Although each participant in an encounter will construe the event somewhat differently, there are general classes of factors in other people that will affect an individual's behavior in the setting. Some of these factors are obvious—the physical characteristics and overt activities of the others in a social setting will often have a major impact on the ways in which an individual behaves. In addition, more subtle factors—for example, the mannerisms of a participant—often play a role.[2]

---

[2] Some major classes of these physical mannerisms include posture, gestures and other movements, voice quality, accent, and so forth.

Another variable of which we are not often aware, but one that does play a role in human behavior, is the physical location of the others in the setting.

In the context of the story, these components of the interpersonal environment had some obvious effects on the participants' behaviors. For example, suppose that the apparent screams sounded to the observing couple as if they were being emitted by a male voice. Had even this one aspect of the interpersonal environment been changed, the events probably would not have unfolded as they did. It is also likely that the young man in the courtyard—even in his inebriated state—would have responded quite differently to the two intruders had they not been dressed in dark blue uniforms and had their guns drawn. A major aspect of the male observer's interpersonal environment was the content and form of his conversation with his wife. What she said and did affected his own behavior towards her and the processes involved in his decision to call the police.

Personal Structure

The nature of individual differences in human behavior—that is, the fact that two people in the same situation can behave very differently—has been a focus of attention in psychology since its inception, and it continues to be one of the major points of contention in the field. Some members of the field would even go so far as to assert that there is no such thing as personality or that we can understand human behavior well enough without resorting to the use of such abstract and amorphous concepts as motivation or ego-functioning. Others would argue with equal fervor that the major determinants of human, and especially adult, behavior are all inside the human mind, while factors in the environment typically have only a minor and rather transitory impact on behavior.[3]

Our position in this controversy lies somewhere between these two extremes. We believe that behavior is determined by a unique combination of situational and personal factors. Thus, people in the same situation will act differently because central features of their *Personal Structures* are different, and therefore, they perceive and respond to the Social Context in different ways. For example, a person's interpersonal environment differs from those of other participants due in part to the unique perspective that the individual brings to the situation. On the other hand, the same person will act differently across situations because differences in environmental variables will affect the individual's behavior. For instance, a person who is typically loud and boisterous at a football game might be the most quiet, unobtrusive person in the office. The Personal Structure of this individual does not change from

---

[3] It should be noted that social psychologists are not the only creatures who make these sorts of assertions. One phenomenon of interest to us, in fact, is the tendency of people to explain their own behaviors and the behaviors of others in terms of personal or situational causes (see the discussion in Chapter 7 of the cue selection process in impression formation).

Because of differences in Personal Structure, people in the same situation can think and behave very differently.

place to place, but the salient environmental cues that interact with the actor's personality do change.

Applying these observations to the major characters in our story provides some insight into the mutual influence of Personal Structure and Social Context on behavior. To the male observer in our story, the scene that was unfolding before him was a source of discomfort in large measure because he was unsure about the right thing to do, and thus, he felt less than totally competent. Factors in his Personal Structure (competence needs, lack of experience with physical violence, and so on) led him to respond as he did to the cues in the Social Context. Similarly, his wife also experienced this sense of inadequacy to some extent, but because of her Personal Structure, this feeling was moderated by the belief that deciding on the appropriate action was more her husband's responsibility than hers.

In considering the behavior of the young woman, we must view her encounter with her date from a very different perspective. Why was she so ambivalent about the situation in which she found herself? First, she probably was motivated by a number of concerns, some of which were mutually antagonistic. On the one hand, the general pattern of behavior that she expressed, starting with her acceptance of the date, indicated a certain motivation for affiliation. That is, like most of us, she was motivated to seek the company of others, especially persons of the other sex; obviously she was not a social isolate or recluse. Moreover, she must have felt some need to be liked and appreciated; she probably cared about what her date thought about her. It is probable that her sexual needs affected her behavior as well. These concerns, working in concert, motivated the young woman to cooperate to some extent with her date's advances. On the other hand, a number of personal factors in the young woman caused her to resist the blandishments of the young man. For example, from her behavior we would assume that at least to some extent, she had learned and accepted the standards of conduct regarding sex that society at that time defined as appropriate for unmarried women. Clearly, this well-established conception of correct conduct conflicted with the social and biological concerns noted above, and this conflict contributed to her ambivalent response.

In contrast, the personal factors in the young man that influenced his behavior were much more in harmony. As was true of his date, the young man was probably influenced by affiliative and sexual motives, as well as a concern for enhancing his sense of self-worth. The socially prescribed activities that he had internalized, however, were consistent with these needs, rather than contrary to them, as was the case of the young woman. Furthermore, it is possible that the degree to which one or more of these motives was aroused in the young man served to bias his judgment regarding the meaning of his date's behavior. That is, he might have misinterpreted her fundamentally ambivalent reactions and might have seen them as unequivocally accepting of his advances. He might have come to the erroneous conclusion that while her lips were saying no, No, NO, her eyes were saying yes, Yes, YES! We must stress that a man with a different Personal Structure probably would have acted differently in this situation. Another male, for example, might have interpreted the young woman's ambiguous behavior as indicating dislike or rejection, and his reaction, in response, could have taken any of a number of forms quite different from that which was observed.

In turning to a more systematic discussion of Personal Structure, we have classified the most relevant components of this core concept into five central categories: evaluative beliefs, motives, affects, faculties, and habits.[4]

Evaluative Beliefs. We will begin our review of the major components of the Personal Structure with a discussion of *evaluative beliefs,* in large part because this phenomenon has been one of social psychology's major concerns. Indeed, the different types of evaluative beliefs and their formation, structure, and change, were for many years the primary focus of the field. While the domain of social psychology currently encompasses a broader range

---

[4] We should note that a comprehensive presentation of personality is beyond the scope and mission of this book. We cannot (nor do we wish to) discuss specifically the many and varied theoretical perspectives that have been advanced to explain individual human functioning, nor can we present a comprehensive summary of the data that empirical research on personality has produced. Instead, in this section and throughout the book, we limit our concerns to those issues and ideas that are of most relevance to the understanding of social behavior. What follows, therefore, is a rather general summary of Personal Structure, which can be used as a framework to discuss the impact of differences among individuals on the behaviors that are of most interest to social psychologists.

of phenomena, the concept of evaluative belief remains a central preoccupation of the field.

In our view, evaluative beliefs are cognitions—that is, thoughts—that have two major elements: (1) an *informational component,* consisting of an idea about an object, person, quality, or event that we hold to be true; and (2) an *evaluative component,* consisting of the judgment of the goodness or badness of the object, person, quality, or event in question. Though the words *good* and *bad* or their synonyms might not be used specifically in identifying one's reaction to a person or thing, evaluations of this type are always implied in these judgments. For example, we might hold the belief that Adolf Hitler was a mass murderer. This evaluative belief has an implied negative judgmental component unless, of course, one positively values mass murder.

There are three major types of evaluative beliefs: *opinions, impressions,* and *norms.* In this book we use the term *opinion* to refer to an evaluative belief about an object, quality, or aggregate of persons; *impressions* are defined here as evaluative beliefs about individuals; and *norms* are rules of behavior that prescribe what we should or should not do in a given circumstance. While intimately tied to one another through the common processes involved in their formation, the three categories of evaluative beliefs rarely have been discussed within a common framework. It is important to understand, however, that at their most basic level, opinions, impressions, and norms merely are different manifestations of the identical psychological process, in that they are all cognitions having an informational and an evaluative component.

This is not to say that opinions, impressions, and norms are psychologically synonymous; they differ in terms of the numbers and types of entities (objects, persons, activities, and so on) to which they refer. As noted, opinions are evaluations of impersonal entities, such as objects, events, groups, or aggregates of people. A given opinion can refer to a singular entity or to a class of objects or persons. For example, we believe that the loud, imitation Hawaiian shirt that our friend, Dan, wears all the time is the ugliest article of clothing that we have ever encountered. This is an opinion about a singular entity—Dan's shirt. On the other hand, we might mistrust Russians and thus have an opinion about an aggregate composed of 250 million people (give or take 50 million or so).

In contrast, impressions are judgments about the goodness or badness of specific individuals. Impressions always are personal; a given impression is invariably directed toward a specific person. Finally, norms are evaluative beliefs about appropriate social conduct.

A more comprehensive example should help to clarify this distinction. Suppose that we have a very negative opinion of "the Russians" (an aggregate of people): "Russians cannot be trusted; they are a sneaky lot who do not play fairly." On the other hand, we greatly admire our nextdoor neighbor, a renowned Russian biochemist who has come to work at our university for a year. This positive evaluative belief is an impression, as it refers to a judgment of the goodness of a specific individual. Moreover, when talking to our new neighbor, we probably would not verbalize our anti-Russian opinions, nor would we knowingly make an ethnic slur about her cultural heritage; we would be constrained in our expression of such an opinion by norms that prescribe the appropriate conduct between neighbors.

Over the years in social psychology, the three forms of evaluative beliefs have been the subject of a great deal of theoretical and empirical inquiry. As noted, however, social scientists typically have examined the forms in isolation of one another, a strategy that has produced three somewhat independent literatures: one on opinions, another on impressions, and a third on norms. As is evident from our discussion to this point, we believe that the three concepts share a common identity—that is, they are all evaluative beliefs—and as such, their formation and change are governed by the same psychological processes. This realization is important, since a recognition of their common underlying bases permits a more integrative approach to their understanding.

Let us now return to our example to see how the three types of evaluative beliefs relate to what transpired in the courtyard. We are tapping only the surface of the multitude of evaluative beliefs that came into play in this story; all social encounters generate, or make salient, a very large number of such cognitions. These examples are provided to illustrate the similarities and differences among opinions, impressions, and norms in everyday life.

Consider one of the beliefs that came about as a consequence of the actions of the legal authorities: the prompt response of the police generated in the author and his wife a very positive opinion of the Evanston police department. In contrast, because the exposure to the particular officers involved in this incident was so brief, the observing couple formed no lasting impression of these specific individuals.

Of course, some impressions might well have been formed as a function of the evening's events. From the actions of the young man in the courtyard that night, we would infer that his impression of his date was favorable—at least until the police arrived. The young woman's impression of her escort is somewhat more difficult to determine, in part because her actions in the courtyard could have been the result of either the operation of norms ("good girls" do not do these things on the first date—and especially not in the courtyard of grandmother's apartment building) or of a mixed impression about her suitor. The operation of norms was more obvious in the observing couple's behaviors. From their words and actions, it was clear that they felt some obligation to at least consider intervening in the potential emergency. The young woman's screams made salient a norm (altruism) that prescribed the active intervention of the observers in what might have been a dangerous situation.

Motives. *Motives* are a second component of the Personal Structure that have been found to be relevant to social behavior. We view motives as the complex set of psychological processes that direct people toward specific end points or goals. These processes operate together, forming a force that activates behavior, and as such, they can be conceptualized in terms of the psychological energy that is associated with, or attached to, a person's goals.

"The only thing that turns my husband on
is a hot pastrami sandwich."

People can differ widely in what motivates them.

In other words, motives are the drives, needs, urges, and concerns that propel an individual to attempt to achieve certain end states.

For example, we all have a need to ingest food. When this need is salient—perhaps because we have not engaged in this activity in the recent past or because we have come upon a plate of Twinkies, our very favorite food—we are likely to act to accomplish this goal: we eat. By doing so, we satisfy the motive, relieve the concern, and so forth.

Of course, not all motives are so easily satisfied. Unfortunately, our plates are not always filled with Twinkies; frequently, situational constraints exist that inhibit the accomplishment of a goal. Under such circumstances, our motives activate us to seek alternatives or substitutes for the desired ends. For example, if we are very hungry and there is no food available, we might watch television, chew gum, read a social psychology textbook, write letters, or perform any of a host of activities that have little, if anything, to do directly with the unsatisfied motive. The activating nature of motives is intriguing, since the psychological energy that they engender often is displaced toward other endeavors.

Moreover, we often are activated by two or more motives whose end states are contradictory. For example, we might feel the urge to eat the 16 Twinkies arrayed before us, but we also feel the desperate need to achieve a body whose proportions are more consistent with our culture's image of physical beauty (or at least adequacy). In this instance, our lips would be saying yes, Yes, YES, while our hips would be saying no, No, NO. In these circumstances, which occur all too frequently, our actual behaviors might represent a compromise between the competing concerns, or a substitute that is not obviously related to either motive. No matter what the behaviors undertaken, however, we assume that they are a consequence of motives, even if the actor is not aware of the motives underlying a specific action, which is often the case. All behaviors are energized, directed, and determined by our needs, urges, and concerns.

While all motives are structurally similar in that they have in common the features of activation and goal direction, the focuses of individual motives can be extremely diverse. For example, compare the sex drive with the need for achievement (the concern for the successful accomplishment of a task): both of these motives are energizing and goal-directed, but their focuses— the particular goal or end point of each—are quite different. A number of theoretical systems have been developed to organize the multitude of human motives that have been identified. Most of these systems posit some distinction between *biogenic motives*—those having an obvious physiological basis (for example, sleeping or eating), and *social motives*—those which are a product of past experience and whose satisfaction is dependent upon factors in the interpersonal environment (for example, achievement or affiliation).

Across cultures, people satisfy their hunger motive in very different ways.

The distinction between biogenic and social motives is somewhat simplistic, because there is a social component in even the most biogenic drives and a biological basis for the most social motives. Consider hunger, a motive whose basis is strongly biogenic. Across cultures, we know that different social learning experiences lead to a wide variation in the expression of this motive. For example, cultures differ with regard to the number of meals that are served in a day and the time at which the major meal is eaten. In addition, there is wide variation in the kinds of substances used to satisfy the motive. In some cultures, eating grasshoppers is a perfectly appropriate means of satisfying hunger, while in others, the mere sight of such "food" would reduce a person's inclination to eat.

Similarly, there are a variety of socially defined rules that govern motive-related behaviors. For instance, in some groups, all food is eaten with the fingers of the right hand, and to violate this rule is a sign of extremely poor breeding. By way of contrast, imagine the reaction that this same practice would generate at an expensive American restaurant. These differences that occur across cultures are important to note, since they suggest that basic biological needs can be substantially affected by social convention. A parallel demonstration could be made to illustrate the effect of biologically based processes on social motives—for example, the role that such drives as hunger and sex play in the development and expression of such motives as affiliation (the need to establish some relationship between one's self and others, to have friends, to be one of the gang, and so on).

Most relevant to social psychology are those motives that have a large social component—affiliation, altruism, dominance, nurturance, achievement, power, sex, and succorance is only a partial list. Clearly, there is a multitude of motives whose goal states integrally involve other people. This large number is not surprising given the social nature of human beings. And that is precisely the point: human beings are thoroughly social animals, and our motives reflect this truism.

Speculation about the motives that were salient in the minds of the actors in the courtyard episode provides some further insight into the factors that determined the behaviors that occurred. For instance, it is most likely that the motive for affiliation was one of the reasons for the young man in our story to arrange the date and for the young woman to accept his invitation. While these actions were quite different, they were undertaken, at least in part, as a result of a similar need.

Another motive that was operative in the events of that evening was curiosity. Why did the author and his wife interrupt their routine to investigate the sounds coming from the courtyard? While the reasons for their behavior were complex, it is reasonable to assume that their activity was motivated to some extent by a need to see the cause of the unusual clamor. We might speculate as well that the curiosity of the other apartment-dwellers was also stimulated, but for them, concerns for self-preservation overcame needs to investigate this novel occurrence.

In analyzing the behavior of the police, it is clear that their actions consisted of a series of well-practiced behaviors that were expected of them. Practice and previous experience with similar episodes probably helped them to suppress whatever tendencies they might have had not to directly intervene, such as the self-serving motives that the author found impossible to resist. The policemen's sense of responsibility and competence overcame whatever motivations for self-preservation they might have sensed.

Obviously, we have only scratched the surface with regard to the number of motivational inferences that could have been derived to explain the actions that occured in the episode. There is a danger in overdoing this approach, however. The overuse of motivational explanations can mask a rather severe lack of understanding of the phenomenon of interest. Merely explaining a behavior with the rather simplistic argument that it was the result of some specific motive does not really explain anything. This type of circular reasoning must be avoided if we are to arrive at some persuasive analysis of human behavior. Of course, the use of motivational explanations does not necessarily imply circularity, but they are quite prone to such criticism. For example, to explain the young woman's actions in the courtyard by inferring that she was motivated by the need to scream would seem absurd. Yet, this statement is no less rational than any other motivational inference made in the absence of supportive evidence. The legitimate use of motivational explanations calls for evidence that supports the hypothesis regarding the probable operation of the motive, in addition to the observed behavior, which is the focus of our explanation.

Affect. The third major component of the Personal Structure, *affect*, has as its identifying feature the experience and interpretation of our own physiological states, especially those that involve the autonomic nervous and endocrine systems. The major subclasses of affect are emotions, moods, and temperament.

Emotion is the outcome of our interpretation of relatively specific and abrupt changes in our internal (body) states. For example, in an objectively dangerous situation (for example, a soldier on a bloody battlefield), one might become aware of a number of major physiological changes—heightened heart rate, increased respiration, the arousing effect of greater adrenalin production—and interpret this set of events as the emotion of fear. Note that it is not the physiological reactions per se, but the changes accompanied by our interpretation of them, that comprise the emotion.

Less clear-cut but more long-lasting physiological events are the basis of a different type of affect, namely mood. As with emotions, there is an interpretational component to the experience of any mood. For example, two people may each experience a similar, somewhat amorphous, long-lasting state of low energy. One person might interpret this mood as being a case of the blues, or depression, while the other might view the mood in a more positive light, such as being relaxed, "mellowed-out," or "cool."

A third subclass of affect is temperament, which is a person's interpretation of his or her characteristic (base-rate) body states. Oscar the Grouch, the Muppet character of "Sesame Street" fame, is an extreme example of someone with a most consistent and simplistic interpretation of his body state: no matter what the situation, the people, or the events, one can always count on Oscar to be grouchy, a description of his temperament with which even he would agree. Temperament is the most typical or characteristic aspect of the affective component of the Personal Structure, since it is not influenced by immediate events.

Though these three types of affect are similar—they are all forms of an individual's interpretations of his or her internal states—their differences are also worth noting. Our three subclasses of affect differ in terms of their duration and consistency over time, and the immediacy of the factors that elicit them. Emotions typically are short-lived reactions to immediate circumstances in which an individual is involved. Emotions usually dissipate rapidly, especially if there is a change in the circumstances that originally elicited them. Moods, in contrast, are more long lasting, and the specific events or circumstances that trigger them often are not as obvious to the actor. Temperament is the most long-term affective state; it represents an individual's typical interpretation of his or her emotional makeup.

It is important not only to compare the three subclasses of affect, but

Even Oscar would agree that he is a grouch.

also to note as well the similarities in, and differences between, the more inclusive concepts of motive and affect. The relationship between these two components of the Personal Structure is a major concern in the psychological study of personality. For our purposes, it is sufficient to point out that motives, like affects, often have an accompanying physiological component; that is, we often employ an observed physiological change to infer our motive state. For example, we interpret the physiological sensations of a dry mouth, constricted throat, and so on, to mean that we are thirsty. Conversely, there can be a motivational component to affects. For example, we can actively behave to produce good feelings and to avoid bad ones.

To demonstrate the manner in which affects can operate in social encounters, let us return to our story. The author recalls quite vividly that the ambiguity of the events in the courtyard gave rise to a series of physiological changes that he and his wife felt as anxiety and, furthermore, that this emotional reaction had a major influence on their behavior. This reaction was one of the reasons that they attempted to reduce the ambiguity by seeking definitions from each other of what was going on and ultimately was a contributor to their decision to call the police. The policemen who answered the call probably felt less anxious than the observing couple, in part because such situations were not novel for them. Thus, the uncertainty that played so large a role in the couple's emotional reactions and subsequent behavior was not nearly so important a contributor to the policemen's responses. This is not to suggest that the police did not experience any emotional reaction to the situation—remember, they came out of their car with their guns drawn. However, the emotions that they experienced—fear for their well-being— probably were quite different from those of the other observers—a combination of uncertainty, fear for their own safety, and fear for the well-being of the young woman. Thus, the same Social Context can produce very different emotional reactions in people.

Similarly, the participants in our drama probably experienced different moods. For example, though we would interpret the young man's physiological condition and subsequent actions as attributable to drunkeness, he probably viewed his own affective state in a very different light. While he might have admitted to having had a few drinks and being slightly tipsy, his likely interpretation of his general body state was that of being in a good mood— at least until the police arrived. His interpretation of his long-term feelings undoubtedly contributed to his lack of awareness of the negative cues that his date was expressing towards his advances. On the other hand, the author's mood was not nearly as euphoric as that of the young man's. The late hour, the interruption of his nightly routine, and the anxiety that he was feeling all subtly contributed to a general sense of being in a bad mood.

This negative frame of mind is not characteristic of the author but was a consequence of the unpleasant events of that evening. On the other hand, if he was characteristically cranky or unpleasant, we might infer correctly that this affective state was a facet of his temperament, rather than an instance of a more transitory mood state. A more direct example of temperament is provided in a consideration of the affective makeup of the author's wife, who can be typified as generally cool-headed and nonexcitable. This calmness was overcome by the events in the courtyard, and because her reaction was not typical of her, it was all the more noteworthy to her husband. The implication of this observation is that temperament is not necessarily a steady state that permeates an individual's every affective reaction; rather, it is the emotional base line that influences responses, but does not determine them completely.

Faculties. The fourth component of the Personal Structure—*faculties*—can be thought of as the abilities that develop as a result of a unique combination of biological predisposition and past learning experiences. Intelligence, the ability to think abstractly, is an obvious example of a faculty, because it represents a set of biologically determined capacities whose development is subject to extensive environmental influences. Aside from this obvious example, it is important to note that such varying talents as dancing ability, interpersonal perceptiveness, and communication skills are also faculties.

Many of the specific abilities that are subsumed under the general heading of faculties have been the subject of extensive social psychological inquiry. As will be discussed in later sections of this book, such faculties as intelligence, cognitive complexity (the ability to perceive and process simultaneously sets of diverse cues, inputs, and information, in arriving at an integrated decision or judgment), perceptual accuracy, and bias have been investigated as variables that affect social behavior. To provide some indication of the relevance of faculties in everyday behavior, let us return to the courtyard episode. Consider the faculty of communication skill as it contributed to the initial interaction that took place between the young couple and that ultimately led to the events in the courtyard. If the young man did not possess a reasonable facility with the specialized language that was used by late adolescents of the time, it is possible that the meeting would never have taken place. On the other hand, if he had possessed greater fluency and persuasive abilities, the encounter in the courtyard might have ended quite differently.

As another example, the faculty of cognitive complexity operated to affect the actions of the observing couple. As noted, complexity is the ability to perceive and process diverse information. In the case of the author and his wife, they possess the capacity to perceive a great many environmental cues, but concerning the courtyard instance, they were unable to efficiently arrive at an integrated judgment. If this faculty had been more limited—had they been more cognitively simple—they might have intervened more quickly, since they would have attended to the young woman's screams, ignoring her laughter and the other contradictory cues. Or they might have attended to the laughter, and disregarded the screams. In either case, a good deal of the available information would not have been perceived, and they would not have been faced with the anxiety-provoking dilemma about the appropriate behavior for the situation. On the other hand, if they had possessed a greater capacity to integrate diverse cues, they also might have acted more quickly.

Habits. The final component of the Personal Structure to be discussed involves well-learned patterns of behavior that are unique to each individual. We have termed these patterns *habits,* since this word, even in its nontechnical sense, connotes the major features of this part of our Personal Structures. Two fundamental learning processes underlie a habit: (1) a habit is composed of a specific chain of behaviors whose connection has been learned; and (2) as a result of past experience, such chains are elicited in response to a specific cue or pattern of cues. Thus, a habit is established when, through learning, a specific set of cues evokes a specific chain of actions.

Once a habitual pattern of behaviors is initiated, we tend to carry out the entire sequence of actions with little self-awareness. It is not that such action sequences are beyond conscious awareness but rather that we typically do not attend to them. For example, consider the sequence of behaviors that constitute a long-term smoker's lighting of a cigarette. If such a person is observed for a number of occasions, a remarkable consistency will be noted in the manner in which this pattern of actions is carried out. Given the consistency, frequency, and relative unimportance of this behavior, it is reasonable to assume that the smoker is not attending very carefully to the actions observed but is engaging in them more or less automatically.

It is also the case that habitual patterns of actions, once initiated, are relatively impervious to modification. This rigidity is due in part to the lack of attention paid to the behaviors themselves. But such resistance to change is due as well to the learning processes through which the habit is formed. As noted, a habit is a learned chain of behaviors in which one behavior in the chain evokes the next behavior in the chain. In the example of the smoker, the habit of lighting a cigarette is part of a larger sequence of behaviors that the smoker has learned. For instance, he might reach for a cigarette every time that he talks on the phone. Even if he is trying to quit and manages to reduce his smoking appreciably, he still finds a lit cigarette in his hand almost every time he is on the phone. These falls off the wagon are a consequence of two forces: (1) the strength of the link between the actions of talking on the phone and reaching for a cigarette; and (2) the strength of the distraction (away from concentrating on not smoking) generated by attending to a telephone conversation.

This last example implicitly suggests another feature of habits—namely, that their degree of complexity can vary. Very simple habits are composed of a small number of specific behaviors: characteristically answering the phone with the word, "Hello," or greeting passing acquaintances with the phrase, "How are you?" are examples of simple habitual actions. More complex chains of behaviors consist of a *series* of simple habits. Such complex habits can be as complicated as a very extensive "script" that is evoked whenever a person finds himself meeting an attractive stranger.

Ironically, since more complex habits are composed of complicated chains of smaller cue-behavior patterns, they are easier to interrupt and to modify. Simply breaking one of the cue-behavior sequences will serve to interrupt the more complex overall pattern of actions. However, complex habits are

Cigarette smoking often is a well-learned part of a larger sequence of habitual behaviors.

more difficult to extinguish entirely. This is so because such complicated patterns of action consist of a number of specific cues and corresponding behaviors that operate in combination. Elimination of only a small portion of these cue-behavior sequences has little impact on the total pattern of actions that are expressed.

Let us now examine the relevance of habit for understanding some of the participants' actions in our story. As noted, the nightly routine of the author and his wife was disturbed by the screams and laughter of the young woman in the courtyard. To the extent that this nightly routine was triggered by a specific cue or set of cues (that is, the author and his wife regularly might have gone to bed immediately after watching the evening news), this set of behaviors could be considered habitual. This habitual aspect of their behavior was in part responsible for the observers' difficulty in interrupting it; the reader will recall that such sequences of action are somewhat rigid and, thus, once engaged, are difficult to short-circuit. As a consequence, the time that elapsed before the observers investigated the disturbance was greater than it would have been had they not initiated their nightly routine.

The same might be said of the behaviors of the young man in the court-yard. For example, his actions probably were a highly stylized, well-learned, and often-repeated sequence of behaviors that he had acquired over a relatively long period of time. The script that he had employed in asking the young woman for a date as well as many of the behaviors that he had emitted during the evening (for example, opening the car door for his date, asking her about her college courses, and so on) were probably expressions of well-learned habits, at least to some extent. His actions at the end of the evening might also have been habitual in nature—that is, he might kiss good-night all the women he dates, without giving much thought to the behavior.

The behaviors of the police provide one of the clearest examples of habit-based actions. Their response to the communication by their dispatcher was the result of an extensive training program. That is, their actions, from the time they received their order to investigate a possible problem to the time at which they had determined the cause of the disturbance, were a set of well-rehearsed and semiautomatic sequences of behaviors. They did not have to think about what to do, they merely engaged in routine. As shown by these examples, habitual behaviors make up a large portion of our day-to-day actions.

Level. Before concluding our formal discussion of the Personal Structure, we should note that the processes and mechanisms that constitute this core concept can vary in terms of importance, salience, and intensity. This dimension of importance has been termed *level* to suggest that high-level processes have more of an impact on our functioning than do those of low levels. Consider, for example, how our own evaluative beliefs vary in terms of their level or importance to us. For many of us, feelings about our parents, our religious beliefs, moral convictions, political philosophy, and so on, can have a strong impact on the way we behave. On the other hand, lower level beliefs—those that have a less important place in our cognitive structures—will have much less an influence on our overt actions.

Level is important when considering motives because it alerts us to the fact that motivation can occur along a continuum ranging from basic needs to superficial concerns. At one end of this continuum are basic needs, characteristic and enduring energizers that shape or define the rewards most relevant to us across a broad range of situations.

For example, the noted psychologist Abraham Maslow made the point that there are persons whose central concern in life is the motive for a predictable, orderly, and safe environment. Such people would derive rewards from features of the environment that others would view as restrictive. Moreover, these safety-oriented people would act to structure their world to be as predictable as possible, regardless of the actual realities of the situation. We might speculate, as an example, that when Richard Nixon was president, he structured his White House environment in a manner that reflected a pervasive safety orientation. Thus, the wire tapping of the Democratic National Headquarters in the Watergate office complex might be viewed as a consequence of the impact of his basic need for safety on the actions of those who served him.

For Tracy Austin, competition is probably a high-level motive.

At the other end of this continuum are superficial concerns that energize us in a very restrictive sense. For example, consider a person who is a mediocre but enthusiastic tennis player. The person might know very well that she will never become another Tracy Austin, but she nevertheless plays to win with all the skill and energy at her disposal. In most other aspects of her life, however, this same woman might be almost completely noncompetitive. Competition is a motive for her, but only in the restrictive environment of the tennis court. For her, then, competition is a superficial concern (for Tracy Austin, however, competition is probably a basic, high-level need).

As with beliefs, differences in levels of motive yield an element of uniqueness across people that helps to explain individual differences in behavior. While it is likely that there exists a set of basic needs that are common to all people, the manner in which these needs are expressed vary in terms of their intensity. Moreover, other, less biologically derived motives can differ widely among people with regard to their level.

In the case of affects, the major implication of level is the extent to which an emotional reaction has motivating properties; low-level affects are less likely than high-level affects to influence behavior. For example, the slight feeling of embarrassment that might occur as a result of stumbling on the sidewalk is a low-level affect, in that it would not increase our vigilance about where we were walking for more than a short period of time. On the other hand, the great embarrassment that might occur as a consequence of making fools of themselves prevents some people from speaking out in public meetings. Level of affect appears to be associated with the perceived intensity of the feelings involved. Because emotions tend to be more volatile than moods or temperament, they are more variable in their level. It is possible to think of instances of high-level mood states, but their occurrence no doubt is less frequent than high-level emotions.

Level is also relevant to understanding the role of specific faculties in determining behavior. People differ regarding the extent to which any given faculty is important to their functioning. For example, we have often heard a person described as a natural athlete. In our terms, this descriptive phrase would mean that the individual so described had great athletic facility. This same person, however, might not really care much about this ability since it has little to do with any behaviors of importance to him. For this person, athletic ability is a low-level faculty. In contrast, athletic ability would be a high-level faculty for most professional football players, as it would play a major role in the successful practice of their craft.

It is important to understand that in this context, the concept of level refers to the centrality or perceived importance of a faculty, not to the degree of skill involved per se. The indifferent athlete has a great deal of skill, but nevertheless, athletic ability is a low-level faculty for him, since he does not care about such endeavors. On the other hand, the ardent but mediocre tennis player is an example of a high level faculty associated with a low degree of skill. Obviously, the degree to which we possess a skill or ability often is related to how important that faculty is to us (that is, its level). There are a number of reasons for this. First, degree of proficiency at any complex skill or faculty is often related to our practicing of the behavior, which is usually a function of level; second, we tend to care about activities that we have worked for; third, we find rewarding the things we do well.

Habits too can vary in terms of their level. The most important habits—those of high level—are patterns of behavior that apply across a wide range of Social Contexts, whereas low-level habits are applicable to a rather restricted set of situations. The behaviors that males or females have learned to be appropriate actions for their sex, as defined by the culture, are examples of high-level habits. These habits have a very major influence on the ways in which men and women relate to each other over a wide variety of situations, as well as an influence on the general Social Contexts in which men and women find themselves. At the other end of this spectrum, in their most extreme form, low-level habits are those patterns of behavior (usually simple) that have little importance for social functioning. The example of the habitual sequence of lighting up observed in many cigarette smokers—tapping the top of the cigarette pack with the end of the cigarette, putting the cigarette in the left side of the mouth, and so on—is an example of one such low-level habit.

Interaction of Core Concepts

To help summarize the material of Chapter 1, the major components of the social field—the core concepts and their subparts—are presented in Table 1.1. However, this illustration and the analysis of the social field that we have presented have as their major disadvantage the artificial division of what is, by its very nature, a complete or wholistic entity. For example, dividing the social field into its hypothetical component parts is a useful exercise, since it allows us to discuss a number of critical aspects of this whole in some logical order. However, it is important to realize that these components never operate in isolation of one another. In actuality, these factors cannot be viewed in isolation if one is to understand the role that situational and personal variables play in social functioning.

In other words, social behavior is the outcome of a multitude of factors that combine in unique ways. Variables within a core concept, as well as across the core concepts, can operate together or in opposition to create behavioral outcomes that could not have been foreseen through an isolated consideration of each component. This interaction of variables produces the variety that is at once so compelling and so maddening a part of the field of social psychology.

In this context, consider the behavior of the young woman in the court-yard. Why did she behave as she did? Why did she engage in the unusual approach-avoidance activity? And why did she do so in such a boisterous manner? Her customary good-night behavior (habits), her level of alcohol consumption (the physical environment and her faculty to consume liquor),

TABLE 1.1
Major Components of the Social Field

I. Social Context
   A. Physical environment.
   B. Interpersonal environment.
II. Personal Structure
   A. Evaluative beliefs.
   B. Motives.
   C. Affects.
   D. Faculties.
   E. Habits.

the darkened and quiet courtyard (the physical environment), her evaluative beliefs about appropriate behavior on first dates (norms), her need for affiliation (motives)—these and other variables determined her actions. And they did so in a very unique manner. If she had not been drinking, she might have acted differently. If her date had acted differently, she would have also. A change in any of these factors—if the courtyard had been well-illuminated, if she had been at the door of her own apartment, if she had possessed a different level of need for affiliation—or in other factors of which we are unaware would probably have had very major repercussions for her behavior.

We shall return to this interactionistic perspective throughout this text. It is emphasized in the present context to illustrate the complexity of the domain of social psychology. We find this complexity to be a challenging adventure, and we have written this book, in part, to share this sense of adventure with our readers.

The Interpersonal Themes of Control and Sentiment

For better or worse, social psychologists have typically studied phenomena discretely and left as unspecified the interrelationships between phenomena. Social psychologists often "discover" a set of human behaviors that they feel should be studied (for example, love, fear arousal, obedience, and so on) and then set out to uncover the variables that determine how or when such behavior is expressed. While this strategy can produce rapid advance within a specific subarea, such progress is not without its costs. One major problem with this approach is that it introduces an element of disjointedness to most reviews of the field. Grasping the underlying processes of the discipline then becomes a very difficult task for the beginning student. We feel that the integrative framework provided by the thematic approach in this book will lessen the difficulty of this task.

Five integrative themes will be presented in this and the following chapter: *Control, Sentiment, Resolution, Consistency,* and *Valuation.*[1] A definition is provided for each of the following themes along with examples of how they operate across diverse areas of social psychology. This material should help you to grasp the essence of the themes and to perceive their utility in integrating the phenomena of the field.

By considering these themes in concert, we underscore our belief that a set of common processes underlies the various phenomena of interest to social psychologists. This chapter is primarily concerned with the themes

---

[1] So as not to burden the reader with what appears to be so formidable an amount of material, we have chosen to divide our presentation of the five integrative themes between two chapters. In many ways this is an artificial division, since the themes are meant to provide a unitary system by which the diverse subject matter of social psychology can be integrated.

whose central focus is interpersonal influence and behavior; Chapter 3 is concerned with the themes that are more relevant to cognitive mechanisms and processes, such as thoughts, beliefs, and opinions. Thus, in this chapter, we deal with themes involving the ways in which people control the behavior of others, and the ways that social encounters generate and result from the feelings that people have for others. In Chapter 3, we present themes that are concerned with the ways in which people think, the determinants of their decisions, and other cognitive phenomena related to social behavior.

THE THEME OF CONTROL

The first theme to be discussed is Control. This theme focuses on the processes and procedures that a person employs to influence another's evaluative beliefs or actions. One type of Control—impingement—involves attempts to modify another's overt actions. Sticking a gun in someone's ribs and asking for his money is an example of one time-honored attempt at impingement. Of course, there are other less coercive but perhaps equally effective instances of such behavior Control. Withholding a reward from a person unless some specified conditions are met ("You won't get the car until you mow the lawn") is a very common form of this tactic of behavior control.

A second type of Control—incorporation—involves the acts undertaken to persuade another to adopt a specific evaluative belief or set of beliefs. Incorporation is especially relevant to opinions and norms, as these types of beliefs are directly involved in long-term behavior control. The reader will recall that opinions are beliefs about objects, events, ideas, or classes of people. Convincing a person that eating meat is unhealthy, for example, would probably have implications for the kinds of foods that the person would eat; such an activity would be an instance of the process of incorporation. Persuading one's parents that good grades are not the sole criteria of success in college is another, perhaps more relevant and well-rehearsed incorporation attempt. Norms, as you will recall, are beliefs involving rules of proper conduct. As such, their relevance to behavior Control is straightforward: inducing someone to incorporate a norm into his or her Personal Structure—for example, "Don't be a litterbug"—has direct and possibly long-term implications for that person's behavior.

Before turning to a more detailed exposition of the two major Control mechanisms, their similarities and differences should be considered. First, while impingement and incorporation can result in behaviors that appear identical, the processes that induce the behaviors are quite different. Behaviors controlled by impingement processes are a result of factors in the Social Context; that is, they are determined by variables that are external to the individual. By definition, behaviors controlled by impingement are performed solely to obtain a reward or to avoid a punishment; the behavior itself is not necessarily valued by the actor performing it. Actions that occur as a result of incorporation, in contrast, are valued by the actor, since they are a result of some internalized belief. They are consistent with the person's ideas of what is good (opinion) or correct (norm).

Second, the definitions of impingement and incorporation do not address the issue of whether or not the Control attempt was successful. The theme of Control is focused on the actions that are employed, whether successfully or not, to affect the behavior of another person or group of people. For example, by our writings in this text, we might attempt to induce the reader to have a very positive opinion of social psychology. For some, this attempt might succeed, while for others, it might fail abysmally. In either case, however, our behavior is an attempt at incorporation. Whether the attempt succeeds or fails is not a relevant feature of this concept. This is not to say that social psychologists are not concerned with the success or failure of Control attempts. Indeed, the study of variables that moderate the success of a Control attempt is a major focus of much social psychological research, to be discussed in detail later in this book.

Third, we should note that impingement processes can lead to incorporation, as diagrammed in Figure 2.1. That is, we sometimes find that a behavior that has been induced by the Control process of impingement becomes, over time, incorporated. Such conversions typically involve a high degree of control over the behavior of the recipient of the impingement.[2] Examples of extreme situational and behavioral control are provided in parent-child interactions, brainwashing situations, marine boot camp training, prisons, and so forth.

We will now explore in detail the subthemes of impingement and incorporation, the two major components of the theme of Control.

Impingement

Surveillance. As noted, the subtheme of impingement refers to the attempted Control of another's overt actions. Typically, such Control is exercised through the use of various forms of psychological and material rewards and punishments. Impingement presumes the ability of the influencer to monitor the activity of the target of the Control attempt; without monitoring, or *surveillance,* the mechanisms of impingement could not be applied and the desired activity most likely would not occur.

To return to the "gun in the ribs" example, consider the absurdity if the stick-up man (or woman) were blind. Such an occupation probably would not be very profitable for a blind person. The attempt at impingement ("Give me your money or I'll shoot"), devoid of the ability to monitor the victim's response, would not have the weight of surveillance behind it and thus would not result in Control of the victim's subsequent behavior.

Though we often are unaware of it, an element of impingement permeates much of our social world. A mother's discipline of her toddler, for example, is usually directed at Control of the child's behavior. Similarly, a professor's assignment of materials to be included on an examination is an attempt to

---

[2] This conversion process will be discussed in detail later in this chapter.

FIGURE 2.1
An Instance of Repeated Impingements Leading to Incorporation

Does Your Mother Still Have to Remind You to Brush Your Teeth?

Control students' actions through impingement. In this case, the surveillance is less immediate and direct, but it is real nonetheless.

Mechanisms of Impingement.   The mechanisms of impingement consist of resources under the control of the influencer, which he or she believes are relevant to the welfare of the target of influence. In their simplest form, these mechanisms involve the physical well-being of the target. For example, a mother's threat of a spanking if her child rides his tricycle in the street

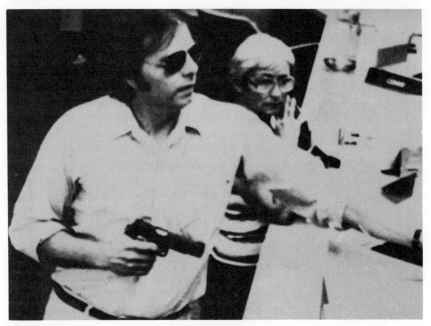

This person was captured (on film) as he engaged in a time-honored tactic of impingement.

is a powerful impingement, since young children view such outcomes as very painful experiences. Similarly, employers who are known to award bonuses for unusually meritorious work performance provide another example of a direct impingement mechanism.

There are, of course, more subtle but equally powerful mechanisms of impingement which are relevant to the psychological well-being of the target. These mechanisms involve outcomes that satisfy or thwart a social motive. For example, the recognition that a target has a strong need for attention provides the influencer with a mechanism—attending or ignoring—that can be used to impinge upon the actions of that individual. Perhaps the most pervasive mechanism of impingement that operates through control of psychologically based resources involves the use of *social pressure*. Social pressure is an explicit or implied threat to reject a person as a result of deviance if he or she does not behave in the desired manner. People who apply social pressure must assume that the target cares about being rejected, about being perceived as deviant, etc.

Investigations of Impingement Mechanisms. Because impingement is so pervasive a part of our daily lives, social psychologists have expended much effort to analyze this phenomenon. Those impingement attempts that involve social pressure have received extensive attention, perhaps because these processes are so uniquely social in nature.

For example, one of the classic contributions in the field was Solomon

"It says if you don't buy at least $10 worth of
merchandise from them, they will give our
name to every catalog house in the country."

Mechanisms of impingement can involve threats to our physical or psychological well-being.

Asch's (1951, 1956) research on the extent to which social pressure can impinge on a person's reports of his or her perceptions. Asch asked groups of respondents to make a series of relatively simple line judgments. Typically, a single line would be presented, and subjects then would be asked which one of the three lines subsequently presented matched the original (stimulus) line. A typical line judgment choice is depicted in Figure 2.2.

As can be seen from this figure, the decisions that Asch asked of his subjects were not really very difficult. In fact, when respondents were studied individually, approximately 98 percent of their judgments were correct. But Asch did not confine his research to the estimates of respondents operating in isolation. If he had, there would have been little of a *social* psychological nature to his research. Instead, he studied the actions of individuals that took place in an interpersonal environment, that is, in the company of other respondents. Furthermore, he controlled the interpersonal environment by employing a number of people to play the role of respondent. Thus, with the exception of a single naive subject, all of the other respondents were accomplices of Asch. They had been trained to apply social pressure by reporting the same incorrect judgment on approximately one third of the choices made.

To lend some reality to this research situation, the reader can consider

FIGURE 2.2
Judgment Stimuli in the Asch Experiments

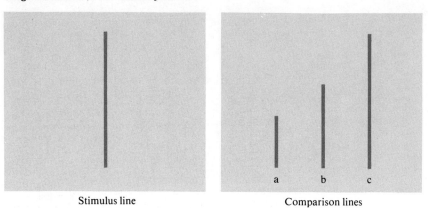

Stimulus line   Comparison lines

what his or her reaction might be as a naive subject in such a demonstration. You arrive at the laboratory promptly at 10 A.M., as scheduled. A few fellow students, whom you vaguely recall seeing around the campus, are already there. Eventually, you, along with seven others, are gathered in the anteroom of the research laboratory. A kindly looking professor (most are) then enters the anteroom and ushers you into his laboratory. Everything looks innocuous enough. You and your fellow students are seated, and the professor explains his study:

> I have asked you here today to help me study the processes involved in the accurate judgment of lines of different lengths. This work has some important implications for various theories of perception, and your cooperation today will help me to unravel, I hope, some of the problems that have cropped up in this field. In this study I will be showing you a single stimulus line, then three others—we call these comparison lines—one of which is the same length as the first. Your task is to tell me which of the comparison lines matches the stimulus line. I will be doing this a number of times. On each trial, each of you is to give your choice, aloud. Please respond in order of seating, from left to right, on each stimulus presentation.

Apparently by happenstance, you find yourself sitting on the far right, and thus you will be one of the last people to respond on each trial.

The professor then presents the first set of lines, as illustrated in Figure 2.2. The correct choice is obviously line *C* and, not surprisingly, each respondent gives 'line *C*' as the answer. The same thing happens on the second trial, when everyone, including you, correctly responds that line *B* most closely matches the stimulus line. It is becoming clear to you at this point that the choices that the kindly looking professor has asked you to make are not really too difficult. Then something strange occurs. On the third trial, the lines are presented, and it is clear to you that the correct choice is line *A*. However, the respondent in the first seat unaccountably reports line *B* as his choice. You grin sheepishly in embarrassment for the poor sap, and resolve that you will not let your own attention wander in such a way. Your sheepish grin begins to fade, however, when the second respondent gives his choice: "Line *B*," he says in a matter-of-fact tone. When the third subject says the same thing, you sneak a quick look back to the "simple" choice situation. It does no good, you still cannot understand how the first three respondents could answer as they had. When the fourth subject's response matches theirs, however, you begin to squirm a bit in your seat—which, as noted, is near the last in line.

Ultimately, what is obviously the incorrent judgment (to you) has been given by every one of the previous respondents! It is now your turn to act. What do you say? If you are like many of Asch's subjects, you say that you agree with the unanimous but incorrect majority judgment. The responses of the others, along with their mere presence in the situation—their ability to monitor your response—impinged upon your actions.

Did you really see what you reported you saw? Asch's research suggests that this probably was not the case for most people. In interviews that Asch conducted after each session, respondents reported that they had answered as they did primarily out of a reluctance to be seen as different or because they were not completely sure of the correct choice by the time it was their turn to respond. For whatever reason, it is clear that most subjects did acquiesce to the social pressure to which Asch had subjected them; in fact, about 75 percent of all subjects in Asch's research did so at least once, and among all subjects, approximately one third of the group-influence attempts were successful. Given the patent transparency of the correct choice (remember that when subjects were tested alone, 98 percent of their answers were correct), the extent of the respondents' acquiescence provides ample testimony to the strength of social pressure as a mechanism of impingement.

Asch's demonstration is a very close analogue to the impingement processes that operate in much of human activity. This phenomenon is so common, in fact, that a fairy tale with impingement as its theme—"The Emperor's New Clothes"—has remained popular for centuries. A more chilling example of the effect of impingement processes on behaviors of extreme importance was provided by President John F. Kennedy's decision to involve the United States in the disastrous Bay of Pigs invasion of Cuba. By his own account, Kennedy was overwhelmed by the apparent consensus on the part of his "expert" advisors. At the meetings called by the president to discuss the feasibility of the invasion, those advisers who initially opposed the plan very soon became aware that they were in the minority, and thus they offered little, if any, overt opposition to it. In the face of what appeared to be the unanimous advice of his most trusted experts, Kennedy decided to commit the United States to this venture, even though privately he harbored serious doubts about the wisdom of this action. Irving Janis (1972) has discussed in detail the processes that operated in this situation and has coined a term—*groupthink*—which graphically describes the force that impingement-based social pressure can bring to bear on interpersonal decision-making processes.

Janis's analysis of the processes that led to the Cuban invasion suggests that even exceptionally important actions (unlike those studied by Asch) are susceptible to the impingement mechanism of social pressure. Stanley Milgram's work on obedience to authority provides further compelling evidence of this power. In his research, Milgram (1963, 1964, 1965, 1974) attempted to determine whether people could be induced through social pressure to administer painful, dangerous electric shocks to another person, certainly an action that most of us would find highly disagreeable and would be most reluctant to perform.

In one of his studies, Milgram brought two subjects into his laboratory and assigned them the roles of either teacher or learner. Milgram explained to the subjects that he was interested in the effect of punishment on learning rates. Accordingly, the teacher was to present a list of word pairs which the learner was to memorize. In his original study, Milgram's participants were placed in different rooms, and their interaction took place via an intercom.

The learner was strapped to a chair, and electrodes were placed on his arm. Milgram instructed the other subject (the teacher) that each time the learner made a mistake, he (the teacher) was to shock the learner and to increase the level of shock with each successive error. The teacher seemingly administered the punishment through a complicated electronic apparatus (see

FIGURE 2.3A
Milgram's Shock Apparatus

Figure 2.3A). As can be seen from Figure 2.3B, which represents the labels attached to each button on the shock generator, the shocks began at a relatively innocuous level (15 volts); but subsequent shocks, ranging to 450 volts, clearly were labeled as dangerous.

The reader can imagine observing one of Milgram's sessions. In this instance, the learner is not doing well. His mistakes are piling up, and the shock level to which he is subjected is becoming rather frightening. When the shock level reaches 200 volts, he complains and asks to be released from the study. After this, his complaints become increasingly louder, more urgent, and more dramatic. After the 300-volt shock level is reached, there is an ominous silence—the learner apparently refuses to, or cannot, respond further. Yet the teacher continues to engage in the task, shocking the now silent learner until the highest shock level has been reached.

What would induce the teacher to engage in such inhuman behavior? Were his acts typical of the other subjects who were assigned the teacher role, or were his actions those of an exceptional thug or a sadist? If they were typical, how were such extreme behaviors induced? Did the experimenter compel the teacher to engage in these repulsive actions by threatening him with dire consequences?

Milgram's research provides answers to these questions, as well as further insight into the nature of human behavior. Before we turn to his results, we must reveal some details of the study that were not disclosed earlier. The learner was not really a naive subject but a talented accomplice of Milgram whose behavior was exactly the same during every session. No shocks were really delivered, but the physical setting and the actions of the learner convinced every subject appointed as teacher that they were causing pain to another. Consequently, most teachers who acquiesced did so with great reluctance. Their continued cooperation often was accompanied by bitter complaints to the experimenter about what they were being asked to do. The subjects almost invariably wanted to terminate the study at the learner's first complaint. To their initial requests to be allowed to stop administering shocks, however, the experimenter merely responded, "Go on." If the teacher

FIGURE 2.3B
Panel Markings on Milgram's Shock Apparatus

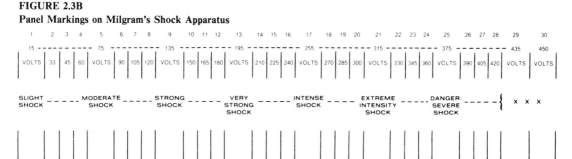

Source: From Milgram, 1974, p. 28.

displayed further reluctance in reaction to the learner's cries, the experimenter said simply, "The experiment requires that you go on."

As a result of this impingement, more than 60 percent of Milgram's subjects complied totally with his wishes—that is, they proceeded to shock the victim up to the most extreme level (450 volts) possible. While these respondents expressed (and, no doubt, felt) great reluctance to do so, they complied nonetheless. It is important also to note that most of the subjects who were unwilling to continue to shock the learner to the highest level (approximately 40 percent of the sample), did, in fact, deliver some shocks.

What could have caused so many apparently normal people to act in such an inhumane way? Clearly, no overt threat was made against them; at most, the experimenter's admonitions vaguely implied that something bad would happen if they stopped the shocks. Yet this subtle impingement had a tremendous impact on respondents' actions. Why?

We believe that subjects were obedient in large measure because Milgram was able to apply a considerable amount of social pressure as a result of his role as scientist. Milgram's postsession interviews with the obedient subjects revealed that one of the principal reasons that they did not quit the experiment was their reluctance to ruin an important scientific study. While they were unhappy about having to deliver painful shocks to another, they were even less happy about the prospect of impeding the progress of science.

A second, related reason was that Milgram's role as a scientist afforded him a great deal of authority and credibility in the eyes of the subjects. The teacher-subjects reported that they assumed that Milgram knew what he was doing, that no permanent harm would result to the learner, and so on. Thus, in saying that the experiment required them to go on, Milgrim brought to bear the whole weight of science, the scientific community, and progress on the shoulders of the reluctant teacher. Under this type of social pressure, it is somewhat surprising that as many as 40 percent of Milgram's subjects refused to acquiesce totally to his demands.

Milgram's work in combination with Asch's studies has three important implications for our discussion of impingement. First, Milgram's study reinforces the major conclusion that we drew from Asch's work—namely, that social pressure can be a powerful weapon of behavior control. If further proof was necessary after the impressive results provided by Asch, Milgram's studies surely provided it.

Second, Milgram's research suggested, as did Asch's studies, that the threatened negative consequences for noncompliance that are an integral part of many impingement attempts need not be drawn explicitly. In neither of these studies were respondents provided with a clear message regarding the consequences of defiance: Asch did not have his accomplices ridicule the naive subject if he did not agree with them; and Milgram never said to his teachers, "If you do not continue, you will do a grave disservice to Science, one of society's most valued enterprises." Instead, the threats in both research situations were implied. No one had to point out the implications of noncompliance to either set of subjects; the imagined consequences of defiance were well understood by all. Those who comply never learn what the actual consequences of transgression might be. The acceptance, without proof, that noncompliance to social pressure has negative consequences is a major determinant of the effectiveness of this mechanism of impingement.

Third, the specific source of social pressure differed in the two sets of studies. Asch used an apparent consensus of judgment (all accomplices reported the same answer for each of the critical judgment trials) to produce impingement pressure; Milgram, on the other hand, implicitly appealed to the prestige and value of science and to the authority of the scientist, to induce obedience to his request.

The extended examples presented used the threat of some negative outcome—social isolation, ridicule, authority displeasure, and so on—for noncompliance with the position or wishes of the influencer. We should reemphasize that not all impingements involve the threat of negative consequences. As discussed earlier, influencers can provide rewards for compliance—bonuses for good work, high grades, sexual favors, and so on—and such reward processes also can operate as strong impingements on behavior. For example, a favorite inducement that parents of adolescents use to persuade their offspring to engage in desirable behaviors (from the parents' standpoint) is the promise of more liberal use of the family car. Such an impingement can have a powerful impact on behavior, although the adolescent might not have a positive opinion about the actions—such as cleaning rooms or washing dishes—that are induced.

Fourth, just as people can use the implied threat of negative consequences as an impingement, they also can attempt to influence behavior by implying that there is a connection between a desired behavior and the resultant reward. Thus, the connection between behavior and reward need not be direct; the impingement can operate so long as such a connection is established in the actor's own mind. For example, legislators often vote for another's pet project with the expectation that the favor will eventually be reciprocated, although no overt or specific promise of such future consideration is made. Nonetheless, support of the bill operates as an impingement on the future behavior of the bill's sponsor.

In summary, impingements are dependent on a target's understanding that there is a connection between his or her actions and a positive or negative outcome. The influencer can explicitly communicate this connection—for example, through threats or promises—or the connection can be implied, or implicitly understood. This perspective suggests that there are four distinct types of impingements, and examples of each have been provided in this chapter.

The promise of the boss who gives bonuses for good work exemplifies an impingement based on an explicitly communicated reward. The legislator who votes for a colleague's bill with the expectation that the favor will be reciprocated exemplifies an impingement based on implicitly communicated rewards. An instance of an impingement based on explicitly communicated punishment is provided by the mother who threatens her toddler with a spanking. Finally, the Milgram and Asch studies are examples of impingements based on implied negative outcomes. Considerable attention was paid to this last type of impingement because we view one of its specific forms— social pressure—as a most important and common behavior control mechanism.

No matter what their specific form, all impingements share two identifying features: (1) the target must perceive that there is a connection between some action and a consequence to his or her welfare; and (2) the influencer must have the means to monitor the target's behavior so that positive or negative consequences can be applied in cases of compliance or noncompliance, respectively.

Incorporation

In contrast to the Control processes of impingement, which are attempts to directly influence overt actions, the processes of incorporation involve attempts to modify the evaluative beliefs of others.[3] As we will discuss in detail in Chapter 6, there are many factors that operate to inhibit a person from acting in accordance with a belief. However, as in the case of impingement, the success or failure of the incorporation to affect actions (or beliefs) is not integral to its definition; what matters is that an influence agent has engaged in some activity designed to modify a target's evaluative beliefs.

Research on incorporation traditionally has focused on three areas that usually have not been linked in the social psychological literature: (1) *conformity,* the private acceptance of the ideas of an influencing agent; (2) *opinion change,* the factors that affect a person's willingness to modify his or her evaluative beliefs about objects, events, classes of people, and so on; and (3) *socialization,* the study of variables involved in the ways that children and adults learn the rules of socially defined appropriate conduct (norms).

Conformity. From the time of Leon Festinger's (1953) classic theoretical discussion of social influence processes, social psychologists have distinguished between the processes of public compliance with an influence agent (impingement), and the private acceptance of that influence (incorporation). All forms of incorporation involve belief change. In the case of *conformity,* the beliefs center on the ideas of correct, successful, efficient actions.

Suppose, for example, that you are an avid, but not very proficient, golfer. You are warming up on the practice tee one Saturday morning before your regular game with your cronies—who lately have been taking a lot of your money by playing better than you—when, by chance, the local golf professional walks by just as you swing and dribble the ball about 20 feet off the practice tee (why do such embarrassing things always happen to you?). He glances your way and says, "You know, you'd do a lot better if

---

[3] The discussion of incorporation is included in this chapter on interpersonal themes, rather than in Chapter 3, because it is usually the case that people attempt to modify the evaluative beliefs of others as a means of controlling their actions.

Golfer on left is practicing exhaling on his downswing.

you exhaled on your downswing." For the rest of the day, it is not surprising that you find yourself consciously attempting to exhale just as you begin to bring the club down towards the ball. Why? The professional is not watching your progress. Indeed, your game might not be any better than it was before you began following his casually given advice. You have accepted this advice, however, and this acceptance affects your behavior even in the absence of monitoring. Behavior control in the absence of monitoring is the feature that distinguishes conformity, and incorporation in general, from impingement.

It is clear from this example that the perceived competence of the influencer plays a vital role in determining the extent to which a belief is changed or accepted. A study by one of the authors of this book (Crano, 1970) demonstrates this influence of expertise on the conformity process. In this experiment, as in Asch's pioneering work, subjects were asked to make a series of perceptual judgments. The judgments involved the estimation of the number of small dots flashed on a screen. The task was designed to be more difficult than Asch's, since the slides were presented for only a short period (five seconds), and there were many dots per slide (an average of 40). Pretesting demonstrated that the subjects who responded in isolation consistently underestimated the actual number of dots presented by an average of 30 percent.

The initial phase of the study made use of two respondents; one participant was a naive subject and the other was an experimental accomplice who was programmed on each judgment to overestimate the number of dots by 30 percent. The goal of the first phase of the study was to determine whether the accomplice's responses had at least impinged on the responses of the real subjects. As might be expected from Asch's findings, they did. When the subjects gave their judgments aloud, they almost always followed the lead of the experimental accomplice and overestimated the number of dots presented on the screen.

Of more importance to our present concerns was the impact of the apparent competence of the confederate. The naive subjects were subtly led to believe that the other respondent was either very proficient or very incompetent at the dot estimation task. This manipulation was accomplished through a staged conversation that took place between the experimenter and his confederate just prior to starting the task. The experimenter appeared to recognize the accomplice and asked him whether he had not already participated in the experiment. The accomplice responded that indeed, he had served in a similar study earlier in the term, and had performed either very successfully ("You probably recognize me because I was the one who won the $9") or very poorly (the word *lost* was substituted for *won*). The experimenter always responded, "Right! That's why you looked so familiar." At this point, the experimenter was forced to explain to the naive subject that the other participant had been in a similar study conducted earlier; people in this earlier study could either win money or lose all that they were initially given, depending on the accuracy of their judgments.

Thus, in some instances, subjects were led to believe that their coworker was very competent at the task—that is, that he or she had been extremely accurate on a task very similar to the one that they were about to undertake—while others were given the opposite impression. This information had a marked impact on respondents' actions. Those subjects who were paired with the "expert" very quickly began to respond in a manner similar to that of their apparently proficient partner; but those whose partner had proved ineffective in the earlier experiment were more resistant to the social pressure that existed in the situation.

Even more interesting were the responses that the naive subjects made during a second phase of the study, when their judgments were made in private. In the initial part of the study, both subject and accomplice gave their judgments aloud after each slide presentation. In the second phase, however, judgments were written, so that neither could know how the other responded. If only the process of impingement had operated in this situation, the private responses of the subjects who had been paired with the "expert" would not have differed from those of the other subjects, since the procedures used in the second phase of the study did not provide the accomplice with the means to monitor the answers of the subject. Contrary to this possibility, however, the private responses of such subjects were not different from the earlier judgments that they had given aloud. That is, they continued to overestimate the number of dots by 30 percent. It was as if the expert were still there, telling them what to do even though he or she could not possibly know the subject's response. The subjects had internalized, or incorporated, the correct response rules that they had learned from their fellow (expert) respondent.

Why were such results obtained? To answer this question, it might be helpful for the reader to once again imagine being in the place of the subject. You are being asked to make a series of judgments about a set of extremely ambiguous stimuli. What factors are available to help you to successfully perform this task? First, of course, there are your perceptions of the stimuli themselves. But this information is such that you have little confidence in its validity. In addition, the task is relatively unique—you have had little, if any, previous experience at performing similar tasks.[4]

A second source of information available to you is provided by the responses of your fellow subject. In the present instance, the knowledge that your coworker is an expert at such judgments gives added weight to the information that he or she provides. A third consideration in your decision making is the increasing realization over trials that there exists a systematic discrepancy between the two major sources of information. Your perceptions of the number of dots, you realize, are considerably lower than those reported by the expert. Once this discrepancy becomes apparent, you are faced with somewhat of a dilemma. Do you trust your own perceptions, or those of the other person? The task in the present case was so ambiguous that you had little confidence in your own judgment; on the other hand, you have access to the perceptual judgments of a person who you believe to be very proficient at the task. Under these circumstances, it is quite reasonable for you to incorporate the expert's response strategy. What originally had seemed to you to be an overestimate became the correct perception. You had learned how to compensate for your own "faulty" perceptions by incorporating a decision strategy that was based on your interpretation of the actions of an expert. In other words, conformity involves the acceptance of another's views about the correct course of action, perception, or solution to a problem, in a given situation.

Opinion change. As noted, opinion change is a second major form of incorporation. This form of control is very similar to conformity, which involves beliefs about useful or adaptive actions. In contrast, opinion change focuses on the influence processes designed to change beliefs that, as noted in the first chapter, are concerned with the evaluation of people, objects, or qualities.

In discussing the processes of opinion change, we are faced with one of the most extensive literatures in social psychology. The literature relevant to opinion change, or persuasion, is so extensive, in fact, that a single research example cannot even begin to capture the diversity of methods and results

---

[4] See the discussion of the theme of Resolution (Chapter 3) for a more complete treatment of the influence of ambiguity on behavior.

contained in it.[5] Nonetheless, one example of a persuasion experiment should prove useful as a first step toward understanding opinion change as an instance of incorporation.

The example is one of the classic contributions of Carl Hovland and his associates in the Yale University Communication Research Program formed shortly after the end of World War II. In this particular study, Hovland and Weiss (1951) wanted to determine the effect that the credibility of a source of communication had on the acceptance of that message. The design of their study was quite simple and the results clear-cut.

In this experiment, subjects were presented with messages about a number of issues. For example, one message that was used advocated the feasibility of nuclear-powered submarines (this research was conducted in the early 1950s, before such vessels were a reality). Two groups of subjects read this communication: for one group, however, the message was attributed to Dr. J. Robert Oppenheimer, a noted and well-respected nuclear scientist; the other group received the exact message, but it was attributed to *Pravda*, the leading newspaper of the Soviet Union.

The point of the study was to determine whether the identical message would have varying impacts on the subjects' beliefs if it was attributed to different sources. As Hovland and Weiss expected, such differences, did in fact, occur: when the message was attributed to Oppenheimer (the credible source), it proved extremely persuasive, while little opinion change was evident among the subjects who were led to believe that the message came from *Pravda*. Through this and many subsequent studies, the immediate impact of communicator credibility on opinion change has been established firmly.

The choice of the Hovland and Weiss (1951) study as our example of opinion change research was purposive, as the variable that they examined—communicator credibility—allows us to make an important point. It should be obvious that credibility has features in common with the variable of competence, or expertise, that Crano (1970) explored in his experiment on conformity. While credibility and expertise were created in very different ways in the two studies, they share some important conceptual features. It appears likely that both mechanisms operate by providing cues to the quality of the information that the influencer is dispensing. One set of cues that people use to infer information quality is the characteristics of the source of the information. In the conformity situation, perceived competence has been shown to be an indicator of information quality; in persuasion, the expertness of the communicator operates in a similar manner. Although the processes of opinion change and conformity long have been studied as separate and discrete phenomena, the observed conceptual similarity between expertise and credibility suggests that they operate through a common underlying process. For this and other reasons, we feel that conformity and opinion change share a common theme, which we have termed incorporation.

In many instances, a change of opinion can have no observable impact

---

[5] The literature of opinion change, or persuasion, is treated in detail in Chapters 4 through 6.

on behavior. For example, after reading a number of technical reports on this year's new cars, you might change your mind about the best car on the road, from Jaguar to Porsche. However, as your total assets are contained in the change purse of your wallet, this opinion change is likely to have little impact on any of your overt actions beyond that of defending your new position to fellow car buffs.

In addition to the constraints that the Social Context (in this case, a lack of money) can impose on the expression of opinion, there exist other, equally powerful factors that can limit the link between opinion and behavior. Components of the Personal Structure, for instance, can limit the impact of opinion change because previously well-learned patterns of activity (habits) can inhibit the overt behavioral manifestation of the new belief. Unless the belief is salient (that is, of a high level), there is a very good chance that well-established response patterns will determine the behavior that is emitted in a given situation.

For example, a man might become very much in sympathy with the goals of the feminist movement in this country. However, because of his well-learned habits of interaction with women, he may, unaware, continue to engage in many acts of sexist discrimination. This same man who professes (and believes in) sexual equality may behave very differently toward his young son and daughter, solely on the basis of their sex. When the son arrives in the house crying over a skinned knee, the father might sympathize but tell him to bear up. When a similar catastrophe occurs with his daughter, he is much more solicitious and overtly affectionate. When confronted with this discrepancy between professed belief and observed action, the father might, as is typical of many people, deny that his behavior was, in fact, discriminatory. In this case, his beliefs would lead him to distort his perceptions of his own actions.

Socialization.   As with opinion change, there is extensive literature in psychology devoted to the study of socialization, the third major form of incorporation. Of long-standing interest to social and developmental psychologists have been the variables that affect the processes by which people, especially children, acquire the appropriate values and rules of behavior (norms) of the groups of which they are (usually new) members. There is a vast literature in this area; however, we will concentrate on a few variables that appear to play a major role in this type of incorporation.

A number of attempts at capturing the major factors involved in the socialization process have been proposed over the years, and of these, the model presented by Jones and Gerard (1967) is perhaps one of the most useful. In their scheme, two central variables mediate the extent to which socialization attempts are successful. Both involve a consideration of the extent to which the target of the Control attempt is dependent upon the influencer. One type of dependency, which Jones and Gerard (1967) have called *effect dependence,* concerns the degree to which the welfare of the target is under the control of the influencer.[6] In the development of their

---

[6] Thibuat and Kelley (1959) termed this power *fate control.*

theoretical framework, Jones and Gerard summarize and interpret considerable evidence to support the assertion that the greater the perceived effect dependence, the more likely the dependent person is to incorporate the values and norms of the person (or persons) who controls his or her fate.

In his brilliant and disturbing psychological analysis of Nazi concentration camps, Bruno Bettleheim (1943, 1979) provides us with dramatic examples of the role that effect dependence plays in socialization. Bettleheim, who was an inmate of a concentration camp, notes that many of the prisoners adopted behaviors that would appear inexplicable, perhaps even bizarre, to casual observers. Many inmates, for example, began to emulate their captors, the vicious Nazi Gestapo guards who constantly brutalized them. For instance, they made feeble attempts to modify their own prison garb in an effort to make them resemble that of their captors. As Bettleheim (1979, pp. 80–81) observed:

> Often the Gestapo would enforce nonsensical rules, originating in the whims of the guards. They were usually forgotten as soon as formulated, but there were always some old prisoners who would continue to follow these rules and try to enforce them on others long after the Gestapo had forgotten about them. These prisoners firmly believed that the rules set down by the Gestapo were desirable standards of human behavior, at least in the camp situation.

For example, Bettleheim reports that on one occasion, a guard forced the prisoners to wash their leather shoes! The guard soon tired of this brutal prank, but one prisoner persisted in this nonadaptive act for many weeks thereafter. Moreover, he chided his fellow inmates for not continuing to do what was appropriate.

There are a number of reasons for this rather extreme form of socialization. In our view, a major determinant of the prisoners' behavior was the almost total control over their fate that the Gestapo guards exercised. Prisoners were constantly reminded of their own powerlessness through the brutal and capricious acts of their captors. All of the basic necessities of life were under the control of the guards. Their captors could do anything to them; they were completely defenseless. Under such circumstances of extreme effect dependence, it is little wonder that the prisoners incorporated the norms of their captors.

Jones and Gerard (1967) termed a second factor in the socialization process *information dependence,* referring to the extent to which a person relies on the information, interpetations, and advice of the socializing agent in coming to grips with the Social Context. As with effect dependence, Jones and Gerard have convincingly demonstrated that as information dependence increases, the likelihood of successful socialization also increases.

In concentration camps and similar environments—custodial institutions such as jails and prisons—the major goal is the isolation of "undesirables" from the rest of society. While, as noted, those incarcerated in such settings often adopt the norms of the captors, such socialization processes rarely are the central concern of the captors. In contrast, there are some situations (which share many of the features of custodial institutions) in which the people in power explicitly and comprehensively attempt to modify the beliefs and subsequent actions of their captives. One of the most dramatic examples of the operation of socialization processes in such settings is *brainwashing*. In this extreme form of Control, a person is subjected to a number of techniques whose central purpose is to change his or her fundamental beliefs.

Some of the tactics that many so-called religious cults use to acquire new members are more subtle cases of the operation of the same socialization processes. The following example provides an illustration of a set of techniques that appear common to the way that such cults recruit potential converts.

AT HOME WITH BELMONT AND THE DIONS

Suppose that while walking down the street one day, you ran into an old acquaintance from your past. You notice that though dressed somewhat

Reprinted by permission *The Wall Street Journal*

"I'd like to see Reverend Moon try to indoctrinate you!"

Not everyone is equally susceptible to incorporation tactics.

strangely and using some peculiar language, she seems happier than you had remembered her as being. She invites you to spend some time with a group of her new-found friends. You agree and soon find yourself in the commune-like setting of the Dions, a cult whose fundamental precept is the notion of the divine inspiration of rock and roll music. You vaguely recall reading about this group some time ago in *Rolling Stone* magazine, and your initial reaction is one of curiosity accompanied by a small dose of anxiety.

The group members all seem quite interested in you and in making sure that you feel at home in their company. Over and over again, members of the group tell you how happy they are that you could be with them and how much they look forward to being with you. After a while, in the face of this series of very pleasant encounters, you decide to accept their invitation to stay for dinner. After the dinner, which was remarkable only because every course was served on old 78 records, the people sitting near you begin to tell you something about their beliefs. Some of what they are saying to you sounds really strange—the "universal 4/4 beat" that permeates the cosmos—while other aspects of their credo, like a belief in the goodness of all living things, appear more reasonable.

Soon you realize that it is very late, and you begin to make motions to leave. This activity sends waves of consternation through the ranks of your new-found friends. One after another of them, including their leader, Belmont, implores you to stay just a little bit longer. After some hesitation, you agree to spend the night with them.

A party of sorts then begins, partly in celebration of your decision to remain. All the while, various bits of the code are being presented and discussed with you. At the same time, continuous rock and roll music is blaring forth from the 16 speakers arrayed around the room. You are quite sleepy, but every time you make a move to retire, it becomes apparent that your absence would put a damper on the fun. Accordingly, you remain awake for the entire night. At about 9 A.M., you decide that you have had enough, and you start for the door. Almost en masse, the group surrounds you, and begs you to stay with them. You explain that you are extremely tired, to which Belmont replies, "If you stay, we'll take care of you, and you'll never feel tired again." For some reason, perhaps because of your depleted condition, Belmont's words bring tears to your eyes (after all, it's your party, and you can cry if you want to). After considerable self-reflection, you agree to put yourself in their hands—at least for the time being. They show you to a bed, and you sink gratefully into a blissful sleep.

Sometime later, you are not sure when, you awaken to the sounds of rock-and-roll music playing softly in the distance. You get up and try to leave, but once again you are surrounded and pressed to remain. The pattern of the first night is repeated for the next few days. Every time you appear to wish to contact someone outside of the group or to leave, a tremendous amount of social pressure is directed against such actions. You never are told explicitly that you cannot leave or cannot phone an "outsider," but it is clear that such actions would displease those around you. As was documented above, such social pressure can have a very strong effect on people's actions.

Slowly, you come to see the people in the commune as your sole contacts with the outside. Moreover, you begin to realize that while you remain in the house, you are entirely dependent on the group for such necessities as food, sleep, and companionship. Further, you realize that almost every minute of your day and night is run according to some prearranged schedule; you have no time to yourself; it seems that someone is always with you, explaining the mission of the group.

After the passage of some time—you cannot tell how much since you have lost track of how long you have been staying with the Dions—you stop having thoughts about leaving. Perhaps of even greater importance, you now understand the nature of the group and have come to see the truth of their beliefs. Ideas that had seemed silly when you first heard them now make a great deal of sense. Finally, you decide that for you, rock and roll is here to stay; you decide to become a full-fledged member of the cult. You renounce your old name, pledge to destroy all your Barry Manilow albums, and begin to actively help your group by seeking out new souls to save.

FACTORS IN SOCIALIZATION

Our somewhat flippant example is provided to portray three processes that operate in the making of a cult member. The basic precondition for these processes to operate is the physical isolation of the potential convert from his or her customary sources of support, both physical and psychological. This isolation puts the convert-to-be in the hands of those who can control the information flow and the necessary physical amenities. In a context such as this, it is fairly easy for influencers to use mechanisms of impingement to control the actions of the novice. As can be seen from our example, many of these mechanisms are focused on insuring that the newcomer does not leave the scene. In the story, the impingement mechanism of social pressure is applied primarily through the actions of the cult members, who are unanimous in their reluctance to see their new friend leave and who carefully monitor the convert's every action.

Once the pattern of being there has been established, the more subtle but long-lasting effects of the incorporation processes can be applied fully. As was portrayed in the story, the Dions had complete control over what the novice heard and saw. This power generated, in Jones and Gerard's (1967) terms, a tremendous amount of *information dependence* in the newcomer. In addition, the very real isolation from the outside world made the novice completely dependent on the cult for satisfaction of fundamental physical and psychological needs; that is, these conditions place the recruit in a state of effect dependence. Taken together, this tremendous degree of information and effect dependence provided the force necessary to insure the new recruit's incorporation of the group's code of beliefs.

A subtle point in the preceding paragraph should be stressed. Notice that the social pressure applied to control the actions of the newcomer, over a period of time, came to modify the newcomer's beliefs; that is, after repeated impingements, the novice stopped thinking about leaving the commune setting. As noted, impingements are focused strictly on those tactics that moderate overt behavior. However, as in the example, there are conditions under which an impingement can have an indirect effect on beliefs (incorporation). These conditions generally involve situations in which the impingement is long-term, subtle, and pervasive.[7] Recent real-life examples, such as the brief political conversion of the kidnapped Patricia Hearst and the mass suicide of hundreds of People's Temple "believers" at Jonestown, attest to the strength of long-term impingements on incorporation and ultimately on behavior.

The related phenomena of brainwashing and religious conversion are extreme examples of some relatively commonplace socialization processes. While somewhat less severe, typical child-rearing practices involve among other processes many of the same techniques. Parents have almost complete effect control over their infants and young children, and their control over the information that is transmitted to their offspring is almost equally as pervasive. Given the long-term nature of the parent-child relationship, the severity of the expression of such Control need not be great to have a powerful shaping influence on the developing child. Finally, it should be noted that other Social Contexts (the Army, fraternities and sororities, medical school, and so on) are similar to the family with regard to the Control mechanisms that such organizations have at their disposal.

This concludes our formal development and discussion of the interpersonal theme of Control, which is focused most specifically on those processes that people use to influence each other's actions in social encounters. In the following section, we turn our attention to a theme that is concerned with the manner in which interpersonal encounters affect people's feelings about one another.

THE THEME OF SENTIMENT

Sentiment, the final theme to be discussed in this chapter, refers to the attachment of positive or negative emotion to other people. As noted in Chapter 1, emotion is a component of our Personal Structure that consists of our interpretations of our physiological states. Positive emotions are those that connote pleasantness or pleasure, and they are motivating because we seek to experience them. Negative emotions are feelings that have aversive, painful,

---

[7] A more detailed discussion of this conversion of impingement to incorporation is presented in Chapter 5.

or other noxious components, and like the positive emotions, they also are motivating, since we seek to avoid experiencing them.

Sentiment involves a specific subset of emotions—namely, *affection* and *repulsion*. A Sentiment relationship is one that produces an emotional reaction in us: if positive, we call this reaction affection (in the broadest sense); if negative, repulsion. Because of the amorphous nature of emotional reactions, it is difficult to deal with Sentiment in a systematic way. However, this theme represents perhaps the major human concern, and as such, it has been explored at length by philosophers and social psychologists as well as novelists and song writers.

Because of its central place in human experience, we would have been remiss had we not included Sentiment among the major themes of social psychology. We will explore some of Sentiment's major implications in Section 3 of this text and thus need not present in detail here the major empirical and theoretical treatments that have focused on this theme. Our goal in the present section, therefore, is to outline the antecedents and consequences of Sentiment and to provide some examples of its operation.

ANTECEDENTS OF SENTIMENT

A number of factors produce affectional and repulsive Sentimental reactions. Some of the antecedents are acute in nature, in that the reaction to the object of the Sentiment occurs rather quickly, sometimes on first meeting. The phenomenon of love at first sight is one example of these acute processes. Other antecedents are of a more long-term and perhaps subtle character. The formation of friendships often involves variables that operate over extended periods. Many sentimental relationships, of course, are the result of both acute and extended processes. We presume that those relationships that are a consequence of only the more acute factors probably are not as persistent as those that share both components. (Often, however, they are lots of fun.)

Acute Antecedents

Cue Similarity.   The variable that perhaps has the greatest impact on acute Sentimental reactions is *cue similarity*. By this term we mean that people tend to have emotional reactions to strangers to the extent that they resemble in some critical ways people from their past with whom they had formed strong Sentimental attachments. In more technical psychological terminology, this process has been labeled *stimulus generalization*. Because emotional reactions typically are not under our voluntary control, cue similarity operates more or less automatically, often without our awareness of it.

For instance, consider the case of a young boy meeting his third-grade teacher for the first time. He feels vaguely uneasy and surprised, because he finds himself strongly attracted to her. He is experiencing what has come to be known as a schoolboy crush. Why? Although he might not be consciously aware of this, the teacher bears a slight physical resemblance to his favorite aunt and wears the same perfume as she wears. Obviously, there are many possible causes for the intensity of the boy's response, but one of more powerful antecedents of the Sentimental reaction no doubt is the similarity between the teacher and the boy's favorite aunt. The teacher is clearly younger than the boy's aunt, and she is shorter, thinner, and so forth, but she resembles her in enough aspects that there are sufficient cues to trigger the emotional reaction in the boy.

As noted, cue similarity can also operate as one of the factors that produce the phenomenon in adults known as love at first sight. This acute Sentimental response to a decidedly novel stimulus is often the result of similarities between the new-found object of affection and a person (or people) from the past with whom the perceiver had strong Sentimental ties. Usually, the perceiver is not aware of the similarities, indeed would argue that no such connection exists. These similarities tend to involve physical cues, because such aspects as physical appearance, voice quality, and posture, are so readily perceived.

Motive Prepotency. A second factor in acute Sentimental attachment is *motive prepotency.* Konrad Lorenz (1966), the Nobel prize winning ethologist, has speculated that the longer a motive remains unsatisfied, the less appropriate a stimulus has to be to trigger it. *Motive prepotency* can contribute to the phenomenon of love at first sight, since the acute responses of the victims of this affliction often result from the prepotency of their deprived affiliative need (i.e., the need to be with someone). The following scenerio illustrates this possibility.

Most of us are familiar with situations of the following sort: Your roommate recently has experienced an end to a long-term romantic entanglement. She has not been on a date since that time, nor has she really had much opportunity to interact with men in any but the most superficial and transitory encounters. After two months of this deprivation, you convince her to accompany you to a party. At the party, she stands around for a while, obviously uncomfortable. She knows no one but you, and nobody is paying much attention to her. After a few minutes, a man walks by and smiles at her as he passes. She smiles back, and a few moments later, he returns with two drinks and offers her one. They spend an hour together making polite conversation, after which the man apologetically explains that he has to leave for work. Later that evening, you are surprised to find that your roommate has found the man of her dreams—after one hour's conversation! How? Cue similarity might have played a part, but the prepotency of your roommate's affiliation need obviously was also an important determinant of her acute affectional reaction.

While it is difficult to scientifically investigate such a powerful but elusive phenomenon, James Pennebaker and his colleagues (1979) have provided an interesting study of the impact of need prepotency on at least one facet of love at first sight, the perceived attractiveness of another person. As might be expected, attractiveness is a major force in the love at first sight phenomenon.

In this study, Pennebaker et al. (1979) asked patrons of a number of different bars to rate the attractiveness of individuals of the other sex whom they had observed that night. Male researchers approached male patrons and asked them to "rate, on a scale from 1 to 10, the women here tonight." Likewise, female researchers approached female patrons and asked for ratings of the men in the bar. Various patrons were queried at three different times: early evening, in the middle of the evening, and just before the bar closed. Subjects' ratings of the attractiveness of the others in the bar were found to vary as a result of the time of night at which they were collected. Summarizing their findings, Pennebaker and his colleagues note in the title of their article, "the girls get prettier at closing time."[8]

If we assume that those persons who responded just before the bar closed had spent the longest time there, then these results well could be attributed to the heightened motive prepotency of these respondents, relative to those measured earlier in the evening. No doubt many of the men and women who participated in the study were at the bar because of a desire for companionship. Those who still were alone at the end of the evening probably felt this need more acutely than those who were queried at the beginning of the evening. Moreover, added to the need prepotency of the "unsuccessful" respondents was the anticipation of a long, lonely night in which their affiliative (and related) needs would remain unsatisfied. At the end of the evening, their chances of altering this unfortunate circumstance were not as good as those of the patrons who, earlier, still had the bulk of the evening before them. For these reasons, motive prepotency enhanced the apparent attractiveness of the respondents' potential companions.

Mislabeled Arousal.   Mislabeled arousal can also play an important role in the development of acute Sentimental attachment. Such arousal is an erroneous interpretation that we make about a physiological reaction. In such instances, we experience some change in our body state while in the presence of another, and we incorrectly label or interpret the feelings that are aroused. For example, the increased heart rate that an individual might experience as a result of an argument with an attractive but aggressive person of the other sex might be misidentified as love rather than anger. This process is related to, but distinct from, motive prepotency: in the latter case, a set of cues triggers a reaction that is disproportionate to the strength of those cues; in the case of mislabeled arousal, the person who experiences the emotion misidentifies the cues that caused it and/or misinterprets the physiological bases of the reaction.

To more fully illustrate the mechanism of mislabeled arousal, let us return to the example of the young woman who fell in love after a brief encounter at a party. Recall that she felt lonely and slightly ill at ease when she arrived. When the young man passed by and smiled in her direction, this act no doubt triggered a complicated physiological response, which at

---

[8] We should add that they found that, from the viewpoint of the female patrons, the boys got prettier, too!

least in part consisted of the body changes that accompany feelings of anxiety. These feelings, however, given the circumstances of their arousal, were mislabeled—the young woman interpreted her physical state as a positive Sentimental response, attraction. In a similar way, she might have experienced some sexual arousal during her conversation with her new acquaintance but misinterpreted these physiological responses as at least somewhat affiliative rather than as entirely sexual in nature. In this instance, lust was interpreted as love.

Reward Expectation. The expectation that another person will be the source of reward or motive satisfaction also can stimulate an emotional reaction in people. Such reward expectations can foster positive reactions in an individual because the anticipation of such rewards is, in itself, a pleasant experience. Furthermore, in a more complicated manner, the expectation can trigger a positive reaction in an individual to the extent that in the past, similar good feelings were associated with experiencing the reward. For example, the young woman who experienced love at first sight in the example probably expected that her new-found friend would provide her with rewards similar in intensity and type to those that she had experienced with her former love. This anticipation was in itself rewarding, and in addition, it motivated her to seek further interactions with the new source of expected reward.

One set of cues that leads to expectations of reward is physical appearance. People use the physical attractiveness of others with whom they have had little past contact as an indicator of the rewards that they are likely to experience if they were to establish an extended relationship with them.[9] Research on the effects of physical appearance on impressions of others supports the observation that this variable does play a role in reward expectation. As Karen Dion, Ellen Berscheid, Elaine Walster Hatfield, and many others have demonstrated, we associate physical beauty with positive personal characteristics, and ugliness with negative traits. We expect that people who are physically attractive also will have Personal Structures that consist of a host of valued and rewarding characteristics—intelligence, loyalty, honesty, charm, warmth, humor, and so on. Since we have learned that associating with people who possess these traits leads to rewarding outcomes, we expect that associating with attractive people will prove to be rewarding. In contrast, people who are physically unattractive often are presumed to be dishonest, stupid, socially unskilled, and so forth; thus, we expect that associating with unattractive people will be unrewarding if not downright unpleasant.

A study by Karen Dion (1972) indicates that people use the physical attractiveness of others to attribute personal characteristics to them. In her study, Dion asked a large number of undergraduate female respondents to evaluate the behavior of seven-year-old children. The descriptions of the children's actions allegedly were random selections from teachers' daily journal

---

[9] We will discuss this issue in detail in Chapter 12, which is concerned with the antecedents and consequences of interpersonal attraction.

Isn't it hard to believe that this beautiful child would intentionally hurt an innocent dog?

reports of classroom and playground disturbances. One of the episodes that Dion presented to her subjects, for example, read as follows:

> At one corner of the playground a dog was sleeping. Peter stood a short distance from the dog, picked up some sharp stones from the ground, and threw them at the animal. Two of the stones struck the dog and cut its leg. The animal jumped up yelping and limped away. Peter continued to throw rocks at it as it tried to move away from him (Dion, 1972, p. 210).

A picture of the misbehaving child accompanied the written description of this and every other incident that was presented. In actuality, the children pictured had nothing to do with the incidents; pictures were chosen to represent a range of attractiveness. Thus some subjects were given a picture of a very attractive child along with the description of the disturbance, while other respondents read the same description accompanied by a photograph of a very unattractive child.

The central question of the research was whether the experimental variation of the children's attractiveness affected subjects' evaluation of the Personal Structures of the misbehaving children. The results of Dion's study in fact demonstrated that the physical attractiveness of the children had a significant impact on respondents' evaluations of them. Antisocial tendencies were much more likely to be seen as consistent aspects of the unattractive children's Personal Structures, while the respondents were more willing to give the attractive children the benefit of the doubt. The destructive actions described were seen as less characteristic of the attractive than of the unattractive children. In addition, attractive children were evaluated as more honest and more pleasant than were their unattractive counterparts. We must reemphasize that these results occurred despite the fact that the actions that were attributed to the attractive and unattractive children were identical; the only difference between the two groups was in the pictures that supposedly depicted them.

Subsequent research (Berscheid & Walster, 1974; Dion, Berscheid, & Walster, 1972; Schneider, Hastorf, & Ellsworth, 1979; Snyder, Tanke, & Berscheid, 1977) has confirmed and extended Dion's findings: we attribute positive and negative personal characteristics to others as a function of their physical appearance. These evaluations have an impact on the rewards that we anticipate from a relationship with another, and hence, they can affect our emotional reactions to the person.

Obviously, the reward expectations that we form on the basis of physical appearance and other variables can be distorted or one-sided. The young woman discussed earlier might have fallen in love with a man she had known for less than two hours, in part because she failed to recall all of the trouble and heartache that her former boyfriends had caused her. Such recollections probably would have been painful—that is, they would have triggered a negative emotional reaction—and so they were avoided. Avoiding unpleasant memories can inhibit the negative emotions that are associated with such unhappy past events. However, this mechanism does not always operate perfectly, and for this and other reasons, negative Sentimental reactions or feelings of repulsion do occur.

Negative Reactions. To this point, our discussion of acute antecedents to Sentimental attachments has been positive in nature. These same basic processes, however, can operate to generate feelings of repulsion. Cue similarity, for example, can produce in us strong negative feelings about another, based on his or her similarity to someone from our past whom we detest. Similarly, the other acute processes involved in Sentiment formation—motive prepotency, reward expectation, mislabeled arousal—can operate to produce negative Sentiments. For the sake of brevity, we will examine evidence related to only one such process—mislabeled arousal.

As empirical research has shown, mislabeled arousal can generate negative as well as positive Sentimental reactions. For example, numerous studies (Barclay, 1971a, 1971b; Donnerstein & Barrett, 1978; Donnerstein & Hallam, 1978; Jaffe, Malamuth, Feingold, & Feshbach, 1974; Zillman, 1971) have demonstrated that sexual arousal can be mislabeled as anger or aggression, and vice versa. Yoram Jaffe and his colleagues (1974) provide a dramatic example of the mislabeling of arousal, in this case, sexual arousal. Male and female subjects in this study read one of two types of materials: one group of subjects was provided with a series of three erotic passages, whereas the other group read a short science fiction selection. This experimental manipulation had the intended effect, as those who had read the erotic material reported feeling more sexually aroused, affectionate, and playful, than their counterparts.

The playful, affectionate mood of the erotically aroused subjects appeared to change, however, when they were introduced into a new Social Context, that of a shock administration task similar to Milgram's, in which they played the role of the teacher. In this second phase of the study, subjects were to shock another participant for his or her mistakes in an experimental task. Subjects were free to choose the shock level that they thought was appropriate, and the average level that a subject used to punish the victim for mistakes was used as a behavioral measure of his or her aggressiveness.[10]

This study yielded a number of interesting results. For example, on the average, male subjects delivered higher shock levels than did females. Of most relevance to our discussion was the finding that the erotically aroused subjects used higher levels of shock in punishing the errors of the victims than did their nonaroused counterparts. Furthermore, this effect could not be attributed entirely to the sexual frustration that the aroused subjects might have felt as a result of their exposure to the erotic materials, since the nonaroused subjects had reported that they felt more frustrated than did the erotically aroused group. Apparently, subjects aroused by the sexually explicit material had mislabeled their reaction when they were placed in the teacher/victim context. It seems reasonable to speculate that the cues in this situation (the shock generator, the experimenter's instructions, and so on) produced in the erotically aroused subjects an alternative interpretation of their internal body states.

Personification.   The last issue to be addressed in our discussion of the acute antecedents of Sentiment involves the object of the Sentiment. Although all of our examples of Sentimental reactions have involved other people as the source and recipient of our feelings, we must note that people can and do react similarly to animals, plants, and even inanimate objects. In our view, the factors that underlie attachment to nonhuman objects are the same as those involved in interpersonal Sentimental relationships. In the case of such attachments (to pets, plants, prized automobiles, and so on) the person tends to humanize or personify the object of the Sentiment. Pets, cars, and plants are given names, spoken to, and treated as if they had human feelings. When an individual personifies an object in this manner, it becomes available for the attachment of Sentiment. The converse also is true: Sentimental feelings for an object can facilitate the personification of the object. At first, a cute little puppy is treated as a cute little puppy; after a few days, it becomes one of the family.

---

[10] As in the Milgram (1963, 1964, 1965, 1974) studies discussed earlier, no shocks ever actually were delivered to the victim (who was an accomplice of the experimenter). The real subjects, of course, did not know this at the time of the experiment.

It's easy to understand why Rolphie is treated as one of the family.

Although we have focused only on the acute antecedents of Sentiment, it should be noted that personification is relevant to both acute and extended antecedents. This observation should be kept in mind when reading the following section, which presents the major extended antecedents of Sentimental attachments.

Extended Antecedents

Opportunity. The most basic of the extended processes that moderate emotional attachment is the opportunity to interact or experience the target of the attachment. The more opportunity one has to deal with the object of a Sentimental attachment, the greater the probability of some (positive or negative) modification of the Sentiment. Homans (1950) asserts that interaction and Sentiment have a reciprocal relationship: positive Sentimental attachment causes one to wish to be with the target of the feeling; and the greater the amount of interaction with another, the more positive the Sentiment generated.

While we find the first part of Homan's assertion reasonable, the second part appears too narrow to us. Intense or extended interactions with another well might produce increased affection. On the other hand, such encounters also can produce intense negative Sentiment, or repulsion. The point of our disagreement with Homans lies in his assumption that people would not interact with someone whom they had grown to dislike. It is obvious that most of us would prefer to avoid such encounters, but the force of circumstance often thrusts them upon us. Sometimes, in fact, such quirks of fate work to our advantage in that we overcome our initial negative feelings and form an affectionate tie with the originally disliked other.

It is difficult to study the impact of opportunity on Sentiment formation systematically since, by their very nature, this and the other extended antecedents of emotional attachment take a considerable amount of time to evolve. To study opportunity and Sentiment comprehensively would require the intensive observation of large numbers of people over many interpersonal encounters; however, social psychologists have begun to examine this process, though in a less protracted and comprehensive fashion than is ideal.

In one of the more interesting of these investigations, Chester Insko and Midge Wilson (1977) constructed a laboratory demonstration in which constraints were placed on the permissible interaction opportunities within three-person groups of subjects. In this demonstration, three subjects were seated facing each other in close proximity and were asked to get to know one another. However, Insko and Wilson imposed some limitations on the conversation flow such that two of the three subjects in a triad were forbidden from talking to each other. That is, subjects A and B had the opportunity to interact with one another; likewise, subjects B and C could converse; but A and C could not. After a period in which they were allowed to interact in this fashion, each subject was asked to indicate in private how well he or she liked the other members of the triad. Interestingly, those subjects who had been allowed to talk with each other liked each other more than those who were not permitted to do so. Thus, even within the limited context of the social psychological laboratory and within the brief duration of the interaction, we find that opportunity had a striking effect on subjects' feelings about one another.

There has been one variable related to opportunity that has been examined rather comprehensively over a long span of years—namely, proximity (Bossard, 1932; Festinger, Schachter, & Back, 1950; Katz & Hill, 1958; Priest & Sawyer, 1967). Proximity refers to the actual geographic distance that separates two potential interactants. Obviously, the greater the distance that separates two people, the less opportunity they will have for interaction.

An example of one such investigation is provided in the work of Robert Priest and Jack Sawyer (1967), who examined friendship patterns among the residents of a 320-man dormitory at the University of Chicago. In this study, which extended over four years, dorm residents were asked every fall and spring to complete a set of questionnaires. Some of the items dealt with respondents' backgrounds but most were focused on issues of friendship choice. For example, each respondent was asked to name his best friend and four men in the dorm whom he liked next best. After this, the respondent was asked to read a complete list of the names of all the men of the dorm and to note those whom he recognized, those whom he talked to at least once a week, and those whom he liked.

Priest and Sawyer then examined the friendship choices in light of the actual physical distance between respondents' dorm rooms and those of all of the other dorm residents.

Priest and Sawyer's study of friendship choices within this dorm yielded a wealth of support for the proximity-Sentiment relationship. For example, responses showed a pattern of decreased liking with increased distance: 93 percent of the respondents indicated that they liked their roommate; 45 percent indicated that they liked their floormates; and only 16 percent indicated that they liked other dorm residents who did not reside on the same floor. Since proximity is a major determinant of the opportunity to interact, it is not surprising that there would be a positive relationship between physical distance and Sentiment in this study. Unlike some other Social Contexts, each dorm resident was relatively free to choose to interact with or to avoid the other 319 men who lived in the same building. Thus, the ease with which such encounters could occur was a major factor in determining the patterns of interaction that actually did take place.

Association. In the description above, we alluded to another important component in long-term attachment processes, namely association. This concept refers to the conditioning processes by which positive or negative feelings become attached to a stimulus person or object. These conditioning processes involve a repeated association between the stimulus object and positive or negative outcomes, which leads to the Sentiment. The association between stimulus and outcomes most often comes about because the stimulus (the other person) is, in fact, the source of the outcomes. Typically, this process results in the establishment of positive Sentiment, as people tend to avoid stimuli that are associated with negative reactions.

Thus, to the extent that a continuing interpersonal relationship is voluntary, it is likely to produce positive Sentiment. If an individual with whom we could interact fails to provide such rewards or, in fact, is associated with negative outcomes, it is unlikely that a continuing relationship would be established or maintained.

Based upon extensive evidence derived from the animal and human learning research literature, social psychologists generally accept the proposition that a person's association with reward or punishment will affect another individual's Sentiment toward that person. Much of this work has been performed by Albert and Bernice Lott. One of their studies should serve to illustrate their general approach.

In this study, Lott and Lott (1960) examined the degree to which positive sentiment was associated with a positive social experience. Three-member groups of children were differentially rewarded for their performance in an experimental game. Some children, in other words, experienced a higher proportion of success than did others. When asked later how much they liked their coworkers, the successful (rewarded) children reported more positive feelings toward the other children in the group than did their unsuccessful (unrewarded) counterparts.

Other studies have replicated the relationship between being associated with a positive outcome and Sentiment. For example, Bridgeman (1972) found that college students who were rewarded for task performance liked the person who dispensed the reward more than did students who received no reward.

Studies of the association between reward and Sentiment typically have been conducted within the rather restricted context of the social psychological laboratory. To lend some real-life substance to the outcomes of this research, consider the following common scenerio. In this situation, two strangers meet, and over the course of time, they become friends. At first meeting, each probably formed a favorable initial impression of the other, due in part to the acute Sentiment processes discussed earlier. Perhaps for this reason, they continued to interact and to engage in activities together. Mutual positive Sentiment between these two people will develop to the extent that they engage in activities they find rewarding. Viewed from the perspective of one of them (call him Ishmael), the fact that the other person laughs at all of his jokes is a very positive outcome for a number of reasons. First, it provides a Social Context in which Ishmael can feel comfortable about telling jokes, an activity that he values. Second, the other's typical response to a joke—laughter—satisfies a number of Ishmael's needs or motives: his need for esteem, affiliation, competence, and so on. Likewise, the fact that both people enjoy the same activities (watching football games, drinking beer) provides each of them with rewards that are experienced in the presence of each other, and enhanced to some degree by their being shared. That is, both probably find it more fun to watch games and drink beer when the other is present.

In a similar way, the extent to which negative outcomes are associated with the stimulus person determines the extent to which negative Sentiment will be attached to that person. In his introductory lectures on social psychology, which both authors were privileged to attend, Donald Campbell provided an interesting example of the development of negative attachment through the association process. While studying the behavior of Navy officers, Campbell noticed a particularly crafty communication tactic that many ship captains practiced. Whenever bad news of any sort had to be announced to the crew of the ship (canceled leaves, extended tours of duty, punishment details, and so on), the captains always delegated this task to their executive officers (their chief assistant on the ship). The men soon associated the "execs" with bad news and grew to dislike them, even though in actuality the execs rarely were responsible for the unpleasantness; they were merely the bearers of bad tidings. On the other hand, the captains were sure to announce whatever good news there was to share with the men. In consequence, the Sentiments of the crew generally were much more positive toward the captain than toward his exec.

Both of our examples of the effects of association are somewhat simplistic, because in most long-term interpersonal interactions, both positive and negative outcomes occur over the course of an extended relationship. The Sentiment that develops typically is a weighted composite of a vast number of positive and negative outcomes. We assume that strong positive Sentiment is the result of an overwhelming ratio of positive to negative associations or outcomes, while less intense feelings are generated by a less disproportionate ratio of positive and negative associations.

CONSEQUENCES OF SENTIMENT

There are three central, interrelated consequences of Sentiment attachment to be discussed here. We will concentrate on positive attachments, perhaps because their consequences are more pleasant to think about than are relationships that are based on negative Sentiments. However, the reader should understand that the general consequences of Sentiment presented apply to negative as well as positive reactions.[11]

Sentiment as a Motivator. One of the most important consequences of Sentiment attachment is that the objects of our affection develop motivating properties; that is, because their psychological presence is a source of positive emotional feelings in us, we seek to generate these feelings by being with positively valued others. For example, people often appear willing to expend a great deal of effort to be with their friends. Why? Because their company is rewarding, and thus their presence is motivating. Conversely, we also are motivated to avoid the aversive reactions generated by objects of repulsion, and we do so by avoiding them physically (not interacting with them) and psychologically (not thinking about them).

Unit Relationships. The second major consequence of Sentiment attachment is the generation of a unit relationship, in Heider's (1958) terms. By unit relation, we mean the formation of a bond between individuals (or between an individual and some object) such that a perceiver, whether a part of the relationship or not, sees the persons in the relationship as interdependent or as constituting a larger whole. Two individuals who are known to have formed a positive and long-term Sentiment relationship are seen by themselves and by those who know them as an entity, or social unit. It is difficult to think about one of these people without thinking of the other. Society can formalize such unit bonds through such institutions as marriage and legal partnerships; while many unit relations are not formalized in this way, they nevertheless have a major impact on social behavior (Jordan, 1968).

An obvious but important implication of the unit bond is that the opportunities for interaction in a unit relationship are appreciably enhanced. This increase in interaction opportunity carries with it the possibility of either positive or negative modifications of the Sentiment relationship. That is, it is in unit relationship situations that Sentiment bonds can be stretched and severed, or stretched and strengthened. For example, most of us know of high school friends who room together their first year at college. Deciding to room together and signing a contract for the dormitory room or apartment were consequences of the unit relationship that existed between them. Living together in this way brings the two friends into much closer contact with

---

[11] Also discussed in detail in Chapter 13 are some of the implications of negative sentiment.

Abe and Marge, who have enjoyed a long term Sentiment relationship, are seen by themselves and others as a social unit.

one another than they had experienced before. This increase in the intensity and frequency of interaction can have one of two consequences. The friendship might become even more solid as a function of the increase in positive Sentiment that develops out of these encounters, or because of the nature of the encounters, the friends might come to like each other less, to dislike or even hate each other.

The Welfare of Others.   The final consequence of Sentiment attachment involves the generation of concern for the welfare of the object of affection. Such concern can be seen as a nonobvious form of self-interest, in that the well-being of a valued other has direct implications for one's own well-being. On the other hand, such concern can be a form of pure altruism, in that one's own welfare is not considered when thinking about the other. A father's concern for his sick child has some self-interested components, but on the whole, this concern often is likely to be altruistic in nature.

A study by Cookie Stephan, James Kennedy, and Elliot Aronson (1977) illustrates that a major consequence of positive Sentiment is the concern for the welfare and feelings of the other. Subjects in this study were sixth-grade students who played a bean bag tossing game. Success was rewarded with candy bars. Children played the game in pairs under conditions that fostered either competition or independence. In the competitive condition, pair members were pitted against each other, such that the child who performed better won the candy. In the independent condition, success or failure was measured against an absolute criterion; thus, either or both of the children in a dyad could succeed or fail at the task. Half of the subject pairs consisted of friends, while the other half was composed of children who knew each other but were not particularly friendly.

For our purposes, the major results involved the attributions that children made to account for their performance. The children were asked, "Do you think that doing well on this test was a matter of luck or skill?" Responses to this question indicated that friends in the competitive condition of the study were less willing to attribute their success to skill than were the children who had succeeded against a nonfriend. In contrast, in the independence condition, the subjects who had been paired with a friend and had succeeded were more willing to attribute their good performance to skill than were the subjects who had defeated a friend in the competitive condition.

These findings demonstrate that the thrill of victory is tempered by issues of Sentiment when the person who is experiencing the agony of defeat is a friend. Subjects were somewhat reluctant to admit that a difference in skill was responsible for their victory over a friend, while this reluctance was not evident when the subject had competed against, and defeated, a nonfriend. This reluctance indicates to us a concern for the welfare and feelings of a friend.

A point closely related to the issue of Sentiment fostering interpersonal concern is the proposition that a sense of empathy develops between those who share strong affectional ties. Empathy in this sense is the sharing of an emotional reaction that another is experiencing. When a person to whom we are attached feels good, we feel good; when he or she feels bad, so do we. This contagion of emotional experience can come about as a consequence of the Sentiment relationship. Thus, Sentiment attachment can give rise to the very human processes of altruism and empathy. On the negative side of the coin, it also should be noted that the attachment of negative Sentiment (repulsion) is responsible for the unfortunately also very human processes of *hostility* and *indifference*.[12]

CONCLUDING REMARKS

This concludes our discussion of Control and Sentiment, two themes whose central focus is interpersonal in nature. In the next chapter, we will turn our attention to three themes whose major emphasis is on the more cognitive features of social experience.

We must emphasize that the classification of themes into cognitive and interpersonal categories was motivated principally by the need to provide readers with chapters of reasonable length. Clearly, we have discussed a number of cognitive factors in the present chapter, just as we discuss many interpersonal issues concerning the cognitive themes in Chapter 3. As we

---

[12] A closer examination of these opposing tendencies is provided in Chapters 12 and 13, respectively.

try to demonstrate throughout this text, what we have labeled *interpersonal* and *cognitive* themes are both relevant to a variety of social phenomena.

Given our attempt at relating these diverse topics, it is important that the organizational structure which we have endeavored to build in this chapter be maintained and integrated with that of Chapter 3.

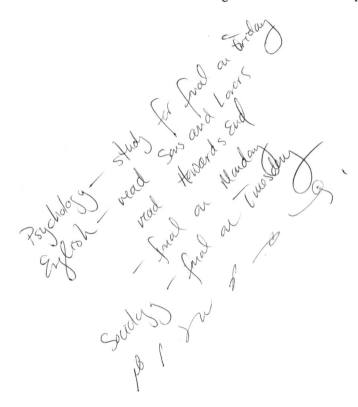

The Cognitive Themes of Resolution, Consistency, and Valuation   3

While the two themes discussed in the previous chapter are concerned primarily with interpersonal activities and relationships, the themes to be presented in this chapter are focused on intrapersonal (that is, internal, cognitive) events. The cognitive themes involve the thought processes that operate when we, as individuals, make decisions about our social behaviors and the environment in which they occur.

In all, we will consider in detail three themes in this chapter: (1) *Resolution*, which is concerned with the impact of ambiguity on our decisions and actions; (2) *Consistency*, which involves processes that lend structure to the complex set of stimuli and events that comprise our social fields; and (3) *Valuation*, which deals with the manner in which we differentially weigh various types of information in order to make decisions and guide behavior.

THE THEME OF RESOLUTION

A variable that pervades many phenomena in social psychology is the degree of uncertainty that exists about the appropriateness of a response, whether the response is a change of belief or an overt action. The magnitude of this ambiguity is a consequence of such factors as the novelty of the situation, the complexity and contradictions in the available cues, the uncertainty of the actor, the low level of the beliefs involved, and so on.

To identify this theme, we have borrowed the term *Resolution* from the field of optics, where it refers to the degree of clarity or focus in the visual field. Similarly, in our social psychological perspective, Resolution refers to the degree of clarity or focus in a given social field—that is, the degree to which the actor perceives that a clear and appropriate response is available.

The processes of Resolution lie at the core of many of the phenomena treated in this text. Resolution is a basic and ubiquitous theme in human decision making and action, and as such, it is relevant to almost all human behavior. In introducing this theme, we present a number of examples, including some derived from the empirical literature of our field. We will begin with another classic study in social psychology: the work of Muzafer Sherif on the formation of response norms in a highly ambiguous Social Context. The variables that affect the manner in which people decide about the correct course of action (or way of thinking) have been a continuing preoccupation of social psychologists at least since Sherif's pioneering work of more than 40 years ago.

The Autokinetic Illusion

Sherif (1936) was interested in discovering the social processes that guide the formation of beliefs and perceptions. To explore this issue, he made use of the *autokinetic phenomenon,* a compelling optical illusion. The autokinetic effect occurs when a person stares at a small pinpoint of light that is presented in an otherwise completely darkened room. After watching the light for a minute or two, it appears to move, even though it is, in fact, stationary. This illusion is so irresistable that even those who know about the effect still "see" the movement. In his studies with the autokinetic effect, Sherif asked subjects to judge the apparent distance that the light moved from its origin.

In the first of his investigations, in which a single respondent was exposed to this illusion a number of times, Sherif (1936) noted that a subject's initial responses varied widely from one exposure to another. With increased exposure to the illusion, however, the respondent's judgments became less erratic. Over trials, that is, the subject's perceptions converged more and more closely on a single value. It was as if the person had formed a response rule which, in effect, guided his or her later perceptions. This consistency of a single person's responses occurred despite the fact that across subjects, the response rules (the single values that each apparently had "decided" upon) differed widely. The rule that an individual developed could not have been a function of the objective reality of the situation since, as explained earlier, the autokinetic effect is completely illusory.

An illustration of the separate estimates of three individual subjects over a series of exposures is presented in Figure 3.1. Note that while the ultimate response rules differ among all three subjects, the general pattern of extreme initial variability, followed by a gradual zeroing in on a more consistent response, characterizes the responses of all three subjects.

Sherif's work may not seem to be of obvious relevance to social psychology, since subjects in his initial demonstration were studied in isolation. His later studies, however, were clearly relevant to understanding interper-

FIGURE 3.1
Illustration of the Response Records of Three Individual Subjects in an Autokinetic Study

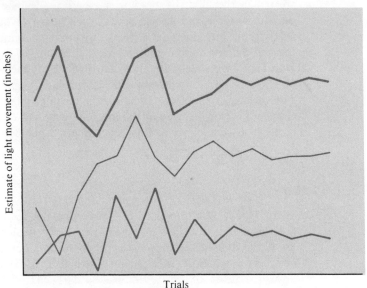

sonal behavior, since they investigated the norm formation process under conditions of high ambiguity (that is, poor Resolution). To do this, Sherif examined the responses of pairs of subjects, rather than those of isolated individuals. When two people were placed together in an autokinetic situation and asked to give their estimates aloud, their response records followed the usual pattern of judgments (see Figure 3.1), with one important exception: both respondents in the typical group condition began by responding erratically, as did the individual subjects, but their judgments soon converged on a value that stayed reasonably constant over the remaining trials (see Figure 3.2). It was as if they had come to some unspoken agreement about the "reality" of the moving light. In other words, a common, socially derived response norm had been created through the combined action of the responding pair.

Sherif further extended his research with an even more interesting demonstration. In this final set of studies, he had a number of pairs of subjects respond to repeated trials of the autokinetic effect so that a response norm would be generated in each dyad. A short time later he took individuals from different groups and paired them in yet another series of exposures to the illusion. Unlike naive subjects, the participants in this demonstration had already formed response norms to guide their perceptual judgments during the previous session. The norms that had been formed, however, were different for each member of the new pair, because each individual had been originally exposed to the illusion with a different partner, and it was during this initial situation that the norm had been formed.

FIGURE 3.2
Illustration of the Response Records of Two Subjects Paired Together in an Autokinetic Study

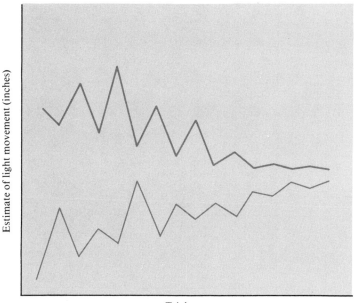

Trials

This study represents an ingenious extension of Sherif's previous research, as it placed in the same Social Context respondents who, as a result of somewhat different past social experiences, had developed dissimilar response norms. The pattern of judgments of these subjects in their new situation was quite interesting. Rather than converging on a common response, as did pairs of subjects with no previous experiences, the experienced subjects followed their own response norm and responded as they had in the earlier session, despite the fact that the expressed judgments of their present coworker differed markedly from their own. A typical response record of such a pair is presented in Figure 3.3.

Resolution and Conformity

The implications of Sherif's results are crucial in order to understand the theme of Resolution. The initial research series demonstrated that individuals attempt to act "correctly" in what is, almost by definition, the ultimately ambiguous situation—the perception of an illusion. Over a series of trials, each subject increased the Resolution of the situation by evolving his or her sense of reality. Each person developed a response rule that best represented what he or she saw, and this norm lent some regularity or certainty to the situation. Moreover, this increase in Resolution made the judgment task much less difficult to accomplish.

FIGURE 3.3
Illustration of the Response Records of Two Experienced Subjects in an
Autokinetic Study Who Were Paired after Acquiring Different Response Waves

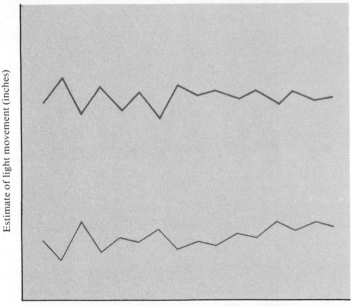

Trials

Sherif's findings strongly suggest that there exists a tendency in humans to seek order or structure in their world. This point will be discussed further when we consider the theme of Consistency. It is sufficient to note here that the disposition to impose structure on our social world appears a persistent human characteristic. Such a characteristic forms the basis of the Resolution process; without it, there would be no need to resolve the ambiguities and inconsistencies in order to derive some meaningful understanding of the social reality.

Sherif's second series of studies, in which subjects made their judgments in pairs, demonstrated the utility of socially supplied information for human decision making. Similarly, Crano's (1970, 1975) study of incorporation discussed in the previous chapter also points out the role that social sources of information play in the process of Resolution. In both of these studies, subjects used the information provided by others to revise their own judgments of the situation. In both studies, subjects had available for their consideration information derived from both perceptual and social sources; since the cues from the environment were not well resolved, however, the information derived from the responses of others was given great weight, and this led to the development of a consistent response rule or norm.

In his theory of social comparison, Leon Festinger made a similar point when he hypothesized that in the absence of firm, objective information, we seek out the more socially oriented definitions of reality to guide our thoughts and actions (Festinger, 1954). Under conditions of poor Resolution—an ambiguous dot-counting task or the autokinetic illusion—people will attempt to decrease ambiguity by using the responses of others in coming to a decision about their own thoughts and behavior.

 The findings of Sherif's third research series are also very relevant to the theme of Resolution. In this set of demonstrations, subjects who had formed response norms in earlier sessions were found to be extremely resistent to the social pressure derived from the expressed judgments of their new coworker.

This fact has two very important implications. First, it suggests that once a social situation is resolved to a degree acceptable to the actor, he or she attaches minimal weight to new cues in the situation. Such discounting of new information leads individuals to respond with some consistency across similar Social Contexts.

This discounting mechanism shields the actor from information overload. In many social situations, we are faced with more data than we can possibly process. In such cases, lack of complete Resolution, if it exists, is a consequence of conflicting and/or ambiguous cues. One common tactic used to increase Resolution involves selective attention to, and processing of, only a subset of the available cues. Sherif's work in his third research series presents graphic evidence of this discounting process in action. Note that the respondents, in making their judgments, used a Personal Structure variable (a norm that they brought with them into the situation) and discounted the information provided by the Social Context (the new coworker's responses). Of course, this particular procedure for weighing cues is not always followed. In many situations, the environmental stimuli are weighted more heavily than are cues derived from the Personal Structure.

A second important implication of Sherif's third set of studies is its relevance to the distinction between the Control mechanisms of impingement and incorporation. Recall that in our discussion of Asch's work in Chapter 2, we questioned the actual perceptions of the compliant subjects. Did they really see what they said they saw? It is not possible to answer this question directly from their responses during the line-judging task, but when Asch interviewed them afterwards, many subjects admitted that they did not really see what they had reported.

In Sherif's work, however, the apparent reluctance of subjects who previously had developed a response norm to change their answers suggests that their actual perceptions were affected in the task that was employed. In other words, Sherif's subjects had incorporated a disposition to perceive reality that was in part a product of the social encounters that they had experienced in the situation. Asch's subjects, on the other hand, did not incorporate a belief, but rather were impinged upon by the actions of the other respondents.

What accounts for this variation? We believe that differences in the degree of Resolution between the two experimental contexts determined the particular process (impingement or incorporation) that was activated. In the highly resolved situation used by Asch (recall that in his studies, the objectively correct response was obvious), there was little chance that the subjects would incorporate a response tendency that was so glaringly discrepant from their perceptions. The Resolution simply was too great. However, in the autokinetic situation, a physical environment of extreme ambiguity, an incorporation of a systematic response disposition, which in effect provided structure or Resolution to the situation, was much more likely. If we can apply this observation to other Social Contexts, it suggests that in general, only impingement will succeed in situations of high Resolution; in situations of poor Resolution, however, both impingement and incorporation processes can, and often do, operate.

Following the Leader

A real-life example may help to illustrate how the Resolution of a social situation affects an individual's behaviors. The anecdote concerns a young journalist who was invited to dine at the White House for the first time. The events of interest occurred during the presidency of Franklin D. Roosevelt. Naturally, the young man was delighted to have received the invitation. He also was extremely anxious to make the proper impression, since he hoped that this invitation would be the first of many. He knew that Roosevelt often would leak important stories to reporters who attended such functions; needless to say, such a scoop could have very positive implications for the blossoming career of an inexperienced journalist. Determined to make a good impression, the reporter decided to imitate the actions of his host, the president. He did so because he felt that by modeling his behavior after that of the central personnage in this drama, he could not go too far wrong.[1]

As the evening progressed, the young reporter became more and more pleased with his imitative tactics. When Roosevelt picked up the third fork on the left, so did he—and as it turned out, so did everyone else. When Roosevelt laughed, he laughed—and so did everyone else. As the dinner wound down, the reporter congratulated himself on his brilliant maneuver. He felt so relaxed, in fact, that he almost began to enjoy himself.

The last course to be served that evening consisted of coffee and a fine brandy. The reporter, as he had done throughout the evening, intently but surreptitiously watched Mr. Roosevelt's actions. At this point, he saw the president begin a somewhat peculiar ritual. The president lifted his coffee cup, and from it, poured a small amount of coffee into his saucer. He followed this curious action by pouring a slightly larger amount of cream into the saucer, and stirring the mixture. The eager young journalist, of course, followed suit. Mr. Rooosevelt then raised the saucer off the table—as did the young man. While in mid-lift, however, the young man watched in growing

---

[1] This is a time-honored strategy in the history of subject-ruler interactions. For example, the lilting sound of Castillian Spanish is the direct consequence of the behavior of courtiers who, centuries ago, adopted a lisp-like pronunciation of standard Spanish because their king had a speech impediment—he lisped.

embarrassment as the president proceeded to place the saucer at his feet where his dog, Falla, waited for his customary treat. We would like to tell you how this story ended, but we do not know how the young man explained to the people at his table why he was holding up a saucer filled with cream and coffee.

The point of this story is that while the Social Context will often provide a number of cues to appropriate behavior, these cues are not always correct. The reporter's general plan of using the Social Context to infer the actions appropriate in the situation, however, was sound. Indeed, the reporter really had little choice in the matter. He could not really fall back on his own Personal Structure (norms, habits, and so on) to guide his behavior, as the situation in which he found himself was almost completely novel. To be sure, he had had extensive past experience with knives and forks—but never White House knives and forks! His imitative strategy would have worked perfectly, except that his source of information proved not to be completely reliable for the purposes at hand. Focusing on a single information source, as did the young reporter, is a heady but often dangerous tactic, and because of this error he failed in his attempts at normalcy. In any event, his behavior is a good example of a commonplace phenomenon: under conditions of uncertainty, we are likely to search for (and sometimes create) cues through which we can increase the degree of Resolution.

Resolution and the Other Cognitive Themes

One additional observation, alluded to in our earlier discussion, should be made concerning Resolution: there is a link between Resolution and the other cognitive themes. The themes of Resolution and Consistency are related, for example, since the poorer the Resolution of a given social situation, the more likely it is that an actor will engage in Consistency-producing thoughts and actions. Through these mechanisms, the actor attempts to create a more orderly and comprehensible Social Context, since such circumstances facilitate the choice of behaviors to be expressed.

Similarly, Resolution is also related to Valuation. There are a multitude of cues to action, both within the actor and within the environment, that are present in any Social Context. In deciding on a course of action, people typically weight these stimuli differentially. This weighing process is Valuation. The poorer the Resolution of a social situation (that is, the fewer in number, the more ambiguous, incomplete, or inconsistent the internal and external cues to action), the more difficult and uncertain is the outcome of the Valuation process.

THE THEME OF CONSISTENCY

As noted, in situations of less than complete Resolution, people often will engage in behavioral and cognitive activities designed to lend structure or Consistency to the ambiguous field in which they find themselves. For this reason, the theme of Consistency is a central focus of much of cognitive social psychology, which is the major subdiscipline of the field that is concerned with beliefs and the processes involved in their formation and change.

In general, Consistency refers to the maintenance of a psychologically appropriate balance among one's beliefs, or between one's beliefs and actions. In discussing this theme, we treat two different types of Consistency: *self/ other Consistency* and *self-Consistency*. Self/other Consistency involves the perceived fit between one's own beliefs and behaviors and the beliefs and behaviors of important others. These important others are usually people in the immediate interpersonal environment; however, they also can include people whose "presence" is purely psychological (such as Jesus, Martin Luther King, or Ronald Reagan), but whose influence on our behavior nonetheless can be pervasive. Self-Consistency refers to our attempts to maintain a personally perceived "fit" among our beliefs, and between our beliefs and actions.

Self/other Consistency

In his theory of interpersonal balance, Fritz Heider (1958) hypothesized that two types of associations could exist between persons, or between people and inanimate objects. He termed one of these the *unit relationship,* a concept introduced briefly in Chapter 2. As noted, unit relationships involve the extent to which the interconnection between people or things is perceived as appropriate or fitting.[2] For example, we would view a loving couple who has been together for many years as forming a unit relationship. We would perceive them as belonging together—their mutual presence would strike us as fitting or right.

The second type of bond that could exist between people—the Sentiment relationship—is a variant of the unit bond, but an extremely important variant. As noted in the previous chapter, the Sentiment bond implies liking and loving, or disliking and hating. In the example of the couple who had been together for a long time, we would assume that a positive Sentiment relationship was taking place. Congruence between the positive (or negative) poles of the Sentiment and the unit relationships implies a certain fit, a balance, what we have called self/other Consistency. So, for instance, a long-married couple who are deeply in love provides an example of a fitting, consistent, or balanced relationship. By the same token, the long-married couple who detest one another seem, to the husband and wife and to observers, unbalanced, nonfitting, or inconsistent. Self/other Consistency thus refers to the balance or fit between the actor and the others in the interpersonal environment.

A slightly more complex form of self/other Consistency occurs in contexts in which more than two persons or objects are involved. For example, suppose that two good friends share a common and intense interest in automobiles. They await each new car season with great anticipation and love to

---

[2] Nehemiah Jordan (1968) has provided a lucid discussion of the unit relationship.

discuss the relative merits of the latest automotive innovations. After having the opportunity to inspect the latest model Corvette, which incorporates a number of radical and controversial features, one friend calls the other and says, "Did you see the new Corvette? It's one of the most magnificent cars that I have ever seen!" To which his friend answers, "Yeah, I read a report of it in *Road and Track,* and I think it's lousy." How will the caller react to his good friend's negative comments? Will there have been any pressure on him to change his opinion? Will there be any pressure on the other to change his?

We believe that at the very least they both might reconsider the reasons for their disagreement about the car. Or, they might converse further, attempting to determine the precise points that led to their disagreement. One or both even might try to convince the other to change his mind. Why? Disagreement among friends is unpleasant. There exists both a positive Sentiment and a positive unit relationship between friends, and thus, a disagreement between them about an important issue generates a condition of self/other Inconsistency in both.

Now think of a similar situation, except in this case, the conversation takes place between you and a person whom you really dislike. Because of circumstances beyond your control, you find yourself sitting next to one another at a concert. In an attempt to make small talk before the show begins, you voice your enthusiasm for the Corvette. This person responds, "I read a report of it in *Road and Track,* and I think it's lousy." Do you think that this response would cause you to reconsider your position, as it did the friends in the example above? We do not think so. While the interchange might be an unpleasant one, it is not likely that it would cause you to rethink your opinion. As a final example, suppose an enemy of yours is critical of Corvettes. This difference in opinion might even bolster your positive evaluation of the car. Finding yourself in disagreement with someone you dislike is not a source of Inconsistency; indeed, if anything, it is an instance of self/other Consistency. Liking a thing that your enemy hates, or hating a thing that your friend hates, is, according to both Heider and our own naive intuitions, appropriate, balanced, or fitting.

Considerable research has examined self/other Consistency and Inconsistency from Heider's balance theory perspective (Crano & Cooper, 1973; Janis & Hoffman, 1971; Lott & Lott, 1961; Price, Harberg, & Newcomb, 1966; Rodrigues, 1967). These studies have specified with some precision the conditions under which Heider's balance formulation most accurately predicts the psychological reactions of people to self/other Consistency and Inconsistency.

The study by Irving Janis and David Hoffman (1971) provides an interesting real-life example of the influence of self/other Consistency on opinions and behaviors. This study was conducted in connection with a smoking clinic at Yale University. In the study, adult volunteers who had indicated a desire to curtail their cigarette smoking took part in a program in which they met in pairs with a clinic consultant once a week for five weeks. The weekly

AMAZING NEW CANCER OPERATION UNVEILED.

The doctor doesn't cut out anything. You cut out cigarettes.

This simple surgery is the surest way to save you from lung cancer. And the American Cancer Society will help you perform it.

We have free clinics to help you quit smoking. So, before you smoke another cigarette, call the A.C.S. office nearest you.

And don't put it off. The longer you keep smoking, the sooner it can kill you.

AMERICAN CANCER SOCIETY

THIS SPACE CONTRIBUTED
BY THE PUBLISHER
AS A PUBLIC SERVICE.

Self/other Consistency is only one of a number of tactics used in the fight against smoking.

clinic sessions provided participants with information about the dangers of smoking and strategies that they could use to break the smoking habit, as well as a period of free discussion between the two subjects. Within this general framework, subjects were assigned to various experimental conditions: members of some pairs were asked to talk with each other daily (the high-contact condition) in addition to attending the weekly clinic meetings together; members of other pairs spoke with one another only at the weekly meeting (the low-contact condition).

Janis and Hoffman designed this study so that different Sentiment relationships would form between the participants in each condition, and their attempts were quite successful. As would be expected on the basis of our previous discussion of the antecedents of positive Sentiment, 7 of the 10 subjects in the high-contact condition reported liking their partner "more and more as I got to know him," whereas in the low-contact condition, only 1 subject of 10 did so.

Moreover, self/other Consistency mechanisms appeared to operate in this Social Context since Janis and Hoffman also found differences in smoking behavior as a consequence of experimental condition. Although all participants appeared to have initially profited from the smoking clinic, reducing the number of cigarettes smoked from a preclinic average of more than 30 per day to less than 10 at the end of the experiment, only those in the high-contact condition had maintained this reduction 12 months later.

A similar pattern of results was found for subjects' opinions about smoking. It is reasonable to speculate that the positive Sentiment that existed between the members of a high-contact pair, in conjunction with their mutually shared desire to reduce smoking, fostered and maintained their strong antismoking opinions and behaviors. In contrast, members of the low-contact condition did not have the advantage of a supportive Sentiment relationship to bolster their antismoking position; thus, self/other Consistency could not operate as strongly as it did in the high-contact pairs.

Self/Other Consistency—Reference Group Theory. Self/other Consistency also can be viewed from the perspective of *reference group theory* (Kelley, 1952; Newcomb, 1943; Stouffer et al., 1949). In this theory, persons are assumed to evaluate both the appropriateness of their behaviors and the goodness of their outcomes by comparing them to the behaviors and outcomes of people with whom they identify (termed *referents* or *reference persons*). Such identification can occur as a result of the perception that these reference persons are similar to us in important ways or that they are worthy of our emulation.

Thus, a reference group for a given individual can be a collection of very diverse persons. Referents can be people who are members of the important social collectives to which the individual actually belongs (the person's church congregation, the members of his or her social club, family, or work group). On the other hand, the referents can be people whom the individual has never met but nevertheless admires and aspires to imitate (for example, members of a select professional group, a particular social or economic class, media stars, or religious figures).

Reference group theory holds that we strive to maintain similarity between ourselves (in terms of behaviors and outcomes) and those whom we identify as our central referents. In the terminology of the present text, this similarity is a form of self/other Consistency. The other, in this case, is typically a composite that we have created, comprised of the relevant qualities of the reference group.

For example, Sam, a young boy, might dream of one day becoming a

HORST SCHÄFER/PETER ARNOLD, INC.

Sam even imitates his hero's fielding posture.

major league baseball player. As part of his dream, little Sam worships his hero, the incomparable Guido Epstein, first baseman for the Mets. The young boy wears Guido's number on his little league jersey, models his batting stance after his hero's, and compares his fielding statistics to those of the all-star. He does not, however, chew tobacco as Guido does, nor is he regularly booked for being drunk and disorderly, as is his hero. These activities are not included as parts of the composite other that little Sam has created from a combination of Guido's actual behavior and his own romanticized vision of the baseball star. Other components of this composite reference could have been derived from aspects of other baseball players who, at one time or another, Sam also admired.

The extent to which little Sam sees his actions on the ball field as meeting the standard that he derived from his reference group is the extent to which he is satisfied with his performance. Sam is satisfied with his outcomes to the extent that he views the rewards he receives in his particular Social Context as commensurate with those that Guido receives in his (Guido wins the MVP in the big leagues; Sam wins it in his six-team little league). The degree to which events do not meet these standards is the degree to which Sam experiences self/other Inconsistency and to which he acts to alter his actions or perceptions. A change of perceptions, for example, can involve a more liberal interpretation of one's outcomes, or the creation of a new reference group.

Balance and Reference Group Theory.   In many ways, balance theory and reference group theory are similar conceptually. Both involve social comparison processes. Balance theory assumes that we compare our evaluation of another (or of some object) with that of a person whom we like or dislike. Similarly, reference group theory posits that we compare our responses and outcomes to those of important others, including our friends and sometimes our enemies—we can have negative reference groups, which help us define our behaviors and outcomes by means of contrast.

Both theories postulate a preference for self/other Consistency. The major distinction between the two is that balance theory limits the domain of relevant others to persons with whom we have established some Sentiment or unit relationship, while reference group theory assumes that any person or collective—real or fictional—can serve as a comparison group. Any other difference between the theories appears to be much more a matter of terminology than of substance. Indeed, so similar are the theories conceptually that each can be translated into the other's language, without violating the formal structure of either.

One of the most impressive real-life demonstrations of the operation of self/other Consistency (as well as other themes) was conducted by Theodore Newcomb more than 35 years ago. In his study, Newcomb (1943) explored the relationship between the political opinions and the interpersonal relationships of a large group of students at Bennington College in Vermont. Bennington is a small, privately funded, liberal arts college for women, located in a beautiful but geographically isolated area of New England. Because it is

*"They sent her to Bennington to lose
her Southern accent, and then she turned her back on everything."*

privately funded, the tuition, fees, and other costs of attending the college
are high. One of the factors that contributes to the high cost of this college
is the experimental nature of the curriculum. Bennington is designed to provide its students with an environment that fosters intense and continual fac-
ulty-student interaction.

As Newcomb conducted his research during the depression of the 1930s,
it is not surprising that the students who attended Bennington at that time
came from wealthy families. As is true today, the political orientations of
people from the upper socioeconomic classes are primarily conservative. Newcomb in fact found this characterization to hold in his sample of respondents
when he measured their political opinions as freshmen. However, the political
orientation of the faculty members of Bennington, many of whom were effective, charismatic teachers, was left-wing. We have here the makings of a
classic case of self/other Inconsistency. The values of the students were in

direct conflict with those of a powerful and competent set of authority figures.

The outcome of this clash of ideas was determined in large part by the particular group that each student chose as her primary referent. Those undergraduates who became campus leaders due to factors in their Personal Structures and the Social Context, also quickly formed positive Sentiment and unit bonds with their professors—in other words, the members of the faculty became a powerful reference group for them. In contrast, the influence of the family as a primary reference group was lessened—the relationship of these students with their family members, particularly the unit bond, was weakened. For these women, the family was no longer viewed as the exclusive source of social, intellectual, and emotional support. The consequence of this shift of identification was a change in political opinion toward that of the faculty's beliefs. In a relatively short period of time, the students discarded their conservative political values and adopted in their place a more left-wing orientation.

The process of opinion change was not limited to the student leaders, although it was most marked in this group. A large portion of the entire student body examined by Newcomb evidenced a similar shift in political values. These more typical students, like the leaders, also came to form Sentiment and unit relationships with the faculty of Bennington, and became less inclined to use family members as referents in social and political matters. In addition, the student leaders became a reference group for these undergraduates as well. Through these self/other Consistency processes that Newcomb chronicled, the political and social belief structure of most of the student body of Bennington was dramatically modified.

It is of interest also to consider the students who proved exceptions to this trend. While relatively few in number, some students resolutely maintained their conservative political ideology. How did these students differ from their more typical counterparts? Though we have no direct proof of this contention, it is probable that important components of these students' Personal Structures differed from those who did change. What we do know, however, is that these exceptions did not shift in their primary reference group. When Newcomb measured the strength of the family ties that each student perceived, he found that these women remained bound most strongly to this fundamental unit. Moreover, he noted that they were more likely to leave school than were the students who accommodated to the prevalent political atmosphere of the college.

Newcomb also explored the long-term implications of the opinion change that these students experienced in their early college years (Newcomb et al., 1967). This followup study, conducted 25 years after the original, demonstrated that the former Bennington students maintained a remarkable degree of belief Consistency over this long passage of time: the majority of them had retained the political and social values that they had acquired at college. For example, compared to a sample of women who were similar to them with regard to socioeconomic status and age, nearly twice as many of the Bennington alumnae voted for John Kennedy rather than Richard Nixon in the 1960 presidential election. Remarkably, the belief changes that were induced during their years at Bennington persisted over time to affect their behavior nearly a quarter century later.

Newcomb's two studies, taken together, raise a number of interesting issues. For example, what are the psychological processes that can account for the rather rapid change in fundamental political philosophy that these women experienced? First, it is likely that the physical environment of Bennington College played a major role in effecting the change in reference groups and the accompanying change in values that occurred. Recall that the college was (and is) located in an isolated locale. This physical isolation no doubt served to generate in the members of the student body a deep sense of separation from their families. This sense of separation, moreover, was quite valid, given that the frequency and duration of the contacts between a student and her family decreased when she entered college. Thus, in this highly restricted situation, the students were more-or-less forced to turn to the people in their immediate interpersonal environment—their sister students and the members of the faculty—for social support.

Note the parallel between the Social Context of Bennington College and those of the brainwashing and religious conversion situations discussed in the previous chapter. The students entering the isolated college setting were placed in a context of rather extreme ambiguity, or poor Resolution. They had been deprived of easy access to their families and removed from the familiar surroundings of their past. The social forces operating in this context were intense. To whom could they turn for definition? Newcomb's data suggest that it was the faculty and the student leaders of the college who became the source of the observed belief changes. The isolated situation was an ideal setting for the activation of incorporation processes since, as noted, incorporation is most likely to occur in contexts of poor Resolution. It is in examples of this type that we can see most clearly the interplay of the themes of Control, Resolution, and Consistency.

Newcomb et al.'s (1967) work is also informative about the conditions that foster persistence of political ideas. As noted, his respondents' beliefs, which were acquired at Bennington, persisted for a span of 25 years. What mechanisms likely are responsible for this remarkable Consistency over time? Again, we must consider the theme of Resolution to understand this pattern. Most of the graduates left Bennington with a well-developed political philosophy; nevertheless, outside the college they probably found themselves once again in a situation of poor Resolution. Any radical change from one status (student) to another (wife, career woman) usually entails some degree of uncertainty. However, unlike the situation that they had encountered in their freshman year at Bennington, the women now had the opportunity to seek out sources of support for their established beliefs. At Bennington, such an option did not exist for long. Although freshmen could turn to each other for support of their old beliefs, the inexorable influence processes that operated there soon made this option unavailable. The isolation of the college enabled the socializing agents (that is, the faculty, who had a strong commitment to left-wing causes) to quickly undermine the existing opinions of their young charges.

Such conditions typically did not exist in the Social Contexts that the young graduates encountered after leaving Bennington. In most of these settings, there existed a wide variety of potential sources of support (referents) among which the graduates could choose. Not surprisingly, they chose those people whose values supported their own. For example, Newcomb et al. found that the majority of the Bennington women married men whose political ideologies were similar to their own.

The point here is that we are not merely passive receptors of the social forces operating in our Social Contexts. We actively structure these contexts to foster Consistency, to increase Resolution of the context, and to resist attempts at Control of our beliefs and actions. It is much more frequently the case that we are actors in, rather than reactors to, our social world.

Self-Consistency

One of the major benefits of self/other Consistency is that it facilitates the maintenance of self-Consistency by providing a source of consensual support for one's important beliefs. Learning that others share our views of reality contributes to our sense that we are rational, reasonable, and valuable human beings. By self-Consistency we mean the tendency of individuals to maintain a balance, or fit, among their beliefs (opinions, norms, and so on).

This balance is not necessarily logical. For example, Ann might be very

WILLIAM D. CRANO

The balance or fit between beliefs is not necessary logical. For Ann, eating health foods and smoking are consistent behaviors.

concerned about good health. She is a strict vegetarian and rarely drinks anything stronger than goat's milk. On the other hand, Ann smokes two packs of Camels every day. These sets of actions might appear as inconsistent or incongruous to a disinterested observer. To Ann, however, they make good sense because of a moderating third belief ("If I quit smoking, I would gain lots of weight, and that would be even more hazardous to my body than smoking"). While we might not agree with this reasoning (indeed, few nonsmokers would), it is sufficient that Ann perceives these beliefs as consistent. Given this condition, Ann feels little pressure to modify this component of her belief system (in this case, the set of interrelated beliefs that constitute her domain of opinions about smoking).

We have provided a simplified example to illustrate our point. In reality, each component of a belief system consists of many more opinions than the small number used here. This general principle of self-Consistency remains the same, however, regardless of whether the domain of opinions consists of two or a multitude of elements; if an individual judges the beliefs in his or her system to be consistent, then any lack of logical validity that might exist in that system is irrelevant. Moreover, under such conditions of perceived self-Consistency, there is little internal pressure to modify the system.

A number of formal models of self-Consistency have been advanced in social psychology (Festinger, 1957; Fishbein & Ajzen, 1974, 1975; Fishbein & Hunter, 1964; Osgood & Tannenbaum, 1955; Rokeach & Rothman, 1965). While there is wide diversity among the details of these theories, they all share a common, basic premise: people strive to create and to maintain Consistency among the components of their belief systems. Furthermore, Inconsistency motivates behaviors that attempt to resolve it. Consistency, or cognitive equilibrium, is viewed as the preferred state of the human organism. Accordingly, when self-Consistency is threatened, or cognitive Inconsistency is experienced, the individual almost invariably will take some actions to alleviate the condition. The specific actions most likely to be undertaken, and their relative effects on cognitive Inconsistency, provide grist for the mills of the varying self-Consistency theories, but their underlying assumptions are similar.

An interesting example of the impact of becoming aware of one's self-Inconsistency is provided by an intriguing study conducted by Milton Rokeach (1971) at Michigan State University. In this study, Rokeach asked his subjects to rank order a series of 18 values (for example, inner harmony, pleasure, happiness, freedom, wisdom, equality, and salvation) in terms of their importance to them. In one condition of his study, Rokeach then asked subjects to look at their own responses and to attend to the relative rankings that they had given to the values of freedom and equality. On the value scale, freedom was defined briefly as "independence, free choice," while equality was defined as "brotherhood, equal opportunity for all." Rokeach suggested that those who considered the former value more important than the latter perhaps were concerned more about their own well-being than they were about the welfare of other people. If the subjects held a view of themselves as humanitarians (and most of us do), then a large difference in the rankings of freedom and equality would be expected to generate a certain degree of Inconsistency. In a second condition, subjects completed the same value survey but were not given Rokeach's interpretation of a discrepancy between freedom and equality. These subjects would not have been expected to experience self-Inconsistency, as the discrepancy between their value rankings and their self-definition as humanitarians was not made obvious to them.

Three to six months later, all of the subjects who had ranked freedom as substantially more important than equality, whether or not they had received Rokeach's interpretation, received by mail a solicitation for support by the National Association for the Advancement of Colored People (NAACP). Cooperating with Rokeach, the NAACP had actually mailed these letters to the subjects that he had specified. Rokeach found striking differences in the responses to this solicitation as a consequence of the condition in which the subjects had participated months earlier. Those who had been exposed to Rokeach's attempt to generate a sense of self-Inconsistency were three times more likely to respond positively to the NAACP's request for support than were subjects who had expressed similar patterns of values but had not heard his interpretation.

Rokeach's findings raise a number of questions that touch on some very fundamental social psychological processes. For example, we might question why an apparently minor experience had such a powerful and long-lasting effect on the opinions and behaviors of a sample of university students. After all, Rokeach's speech was presented to subjects in groups; it was not directed toward any individual in particular. In addition, the measurement of belief change was so separated in time and context from the experimental session that the subjects could not possibly have suspected that their behavior was being monitored. As you recall, however, the monitoring of behavior is necessary for impingement, but not incorporation, to operate. This fact, coupled with the long-term impact of Rokeach's manipulation, suggests that the processes invoked in this study were incorporative in nature.

A second issue raised by Rokeach's study concerns the role that level of beliefs plays in moderating the force of Inconsistency. As noted, level refers to the centrality or importance of a specific element in the Personal Structure. Rokeach's survey of values was designed to measure rather central (high level) opinions. His results suggest that if we can evoke a sense of Inconsistency about important beliefs, the resulting lack of Resolution in the Personal Structure will have important and potentially long-term implications for an individual's behavior. On the other hand, evoking a sense of Inconsistency on less central (lower level) beliefs should have much less of an impact on the belief structure and consequent actions of the individual.

It is reasonable to speculate that among the most high level beliefs that people possess are their impressions about themselves—that is, their self-concepts. Elliot Aronson (1968, 1980), for example, has proposed that Resolution and Consistency operate only in situations involving Inconsistency between behaviors or beliefs concerning the self. In Rokeach's study, it could be that the Inconsistency, induced in some subjects by the interpretation of their value rankings, threatened their impressions of themselves, an important aspect of their Personal Structure.

Though difficult to do in an experimental laboratory, there have been scientific attempts to manipulate persons' impressions about themselves, and these studies have produced results consistent with the speculations of Aronson (1968, 1980). In examining this work, it is important to keep in mind that any beliefs about the self that can be induced in a short-term laboratory study are not likely to be central or important. With this limitation in mind, let us consider an experimental attempt to manipulate a belief about the self, which was conducted by Aronson and Carlsmith (1963).

In this study, the investigators manipulated subjects' self-impressions by employing a photo-rating task with which the subjects could have had little prior experience. The task itself was fairly straightforward; respondents were simply to look at pairs of photographs of human faces and identify in each pair the picture of the "diagnosed schizophrenic." Since all pictures were taken from a Harvard University yearbook, this task was probably more difficult than it initially might seem. At the very least, the task was ambiguous, and thus it allowed the experimenters to give subjects any feedback about their performance that they wished.

Accordingly, Aronson and Carlsmith induced different self-impressions in two groups of subjects. In one group, the subjects were given feedback to indicate that they were highly successful in their judgments on the first 40 pairs of pictures. The subjects in the other group were told that they had performed very poorly. On the next 10 trials, the experimenters provided information that was either congruent with or discrepant from the respondents' self-impressions which had been generated over the first 40 judgment trials.

To make things even more interesting, the experimenters then told the subjects that because of an equipment breakdown, their last 10 judgments were not recorded and these trials would have to be repeated using the same photographs. The experimenters presumed that the subjects would be able to remember their choices (and whether or not their choices were "correct") and thus could maximize their score if they desired to do so.

Results of this study indicated that those subjects with a positive self-impression of their ability on the task were more likely to maximize their scores than were those with a negative impression. For the former group of subjects, a good score was consistent with the self-impression that had been induced during the earlier trials. Among those for whom a negative self-impression was induced, however, a high score was not consistent, and they proved much less likely to change their ratings to enhance their performance. These findings, as counterintuitive as they might appear, have been replicated in other studies as well (Aronson, Carlsmith, & Darley, 1963; Taylor & Huesman, 1974).

We would speculate that the subjects of Aronson and Carlsmith behaved the way they did because the task itself was not perceived as very important. Thus, poor performance probably did not impinge upon an individual's central self-impression of general competence, an impression that most of us attempt to maintain. If the task performance were an important aspect of a respondent's self-identification (for example, if the individual were interested in becoming a clinical psychologist), we would expect that poor performance would have generated a good deal of self-Inconsistency, and this Inconsistency would have compelled the individual to better his or her performance, especially on the final set of picture judgments. Trope (1979) has provided evidence consistent with this expectation.

As noted at the outset of this section, Consistency has been one of the central concerns of social psychology for many years. The reasons for this preoccupation are many. For example, Roger Brown (1965) has suggested that a Consistency framework is the most likely perspective to organize the diverse set of information that forms the substance of social psychology. Perhaps more importantly, Consistency is integrally related to other central processes (themes) that play so important a role in determining social behavior across a variety of contexts. For example, as we have demonstrated, Consistency processes form a powerful mechanism of incorporation. In addition, the force for Consistency is, in itself, a compelling example of the tendency in people to maximize the Resolution of their social fields. Likewise, Consistency can be a determinant of the outcome of the Valuation process, the theme to which we now turn our attention.

THE THEME OF VALUATION

Earlier, we briefly touched on the theme of *Valuation,* which, like the others, plays a fundamental role in the manner in which people think and behave in social settings. Valuation refers to the tendency of individuals to weight the cues available to them and use these values to come to a conclusion or a decision to act. The cues to which we assign weights or values are derived from both the Social Context and the Personal Structure.

The overriding purpose of Valuation, as we view it, is the maximization of one's physical or psychological welfare. This process can be likened to an accountant's cost/benefit analysis: the individual compares the potential rewards or benefits of a given behavior to the costs involved in implementing it; the ratios of costs to benefits are then compared across a number of potential behaviors, and the most "profitable" outcome is chosen.

We assume that a similar, if perhaps less self-conscious and purposive, process occurs in our day-to-day behavior regarding a whole range of decisions and actions. With this brief introduction, let us turn to a consideration of the major facets of the informational cues employed in the process of Valuation.

Weighting of Cues

The course of the Valuation process entails a series of preliminary decisions or judgments concerning the cues or information available. The first decision involves the weight that we give to a specific cue or piece of information, or the extent to which we view the cue as an important element in our decision-making process.

For example, suppose that a person were to tell us that the nuclear plant near our town was about to spew atomic waste over the surrounding area. How would we deal with this information? First, we would look for cues to tell us how much attention we should pay to this startling revelation and therefore evaluate the importance of the information. To do this, we would begin to evaluate the background or contextual cues that accompanied the message. For example, we would evaluate the source of the message by processing the cues concerning his qualifications to make such a statement. Was he an internationally acclaimed nuclear physicist? Was he the sensationalist journalist for the local newspaper? Was he obviously inebriated? Was he dressed to look like a gigantic chicken? Any of these possibilities would have an impact on the weight that we would assign to the information he gave us.

Other cues also would be processed, for instance, those concerning the appearance of the plant. Was the sky above the plant glowing green, or was it merely filled with black smoke, as usual? In this instance, we would be using cues in the physical environment to corroborate or refute the information. A third source of cues is provided by the interpersonal environment, that is, the reactions of those around us. Suppose that after hearing the warning, the person standing next to us announced her intention to leave immediately for Bermuda. If this person were the head of the physics department at the local college, her response probably would have a different impact

In valuating the warning about the radiation leak, one might look in the direction of the plant. Was the sky above the plant glowing green, or was it merely filled with black smoke, as usual?

on our interpretation (and utilization) of the news than if she were the acknowledged town crackpot.

A fourth source of cues might come from our own Personal Structure.
For example, we might be the president of the power company, and for
many years a believer in, and a strong advocate of, the use of nuclear energy.
On the other hand, we might be an active member of the area's antinuclear
coalition. Finally, we might have strong security needs. In this last circumstance, we would be much more likely to heed the warning implicit in the
communication, even in the absence of supporting evidence.

Focal and Contextual Cues. The example that we have discussed provides an illustration of the manner in which we weight a given cue. It should
be clear that this cue-weighting process cannot be accomplished without
the consideration of a number of other cues. The information whose importance we are evaluating is the focal cue, and the cues that are used in arriving
at this judgment are the contextual cues. Assigning weights to focal cues
in this manner is one of the major components of the Valuation process.

It should be noted that in some ways, the distinction between focal and
contextual cues is arbitrary. For example, a piece of information that serves
as a contextual cue can, in itself, be a focal cue. The behavior of the person
near us, for instance, which we used as a contextual cue in the evaluation
of the warning, was also a focal cue, because we used information about
the person (professor versus crackpot) to evaluate the inherent information
value of her response. Conversely, a focal cue can serve as a contextual
cue in one's decision about the importance of another piece of information.
Our judgment about the warning given us, for example, might be used as
a contextual cue to determine the weight that we give to the sound emanating
from the direction of the plant. Is it the lunch whistle that we hear or the
first notes of Gabriel's horn?

With this example in mind, we can turn now to a more formal discussion
of the factors involved in determining the weights we assign to cues in the
Valuation process. This issue is an important topic in cognitive social psychology, and it has stimulated considerable empirical and theoretical work. We
will present below a summary of the most important determinants of cue
weight and the role of cue weighting in the Valuation process.

Association. Association, discussed earlier as one of the antecedents
of Sentiment, also plays an important role in the cue-weighting process. The
weight that a person places on a cue is, in part, a result of its psychological
association with past experiences. If a source of a cue has been previously
associated with positive outcomes, then the cue will be weighted more heavily
than if the source has been linked with failure, or if its links with positive
or negative outcomes have yet to be established. It appears that association
affects people's perceptions of the quality of the cue under consideration.
The regularity with which positive or negative outcomes have been associated
with a given cue provides an indication of that cue's information quality.

It is interesting that the association need not involve skills or attributes
specific to the cue of interest. In many instances, positive or negative traits

completely irrelevant to the task under study have been found to influence people's behavior. For example, in their study of social behavior in juries, Strodtbeck and Mann (1956) found that jurors with high status occupations were most likely to be chosen as jury foreman. If we think about this for a moment, it should be clear that one's occupational status is a very poor predictor of the qualities desired in the ideal jury foreman (fairness, openmindedness, ability to ensure that all viewpoints are heard, and so on). Nevertheless, such logically irrelevant qualities are used frequently in the cue-weighting process when people are forced to make a decision or take an action. Associations of this kind have been widely studied in social psychology. Communicator credibility (in opinion change studies), expertise (in conformity studies), and leadership (in small group studies) are just a few examples of the Social Contexts in which this process has been studied.

Redundancy. A second factor affecting the weight assigned to a focal cue is redundancy. This term refers to the degree to which a piece of information (cue) tells us something that we do not already know. The less redundant the information, the greater its weight is likely to be in the Valuation process. Robert Wyer (1974) has discussed this factor at great length and has shown that redundancy does indeed diminish the impact of a specific cue on a decision.

A good example of the impact of redundancy on decision making is provided in the work of Asch (1956), discussed in Chapter 2. In an extension of his work on compliance (see pp. 40–44), Asch varied the number of experimental accomplices who were employed to give the incorrect perceptual judgments from 2 to 15. As might be expected, increasing the number of confederates resulted in an increase in compliance rates—but only up to a point. Increasing the number of confederates beyond three had no appreciable impact on compliance rates. Why?

We believe that the responses of the 4th through 15th accomplices were essentially redundant with the information provided by the first three. The response of the second was helpful in that it corroborated that of the first; likewise, the answer of the third accomplice corroborated and lent additional credence to those of the first two. Beyond this point, however, the simple repetition of the same response added no new information.

Clarity. A third factor that influences the weighting process is the extent to which a given focal cue is clear or unambiguous in the information that it provides. The greater the *clarity* of the cue (that is, the less its ambiguity), the more readily we can assign it a specific weight in our decision-making process.

Suppose, for example, that you were to call a person and ask him or her to go with you to the corner bar for a beer or two. The person replies, "Gee, that sounds like fun, but I can't—too busy." If the person you called were a good friend, you probably would find this message relatively unambiguous. Your friend would have liked to go but simply could not. However, if you were not well acquainted with the person whom you called (someone whose name and number you copied off a bathroom wall, perhaps), your interpretation would be much less certain. Was the person really busy, or did he or she simply not want to go out with you? It is difficult to say for certain. The clarity of the cue in this Social Context is not great, and thus, its implications for your future actions are not obvious.

It should be noted that the concepts of clarity and Resolution are distinct. Clarity refers to the degree of ambiguity of a single cue; in contrast, Resolution refers to ambiguity on a much larger scale, which might consist of hundreds of cues. Cue clarity is a component of Resolution, but only one of many.

Motive Relevance.   The extent to which a cue is associated with a need in the perceiver will also have an impact on the degree to which the cue is weighed in the Valuation process. Cues that are relevant to a motive that is already salient in an individual will be weighted more heavily than those that are irrelevant.

A study by John P. Wilson (1976) provides a good example of the effect that motive relevance can have on the cue-weighting process. In this study, Wilson examined two distinct types of people identified by means of a personality test that had been developed by Joel Aronoff (1967). One group was composed of safety-oriented subjects, that is, their Personal Structures were such that they were very concerned with order and prediction in their social fields. Because of this basic motivation, safety-oriented individuals are people who avoid displaying initiative or taking risks, preferring instead to blend into the social background. Wilson's other group was composed of esteem-oriented subjects. These people were motivated to display competence and to receive positive feedback about their behaviors. Esteem-oriented persons are risk takers, preferring to chance failure rather than accept second place. Both of these basic motives were identified by Abraham Maslow and discussed at length in his classic work, *Motivation and Personality* (Maslow, 1970).

Having identified persons with these two different motivational orientations, Wilson placed them in a Social Context in which they had to decide whether or not to investigate an ambiguous event that might reasonably be construed as an emergency. In one part of his study, each person was paired with an accomplice of the experimenter, who played the role of another subject. Both the real subject and the accomplice were placed together in a room, ostensibly to complete some questionnaires. While doing so in the experimenter's absence, they heard a loud crash from the next room; this noise was followed immediately by the sound of a human voice crying out in pain. In these conditions, the accomplice always rushed to the door upon hearing the crash. In other conditions, subjects were exposed to the same potential emergency, but they heard these noises while alone.

Safety- and esteem-oriented subjects differed markedly in their weighting of the available cues when deciding whether or not to investigate the disturbance. The safety-oriented subjects needed to see the actions of the other subject before they would intervene. When alone, they rarely investigated the crash. However, when the other person was present, they modeled their behavior after his by following him to investigate the noise. The esteem-oriented subjects, on the other hand, reacted in a very different way. They tended to investigate if anything were wrong whether they were alone or in the company of the accomplice. In other words, they focused on the noises from the next room rather than on the actions of the other person.

A number of cues were available to the subjects in Wilson's experiment. It is of interest that some people weighted the actions of a fellow subject more heavily, whereas others attended more closely to the commotion in the next room. These differences in cue-weighting could be predicted on the basis of the subjects' basic motivational orientation. The safety-oriented persons opted for the least risky course of action: to stay seated and not get involved when they were alone; and to mimic the behavior of their fellow subject when he ran to investigate the commotion in the next room. In contrast, the esteem-oriented subjects appeared to see the potential emergency as a chance to display their competence. When alone, the esteem-oriented subjects were much more likely to help than were the safety-oriented subjects placed in the same Social Context. If anything, they tended to help somewhat less when the accomplice was present and took action than when they were alone, perhaps because they felt that there was less opportunity to display their competence when another person was sharing the glory of the rescue.

For our purposes, Wilson's study clearly demonstrates the operation of motive relevance on the cue-weighting process. The different pattern of responses of the two types of subjects in the presence or absence of the accomplice strongly suggests that their basic psychological motivation played a role in the weighting of the cues potentially provided by the other's behavior. In general, we might postulate that cues that fit, or are consistent with, our high level needs will have a greater influence (that is, they will weigh more heavily) on our decisions and actions than will cues that are irrelevant or antithetical to these needs.

Belief congruence. *Belief congruence* operates in the cue-weighting process in a manner similar to that of motive relevance. The more a cue is consistent with a person's system of beliefs, the greater the weight it will likely be assigned in that person's Valuation process. If a person provides you with some novel information that you could have expected or predicted on the basis of your beliefs, you would be likely to weigh that cue more heavily than if this information were contrary to, or inconsistent with, these expectations.

An interesting example of the operation of belief congruence is provided in the study by Efran (1974). As noted earlier, there is much research (Berscheid & Walster, 1978; Dion, 1972; Dion, Berscheid, & Walster, 1972) which demonstrates that people associate positive traits and behaviors with physical attractiveness; that is, they hold the opinion that beautiful people are good people; they also hold the inverse opinion, that ugly people are bad people. Efran made use of this commonly held belief in his study of the attribution of guilt and innocence. In a simulated jury study, all subjects read the same narrative about a college student who had been accused of cheating. They were asked to read the transcript as if they were members of the panel charged with deciding the extent to which the accused was guilty and the harshness of penalty for the transgression. In addition to the transcript, each subject received a photograph of the supposed defendant. Actually, Efran employed a number of different photographs, all of which had been rated earlier by a panel of judges as depicting either an attractive or unattractive person. He found that the physically attractive defendants were judged as being less guilty than were the unattractive defendants; in addition, the attractive defendants received lighter penalties.

This study illustrates very well the impact of belief congruence on the cue-weighting process. The negative information available in the transcript was weighed less heavily when it was associated with an attractive defendant, because these cues were inconsistent with the general and widely held belief that beautiful is good. When the defendant was unattractive, the negative information was consistent with beliefs, and the cues presented in the transcript were accepted more readily and led to much harsher judgments.

Interaction of Cue-Weighting Processes.   As with most social psychological processes, the factors that affect cue weighting do not operate in isolation of one another. Motive relevance, cue clarity, association, and so forth, tend to combine in unique ways to affect the weight given to any particular focal cue in the social field.

One example of such a combinational or interactive process might involve association, clarity, and belief congruence. Suppose you believe that you should attempt to maximize your rather meager estate. There are a number of ways, of course, to go about this. Some of these potential means (the state lottery, Las Vegas, and so on) appear to be too risky. Others seem very sound, if somewhat low in return (savings bonds, bank accounts, and so on). Buying stocks, however, lies somewhere between these poles in your opinion. You see both good and bad features in this option.

By chance one evening, an acquaintance stops by your barstool and tells you, "Sell your car and invest the money and everything else you can get your hands on in Akron Fruit." If this source were the financial whiz of the largest brokerage house in town, his association with past financial successes would operate to clarify your belief in the profitability and wisdom of playing the stock market, thereby enhancing the belief congruence of the cue to invest. On the other hand, if the source were a well-known fool, his utterance would help to confirm your belief that investing in the stock market was not your best option.

Although the outcomes of these two possibilities differ as a function of the source of the cue, the processes that operated in each are the same. In both, association, clarity, and belief congruence interacted in your determination of the weight that was accorded the information. Variations in association (that is, the credibility of the source of the message) clarified your beliefs in different ways, resulting in the differential weighting of the cue as a function of belief congruence. In both instances, the weighting processes acted on one another in a reciprocal way, mutually enhancing their respective influences.

Response Options

Interacting simultaneously with the cue-weighting process is a second component of Valuation, namely the identification of response options. Response options are the behaviors (overt and covert) that an actor perceives as available in a given situation. We often enter a situation with one or a set of response options already in mind. However, the pattern of cues available to us in the situation will often alert us to the existence of feasible alternatives to our original plan of behavior. It is also likely that our initial inclinations will affect our cue-weighting processes by inducing us to judge as more important those cues that are relevant to, or consistent with, them. In any event, an integral part of the Valuation process is the determination of the response options available to us in a given Social Context.

The processes that influence the perception of response options are basically the same as those that affect the weighting of cues. Association, redundancy, clarity, motive relevance, and belief congruence operate in the identification of behavioral options to be considered in Valuation. Of all the factors that affect the perception of response options, motive relevance is perhaps the most influential. If the overriding goal of Valuation is the optimization of outcomes in terms of cost/benefit ratios, it follows that options relevant to our important needs would be most easily recognized and least likely to be dismissed.

For example, the reader can imagine (if possible) having just completed a satisfying dinner in the dormitory dining room. You return to your room and find your roommate about to leave for town. As you throw your coat on the floor, you cannot help but notice your psychology text lying open on the desk. These two sets of cues (textbook, roommate leaving) will be weighed differently, and will generate different response options, in large measure depending on your motive state. If you are in need of companionship, you will focus on interpersonal response options (going out with your roommate, calling another friend, and so on); if your need for achievement were particularly acute this evening, the open book might serve to remind you of the forthcoming midterm examinations, and bring to mind other options (studying psychology in your room, going to the library, and so forth). Suppose, however, that both motives are salient. In that case, the aforementioned response options also would likely come to mind, along with a series of alternative actions. For example, you might try to convince your roommate to accompany you to the library, or you might think of getting together with your partner in chemistry lab to go over preparations for the next report.

Cue Distortion. To this point, we have presented the Valuation processes as if they were perfectly reliable—that is, as if our cue weighing and response option perceptions always optimized the quality of our outcomes. Unfortunately, such is often far from the case. We often misread cues and overlook obvious and worthwhile options that follow from the cues. Mere chance is not the only cause—perhaps not even the major cause—of unreliability in the perception of response options. There are biasing variables that systematically affect the quality of our Valuations. On common contributor to unreliability of our perceptions of response options resides in the dynamic nature of the Valuation process itself: in many circumstances, we reevaluate the importance of cues as information accumulates, discarding some options while generating new ones. With the accumulation of information and the accompanying change in cue weighting that follows, however, previously discarded options will sometimes become relevant. However, once they are discarded, options typically are not brought back for reconsideration. Thus, the option that would have been the most useful among a set of possibilities is not psychologically available for consideration.

A young person's choice of a university provides a good example of this problem. The student begins the search with some notion of the ideal college. After reading innumerable college brochures, talking with advisors and friends, and a good deal of thinking, a new picture of this ideal emerges in her mind. In her initial vision, she might have placed great weight on the geographic location of the institution, and therefore discarded from consideration a number of universities that did not fall within her preferred boundaries. Over time, however, her cue weighting changes, and geography becomes a less important consideration; instead, now she is concerned more with the schools' science curriculum and laboratory facilities, since she has come to realize that these factors will play an important role in the achievement of her goal to become a surgeon. Unfortunately, some of the schools that she had earlier dismissed from consideration on the basis of the geographic cue (which is no longer an important feature to her) might have fulfilled her newly realized needs better than any of the options that she now perceives as available. But these previously rejected alternatives (response options) simply are not reconsidered; the quality of her ultimate decision, therefore, is adversely affected.

In addition to a change in the weight of the cues that are processed, a second factor hinders the development of the most appropriate response options. This problem involves biases that prevent us from perceiving an option as it really is. A classic theme in romantic literature illustrates this very point: the girl nextdoor serves as the major source of comfort to the hero as his search for the perfect woman goes from bad to worse to disastrous. Because of their particular past histories of interaction, his present impression of her has a large component of unreality—he does not see her as she actually is but as she was, perhaps many years ago.[3] In the movies, the truth almost invariably dawns on our myopic hero, who comes to realize that the girl of his dreams was there all the time. Unfortunately, life is not always like the movies.

In this example, a viable response option was not recognized because a belief that had developed over time was no longer valid. In this way, the

---

[3] Typically in such stories, the young woman is not nearly so blind.

option was rendered unavailable to the perceiver and, as a result, his Valuation of his Social Context was less useful to him than it could have been.

An empirical example of the influence of biased expectations on subsequent perceptions is provided in a study conducted by William B. Swann, Jr. and Mark Snyder. In a cleverly designed experiment, Swann and Snyder (1980) brought groups of three subjects into their laboratory and assigned one of them the job of teaching a card trick to the other two. After the "teacher" had learned the trick himself, he was provided with information regarding the general competence of the other two participants by the experimenter, who showed him their responses to a background questionnaire. Actually, the teachers were shown two questionnaires that had been prepared beforehand by Swann and Snyder: on one, the respondent was pictured as a very bright pre-law major; on the other, the respondent was shown to be a sociology major with a mediocre grade-point average. The instructor was given 10 minutes to teach the trick to both students.

Afterwards, Swann and Synder tested students' actual performance on the card trick, and obtained measures of teachers' impressions of the students with respect to how quickly each caught on to the card trick. Interestingly, teachers' impressions of students were affected more by the cues provided in the bogus questionnaire than by the students' actual performance! Teachers more positively rated the pupils whom they expected to have high ability, although these subjects were often outperformed by their "low-ability" counterparts.

It appears that the teachers undervalued the cues provided by subjects' actual behavior and overvalued the initial information obtained from the pupils' supposed questionnaire responses. This cue distortion could have had an unfortunate limiting effect on teachers' response options if, for example, Swann and Snyder had asked the teacher to choose a student to perform the card trick, with the understanding that the teacher would receive $15 if his student performed without error. No doubt, most teachers would have chosen the "high ability" student, whom they believed (often incorrectly) to be the better performer.

Valuation Outcome

At some point in the reciprocal processes of cue weighting and the discovery of available response options, a person must make a decision or judgment about the behavior (action or belief) to be undertaken. The behavior taken is the *Valuation outcome,* and represents an integration of cue weights and response options that, in the actor's perception, maximizes his or her cost/benefit ratio. In the ideal case, Valuation outcome involves an attempt to predict the positive and negative consequences of implementing each response option. This prediction is based on a consideration of the weighted cues available in the situation.

Consider a fairly simple if somewhat extreme situation. While you are walking down a dark street one evening, you become uncomfortably aware that you are not alone. This realization occurs to you because someone has just jabbed a hard object in the small of your back and said, "Gimme your money." In this situation, the cues available for interpretation or weighting are rather minimal. So, too, are the options that come to mind: you develop two rather quickly—hand over the money and hope for the best or do something more drastic like run (and hope for the best). Obviously this does not exhaust the possibilities; for example, you might turn and fight, and so on. However, the two options that came to your mind exhausted the possibilities that you could imagine. You weight the available cues, which include the fact that you are practically alone (an important cue), unarmed (also important), and that someone has stuck a gun in your ribs (extremely important). On the basis of this cue weighting, you develop the options noted above, and attempt to predict the likely consequence of each outcome in terms of your welfare. Your life happens to be of greatest concern to you, and in your judgment, the strategy of acquiescence seems the most likely to foster its continuation. Accordingly, your Valuation outcome consists in handing your money to the thief.

Most social circumstances, of course, are much more complex than the example presented above. Typically, there are many more cues and many more response options available, all leading to much more ambiguity than that portrayed in the story. The conditions of the ideal Valuation outcome seldom are realized because (1) the number of relevant cues available is not optimal; and (2) the outcome of the cue-weighting process does not often so clearly favor one response option over all others. In other words, for any given set of possible response options, we can have too few cues on which to base our Valuation, or we can have so many cues available, relative to the possible options, that we cannot process them efficiently. In either case—under conditions of insufficient cues or information overload—the quality of our Valuation outcome suffers.

In addition, time constraints can limit the quality of our Valuations. Too little time—as might have been the case in the robbery example—leads to decisions which usually are not based on a complete exploration of all of the response options and informational cues available. On the other hand, too much time can breed indecision. Clearly, one possible Valuation outcome is the failure to make a final judgment. This outcome, which is typically of low quality, is frequently encountered in judgment situations in which there is information overload or in which the time constraints on the decision are so long-term as to be meaningless. This "decision by indecision" removes the response outcome from the actor's control and places it in the hands of fate.

INTEGRATIVE THEMES AND THE CONTENT OF SOCIAL PSYCHOLOGY

This concludes our two-chapter discussion of the central, integrative themes in social psychology, as we view them. Judging from the diversity of the topics covered and the examples provided, the themes touch on a great many facets of the discipline of social psychology. Indeed, in our own view, the themes discussed in these chapters organize all of the important aspects of social psychology.

In the chapters that follow, we will attempt to expose the reader to the major substantive areas of the field as they have been traditionally treated. We will discuss the relevance of various themes as we present this substantive material. These thematic analyses are provided to help the reader understand the underlying processes that lie at the heart of so many social phenomena.

2

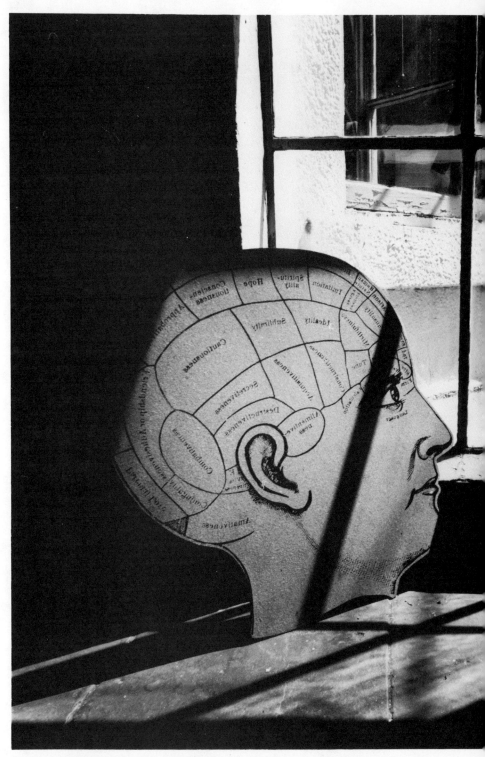

Beliefs and Their Consequences

The first section of this book presented the basic organizational structures—core concepts and integrative themes—that summarize and integrate the diverse areas of social psychology. We now are in a position to apply these organizational structures to the many facts about social phenomena discovered by researchers in the field. This activity will occupy our attention for the remainder of this text.

In this section, we explore the study of evaluative beliefs, a major preoccupation of social psychologists. Comprised of Chapters 4 through 8, this section presents a discussion of the central issues surrounding two specific types of evaluative beliefs—opinions and impressions. Norms, the third major type of evaluative belief, are discussed in detail in the final section of this book, which considers interpersonal encounters.

In Chapter 4, the fundamental principles of opinion formation and change are presented. Chapters 5 and 6 extend the material presented in Chapter 4 by considering the mutual interplay of opinions and social behaviors. In Chapter 7, we turn our attention to the variables that influence impression formation, the process by which we valuate the goodness or badness of others. Chapter 8, which completes this section, is concerned with the behavioral implications of impressions.

Opinion Formation and Change   4

Opinions—our evaluative beliefs about objects, classes of people, ideas, and events—have been the focus of intense attention in social psychology for at least the past 30 years. This type of evaluative belief has been called a number of different names—opinion, attitude, value, belief, and acquired behavioral disposition. In fact, Campbell (1963) listed 76 distinct terms that have been used to represent the general concept that we call *opinion*. Whatever the specific label employed, the principal determining characteristic of this form of evaluative belief is the same. All of these terms refer to a belief that implies some judgment about goodness or badness. In this chapter, we will review the variables that affect the ways that people develop opinions, and the factors that govern the likelihood that such opinions, once formed, will change.

HOVLAND'S THEORY OF PERSUASION

We will begin our review of work on opinions with the program of research that Carl Hovland and his associates conducted at Yale University (Hovland & Janis, 1959; Hovland, Janis, & Kelley, 1953; Hovland, Lumsdaine, & Sheffield, 1949; Rosenberg & Hovland, 1960; Sherif & Hovland, 1961). We start with Hovland's research because in many ways, it has laid the foundation for much of what is known today about opinion formation and change.

Hovland's theory is based on the assumption that people change their opinions as a result of receiving new information that is inconsistent with their established beliefs. If the new information is convincing, the people receiving it are expected to modify their beliefs. However, not all new information produces opinion change, and Hovland conducted considerable research in an attempt to isolate the factors that determine the effectiveness or ineffectiveness of a potentially persuasive communication.

In developing the theoretical framework that guided his research, Hovland speculated about the preconditions necessary for opinion change and the characteristic responses of those who are the targets of persuasion attempts. For example, he assumed that a persuasive communication, if successful, stimulates two distinct reactions in targets: (1) the information presented induces the person to question his or her established or existing belief; and (2) the information provides an answer to the question that it raised (this answer is called the recommended opinion).

Hovland also suggested that persuasive communications induce people to carry on an internal debate with themselves; they literally argue with the new information and contrast their own opinions with the new position advocated by the communication. This process is called counterargumentation. When counterarguing, people consider the pros and cons of each position and then decide either to maintain their original belief or to change their opinion in the direction of the new position advocated in the message.

For example, suppose that you believe that your composition course was an utter waste of time. You detest writing essays and like receiving evaluations on them even less. You feel that this course has done little to further your goal of becoming a successful electrical engineer. One day, you decide to attend a meeting of the Future Engineers of America—a campus organization to which you belong—mainly because you are particularly fond of the milk and cookies that the club always provides at these functions. Upon your arrival at the meeting, you are surprised to learn that the guest speaker is a professor from the English department. The topic of his speech is "Effective Communication and the Successful Engineer."

You listen politely while munching on your cookies as the professor

"Certainly can't argue with that."

People will change their opinions to the extent their efforts to counterargue a persuasive message are unsuccessful.

For many people in the audience, the professor's talk about the need for effective communication has caused them to question their established beliefs.

presents some information that you had not heard before. He cites studies that have shown that the ability to communicate effectively, especially in writing, creates a major difference between engineers who are promoted into higher management positions and those who are passed over. For this and many other reasons, the professor concludes, it is worthwhile for engineering students to take advantage of the writing courses offered at the university.

During the speech, you cannot help but notice the discrepancy between the professor's position and your own opinion regarding the composition course in which you are enrolled. In Hovland's terms, his communication has caused you to question your own established belief. As the speech progresses, you silently begin to attempt to refute the points made in the speech. This process of counterargumentation is not successful, however, since the professor's "facts" appear to be based on solid research evidence, whereas your opinion is based primarily on your lack of enthusiasm for writing essays.

After the speech, you find your opinion about the course somewhat altered; while you still think that writing will never be a pleasant activity, it now appears that learning to do it well will prove rewarding in the long run. Thus, you vow to approach your composition course with somewhat more seriousness in the future.

Figure 4.1 presents a graphic illustration of Hovland's speculations about the processes involved in opinion change, specifically as they apply to your experiences while listening to the speaker's persuasive communication.

It should be noted that the cognitive themes discussed in Chapter 3 are relevant to Hovland's ideas about the processes involved in opinion change. In our terms, to be successful a persuasive message must lower the Resolution of a person's set of opinions—that is, it must stimulate in the receiver of

FIGURE 4.1
Diagram of Hovland's Model of Communication and
Opinion Change

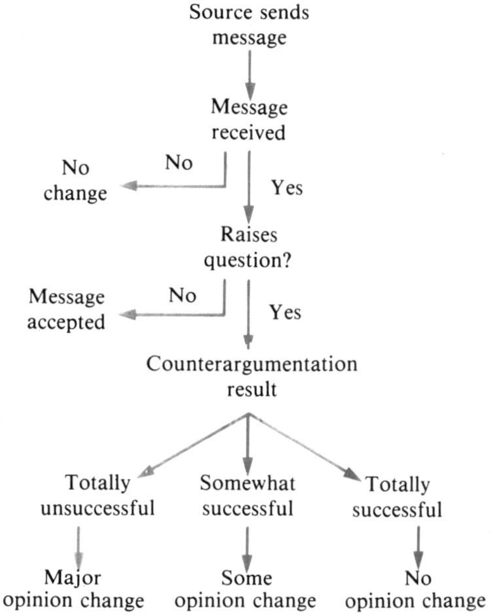

Attack opinions

Source sends
message

↓

Message
received

No ← No | Yes
change

↓

Raises
question?

Message ← No | Yes
accepted

↓

Counterargumentation
result

Totally   Somewhat   Totally
unsuccessful   successful   successful

↓   ↓   ↓

Major   Some   No
opinion change   opinion change   opinion change

the message (the target) some doubt or ambiguity about the correctness of his or her beliefs. Research (Trope, 1979) has shown that ambiguity of this type is an unpleasant state; accordingly, under such circumstances, processes involving Valuation are activated to reestablish a satisfactory level of cognitive Resolution. The conclusion (Valuation outcome) a person reaches is what Hovland termed an *opinion*. When the Valuation outcome results in a modification of a previously held belief, which then becomes incorporated as the individual's new opinion, *opinion change* has occurred.

Hovland's research on opinion change focused on the factors affecting the weight that people apply to the various cues encountered when they are confronted with a persuasive message. He postulated that the cue-weighting process which determines the persuasive power of a communication— that is, the extent to which a message successfully modifies a person's opinion—is affected by four general classes of factors that may be present in the persuasion setting: (1) the characteristics of the source of the message; (2) the variations in the setting in which the communication is presented; (3) the specific form and content of the message; and (4) the components of the target's Personal Structure.

We view these factors as cues that influence the weight accorded either the target's established opinion or the new position advocated by the message. In the sections that follow, we will discuss each of these classes of variables and provide research examples of their effects on opinions.

THE SOURCE OF THE COMMUNICATION

In developing his theory, Hovland hypothesized that the characteristics of the *source* of a communication have a considerable impact on the extent to which its message influenced people's opinions. In his perspective, a source could be a specific person (President Reagan), a more global collective of people (Princeton undergraduates), or an impersonal transmitter of information (the *New York Times*); in fact, any medium that provides information could, and often does, serve as a source of a persuasive communication.

Hovland distinguished between two features of a source that might affect people's susceptibility to its message: (1) the source's expertise; and (2) the source's trustworthiness or objectivity.

Expertise. *Expertise* refers to the credentials of the source of a communication which, in turn, bear on the apparent validity of that source's assertions about an opinion object. In short, evaluating the expertise of a source involves a judgment about the qualifications of the source for making the assertions contained in the message. A well-known nuclear physicist discussing the latest trends in atomic weaponry provides an example of an expert source. Such a communicator should be a good source of well-informed observations, and as such, his or her statements could prove very influential in shaping opinions.

However, expertise varies as a consequence of the issue. So, for example, if the physicist were to offer his opinion on the probable winner of the Super Bowl, his prediction would be viewed as no more expert than that of any

For most people, Albert Einstein is regarded as an expert in the areas of science and mathematics.

other intelligent football fan. As such, his prognostication about the outcome of the big game would be less persuasive than would his expressed opinion about nuclear weaponry.

Trustworthiness. *Objectivity,* or *trustworthiness,* is a quality related to the apparent manipulative intent of the source: a source is trustworthy to the extent that he or she is judged as having nothing to gain by a person's acceptance of the message. For example, consider the credibility of a witness in an embezzlement trial who testifies against the defendant. If the witness was a business partner of the defendant and stood to gain control of their company if the defendant was convicted, his testimony would be considered less credible than if he had nothing to gain from his partner's incarceration. In Hovland's terms, such a witness would not be perceived as trustworthy if the information he was communicating was viewed as self-serving.

While the characteristics of source expertise and trustworthiness are often related, they can exist independently of each other. It is possible to be trustworthy without being an expert or to be an expert without being trustworthy. For instance, suppose that the nuclear physicist in the example strongly advocated the development of a specific type of advanced missile system. It seems reasonable that we would be more persuaded by his arguments if it appeared that he had nothing to gain by our agreeing with his views. On the other hand, if he owned the patent on the weapon system or worked for the company that did, his arguments would be much less persuasive.

As noted in Chapter 2, Hovland used the term *credibility* to represent those qualities in the source that increase the likelihood that he or she will be believed. The most highly credible source is one that (1) appears qualified to make valid assertions about the topic of the communication; and (2) has little if anything to gain by another's acceptance of the message. Communications of a highly credible source (one who combines both expertise and objectivity) are thought to have more impact on other persons' opinions than those of a source who does not share these qualities. The research of Hovland and Weiss (1951), cited in Chapter 2, as well as later work—reviewed extensively in the literature (Giffin, 1967; McGuire, 1968; Petty & Cacioppo, 1981; Schweitzer & Ginsburg, 1966; Zimbardo, Ebbesen, & Maslach, 1977)— lend general support to this theoretical proposition.

As noted earlier, it appears that cue weighting, as a consequence of association, underlies the source credibility effect. When a source is associated with high-quality information, that source's affect on the Valuation process is enhanced. Thus, any procedure or characteristic that increases the apparent quality of a cue will result in greater impact on opinions. We come to understand, through many experiences, that experts provide information of high utility. For example, we have learned to seek a doctor's advice when we are ill, and such advice is often associated with positive outcomes. Experiences of this sort lead to a generalized association between expertise and cue quality. Thus, when we accept a source as an expert, we tend to weigh the information that this person provides more heavily than that provided by a source which does not have this quality.

Other Source Characteristics. In his work, Hovland concentrated on credibility as a major determinant of a source's impact on opinions. However, it would be a mistake to conclude that credibility is the only important characteristic of a source. From our more general perspective, we would expect that almost any characteristic associated with valued outcomes would enhance the persuasive impact of a message, whereas any characteristic associated with negative outcomes would diminish such an effect. Evidence in support of this hypothesis is provided by a number of studies (Aronson & Golden, 1962; Chaiken, 1979; Eagly & Chaiken, 1975; Hall, 1980; Miller, Maruyama, Beaber, & Valone, 1976). For example, Aronson and Golden (1962) found that sources who possessed socially valued traits (high status, neatness, and so on) were more persuasive than sources who possessed undesirable characteristics (sloppiness, obesity, and so on), even when these qualities were irrelevant to the issue of the communication. Likewise, Chaiken (1979) found that physically attractive sources were more persuasive than were their less attractive counterparts.

Advertisers long have been aware of the general effect of association on persuasion. Why else would they pay large sums of money to induce celebrities to endorse a product? For example, Robert Young, the actor who for many years played the television role of a kindly and competent physician, Dr. Marcus Welby, was hired by a well-known food producer to advertise its brand of decaffeinated coffee in TV commercials. The company no doubt hoped that the association of Young with his role as a doctor would enhance the effectiveness of their advertising campaign. Young is not an authority on coffee, nor is he necessarily any more trustworthy than the rest of us— obviously, he did not provide his services for free. Thus the company appeared to hire him in the hopes that his past association with favorable outcomes (in the role of Dr. Welby) would make him a most persuasive source for their message. Evidence of the correctness of this assumption is provided by the fact that Young has been retained by the coffee company as its spokesman for a number of years.

THE SETTING OF THE COMMUNICATION

A second factor that Hovland hypothesized as having an impact on persuasiveness is the setting in which the communication is delivered. To understand the reason for Hovland's assumption, a brief reconsideration of his theory of persuasion is in order.

Recall that in Hovland's view, when confronted with a persuasive message, people engage in an internal debate, contrasting their established beliefs with the recommended opinion. Furthermore, he suggests that factors in the setting moderate a person's ability to counterargue, and thus, could have a profound impact on opinion change.

For example, suppose that an experimenter were to develop a persuasive communication and present it in conjunction with a very complex task to which subjects had to devote almost their entire attention. If the experimenter could subtly introduce a message, it is possible that subjects would be extremely susceptible to it. Why? Because they would find it very difficult to resist (to counterargue) the communication since, given the demands of the task, their normal abilities for counterargumentation would be inhibited.

Situational Distractions and Opinion Change

Leon Festinger and Nathan Maccoby (1964) conducted a study that provides indirect evidence supporting the hypothesis that distracting conditions affect opinion change. In this experiment, two groups of subjects listened to a series of very strong arguments against the fraternity system on American campuses. In one condition of the study, the antifraternity communication was paired with an antifraternity film; in the other condition, subjects heard the same verbal message while viewing a film, but in this case, the film had nothing whatever to do with the anti-fraternity sound track—it consisted of a series of abstract art prints. After having been exposed to these communications, subjects' opinions toward the fraternity system were assessed via a standardized questionnaire.

One might assume that since the respondents in the distracting art film condition could not easily attend to the content of the persuasive message, they would be less likely to change their opinions. In fact, however, the opposite occurred: those subjects who had seen the abstract art film were more influenced by the concurrent antifraternity "sound track" than those who had received the more standard persuasive message consisting of the same antifraternity message paired with an antifraternity film.

While, at first glance, these results are somewhat startling, Hovland's theory provides one explanation for them. From his perspective, the greater distraction which took place during the abstract art presentation made counterargumentation more difficult, and thus, opinion change more likely. For this reason, respondents in this condition of the experiment would be more susceptible to the antifraternity message than those in the more standard communication condition.

Direct evidence that distraction can inhibit counterargumentation was provided in an ingenious experiment conducted by Richard Petty, Gary Wells, and Timothy Brock (1976). The investigators reasoned that if Hovland's theory were correct, a relationship would exist between the quality of a message and the effects of distraction on opinion change. If a belief discrepant message were very poorly reasoned and very unpersuasive, distraction would enhance its impact. Under distracting conditions, people would be unable to closely analyze the communication, spot its weaknesses, and ultimately reject it and maintain their established opinions. On the other hand, distractions would lessen, rather than enhance, the effect on opinion change of a well-reasoned persuasive communication. When distracted, people would find it more difficult to concentrate on the communication and therefore would be less likely to realize that the position advocated was a reasonable one and difficult to refute. Thus, the experimenters reasoned that distractions would be likely to reduce the persuasive impact of high-quality messages.

To test the hypothesized relationship between message quality and distraction, Petty, Wells, and Brock (1976) composed two messages that varied in the quality of their arguments. Both messages argued for a 20 percent tuition increase at Ohio State University, the site of their investigation. The high-quality message was logical, easily defensible, and compelling: it stated that the hike in tuition was recommended after two years' study; that Ohio provided less aid to higher education than any of the other 49 states; and that it had been proven that such an increase in fees would upgrade the quality of the university, thereby resulting in an increment in the average salary of Ohio State's graduates.

The low-quality message made similar arguments but advanced them in a much less compelling manner: it stated that a tuition increase was recommended after only two months' study; that Ohio rated 10th nationwide in state expenditures for higher education; and that such an increase would allow the university to install better lighting in the classrooms, thereby reducing the frequency of students' headaches!

One of these messages was presented to each subject. In order to study the effect of distraction on opinion change, Petty, Wells, and Brock (1976) asked their respondents to perform an additional task while listening to the message. During the course of the tape recorded presentation, subjects were informed that the letter X would be flashed somewhere on a screen that had been placed before them, and they were to count the number of times the letter appeared while they listened to the message. To vary the degree of distraction of this task, the investigators flashed either 0, 4, 12, or 20 Xs per minute during the presentation of the persuasive communication. Presumably, subjects who had to deal with the incidental stimulus every three seconds would find the task more distracting than those who saw the stimuli much less often.

The experimenters expected that the more rapid the presentation of the incidental stimuli (the Xs), the more distracting would be the task. This expectation was confirmed. As Petty, Wells, and Brock (1976, p. 878) observed, "the faster the Xs flashed on the screen, the more distracted subjects reported feeling."

The findings of Petty, Wells, and Brock (1976) supported Hovland's hypotheses regarding the relationship between distraction and opinion change. Those subjects who heard the low-quality message were more persuaded if they were distracted, whereas under conditions of less distraction, respondents were very resistent to the communication. On the other hand, those respondents who heard the high-quality message were more likely to be influenced under conditions of less distraction. When the situation was extremely distracting, the very persuasive arguments of the high-quality message could not be processed by the recipients, and thus, opinion change in this condition was minimized.

Additional results collected in the study also supported Hovland's theory.

For example, after hearing the message, respondents were asked to try to list all of the thoughts that they had during its presentation. Those who had been subjected to the conditions of less distraction listed significantly more counterarguments than those respondents who had been very distracted. The results of Petty, Wells, and Brock (1976) are consistent with the findings of other investigations (Insko, Turnbull, & Yandell, 1975; Keating & Brock, 1974; Lammers & Becker, 1980; Petty & Cacioppo, 1979; Watts & Holt, 1979).

Other Effects of the Setting

There are a number of other findings in the opinion change literature, some of which are presented in the following pages, which also support Hovland's contention that factors in the setting can influence persuasion. While the variables that we discuss do not involve distraction per se, they all affect the likelihood or ability of people to defend their beliefs against the opinion recommended in a persuasive communication. According to Hovland's theory, almost any factor that inhibits counterargumentation will result in greater opinion change. These variables can operate in very subtle ways, and because of this, people often find it very difficult to defend themselves against them. Two general examples of such subtle contextual factors will now be presented.

Role Playing and Opinion Change.   Evidence of the inhibition of counterargumentation by subtle factors in the setting is provided in studies of the influence of role playing on people's beliefs. A number of investigators have shown that when subjects are induced to play a role, quite often they later change their beliefs to be more consistent with the role they have played (Collins & Helmreich, 1970; Elms, 1966; Greenwald, 1969, 1970; Janis & Mann, 1965; Matefy, 1972; Zimbardo, 1965). Results of this sort occur even when the role is contrary to the individual's established opinions. This effect is especially likely to occur when the means used to induce a person to role play are subtle rather that blatantly coercive.

A striking example of the impact of role playing on opinions and behaviors is provided in the study of Janis and Mann (1965). In this investigation, female smokers were asked to play the role of a person whose doctor (played by the experimenter) had just informed her that she had developed lung cancer. The subjects, who were given a set of recommendations by the "physician," were encouraged to express the emotions that such a patient would experience, to act out all of the horrified reactions that such a diagnosis might generate. Other female smokers did not role play, but were assigned to the control condition; each of them heard a different tape-recording of one of the doctor-patient interactions.

The results of this study showed that the women who actually had played the role of the lung cancer victim felt more vulnerable to this disease and were more determined to quit smoking than were subjects in the control group. Even more impressive were the findings of the followup study conducted by Mann and Janis (1968) 18 months after the original experiment.

In this later study, the investigators found that the women who had been assigned to the role-playing condition in the original experiment were smoking much less than were the control group participants. Apparently, the role-playing group had incorporated an opinion about smoking that had had a long-term impact on their actual smoking behavior.

In explaining these results, proponents of Hovland's theory would observe that the women in the role-playing condition of Janis and Mann (1965) were less likely to counterargue, since their part in the experiment masked the fact that they were in a persuasive context. Moreover, they well might have been distracted by the demands of playing the role of a cancer patient. Thus, they were less able to resist the communication delivered them by the experimenter (doctor), since they were less defensive about the doctor's persuasive message and therefore less inclined to counterargue his recommendations. Under such circumstances, they were much more vulnerable than control group subjects to the opinion change influences that were brought to bear on them, and all the more likely to change.

"Overheard" Communications

One of the more insidious ways that the Social Context in which a cue is presented can affect people's opinions—without their knowing that they are in an influence situation—is illustrated in a study performed by Elaine Walster and Leon Festinger (1962). In this experiment, the investigators demonstrated that people were extremely susceptible to persuasive messages in circumstances in which the intention of the communicator was hidden. Subjects in this study were students in an introductory psychology class at the University of Minnesota. As part of their introduction to the field, they were taken on a guided tour of the psychology laboratory facilities, including the one-way mirror research rooms, which allowed experimenters to unobtrusively observe their subjects as they interacted.

As luck would have it, one of these rooms was occupied by two graduate students who were talking about common misconceptions about the dangers of smoking. One group of students from the touring class could see and hear these two people, who apparently were "unaware" that they were being observed. In their conversation (which actually was staged), one of the speakers argued that there was really no definitive evidence linking smoking to lung cancer. The other group of students from the introductory course witnessed the same episode, but were informed that the interacting dyad knew that they were being observed and were there in order to show the students how the mirrors and hidden microphones worked.

In class one week later, all students' opinions were assessed regarding the dangers of smoking, as well as their beliefs regarding the possibility of a causal relationship between smoking and lung cancer. This opinion measure was imbedded in an extensive questionnaire on health-related issues. At this time, no mention was made of the prior week's laboratory tour, which presumably the students had forgotten. The results of this study were very interesting:

those people who had "overheard" the prosmoking communication were much more persuaded by it (that is, they were much less convinced of a relationship between smoking and cancer) than those who knew that the message was staged for their benefit. The overheard message was somehow more convincing than the same message when it was known to be staged.

The results of Walster and Festinger's (1962) experiment are relevant to Hovland's conception of the effect of the trustworthiness of a source during persuasion. When a person overhears information of one sort or another, such information arouses less suspicion regarding the persuasive intention of the source of the message, and thus is accepted more readily as true or accurate. Charles and Sara Kiesler (1964) have provided evidence which indicates that merely knowing that a person is attempting to persuade lowers that source's effectiveness as an opinion change agent. The extent to which persuasive communications appear self-serving seems to influence their effectiveness, but it is also likely that any overt attempt to persuade will, to some extent, lower the perceived trustworthiness of the source, no matter the source's reasons for the attempt.

Message-Audience Incongruity

An extension of this reasoning has been examined in a number of studies in which some *message-audience incongruity* exists (that is, there is a difference between the position advocated and the established opinions of the audience to whom the message is delivered). If we consider the audience to be an important part of the Social Context, then it is clear that known characteristics of the people who make up this aggregate can serve as factors in the cue-weighting process. For example, knowing that an audience is hostile to a speaker's position should bear on one's hypotheses about the speaker's true beliefs concerning the issue. We would have greater confidence that a speaker is sincere if he or she is willing to deliver a communication to an audience whose beliefs are known to be antithetical to those presented. Why? Because we feel that those who are willing to subject themselves to potentially uncomfortable encounters simply to present their opinions must really believe in the correctness of their positions.

One of the most telling proofs of this observation is illustrated in the life and death of an early Christian martyr, Sebastian.[1] Like many of the early Christians, Sebastian, a Roman soldier, was not born into the faith but converted to it some time in his early adulthood. By the time of his conversion, Sebastian was a high-ranking officer in the employ of the emperor. In fact, as the story was told, Sebastian was one of Caesar's favorites, having access to the court and to the emperor's ear.

---

[1] As one of the authors of this text attended St. Sebastian's grade school, the story of this saint was an oft-told lesson about courage and sacrifice. Of most relevance to present concerns, however, is the reaction that the story of Sebastian stimulates on the part of the listener, since it serves as an excellent example of the processes by which we infer another's level of commitment to a belief.

To be a high-ranking soldier in the Roman legions as well as an advisor to Caesar was quite unusual for a Christian in those days. At the same time that Sebastian carried out these duties, he also secretly practiced and professed his faith with his fellow Christians. If these facts were all that we knew of his life, we might question the sincerity of his religious beliefs. This is true especially in light of the activities that typified life in the emperor's palace: palace life in those days was exceptionally decadent; to apply current standards, palace activities would be rated XXX. Sins of the flesh were not only practiced but refined to an art form. While Sebastian did not partake in these diversions, he could not avoid witnessing them.

Obviously, the palace was not the type of place that an early Christian could tolerate for long, if he really believed the tenets of his religion. On the other hand, overt objections about this dissolute lifestyle could result in some very unappealing consequences. As the story goes, Sebastian objected, and the consequences were unappealing. In fact, Sebastian confronted the emperor in front of the assembled court and berated Caesar for the decadence of the life that he was leading. The emperor, after hearing what Sebastian had to say, quickly devised an appropriate response: he ordered his guards to use Sebastian's body for archery practice.

It is obvious that Sebastian was reasonably committed to Christianity. Why else would he have confronted the emperor, knowing that he was taking some risk in doing so? Still, the risks were not completely clear: he might have thought that the emperor would scold him, banish him, or put him on unemployment compensation, and for this reason, our estimate of the level of Sebastian's faith is somewhat tentative. Certainly, Sebastian's courageous actions could be interpreted as indicating high commitment. On the other hand, it could be that Sebastian's outburst was a result of his being prodded by his Christian friends to protest the emperor's lifestyle and not the consequence of an incorporated, high-level belief. Sebastian might have felt that his admonitions would stimulate only a very mild rebuke from the emperor, an acceptable price to pay in order to demonstrate his strong faith to his fellow Christians.

Sebastian's later actions, however, provide irrefutable evidence that his behavior arose from a set of extraordinarily high-level religious beliefs. You see, Sebastian did not die from the multiple arrow wounds inflicted on him by the emperor's henchmen. He was spirited away by his friends and nursed back to health. As soon as he was able, Sebastian returned to the palace and once again lectured the surprised but unrepentant emperor. This time, the emperor made sure that Sebastian would not bother him again, and thus, Sebastian became St. Sebastian.

The social psychological moral of this story is almost as straightforward as the religious one. By observing his willingness to knowingly suffer for his beliefs, we infer with great confidence that St. Sebastian had truly incorporated the Christian credo. Such an inference can have a powerful impact on our own beliefs. This man's willingness to give his life for a religious conviction cannot be readily dismissed. Obviously, Sebastian's behavior was far from self-serving, and he was convinced of the truth of his position.

Sebastian's perseverance in the face of a hostile audience
increased the cue quality of his actions.

Both of these factors make it more difficult to dismiss the message contained
in Sebastian's actions. Sebastian's perseverence in the face of a hostile audience
tends to increase the perceived cue quality of the information provided by
his actions.

The social psychological laboratory has yielded evidence consistent with
this interpretation of Sebastian's sacrifice. While the circumstances examined
were somewhat less extreme, a study by Judson Mills and Jerald Jellison
provides graphic evidence that the Social Context of an apparently sympathetic or hostile audience can have a strong effect on the perceived cue quality
of a message. In this experiment (Mills & Jellison, 1967), respondents were
asked to read a persuasive message that argued for a tripling of truck licensing
fees. Two groups of respondents read the identical speech, which was attributed to a candidate for the Missouri legislature. The only difference between
the two samples of respondents was that one group had been informed that
the speech had been originally delivered to a meeting of a local union of
railway workers, while subjects in the other group were told that the speech
had been presented to an assembly of long-haul truckers at their local union
hall. After reading the speech, all respondents were asked to report their
impressions of the speaker, to answer a set of factual questions concerning
the presentation, and to give their personal opinions regarding the truck
tax proposal.

The variations in treatment in this study were undertaken to create two different perceptions in the respondents with regard to the Social Context in which the message was delivered. In the condition in which the audience allegedly was composed of railway workers, the respondents were expected to view the source's message as consistent with the biases of this audience. Thus, the Social Context was such that the communication could have easily been self-serving. Since the message presumably met with widespread approval, it would be a reasonable assumption that the communication was a simple attempt on the part of the speaker to ingratiate himself with the audience. Such a presentation obviously was politically expedient, as the favorable impression created by the candidate through his speech would be expected to translate into votes for him on election day.

In contrast, a much different Social Context existed when the speech supposedly had been given to a union hall filled with truck drivers whose economic well-being would be damaged if the licensing proposal were enacted. In this instance, the speech obviously was not consistent with the established opinions of the audience, and it clearly was not politically expedient to voice these views. At a minimum, the candidate was taking a political—and perhaps physical—risk by presenting his position to an audience of teamsters.

Some parallels can be drawn between this study and the life and death of St. Sebastian. Advocating an increase in trucking fees to a group of railway workers who would profit from such a law is analogous to the situation in which St. Sebastian spoke to an assembly of his fellow Christians. Under these circumstances, the Social Context tells us very little about the sincerity of St. Sebastian or of the political candidate. The same set of cues (the speakers' words) is evaluated quite differently when we know that they were uttered to a hostile audience, whether the audience was the Emperor's court or a group of disgruntled truckers.

The Social Contexts arranged by Mills and Jellison produced very different reactions in the respondents. First, the respondents' impressions of the speakers were very different, despite the fact that in each communication condition, the speaker was described in identical terms and had given the identical speech. Subjects' impressions of the speaker were much more positive when his presentation was made before a hostile audience. These respondents perceived the speaker as less cynical and opportunistic, and more honest and sincere, than did those who thought that the speech was delivered to the sympathetic audience.

Given these differences in the respondents' evaluation of the speaker, it is not surprising that their opinions were also influenced by the Social Context in which the speech was delivered. Subjects who thought that the presentation was made to a hostile audience were much more persuaded by it. In explaining their findings, Mills and Jellison (1967) stressed differences in respondents' evaluations of the source of the communication as an important determinant of his effectiveness. Obviously, a speaker who is viewed as honest and sincere will be more credible, and hence more persuasive, than one who appears to lack such qualities. By presenting a communication to a hostile audience, the credibility of the source was enhanced, and this enhanced credibility resulted in greater opinion change.

Interpersonal Environment and Opinion Change

To this point, we have confined our discussion of the impact of the setting to impersonal factors. Overheard communications, audience-message incongruity, role playing, and distraction are contextual variables, but none of these factors derives its impact directly from aspects of the interpersonal environment, that is, from those around us. In this section, we will present evidence that demonstrates clearly that the behavior and apparent opinions of those around us can exert a strong influence on our own evaluative beliefs.

Straightforward evidence that the opinions of others can have an impact on our own beliefs was obtained by Richard Crutchfield. In his work, Crutchfield (1955) refined the procedure used by Asch (1951), discussed in detail in Chapter 2, to study the impact of information about the opinions of others on a subject's own beliefs. Crutchfield's method of providing participants with controlled information about their interpersonal environment was simple, but very effective. In his research, he gathered groups of five subjects, and assigned each subject to a separate cubicle; each cubicle contained a panel of lights and switches. One of the tasks that Crutchfield employed required that respondents give their opinions about a number of topics by pressing the appropriate switch provided them on their control panels. He informed each group that subjects were to respond individually, in a specified order. Through the lights on the panel, subjects were informed of the opinions of others who supposedly had responded before them. In actuality, all subjects were told that they were the last to respond, and hence, were privy to the opinions of all of the others in their group. These opinions were fictitious and were completely controlled by Crutchfield.

In some conditions, subjects thought that their fellow respondents in the other booths were unanimous in their opinion on an issue. In these circumstances, subjects displayed a strong tendency to express views that were consistent with this consensus position. For example, when they responded without knowing the opinions of others, only 19 percent of Crutchfield's subjects agreed with the rather extreme statement, "Free speech being a privilege rather than a right, it is proper for a society to suspend free speech whenever it feels itself threatened." However, when subjects thought that all four of the others in their group had agreed with this statement, 58 percent expressed a similar opinion.

The unanimous views of the other respondents gave subjects in Crutchfield's research a cue as to the most appropriate position to adopt. This cue weighed heavily in respondents' Valuation processes for two reasons. First, the Social Context of this laboratory task was poorly Resolved for most respondents, who probably had not thought much about such issues as free speech, national security, and their mutual interplay. In such circumstances, we tend to rely upon any available cues to guide our decisions. In the present instance, a very salient set of cues was provided by the consensual judgments of the others in the group. Second, as noted in Chapter 3, people appear to strive for self/other Consistency. In the present context, this tendency would also act to influence the opinions of individual respondents.

To illustrate the roles that the interpersonal environment, Resolution, and self/other Consistency play in opinion change, consider the likely thoughts of one of the young men who served as a subject in Crutchfield's study. As with most undergraduates, his knowledge and past experience have provided him with little expertise in the experimental task. The issues under study were not topics to which he had devoted much thought. On what criteria was he to base his opinions? Obviously, confidence in his own spur-of-the-moment judgments was not great, but in the absence of other cues, they would have to serve as the bases for his beliefs. However, when additional cues (the judgments of others) were available, they provided a consistent picture of "reality," and thus, they weighed heavily in the subject's Valuation processes.

In addition, the people who were the source of the cues were very similar to the subject—they were his peers. Thus, concerns with self/other Consistency added to the subjects' tendency to advocate a position similar to their fellow participants. In contrast, if the other respondents in the group were very different from the subject, issues of self/other Consistency would prove less relevant. For example, suppose that for some reason, the respondent had been grouped with six Chinese rice traders who had just arrived in the country that morning. Since these people are not a reference group for the respondent, their unanimous opinions would have had much less impact on his own beliefs. There would have been little reason to expect the operation of self/other Consistency forces under these circumstances.

Research by David Myers and his colleagues has shown how the interpersonal environment provided by our reference group can shape our opinions. For example, in one of these studies, Myers, Wojcicki, and Aardema (1977) elicited the cooperation of a local church group. The researchers had a subset of the group complete an opinion questionnaire. Three weeks after the initial administration of the questionnaire, information about the more extreme responses obtained in the initial sample was provided to a second group of people from the same church; other church members were given no information regarding the responses of their peers. Immediately thereafter, the original opinion questionnaire was administered to these two groups of respondents. The results indicated that knowing the extreme opinions of one's fellow church members had a dramatic effect on respondents' own expressed opinions. The opinions of respondents who had been exposed to the extreme views of their fellow parishioners were much more extreme than were those of the subjects who had not been provided with such information.

It is important to note that this findings cannot be attributable to the operation of impingement processes. In Crutchfield's research, subjects well might have been influenced by the interpersonal environment to state views consistent with those of the majority—views with which they did not truly agree. In Myers' work, however, respondents knew that their individual opinions would remain confidential. As we have noted, in the absence of monitoring, impingement cannot occur. Thus, the opinions of Myers' respondents appeared to be strongly influenced by the information that they had been given about the opinions of their peers. Other research by Myers and his colleagues (Lamm & Myers, 1978; Myers, Bruggink, Kersting, & Schlosser, 1980) provides additional supporting evidence.

ASPECTS OF THE COMMUNICATION

In addition to the characteristics of a source of a communication and the setting in which the communication is delivered, a third set of factors that determines opinion change involves the general form and content of the communication itself. Message content encompasses a wide variety of communication characteristics, many of which have been extensively studied in social psychology. Many diverse variables have been shown to wield a powerful impact on opinion formation and change: the emotional content of the presentation (Janis & Feshbach, 1953); the order in which information is presented in a message (Crano, 1977); whether or not the message contains an explicit conclusion (Hovland & Mandell, 1952); the specificity of the actions or beliefs advocated (Fishbein & Ajzen, 1975); whether or not some points contrary to the advocated position are presented (McGinnies, 1966); and the grammatical form of the messages themselves (Petty, Cacioppo, & Heesacker, 1981).

As illustrative examples of the research that has been undertaken in this area, we will briefly review work on three message variables: (1) the impact on opinion change of drawing an explicit conclusion; (2) the effects of fear-arousing appeals; and (3) the more long-term influence of message content on resistance to subsequent persuasion attempts. These three topics vary widely in the amount of research that they have stimulated; conclusion drawing in a communication has been the focus of relatively few investigations, whereas the effects of anxiety-arousing appeals have been studied at great length. The amount of research on resistence to opinion change as a function of past messages lies somewhere between these two extremes.

We will begin with a discussion of conclusion drawing. The findings surrounding this effect are relatively straightforward; at the same time, they provide a clear example of the impact of message factors on opinions.

Drawing A Conclusion

The question addressed in research of this type concerns the advisability of drawing a conclusion in a message, along with the usual persuasive information. Should a communicator draw an explicit conclusion, or should he or she allow the targets to do this for themselves? This issue was investigated in a study by Hovland and Mandell (1952). In this work, the experimenters assigned their respondents to one of two different experimental conditions. In both conditions, respondents listened to a tape-recorded communication which discussed in an informative and nontechnical manner the advisability of a devaluation of the American dollar. For one group, the message led to a conclusion which the communicator stated explicitly—namely, that the dollar should be devalued. For the other group, the message was the same except that the explicit conclusion was omitted.

While both forms of the message were reasonably effective in inducing opinion change, the presence or absence of a conclusion also had an impact on respondents' beliefs. More than half of the subjects who heard the explicit conclusion changed their opinion in the direction advocated; in contrast, less than one third of the group not presented with an explicit conclusion changed in this manner. Later research on this issue (Ferris & Wicklund, 1974; Thistlethwaite, de Haan, & Kamenetsky, 1955) has yielded additional information regarding the manner in which conclusion drawing in a communication affects opinion change. To some extent, these studies supplement and extend the basic findings of Hovland and Mandell (1952); however, the straightforward relationship between explicit conclusions and opinion change uncovered by the original experiment remains unchallenged.

It seems likely that Resolution is the primary underlying process by which conclusion drawing in a communication influences opinion change. Persuasive messages often contain a large number of diverse facts and statements of opinion. The task of integrating such information can be formidable, especially if the topic is one on which the targets are not well-versed. Since the audience must weigh rather diverse bits of new information, the communication situation can be one of low Resolution. By drawing a conclusion, the communicator reduces this ambiguity, providing a convenient summary of the details contained in the message. This increased Resolution facilitates the act of Valuation inherent in the opinion-change process by increasing the audience's ability to comprehend the information presented (Thistlethwaite et al., 1955). Obviously, information that is understood weighs more heavily in a person's decision about the validity of an argument or the propriety of an opinion than does information that is not fully comprehended.

Fear-Arousing Communications

In contrast to conclusion drawing, the effects of fear-arousing communications on opinion change have stimulated a considerable amount of research. The central question here involves the relative differences in persuasiveness of emotionally arousing versus nonarousing communications.

Much of the research on fear arousal is patterned after an early study of Irving Janis and Seymour Feshbach performed more than 30 years ago. In this study, the investigators presented their subjects (high school students) with one of three different communications regarding dental hygiene. The persuasive appeals were presented in the form of a 15-minute lecture accompanied by illustrative slides. The information presented in the three message conditions was basically the same, but the conditions differed markedly in their degree of gory details and personalized threats.

In the highly fear-arousing condition, subjects were informed of the painful consequences of neglecting to brush their teeth properly and use the appropriate type of toothbrush, and so on. These words of warning were accompanied by a series of rather gruesome slides depicting in graphic detail the consequences of poor dental hygiene.

Some of the threats made in this condition were extraordinary: "If you ever develop an infection of this kind from improper care of your teeth, it will be an extremely serious matter because these infections are really dangerous. They can spread to your eyes, or your heart, or your joints and cause secondary infections which may lead to diseases such as arthritis, paralysis, kidney damage, or total blindness." Of course, these words were accompanied by slides that dramatically displayed the aversive consequences of poor dental hygiene.

In the other extreme (the low fear-arousing condition) subjects learned of the development of teeth and were shown slides of healthy teeth, x-rays of teeth with cavities, and so on.

Immediately after the presentation, subjects' reactions to the materials presented in the communications were assessed. As expected, the gory, personalized threats of the highly fear-arousing message did induce greater anxiety than did the moderate or low fear-arousing communications. In addition, one week after being exposed to one or another of these messages, subjects'

RADIOGRAPHY MARKETS DIVISION, EASTMAN KODAK CO.

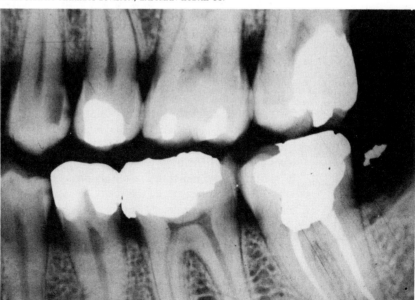

An example of the materials used in Janis and Feshbach's low fear-arousing condition.

opinions about issues of dental hygiene were tested. In this session, Janis and Feshbach (1953) found that the students who had been subjected to the highly fear-arousing message were least likely of all three of the groups tested to have followed the advice originally presented. In addition, subjects in the highly fear-arousing condition were most susceptible to a countercommunication that argued against the major premise of the original message.

In explaining their results, the experimenters argued that the highly fear-arousing message caused subjects to respond defensively and thereby to avoid thinking about it. Over time, such defensive reactions would offset the possible impact of the persuasive message on receivers' behavior.

This interpretation was consistent with the findings of a later study by Janis and Terwilliger (1962). In this experiment, groups of smokers were provided with one of two communications regarding the dangers of smoking. In the low fear-arousing communication, subjects were given 15 paragraphs attributed to medical authorities which argued that the risk of cancer could be reduced if smokers reduced their use of tobacco. The highly fear-arousing message contained 7 paragraphs in addition to the original 15. These added messages discussed the life-threatening aspects of lung cancer.

An intriguing aspect of this study derived from the measures gathered as subjects read each of the messages. After each paragraph, subjects were asked to verbalize their reactions to the information presented. An analysis of these reports revealed that subjects in the highly fear-arousing condition were more frightened than their counterparts; in addition, they were much more likely to reject the information presented them; as a consequence, these respondents were less likely to change their opinions regarding smoking. Janis and Terwilliger (1962) argued that these results supported their "defensive reaction" explanation of the effects of fear-arousing communications. Apparently, a very frightening or threatening message results in a rapid and vigorous counterargumentation response; this reaction, in turn, weakens the effect of the communication on the opinion of the receiver.

The results of the two studies by Janis and his coworkers present a somewhat simplistic picture of the effects of fear arousal on opinion change. In their studies, fear arousal was extreme, and it usually focused on a highly involving issue. It is reasonable to speculate that in such circumstances, people become so frightened that they cannot process the information that might have persuaded them. In contrast, it is likely that when the fear-arousing properties of the message are not as great and/or the subjects' involvement in the issue is not extreme, the relationship between fear arousal and opinion change might be reversed. Under these circumstances, that is, the greater the fear-arousal properties of a message, the more likely it is to persuade. A number of investigations have supported this speculation (Evans, Rozelle, Lasater, Dembroski, & Allen, 1970; Higbee, 1969; Leventhal, 1970; Millman, 1965; Rogers & Thistlethwaite, 1970).

A study by Millman (1965) has provided some evidence that supports the interpretation that arousal facilitates opinion change, but only up to a point; if arousal becomes too extreme, it is likely to evoke defensive reactions to the communication, resulting in decreased message effectiveness. In his study, Millman coupled a persuasive message with an extraneous threat to the receivers of the message, whose level of chronic anxiety had been assessed through a standard psychological measure of this Personal Structure characteristic. The extraneous threat was designed to heighten the preexisting anxiety levels of the respondents, although it was not directly connected with the communication presented. The results of Millman's experiment demonstrated that for people who were chronically anxious, the increased fear arousal inhibited opinion change; however, for those whose chronic anxiety level was low, the introduction of the extraneous threatening stimulus enhanced persuasion.

An investigation by Insko, Arkoff, and Insko (1965) further illustrates that fear arousal, if not extreme, can have a facilitative effect on opinion change. We present this study because in many respects, it is very similar to that of Janis and Terwilliger (1962). However, the Insko et al. (1965) study differed from Janis' work in one important regard: in the Insko study, the anxiety level of the subjects concerning the issue of the communication was only moderate. In their study, Insko et al. exposed a group of nonsmoking junior high school students to either a highly fear-arousing or a low fear-arousing antismoking message. They found that the highly fear-arousing message had a greater effect on subjects' opinions than the low fear-arousing communication. In a discussion of this study, Insko (1967, p. 39) reports that subjects who had been exposed to the more arousing message were much more likely to respond negatively to items such as "Will you ever try smoking cigarettes?" and "Will you become a regular smoker?"

Similarly, in a series of very carefully designed experiments, Howard Leventhal and his colleagues (Leventhal, 1970, 1974; Leventhal, Jones, & Trembly, 1966; Leventhal, Singer, & Jones, 1965; Leventhal, Watts, & Pagano, 1967) found results that generally were consistent with those of Insko et al. (1965). For example, in the study by Leventhal, Singer, and Jones (1965), both highly fear-arousing and low fear-arousing messages regarding the dangers of tetanus were presented to Yale University undergraduates. The communications varied considerably with respect to the fear-arousing nature of the materials presented. The highly fear-arousing message, for example, included color pictures of a tracheotomy, of patients with tubes inserted in various parts of their bodies, and so on.

The results of this study disclosed that those who had received the highly fear-arousing message were more fearful about tetanus and had more favorable opinions toward tetanus injections than students who had read the low fear-arousing message. Subsequent investigations by Leventhal, Jones, and Trembly (1966), and Rogers and Mewborn (1976), among others, have presented results consistent with the general findings of Leventhal et al. (1965).

As noted above, the results of work such as that of Leventhal et al. are not contradictory to the findings of Janis and his colleagues, especially if we consider the differences in fear arousal that the various procedures likely evoked. Recall that in the Janis and Terwilliger experiment, the sample consisted principally of a group of long-term smokers; in the Insko et al. (1965) study, however, the respondents were nonsmoking seventh-grade school children. It seems likely that subjects' differential experience with the activity in question—smoking—was the major determinant for the different results that were obtained in the two studies.

It is reasonable to postulate that the smokers in the Janis and Terwilliger study might have been more than a little apprehensive about the implications of this practice for their health, even before the experiment began. Given this circumstance, it is probable that a large increase in arousal—which would be evoked by the highly fear-arousing message—would prove extremely noxious, since it would add to an already uncomfortable level of anxiety. If this were the case, then subjects in the highly fear-arousing condition of the study would be expected to counterargue the persuasive communication with a good deal of vigor, and in doing so, they would avoid or counteract the threatening implications of the communication.

Smokers in the low fear-arousing condition, however, would not be expected to raise such a strong defense against the message presented to them. While these subjects' preexisting levels of apprehension on this issue would be similar to those of the smokers in the other group, the increase in anxiety caused by exposure to the low fear-arousing message would not heighten their fears to an intolerable level. Accordingly, the low fear-arousing communication would be expected to prove to be the more persuasive in this study. This was the exact result obtained by Janis and Terwilliger (1962).

The situation was quite different in the Insko et al. (1965) experiment. It is unlikely that the nonsmoking seventh-graders were greatly concerned about the impact of this habit on their health. In this circumstance, the arousing message would be expected to prove more effective, since it would be more motivating than the low fear appeal, but would not be so arousing as to cause defensive reactions on the part of the audience.

Research by Leventhal and his colleagues provides additional insight into the complex relationship between the fear-arousing properties of a message and subsequent opinion change. In his research program, Leventhal (1970) demonstrated that fear-arousing messages that offered a possible solution to the negative consequences depicted were very effective in inducing opinion change. Apparently, while a fear-arousing message heightens arousal, an accompanying solution sufficiently moderates this reaction and so inhibits defensive reactions. Thus, anxiety is raised to the point that it motivates opinion change, but not so high that it is intolerable to the respondent. In the absence of a solution, however, fear-arousing messages often lead to defensive reactions, which inhibit opinion change.

In summary, the combined work of Janis, Insko, Leventhal, and Millman, suggests that fear-arousing communications affect the Valuation process in a somewhat complicated manner. It appears that heightened arousal increases the weight that people accord to the information provided in the communication; thus, heightened arousal is positively related to opinion change. However, beyond some arousal threshold, it seems likely that the individual will become

FIGURE 4.2
The Relationship between Level of Fear Arousal and Opinion Change

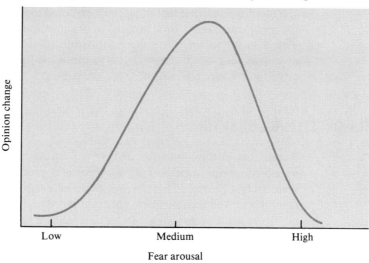

so uncomfortable that the information associated with this discomfort is summarily dismissed; thus, under such circumstances, increased fear arousal does not induce opinion change. A graphic depiction of this complex relationship is presented in Figure 4.2. As shown in the figure, the persuasive power of a communication increases with increasing fear, but only up to a point; opinion change begins to diminish sharply when arousal level passes beyond some threshold value.

Belief Inoculation

Another focus of investigation about message factors in opinion change involves the manner in which the content of one message can influence a person's resistance to later attempts at persuasion. This work, performed primarily by William McGuire and his colleagues (and summarized in McGuire, 1964, 1969) demonstrated that exposing subjects to a message that indicated the kinds of arguments that they would face in a later communication tended to "inoculate" them against the persuasive power of that appeal. Merely providing the subjects with arguments that supported their opinions, in the absence of the warning, was not nearly so effective in promoting resistance to opinion change.

These findings are compatible with Hovland's theory of opinion change: those subjects who were provided with some indication of the kinds of appeals that were to be used against their established opinions were much better able to defend themselves against attempts to persuade them (that is, better able to construct effective counterarguments) than those who first encountered the opinion-Inconsistent information in the persuasive message itself.

It should be noted that the inoculation phenomenon involves factors in both the message and the target. In one sense, that is, McGuire studied the effect of a message factor, since he explored the impact of new information that was transmitted to a person. In another sense, he was also concerned with a target factor, since the information that he originally provided had an impact on targets' susceptibility to subsequent persuasive messages. Other target-based variables will now be considered.

FACTORS IN THE RECEIVER

Recall that in the discussion of Personal Structure presented in Chapter 1, we noted a wide variety of mechanisms and processes in people that affect their social behavior. These processes include habits, motives, evaluative beliefs, affects, and faculties. Some of these processes, depending upon variations in the Social Context, enhance an individual's susceptibility to persuasion; in other circumstances, these processes appear to enhance resistance to the persuasive message.

For example, much research has demonstrated that existing high level opinions are extremely resistant to change under most circumstances. Conversely, we expect that a person with strong security motivation would be susceptible to persuasion, especially if the source of the communication were an authority figure. Consistent with this expectation, Ward and Wilson (1980) found that people with high level security needs were more easily influenced by the expressed opinions of others than were those with lower level security needs.

It is impossible in a brief section to summarize all of the possible effects that specific Personal Structure characteristics can have on people's susceptibility, or resistance, to opinion change. Fortunately, Sherif and Hovland (1961) have developed a set of concepts that satisfactorily summarize the components of the Personal Structure that mediate persuasion. They termed this approach *social judgment theory*.

Social Judgment Theory

In collaboration with Sherif, Hovland extended his theory of opinion change to encompass some ideas about the role of the target's belief system in persuasion. In the earlier version of his model, the target was conceived as a passive receiver of information whose ability to counterargue was often determined by external forces such as situational distraction and message content. Indeed, in their book, *Personality and Persuasibility,* Hovland and Janis (1959) focused on a single characteristic of the Personal Structure: the target's susceptibility to persuasion. As in Hovland's earlier work, the target was viewed as a passive receiver of information. Some receivers—those characterized as high in persuasibility—were easy victims to almost any persuasive attempt; others—those low in persuasibility—could rarely be convinced of anything.

As one amusing example of high persuasibility, an acquaintance of ours once told the true story of an exchange student from Jamaica who, when new to this country, apparently had no resistance whatsoever to persuasion. While driving from Florida, where he entered the country, to Michigan, where he was to attend school, this young man encountered a number of signs along the way extolling the virtues of the various fast-food restaurants ("The World's Juiciest Hamburger") and other roadside attractions ("Don't Miss Crystal Cave, One of Nature's Most Beautiful Natural Wonders"). He took the messages of these signs literally and could not resist stopping at most of the establishments whose billboards promised an exceptional experience. Who could pass up the opportunity to eat the world's juiciest hamburger?

Needless to say, he arrived two weeks late for classes, with much of his savings dissipated and a sense of bewilderment about the American way of advertising. In contrast, most of us who are raised in this culture are at least somewhat less gullible than the young Jamaican, although as Hovland and Janis (1959) noted, people do differ in their relative susceptibility to persuasion.

Through studying the issue of persuasibility, Hovland and his colleagues confirmed that people do differ in terms of gullibility. However, they also found that an individual could vary in persuasibility because of factors such as involvement in the topic of the communication, level of commitment to established beliefs, and so on. Thus, in a subsequent theoretical model, Sherif and Hovland (1961) expanded their perspective to take into account the fact that a myriad of features, including the target's Personal Structure, can influence susceptibility to persuasion attempts. In this expanded model of persuasion, they employed three central concepts—the *latitudes of acceptance, rejection,* and *noncommitment*—to represent the Personal Structure variables that affect the process of opinion change.

Opinion Latitudes. From personal experience, we know that most evaluative beliefs are not discrete points on the continuum of all possible opinions surrounding an issue; rather, our opinions might be described more accurately as summary statements of a range of positions about an issue that we are willing to accept. Sherif and Hovland (1961) recognized this fact and incorporated this view into their theory. In doing so, they defined the range of positions that an individual finds acceptable as his or her latitude of acceptance.

For example, suppose that a person held a positive opinion about the Democratic Party. A statement that best characterized this opinion might be, "The Democratic Party provides the best representation for all the people of this country." At the same time, this person probably would subscribe as well to a host of other positive statements regarding the party: "The Democrats are the party of the 'little people,' " and "The Democratic Party is the most sensitive to the problems of the disadvantaged."

Just as there is a range of positions on an issue that an individual might find acceptable, there also exists a range of positions on a topic that an

It is likely that almost any message favoring abortion, even slightly, would fall into these women's latitude of rejection.

individual might find unacceptable: "All political parties, except the Democratic Party, should be outlawed," or, on the other side of the opinion dimension, "History attests to the fact that the Democratic Party is the country's most corrupt political organization." Sherif and Hovland termed this range of unacceptable positions the individual's latitude of rejection. These concepts—latitude of acceptance and latitude of rejection—are graphically illustrated in Figure 4.3.

As suggested in Figure 4.3, not all opinion-relevant positions on an issue are subsumed within a person's latitudes of acceptance and rejection. Sherif and Hovland (1961) referred to the remaining points on the opinion continuum as a person's *latitude of noncommitment.* The latitude of noncommitment represents those positions that an individual neither accepts nor rejects. Such

FIGURE 4.3
Possible Range of Positions Toward Some Issue or Object

[rrr][aaaaafaaaaa][nnnnnnnnnnn][rrrrrrrrr]

Favorable pole   *Unfavorable pole*

where:
    r = A rejected position
    a = An accepted position
    n = A neutral position
    f = Most favored position

positions are viewed by the individual as neither particularly laudable nor particularly odious, and hence are subject to change.

Assimilation and Contrast.   When a persuasive communication advocates a position that falls within a person's latitude of acceptance, the individual views it as more congruent with his or her position than is actually the case. Sherif and Hovland called this tendency to distort the meaning of such a message an *assimilation effect.* Assimilated messages defuse the receiver's defenses, but their impact is relatively minor, since they are perceived as calling for little change.

Of course, a communicator can miss the mark to such an extent that his or her message falls within the receiver's latitude of rejection. In this circumstance, social judgment theory predicts a *boomerang effect,* in which the receiver changes his or her opinion, but in the direction opposite to that advocated in the persuasive message. A factor that contributes to the boomerang effect is the tendency of people to distort the meaning of such messages and to perceive them as being even more antagonistic to their opinions than they actually are.

Sherif and Hovland called this type of distortion a *contrast effect.* Contrast effects occur in the persuasion process when a communication advocates a position that falls well within the target's latitude of rejection. In such an instance, the communication's effect is opposite to that intended by the communicator. Research has generally provided support for the operations of both assimilation and contrast effects (Dawes, Singer, & Lemons, 1972; Hovland et al., 1957; Judd & Harackiewicz, 1980; Lord, Ross, & Lepper, 1979; Sherif & Hovland, 1961; Ward, 1966; Zavalloni & Cook, 1965).

Social Judgment and Opinion Change.   This model suggests that people do not readily undergo radical, dramatic shifts in belief—the processes of conversion discussed in Chapter 2. It is extremely rare for a single persuasive communication to cause a person to accept a position that was previously within that person's latitude of rejection, or to reject a previously acceptable view. More typically, change occurs when opinions that once were within a person's latitude of noncommitment now fall within that person's latitude of acceptance or rejection. It is also common that a persuasive communication will influence a person to change an opinion so that what was an accepted (or rejected) position now falls within the latitude of noncommitment. While extreme shifts of opinion can occur in this framework, they tend to be the result of a gradual process involving a series of small-scale modifications in opinion.

A major implication of the theory is that to achieve maximum opinion change, a communicator should construct a persuasive message so that it falls somewhere within the boundaries of the receiver's latitude of noncommitment. On the one hand, such a message would avoid the receiver's latitude of rejection and, as such, would not strongly engage his or her defenses. The receiver would probably counterargue the persuasive communication in this instance, but not so strongly that the position advocated in the message would be completely rejected. On the other hand, the message also would

FIGURE 4.4
**Recommended Message Placement in Social
Judgment Theory**

[rrr][aaaaafaaaaa][nnnnnnnnnnnCn][rrrrrrrrr]

Note: C refers to the position advocated in
the communication, placed within the individual's
latitude of noncommitment so as to stimulate maximal opinion change.

fall beyond the receiver's latitude of acceptance, where, because of assimilation
and other processes, there is minimal impetus to change. Thus, as illustrated
in Figure 4.4, it is when the communication falls within the target's latitude
of noncommitment that at least some opinion change is most likely to occur.

Ego-Involvement and Latitude Width

Sherif and Hovland's (1961) theory is relevant to understanding the role of
Personal Structure variables in persuasion: factors within the person determine, to a large extent, the widths of these various latitudes which, in turn,
determine the susceptibility of the individual to a persuasive communication
on a given issue.

For example, the relevance of an opinion to one's high level motives
will undoubtedly affect latitude width. Consider a person with a strong motivation to achieve. If this individual, though quite intelligent, did not perform
well in standardized testing situations, she would be very reluctant to accept
any communication which argued that such tests were valid predictors of
success. Given this high level of motivation, any position that would imply
failure would fall within the person's latitude of rejection. This region would
be very wide in relation to the other latitudes. Thus, any communication
antagonistic to the receiver's high level motive would tend to stimulate a
boomerang effect.

In developing their theory, Sherif and Hovland (1961) used the term
ego-involvement to summarize all of the Personal Structure determinants of
latitude width. This term subsumes a host of variables, all of which refer
to the level of an issue for an individual. As defined by Sherif and Hovland
(1961, p. 197), ego-involvement refers to "the intrinsic importance of the
issue" for an individual, reflecting his or her "abiding stand on the issue."
Research (for example, Eiser & Stroebe, 1972) has demonstrated that the
more ego-involving the issue (that is, the more relevant it is to high level
beliefs), the wider are persons' latitudes of rejection and the more constricted
are their latitudes of noncommitment.

In many ways, the basic tenets of social judgment theory make intuitive
sense. People who are extremely involved on an issue are rarely open to a
wide range of alternative positions about it. They are difficult to sway, as
would be expected given their narrow latitudes of noncommitment and rela-

tively broad latitudes of rejection. Positions at variance with their established opinions are likely to be seen as even more discrepant than is actually the case and, as such, judged as unacceptable, perhaps intolerable.

For example, consider a young man who is extremely involved in his religion. This man would probably judge positions even slightly at variance with his as foolish or intolerable. In terms of the social judgment model, this man's latitude of rejection would be expected to be quite wide relative to his latitude of acceptance, and his latitude of noncommitment would be constricted. Under these circumstances, communications urging a change of opinion would not be likely to succeed.

In contrast, in considering another issue, the same young man might have a wide latitude of acceptance relative to his latitude of rejection. For instance, he might be very unconcerned about presidential politics, thus he would find it necessary to reject only a small portion from the possible range of opinions on this issue. Variations in this man's latitudes of acceptance and rejection that are a result of the issue under consideration are illustrated in Figure 4.5. From this illustration, it should be clear that high level opinions will be the most difficult to change. In these conditions, a receiver's latitude of rejection is wide while the latitude of noncommitment is correspondingly narrow. Therefore, there is a much greater possibility that a persuasive message will advocate a position that falls within the latitude of rejection when highly involving opinions are the focus of the communication.

Ego-Involvement, Discrepancy, and Change

Research investigating the predictive implications of Sherif and Hovland's social judgment model has generally provided evidence supportive of the theory. A review of a few of the many studies in this area will provide some insight into the general trends in this field.

In one of the earliest studies of the effect of ego-involvement on the relative widths of subjects' latitudes of acceptance and rejection, Hovland, Harvey, and Sherif (1957) provided a sample of Oklahoma voters with a series of nine statements which summarized a wide range of possible opinion positions regarding the prohibition of alcoholic beverages in their state (an issue on an upcoming ballot). Respondents were asked to indicate which statement best represented their opinion, which of the others were acceptable

FIGURE 4.5
Variations in Widths of Latitudes of Acceptance,
Noncommitment, and Rejection

High involvement issues:
    [rrrr][aaaaafaaaaa][nnnn][rrrrrrrrrrrrrrrrrrrrr]

Low involvement issues:
    [rr][aaaaafaaaaa][nnnnnnnnnnnnnnnnnnn][rrr]

to them, which statement was most unacceptable, and which of the others also were unacceptable. Hovland, Harvey, and Sherif (1957) found that the more extreme the respondent's most acceptable position (an indicant of the subject's level of belief on an issue), the wider his or her latitude of rejection. This relationship was evident whether the respondent was in favor of or opposed to prohibition. Findings generally consistent with these results have been reported by Eagly and Telaak (1972); Sherif, Kelly, Rodgers, Sarup, and Tittler (1973); Sherif, Sherif, and Nebergall (1965); Sherif and Sherif (1967); and Whittaker (1963), among others.

What of the relationship between communication discrepancy and opinion change? On this point, the findings for the most part also are in agreement with the theory. Though only a small number of experiments have directly measured respondents' latitudes of acceptance, rejection, and noncommitment, these have quite consistently yielded findings that supported the social judgment model (Eagly, 1967; Hovland et al., 1957; Peterson & Koulack, 1969).

One such experiment, performed by Paul Peterson and David Koulack, provides an example of this type of research and the results typically found in this area. In the late 1960s, these investigators surveyed the opinions of a group of undergraduates about the war in Vietnam, using a procedure that allowed them to derive each respondent's latitudes of acceptance and rejection on this issue. Three weeks later, they brought these respondents back into their laboratory and asked them to write a 500-word essay which advocated a position on the war which was discrepant from their own. For some, the opinion that they were to support in the essay was only slightly different from their most favored position, as measured earlier; for others, the opinion to be supported was moderately discrepant; whereas a third group was asked to defend an opinion that was very different from their own position on the Vietnam war.

As shown earlier, asking people to role play in this manner can be an effective means of altering their opinions. In Peterson and Koulack's (1969) experiment, the effectiveness of this technique was found to depend on the distance between subjects' original opinion and that which they advocated in the essay. As predicted on the basis of social judgment theory, there was an increase in opinion change with increased distance from the most favored position, but only up to a point; when the position that subjects had to advocate fell clearly within their latitude of rejection, the essay writing produced little, if any, shift in opinion.

In addition to studies that have demonstrated the relationship between opinion latitudes and opinion change, another body of evidence supports a similar link between ego-involvement and opinion change. One example of this type of research is provided by Ramon Rhine and Laurence Severance. In this experiment, Rhine and Severance (1970) asked California college students their opinions on two issues of markedly different importance to them. The high-involvement issue concerned students' views on charging tuition in the California college system, a topic being considered at that time by state officials which was a source of considerable student agitation (at this time, no tuition was charged citizens of the state for attending public colleges and universities). The low-involvement issue dealt with the amount of new park acreage that should be developed in Allentown, Pennsylvania.

In their research, Rhine and Severance first measured respondents' latitudes of acceptance, noncommitment, and rejection to various amounts of tuition and park acreage. Consistent with social judgment theory, the widths of these latitudes varied, depending on the respondents' levels of involvement with the issues. For the park acreage issue, the respondents displayed very wide latitudes of noncommitment and correspondingly narrow latitudes of rejection. In contrast, for the high-involvement tuition issue, the widths of the respondents' latitudes of noncommitment were quite narrow, whereas their latitudes of rejection were very wide.

In addition, this experiment exposed respondents to one of two persuasive messages. For some, the message advocated the institution of tuition in the state universities (the high-involvement issue); for others, the message was concerned with park acreage (the low-involvement issue). Within each of these issue conditions, the discrepancy between the students' existing opinions and the position advocated was varied as well. Thus, for some respondents, the message advocated a position that fell within their latitudes of acceptance; for others, the position advocated clearly fell within their latitudes of rejection; for still others, the message fell somewhere between these extremes.

The results of this study (presented in Figure 4.6) were consistent with the predictions of social judgment theory. Under low-involvement conditions (the park acreage issue), the more extreme the discrepancy between respondents' initial opinions and the position advocated in the persuasive message, the greater the opinion change. In contrast, under high-involvement conditions, the smallest discrepancy (which was within respondents' latitudes of acceptance) produced little change. As message discrepancy increased, opinion change increased for those advocated positions that were within respondents' latitudes of noncommitment. When the message advocated a view that fell within the subjects' latitudes of rejection, however, the amount of shift in opinion dramatically decreased.

In summary, the results obtained in this study indicate that the impact of a persuasive message on opinion change varies as a consequence of the latitude into which the advocated position falls, and that the widths of the three latitudes vary as a result of differences in ego-involvement. Additional research (Eagly, 1967; Freedman, 1964) has yielded similar supportive evidence that other Personal Structure variables related to ego-involvement affect the relationship between discrepancy and opinion change.

As this research has shown, the theory of social judgment provides a comprehensive picture of the effects which the many factors that reside within an individual can have on opinion change. The evidence summarized suggests that Personal Structure factors determine persons' reactions to persuasive

FIGURE 4.6
Relationship between Discrepancy and Opinion Change under High and Low Involvement

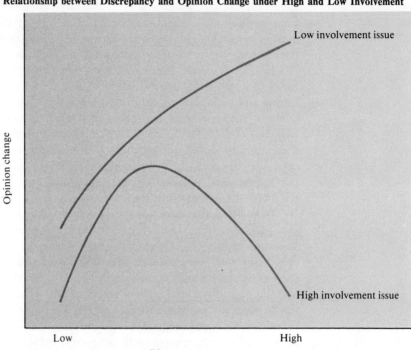

Source: Adapted from Rhine and Severance, 1967.

communications by affecting the widths of the three latitudes. Similarly, information has been presented concerning the other major classes of variables (source, setting, message) that Hovland first identified as crucial determinants of opinion change.

To this point, we have considered each of these factors as if they operated independently of one another. In fact, all four factors—source, setting, message, and target—act in concert to affect persons' responses to persuasive communications. To provide a more accurate, if more complicated, picture of the interactions of these variables, we will discuss in the following section some studies that examine the effect of more than one type of opinion-change factor. A closer consideration of the research discussed earlier in this chapter reveals that much of this work had simultaneously investigated more than one of the major opinion-change factors. On the following pages, these studies will be reviewed from this more inclusive perspective, as will be other relevant research involving the interaction of these major sources of influence on persuasion. In doing so, we will examine representative research examples which address some of the issues that long have been of major concern in the study of persuasion.

INTERACTIVE EFFECTS OF SOURCE, SETTING, MESSAGE, AND TARGET

Interaction of Source and Setting

Earlier, we discussed the research of Mills and Jellison (1967), in which the same message—an argument advocating an increase in truck licensing fees—was differentially persuasive according to the audience to which it purportedly had been delivered. Recall that the speech was more persuasive to respondents who thought that it had been presented to a hostile audience. These findings were presented as an example of the effect of the Social Context on opinions. A closer examination of this study indicates that information about the audience did not directly affect opinions, but rather influenced respondents' perceptions of the credibility of the source of the communication, and that it was this latter factor—source credibility—which was responsible for the obtained results. This relationship is graphically illustrated in Figure 4.7. In Hovland's terms, a setting factor influenced subjects' perceptions of a source factor which, in turn, influenced their opinions. This experiment demonstrates the ways in which two of the major factors involved in the persuasion process operated in concert to mediate opinion change.

Interaction of Source and Message

In research that paralleled that of Mills and Jellison (1967) to some extent, Koeske and Crano (1968) examined the interactive effects of source and message on persuasion. This study demonstrated that opinion change could be enhanced when a communicator provided a message that was inconsistent not with the opinion held by the audience, but with his or her own well-known position on the topic.

In this study, the experimenters asked a group of 78 Northwestern University undergraduates to read a 17-page booklet which contained a number of factual statements, one to a page. After reading a statement, subjects were to indicate the extent to which they agreed with it by marking an opinion scale provided for that purpose. For some of the respondents, a source was paired with each statement; for the others, no source attribution

FIGURE 4.7
Sequential Effects of Social Context on Source Credibility and Opinion Change

Social context	Communicator credibility	Opinion change
Hostile audience ⟶	High ⟶	Yes
Supportive audience ⟶	Low ⟶	No

Source: Based on Mills & Jellison, 1967.

was made. Typical pairing of source and statement and the rating scale used in this study are as follows:

> ". . . In order to be really effective, our foreign aid program should be almost completely redesigned and massively increased in scope."
>
> Senator J. W. Fulbright

: __ : __ : __ : __ : __ : __ : __ :

Strongly	Strongly
disagree	agree

Subjects responding in the "no source" condition of the experiment were given the same statement and response scale, but the source's identification—in this case, Senator Fulbright—was omitted.

In attempting to determine whether the consistency or inconsistency of a source's statement and its established position affected the persuasiveness of a message, Koeske and Crano (1968) built two critical source-statement comparisons into their study. One of the sources chosen for the experiment was General William Westmoreland, the commanding general of the U.S. Armed Forces which, at that time, were engaged in the bloody conflict in Vietnam; the other source was Stokely Carmichael, a noted civil rights activist whose slogan "Black Power" had gained him considerable notoriety in the press at that time. For each source, two statements were devised; one of these was obviously consistent with the source's known position, the other was inconsistent, but still plausibly stated by the source. The source-consistent and source-inconsistent statements that were attributed to Westmoreland or Carmichael are presented in Table 4.1.

The central question in this research was whether the persuasive power of these statements varied as a result of their attribution to a congruous or incongruous source. In other words, do the factors of source and message combine to produce opinion change that differs from the effect of either variable taken separately? To answer this question, the ratings of respondents in the "no source" group were compared with those of the "source present"

TABLE 4.1

Congruous and Incongruous Source-Statement Pairings (from Koeske & Crano, 1968)

	Source	
Message Type	*Westmoreland*	*Carmichael*
Incongruous	Generally speaking, the number of U.S. casualties in the Vietnamese conflict has far exceeded that reported in the U.S. press.	Often Negroes have not taken the initiative necessary to benefit from civil rights legislation.
Congruous	U.S. bombing of North Vietnam has partially reduced the influx of men and military supplies to the South.	There are many documented reports of police brutality in Negro neighborhoods.

group. The ratings of the "no source" subjects provided an estimate of the inherent persuasiveness of a statement.

To illustrate this comparison process, consider this statement from Table 4.1: "Often, Negroes have not taken the initiative required to benefit from civil rights legislation." When this statement was not attributed to a source, the subjects who read it found it rather unpersuasive (on a scale from 1 to 7, with higher numbers indicating greater agreement, this statement was rated 3.7). However, when the same statement was attributed to Stokely Carmichael, it was found to be somewhat more persuasive (the average agreement rating was 5.1).

Interestingly, when a message is congruent with the source's apparent bias, the message's persuasive power tends to decrease. For example, consider this statement: "There are many documented reports of extensive police brutality in Negro neighborhoods." When not attributed to a source, this statement was found to be very credible by the subject sample; however, when this same statement was attributed to Stokely Carmichael, it was found to be less credible (its mean agreement rating dropped significantly). This pattern of findings was also obtained in the statements allegedly made by Westmoreland.

Other research that has examined different source and message variables has also demonstrated ways in which these factors interact to affect opinions. For example, a number of studies have shown that source credibility can mediate the impact of message content on low level opinions. If the source is highly credible, there is a strong relationship between message discrepancy—the extent to which the advocated position differs from the existing opinion—and opinion change. Conversely, when source credibility is low, there is little relationship between discrepancy and opinion change. However, when there is a moderate level of source credibility, the relationship appears curvilinear—that is, discrepancy and opinion change are positively associated up to a point, with greater discrepancy resulting in greater change; after this point is reached, however, increasing discrepancy between message and opinion typically results in decreasing opinion change. While no single study provides support for all aspects of the relationships described here, the combined work of Aronson, Turner, and Carlsmith (1963), Bochner and Insko (1966), Brewer and Crano, (1968), and Wood and Eagly (1981) supports the idea that a source and its statements interact to affect opinion change.

Interaction of Source and Target

Many years ago, Solomon Asch (1948) asked subjects to give their opinion about the following statement: "I hold that a little rebellion now and then is a good thing." For some respondents, the source of the statement was identified as Thomas Jefferson; for others, the statement was attributed to V. I. Lenin. As might be expected, subjects expressed a more positive opinion of this assertion when they thought Jefferson was its author. Asch attributed this result to differences in the meaning that subjects attached to the statement as a function of its source. As such this study illustrates the operation of a source factor on persuasion.

Suppose, however, that we were to extend this study by examining two very distinct groups of respondents. One of our groups would consist of American college students, as in the original investigation; the second group would be comprised of members of the Soviet Politburo. In this case, we would expect rather large differences in the two groups' reactions to the message as a function of the source to which it was attributed. The college student sample would be persuaded much more by the communication if it were attributed to Jefferson; the Politburo members, on the other hand, would be more likely to subscribe to the position advocated in the message if they thought it had been espoused by Lenin. This imaginary study is an example of the interaction of the factors of source and target on opinion change.

A more concrete example of this interactive relationship is discussed by Milton Rokeach in his impressive work on dogmatism. In this work, Rokeach (1960) demonstrated that dogmatic respondents—that is, those whose Personal Structures inclined them to be rigid and close-minded—were greatly influenced by a message in the form of an assertion made by an authority figure (for example, a well-known general). Respondents who were not dogmatic, on the other hand, were more likely to be persuaded by a message which presented a logical case for its position.

Interactions of Setting with Message or Target

The study by Petty, Wells, and Brock (1976) was described earlier as a demonstration of the impact of distraction—a factor in the setting—on opinion change. Recall, however, that in this study, the effect of distraction differed as a consequence of the quality of the message presented. High-quality messages were less effective and low-quality messages more effective under distracting conditions. The opposite pattern was found when distraction was minimal. These findings suggest that setting and message factors interact in determining opinion change.

Similarly, in presenting the effects of fear arousal on opinion change, we cited a study by Millman (1965) to illustrate the point that variations in the initial arousal level of an individual moderate the impact of additional arousal on opinion change. More specifically, Millman's study demonstrated that an extraneous threat—a factor in the setting—can interact with a respondent's chronic anxiety level—a Personal Structure characteristic—in affecting susceptibility to a persuasive message. This investigation provides a clear example that the impact of factors in the Social Context—the level of threat in the setting—can be moderated by factors in the target of the communication.

Interaction of Message and Target

An early study by Hovland, Lumsdaine, and Sheffield (1949) provides a good example of the interaction of message and target in opinion change.

In this study, undertaken during World War II, groups of soldiers who initially either favored or opposed the position of a communicator about the likely length of the war were presented with one of two messages. For some, the message presented only evidence consistent with the communicator's point of view. For others, the message strongly favored the communicator's position on the issue, but also contained some arguments contrary to his view. The results demonstrated an interaction between the Personal Structure variable of the targets' initial belief and the type of message employed. One-sided messages were more persuasive among those who initially were inclined to agree with the position advocated, whereas two-sided messages were more effective when employed among respondents who initially were opposed to the communicator's views.

It should be noted that the fundamental premise of social judgment theory is that message and target factors interact to influence the effect of a persuasive message on opinions. For example, as noted, the work of Rhine and Severance (1970) has demonstrated that the impact of a specific message depends upon such Personal Structure variables as the target's ego-involvement on the critical issue and the widths of his or her latitudes of rejection, noncommitment, and acceptance.

More Complex Interactions of Factors in Persuasion

Our discussion of the ways in which persuasion factors interact was designed to provide some insight into the complexity of the processes involved in opinion change. We have considered the operation of the factors that Hovland implicated as critical in persuasion both in isolation and in combination. However, the various combinations possible among source, setting, message, and target factors paint an even more complex picture. A single example should suffice to provide some idea of the rich and multifaceted nature of the opinion-change process.

Interaction of Setting, Message, and Target. In their investigation of the impact of overheard communications on opinion change, Walster and Festinger (1962) provide an example of an interaction of setting, message, and target factors in persuasion. In an extension of their first study, discussed earlier, Walster and Festinger (1962) found that a respondent's level of ego-involvement in the topic of the overheard message affected its persuasive impact.

Subjects were presented with two messages which supposedly were the tape-recorded discussions of two therapists who were awaiting their next patients. One of these communications argued that student husbands should spend more of their time at home. The second message suggested that unmarried female students should be given the opportunity to live off campus (when the study was undertaken, this was not a common practice).

The marital status of the subjects who heard these messages was related to the impact that the communications had on their opinions. The communication about student husbands was more persuasive for married women when they thought that they were listening in on therapists who supposedly did not know they were being overheard. In contrast, the manner of presentation of this same message (overheard versus normal) had little impact on the opinions of single women. On the other hand, single women were more persuaded when they overheard the communication which argued that unmarried women should be allowed to live off campus; they were less persuaded when the message was not presented as having been surreptitiously tape recorded.

These results indicate that factors in the setting—whether the message is overheard or presented directly as a persuasive communication—can affect the impact of a message. The impact of the message, in turn, is dependent on relevant personal characteristics of the target. Obviously, a very complicated pattern evolves when the effects of three different factors are mutually dependent upon one another. However, the picture suggested by this example of an interaction of setting, message, and target factors is more representative of the manner in which persuasive communications operate in the real world.

CONCLUDING REMARKS

We expect that the examples presented to this point have convinced you that the processes of opinion formation and change often involve a multitude of variables whose effects are mutually interdependent. While this fact complicates things somewhat, the reader should not be blinded to the more basic idea that has been the underlying integrative feature of this chapter—namely, the relevance of the theme of Valuation for understanding opinion change as an incorporation process. All of the factors discussed may be viewed from the perspective of the cognitive operations in which an individual engages while reacting to a persuasive message.

We conceive of opinion change as a Valuation process that involves two focal cues: (1) the position advocated in the message; and (2) the initial opinion position of the target. Other variables (for example, source, message form, and so on) are contextual cues that influence the weight applied to these two positions. Under some circumstances (for example, high ego-involvement), contextual cues will lead the target to weight the focal cue of initial opinion position much more heavily than that of the advocated position. In this case, very little opinion change in response to the message will be evident.

In other circumstances (for example, those involving a source of extremely high credibility), the relative weights of the two focal cues will tip in the opposite direction; that is, the position advocated in the message will be accorded greater weight than the target's initial opinion, and this differential weighting will lead to an incorporation of the position, or part of the position, advocated in the persuasive message. In other words, a change of opinion will take place. We believe that conceptualizing opinion change as an example of incorporation produced by the Valuation process allows one to make a more informed estimate of the probable impact of any of a host of persuasion variables.

We have presented a wealth of complicated material in this chapter. However, to this point, our discussion has been limited to the processes of opinion formation and change, per se, and has not dealt with the relationship between these processes and overt actions. This important topic is considered in detail in the two chapters that follow. Chapter 5 reviews the theory and research evidence concerned with the impact of overt behavior on opinions. Chapter 6 considers the reverse relationship—namely, the effect of opinions on overt behavior.

Beliefs and Overt Actions: 5
I. Effects of Behavior on Opinions

The previous chapter dealt with theories and research findings concerned with the development, maintenance, and change of opinions. From this presentation, it is apparent that enormous attention has been devoted to these topics. Despite the scope of the materials covered, however, one very important determinant of opinion and opinion change remains to be considered—namely, the effect of our own actions on our evaluative beliefs, a topic to which we now turn our attention.

The traditional view of the relationship between opinions and overt actions holds that such beliefs are major determinants of the ways that people behave. For years, this basic tenet was a motivating force for much of the empirical research on opinions presented in the last chapter. Obviously, social psychologists would not have studied opinions with such vigor unless they had accepted the idea that these beliefs had some systematic influence on persons' subsequent actions. Evidence directly related to the proposition that opinions cause actions will be presented in Chapter 6, and there is much in that chapter to support the classic view. In the present chapter, however, the reverse possibility will be examined: the proposition that actions can affect opinions.

By the middle 1950s, the traditional assumption of a causal relationship between opinions and behavior had become so well entrenched that it was one of social psychology's most widely accepted principles. In 1957, however, Leon Festinger proposed a theory whose principal assumption about the link between opinion and action was directly opposite to that of the traditional view. In his theory of cognitive dissonance, Festinger (1957) asserted that actions caused opinions, rather than the reverse. His model was a radical departure from the perspective that had been accepted for so long in social psychology. His theory caused so much controversy and had such a major impact on the field that a large portion of the subsequent work in social psychology has been addressed to the many issues that his model raised. For this reason, we will begin our discussion of the influence of behaviors on beliefs by examining Festinger's landmark theory.

FUNDAMENTALS OF DISSONANCE THEORY

Festinger's theory of cognitive dissonance is deceptive. The theory appears simple and straightforward, yet its basic tenets often lead to predictions that are contrary to our intuitions about human behavior. A major factor in the theory's disarming simplicity is that as originally formulated, it consisted of only three fundamental premises. When considered separately, each of these seems quite reasonable, as their paraphrasing here should attest:

1. People are sensitive to imbalances or Inconsistencies among their beliefs, or between their beliefs and actions;
2. Such perceptions of imbalanced or dissonant relationships are uncomfortable, and thus motivate the perceiver to modify the dissonant elements in order to restore a state of Consistency or balance;
3. These modifications can take one of two forms: (1) people can attempt to change the beliefs that they perceive as contributing to their feelings of dissonance; or (2) they can attempt to change the actions, or consequences of those actions, that they perceive as inconsistent with their established beliefs.

As noted, each premise, in itself, is straightforward; when combined, however, the three generate some startling predictions, as the following example demonstrates.

THE FORBIDDEN TOY STUDY

In an interesting experiment conducted by Elliot Aronson and J. Merrill Carlsmith (1963), primary-grade school children were individually escorted into a playroom and shown five different toys—a battery-powered tank, a steamshovel, a set of plastic gears, a fire engine, and a set of pots and pans. After a short period in which the child could examine the toys, each was asked to rate them in terms of their desirability as playthings. After the child made these ratings, the experimenter placed the second-ranked toy on a table. The remaining toys were spread on the floor.

The experimenter then said:

> I have to leave now for a few minutes to do an errand. But why don't you stay here and play with these toys while I am gone? I will be right back. You can play with this one [*pointing*], this one, and this one. But I don't want you to play with the———[*indicating the second-ranked toy*].

In Aronson and Carlsmith's study, each child was allowed to play with the toys before rating them.

To induce compliance, the experimenter made one of two "threats": in the severe threat condition, the child was told that the toy could not be played with, and if it were, the child would not be allowed back, would be seen as a baby, and so on; in the mild threat condition, the experimenter simply said that he would be annoyed if the child played with the toy.

None of the children in either of these conditions played with the forbidden toy after the experimenter had withdrawn from the playroom, although they all played with the other toys available. Apparently, both admonitions were sufficient to dissuade the children from risking the wrath of the experimenter; besides, other toys were available. After 10 minutes, the experimenter returned to the room and asked the children once again to rate the toys.

Imagine for a moment that you are a doctoral candidate in social psychology attempting to pass your comprehensive examination. Your professor presents you with the information from Aronson and Carlsmith's (1963) study and asks you to predict the reactions of the children to the forbidden toy. What effect (on the subjects' opinions toward the toy) if any, did the differences in the severity of the threats have?

Some people would guess that the children who had been severely threatened would downgrade the toy in the reevaluation. Others might guess that either threat would lower the desirability of the forbidden toy. Still others might hypothesize that both types of threats would increase the children's desire for the toy—the old forbidden-fruit phenomenon. If your studies had included a consideration of dissonance theory, however, you would have developed very different predictions.

First, you would have asked yourself, "In which of the experimental conditions was a state of cognitive dissonance more likely to have developed in the children?" After some thought, you would correctly surmise that there was greater dissonance generated in the mild threat condition. Why? Because the experimenter's admonition in this condition was a weaker impingement attempt than were the words that he had used to elicit obedience in the severe threat condition. Yet, the children in the mild threat condition did not play with the forbidden toy after being told not to do so. Thus, they held in their minds two beliefs that were dissonant—the opinion that the toy was a highly desirable plaything and the knowledge that they did not play with it, even though the threat was quite mild.

The children in the severe threat condition, on the other hand, probably experienced much less dissonance than had their counterparts who were given the mild impingement. Why? Because the relevant cognitions that they held were less contradictory and more balanced. The children who had been threatened severely also did not play with the desirable toy, but they had a good reason for their decision—the explicit negative consequences that the experimenter promised should they violate his dictum. Thus, you would conclude that the children in the mild threat condition experienced more cognitive dissonance than did those whose behavior had been severely constrained.

You next turn your attention to the question of how the children who had been threatened mildly could reduce the dissonance that they were experiencing. It is clear that they could not turn back the clock and relive the experience. An action, once performed, cannot be undone—but it can be distorted in one's mind. Thus, one possible way of reducing the dissonance would involve a distorted recollection of past experiences. In other words, the children in the mild threat group might have (incorrectly) "remembered" having been severely threatened. A second possible mechanism by which the mildly threatened children could reduce their dissonance would entail a change of opinion about the desirability of the toys. They might tell themselves that they had not bothered to play with the forbidden toy during the experimenter's absence because after thinking about it, they found it less desirable than they had initially judged it to be.

If adopted, either dissonance-reducing tactic—distortion or opinion change—would lead the children to devalue the toy on the second rating. Thus, in developing your answer to the professor's question, you must decide which of these two basic tactics the children would most likely adopt. It makes intuitive sense to you (as it did to Festinger) that people would use the tactic that was easiest to implement. In the present case, it seems that the children would find it easier to change their opinions about the toy than it would be for them to forget and distort what had actually happened. Thus, you would predict that the children in the mild threat condition would change their opinions about the forbidden toy's desirability as a plaything. The children who had been severely warned about playing with the toy, however, would not have had to go through this reevaluation process, because they did not experience much dissonance between their favorable opinion of the toy and their failure to play with it.

This brilliant reasoning predicted exactly the results of Aronson and Carlsmith's (1963) study, as well as the similar findings of later work (Ebbesen, Bowers, Phillips, & Snyder, 1975; Freedman, 1965; Lepper, Zanna, & Abelson, 1970; Ostfeld & Katz, 1969; Pepitone, McCauley, & Hammond, 1967; Turner & Wright, 1965). A substantial number (36 percent) of the children in the mild threat condition decreased their evaluation of the previously forbidden toy on the second ranking; in contrast, none of the children in the severe threat condition did so. The summary implication of this research is that Inconsistencies between two beliefs ("I liked that toy, but I didn't play with it") can result in the modification of one or the other of them ("I really didn't like the toy all that much, and that is why I didn't play with it").

At first glance, one might expect that the level of threat should have no bearing on opinion. Or, one might expect that the threat would generate negative feelings in the child and that these feelings would become associated with the object of the threat (the forbidden toy). Under this circumstance, the more severely threatened the child, the less favorable would be his or her subsequent evaluation of the toy. Yet, neither of these outcomes was observed. Instead, the more mild threat produced the greater opinion change. From the perspective of dissonance theory, this result makes good sense. Opinion change occurred because compliance to the mild threat generated the greatest amount of cognitive dissonance, and a reevaluation of the toys apparently was the most efficient means of reducing this aversive state.

Predictions of the type that stimulated Aronson and Carlsmith's (1963) study generated a considerable amount of attention in social psychology. The exploration of the boundaries of Festinger's (1957) theory became a major thrust of empirical work on opinion change and related topics. In the following section, we will discuss some of the major research areas to which dissonance theory has been applied.

AREAS OF DISSONANCE RESEARCH

Such diverse phenomena as doomsday cults (Festinger, Riecken, & Schachter, 1956), rats running down a straight alley maze (Lawrence & Festinger, 1962), initiation ceremonies (Aronson & Mills, 1959), and job-related opinions (Festinger & Carlsmith, 1959) have been viewed from the vantage point of dissonance theory. A detailed summary of the extensive research literature that has developed around dissonance theory would constitute a book in its own right (Brehm & Cohen, 1962; Wicklund & Brehm, 1976). Rather than undertake a comprehensive review in this section, we will attempt to distill the major lines of empirical research on the theory that have developed over the years.

In general, three overriding phenomena have occupied the attention of dissonance researchers; effort justification, free choice (or post decision regret), and forced compliance (or counterattitudinal advocacy—advocating a position at variance with one's true belief). In the following pages, we will discuss the essential features of each of these phenomena and provide examples of typical studies that have been undertaken to investigate them.

Effort Justification

Dissonance theory presumes that people must justify to themselves any effort that they have expended or work that they have performed to the extent that obvious extrinsic reasons for these efforts are not immediately apparent to them. The expenditure of effort in the absence of a sufficient extrinsic reward theoretically is dissonance arousing, as the following example illustrates.

RUNNING AROUND WITH JOEL

Take jogging. (Please!) As we see it, this is a painful, boring, and sometimes dangerous pastime, whose extrinsic rewards are clearly more long-term than immediate.[1] Consider Joel Break, a middle-aged, somewhat pudgy businessman from Long Island. After a particularly disheartening interchange with his physician, Joel decides to get his body in order. To this end, among other things, he starts to jog. At first, the pain of his sore feet, stiff muscles, and aching lungs all meld into a single chord of agony.

After a short while, however, Joel's body becomes acclimated to the increased activity level, and he finds this pastime somewhat less aversive. However, it is still painful, time-consuming, and somewhat boring. As time goes by and Joel continues to jog every day, a funny thing happens. He comes to the realization that he likes jogging! He no longer jogs solely for reasons of health—he has already reached his ideal weight. Instead, he continues to jog in large part because he likes it, and finds that when he cannot perform his daily ritual of running five miles, he feels disappointed. Why?

One of the many reasons underlying Joel's curious change of opinion regarding jogging was probably based on the need to justify his effort to himself. While he realized that jogging in the long run might do him some good (for example, prolong his life), the short-term effects of this action were, initially, almost entirely negative. He might have received some pleasure from knowing that after a few weeks of jogging he could run a half mile without fainting, but this was probably small consolation for the blisters that had developed on both his feet. Of course, Joel's jogging provided him other extrinsic rewards—he might have enjoyed the compliments that he received on his weight loss as well as his wife's positive comments on his increased stamina—but an objective observer of Joel's relative costs and re-

---

[1] It should be obvious that neither author engages in this aberration.

"... in sickness and in health, when in top condition and when out of condition. ..."

Cognitive dissonance can lead to positive evaluations of actions that require considerable effort.

wards with respect to this action might not understand why he persisted in jogging. It simply does not appear to be worth the effort expended.

In terms of extrinsic rewards, such an assessment is probably correct. Precisely such an issue might have given rise to the development of cognitive dissonance in Joel. Consider the competing cognitions with which probably all joggers, including Joel, ultimately must contend. On the one hand, Joel thinks of himself as a logical, rational individual; on the other hand, he does not like the physical pain that often accompanies jogging. Yet, he continues to subject himself to this experience! He searches for reasons for his actions, and while he finds some (as noted above), they are insufficient to justify the behavior. These judgments are clearly in conflict, and thus Joel is in a state of cognitive dissonance, which is unpleasant and must be resolved.

To resolve this internal conflict, Joel has two major alternatives: (1) as has been the case for many former runners, he can quit; or (2) he can reevaluate the intrinsic worth of this activity and decide that it is fun and valuable in and of itself, and therefore worth the effort. At this point, the cognitive conflict has been resolved. The efforts that Joel now expends on jogging are well justified, at least in his own mind. Without such an *effort justification* process, the activity could not have persisted.

The process of effort justification is a fairly ubiquitous one in our daily lives, and as such, it has been described and explained within the context of a number of theories of social behavior.[2] Because of its relative impact on so many human endeavors, it is not surprising that there have been a number of attempts at demonstrating effort justification phenomena in the more controlled environment of the research laboratory. The study of Aronson and Mills (1959) is perhaps the best-known example of such laboratory research.

The Sex Discussion Club.   This study is a classic. In this research, Aronson and Mills (1959) recruited female volunteers to participate in a discussion group whose continuing focus was the many facets of sexuality. The undergraduate women who expressed an interest in joining the club were told that because of the nature of the materials to be considered, each potential member would be asked to take a screening test to ensure that she could contribute to the discussion in a frank and uninhibited manner. The screening test took one of two forms: a mild form, in which the women were asked to read aloud a series of mildly suggestive words (for example, *petting*); and a severe form, in which the women were asked to read aloud a series of sexually explicit words and passages from pornographic fiction. After this experience, each subject was allowed, via intercom, to listen to an ongoing meeting of the sex discussion club. This meeting was, in reality, a tape-recorded enactment by experimental accomplices of a boring discussion of the secondary sex characteristics of lower animals.

The central issue of this research was the effect of the two screening tests on the subjects' opinions of the discussion that they had been allowed to monitor. Dissonance theory predicts that the more severe the screening experience—that is, the more psychological effort the women had to expend to join the group—the greater the dissonance they would experience listening to the boring discussion. The respondents who had to read the more explicit materials had expended a great deal of effort to join the sex discussion group, and in return, they had merely received the opportunity to listen to some conversation on the relatively uninspiring topic of the physical attributes of animals. In such a circumstance, we would expect that cognitive dissonance would evolve—too much effort had been expended for too little gain. In contrast, the women who had experienced the innocuous screening test probably felt little need to justify the efforts that they had expended to join the discussion group, as they in fact had done very little. Accordingly, while they also might have been disappointed with the discussion, they probably did not experience cognitive dissonance, since it had cost them very little psychological energy to have participated to that point.

Since the women in the severe screening condition experienced more cognitive dissonance than their counterparts in the mild screening group, they would feel greater pressure to resolve the dissonance that their experiences had generated. How could they do this? One obvious way would entail a more positive evaluation of the discussion that they had monitored. In

---

[2] For example, see Gordon Allport's (1961) discussion of functional autonomy, which in many important ways, is consistent with the dissonance theory explanation of effort justification.

this way, their efforts to join the discussion group would be justified, and their dissonance reduced. The results of the Aronson and Mills (1959) study were consistent with this expectation. The women in the severe screening condition expressed opinions that were more favorable to the discussion and the discussion group than did the mildly screened subjects. Other laboratory experiments in this subarea of dissonance research (Freedman, 1963; Gerard & Mathewson, 1966; Schopler & Bateson, 1962; Wicklund, Cooper, & Linder, 1967; Yaryan & Festinger, 1961; Zimbardo, 1967; Zimbardo, Weisenberg, Firestone, & Levy, 1965) have provided results consistent with the general expectations of the theory. Thus, there is a reasonable amount of evidence indicating that actions based on insufficient external justification can lead to opinion change.

Free Choice (Postdecision Regret)

An interesting corollary of dissonance theory is that almost any decision between two or more alternatives involves some postdecision regret. The inability to possess the rejected alternatives is hypothesized to produce dissonance. Obviously, extremely clear-cut decisions probably involve little, if any, dissonance: for example, if a gunman were to ask you, "Would you like me to shoot you?" your negative response would probably not involve much dissonance—unless you were feeling particularly depressed at the time. However, most decisions that we make do not involve such clear-cut choices, and thus, according to Festinger's theory, some dissonance is aroused subsequent to almost any choice that we make.

As might be expected, the greater the similarity between alternatives in terms of their overall composite evaluations, the greater the postdecision regret. For example, suppose that you were accepted for admission at two colleges. If you evaluated these colleges very similarly in terms of their overall desirability, then whatever your choice, some dissonance would be aroused as a result of the lost opportunity to attend the other school. However, if the colleges were quite dissimilar in terms of your net evaluation of them, you would feel much less postdecision regret about your choice.

The Gift of Choice. Jack Brehm performed one of the first experimental demonstrations of the operation of postdecision regret in a *free choice situation*. In this study, Brehm (1966) asked female college students individually to evaluate a number of small, inexpensive consumer items, such as a coffee pot or a silk-screen print. For their participation, the women were promised that they would be allowed to choose between two of these items, as specified by the experimenter. In the condition designed to arouse considerable postdecision regret, the subject was allowed to choose between two items that she had rated very similarly; in the condition in which little dissonance was expected to be generated, the choice involved items that the subject had evaluated very differently. After the chosen item was presented to the subject, she was asked to read some material about it and to rate once again all of the earlier alternatives.

"I gave up on politics when no matter who I
voted for, I regretted it."

*Postdecisional regret can cause us to change our beliefs or
modify our behaviors—whatever is easier.*

As noted, the theory hypothesizes greater cognitive dissonance in the
condition involving the choice between very similarly rated alternatives. Thus,
the women in the condition that presented them with the more difficult choice
would be expected to experience more dissonance than those subjects in
the disparate alternatives condition. How would the dissonant subjects reduce
the Inconsistency? One of the few feasible means available in the context
of the experiment would entail a modification of their original evaluations,
such that the rejected alternative was no longer seen as similar in appeal
to the one chosen. Accordingly, we would expect that the women experiencing
high dissonance would enhance their evaluation of the chosen object or devalue the rejected alternative. In fact, the subjects in the highly similar choice
condition of Brehm's (1966) study did both.

In the dissimilar choice condition, little dissonance was aroused and
hence there was little need for the women to reevaluate either of their alternatives. We would expect, therefore, little difference between these women's
predecisional and postdecisional evaluations. This expectation was also confirmed. Later studies, conducted both in the laboratory and in naturalistic
field settings, have yielded results that are congruent with this aspect of
the theory (Knox & Inkster, 1968; Walster, 1964; Younger, Walker & Arrowood, 1977).

Forced Compliance (Belief-Inconsistent Actions)

In some ways, all dissonance phenomena involve an Inconsistency between
a belief and an action. In effort justification research, for example, the locus

of aroused dissonance is between the belief that "I am a reasonable person," and the knowledge that "I have just expended a great deal of effort on an activity whose extrinsic value is not established in my mind." In studies of postdecision regret, subjects are faced with a similar dilemma—they liked the alternatives provided them but rejected one in favor of another. This conflict between beliefs and actions is the force behind all dissonance research.

At the core of this area of research, however, are studies that have directly induced subjects to perform, *apparently of their own free choice,* a meaningful action that is antagonistic to one or more of their well-established opinions or other beliefs. Such belief-Inconsistent behavior is hypothesized to produce dissonance in the actor to the extent that (1) the actor cannot find sufficient external justification for such behavior; and (2) the opinions that have been violated are an important component of the actor's belief system. To observe the interaction of these necessary conditions for dissonance production, consider the following example.

MILO AND THE KOOLS

Milo Reams is the 13-year-old son of LeRoy and Gretchen Reams, a middle-class couple who live in Tarzana, California. Among other things, young Milo has been taught to avoid the menace of tobacco. He has learned from his parents that smoking is not only a smelly and disgusting habit, but a dangerous one as well. It is early autumn, just after Milo has returned from a summer at camp. On the first day of the new school year, Milo and three of his pals decide to visit the home of their good friend Waldo Precourt to listen to the record albums that Waldo had acquired over the summer. While listening to the albums in Waldo's room, one of Milo's friends pulls a pack of Kools from his jacket pocket and lights up. A second friend takes the pack and does likewise. Soon, all of the boys in the room, with the exception of Milo and Waldo, have a lit cigarette in their hands. Waldo then says, "Milo, will you pass me the pack?" As he does so, Milo also takes a cigarette, and while feeling somewhat nervous, lights up. Like his friends, Milo proceeds to puff away on the cigarette, suppressing his urge to cough all the while.

How does Milo evaluate the Kool that he smoked? To answer this question, we must consider the context in which this belief-Inconsistent action took place. Four conditions are necessary for the arousal of cognitive dissonance.

First, we might consider whether or not the opinion that Milo violated was important to him. As noted in the beginning of the story, it was—Milo had been socialized to believe that smoking was a bad habit for a number of reasons.

Second, we need to know if the belief-Inconsistent action was meaningful to Milo. Again, we believe that it was—in fact, we are sure of it, since we composed the story. Milo's action had real consequences; it was a real cigarette that Milo smoked, not a bubble gum imitation.

ERIKA STONE/PETER ARNOLD, INC.

As "Milo and the Kools" illustrates, actions resulting from social pressure can have long-term effects, especially if these behaviors are dissonance arousing.

Third, we must know whether Milo felt that his smoking was undertaken voluntarily. Did he feel so forced by his pals to smoke that he did not see any alternative? Probably not, as none of them put the slightest overt pressure on him to light up.

Fourth, we must determine if there were any other features in the Social Context that Milo could have used for a justification of his action. In this case there is one—all of his friends were smoking, and he might have felt ill-at-ease had he not also done so.[3] However, did Milo perceive this justification as sufficiently compelling to explain this behavior to himself? If he did not, then our friend Milo would find himself in a state of (probably great) cognitive dissonance.

How could Milo reduce the dissonance that resulted from his belief-discrepant behavior? Potentially, there are a number of means available to him. For example, he might think about trying to undo what he had done. In the present case, however, this is impossible, as he could not unsmoke the cigarette. Or he could decide that a single cigarette was not going to hurt him as long as he never smoked again. It is likely that this tactic would take some of the sting out of his belief-discrepant behavior. Alternatively, he might change his opinion somewhat regarding smoking. That is, he might come away from this experience thinking that cigarette smoking might not be so bad after all. Of course, all of these reactions presume the existence

---

[3] Recall Asch's work on impingement, presented in Chapter 2, as well as our discussion of self/other Consistency in Chapter 3.

of dissonance. It must be stressed that if any of the four necessary conditions noted above were not met, then Milo would probably have experienced little, if any, cognitive dissonance.

With the point of this story in mind, we will now turn to an example of the systematic research that has been conducted in the area of belief-Inconsistent actions.[4] We have chosen as our illustrative example the investigation of Festinger and Carlsmith (1959), possibly the single most influential experiment in the development of dissonance theory as a focus of empirical inquiry.

Lies and Money. In the Festinger and Carlsmith study, subjects worked individually for approximately 30 minutes on two extremely boring tasks. In the first task, for example, the subject was given a large board to which numerous free-turning pegs were attached and was asked to rotate each peg 90 degrees left, then 90 degrees right. The experimenter ostensibly was timing the subject during this nonsensical activity. Imagine doing this for 15 minutes!

The other task was no more interesting. This time, the subject was given a pegboard and asked to place empty thread spools on each of the pegs; when the board was filled, the subject was to remove the spools. After completing the task, the subject's time was recorded by the experimenter, and the subject was to repeat the activity over and over for the remainder of the session.

When the session was over, the experimenter explained that he was interested in the effects of prior expectations on the performance of the two tasks that the subject had just completed. The experimenter further explained that in another condition of the study (obviously not the one in which the subject had just participated), research participants were told by a paid confederate posing as an experienced subject that the tasks which they were about to perform were fun, interesting, and exciting. The experimenter continued to say that his assistant, who usually played the role of the experienced subject, was unable to work that day. The experimenter then asked the subject if he might wish to earn some money by filling in for the missing assistant and convincing a waiting subject that the tasks about to be performed were interesting and fun. The experimenter stated that he could pay the subject the amount that he regularly gave his assistant. The amount of money promised was the major manipulation of the experiment—in one condition, the subject was told he would be paid $1; in the other condition, the subject was promised $20. All subjects in both conditions agreed to tell the next participant in the study that the boring tasks were, in fact, fun and interesting.

The subject, now in the role of the experimental assistant, was then led into another room where he confronted a waiting subject (a woman who was actually an accomplice of the researchers). When the subject stated

---

[4] Studies of dissonance induced by belief-Inconsistent actions constitute the bulk of the dissonance literature, and therefore, a multitude of possible research examples could have been used as our central illustration of such work (see, for example, Brehm & Cohen, 1962, or Wicklund & Brehm, 1976). As we have done in previous instances, we have opted to summarize a "classic" study.

that the experiment was interesting and fun, the accomplice replied that she had heard that it was boring. This forced the newly recruited assistant to insist that, to him, the tasks were fun, unusual, novel, exciting, and so on.

After the subject-assistant had completed his attempt at persuasion, the experimenter asked him to perform one last service. The psychology department, the experimenter explained, required that subjects complete a form that assessed their reaction to their research experience. Accordingly, the subject was given a brief questionnaire concerning his opinions of the peg-turning and spool-assembling tasks that he had performed in the study.

The prediction derived from dissonance theory is reasonably straightforward in this case but still somewhat contrary to our intuitions. One might expect that the more an event is associated with positive outcomes, the more likely a positive opinion regarding the event would develop.[5] Thus, subjects paid $20 would be expected to have formed a more positive opinion about the study than those who were to be paid only $1. Dissonance theory, on the other hand, generates the opposite prediction. Subjects who were paid only $1 to perform an action that was clearly contrary to their opinions (that is, voluntarily professing that the boring tasks were, in fact, enjoyable) should have generated a certain degree of dissonance. The other subjects—those promised $20—would not have felt as much dissonance, because the monetary reward was sufficient to justify their behavior to themselves.

To highlight the difference in dissonance level that the two payment amounts probably generated, consider the likely thought processes of a subject who had been paid $1 for performing the belief-discrepant action. His initial reaction to the tasks was not favorable. However, he told another person that the tasks were fun. The subject believes that he is a reasonable, logical, and truthful individual; why, then, did he describe the tasks in a positive way? Was it for the money? No. In thinking about it, it is clear that the promise of 1 measly dollar was not sufficient to induce him to perform such a belief-discrepant act (although a $20 reward probably was sufficient for those lucky enough to be promised that amount). Was he forced to perform this deception? No, the experimenter only had asked him to do so; he could have refused.

These reflections, in which dissonance theory assumes people engage, place the subject who is paid $1 in an uncomfortable state of cognitive dissonance, and, as will be further discussed, there is evidence that dissonance is a motivating force that activates people to seek to reduce it (for example, Zanna & Cooper, 1976). In the present circumstance, however, there was only a very limited number of means by which the subject could reduce his dissonance. One possibility, perhaps the most feasible, was to reevaluate his original opinion about the tasks. If that opinion were not so negative, then telling another that the activities were fun and enjoyable would not

---

[5] Indeed, as will be further discussed, this premise is a major feature of alternative theories about the action-opinion link.

be such a belief-discrepant action, and the dissonance would thus be reduced.

The results obtained in this study confirmed the predictions derived from dissonance theory. As expected, opinions expressed by subjects who were to be paid only $1 for their belief-discrepant actions were significantly more favorable toward the tasks than were the opinions of subjects promised $20. These basic findings have been replicated and extended in many subsequent studies (Brock & Buss, 1962; Carlsmith, Collins, & Helmreich, 1966; Cohen, 1962; Collins & Hoyt, 1972; Cooper & Worchel, 1970; Crano & Messé, 1970; Davis & Jones, 1960; Gerard, Conolley, & Wilhelmy, 1974; Linder, Cooper, & Jones, 1967; Reiss & Schlenker, 1977; Wicklund, Cooper, & Linder, 1967; Zimbardo et al., 1965).

ALTERNATIVE MODELS OF THE ACTION-OPINION LINK

As noted earlier, the theory of cognitive dissonance stimulated considerable controversy despite the extensive evidence amassed in its support. A number of social psychologists did not share Festinger's basic view of human nature (Bem, 1965; Chapanis & Chapanis, 1964; Rosenberg, 1965; Tedeschi, Schlenker, & Bonoma, 1971), and raised a series of conceptual and methodological objections to both the theory and the research that it stimulated.

It should be noted, however, that the models proposed as alternatives to dissonance theory shared with it one basic premise—namely, that actions can affect beliefs. In fact, this fundamental phenomenon had been demonstrated before Festinger (1957) proposed his model. For example, as early as 1954, Janis and King showed that subtly inducing people to engage in activities that were contrary to their opinions (by having them play a role) produced opinion change. However, dissonance was the first model to systematically speculate about the various factors that determined the action-opinion link, and it was this theory that stimulated systematic exploration of the variables that affected this link. This exploration primarily took the form of attempts to verify dissonance theory or to disconfirm it and support other theoretical positions. In the following sections of this chapter, we will turn our attention to some of these alternative explanations that were advanced to explain the influence of behaviors on beliefs.

REINFORCEMENT-BASED MODELS

Many of the models that present an alternative to dissonance theory are based on more traditional learning theory perspectives on opinion formation and change. For example, one of the generally accepted principles of learning that is seen as relevant to opinion formation and change is secondary reinforcement, the process by which neutral cues take on values because of their past associations with rewards or punishments (Reynolds, 1968; Staats, 1975).[6] Just as our feelings about people can be affected by their associations with positive or negative outcomes, our opinions can be influenced in much the same manner. An opinion is strengthened when the action associated with it leads to a positive outcome. Similarly, when opinion-based behaviors are followed by negative outcomes, the opinion becomes more negative.

There is persuasive research evidence that supports this position (Cohen, 1964; Das & Nanda, 1963; Staats & Staats, 1958; Zanna, Kiesler, & Pilkonis, 1970). In the study by Zanna, Kiesler, and Pilkonis (1970), for example, female subjects were paid to take part in an experiment in which they were to receive a series of electric shocks. Each shock trial, lasting one second, was initiated by the experimenter's reading an adjective, and it was terminated by his reading another adjective. After a series of such trials, the subjects were asked to take part in another study of their opinions about words, which was conducted by a different experimenter. The two adjectives that had been used in the previous experiment to signal the onset and offset of shock were included in the list of words that the subjects were to evaluate.

The findings of this study indicated that subjects evaluated an adjective more negatively when it had been previously used to signal the onset of the shock, while the reverse was true of an adjective that had been used to announce the termination of the shock. Moreover, Zanna, Kiesler, and Pilkonis (1970) demonstrated that this effect generalized to words that were similar in meaning to the critical stimulus adjectives; for instance, if the onset word had been *light*, the word *white* was also devalued, although it had not been used to signal the shock. These results are consistent with the association hypothesis that opinions are affected by the outcomes of belief-related actions.

A real-life example of this process might help to illustrate further the ways in which association affects the link between actions and opinions. Suppose that every time you visit your nextdoor neighbor's house, his dog bites your ankle. This occurs with distressing regularity. We would predict that you would come to negatively evaluate this animal. Not so obvious is the strong possibility that your negative evaluation would also generalize to your next-door neighbor's house, his furnishings, and perhaps even the neighbor himself. In this case, your experiences have affected your beliefs. Such a series of events, like the findings of Zanna, Kiesler, and Pilkonis (1970), support the proposition that the outcomes of belief-related actions can affect the belief itself, a hypothesis that is congruent with learning-based theories of opinion formation and change.

In contrast, dissonance theory would predict that such experiences could have a very different effect on your opinions. If, despite his intemperate dog, you continually returned to your neighbor's house of your own free

---

[6] We discussed this process in Chapter 2 when we noted the role that associations of this type play in the formation of Sentiment relations.

will, dissonance theory would predict that you would come to positively evaluate the dog, the house, and the neighbor! Why? Because returning of your own volition to a scene of discomfort would be extremely inconsistent (dissonant) with your fundamental impression of yourself as a reasonable, logical individual. To resolve this inconsistency, you would have to either change your self-impression (a very difficult and unlikely modification) or reevaluate your opinion of the Social Context of your neighbor's house so as to justify the pain involved in entering it, perhaps through a modification of your opinion regarding the value of your visits.

It is extremely important to note that while the dissonance and learning-based predictions of your ultimate beliefs regarding your neighbor and his dog are diametrically opposed, the underlying causal premise thought to operate is the same in both cases—namely, that experiences can determine opinions.

A specific learning-based alternative to the dissonance model of opinion structure and change was proposed by Milton Rosenberg, who developed a theoretical framework based on Hovland's earlier work. Rosenberg's (1965) approach formally specified learning-based processes of opinion formation and change, of which association with reward or punishment is just one component. This model, which he termed the theory of *affective-cognitive consistency,* explicitly postulates that the opinions formed on the basis of our actions will be consistent with the affective outcomes of the actions. In other words, if we are punished for a specific behavior, our opinion of that behavior will be negative; if rewarded, our opinion will be positive; and, finally, the greater the reinforcement, the more extreme the opinion that is formed.

To Bowl or Not to Bowl—That was the Question. In applying his theory to a situation involving the modification of relatively strong opinions, Rosenberg (1965) took advantage of an actual set of events that had caused the students at the Ohio State University considerable anguish. As was customary in those days, the Buckeyes once again had won the Big Ten football championship. Traditionally, this achievement carried with it the distinction of defending the Big Ten's honor against the champions of the Pacific Coast Conference in the Rose Bowl.

During this particular year, however, there was no formal contract between the two conferences that specified the representatives of the two football leagues. The contract had expired the previous year, and the processes of renegotiation had not yet been completed. Thus, a decision was to be made regarding the teams' participation; and in the case of the Buckeyes, the faculty committee in charge of athletic affairs decided against Ohio State's participation. Rumors circulating at the time of this decision attributed the committee's actions to a fear that the Ohio State University was getting a reputation (undeserved, of course) as a "football factory."

As might be expected, the committee's decision generated a good deal of negative reaction at Ohio State. Indeed, the opinions of the overwhelming majority of students of the university were extremely negative toward the faculty committee's action. It was in this Social Context that Rosenberg opportunistically conducted this study.

The general procedure of Rosenberg's (1965) experiment was reasonably straightforward. Subjects individually reported to Rosenberg's office and upon arrival, found him on the phone. He interrupted his conversation, turned to the subject, and said that he would be off the phone in a moment and that in the meantime the subject should take a seat in the hall. He assured the subject that the study would take only a few minutes, much less time than the subject had committed to it, so that the delay would not prove an inconvenience. Apparently as an afterthought, Rosenberg then mentioned that a graduate student in communications, whose office was on the next floor, had asked him earlier if he knew of any undergraduates who would like to make some money by participating in some research, which would take only a small amount of their time. Rosenberg feigned ignorance of the details of the study, and suggested that the subject might wish to investigate the possibility of participating in the communications experiment instead of simply waiting in the hallway while he finished his telephone call.

The subjects almost invariably followed this suggestion. Upon arrival at the communication student's office, each subject was told that the study was an attempt to construct a questionnaire about the faculty athletic affairs committee's recent decision to pass up the Rose Bowl. To do this, the student explained that he needed a number of essays, both favorable and antagonistic toward this decision. He further told the subject that he had enough anti-faculty essays, and that although he was fairly certain of the subject's opinion about the committee's actions, he nevertheless needed some profaculty essays. If the subject was willing to write such an essay, which would take only 5 to 10 minutes to complete, he would be paid for this time. After the subject agreed to do so (all did), he was told the amount that he would be paid for his efforts. In the low-incentive condition of the study, the subject was promised 50 cents; in the high-incentive condition, the subject was promised $5. After completing these business arrangements, each subject wrote a pro-faculty committee essay and was paid the agreed-upon amount.

After receiving his money, each subject returned to Rosenberg's office, where he was asked to complete a brief questionnaire devoted to various campus-related issues. One item of the scale asked respondents to indicate their opinions about the faculty committee's decision. This item on the questionnaire constituted the primary measure of subjects' opinions.

If reinforcement processes operate to modify opinions, as Rosenberg and others have theorized, then there should have been a positive relationship between the amount of money associated with writing an essay in favor of the faculty decision and the subjects' opinions on this issue. In other words, Rosenberg expected that those paid $5 for writing the profaculty essay would be less negative toward the faculty's decision than those paid only 50 cents. The results that Rosenberg obtained in this study were consistent with his expectations. Those paid more for writing in support of the faculty's decision were more favorable in their opinions toward it, as reflected in their responses on the questionnaire. Later research (Crano & Messé, 1970; and Linder, Cooper, & Jones, 1967) replicated this pattern of results.

Although these findings might strike the reader as reasonable, even obvious, they caused a good deal of consternation among the proponents of dissonance theory. This was so because Rosenberg's (1965) results were completely incompatible with the predictions derived from dissonance theory, which had been supported by studies such as that of Festinger and Carlsmith (1959), discussed earlier in this chapter. This inconsistency can be resolved, however, through the utilization of a perspective that we have advocated throughout this text—namely, that it is short-sighted to believe that any single psychological process can account for all of the complexities of human behavior. Instead, a major goal of social psychology should be the specification of the conditions under which a given process—dissonance, reinforcement, and so on—operates. Both reinforcement and dissonance theory are, under appropriate conditions, accurate predictors of human behavior. It is our goal in the following sections to specify these conditions.

Reinforcement and Dissonance Theories: Resolving the Controversy

Before discussing the variables that appear to determine the relative strengths of dissonance and reinforcement effects on opinions, we need to summarize the major factors that govern the amount of dissonance generated by an inconsistency between actions and beliefs. Studies in the areas of dissonance research, reviewed above, have shown that cognitive dissonance is most likely to occur (and thus to influence beliefs most strongly) only when actors, upon reflection, perceive that (1) they were reasonably free to choose among the options that had been available to them; (2) such options had real consequences for their welfare or that of other people; (3) at least some of the inconsistent beliefs were important to them (for example, high level opinions); and (4) there was insufficient external justification at the time that they had acted to fully explain to themselves what they had done. Dissonance is not likely to be aroused in the individual unless all of these conditions are met, at least minimally. If these conditions are not met, then other processes (for example, reinforcement) are likely to exert much greater influence on behavior than will dissonance.

You should have noticed from the previous presentation that the manipulations employed in the studies of Festinger and Carlsmith (1959) and Rosenberg (1965) were quite similar. Both varied the amount of money paid to the subject to perform a belief-discrepant activity. Yet, the findings of these studies were directly contradictory: Rosenberg found evidence for a reinforcement, or incentive effect (the greater the reward, the more favorable the opinion); Festinger and Carlsmith found dissonance, or a reverse-incentive effect (the greater the reward, the less favorable the opinion).

Subsequently, a number of studies have been conducted to help explain this discrepancy; some of these will now be presented. This research has shown that minor but conceptually important differences in the experimental procedures used in the studies of Rosenberg (1965) and of Festinger and Carlsmith (1956) were responsible, at least in part, for the variation in their findings.

Commitment. For example, Linder, Cooper, and Jones (1967) demonstrated that procedures in Rosenberg's (1965) study reduced the possibility that dissonance would be generated, since subjects in this experiment were induced to *commit* themselves to the belief-discrepant task before they knew the amount that they would be paid (that is, the subjects walked to the essay-writing experiment before knowing what it was all about). This subtle aspect of Rosenberg's procedure no doubt served to raise the subjects' sense of external justification for their actions, irrespective of the amount of money that they were paid for their work. Such an increase in justification would, of course, reduce the dissonance generated in subjects, even in those who were paid very little.

Time. A second important variable that mediates the experience of cognitive dissonance is the *time* at which we become aware of the Inconsistency (Crano & Messé, 1970; Miller, 1968; Walster, 1964; Wicklund & Brehm, 1976). A belief-discrepant action that took place in our lives many years ago, for example, is probably not very motivating, no matter how important the Inconsistency might have been had it been recognized at the time of its occurrence. Similarly, we would expect that even a relatively minor belief-discrepant action would have an intense, if short-lived, motivational component if we were made immediately aware of the Inconsistency.

Such temporal processes appear to have played a role in many of the laboratory studies of the link between action and opinion. Most research in this area employed an experimental procedure in which the effects of dissonance on opinion were assessed immediately after the dissonance had been induced. Such a procedure has two potentially important consequences: (1) it raises the probability that subjects would attend to the discrepancy between their beliefs and the actions that they had just taken; and (2) it is likely to assess subjects' opinions when the dissonance generated in the experiment is maximal. Both of these factors would serve to maximize the effect of dissonance processes in moderating the action-opinion relationship.

A study demonstrating these points was conducted by Crano and Messé (1970). This experiment, like that of Linder et al. (1967), was designed to integrate the apparently contradictory findings of studies such as Rosenberg's (1965) on the one hand, and dissonance research of the type performed by Festinger and Carlsmith (1959) on the other. The reader will recall that in his study, Rosenberg had subjects perform the belief-discrepant essay-writing task in a room different from the one used in the opinion measurement portion of the experiment.[7] As has been known since the days of Aristotle, however, a separation in space also implies a separation in time. Rosenberg's procedure of necessity produced a delay between the time at which the subjects

---

[7] Rosenberg did this in an attempt to minimize subjects' suspicion that the paid essay-writing task was designed to affect their opinions.

finished their essay (were paid, signed the pay voucher, walked down to his office, and so forth) and the time at which they answered the crucial items on the opinion questionnaire.

The passage of time, however, can have important effects on the impact of dissonance induction. This is especially true in the Social Context of the experimental laboratory, where the amount of dissonance generated is unlikely to be great, since the level of the opinions involved is often not high, and the behaviors induced usually are not that important to subjects. Thus, when he increased the time between the task (writing a belief-discrepant essay), and the measurement of its effect on opinion (answering the questionnaire), Rosenberg might also have inadvertently weakened the possibility of detecting any consequences of the dissonance that the task might have aroused.

To test this possibility, the authors of this book conducted an experiment similar to Rosenberg's belief-discrepant essay-writing study. In our investigation (Crano and Messé, 1970), undergraduate volunteers were brought into our laboratory and asked to write an essay favoring the abolition of student draft deferments. Not surprisingly, preliminary tests had revealed that the overwhelming student opinion toward the abolition of deferments was negative. Moreover, we felt that this issue would be highly involving to subjects for a number of reasons, not the least of which was the fact that at the time, the United States was engaged in the war in Southeast Asia.

Subjects were given one of two incentives for writing their essay. Some were promised $5, while others were offered 50 cents. All subjects, no matter what the incentive condition, wrote the belief-discrepant essays. After completing the essays, subjects were divided further into two additional experimental conditions. Some subjects, immediately upon finishing the essay, completed a questionnaire containing items tapping opinions relevant to the student deferment issue as well as other topics. This condition replicated that of the "typical" dissonance experiment (Cohen, 1962; Festinger & Carlsmith, 1959; and so on). Other subjects, immediately upon finishing the essay, completed a figure-drawing task; therefore, they did not begin to answer the opinion questionnaire until approximately 20 minutes had elapsed. This condition was meant to mimic the temporal lag that Rosenberg (1965) had inadvertently built into his experiment.

To summarize, this study combined two different incentives (50 cents or $5) with two different times of opinion measurement (immediate or 20-minute delay). Variations in the times of opinion measurement were examined, as it was our hypothesis that the temporal separation of the opinion-modifying action (writing the belief-discrepant essay) from the opinion measurement had affected Rosenberg's results.

The results obtained in our experiment confirmed these expectations. In the conditions involving the immediate measurement of opinions, the classic reverse-incentive dissonance effect was observed—that is, when opinions were measured immediately after the essay was completed, those subjects paid the lesser amount reported more favorable opinions toward the abolition of student draft deferments than those paid the greater amount. When the opinion measurement was delayed, however, the findings mirrored the reinforcement effect obtained by Rosenberg (1965)—that is, when opinions were measured 20 minutes after the essay was completed, the subjects paid the greater amount expressed more favorable opinions toward the drafting of undergraduates than did those paid the lesser amount.

Repetition.   A third important variable that mediates the relative strength of dissonance and reinforcement effects is *repetition*. While the effects of this factor were not examined in the research discussed above, an extensive literature across areas of psychology demonstrates the impact of repetition on the acquisition of behaviors. As noted earlier, the attachment of positive and negative evaluations as a result of repeated associations with corresponding positive and negative outcomes is well documented in the field of social psychology (Midlarsky & Bryan, 1967; Miller & Dollard, 1941; Staats, 1975; Staats & Staats, 1958; Zanna, Kiesler, & Pilkonis, 1970).

On the other hand, studies that have demonstrated the reverse-incentive effect have tended to focus on a single (that is, the first) instance of an association of a reinforcement with a behavior. Under such circumstances, it is not surprising that the greater reinforcement did not produce a more extreme evaluation. Over numerous repetitions, however, we would expect an increasingly extreme evaluation to occur. This is not to deny the possibility that strong associations can form after a single trial, but rather, it assumes that repetition is by far the more reliable means of modifying opinions through reinforcement.

In summary, the results of the studies cited here support our contention that both reinforcement and dissonance processes can operate to determine the impact of behavior on opinions. Again, we must stress that the crucial issue is not *whether* one or another of these central models of cognitive functioning operates, but *when* they operate. We will return to this position in discussing the factors that appear to influence the relative strength of dissonance and self-perception, the second major alternative explanation of the behavior-opinion link.

SELF-PERCEPTION THEORY

Of all the theoretical perspectives that have been developed as alternatives to dissonance over the years, probably none has proved so influential as Bem's (1965, 1967, 1972) theory of self-perception. Bem (1965) originally proposed the theory of self-perception as a simplified explanation for the findings that typically were interpreted as consistent with the tenets of dissonance theory. Since that time, however, this model has played a more general role in social psychology. Recent trends in the field—which have come to be subsumed under the general heading of attribution theory—have emphasized the importance of understanding the extent to which our perceptual and cognitive processes shape social events, and vice versa. Bem's theory was one of the initial forces in this movement and still plays a part in its ongoing development.

Self-perception theory is based on the general philosophical position of B. F. Skinner, the noted learning theorist. Skinner maintains that there is little need to speculate about internal psychological processes to understand the behavior of humans and other animals. Skinner's framework concentrates solely on overt behavior and makes no assumptions about the internal cognitive factors that might have influenced these actions. In translating Skinner's philosophy to the social psychological arena, Bem, like Wicker (1969), questioned the utility or necessity of concepts such as attitude or opinion. These constructs necessitate, or at least presume, the existence of *internal cognitive processes,* and as such, are seen within the general Skinnerian philosophical framework as superfluous. Bem (1965, 1972) contended that we can understand the link between our actions and many of our opinions without appealing to such amorphous, mentalistic concepts as dissonance, motivation, and so on.

In Bem's (1965, 1972) scheme, some evaluative beliefs are nothing more than explanations that people create after the fact in response to questions about their earlier actions. Bem postulated that people often view their own overt actions in much the same way that they view the actions of others—that is, they attribute internal or external explanations to their own actions in the same manner that they interpret the observable actions of others. For example, if we were to ask an individual to state his or her evaluative belief about a specific object (possibly another person), the individual might review his or her previous behaviors toward that object—the cues in the Social Context in which the behavior occurred—and from this information, create the requested explanation.

The question of evaluation need not be explicitly stated nor posed by another person. We can, for example, interpret a quizzical glance from another as a question about our actions. In responding to this question, the explanation that we create is often a belief. For example, in response to a question from your roommate as to why you spent the last three hours studying social psychology, you might assess your own behaviors and reply, "I studied the material because it is interesting." Thus, according to the theory, when self-perception processes are activated, opinions and actions are linked because beliefs are nothing more than the post hoc interpretations of past behaviors.

An example will help to clarify Bem's theory. Suppose that you were standing in line at a long buffet table piled high with an assortment of appetizing foods. As you pass down this line, grabbing whatever strikes your fancy, you happen by a huge platter filled with a large assortment of rolls—sesame, onion, pumpernickel, and zucchini rolls, to name just a few. You nonchalantly pick a sesame roll and put it on your plate, which is already groaning under the strain. You finish your voyage through the line, and, with knees buckling from the weight of your burden, you struggle to an open table. As fortune

Self-perception can influence the opinions that people express about the food that they chose (or rejected) from a buffet.

would have it, the person sitting to your immediate left is a social psychologist. She looks at your plate, suppresses a look of amazement, and asks, "What kind of rolls do you like?" You are taken aback for a moment, because you have not thought much about this issue—you tend to think of food mainly in terms of quantity rather than type. After some brief deliberation, you respond, "I like sesame the best, don't you?"

Why did this response come to mind? From a self-perception perspective, we would interpret the events as follows. As noted, the theory postulates that people interpret the causes of their behaviors much as they would those of others. To begin this process, we would consider the Social Context in which the relevant behavior occurred. Did components of the context place any constraints on your behavior in choosing a roll? In this case, it does not appear that the context was constraining. There were many different types of rolls available; no one insisted that you try the sesames; you had not noticed the three people ahead of you take sesame rolls; and so on. In other words, there were no obvious outside impingements on you to take the particular variety that you did.

In the absence of such external (or contextual) cues, we tend to interpret the observed behavior as being a consequence of internal (Personal Structure) variables. That is, we would likely assume that you took the sesame roll because of your favorable opinion toward them, relative to the available options.[8]

The principal assumption of self-perception theory is that the processes that affect observers' judgments are identical to those that affect the actor's judgment of his or her own behavior. In this instance, you would be expected to make attributions about your opinion regarding sesame rolls in exactly the same way that we, the observers, did—that is, you would conclude that the reason you took the sesame roll was because you like sesame rolls more than the others that were available. This response, literally created on the spot, becomes for the moment your statement of *opinion*. It is important to note that this opinion is subject to constant revision—as are all of your opinions—as a function of your subsequent interpretations of your actions.

It should be clear from your own experiences that beliefs are not always a consequence of self-perception processes. For example, you would not expect that long-term Sentiment relationships would be an outcome of circumstances that have little to do with the development of feelings of attachment. If asked, "Do you like Joe Smith (your best friend)?" it is unlikely that you would reply, "I guess I do, I was just with him." The fact that you have been friends through thick and thin for so many years is the basis for your response, not your most recent interaction. Moreover, your most recent interaction might very well have been the result of your positive beliefs about Joe. Indeed, to have actively sought out Joe presumes the existence of a positive belief about him.

Bem recognized the fact that all beliefs are not the result of the operation of self-perception processes. Accordingly, he observed (Bem, 1972, p. 2) that self-perception processes were likely to operate "to the extent that internal cues are weak, ambiguous, or uninterpretable." A study by Michael Scheier and Charles Carver (1980) provides support for this conclusion. In their research, Scheier and Carver (1980) measured the extent to which a large number of potential subjects characteristically attend to their own beliefs. A sample of those who scored high or low on this measure were then induced to write an essay that was contrary to an opinion they held.

The researchers found that those who characteristically put great weight on their established beliefs were not likely to change their opinions in the direction of the essay they had written, whereas those who were typically more influenced by contextual forces were more likely to change in the direction that they had advocated in the essay. Thus, it appears that the less weight people accord their established evaluative beliefs about an issue, the more likely their expressed beliefs are to be affected by their most recent behaviors.

---

[8] This reasoning is one instance of the general processes involved in the attribution of causality, which are discussed in detail in Chapter 7. For the moment, your intuitive grasp of this process is all that is necessary for an understanding of the self-perception position.

Self-Perception Theory versus Dissonance Theory

To this point, we have not specifically contrasted self-perception and dissonance theory. The two approaches differ fundamentally with regard to their assumptions about the basic mechanism underlying the link between actions and opinions. Dissonance theory postulates that people are concerned with maintaining self-Consistency, and thus find a lack of it between beliefs and actions to be aversive (and therefore motivating). On the other hand, self-perception theory maintains that beliefs are products of the ways that we process information, which are derived from our Personal Structures, our own actions, and the Social Contexts in which those actions took place. Within the framework of self-perception theory, it is unnecessary to assume the existence of a motivation such as the need for Consistency to account for the positive relationship between actions and opinions.

In his attempt to demonstrate that an information-processing approach was a viable alternative to dissonance theory, Bem conducted a number of intriguing experiments whose general designs mimicked those of the classic dissonance studies. In these studies, Bem demonstrated that he could produce effects that traditionally had been attributed to cognitive dissonance in circumstances in which subjects should have experienced no dissonance.

As noted, self-perception theory postulates that we attribute our opinions about objects on the basis of our actions toward those objects, much as other people infer our opinions by observing our actions. Bem reasoned that if others could correctly infer the opinions of an actor simply by knowing the circumstances in which the actor's opinion-relevant behavior occurred, then we could assume that parallel processes of *self*-observation similarly affect the actor's perception of his or her own beliefs.

Interpersonal Replications. An impressive example of the possible operation of such self-identification processes was provided in Bem's simulation of the Festinger and Carlsmith (1959) experiment discussed earlier in this chapter. In one of a series of studies that Bem termed his *interpersonal replications,* subjects listened to a tape recording of what purportedly occurred to one participant when he took part in the Festinger and Carlsmith dissonance experiment. First, the observers overheard the experimenter explain the nature of the spool-placing and peg-turning tasks. As in the original study, these tasks were described in a straightforward, nonevaluative manner. Then the observers heard the experimenter explain about his missing accomplice and offer the subject either $20 or $1 to substitute for him and favorably introduce the study to a waiting subject. The observer-subjects heard the participant agree to do so (no matter what the amount of the incentive), and listened as he ostensibly extolled the virtues of the boring tasks to the dubious subject. In every regard, except for differences in incentive, the tape recordings that observer-subjects heard in the two conditions of the simulation study were identical. All observer-subjects in Bem's study were then given an opinion questionnaire that was identical to the one used in the original experiment and were asked to respond to it as did the subject whose experience and actions they had just monitored.

The issue here is intriguing: if the naive observers in Bem's (1965) study could accurately predict the professed opinions of subjects in the Festinger and Carlsmith (1959) experiment, this would imply that the cues present in the Context of the actual study were sufficient to account for the variation in opinions that were expressed by the real subjects. In other words, if outside observers could predict that subjects who were to be paid only $1 would report a more favorable evaluation of the experimental tasks than did those who were promised $20, we could assume that the subjects found sufficient cues in the Context of the experiment (including their own actions) to make a similar attribution about their own opinions. We would not need to postulate a motivational process like the arousal of cognitive dissonance to explain the reverse-incentive effect that was observed in the Festinger and Carlsmith study.

The results reported by Bem were consistent with self-perception theory. That is, although they merely observed the experiences of a participant in the Festinger and Carlsmith experiment, Bem's subjects accurately predicted the participants' responses to the opinion questionnaire, based on inferences they made from the available contextual cues.

From these results, Bem inferred that the original subjects of the Festinger and Carlsmith study had processed such information in a similar manner. Thus, the opinions that were reported in the original study might well have been the result of a cue-weighting Valuation process (self-perception), not the outcome of a motivational process (dissonance reduction).

Overjustification Effects. Studies of the effects of *overjustification* on opinions have also yielded findings that are more compatible with self-perception theory than with dissonance theory. Overjustification refers to a set of conditions in which incentives are employed to prompt an action that probably would have taken place voluntarily (that is, without the impingement). From the perspective of self-perception theory, overjustification provides an actor with an overabundance of cues by which to explain his or her behavior. In such circumstances, the actor often will use only a portion of the available information—usually the most salient cues—to attribute causes (including opinions) for the action. This process can result in the replacement of what is an established intrinsic reason with an extrinsic justification for an act.

Parents and other guardians of young children often make use of overjustification by pretending to forbid actions that the child had no intention of performing in the first place. They employ this tactic—which is popularly known as using *reverse psychology*—to subtly induce the child to behave as they (the parents) really wish. For example, in the movie *Mary Poppins,* the governess, Mary, induces her two young charges to settle down to sleep by pretending that she wishes them to stay awake so that she can sing to them. In this scene, she sings the lullaby, "Stay Awake," and they promptly fall asleep.

It perhaps is easier to demonstrate the reverse effect of overjustification—

that is, to lower a person's intrinsic interest in an action by providing positive external reasons for engaging in it. There have been a number of successful laboratory demonstrations of this phenomenon, and one of the most clear and compelling of these is the study by Lepper, Greene, and Nisbett (1973). In this experiment, the researchers observed the free play behaviors of a number of nursery school children. After a short time, the experimenters identified those children who, from their overt behavior, appeared to like to use art materials. In a later session, these children were individually asked to play with some drawing equipment in the guise of helping to market-test some new products. The children were randomly assigned to one of three conditions: in one condition (the control), children tested the materials, gave their evaluation of them, and were thanked for their help; those children assigned to a second treatment (the crucial expected reward condition) were told before they tested the materials and evaluated them that they would be rewarded for their services; a third group (the unexpected reward condition) received the same extrinsic reward as the second, except it was given to them as a surprise, after they had finished their evaluations.

After the testing session, each subject's behavior once again was monitored in a free play situation in the school. The results of these later observations indicated that of the three groups of children, only those in the expected reward group—the children who were rewarded for engaging in behaviors that prior observation had indicated they enjoyed, and would probably have performed anyway—decreased their use of art materials. The behavior of the other two groups of children was not affected by the experimental treatment. Apparently, the impingement of the expected reward overjustified the previously enjoyable behavior for the second group. Their diminished interest cannot be attributed to either their participation in the rating study, or to receiving the reward, per se, as one or both of these factors were present in the other two experimental conditions.

Self-perception provides a reasonable explanation of these findings and of those of the many other studies that have replicated and extended these results (Anderson, Manoogian, & Reznick, 1976; Boggiano & Ruble, 1979; Deci, 1975; Deci & Ryan, 1980; Folger, Rosenfield & Hays, 1978; Lepper, 1981; Lepper & Greene, 1978; Ross, 1976; Scott & Yalch, 1978; Sivacek & Crano, 1980; Smith & Pittman, 1978). This information-processing approach postulates that, just as we use available information to interpret the behaviors of others, we use available cues to make attributions of causality about our own behavior. In the Lepper, Greene, and Nisbett (1973) study, this process would affect the self-perceptions of the children who had expected and received a reward for their play with the art materials. Based on the findings of this study, these children probably attributed their actions to the reward rather than to their previously established interest in artwork. The other children would not have formed such self-perceptions, since they were not induced to play with the material through the promise of an (unnecessary) extrinsic reward; thus, these extrinsic reasons were not a part of their cue-weighting process.

Dissonance theory, on the other hand, is mute with respect to the overjustification phenomenon. There is no cognitive conflict created in the typical overjustification situation. People are not induced to behave in a belief-discrepant fashion, but rather they are reinforced for actions that are, themselves, intrinsically reinforcing, or belief-congruent. Under such circumstances, there is no pressure from dissonance to modify the critical opinions. Moreover, with his interpersonal replication studies, Bem demonstrated that there was a reasonable alternative explanation to the dissonance theory interpretations of the link between actions and opinions, one that did not postulate a motivational basis for opinion change.

Other research, however, has provided evidence that inconsistencies between established beliefs and actions in fact can be motivating, findings that are contrary to the tenets of self-perception theory. We will now review some of this research.

Arousing Properties of Dissonance. Perhaps the most persuasive evidence that under appropriate circumstances, inconsistencies between beliefs and actions can be arousing is provided by the work of Mark Zanna, Joel Cooper, and their associates (Cooper, Fazio, & Rhodewalt, 1978; Cooper, Zanna, & Taves, 1978; Higgins, Rhodewalt, & Zanna, 1979; Zanna & Cooper, 1974, 1976). Two examples of this creative work follow.

Zanna and Cooper (1974) induced subjects to write an essay supporting a position that was contrary to their opinions. Even though they were in favor of allowing controversial speakers to appear on their campus, the students were induced through rather subtle impingements to write essays supporting a ban on such activity. This general research model has been used extensively to examine the variables that affect the link between actions and opinions (Crano & Messé, 1970; Rosenberg, 1965).

Zanna and Cooper had an additional feature in their study, one that was crucial to the question of whether or not inconsistency is motivating. They gave all subjects a pill whose expected effects were described to subjects in a number of different ways, depending upon the particular experimental condition to which they were assigned. Although the pill was composed of milk powder, and thus could have no pharmacological consequences (in medical research, such a pill is called a placebo), it was variously described to subjects as (1) a drug that would cause them to be aroused and tense; (2) a drug that would relax them; or (3) a drug with no side effects.

After writing the essays, subjects were asked their opinions on a number of campus issues, including the one that was the topic of their essay. The major point of this study was to determine in a reasonably direct way whether people became aroused under conditions in which dissonance, theoretically, should be created. Subjects' expectations about the effects of the pills were manipulated to determine whether or not they actually felt physiological changes that could be attributed to the effects of the drug (even though these changes were really caused by the dissonance induction).

The crucial test of dissonance arousal was the extent to which subjects changed their opinions as a function of the expected effect of the drug. In the experimental condition in which subjects expected to feel aroused by the pill, there was little opinion change. Apparently, the discomfort that subjects felt as a result of writing the opinion-discrepant essay was misattributed to the expected effects of the pill. In the condition in which subjects were told that the pill would produce no side effects, a moderate amount of opinion change occurred. In the condition in which subjects expected the pill to relax them, a great deal of opinion change occurred. Why? In this last variation of the experiment, subjects expected to be calm (because of the pill), but were, in fact, aroused (by the dissonance generated by their opinion-discrepant essay). This difference between their expectations and the way they actually felt caused them to overemphasize the degree of stress that they were experiencing. This overemphasis, in turn, caused them to attempt to reduce this aversive arousal in extreme ways. Thus, they displayed greater opinion change than did subjects in the "no side effect" group (who presumably experienced a similar amount of dissonance as a result of their essay).

The major point of presenting this study is not to burden the reader with the somewhat complicated results that were obtained, but rather to demonstrate that dissonance can be arousing. There appear to be no other reasonable explanations for Zanna and Cooper's findings. The pill was a neutral substance, and could thus produce no real physiological reactions. Yet, subjects who engaged in opinion-discrepant actions obviously felt some emotional distress. The distress was a consequence of their behavior, whether they attributed it to the drug that they had taken or to the essay that they had written.

In a complementary study, Cooper, Zanna, and Taves (1978) demonstrated that dissonance was not felt when subjects were given a mild sedative. Under such conditions, there was no difference in opinion change between subjects who were forced to behave in a opinion-discrepant manner (the low-dissonance condition) and those who were subtly induced to do so (the high-dissonance subjects). The manipulation of perceived freedom of choice did produce differences in opinion change among subjects who were not given the relaxant, as predicted by dissonance theory. These findings have been supported, in substance, by other studies (Drachman & Worchel, 1976; Pallak, 1970; Pallak & Pitman, 1972; Pittman, 1975; Waterman, 1969).

Integration of Dissonance and Self-Perception Theory

Bem originally proposed his self-perception model as a straightforward and parsimonious substitute for dissonance theory. However, the work of Zanna and Cooper (1974, 1976), among others, demonstrates that self-perception cannot account for all, or perhaps even any, of the findings typically viewed from the perspective of dissonance theory. The lack of a motivational component in self-perception, while appealing from the standpoint of simplicity, does not appear to accurately describe the processes of opinion formation and change. People are bothered by Inconsistency, and this aversive motive state has implications for the relationship between their actions and their beliefs.

This conclusion, however, is not to deny completely the utility of information-processing approaches for understanding opinion formation and change. For example, as noted, dissonance theory cannot explain the results of the many studies that have demonstrated overjustification effects. Thus, it is crucial to identify the variables that specify the conditions under which dissonance or self-perception seem most likely to operate. We are convinced that self-perception processes are likely to have their greatest impact in Contexts involving low level (noncentral or unimportant) beliefs, whereas dissonance processes seem particularly applicable to conditions in which the actor perceives inconsistencies between behaviors and high level opinions.

A study by Shelly Taylor (1975) provides very compelling evidence that self-perception effects are most common in situations involving low level beliefs. In her research, Taylor asked female subjects to rate the attractiveness of a set of males depicted in a series of photographs. Half the women did so with the expectation that they would be meeting some of the men pictured; this manipulation was designed to increase the importance of the ratings for these women. The other women in the sample were not led to expect to meet the men; thus, their judgments should have been less important to them. Taylor also gave some of the subjects false physiological feedback which indicated that they had been aroused by a particular stimulus person—one that, in fact, each had rated as highly attractive.[9] She then asked these subjects again to rate the attractiveness of each of the men in the pictures.

Of most interest to our present concerns was the difference in ratings obtained as a function of the importance of the judgments. In the low-importance condition (in which the subjects had no reason to think that they would meet the men pictured), the false physiological feedback manipulation influenced the women's second ratings. They substantially increased their initially positive evaluations when they were "informed" of their arousal. This finding is congruent with the principles of self-perception theory. However, in the high-importance condition (in which the subjects expected to actually meet the men who were pictured), the feedback of apparent arousal did not increase attractiveness judgments. For these women, self-perception processes did not operate.

Similarly, a recent review of the research involving the overjustification effect (Lepper, 1981) suggests that this phenomenon is most easily observed in children—although it has been demonstrated in adults as well (cf. Deci & Ryan, 1980). It is probable that this effect occurs most reliably in persons who have a poorly resolved set of relevant beliefs; such a condition is most likely to occur in those possessing low level opinions, and in those people (for example, young children) who have yet to form a well-resolved belief system.

In addition, there is some evidence that dissonance theory has its greatest

---

[9] Note that there is no dissonance induced in such a circumstance.

relevance when the beliefs involved are of a high level (Ehrlich et al., 1957; Rokeach, 1971; Walster, 1964). Indeed, the theory explicitly states that little dissonance will be generated by perceived inconsistencies among unimportant (or low level) opinions. Aronson (1968, 1980) has persuasively argued that the theory finds its greatest predictive power in those situations involving persons' most closely held beliefs—their self-impressions (beliefs about themselves). Thus, as with self-perception theory, it appears that level of belief also moderates the operation of dissonance processes. In the present instance, however, the theory demands high level beliefs to be maximally effective.

CONCLUDING REMARKS

This concludes our discussion of the impact of actions on opinions. Although we devoted considerable attention to this important issue, it is only one subset of a more general area of concern—namely, the variables that determine the formation, maintenance, and change of opinions. Thus, the material presented in this chapter should be viewed as a continuation of the exploration of an important issue begun in Chapter 4. In the next chapter, we will extend this exploration into somewhat new territory: the consequences of opinions for overt behavior.

Beliefs and Overt Actions: 6
II. Effects of Opinions on Behavior

In Chapters 4 and 5, we discussed the formation and change of opinions, per se. The research on opinion change that was described in those chapters explored the variables that affect the stability of our evaluative beliefs, including the ways in which actions influence such cognitions. Thus, we concentrated almost exclusively on the factors that moderate the incorporation and maintenance of beliefs, without remarking in any detail about the possible consequences for overt action that such changes might engender. Almost all this work, however, is based on an underlying premise that a causal link exists between opinions and actions. This fundamental proposition is the central concern of this chapter.

It seems obvious that the opinions we hold affect our actions. For example, if a person's favorite flavor of ice cream is chocolate, then it seems reasonable to expect that he or she would order this flavor more often than not. However, as is noted repeatedly in Chapter 5, people often engage in actions that are inconsistent with their established beliefs. Indeed, one of the basic preconditions for the operation of cognitive dissonance is the realization that there is an Inconsistency between one's beliefs and actions. Since the study of such Inconsistencies has received so much attention in the field of social psychology, we will begin this chapter by considering the evidence that argues against the assumption of a causal link between opinions and behavior.

Negative Evidence

Early Research. The early research that attempted to examine the causal relationship between opinions and actions generally did not yield strong support for the existence of this connection. What has come to be seen by some as the traditional finding in this area was probably first reported by LaPiere (1934) in one of social psychology's most frequently cited studies. While LaPiere's research has been criticized as having some major shortcomings, it nonetheless provides a means by which a number of important concepts can be introduced. Thus, for our purposes, LaPiere's (1934) study provides a framework for discussing important issues regarding the link between beliefs and actions.

In his study, LaPiere traveled throughout the United States accompanied by a Chinese couple. He was interested in determining the extent to which people's actions—in this case, their treatment of his travelling companions—appeared to reflect their underlying opinions. During their travels, the three visited approximately 250 restaurants and motels and were provided service in all but one. Interestingly, however, when LaPiere later contacted the managements of these establishments by mail, nearly 90 percent of those that responded (about half of the total) said that they would not provide service to an Oriental.[1]

LaPiere's study is often taken as a straightforward demonstration that opinions and actions need not stand in a simple, one-to-one relationship to one another. However, while LaPiere's findings are apparently clear-cut, critics have noted that there exist a number of methodological flaws in his study that call the validity of the results into question. For example, as Triandis (1971) pointed out, it is quite possible that the agents of the hotels and restaurants who replied to LaPiere's written inquiry were not those who actually met and served LaPiere and his Chinese companions. That there is little consistency between one person's opinions and another person's actions should not prove too surprising.

There is another possible reason why LaPiere failed to detect an opinion-behavior link, and this reason has implications for understanding both the basic nature of opinions and the manner in which they can be conceptualized and measured. As will be discussed in greater detail in Chapter 11, sociologists and organizational psychologists distinguish between the *formal rules* of an organization and the *personal beliefs* held by its members. Formal rules are the regulations and codes of ideal conduct that every member of an organization is supposed to follow. Typically, however, there is tremendous variation in the extent to which the authorities in the organization are concerned with enforcing these rules. For example, many industrial and commercial organizations have rules that permit employees to smoke only in designated areas. Some companies strictly enforce such rules, while others do not.

Consider two such companies: in one of them (company X), the antismoking ordinance is stringently enforced, while in the other (company Y), it is not. If we were to monitor the smoking behavior of the employees of these two firms, we probably would notice a considerable difference between them: there would be a much greater incidence of smoking in company Y. However,

---

[1] It should be noted that at that time, opinions unfavorable to Orientals were quite common in the United States.

184

JOEL GORDON

Formal rules are not equally enforced across different organizations.

if we were to write the public relations departments of each company and ask if smoking on the job is permitted, it is likely that we would receive the identical answer from both—it is forbidden. The formal answer has more to do with the companies' policies than it does with the actual beliefs (or actions) of their employees. The report that we obtain is not necessarily a distortion—it is an accurate portrayal of a formal rule—but it has little, if anything, to do with the personal beliefs of the individuals who belong to the organization, and it only affects the behavior of those individuals when it is enforced (or monitored) within that Social Context.

Returning to LaPiere (1934), we can see that one possible reason for his failure to find a strong opinion-behavior link can be attributed to the fact that those employees who responded to the mailed query were reporting the formal company policy rather than any individual employee's personal opinion. In explaining LaPiere's results and similar findings of later research (Kutner, Wilkins, & Yarrow, 1952), Dillehay (1973) has noted that in formal organizations, there is often a gulf between company policies and employee actions. Under such a circumstance, a lack of correspondence between employee opinion and action is to be expected. Moreover, discriminatory company policies would guide the actual behaviors of the employees only to the extent that the management of the hotels took steps to enforce these rules. That is, if the company strictly monitored its employees' actions and punished clerks who were caught ignoring the rules against serving Orientals, then it is likely that few employees would disobey this edict. Such impingement would be effective regardless of the personal beliefs of the employees who were charged with enforcing the company's discriminatory policies.

Of course, Consistency between personal opinions and company regulations can occur, but only if at least one of three preconditions is met. First, the processes of self/other Consistency can operate to induce people to seek Social Contexts in which there is support for their beliefs. Thus, it is possible that a potential employee who held negative opinions about Orientals would be interested in joining an establishment whose well-known policies discriminated against this ethnic group.

The process of incorporation is a second possible determinant of self/ other Consistency in these situations since, as noted in Chapters 2 and 5, a person can come to hold an opinion as a consequence of repeated impingements on his or her behavior. A desk clerk in LaPiere's study, for example, might come to believe, over time, that the discriminatory actions that he was induced (by the hotel management) to perform did, in fact, represent his own true opinion.

Third, it is also possible that an individual clerk's beliefs were, by chance, consistent with the policy of the hotel. Under this circumstance, there would be a positive association between opinion and formal rule, but this association would not be an example of a true cause-effect relationship. On the other hand, such a chance occurrence might encourage the employee to remain with the organization, since the Social Context of the work setting would provide him or her with the opportunity to express established beliefs. In any event, very few of the clerks in LaPiere's study displayed such self/ other Consistency.

Thus, there is little evidence that any of these processes had a major impact on behavior in this instance. However, as noted, there is considerable evidence to demonstrate the force that incorporation, self/other Consistency, and even chance can exert on social acts, and it might be expected that these processes would, in many instances, play a determining role in people's behaviors. They simply did not appear to operate in the context of LaPiere's study.

In short, it does not appear that LaPiere really investigated the variables that he intended to study. There are a number of ways by which opinions can be measured. Some of these procedures incorrectly ask people to report their perceptions of their Social Contexts ("Does your hotel have a rule against accommodating Orientals?") rather than their personal beliefs ("How do you personally evaluate Orientals?"). Questions that tap persons' perceptions of their Social Contexts are not really measuring their opinions, as we have defined them. In his study, the questions that LaPiere asked were probably perceived by the hotel employees as inquiries about their companies' formal policies regarding Orientals rather than about their personal opinion of this ethnic group. These people might have truthfully answered LaPiere's questions, but the questions themselves might have elicited information that was not really relevant to the central issue of the research—namely, the relationship between personal opinions and subsequent behaviors.

Given that LaPiere's study was flawed, it has little to say about this relationship. However, his study does provide some interesting insights into the forces that constrain people's actions in interpersonal encounters. Consider the forces that might have operated on the typical desk clerk in LaPiere's study. In one circumstance, this individual might well have known the company policy against renting rooms to Orientals. When LaPiere's troupe arrived at his desk, the clerk was faced with a real dilemma: to refuse them service or simply to go through the usual motions of the innkeeper. As will be further discussed, strong forces operated to induce the clerk to accept the Chinese couple. Moreover, there appeared to be no strong inpingement by the management (for example, a threat of severe negative consequences) for breaking with the formal company rule. The outcome of all of these factors would result in the clerk's renting the couple a room, no matter what his personal opinion might have been.

A portion of the findings from Milgram's (1974) work on obedience, discussed in Chapter 2, is particularly relevant to the factors that appear to have influenced the decisions and actions of LaPiere's hotel clerks. In one modification of his basic research procedure, Milgram varied the number and intensity of the cues provided by the learner-victim. In the conditions described earlier, the victim and teacher were located in different rooms. Thus, the cues provided the teacher were limited to the victim's verbal reports—if we can be permitted to call screams and pounding on walls verbal reports. In other conditions that Milgram explored, the victim and teacher were in the same room, and thus visual as well as auditory cues were present. In the most intimate teacher-learner condition, the teacher-subject actually had to force the victim to place his hand on an electric grid after he had made a mistake on the bogus learning task.

The manipulation of the victim's presence had a marked effect on subjects' actions. The degree of obedience to the experimenter's instruction to shock the learner for his errors was strongly influenced by the immediacy of the victim. The greatest degree of obedience occurred when the victim was not physically present; the least occurred when the subject had to force the learner's hand onto the shock plate.

The implications of these findings for an informed interpretation of LaPiere's results are straightforward. The Social Context that LaPiere's Oriental couple presented the hotel clerks was analogous to the situation of a teacher-subject in Milgram's study who had to decide how to act under conditions in which the victim, but not the experimenter, was present in the room.

The physical presence of LaPiere's Oriental couple who requested service, for example, was a more immediate and impressive cue than was the poorly monitored formal rule of the organization, just as the dramatic behavior of the victim in Milgram's "learner in the same room" condition was a greater impingement than the experimenter's rule that the subject continue to perform his job.

Even if we assume the unlikely case that the same hotel employee who dealt with LaPiere in person was also the one who corresponded with him, we might expect a pattern of findings similar to that reported, given Milgram's results: corresponding via mail (in LaPiere's study) is comparable to the teacher's only hearing his victim (in Milgram's study). Both settings (the correspondence condition and the "victim out of room" condition) severely limited the number of cues available from the persons in need (the victim and the travelers). In this circumstance, other cues (the formal rules, the demands of the job, and so on) would weigh more heavily in the Valuation process. Conversely, in the settings in which the cues provided by the supplicants were more compelling (that is, in the face-to-face conditions of both demonstrations), the relative impact of the formal rules was greatly diminished. Under these circumstances, the Valuation outcome was a function of the more immediate and intense interpersonal cues.

In a second modification, Milgram (1974) manipulated the experimenter's presence in the Social Context of the experimental room. In the condition discussed in detail in Chapter 2, the experimenter was always present in the room, and thus the teacher-subject could see that his behavior was being monitored. In a second condition, the experimenter was not present during the time the teacher and learner actually were performing the task. After the experimenter had given the pair their instructions, attached the learner to the shock apparatus, and so forth, he went to a separate room and communicated with the subject via an intercom. Milgram found that the presence of the experimenter also had an impact on obedience; there was less obedience when the experimenter was absent from the room during the learning task.

Milgram's manipulation of experimenter presence also has parallels in LaPiere's investigation. For example, it is likely that the clerks' day-to-day actions were not well-monitored in most of the service establishments that LaPiere contacted. If they had been, we would have expected a much greater refusal rate. The moderating effect of the ability to monitor compliance with the formal rule was amply demonstrated in those conditions of Milgram's study that varied the physical presence of the experimenter. As noted, compliance was appreciably diminished when the authority figure was not in the room, and apparently could not monitor the teacher's behavior. We assume that this circumstance closely paralleled the situation in which LaPiere's clerks typically found themselves. In most cases, it was unlikely that the clerks' behavior would be directly monitored by their superiors. The Social Context of the typical hotel is such that room clerks are reasonably autonomous while carrying out their duties. The manager or owner is usually not physically present in the lobby area and rarely oversees the check-in procedure.

Interestingly, many of Milgram's subjects lied to the experimenter in the condition in which the two communicated via an intercom. Often, the subjects reported to the experimenter that they were shocking the learner at the level required when, in fact, they were administering a much lower level of shock or were not shocking the victim at all. This type of deception was probably practiced by the hotel clerks of LaPiere's study as well. When asked by company executives if they were following the procedures of the hotel with regard to the exculsion of "undesirable" customers, it is likely that the clerks reported that they were behaving toward Orientals in a manner that was consistent with the organization's established guidelines. We know from LaPiere's findings, however, that this was far from the case.

Even if LaPiere had measured the personal opinions of the clerks, however, there remains a good possibility that the resultant findings would not have been much different from those that he reported. As shown below, the actual relationship between an individual's opinions and actions is moderated by a number of factors, including, for example, the extent to which such beliefs are consistent with (or at least not contrary to) constraining factors in the Social Context.

There is yet another possibility to consider in evaluating the implications of LaPiere's work. Suppose that every single clerk encountered by LaPiere and his associates in the 250 establishments that they visited possessed a negative opinion about Chinese people. Would this have made a major difference in the results that were obtained in this study? We do not think so. Why? Because in addition to this opinion, the clerks probably held in common a number of other beliefs (especially norms) that would have operated against the overt expression of their biased opinions. For example, all of these people probably learned to be polite as young children. As clerks, they also had learned that creating ugly scenes in the lobby of the hotel also was not company policy—indeed, they probably viewed a brawl in the hotel's lobby as a more negative outcome than the prospect of having a couple of Chinese people occupy the worst room in the house.

In general, the extent to which a clerk would express his negative opinion in terms of overt behavior is governed by the levels that this opinion and the relevant norms occupy in his Personal Structure. If, in fact, the anti-Chinese opinion was a central feature of his belief system, then the force of the norms probably would not have been sufficient to suppress the desk clerk's opinion-consistent action (refusal to accommodate the couple). On the other hand, if the level of the opinion was peripheral—as it probably was in most cases—then the opinion-norm conflict would have been resolved in favor of the norm (the couple would be accommodated).

As noted earlier, the extended discussion of LaPiere's (1934) work raises a number of points that are relevant to much of the material to be presented in this chapter. The issues of impingement versus incorporation, beliefs versus Social Context, and opinions versus norms are central to our discussion of the factors that mediate the degree of correspondence between opinions and overt actions. To explore this issue more fully, we will now turn to some of the more contemporary investigations of the opinion-action link. We will begin with a review of some of the studies that, like LaPiere's research, did not demonstrate this linkage. We will then discuss some conceptual and methodological implications of this work, leading to a discussion of the literature that supports the classic assumption that opinions do, in fact, influence actions.

Contemporary Findings. In the late 1960s, a number of reviews of the empirical work relevant to the question of the link between opinions and actions (Kiesler, Collins, & Miller, 1969; Wicker, 1969) concluded that there was no consistent evidence in favor of the idea that opinions influence overt behaviors. On the pages that follow, we will present a detailed discussion of some representative studies that comprise this literature.

A study that captures the flavor of work in this area was conducted by Leventhal, Jones, and Trembly (1966). This experiment investigated the extent to which opinion change induced through fear arousal affected subsequent actions. As reviewed in Chapter 4, the effects of variations in the amount of fear that a persuasive message induces, under appropriate conditions, is directly related to opinion change.[2] The work of Leventhal et al. (1966) demonstrated that increasing the fear-arousing properties of a message could increase its persuasive power. In addition, however, the researchers studied the implications that fear-induced opinion change might have on actions that could reduce the fear that was generated by the communication.

As in much of Leventhal's work on fear arousal and opinion change, the topic used by Leventhal et al. (1966) was the danger of tetanus. In this experiment, two written messages, which varied in terms of the vividness of the language used to describe the problems associated with a tetanus infection, were presented to groups of subjects. Leventhal et al. found, as did other researchers, a positive relationship between fear arousal and opinions, as measured by subjects' responses on an opinion scale. Unlike most other researchers in the general area of communication and persuasion, however, these investigators also took the next reasonable step—that of determining the extent to which the measured impact of the messages on subjects' reported opinions was realized in their actual behaviors.

In this study, Leventhal and his colleagues informed all subjects that special arrangements had been made with the school's health service to inoculate anyone who wished to be protected against tetanus, free of charge and with no undue delay (six nurses, no waiting). Subjects were given explicit information about the ready availability of this service and specific directions for obtaining it. To determine the relationship between expressed opinions and actual behaviors, these investigators monitored health service records to determine which of the subjects, in fact, took advantage of the offer and went to the service to be inoculated. Contrary to the expectations that one

---

[2] These appropriate conditions include an upper limit on the shock value of the material (recall that a communication can be so frightening or repugnant that it cannot be processed by the receiver), and the implied or explicit provision of a tactic for alleviating the fear.

might derive from assuming a link between opinions and actions, Leventhal et al. found no systematic relationship between expressed opinions (that tetanus inoculation was an important component of good preventive health) and overt actions (actually getting immunized against the possibility of tetanus infection).

Findings of this sort are far from unusual. Indeed, Alan Wicker (1969) concluded on the basis of more than 40 studies of the opinion-action link that such research demonstrated, at most, a weak relationship between expressed opinion and actual overt behavior. In light of these results, he further concluded that it might be reasonable to dismiss the entire concept of opinion and focus instead exclusively on behavior per se.

There are, of course, alternative ways of interpreting the apparently negative results yielded by many studies of this type. For example, Calder and Ross (1973) discussed three reasons—all involving the level of opinion—why there is often a lack of relationship between beliefs and actions. First, they observed that it is easier to induce a person to verbally express a statement of opinion than it is to induce that person to actually act on the opinion. For example, it is much easier to induce obese persons to express a negative opinion toward overeating than it is to get them to reduce their caloric intake (that is, to express the opinion behaviorally).

Second, Calder and Ross speculated that new or changed opinions are unlikely to be expressed in overt behavior because acting on them conflicts

'My next tune makes a statement about our high-technology, energy-consuming society."

It often is easier to express an opinion verbally than to act on it.

with other well-established habits. For example, many older people learned to drive a car before the advent of seatbelts. Although they might now accept the belief that seatbelts can reduce the probability of serious injury in the event of an accident, they often fail to use them. Why? Because their habitual behaviors associated with driving a car had been acquired over a long period of time, were well practiced and well learned, and as such, became almost second nature in their expression. Unfortunately, such patterns of behavior became well established before the formation of positive opinions about seatbelts. Consequently, the behaviors that follow from the newly established opinion—to buckle up before starting the car—conflict with rather fixed and rigidly performed sequences of behaviors. Under such circumstances, it should not be surprising that even well-intentioned actors would fail to express recently incorporated opinions in their actual behaviors.

Calder and Ross's third point involves the transitory nature of many opinions. As we have frequently noted in this text, we hold numerous beliefs that are relatively low level, that is, noncentral or unimportant to us. These are less likely than high level opinions to be supported by other aspects of an actor's Personal Structure. They are, in essence, isolated cognitions that, while accepted, have few implications for other components of the belief system. Of most relevance is the notion that low level opinions are easily formed (and easily changed), and thus do not persist for a sufficient period of time to be consistently expressed in overt behaviors. If a great many of the studies that have been undertaken in this area of research have focused on low level beliefs—and the material presented in the last two chapters would support this premise—then it is not surprising to find a lack of support for the proposition that opinions cause actions.

The findings of Leventhal, Jones, and Trembly (1966), for example, can be interpreted as being consistent with the position of Calder and Ross (1973) concerning the transitory nature of many opinions. It is likely that many of the subjects of Leventhal et al. were concerned about tetanus at the conclusion of the experimental session; however, it also is likely that only low level opinions were induced in the experimental context. It is true that people often are concerned about the general state of their health; it is not clear, however, that the subjects in this study saw tetanus as an immediate threat. They had never had tetanus themselves, and they probably knew no one who had ever contracted this disease. The new opinion, in other words, was not well integrated with other, more central health-related beliefs. As such, its salience probably was very transitory, perhaps limited to the time that they had spent in the room where they had read the message about tetanus.

Though not mentioned explicitly by Calder and Ross (1973), there is a fourth possible explanation for the failure of many studies to demonstrate a strong link between opinions and actions. It involves our core concept— the Social Context. With few exceptions, it is probable that the opinions that can be induced in a short-term, social psychology experiment are of low level. That is, while a subject's belief system is changed through such

Even if the blood and gore in a war movie makes the dangers of tetanus salient, we might not be able to act on this belief.

experiences, the opinions that are affected are typically not of central relevance. For this reason, it is likely that the salience of the new opinions is limited to the circumstances in which they were induced—that is, to the Social Context of the experimental laboratory in which, for example, the threat of tetanus was vividly portrayed. *Salience,* in this case, refers to the extent to which the opinion intrudes on the subject's conscious attention.[3]

It seems likely that the salience of the opinion regarding tetanus immunization influenced the findings of Leventhal et al., because salience was limited by the low level of the belief. There is little doubt, for example, that while they were in the context of the experimental laboratory, subjects thought very seriously about the dangers of tetanus, and its prevention; however, when they left this context, the salience of tetanus immunization sharply decreased, and the issue became a much less pressing and immediate concern.

This is not to say that the opinion itself did not persist. It could well be that the opinion induced by Leventhal et al. remained an element of many subjects' belief systems for a long while. If asked at some later point, these individuals would be likely to say that tetanus immunization was a reasonable and important procedure. However, they also might say that as

---

[3] The term *salience* comes from the Latin word for salt. Just as salt intrudes on our taste buds, a salient opinion intrudes on our conscious thought processes.

yet they had not been immunized—they just never seemed to find themselves thinking about this issue when they could act on it. Thus, the behavioral expression of the opinion might never occur, because the belief does not come to mind under suitable conditions, nor is it attended to long enough to result in the specified behavior.

Subjects from the Leventhal et al. experiment, for example, might think about their experience while watching a war movie on TV in which soldiers are being wounded and maimed. The blood and gore portrayed on the screen might make salient again the dangers of tetanus that were emphasized in the experiment in which they had recently participated. The conditions surrounding the intrusion of the opinion on subjects' consciousness, however, are such that its behavioral expression is extremely unlikely. Very few people in this circumstance would get up and run to the health center at the conclusion of the late show.

It should be noted that in some instances, fate intervenes to raise the salience of a low level opinion. For example, if a subject of the tetanus study had stepped on a nail a few weeks later, it is likely that this unfortunate occurrence would have raised the level of the relevant opinion, at least temporarily. Under this circumstance, the now higher level opinion might well stir the individual to take precautionary measures by being inoculated. This would be less likely if the individual had not been recently exposed to the information provided in the experiment, since he or she would be more likely to dismiss the nail puncture as a minor wound.

Positive Evidence

The literature surrounding the tenuous linkage of opinions with their behavioral expressions was viewed with some embarrassment by social psychologists of the 1960s. The pessimistic conclusion that at most, opinions were weakly linked to behavior was usually accepted by the people who worked in the field. It could be, however, that this pessimistic interpretation of the findings of LaPiere (1934) and Leventhal, Jones, and Trembly (1966) was too readily accepted. The factors that might have mediated the opinion-action link, many of which have been noted here, often were not considered. A reevaluation of this issue has taken place in recent years, however, thanks in large part to the work of Martin Fishbein and Icek Ajzen. Fishbein and Ajzen (1975) noted the imprecision of much past research and suggested improvements for examining the opinion-action link. In addition, other researchers have explored the impact of a number of factors that moderate the overt expression of opinions (Bagozzi & Burnkrant, 1979; Bentler & Speckart, 1979, 1981; Davidson & Jaccard, 1979; Fazio & Zanna, 1978; Jaccard, Knox, & Brinberg, 1979; Kahle & Berman, 1979; Regan & Fazio, 1977; Rokeach, 1973; Sherif, Kelly, Rodgers, Sarup, & Tittler, 1973; Schwartz, 1979; Sivacek & Crano, 1980; Weigel & Newman, 1976). In the following sections, we will discuss six major factors that this work has identified.

Factors that Moderate the Opinion-Action Link

Specificity. One of the major points of Fishbein and Ajzen (1975) concerns the necessity of matching the degree of *specificity* of the measured opinion with that of the potential behavioral expression of the opinion. They argued that it is inappropriate to examine the relationship between an opinion that was measured at a general level and a very specific action that might logically follow from that opinion (but that might be affected by a number of other factors as well).

For example, if we asked an individual to give us his opinion about ice cream, we might find no relationship between his answer ("I love it!") and his behavior when offered two scoops of Sealtest kielbasa crunch ("No thank you"). This particular (that is, specific) behavioral test of the opinion might be inappropriate—kielbasa crunch might be one of the few flavors of ice cream that the respondent finds unappealing, or Sealtest might be one of the few brands that this connoisseur will not sample. On the other hand, the respondent might have expressed a negative opinion towards ice cream in general, but might have eaten the dish of kielbasa crunch because he had not eaten in three days and would have eaten anything as long as it came on a plate; or, kielbasa crunch might happen to be the only ice cream flavor that this person finds worth eating. Thus, while the subject's general opinion about ice cream might have been validly measured, the generality of the measure conflicts with the specificity of the examination of the opinion's behavioral expression. Consequently, no link was found between opinion and action in this instance when, in fact, one well might have existed.

The role that specificity plays in mediating the overt behavioral expression of opinions has been noted in a number of empirical and theoretical treatments, in addition to that of Fishbein and Ajzen (Crespi, 1971; Weigel, Vernon, & Tognacci, 1974). Weigel et al. (1974), in fact, provided a clear-cut demonstration of the moderating effect of specificity in their study of the link between opinions about ecology and actions designed to protect the environment.

In this study, a group of respondents were asked their opinions about environmental problems at three levels of specificity. At the least specific level, subjects were asked to state their opinions about environmental problems in general. At the middle level, specificity was tapped via opinion questions dealing with specific ecological problems that are typically of concern to environmental organizations such as the Sierra Club. At the most specific level, opinion measures were concerned with respondents' evaluations of the Sierra Club.

Five months later, these subjects were sent a request by the Sierra Club for their support and membership. In this manner, Weigel et al. (1974) could examine the relationship between professed opinions and the outcome of this appeal for support. They found no systematic relationship between subjects' general opinions toward environmental issues and their responses to the request, and only a weak relationship was found between respondents' overt behavior and opinions measured at the middle level of specificity. However, opinions measured at the most specific level were found to predict subjects' subsequent behavior with a reasonable degree of precision. Clearly, the degree of correspondence between the specificity of the opinions that were measured and the specificity of the subsequent actions plays a major role in the determination of the opinion-action link. Other research (Bagozzi & Burnkrant, 1979) has yielded results consistent with this observation.

Moreover, we would expect the reverse to be true—that is, that more general opinions would be better predictors of general patterns of behavior than would specific opinions. For example, a person's established opinion towards the Democratic party would be a better predictor of her voting behavior over a period of years than would her specific opinions of a specific set of candidates. That is, like many "confirmed" Democrats, she might well have voted for Ronald Reagan over Jimmy Carter in the 1980 presidential election; this action, however, might have been her sole deviation from party ranks over decades of voting. Thus, a measure of her specific opinions about Reagan and Carter, while accurately indicating her actions in the 1980 presidential election, would have yielded an incorrect prediction of her general pattern of long-term voting behavior. It would not have accurately predicted her choice of candidates in the other political races held in 1980, nor her behavior in previous and subsequent elections. In this instance, her more general opinions about the Democratic and Republican parties would have been better predictors of her general voting behavior, although they would not have been specific enough to pinpoint her vote in the 1980 presidential election.

Intentionality. A second major mediator of the opinion-action link concerns the extent to which the opinion measurement assesses, at least in part, the respondent's *intention* to take some belief-relevant action. It is one thing to have an opinion about something, another to have the intention to act on it. For example, we might strongly believe (that is, hold the opinion) that nude bathing should be allowed on public beaches. However, there might be a number of reasons why we would not personally intend to act on this opinion. For example, we might be too shy; our past training might make it difficult to overcome our initial sense of embarrassment; we might have a very negative self-image concerning our bodies, or parts thereof, and so on. Any or all of these circumstances would weaken the relationship between opinion and this particular opinion-consistent behavior. However, the opinion well might predict our actions with respect to protecting or supporting other persons' rights to nude bathing.

The Fishbein and Ajzen (1975) formal model of the link between opinion and action contains a specific intentionality component; their research has shown, in fact, that additional information about a person's intention to behave toward the object of an opinion permits a better prediction of the person's actions than does knowing only the person's opinion. In the above example, for instance, knowing the bather's opinion about nude bathing would not have provided much useful information about his or her ultimate action on the beach. However, knowing this person's intention (to cover or to un-

It is one thing to have an opinion about nude bathing, and another thing to act on it.

cover), as well as his or her opinion, would provide an accurate forecast of future actions. Research (Fishbein & Ajzen, 1975; Jaccard et al., 1979) has demonstrated the importance of intentions as mediators in the link between opinions and actions.

Note that the statement of intentionality sometimes, but not always, contains within it an inference about the underlying opinion. Measuring the intention, in other words, does not always provide an accurate estimate of opinion. A person might support nude bathing but not engage in it; or a person might not support it but engage in it anyway (for example, because of the impingement of social pressure).

Ambiguity. A third factor that can mediate the opinion-action relationship is the degree of ambiguity in the relevant components of the actor's belief system.[4] We are less likely to act on ambiguous opinions, primarily because we feel that they are likely to result in unexpected or unintended outcomes. Thus, ambiguous opinions are accorded less weight in the Valuation process. In contrast, with unambiguous (clear or well-resolved) opinions, the appropriate behavioral link is obvious to us, as are the most likely consequences of the various behavioral alternatives that are available. As such, this type of opinion is weighted more heavily in deciding on appropriate actions.

---

[4] As noted in Chapter 3, there is a distinction between the ambiguity of a specific opinion or cue and that of Resolution, which refers to the ambiguity of a number of beliefs or components of the context. For present purposes, however, this distinction is not crucial.

For example, suppose that we hold some very unequivocal (highly re-solved) opinions about different kinds of music. Classical music, especially Italian opera, is very much our favorite type, whereas we find country and western music intolerable. On the other hand, our opinions of rock and roll and jazz are somewhat more ambiguous, although we might favor jazz to some extent. When given the choice between two radio stations—one playing one of Puccini's most popular operas, *Tosca,* and the other playing Willie Nelson's latest cowboy lament—our behavior will be readily predicted from our well-resolved opinions. We are certain that we shall enjoy the broadcast of *Tosca* and are equally sure to abhor the country and western tune. In fact, given the choice between Willie Nelson and nothing, it is likely that we would turn the radio off, because we know that listening to this music will be aversive.

On the other hand, we would be less sure of a decision if we were given the choice between a station that features the tops in rock and one devoted to jazz. This is so because we are less certain that one of these alternatives would be more rewarding than the other, given that our opinions about these two forms of music are less clear. As such, they would not weigh heavily in our Valuation, and other external issues would be more important in determining our action. Thus, we might choose to listen to the rock program because the station broadcasting it provides better reception, or the disc jockey playing the music is particularly entertaining. Schwartz (1979) has provided research evidence that is congruent with this expectation.

As discussed in Chapter 5, engaging in a behavior that is inconsistent with a belief has implications for the belief itself and, consequently, for future actions. The degree of Resolution of a belief system is increased through actions that result in varying degrees of positive or negative outcomes. Thus, if we thoroughly enjoyed the rock program, this experience would decrease the ambiguity of our opinion about this style of music. As such, the next time we are faced with a choice, we are more likely to choose rock over jazz.

Experience with belief-relevant people, objects, or events should affect the relationship between these beliefs and later actions, because such experi-ences are likely to increase the clarity of our opinions and impressions. It seems reasonable to speculate that people who have had direct experience with an object of a belief would be more certain of their evaluation of that object. Robin Vallacher confirmed this hypothesis in a study in which he asked undergraduate subjects to report their evaluations of two targets—their best friend, and a stranger whom they had observed for a brief period. He also asked the respondents to indicate how certain they were of their evaluative beliefs. As might be expected, Vallacher's (1975) subjects were more certain of their beliefs about the person with whom they had the greater amount of experience (their best friend) than they were about their evaluations of a person with whom they had little experience (the stranger).

Moreover, opinions are more likely to determine later actions to the extent that these evaluations are based on experiences with the object of

"I don't have any opinions on politics but I'd be happy to give you my opinion of the neighbors."

People are more certain of their beliefs about objects with which they have had some direct experience.

the opinion. For instance, we might hold a negative opinion about marijuana smoking even though we might never have indulged in this behavior. Indeed, our total experience with this issue might have been gleaned from the pages of *Readers Digest* and from lectures given by local drug-enforcement officials. In this case, our opinion would be a less accurate predictor of our actual behavior at a future time than if we held this same negative opinion, but had actually tried the drug and had found the experience unsatisfying or undesirable. Prior experience provides us with firmer ground on which to base an opinion. In the absence of such a grounding, the opinion, while real, is less certain and thus less likely to be expressed behaviorally.

Systematic research evidence shows that the extent to which an actor has had first-hand experiences that are relevant to an object of opinion enhances the likelihood that he or she will behave in a belief-consistent manner. In a review of the literature on the link between beliefs and actions, Fazio and Zanna (in press) proposed that opinions formed as a consequence of experiences that are directly relevant to the evaluative belief are almost always more predictive of later related actions than are opinions formed without this direct behavioral experience. An example of the operation of experience on the opinion-action link is provided in an interesting study conducted by Regan and Fazio (1977).

In this experiment, the opinions of Cornell University students toward overcrowding in the dormitories were assessed. At the time of this study, Cornell University had admitted to its dormitories more students than there were available rooms. Accordingly, some unfortunates found themselves occupying a cot in their dormitory's lobby during their first few weeks of college. Opinions about overcrowding were measured in two groups of students: those who had been subjected to this indignity, and those who had not.

Both groups were found to be equivalent in their (very negative) opinions regarding this nefarious practice. However, when the subjects were asked to work to eradicate overcrowding in the dormitories of their school, Regan and Fazio found a substantial difference between the proportion of volunteers from the two groups. As might be expected, those who had direct experience with "lobby living" (and had expressed a negative opinion about the practice) were three times as likely to volunteer than were those who expressed an equally negative opinion, but who had never been forced to do time in the lobby.

Regan and Fazio (1977) replicated these findings in a second study that involved assigning subjects to different levels of experience on a puzzle-solving task. This study also found that expressed opinions were tied to subsequent behaviors as a function of experience. In other words, the opinions of subjects about the puzzle task predicted their subsequent willingness to work very meticulously on other puzzles if they actually had prior experience with the task. Conversely, there was little systematic relationship between the opinions and actions of those subjects who had had no direct experience with the puzzle-solving task (those who had received only a verbal description of the puzzles). Other research (Fazio & Zanna, 1978a, 1978b; Fazio, Zanna, & Cooper, 1978; Synder & Tanke, 1976) has supported this finding.

Merchants frequently take advantage of this phenomenon by providing a potential buyer an opportunity for direct experience with the product they wish to sell. They do this because their intuition suggests to them that such exposure to their product lowers the ambiguity of the customer's opinion about it, thereby strengthening the opinion-behavior relationship and increasing the likelihood of a sale. For instance, new car dealers will often urge undecided customers to test-drive the car they are considering. Dealers do this because they think that the experience of driving the car will increase potential buyers' confidence in their postive evaluations of the product.[5] In this case, the merchants' intuitions are consistent with the social psychological evidence. In our terms, such a sales tactic helps to lower the ambiguity of customers' opinions, and thereby increases the impact of these opinions on their decisions to buy the product. By enhancing opinion clarity in this way,

---

[5] The dealer begins with the assumption that the buyers' initial opinions are favorable, if tenuous, or the customers would not be in the showroom in the first place.

PHILIPPE LEDRU/SYGMA

While such religious rallies are commonplace, we know of no marches for Ultra-Brite.

the merchant increases the likelihood that buyers will exhibit opinion-consistent behavior. Given that the original opinion is often somewhat positive (if vague), this tactic does, in fact, promote sales.

Level. A fourth factor that has an impact on the opinion-behavior link is the *level,* or centrality, of the belief. As noted earlier in this chapter, Calder and Ross (1973) discussed a number of reasons why there often is little relationship between overt actions and low level opinions. Clearly, the more important an opinion is to an individual, the more likely it is that the opinion will be linked to some form of behavioral expression. For example, think about two beliefs that you might hold: your opinion about your usual brand of toothpaste and your opinion about your religion. Let's suppose that like most people, the toothpaste that you use is not a very important concern, although you do have a definite favorite (a low level opinion). On the other hand, suppose that your religion is an extremely important factor in your life (a high level opinion).[6] It is self-evident that one's resistance to impinge-

---

[6] Of course, many people are indifferent to religious issues, and some are very concerned about their choice of toothpaste, but for the sake of our example, we shall presume that religious beliefs are, in most cases, much more important than opinions regarding brands of toothpaste.

ment attempts would be greater in the case of the more central belief (Bentler & Speckart, 1981; Kahle & Berman, 1979). People in the recent past have died rather than renounce their religious convictions; we know of no one who has died defending his or her choice of toothpaste.

In addition to fostering resistence to impingement pressures, level also has a more direct implication for the relationship between opinions and action: the more central the belief, the more likely it is that it will be expressed behaviorally. Almost by definition, high level beliefs carry with them some form of behavioral commitment. In research concerning this observation, Sherif, Sherif, and Nebergall (1965) estimated the level of respondents' political opinions by measuring their tolerance for a number of statements regarding their personal political preferences. This research was conducted within the framework of social judgment theory, as discussed in Chapter 4. In this study, respondents identified, from a group of nine statements (presented in Figure 6.1), the one item that best represented their true feelings about a political issue. Then they indicated other items which fell within their latitude of acceptance but which were not their most preferred position. Then they identified their least preferred position, as well as other items that fell within their latitude of rejection.

For our purposes, this procedure yielded a number of indicators of the level of the respondents' opinions. For example, Sherif et al. present evidence that the more items that a respondent identified as unacceptable—that is,

FIGURE 6.1

Items Presented to Respondents before the 1960 Presidential Election (from Sherif et al., 1965)

A. The election of the Republican presidential and vice presidential candidates in November is absolutely essential from all angles in the country's interest.

B. On the whole, the interests of the country will be served best by the election of the Republican candidates for president and vice president in the coming election.

C. It seems that the country's interests would be better served if the presidential and vice presidential candidates of the Republican party are elected this November.

D. Although it is hard to decide, it is probable that the country's interests may be better served if the Republican presidential and vice presidential candidates are elected in November.

E. From the point of view of the country's interests, it is hard to decide whether it is preferable to vote for presidential and vice presidential candidates of the Republican or the Democratic party in November.

F. Although it is hard to decide, it is probable that the country's interests may be better served if the Democratic presidential and vice presidential candidates are elected in November.

G. It seems that the country's interests would be better served if the presidential and vice presidential candidates of the Democratic party are elected this November.

H. On the whole, the interests of the country will be served best by the election of the Democratic candidates for president and vice president in the coming election.

I. The election of the Democratic presidential and vice presidential candidates in November is absolutely essential from all angles in the country's interests.

the wider the subject's latitude of rejection—the more important was the issue to that person; similarly, the more extreme the most acceptable item, the higher the level of the opinion. As noted in Chapter 1, other evidence (Rokeach, 1960) indicates that the higher the level of an opinion, the more extreme it tends to be and the less acceptable are deviations from it.

In their research, Sherif et al. (1965) uncovered a number of interesting relationships. Of most relevance to our present concerns is their finding that the higher the level of a person's political opinion, the more likely he or she was to be engaged in organized political activities. Thus, the more statements of political beliefs (see Figure 6.1) that an individual found unacceptable, the more likely he or she was to have joined either the Democratic or Republican party. Additional evidence for these observations has been provided by Sherif et al. (1973), who found that the more ego-involving the issue (the higher the level of the belief), the greater the correspondence between opinions and actions.

Vested Interest.   Vested interest, a concept related to level of opinion, also appears to play a role in determining the extent of opinion-behavior consistency. Vested interest refers to the extent to which a person perceives an opinion to be associated with his or her well-being. The greater the perceived vested interest of one's opinion, the stronger the link between that opinion and one's overt actions. This relationship holds because vested interest is the major criterion that people use in the Valuation process. That is, as noted in Chapter 3, the extent to which people perceive an outcome as affecting their welfare has a major impact on the decisions that they reach regarding the best action to take in a given situation.

A clear, if obvious, example of the operation of this factor on opinion-behavior Consistency occurred when the people of Florida were asked to vote on whether or not casino gambling should be legalized in the Miami area. This referendum, which ultimately was to fail, attracted a large number of supporters and opponents. Not surprisingly, those who stood to personally gain or lose from the legalization of gambling were the most active in the political campaign that preceded the election. The hotel owners and others who stood to directly benefit from an increase in tourism were the major financial backers of the referendum. Those whose vested interests were served by a maintenance of the status quo (that is, permanent residents of the Miami area, retirees, clergy, and so on), however, were most likely to work actively against the referendum. Other people with opinions similar to one of these extreme groups did not work actively in this campaign. Indeed, some of them did not even vote. Why? Because their welfare was not as directly tied to the outcome of the election as was that of the activists.

A research example of the operation of the effect of vested interests was provided in a field study by Sivacek and Crano (1980). At the time of this investigation, the state of Michigan held a referendum that proposed to raise the legal drinking age from 19 to 21 years. As might be expected, the prevailing opinion on the college campuses of the state was very antagonistic to this change. Indeed, in an opinion survey conducted at Michigan State University, 70 percent of the student respondents to this poll were opposed to the goal of the referendum. Note, however, that whatever their opinion, not all of the students would be affected equally by the change; though most of the people surveyed had negative opinions about the proposed change, those students who were already 21 years old would not be seriously inconvenienced if the drinking age were raised. On the basis of our discussion, we would expect a greater correspondence between antireferendum opinions and behavior among the younger students, since the vested interest in this issue was far greater for them than for older respondents with identical opinions.

The Michigan referendum provided Sivacek and Crano (1980) with an opportunity to assess the impact of vested interests on the behavioral expression of opinions in a naturalistic setting. To accomplish this, they measured the opinions of a large number of randomly selected college students at Michigan State University. In addition to opinions, information was also collected concerning each respondent's age and previous experience with bars and drinking. Two weeks later, all of the subjects who had been originally contacted were called by a representative of a fictitious antireferendum organization and asked to volunteer to call others and encourage them to vote against the referendum.

The respondents who had expressed opinions opposing a change in the drinking age in the original survey were identified and classified according to their degree of vested interest in this issue. In this case, vested interest was determined by the respondents' ages: those who would not be able to legally drink in bars for at least two years as a result of the law change were defined as having high vested interest; those who would be at least 21 years old by the time that the change took effect were classified as having low vested interest; and those between these extremes were defined as having moderate vested interest.

Of course, there were no differences between the three groups in terms of their expressed opinions, as only those who opposed the change in the law were included in this analysis. Interestingly, there also were no differences between the three groups in terms of their reported consumption of alcoholic beverages and their patronage of drinking establishments. However, the differences in volunteer rates between the three age groups were substantial. As Sivacek and Crano reported, more than 47 percent of the youngest respondents (those with high vested interest) volunteered to work to defeat the referendum. In contrast, 26 percent of the moderately invested subjects volunteered, whereas only 12 percent of the oldest subjects (those with lowest vested interest) were willing to work to defeat the referendum. These findings clearly demonstrate that vested interest can be a powerful moderator of the extent to which opinions are expressed in overt actions.

It is important to understand that the contribution of vested interest to opinion level is independent of the extremity of the opinion. As Sivacek and Crano demonstrated, while all subjects shared identical (extreme) opinions about the change in Michigan's drinking age, they manifested very different subsequent actions as a result of variations in the degree to which the law change would personally affect them.

Self-Monitoring. The final moderating factor to be discussed regarding the link between opinions and behavior involves Personal Structure. Mark Snyder and his colleagues (Snyder, 1974, 1979; Synder & Monson, 1975; Snyder & Tanke, 1976), and others (Bem & Allen, 1974) have noted that people differ in the extent to which they act consistently across different Social Contexts. Snyder has identified this difference in Personal Structure as *self-monitoring,* a term that refers to the extent to which a person uses feedback from the Social Context as an indicant of the appropriateness of his or her actions. High self-monitors act in accordance with their reading of the situation in which they find themselves and in response to the reactions that their behaviors elicit from others. In other words, the elements of the Social Context are heavily weighted in determining the actions of high self-monitors, whereas internal factors such as opinions and impressions are less influential in their Valuation processes. In contrast, low self-monitors are guided by their own evaluative beliefs more than by the cues in the Social Context—that is, they do not monitor their own behavior in light of what may be relevant cues in their Social Contexts.

As might be expected, these two types of people act very differently in response to situational cues, even when the behaviors involved are rather trivial in nature. For example, McGee and Snyder (1975) found that people who salted their food before they tasted it tended to be low self-monitors,

A behavioral test of self-monitoring: Confronted with this appetizing steak, would you be likely to salt it before or after you taste it?

whereas high self-monitors tended to taste their food before seasoning it. The salience of this observation is clear: in low self-monitors, internally derived cues are given great weight, although relevant and potentially useful environmental cues are available. Conversely, high self-monitors make great use of these contextual cues before acting, but they often underweigh internal cues such as opinions and other evaluative beliefs.

To measure the extent to which people differ regarding their tendency to monitor themselves, Snyder (1974) developed a questionnaire of 25 items designed to assess the various components of this trait. A few of these items are provided in Figure 6.2.

Snyder and Swann (1976) provide clear-cut evidence to support the contention that the opinion-behavior link is mediated to some extent by variations in the trait of self-monitoring. In this study, undergraduates who had been categorized with respect to their degree of self-monitoring were asked their opinions about affirmative action. Two weeks later, they took part in a mock trial in which they played the role of jurors. They were asked to render a verdict in a case involving a female job applicant's sex discrimination suit against an employer who had rejected her in favor of a male. Subjects were told that the applicants had applied for the position of assistant professor of biology at the University of Maine. They were provided with information about the qualifications of the two applicants as well as the arguments advanced in court by both attorneys. They were then asked to render their verdict, as well as to provide their reasons for this decision.

The central question of this study was the extent to which subjects' pretrial opinions about sex discrimination were related to their actions as jurors. Interestingly, only among the low self-monitors was there a strong relationship between opinions and decisions. The actions of these individuals, who characteristically weigh internal cues quite heavily when making decisions, were systematically related to their opinions. In contrast, no appreciable relationship existed between the opinions and actions of the high self-monitors.

FIGURE 6.2
Some Selected Items from Snyder's (1974) Self-monitoring Scale

(This scale consists of 25 true-false, self-descriptive statements. For each item, respondents indicate whether the statement is true or false about themselves.)

1. I am not always the person I appear to be.
2. I can only argue for ideas which I already believe.
3. In order to get along and be liked, I tend to be what people expect me to be, rather than anything else.
4. I rarely need the advice of my friends to choose movies, books, or music.
5. In different situations and with different people, I often act like very different persons.
6. My behavior is usually an expression of my true inner feelings, attitudes, and beliefs.

Note: High self-monitors would tend to answer true to the odd-numbered items and false to the even-numbered statements. Low self-monitors would manifest the opposite response pattern.

These people were influenced by the various pieces of evidence provided them, and barely affected by their initial beliefs.

The general implications of Snyder's conception of self-monitoring for the opinion-behavior link are reasonably straightforward. Low self-monitors are likely to display opinion-consistent actions across a wide variety of contexts, even in the face of rather strong environmental impingements that would operate to weaken the opinion-behavior link in other people. Conversely, high self-monitors are likely to show little opinion-action consistency, since they are highly susceptible to the impingements of the Social Context.

Concluding Remarks on Opinion-Behavior Consistency

As noted earlier, attitude researchers over the years have defended the study of beliefs by asserting that opinions affect actions. Until recently, however, the accumulation of supportive evidence for this position has seemed insufficient to justify such professions of faith. The work of Fishbein and his colleagues was the beginning of a more sophisticated reexamination of the opinion-action link. A number of subsequent theoretical and empirical advances have identified the conditions under which the linkage would be expected to occur—or not to occur. In this chapter, we have distilled the insights generated by much of this work, and have discussed the variables that appear to have had a major impact on the relationship between opinions and overt behavior.

Most of the empirical explorations in this area, including the specific studies discussed, have examined potential moderators in isolation. We know from long experience that if research is limited to such an approach, it produces an incomplete picture of the social reality (see Campbell & Stanley, 1963). The research that constitutes the opinion-behavior literature is only a positive first step toward understanding this relationship. The next logical step will begin to explore the manner in which the important variables that we have identified (and those that have yet to be discovered) combine or interact in their operation on the opinion-action relationship.

While this step has yet to be taken in any systematic manner, we can speculate on the interactive effects that are likely to be uncovered by future research. To begin, consider the findings of Regan and Fazio's (1977) study of students' opinions about "lobby living" in the dormitories of Cornell University. Their explanation is a reasonable one—that actual experience with such living accomodations strengthened the link between opinion and action. But, it is also possible, given the results of Sivacek and Crano (1980), that vested interest moderated the relationship as well. To be sure, students who had experience with the issue had a firm basis for their opinions. But it is also true that it was in their best interests to effect a change of living arrangements. Thus, it is likely that both moderators could have combined in unique ways to generate the results that Regan and Fazio (1977) produced.

It is also possible to speculate about another potential relationship between moderators of the opinion-behavior link. The extent to which specificity is a moderator of the link between opinions and actions appears to be dependent on the level of the opinion. A very high level opinion is likely to have a pervasive effect on a great many related actions. Whether we measure such an opinion very specifically or rather generally would probably make little difference in the strength of its relationship with the actions of interest. For example, suppose that you are a staunch Democrat whose opinions about this political party are of a high level. In this case, either an assessment of your opinion of the Democratic Party in general or a measure of your evaluation of a specific Democratic candidate would yield equally accurate predictions of your behavior toward the candidate in the next election—you would vote for the candidate. Had you possessed lower level opinions, however, the degree to which the specificity of your opinion and your allied behavior correspond should be an important determinant of Consistency. In this case, since your pro-Democratic opinion is not of very high level, this opinion would not be as good a predictor of your voting behavior as your more narrow opinion about a specific Democratic candidate.

Similarly, the extent to which an actor characteristically self-monitors his or her behaviors should also mediate the effect of specificity correspondence. Specificity correspondence is likely to be a crucial factor when the opinion-action relationship is examined in high self-monitors, but it should be relatively inconsequential when the link is explored in low self-monitors. For example, the reader can imagine being a low self-monitoring subject in Snyder and Swann's (1976) mock jury study with a positive opinion about women's rights. Knowing your positive opinion in a general sense about this issue would be just as useful in predicting your verdict as knowing your more specific evaluation of the case made by the woman who filed the sex discrimination suit. In contrast, if we, as jurors, were high self-monitors who shared exactly the same general opinion as you regarding women's rights, the prediction of our behaviors would be much more problematic. In this case, you would need to know our specific evaluations of the case materials before being able to predict our verdicts with any degree of certainty. Since high self-monitors typically attend to external, contextual cues more than to their own established beliefs, the general opinion would not prove to be a useful guide to our subsequent actions.

Many more speculations could be devised concerning the interactive nature of the moderators of the opinion-action linkage, but such an exercise in the absence of empirical evidence is premature. The point that we wish to make here is one that we have stressed throughout this text—namely, that social phenomena are complicated and the variables that affect them rarely operate in isolation of one another. This is almost certainly true in the case of those factors that determine the strength of the opinion-behavior relationship.

SOME CONCLUDING WORDS ON OPINIONS

This concludes our discussion of opinions, a topic that has occupied our attention in the past three chapters. The study of this type of social cognition is a major activity of social psychology and has been so since the inception of the discipline. Given our position that a small number of themes appear to underlie a wide range of social phenomena, it is reasonable at this point to recapitulate the relevance of these general processes for understanding opinions.

Incorporation (a subtheme of Control) and the variables that affect it are the focal concern of most of the processes studied in this review of opinions. By definition, opinions are incorporations of our experiences with the physical and interpersonal environments. Chapter 4, for example, dealt with the manner in which opinions were modified through the incorporation of new information and evaluations. Chapter 5 discussed the conditions under which one's own actions could be mechanisms for incorporation, thereby serving to modify one's own belief system. The present chapter focused on the variables that determined the extent to which the products of incorporation processes affect behavior. Any discussion of the factors that determine the growth, stability, and change of opinions, as well as their behavioral consequences, must involve some aspect of incorporation.

By way of contrast, impingement—the second major component of Control—appears to play a somewhat more limited role in opinion development, change, and expression. As noted in Chapters 4 and 5 (as well as earlier in the text), impingement can lead to incorporation under the appropriate circumstances. Chapter 5 specifically discussed some of the variables that have an impact on the transformation of impingement to incorporation. We noted the conditions under which impingement can lead to belief change, and those under which such behavior control leads to the opposite outcome—namely, resistance. In Chapter 6 we have discussed impingement processes primarily from the perspective of the ways in which such control tactics can inhibit the expression of a specific opinion.

Given that opinions are cognitions, it is reasonable that the three cognitive themes of Resolution, Consistency, and Valuation are also crucial to our understanding of this type of evaluative belief. While a detailed restatement of the relevance of each of these themes is not necessary, their functions in the development and maintenance of opinions can be briefly reviewed.

Resolution is important for two reasons. First, as we have emphasized often, the degree of Resolution of a person's belief system is directly related to that person's resistance to opinion change—that is, the greater the Resolution, the less susceptible is the set of opinions to modification. Second, the lower the Resolution of the Social Context, and the greater the Resolution of the actor's belief system, the more likely that person is to engage in opinion-consistent behaviors and the less likely that person is to be influenced by situational cues.

The two major components of Consistency—self-Consistency and self/other Consistency—are also relevent to the issues discussed here. For example, implicit in our treatment of the influence of prior actions on people's subsequent beliefs (Chapter 5) is the idea that people attempt to maintain some degree of Consistency between their beliefs and behaviors. As noted, self/

other Consistency influences the extent to which the impingement attempts of others lead to incorporation of the underlying belief.

Finally, Valuation—the set of processes involved in decision making—is germain to numerous aspects of opinion development and expression. The variables that affect the weight which we accord to a specific source, for example, determine the extent to which opinions are modified. Likewise, the weighting of various cues in the Social Context and Personal Structure influences the degree to which opinions are expressed behaviorally. Moreover, as noted throughout this section, judgments concerning the desirability of an outcome—a major Valuation process—can affect both opinions and the extent to which such beliefs influence our actions.

The remaining theme—Sentiment—has played a minor part in our discussion of opinions. It was noted in passing that Sentiment can affect the strength of one's concerns with self/other Consistency, and thereby, can play an indirect role in shaping opinions. In contrast, the other themes have been viewed as much more pervasive in their relevance to opinion development and change. While Sentiment does not appear to be crucial to our understanding of opinions, it is extremely relevant in the study of interpersonal relationships per se, a fact that is to be demonstrated in the third major section of this book (Chapters 9 through 13), which reviews the variables that affect, and result from, short-term and long-term social encounters.

Forming Impressions about People

7

A major assumption that underlies the material in this text (and our choice of careers) is that most of us are preoccupied with social relationships. One consequence of this concern is that we tend to spend a great deal of time thinking about our encounters with people. Many of these thoughts probably involve beliefs about particular people, which in turn, often serve as the bases for judgments of these persons' worth, value, goodness, and so on. It is not surprising, then, that such evaluative beliefs, or impressions, have been studied extensively in social psychology. This chapter integrates the major products of this work—the information that has been accumulated about the factors that influence the formation and maintenance of impressions.

Almost any information, no matter how fragmented or trivial, can be used to develop an impression. For example, even a brief newspaper account can be the basis for forming an evaluative belief about a person, as the following article, which appeared in the business section of a large metropolitan newspaper, illustrates:

> Sharlene Kruger was named manager of training for Cadillac Plastic. She will be responsible for developing and administering training programs for corporate and field operations personnel. Before joining Cadillac Plastic, Kruger held a variety of positions in education, government, and business (*Detroit Free Press,* April 12, 1981).

From this small amount of information, we can, and often do, form judgments about the person described—how ambitious, smart, hard-working, or competent she might be—and these judgments contribute to an overall evaluation of her. Of course, other impressions are based on considerably more information about the target person—that is, information that is acquired about someone as a consequence of repeated interactions with that person.

COMPONENTS OF THE IMPRESSION-FORMATION PROCESS

As noted throughout this book, the theme of Valuation is central to any consideration of the manner in which people form any evaluative beliefs. In our view, the Valuation processes that result in an evaluative belief about a specific individual (an impression) can be characterized as a three-stage sequence of judgments: (1) cue selection and weighting, (2) trait inference, and (3) general evaluation.

In the first phase of this process—that of cue selection and weighting—the person forming the belief—the observer—surveys the cues that are potentially available and assigns weights to them. These weights refer to the importance that these cues are accorded in the formation of the impression. Whether or not a given cue provides some insight about the 'true nature' of the individual whom the observer is attempting to evaluate—the *target*—is the central issue for the observer at the cue selecting and weighting stage.

For example, suppose that a friend of yours has just introduced you to a man, Norman. This person smiles, nods his head, and says, "Hi." You respond appropriately, and as a result, you and he engage in a brief conversation. As this encounter progresses, you cannot fail to notice that Norman's body is adorned with what appears to be some very expensive jewelry—rings, bracelets, and neck chains. In addition, over the course of this conversation, Norman says some of the wittiest remarks that you can recall ever hearing. Moreover, as you are talking, he mentions that one of his favorite pastimes is hunting deer.

Despite the sketchiness of this description, this hypothetical encounter furnishes a large number of potential cues, which you might use to form an impression of your new acquaintance. However, these cues differ regarding the amount of information that they present about the target's true nature. Some cues, for example, are of no help whatever, because they tell you almost nothing about Norman as a person. His behavior during your initial exchange of nods and hellos tells you only that he has mastered the rudiments of the introduction ritual and nothing more. On the other hand, the cues that Norman displayed over the next few moments of the interaction are more useful to you in your attempt to develop an impression of him. Thus, you would tend to disregard some of the cues that are present in the context of the interaction, whereas you would weight heavily some of the others, depending on the extent to which you judge that a given cue provides you with insight about Norman's true nature.

Obviously, cues can be overlooked, even if they could have provided important information. The tremendous number and variety of cues that are present in almost any encounter preclude the possibility that we can attend to and consider all of them in the Valuation process. Thus, important cues that are overlooked weigh no more than those that you, as the observer, have perceived but intentionally disregarded—they would be accorded no weight in your impression of the target.

In summary, the cue-selecting stage of the impression-formation process involves the incomplete perusal of the social field, and the choice of cues that will be considered when forming evaluative beliefs about the target. Some cues are overlooked, others are disregarded, whereas others are judged to be useful information about the target. These last cues are employed in the next phase of the impression-formation process.

In the second stage of the impression-formation process—that of trait inference—the observer uses the cues that were selected as bases for inferring various characteristics, qualities, or traits in the target. Thus, from Norman's remarks—which you judged to contain valuable clues regarding his personality—you would be likely to infer that he was witty, and, perhaps even further, that he was bright, sociable, and charming. You would be less likely to infer from the cues available to you that he was athletic, ambitious, nurturant, or musically talented. The specific Valuations that you make are an illustration of the operation of the processes involved in the trait inference stage of impression formation.

Trait inferences can vary with respect to the extent to which they are supported by observable data. Observers often assume that the target possesses certain traits on the basis of less than complete evidence. Some qualities can never be directly observed, since they involve characteristics of the target's Personal Structure, and thus, can be inferred only on the basis of the target's appearance and actions. In contrast, other qualities are somewhat more directly verifiable.

In our example, you inferred that Norman was witty, based upon some statements that he made in your initial interaction. However, you could be wrong in this trait inference. Norman, in fact, might not be at all witty; he might have memorized a series of opening lines to ease him through introductions, since he is incapable of spontaneously generating funny remarks (the defining characteristic of wittiness). From your observation of a small sample of Norman's behavior, you had inferred that he possessed a Personal Structure characteristic that, in fact, might not be true of him.

Even qualities that can be observed somewhat more directly involve an element of uncertainty. For example, you could not help but notice that Norman was wearing some very expensive-looking jewelry. From such cues, you reasonably might infer that he was wealthy. This quality of economic affluence is more easily verifiable than those of a more subtle and internal psychological nature. Even in this instance, however, your inference could be incorrect, since it is based only on the cues that are available to you in your encounter with Norman. Conceivably, his jewelry could have been fake, borrowed, rented, or stolen.

Another important feature of this second phase of the impression formation process is that the traits an observer infers in a target can vary with regard to the sign (positive or negative) and the magnitude of their value. Traits have positive value if the observer believes them to be rewarding and worthwhile qualities, and negative value if the observer finds them reprehensible or aversive. The magnitude of these values, whether positive or negative, depends on two factors: (1) the extent to which the traits are important to the observer, that is, the extent to which they are high level concerns; and (2) the observer's estimate of the extent to which the target possesses the trait (for example, Norman's wittiness might be judged as slight, moderate, or extreme).

To return to the example, suppose that wittiness is a rewarding quality to you, in that you appreciate and enjoy spontaneous, funny remarks. Furthermore, you have inferred that Norman was very witty. As such, your inference that Norman possesses a sharp wit, along with the importance of this trait to you, would result in a very favorable evaluative belief about him. In addition, you might have inferred that Norman was moderately rich; but, if economic affluence is not an important trait to you, this quality would not be valued very highly. In this case, no matter how great you estimated Norman's wealth to be, this characteristic would have little influence on your evaluative belief about him. Finally, you might have inferred that Norman possessed qualities that you find reprehensible (for example, callousness toward our furry friends). This trait would lead to a negative evaluative belief about him, to the extent that you view his callousness as extreme, and to the extent that the welfare of wild animals was an important (high level) concern of yours.

The various traits that are inferred in this phase and their accompanying values serve as bases for the decisions the observer makes in the third stage of the impression formation process—that of *general evaluation*. In this last phase, the observer attempts to integrate the distinct, trait-related evaluative beliefs into a more general, global impression of the target. This general evaluation stage involves a Valuation process, in which the observer combines the various trait values derived earlier to form an overall belief about the target's worth (that is, goodness or badness).

Consider again your reaction to Norman. On the basis of your encounter, you inferred that he was very witty, somewhat rich, and moderately callous towards the plight of wild animals; these characteristics had value for you as a consequence of their perceived importance and your estimate of the extent to which Norman possessed them. Suppose for the sake of this example that the value associated with a trait can range from -100 (very reprehensible) to $+100$ (highly appreciated). In this case, Norman's wittiness has a value of 85, his affluence a value of 3, and his callousness to animals a value of -40. Combining these into a composite results in an average value of 16 ($[85 + 3 - 40] \div 3 = 16$).

Clearly, observers differ in the way in which they combine trait values into an overall composite impression. Indeed, there is considerable controversy in social psychology about the precise manner in which such information is integrated into a composite. However, there is evidence (to be presented later in this chapter) which indicates that people average trait values when developing overall impressions.

Figure 7.1 illustrates the three-stage process of impression formation just described. This model is a framework for presenting the major variables that appear to operate at each stage in the development of this type of evaluative belief. However, one additional point should be made before turning to this more detailed discussion. The stages of cue selection, trait inference, and general evaluation have been portrayed as discrete processes that always follow a specific sequence. In fact, such is probably not the case. As indicated in Figure 7.1, there is no clear demarcation between the adjacent stages of impression formation. The processes of cue selection evolve into trait inferences which, in turn, become the integrated composite impression. Certainly, most people do not consciously think, "I am through selecting cues; now I shall begin to infer traits from them."

Moreover, the outcomes of the later phases of impression formation can reactivate earlier processes. So, a specific trait, inferred on the basis of one or more cues, can induce the observer to reexamine the Social Context for additional evidence that may corroborate his or her judgment. For example, suppose that in your interaction with Norman, you form the belief that he is rich; this belief is based on your noticing his jewelry. To validate this inference, you might search for other cues (that is, return to the cue-selection

FIGURE 7.1
Model of Impression Formation Process

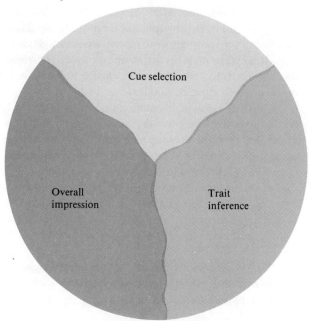

phase) that you had originally overlooked or disregarded. Now, you might look more closely at the quality of Norman's clothes, his shoes and briefcase, and the cut of his hair. Similarly, a general positive impression can induce an observer to make additional trait inferences that are consistent with this overall belief, as well as to search the context for additional corroborating cues.

Having presented a broad outline of the processes that typically are involved in impression formation, we can now explore the major variables involved in each of the three phases in the formation of this type of evaluative belief. We will begin with an extended discussion of how impressions are formed in the context of an initial encounter with a target. Such first impressions have been studied extensively by social psychologists, in large part because they have a major effect on the impressions that will later develop as a result of more extensive experience with the target. We will then discuss the manner in which first impressions and other variables such as Sentiment relationships influence the development of later impressions.

PROCESSES IN THE FORMATION OF FIRST IMPRESSIONS

Cue Selection

The bulk of this chapter will deal with a discussion of the factors that influence persons' selection of the cues they employ in forming impressions of others. We have intentionally concentrated on the initial phase of the impression formation process, since the other phases of this process are built upon the outcome of cue selection.

As noted earlier, observers can use almost any cue in the Social Context of an encounter as a basis for forming impressions of a target. There are direct cues (derived from an actual encounter with a target) and indirect cues (derived from information about a target that is provided by other means, such as other people or news media). Studies in impression formation have varied with regard to both the directness and the number of cues presented to observers.

Social psychologists have investigated impression formation under widely varying contexts. In some of these, the information provided is both direct and extensive (Edelman & Hampson, 1981; Feldman, Higgins, Karlovac, & Ruble, 1976; Krauss et al., 1981; Olson, Barefoot, & Strickland, 1976); in others, very minimal indirect cues are supplied (Smith & Miller, 1979; Srull & Wyer, 1979; Wegner, Kerker, & Beattie, 1978). When taken together, such research has shown that observers can, and do, form impressions of targets, regardless of the nature or extent of the information provided them. Almost any set of cues seems sufficient to activate impression formation responses in observers. Thus, it appears that such processes are well-practiced behaviors by most of us, easily elicited by even the most ephemeral of stimuli.

Of course, in most real-life Social Contexts, observers have an abundance of cues to consider when forming an impression of another. In contexts in which minimal information is provided (a characteristic of many experimental studies in this area), observers are forced to search for relevant cues in forming an impression of the target. In contrast, as Major (1980) has demonstrated, in many ordinary circumstances in which an extensive number of cues are available, the observer must search among them and decide which should be considered in the impression-formation process.

As noted earlier, the major criterion in this cue-selection process appears to be the extent to which the cue can be thought to reflect the true nature of the target person. In this sense, observers must evaluate the likelihood that a cue (the target's appearance or actions) reflects personal causation and personal responsibility on the part of the target. In this framework, personal causation refers to the observer's judgment about the extent to which the actions or characteristics of the target, rather than other factors in the context, have led to the occurrence of some event. Similarly, personal responsibility refers to an observer's assessment that an outcome was the result of some volitional (willful) behavior on the part of the target, rather than an action that was beyond his or her control.

A number of social psychologists (Brewer, 1977; Fincham & Jaspars, 1980) have speculated about the variables that influence observers' perceptions of a target's personal responsibility for an event, and their conclusions are compatible with the approach that we have adopted. Marilynn Brewer (1977), for example, has theorized that observers' attributions of a target's responsibility for the occurrence of some event are related to two factors: (1) the observers' estimates of the extent to which, in the absence of the target, other forces in the Social Context would have caused the event to occur; and (2) the observers' estimates of the likelihood that in general, actions similar to those that the target displayed often result in the outcome that actually occurred.

An example should help to clarify the meanings of personal causation and personal responsibility as used here. Suppose that you were walking down the street, and as fate would have it, you see a car driven by an elderly man run into a pedestrian crossing the street. Furthermore, a social psychologist rushes up to you at that moment and asks you for your impression of the driver of the errant car.

To provide a reasoned answer to this query, you would first have to decide the extent to which the driver caused the collision. That is, you must identify the factors that led to this occurrence, judge their importance in precipitating the event, and decide the degree to which they were attributable to the driver. For example, you would consider the state of the physical environment (Was it raining, icy, clear?); the appearance of the driver (Did he have a heart attack just before the collision? Had he been drinking?); the condition of the automobile (Did the front tire blow out immediately before it hit the pedestrian?); and the actions of the pedestrian (Did she step out between two parked automobiles into the path of the oncoming car?), and so on.

As Brewer notes, your judgment of the extent of the driver's responsibility for this accident will largely depend on factors in the Social Context.

These self-generated questions reflect an underlying concern about the extent to which the driver, by his actions, personally caused the event to unfold as it did. In other words, you must decide the degree to which factors related to the driver led to the collision. Suppose that this event occurred on a dark, rainy night, on a street dotted with patches of ice. When you first notice the car, it is traveling at a reasonable speed (for the road conditions), and appears to swerve out of control only after the left front tire suddenly explodes. The noise of this explosion draws your attention to the driver of the car, who suddenly grabs his chest and apparently loses consciousness while the car is still moving. In these circumstances, it is unlikely that you would attribute any personal cause for the accident to the driver.

On the other hand, suppose that the collision occurs on a clear, dry day, that the street is in perfect condition, that the car's tire does not blow out, and that the pedestrian is hit in the middle of a crosswalk while crossing with the light. Moreover, you notice that the car is traveling at an excessive rate of speed for a city street. In this case, you would be much more likely to attribute personal causation to the driver for what had transpired.

As noted, however, perceptions of personal causation do not always imply perceptions of personal responsibility—although personal responsibility does imply personal causation. An actor's behaviors can cause an event to occur, but these behaviors can be the result of forces that are beyond the actor's control. In this case, we judge the actor's behavior as causing the event, but we do not view the actor as being personally responsible for it. On the other hand, the actor can behave purposefully in a manner that contributes in some way to the occurrence of an event. In such instances, we tend to view the actor as being personally responsible for the event, since some intentional action on the actor's part led to the occurrence of the event.

As noted, the concepts of personal causation and responsibility are related but not identical, and their difference is important in order to understand impression formation. When forming an impression of a person, it is likely that we weight cues differentially as a consequence of our perception of the target's personal causation and personal responsibility. We tend to weight most heavily those cues for which the target appears personally responsible and weight less heavily cues that appear personally caused in the absence of personal responsibility. We accord the least weight to cues that appear to be a consequence of events with which the actor has no association.

Returning to the example, it is likely that you would think about the extent of the driver's personal responsibility for the collision if you have concluded that his actions—at least to some extent—caused the car to hit the victim. In other words, once you have assumed some degree of personal causation on the part of the driver, you then consider the degree to which intentional actions on his part were responsible for the collision. You do this to facilitate your judgment concerning the extent to which the driver's actions reflect on his personal qualities, and thus are cues relevant to your impression of him.

For instance, you would attribute more personal responsibility to the driver if there was evidence that he was intoxicated or that he was willfully negligent in maintaining the condition of his car. If all four of the car's tires were treadbare, you might judge that the driver was at least somewhat negligent in the upkeep of the automobile, and that this failing on his part was responsible for the crash. As negligence implies intentionality (that is, he could have bought new tires or parked the car until he had saved enough money to put it in good order), this factor would suggest an increase in personal responsibility for the event that you witnessed.

In the case of negligence, the intentional activity (ignoring the car's condition) occurs at a time removed from the observed event (the collision); yet, it still contributes to the actor's responsibility. Other incidental but intentional activities (for example, drinking) might also be contributing factors in the observed event. In this sense, knowledge of intentional behaviors that have effects on the observed event, but are really incidental to it, heighten the observer's perception of the actor's personal responsibility for what has happened.

Of course, the strongest attributions of personal responsibility involve situations in which an observer judges that an event has resulted directly from the actor's premeditated behaviors. For example, suppose that you knew that the woman crossing the street in the story was the driver's former wife, whose alimony payments were a source of considerable aggravation to him. It might be reasonable to surmise in such circumstances that the collision was something less than accidental—especially if you had observed the driver waiting in his car nearby until his ex-wife had ventured onto the crosswalk. Under these conditions, you probably would allow the driver's actions to weigh heavily in your impression of him.

There is empirical evidence that supports our contention that perceived personal causation and personal responsibility affect cue selection and cue weighting, the processes that constitute the first phase of impression formation. Miller, Smith, and Uleman (1981) have demonstrated that people judge the relevance of potential cues in forming an impression about a target primarily in terms of the target's personal responsibility for displaying the cues. In other words, observers' judgments that the target's behavior is a consequence of factors in the target's Personal Structure are based on the observers' perceptions that the target is responsible for the behavior and is free to choose whether or not to engage in it.

Other research has shown that observers are more likely to infer traits in a target when they perceive the target as personally responsible for the potential cues. Strickland (1958), for example, had subjects supervise two workers while they performed a task. The supervisors could impinge on the behavior of the workers by fining them for not performing up to a standard. However, the experimenter arbitrarily allowed the subjects to monitor the behavior of one worker (worker A) much more thoroughly than they could that of the other (worker B). At the end of the work period, subjects learned that both workers had performed about equally well. Subjects then were asked to rate the two workers on a number of dimensions. Of most interest, the subjects reported that they perceived worker B's behavior as more influenced by his Personal Structure characteristics (for example, his trustworthiness) than was worker A's behavior, whose actions were seen as being more influenced by contextual forces (the subject-observer's ability to impinge on the target's behavior).

In interpreting these results, it is important to keep in mind that the potential cues that the workers provided were very similar: the performance of both workers was essentially the same. Thus, it is likely that the inclination of the subjects to utilize these cues (the performance of the workers) in making trait inferences was a result of their judgments about each worker's level of personal responsibility for his actions. In one case, the target (worker A) was closely monitored by the subjects; as a consequence, they were reluctant to attribute internal, Personal Structure causes to his performance. On the other hand, subjects were more willing to make such trait inferences when the behavior of the target (worker B) could not be attributed to the external constraint of their impingement. Other studies have yielded results that are consistent with the position that cues are weighted more heavily in the impression formation process when they are viewed as being a consequence of the target's freely expressed behaviors (Hastorf, Kite, Gross, & Wolf, 1965; Jones & Harris, 1967; Kruglanski, 1970; Thibaut & Riecken, 1955).

There also is empirical evidence that observers select and weight cues resulting from events that a target is perceived as having caused, but for which he or she is not personally responsible. Lee Ross and his colleagues have provided a number of examples of this type of cue selection in the impression formation process. In one such experiment (Ross, Amabile, & Steinmetz, 1977), subjects were assigned one of three roles in a quiz of general knowledge. One subject of each pair was randomly assigned to the role of questioner, whose job it was to stump the other subject (the contestant). The third subject was to act as an impartial observer of the interaction.

The questioners were encouraged to draw items of the most difficult and esoteric nature from their own fund of knowledge. Obviously, they had a great advantage over the contestants, who had to attempt to answer them. (For example, suppose that the questioner were an expert in the Chinese game of "Go." He or she could base questions on this topic, confidently assured that most people would not be able to answer them.) Needless to say, the questioners were much more successful than the contestants in this unequal test. In any event, after the contest was completed, the observers were asked to rate each of the participants in terms of the trait of knowledgeability.

The importance of this study for our concerns is that it provided a context in which the interactants caused an outcome to occur but were not personally responsible for it. Though the contestants "caused" the outcome (that is, they really did not answer many questions correctly), they could not be seen as personally responsible for it, since the game was rigged against them. Similarly, the questioners' superior performance was "caused" by their ability to stump the contestant, but this facility was derived primarily from a chance event—their random assignment to a role that conferred a strong advantage on them. Thus, their questions caused the outcome, but their ability to ask the questions was not an outcome for which they were personally responsible.

The results of this study indicated that the observers' impressions of the questioner and the contestant were affected by the perceived personal causation fostered by the outcome of their interaction. Despite the obviously biased nature of this game, the observers inferred that the questioners were much more knowledgeable than were the contestants. Thus, even though the observers must have known that the cards were stacked against the contestants in the quiz, and in favor of the questioners, they nevertheless employed the cues available to them in making inferences about the trait of general knowledgeability.

To summarize, it appears that observers select and weight cues as a consequence of the cues' apparent relevance for understanding the Personal Structure of the target. The perceived relevance of a cue is determined by the extent to which it appears to be the result of outcomes that a target has personally caused, and for which he or she personally appears responsible. Cues associated with the perception of personal responsibility are weighted most heavily in the impression formation process, whereas those that appear unconnected to the target's personally caused actions are considered the least relevant to understanding the target. Of course, there are many other factors that mediate the tendency in observers to perceive cues as relevant or irrelevant to their attempts to form impressions of targets. We will now discuss some of these factors, focusing on those that have received the most attention in the field of social psychology.

FACTORS IN THE TARGET

Target Identity: Self versus Other

One of the major determinants of the outcome of the cue selection and weighting process involves the identity of the target. In the research presented to this point, the person forming the impression (the observer) and the actor who was the object of the impression (the target) were different people. This need not be so, however; as noted in Chapter 1, a very important set of evaluative beliefs for us concerns our impressions of ourselves. The manner in which these self-impressions are formed often parallels the way in which impressions about others evolve. For example, the perception of personal responsibility tends to have the same impact on cue weighting and selection when forming or modifying one's self-impression as it does when forming impressions of others. Research (Krovetz, 1974; Lefcourt, Hogg, Struthers, & Holmes, 1975) has demonstrated that people are more likely to attribute their behavior to Personal Structure factors when they view themselves as being personally responsible for the outcome of their actions. Such findings are similar to those cited above (Strickland, 1958) regarding the influence of responsibility on observers' evaluations of other people.

While the general processes of cue selection and weighting are similar whether the target of the impression is the self or another person, research has uncovered some important differences which result from the identity of the target. Jones and Nisbett (1972), for example, have concluded that people tend to perceive an event as relatively less affected by factors in their own Personal Structures than by contextual forces; in contrast, they tend to assume that personal characteristics play a relatively greater role in causing the actions of other people. As such, observers tend to judge the cues generated in an event as less relevant to their self-impressions than to their impressions of others. Empirical research has yielded considerable evidence consistent with this position.

For example, Jones, Rock, Shaver, Goethals, and Ward (1968) had subjects observe, or take part in, a test of mental ability. The experimenters constructed the test so that subjects answered about half of the items correctly. Results indicated that when subjects were observers, the cues provided by the performance of the other subject had a strong affect on their impressions of that person. In contrast, when the subjects themselves took part in the task, they were less influenced by the potential cues provided by their own performances, and instead attributed their actions more frequently to contextual factors (that is, to the difficulty of the items used). Other studies have provided considerable support for this actor-observer difference in cue selection (Goldberg, 1978; Hansen & Stonner, 1978; Harvey et al., 1975; Janoff-Bulman, Lang, & Johnston, 1979; Miller, 1977; Nisbett, Caputo, Legant, & Marecek, 1973; Storms, 1973; Taylor & Koivumaki, 1976).

Social psychologists have provided a number of explanations for the tendency in actors to discount the cues provided by their own behavior when forming or changing their self-impressions. We will examine two of these theories—self-consistent cue selection and perspective differences—to provide a sample of the work in this area.

Self-Consistent Cue Selection

One of the explanations advanced for the tendency of people to perceive cues from an event as less related to factors in themselves—and therefore less relevant to their self-impressions—involves the concern with maintaining a self-consistent and positive self-impression, a motive discussed throughout this text. As noted in Chapter 3 and elsewhere, results from a considerable number of studies have indicated that people strive to maintain a positive self-presentation so much that they accept evidence that contradicts this impression only when it is strong and unequivocal (Aronson, 1968; Felson, 1981; Frey, 1978; Ross & Sicoly, 1979; Roth & Kubal, 1975; Schlenker, 1975; Snyder, Smoller, Strenta, & Frankel, 1981; Ungar, 1980; Weary, 1980). In many contexts, the consequences of an event in which we have taken part are not completely clear, at least not immediately. Thus, we are often somewhat reluctant to perceive ourselves as responsible for what has transpired, especially if the outcome might be negative. To accept responsibility under such negative or ambiguous circumstances might ultimately prove inconsistent with a positive self-impression and thereby activate concerns with self-Consistency.

In a related area, Rosenberg and his colleagues (Duncan, Rosenberg, & Finklestein, 1969; Rosenberg, 1968) have shown that apprehension about potential negative evaluations influence persons' actions and beliefs. Rosenberg's research suggests that when we are uncertain about the implications of our actions, we tend to be conservative in attributing personal causation and personal responsibility. As a consequence of this self-defensive strategy, we are less likely to judge cues derived from an event as relevant to our self-impression. When forming impressions of other people, of course, concerns about evaluation are much less salient; thus, we are more inclined to make such evaluative judgments and to perceive cues as indicative of their Personal Structures.

The findings of the study by Jones et al. (1968), noted earlier, are consistent with these speculations. Recall that in this study, all participants were told that they had been correct on half the items of the mental ability test that was administered to them. Observers (people who did not take the test but merely monitored the performance of a target) were more likely to perceive the participants as having caused the outcome than were the participants themselves, who tended to attribute their actions to external, situational factors.

It is important to note that a score of 50 percent (received by all participants) was ambiguous. In the absence of any additional information, it was difficult for participants to conclude that they had performed well or poorly on the test. In this instance of low Resolution, the conservative strategy for cue selection would be to attribute outcomes to circumstances beyond one's control. On the other hand, observers were not encumbered with concerns about the evaluative meanings of participants' test performances; as such, they were more willing to attribute actions to factors in the participants' Personal Structures. The results of other research on actor-observer differences in impression formation, cited earlier, are consistent with this position.

The manner in which concerns about maintaining a positive self-image affect the cue-selection process is shown most clearly in studies in which the outcome of the actor's performance is unambiguous—that is, in situations in which it is clear that the target's behavior has resulted in either a positive or negative outcome. Studies have shown that actors tend to view their own performance as indicative of Personal Structure characteristics when the event in which they have participated has resulted in a positive outcome; actors are more likely to disregard these potential cues and attribute the outcome to external, contextual forces when the outcome is negative. In contrast, observers are inclined to view the behavior of a target as indicative of Personal Structure characteristics, irrespective of the outcome of the event (Arkin, Gleason, & Johnson, 1976; Eisen, 1979; Fitch, 1970; Frieze & Weiner, 1971; Gould & Sigall, 1977; Lau & Russell, 1980; Miller, 1976; Snyder, Stephan, & Rosenfield, 1976; Streufert & Streufert, 1969; Wortman, Costanzo & Witt, 1973).

Eisen (1979) conducted an experiment that clearly illustrates the influence on cue selection of persons' concerns with maintaining positive self-impressions. In this study, subjects completed a personality-achievement inventory. Half the subjects were given feedback about their own answers; for some, the interpretation of their responses was positive, whereas for others, it was negative. The remaining subjects were given this same type of feedback about the responses of another person, but not about their own responses. After receiving this information, the subjects were asked to judge the extent to which the test results reflected Personal Structure characteristics.

The results of Eisen's (1979) study demonstrated that actors were less likely to explain their own answers in terms of Personal Structure factors when they had received negative feedback about these answers than when they had received information that reflected positively on them. On the other hand, the judgments of those subjects who were given feedback about the answers of another respondent were not influenced by the positivity or negativity of the feedback. These results are consistent with the proposition that there is a self-defensive component in the cue-selection process when self-impressions are involved. People appear to consider the extent to which a cue is consistent with their positive self-image when judging its relevance to evaluative beliefs about themselves (their self-impressions).

The influence on cue selection of concerns with the maintenance of a positive self-impression is not limited to judgments about one's own actions. Research has shown that when the behavior of others reflects on the observer, he or she is likely to interpret such information defensively (Buldain, Crano, & Wegner, in press; Carver, DeGregorio, & Gillis, 1980; Chaikin & Darley, 1973; Johnson, Feigenbaum, & Weiby, 1964; Shaver, 1970; Weary, 1980). For example, Shaver (1970) has noted that we tend to underweigh negative cues of others when these others are similar to us.

In an interesting field study that makes a related point, Carver et al. (1980) asked the head coach of a college football team and his assistants to estimate their players' abilities and efforts both before and at the midpoint of an unsuccessful season. As Carver et al. (1980) note, the head coach perceives his job primarily in terms of recruitment and the team's development over the span of many years. The role of the assistant coach, on the other hand, is concentrated much more on present concerns—working with players to polish their skills and increase their motivation to win. These role differences are relevant to the issue of self-impressions, since they determine the type of cues that reflect on the competence of the different coaches. Thus, during a losing season, the head and assistant coaches would be motivated to select different cues to explain this unfortunate turn of events. The results of this

DON IVERS/JEROBOAM, INC.

Concerns about maintaining a positive self-impression can cause the head coach and his assistant to evaluate their players very differently.

study suggest that the observers (the coaches) selected and weighed cues when evaluating the targets (the players) so that these evaluative beliefs would be consistent with their own positive self-impressions.

The head coach's impressions of his players dramatically changed over the course of the season, and these changes in evaluative beliefs strongly suggest that the head coach was utilizing and weighing cues in a self-defensive manner. His perception of his players' abilities actually become more positive, a judgment that reflected favorably on his skill in attracting talented athletes; he was, after all, responsible for recruitment. However, to make his impressions of the players consistent with the undeniable fact that they had lost most of their games, he also utilized cues that he interpreted as indicating low effort on their part. Since motivating players to perform on a day-to-day basis was not a major responsibility of the head coach, such a belief is also self-defensive.

The judgments of the assistant coaches, on the other hand, displayed the opposite pattern; their evaluations of the players' natural abilities became less positive, whereas they increased their ratings of the players' efforts. Again, this pattern reflects a concern with self-Consistency. Since the assistant coaches were responsible for motivating players, they were reluctant to attribute the losing season to their failure at this job. On the other hand, since the assistant coaches were less responsible for recruitment, they could use their perceptions of the players' lack of natural ability as a means of justifying their impressions in the face of the team's losing record. To complete the picture, we should note that in a separate study, Felson (1981) found that football players themselves, when judging their own abilities, selected cues that would allow them to maintain positive self-impressions.

In summary, there appears to be considerable evidence that a concern with the maintenance of a positive self-image affects cue selection. However, there is also evidence that people do not always select and weight cues in a self-defensive or ego-enhancing manner (Ross et al., 1977; Stevens & Jones, 1976). In addition, some research has shown that the tendency for people to discount cues as irrelevant to their own self-impressions can be moderated (Miller, Gillen, Schenker, & Radlove, 1974; Wolosin, Sherman, & Mynatt, 1972).

Thus, there appear to be other factors in the observer in addition to concerns about maintaining Consistency with a positive self-impression, and these factors can affect cue selection differences in forming impressions about the self and about others. One major category of such factors involves differences in the perspectives that the observer brings to the context.

Perspective Differences

The vantage point, or *perspective,* from which an observer judges the relevance of an event often differs as a result of the target's identity (that is, whether it is the self or another person). These differences in perspective appear to be affected by three related factors: (1) the amount of knowledge the observer has about the target prior to the event being observed; (2) the different concerns of actors and observers; and (3) the different ways in which observers typically monitor their own behavior and that of others.

Knowledge. The first of these factors—the amount of knowledge that the observer has about the target—has been hypothesized to be a major influence on cue selection in impression formation (Harvey, Towne, & Yarkin, 1981; Monson & Snyder, 1977). Amount of prior information has an effect on cue selection because people are much less likely to assume that an event reflects Personal Structure characteristics when they have a great deal of knowledge about the target's inclinations and past behaviors. Obviously, this set of circumstances arises most often when the observer and target are one and the same person. We know much more about ourselves and our own past histories than we do of most other people.

In contrast, when knowledge about a target is primarily limited to information derived from the immediate event (this would occur, for example, when observing a stranger), people are likely to assume that cues reflect features of the target's Personal Structure, and therefore, are relevant to their impressions of that person. Thus, lack of knowledge about the target has this effect on cue selection because observers in such circumstances have fewer alternative explanations available for interpreting the behavior of the target.

In fact, most research on cue selection—which involves the extent to which a cue is judged to reflect a Personal Structure characteristic—has created conditions that maximize the impact of knowledge differences. Typically, subjects are asked to form an impression of either themselves or a complete stranger. In the latter case, observers have no information about the target other than that available from the experimental context. It is not surprising that empirical research has shown that observers in these circumstances are more likely to view the behavior of others as relevant to these targets' Personal Structures than they are to perceive their own behavior in this fashion.

The effect of knowledge on cue selection has been principally explored within a theoretical framework developed by Harold Kelley. In his model, Kelley (1967, 1971, 1972a, b, 1973) distinguished three forces—consistency, distinctiveness, and consensus—which mediate persons' estimates of the extent to which features of the Personal Structure affect a target's behavior. The first two terms involve knowledge of the target's past behavior. Consistency refers to the extent to which an actor behaves in a similar manner across time and Social Contexts. Distinctiveness, on the other hand, refers to the extent to which an actor expresses different behaviors toward different entities (different people or objects).[1]

An example should illustrate the manner in which knowledge about

---

[1] Consensus—the extent to which different targets in a context display the same cues—is more relevant to contextual influences on cue selection. For this reason, we defer discussion of this factor to a later section of this chapter.

consistency and distinctiveness can affect cue selection processes in impression formation. Suppose that we see John argue with a waiter about his dinner bill. If we know that John has displayed this type of behavior only rarely in the past—to the best of our knowledge, he almost never has disputed charges, no matter what the context, nor has he been argumentative with service personnel—it is unlikely that we would judge his outburst as indicative of factors in his Personal Structure (such as arrogance, contentiousness, stinginess, and so on). In other words, we would probably assume that features in the particular context elicited this unusual behavior from John, and thus, we would not be likely to interpret his actions as cues in forming or changing our impression of him. However, if we possessed no knowledge about John's past actions, it is possible that we would judge his behavior as reflecting his Personal Structure.

Mark Snyder and his colleagues have gathered compelling evidence which indicates that people differ regarding the extent to which they see their own behaviors as varying across contexts and entities (Snyder, 1974, 1976, 1979; Snyder & Monson, 1975; Snyder & Swann, 1976; Snyder & Tanke, 1976). Of most relevance, Snyder (1976) has shown that people who characteristically perceive their behaviors as low in consistency and high in distinctiveness *(high self-monitors)* typically judge their own actions as being influenced by contextual forces, and thus, not as indications of factors in their Personal Structures. Given the consistent findings that people tend to attribute their own behaviors to contextual factors (see pp. 221–224), it seems that most people are at least somewhat sensitive to the inconsistencies in, and the distinctiveness of, their own behaviors—in other words, most people self-monitor, at least to some extent.

On the other hand, in the absence of knowledge of other persons' past behaviors, observers appear to assume that targets' actions reflect high consistency and low distinctiveness, and thus are indicative of Personal Structure. Hansen and Lowe (1976) found that subjects were more likely to consider the consistency and distinctiveness of an action when they were judging the relevance of their own behavior than when they were judging that of others.

Similarly, in a study discussed earlier, Eisen (1979) found that when subjects were given negative feedback about the performance of a target, they were more likely to perceive this information as characteristic (high consistency, low distinctiveness) if another person was the target than if they themselves were the target. However, when observers were given explicit information that led them to assume that the target's actions were atypical (distinctive and inconsistent with past behaviors), they judged the other person's behavior as less reflective of Personal Structure characteristics. Other research (Kuiper & Rogers, 1979; Lau & Russell, 1980; Pyszczynski & Greenberg, 1981) has yielded findings that also are consistent with the idea that behaviors assumed to be typical of a target are weighted more heavily in impression formation processes.

Different Concerns of Actors and Observers. A second factor in cue selection which involves the perspective of the observer concerns the question that the observer is attempting to answer when judging the behavior of a target. There appear to be two general types of questions that most frequently are issues for observers: (1) those that involve the cause of an act (Why did Jim strike out?); and (2) those that involve the reason for the outcome of an act (Why did the strike out occur?). We tend to ask the former question when judging the actions of others and the latter when judging our own behavior. This difference has implications for the cues that we select in forming and changing impressions.

When we encounter and become acquainted with another person, we usually are interested in understanding the causes of his or her actions because impression formation is a high level concern for us. In many ways, "a stranger in our midst" is a source of some difficulty for us, because he or she lowers the Resolution of our interpersonal environment. In an attempt to restore a satisfactory degree of Resolution, we try to acquire an understanding (that is, form an impression) of the stranger, and thereby gain some sense of the other person as a more predictable and stable part of the Social Context. Believing that a person is kind, intelligent, and impulsive provides us with a sense that we can predict the person's behavior in a variety of encounters. This sense of predictability, in turn, makes the context more highly resolved for us. In contrast, when we examine our own behavior, we tend to have a different question in mind. Usually, we are reasonably confident that we can predict our own behavior. Therefore, we tend to perceive sources of uncertainty in a context as arising from external factors. Thus, we typically consider our own behaviors with respect to their outcomes and the reasons that these outcomes unfolded as they did.

For example, suppose that we "know" that we are considerate of the welfare of others. Our roommate comes storming out of the bathroom, chiding us for using all the hot water, just when he (or she) wanted to get ready for an engagement. In this circumstance, our action appears to have hurt another person. Most likely, we would interpret this unfortunate outcome not as a reflection of our general lack of consideration, but rather as an occurrence for which there was sufficient external reason. In this sense, we might very well admit that our actions contributed to (that is, to some extent, personally caused) the outcome, but we probably would conclude that we had not intended to inconvenience our roommate (that is, we would deny personal responsibility for the outcome of the act). Furthermore, we probably would perceive the outcome—the lack of hot water—as being a result of a number of contextual factors: no clock in the bathroom, a faulty hot water heater, a lack of awareness that our roommate needed to take a shower, and so on.

In summary, by the time we are adults, most of us have a well-formed, high level self-impression. As noted in Chapter 3, beliefs of this type are extremely resistant to change, and as such, are unlikely to be influenced by a single, isolated event. Thus, we rarely judge cues in a context as providing further insight into our Personal Structures. Instead, we are concerned about understanding the reasons for the outcomes of our actions, especially when the outcomes are unexpected. As a consequence, we are inclined to utilize available cues as indicants of what went right or wrong rather than as reflections of our intentions. In contrast, when judging the actions of others, we are more likely to question their motives and intentions as a means of developing and verifying our impression of them. With such a perspective, cues are more likely to be perceived as relevant to the target's Personal Structure. This line of reasoning is consistent with the theoretical work of Buss (1978, 1979), Forsyth (1980), Hamilton (1980), Harré and Secord (1972), and Miller and Norman (1975).

Empirical research has yielded some support for the idea that people view cues as answering different questions, depending upon the target's identity (Hansen & Stonner, 1978; Hoffman, Mischel, & Mazze, 1981; Miller, Norman, & Wright, 1978; Pyszczynski & Greenberg, 1981; Srull & Wyer, 1980). An investigation by Hansen and Stonner (1978) illustrates how such perspective differences can influence cue selection. In this research, the experimenters divided subjects into two conditions: some had to make a series of auditory discriminations, whereas others merely observed another subject performing this task. Feedback about performance was provided to both actors and observers. Some actor-observer pairs were led to believe that the actor's performance was better than average, whereas others were informed that the performance was worse than average. All subjects were then asked to judge the reasons for the actor's performance and to predict his or her future performance on a similar task.

The results of this study indicate that actors and observers can use the same set of cues to answer somewhat different questions. As in other studies, actors perceived their performance to be a result of task difficulty (a contextual feature) more than a reflection of ability (a personal characteristic), whereas observers were more likely to attribute the performance to the actor's ability. Moreover, Hansen and Stonner's (1978) findings regarding subjects' predictions of actors' future performances suggest that these differences in the interpretation of cues reflect different concerns. They found that observers used actors' performances in the auditory discrimination task as bases for predicting future successes. In contrast, actors did not base their predictions of their own future performances on how well they had done.

In summary, observers seemed concerned with increasing the Resolution of the experimental context by establishing a sense that they understood the actor, and thereby could predict that person's behavior; actors, on the other hand, appeared more intent on explaining the outcome of this event. In other words, observers seemed to be asking the question, "How good is this person on tasks of this type?" while the actor was asking, "Why did my behavior in this situation result in the outcome that occurred?"

Self-Focus and Other-Focus.   Related to the different types of questions that appear to guide the cue selection of actors and observers is the issue of *differential focus of attention*. Given that actors are less concerned about forming an impression of themselves, it follows that they would overlook, disregard, or interpret differently cues that other observers of their behavior would find indicative of Personal Structure characteristics. Similarly, observers typically are interested in forming an impression of the other and thus tend to overlook, disregard, or interpret differently cues that the actor would use to explain the outcome of his or her behavior. However, some circumstances promote disruptions of this typical pattern of focus of attention, and such situations are useful because they yield some insight into the manner in which differences in *self/other focus* affect cue selection.

The idea that circumstances can influence actors to shift their focuses of attention away from the issue of outcome explanation and toward self-impression has been developed primarily by Shelly Duval and Robert Wicklund. In their theory (Duval & Hensley, 1976; Duval & Wicklund, 1972; Wicklund, 1975, 1979; Wicklund & Frey, 1980), Duval and Wicklund outline a number of conditions that are likely to increase *objective self-awareness*—the tendency to treat oneself as an object, or to monitor one's own behavior in a manner similar to that of an outside observer. Moreover, they suggest that this shift in attention from outcome to self has implications for a number of phenomena, including cue selection. They hypothesize that increasing objective self-awareness would increase the likelihood that actors would perceive their behaviors as reflecting factors in their own Personal Structures, and thus, as relevant to their self-impressions, a prediction for which there is considerable empirical support (Arkin et al., 1980; Buss & Scheier, 1976; Duval & Wicklund, 1972; Hull & Levy, 1979; Sherrod & Farber, 1975; Storms, 1973; Touhey, 1972b; Wegner & Finstuen, 1977).

For example, Storms (1973) videotaped pairs of subjects as they interacted, and then allowed each member of the pair to watch the videotapes of their conversation. Two sets of recording equipment were used in each session, so that a separate tape could be made of each actor's behavior. Some subjects watched the tape that focused on their coworker, whereas others were shown the tape of themselves. In the former condition, subjects could review the interaction from their original perspectives; however, in the latter condition, the perspectives of the subjects shifted in such a way that they now viewed themselves from the perspective of an outside observer (that is, they became self-focused).

All subjects, regardless of whether they had viewed a self-focused or an other-focused tape, were asked to state their reasons for the behaviors which they had displayed in the encounter. The results indicated that subjects' self-reports of their cue selections and interpretations were consistent with Duval and Wicklund's (1972) model. Subjects who viewed the videotape of the other were more likely to explain their own behavior in the usual way— that is, to perceive their actions as reflecting situational forces. In contrast, subjects who viewed the tape designed to raise their self-focuses attributed their actions less to contextual factors and more to characteristics in their own Personal Structures.

On the other side of the coin, research has examined the impact on cue selection of inducing observers to shift their attentional focuses when judging another person (Baxter, Hill, Brock, & Rozelle, 1981; Gould & Sigall, 1977; Hamilton, Katz, & Leirer, 1980; Hoffman et al., 1981; Wells et al., 1977). This work has demonstrated that when observers are induced to perceive an event "through the eyes" of the actor (the target), they are less inclined to judge cues as indicative of the target's Personal Sturcture.

For example, Gould and Sigall (1977) had subjects watch a videotape of a first encounter between a man and woman. They were told that the man was attempting to make a good impression on the woman. Their task was to form an impression of the man (the actor). Subjects also were informed that based upon the female's rating of him, the actor had either succeeded or failed in his mission.

As the experiment has been described to this point, it would be expected from the research discussed earlier that observers would perceive the actor's behaviors as reflecting characteristics of his Personal Structure, regardless of the outcome of his efforts. These results were, in fact, obtained when subjects were instructed merely to observe his behavior. However, the judgments of observers were markedly different when they were asked to empathize with the male actor in the encounter—to view the interaction from his perspective. When given these instructions, the subjects' responses mirrored those that are typically found in studies of self-impressions that result from successful or unsuccessful encounters (Eisen, 1979). Subjects were likely to judge the actor's behavior as reflecting Personal Structure characteristics only when they thought he had succeeded. When the actor's efforts were portrayed as unsuccessful, the empathic subjects perceived his actions as resulting from situational forces.

There are other reasons for observers to view another person from the perspective that they usually apply to themselves. For example, as noted earlier, Kelly Shaver has speculated that people are less willing to form an impression of someone when this belief might result in a subsequent sense of self-Inconsistency. He reasoned further that people will be reluctant to use cues to form impressions of others when (1) they witness a negative event involving a target who is like them in some important way, and (2) they estimate that there is some possibility that they could find themselves in a similar predicament. Shaver's work (1970) as well as that of others (Buldain et al., in press; Cunningham, Starr, & Kanouse, 1979; Wolfson & Salancik, 1977) has yielded consistent support for the proposition that observers will shift their focus of attention in the service of belief Consistency.

To summarize, it appears likely that differences in observers' focuses of attention can have a major effect on the cues that they select and weigh when forming or modifying impressions. Under ordinary circumstances, observers are not self-focused when they think about their own actions. An actor tends to consider his or her own behaviors in terms of their relevance for understanding the outcomes of events, while others interpret an actor's behaviors as possible cues that are indicative of the actor's Personal Structure characteristics. When people's focuses of attention are directed toward themselves, they are more inclined to perceive their behaviors as do outside observers—that is, as relevant to their Personal Structures and therefore relevant to their self-impressions. Conversely, observers who are induced to empathize with a target tend to perceive the actor's behaviors much as they do their own—they focus on the outcomes of the behaviors rather than on the behaviors themselves. Thus, they see impression formation as a less relevant issue in such contexts, since the actor's behaviors are not viewed as indicative of Personal Structure features.

Target Appearance: The Case of Sex

As noted, observers can perceive almost any facet of a Social Context as a source of cues relevant to their impressions of a target. One of the more obvious sources of cues is the appearance of the target, a factor that has received considerable attention in research on impression formation. Social psychologists have investigated the ways in which such diverse aspects of appearance as sex, race, physical attractiveness, dress, hair color, body build, and countenance influence our evaluative beliefs about others (Berscheid & Walster, 1978; Brigham, 1971; Carducci, Cozby, & Ward, 1978; Deaux, 1976; Lawson, 1971; McKee & Sherriffs, 1957; Richardson, Hastorf, Goodmen, & Dornbush, 1961; Sleet, 1969).

Rather than discuss all of the possible target appearance variables, we will focus on one of them—sex.[2] The sex of a target appears to influence cue selection—as well as the other components of the impression formation process—in a number of related ways. Most directly, sex often serves as a cue unto itself—that is, as discussed below, an observer often uses targets' sexual characteristics as cues when inferring traits and forming more global impressions about them.

The sex of the target also influences observers' judgments about the relevance of the target's actions to impression formation. For example, in a series of experiments, Kay Deaux and her associates have demonstrated that people tend to interpret differently the successes or failures of males and females. In one of these studies, Deaux and Emswiller (1974) asked subjects to observe another person working on a visual perception task and to score his or her performance. The task was reasonably straightforward: the worker was shown a series of blurry slides and asked to attempt to identify the objects pictured on them. Two sets of slides were used; one set depicted objects associated with stereotypically masculine activities (such as car repair), whereas the other presented stereotypically feminine objects (such as kitchen equipment). All subjects were led to believe that the worker had done well on this object identification task. They were then asked to evaluate the quality

---

[2] This decision was made for two reasons: first, the processes which underlie the effect of appearance on cue selection are much the same, regardless of the particular facet of the target's appearance; second, the study of a single appearance variable allows for a more intensive and integrative examination of the ways in which such factors operate in the impression formation process.

of the worker's performance and to judge the extent to which this person's activities reflected Personal Structure attributes.

Recall that similar research, presented earlier, demonstrated that observers tend to perceive a target's task activity as indicative of the target's Personal Structure. Deaux and Emswiller (1974) found that subjects tended to judge the workers in this fashion, with one important exception—in all conditions but one, targets' behaviors were viewed as reflecting their ability; however, when a female target performed well on the task that involved masculine objects, both male and female observers viewed her performance as due to circumstances beyond her control. In other words, a female's success at a male-oriented task was not interpreted as indicative of any personal traits that she might possess, and therefore, it was discounted in the impression formation process. The findings of other research have also suggested that the sex of the target affects observers' cue selection and cue weighting (Costrich, Feinstein, Kidder, Maracek, & Pascale, 1975; Deaux & Taynor, 1973; Feather & Simon, 1975; Feldman-Summers & Kiesler, 1974; Larrance, Pavelich, Storer, Polizzi, Baron, Sloan, Jordan, & Reis, 1979; Richardson & Campbell, 1980; Spence, Helmreich, & Stapp, 1975a,b; Taynor & Deaux, 1973, 1975).

Target Actions: Unique or Extreme Behaviors

Obviously, the appearance of the actor is not the only category of target variables that affects cue selection. Another major influence on this phase of impression formation is the target's actions. Edward Jones and Keith Davis (1965) have proposed a model of the cue-selection process that pays particular attention to the behaviors that targets express and the variables that moderate the potential impact of these behaviors on observers' impressions. They postulate that observers will perceive that a target's actions are relevant cues to the target's Personal Structure to the extent that these behaviors are discrepant from those of the typical person or from what norms (beliefs about appropriate conduct) prescribe for that context. A subsequent formulation of this position (Jones & McGillis, 1976) emphasizes the role that unpredictability plays in judging the relevance of a target's actions; we judge persons' behaviors to be relevant to our impressions of them to the extent that their actions violate our predictions about how people in general will act.

An example should illustrate the idea that unpredicted, extreme, or unusual behaviors are selected and weighted more heavily in the impression formation process. Suppose that you are a member of an audience at a public event. Suddenly, a man sitting near you jumps to his feet and begins to scream expletives at the scene that is unfolding before you. If you both were part of a crowd at an exciting football game and your team had just fumbled the ball on its own one-yard line, you might find his behavior relatively uninformative with regard to his Personal Structure. At most, his actions would tell you that he was an ardent fan who cared about the outcome of

Your impression of a man screaming expletives would differ as a consequence of the Social Context in which his actions take place.

the game. In this case, he was only one of the many spectators (no doubt, including yourself) who were screaming their displeasure at this unfortunate turn of events.

On the other hand, suppose that the man expressed the same behavior in a different context—namely, a movie theater. In fact, one of the authors of this text witnessed just such an event. In the movie *Little Big Man,* a story that relates the destruction of the Sioux nation at the hands of the U.S. Army, there is one especially arousing scene in which the cavalry attacks an Indian village and mercilessly slaughters all of its inhabitants, who at this time were women, children, and the elderly. As this scene unfolded, a member of the audience who was sitting a few rows away from the author jumped up and began screaming obscenities and shaking his fist at the screen. While these actions were very similar to those of the football fan just described, in this instance the behaviors weighed very heavily in the author's judgments about the target and the traits that he was likely to possess.

The crucial difference between these two episodes was the perceived uniqueness and unpredicted nature of the behaviors as a result of the Social Context in which they were expressed. In the context in which the actions of the target were unusual or extreme (in the movie theater), they were taken as very informative about his Personal Structure. In the context in which such actions were common (the football stadium), the cue value of the target's actions was perceived to be minimal.

A number of theorists in addition to Jones and his associates have commented on the importance of unusual, counternormative, prominent, or unpredicted behaviors as cues in impression formation (Goffman, 1963; Kelley, 1972a; Taylor & Fiske, 1978). Taylor and Fiske (1978), for example, hypothesize that we perceive a target's behaviors as providing useful cues to the extent that features in the target or in the context call our attention to (make salient) these actions. Salient cues tend to be dramatic, easily noticed features of the Social Context. While varying in specific details, all of the theoretical frameworks appear to emphasize the prominence of a behavior as a mediator of its perceived utility for impression formation.

There has been an extensive amount of research on the impact of behavior prominence—or salience—on cue selection and weighting. Relatively comprehensive reviews of this phenomenon have been provided by Wegner and Vallacher (1977), Taylor and Fiske (1978), Schneider, Hastorf, and Ellsworth (1979), and McArthur (1980). We will now present a representative sampling of the work that has been conducted on this issue, and in doing so we will discuss two related sources of behavior prominence: unexpectedness and vividness.

Unexpectedness. As noted, one of the major mediators of behavior prominence is the extent to which observers perceive targets' actions as atypical, or unexpected. A study by Jones, Davis, and Gergen (1961) provides a good illustration of the effect of unexpectedness on the selection and weighting of cues. In this study, subjects played the role of a personnel director and listened to the tape-recorded interview of a male job applicant. The job being sought was either that of a submariner or of an astronaut. Before beginning their task, the subjects were told that applicants had been informed of the type of traits that were optimal for the job. Subjects who were to observe an applicant for the submariner job were informed that he had been told prior to the interview that it was desirable for submariners to possess the abilities to get along with others, to conform to rules, and so on. Similarly, subjects who were to listen to the applicant for the astronaut position learned that those who applied for this job had been told that an astronaut should be autonomous and independent—the type of individual who could function well by himself.

Jones et al. (1961) prepared two tape recordings for this experiment. In one, the job applicant depicted himself as autonomous and independent (desirable traits for an astronaut but not for a submariner), whereas in the other, he portrayed himself as extroverted and conforming (desirable traits for a submariner but not for an astronaut). Both tapes were used in each of the applicant conditions. This procedure resulted in some subjects hearing an applicant whose self-description was consistent with the demands of the job for which he was interviewing, whereas others heard an applicant describe himself in an unexpected and undesirable (for the job being sought) manner.

After listening to the interview, subjects indicated the extent to which they thought the target's behavior reflected Personal Structure characteristics.

The results of this experiment were consistent with the hypothesis that a target's unusual or unexpected actions are more likely to be selected and weighted in the impression formation process. Subjects who heard the job applicant describe himself in a manner that was inconsistent with the specifications of the job were more likely to perceive this behavior as indicative of the applicant's Personal Structure than were subjects who listened to an applicant describe himself as they expected he would. Moreover, subjects who observed the unexpected actions expressed more confidence in their impression of the applicant.

Note that these results parallel those of the experiment by Mills and Jellison (1967), discussed in Chapter 4. Recall that in this study, subjects were more likely to perceive a speaker as honest and trustworthy when he had presented a speech to an audience that was hostile to his message. Other research has disclosed similar effects of unexpected target behaviors on impression formation (Hastie & Kumar, 1979; Messick & Reeder, 1972; Newtson, 1974; Reeder, Messick, & Van Avermaet, 1977).

A study by Pysczynski and Greenberg (1981) provides a consistent, if somewhat different, perspective on the manner in which violations of observers' expectations can affect cue selection. In this study, male subjects were informed that they were to take part in a discussion task with a female. Before the discussion began, however, all subjects overheard the experimenter ask their coworker (actually an experimental accomplice) to perform either a small or a large favor for him. The accomplice either refused or complied with this request. The experimenter then returned to the subject and gave him a choice of information about the coworker's Personal Structure that was derived from her responses on a questionnaire that she had completed earlier. This self-report included information concerning her inclination to be helpful to others, her tendency to be acquiescent, her mood, her musical tastes, her future plans, her hobbies, and so on.

The results of this research demonstrated that the target's unexpected response to the experimenter's request for assistance—refusing a small favor or agreeing to a major request—increased the likelihood that subjects would ask for information about her that was indicative of Personal Structure characteristics. In other words, subjects were more likely to be interested in knowing about the accomplice's self-reported helpfulness and acquiescence than about her hobbies and musical tastes when she had responded unexpectedly to the experimenter's request. It is interesting that the most frequently requested information concerned the accomplice's mood, a possible clue to the consistency or regularity with which she displayed her unusual behavior.

Extremity of behavior can be considered a special case of unexpectedness. Extreme cues are features of the target or context that are noteworthy because of their excessive strength, frequency, or severity. In other words, extreme cues are unexpected because of their magnitude. Recall for a moment the football game discussed earlier. Suppose that you witnessed someone in the

Features in a target can be prominent as a result of their uniqueness or novelty.

stands quietly reading a book, regardless of the excitement that was taking place around him. You would be apt to take note of this person because his behavior was so unexpected in this context. On the other hand, you would expect spectators to express some emotion during the game—but only up to a point. Behaviors that pass beyond this boundary carry with them added cue value, since they too are unexpected. Thus, you would likely notice the person in the next row whose incessant yelling and screaming continued from the opening whistle of the game until the final gun. As such, you would be likely to perceive her actions as relevant to her Personal Structure. Research on the impact of extremity on cue selection (Fiske, 1980) has provided support for this position.

Vividness.   Features in the target can be prominent or noticeable as a result of their uniqueness or novelty, or because factors in the context cause the target to be differentiated from other components of the interpersonal environment. We have summarized the variables that highlight the target in this manner under the general term of vividness. Research, especially that of Leslie McArthur, Susan Fiske, Shelley Taylor and their colleagues, has shown that the vividness of a target affects the likelihood that observers will form an impression based on the target's actions.

For example, McArthur and Post (1977) undertook a number of different manipulations to enhance the noticeability of a target person. In their research, subjects were asked to observe the videotaped conversation between two individuals who supposedly had just met. The vividness of these two actors was varied by a number of different contextual factors. In one condition, for example, one of the actors was seated in a bright light, and the other was in the shadows. In another condition, subjects saw a target rocking back and forth in a rocking chair, while the other was seated in an ordinary chair. In yet another condition, one of the actors wore a brightly patterned shirt, while the other's was a dull grey. After viewing the targets interacting, subjects were asked to judge the extent to which each actor's behaviors reflected Personal Structure characteristics. The results consistently demonstrated that the more vivid the target, the more likely the target's behavior was judged to be based on personal traits and therefore to be relevant to forming an impression of this person.

From this study, as well as other research (McArthur & Solomon, 1978; Smith & Miller, 1979; Taylor, Crocker, Fiske, Sprinzen, & Winkler, 1979; Taylor, Fiske, Etcoff, & Ruderman, 1978), it appears that vivid cues increase the likelihood that observers will take increased note of their source—the actor displaying the cues. In many cases, this heightened attention results in a greater weight being placed on other cues that this target expresses, and these cues are thus more likely to influence observers' impressions of the target. However, it is possible that more careful monitoring of a target will have the opposite effect on cue selection—that is, when observers attend

"What did you expect a financial wizard to look like?"

Vivid cues can influence observers' impressions.

very carefully to a target, their judgments about that person might be more reasoned, considered, or better informed. These judgments, in turn, might lead observers to conclude that the events that transpired were not informative with respect to the target's Personal Structure.

Some empirical research has demonstrated that target vividness can decrease observers' inclinations to perceive cues relevant to the impression formation process. For example, in some of the studies of the McArthur and Post (1977) program of research, greater vividness in a target appeared to cause observers to perceive cues as less relevant to the target's Personal Structure. A close examination of studies that have produced results of this type reveals that in such cases, the vivid actor often appears to be constrained by the variable that imparts prominence to him or her. For instance, observers might well perceive that a man who is wearing a very distinctive tie or shirt is constrained in his actions because he feels so visible to his fellow actors in the context. In this circumstance, the behaviors of the vivid target would be viewed as less informative about his or her Personal Structure.[3]

Some Concluding Remarks on Target Effects in Cue Selection

In this section, we have reviewed the factors in the target that influence the manner in which observers select and weight cues in impression formation. As noted, however, the study of impression formation does not lend itself to clean demarcations between the types of processes or the classes of variables that are investigated. Thus, the many target variables that influence cue selection also play a major role in the two other phases of the impression formation process—trait inference and general evaluation.

Similarly, as also noted, variables such as target characteristics do not operate independently of the other variables affecting impressions. Targets behave in a Social Context and are perceived by observers who are active seekers and processors of information. Thus, factors in the observers and the context, as well as those in the target, combine to influence the impression that is ultimately formed. This last point is seen most clearly in our review of the effect of target identity on cue selection, in which we noted that the target and observer are often one and the same person. In this circumstance, it obviously is not possible to separate the target from the observer.

Nevertheless, for convenience and simplicity, we have separated our discussion of impression-formation processes into broad categories (cue selection, target factors, observer effects and so on), although much of the material that we present in one category could have been presented in another. The reader should keep this observation in mind while studying the material presented in subsequent sections of this chapter.

---

[3] There is some rational basis for this type of reasoning by observers. Empirical research, in fact, has demonstrated that actors' perceptions of their visibility tend to constrain their actions. These findings will be discussed in detail in Chapter 10.

FACTORS IN THE OBSERVER

As noted earlier, a major set of moderators of impression formation processes involves characteristics in the Personal Structure of the observer. A number of studies have demonstrated that observers differ in terms of the number and types of cues that they select in forming impressions. Some people, for example, consistently appear to utilize an extensive amount of information about targets, whereas others seem to base their impressions of others on only a few cues. Moreover, observers seem to focus differentially on certain cues and to weight them heavily in impression formation; however, people differ regarding the types of cues that take on this centrality or importance for them.

In a pioneering study of observer differences in cue selection, Gollin (1954) had subjects watch a film that portrayed five episodes in the life of a young woman. These episodes conveyed a large and varied amount of information about the woman. After viewing the film, subjects were asked to write descriptions of the woman they just had observed. Gollin (1954) found that some subjects' descriptions, including their impressions of the woman, were very comprehensive—they employed a great many of the cues presented in the film. In contrast, other subjects used much lesss of the potentially available information in their descriptions. And, as might be expected, the subjects' impressions of the woman were highly related to the number and type of cues that they noted in their descriptions. Other research (Kaplan & Crockett, 1968) has yielded additional support for the idea that observers differ in the number of cues they select in forming an impression of a target.

Empirical research has also suggested that many observers do not select cues at random, but rather utilize information that is relevant to Personal Structure characteristics in the target that are important to them. For example, Messé, Stollak, Larson, and Michaels (1979) asked subjects to view a videotape of excerpts from a number of encounters between an adult and a child. After viewing these scenes, the subjects were asked to report the number of positive and negative behaviors that they had observed the child displaying, with a maximum total of 25 behaviors of each type.

Results indicated that the observers varied widely in the number of positive and negative actions that they "saw." While the majority of observers saw a number of behaviors of each type, many others in the sample were biased in their perceptions, since they saw much more of one type of behavior than of the other. In fact, some subjects saw the target child display 25 negative behaviors, but not a single positive behavior; for others, this ratio was reversed—they saw only positive behaviors. Moreover, observers' biases in the cues they selected about the child were related to their evaluations of the adult who was also shown in the videotape. The positively biased perceivers were more likely to evaluate the adult target favorably, whereas the reverse was true for the negatively biased subjects. The findings of other research also support the observation that people can display consistent biases in cue selection (Dornbusch, Hastorf, Richardson, Muzzy, & Vreeland, 1965).

Set

The tendency of some observers to attend consistently to certain types of cues when forming impressions has been termed a *set*. By set, social psychologists mean a predisposition on the part of a person to perceive different people or objects in a similar or consistent manner. Sets are a result of factors in the observer's Personal Structure—such as beliefs, faculties, and motives—which color the individual's perception of his or her social world. We will now present some of the research that has shown that sets induced by differences in these factors can play a major role in observers' cue selection processes.

Beliefs. Social psychologists have often studied the impact of sets on observers' cue selection processes by inducing in subjects a sense that one or more of their opinions are relevant to some target. Observers are induced to assume that the target possesses some feature about which they have an established belief, and this set influences them to selectively attend to cues that the target displays.

For example, research by Claudia Cohen (1981) has shown that providing subjects with belief-relevant information about a target before they observe the target increases the number of cues to which they attend. In this study, subjects viewed a 15-minute videotape showing a man and woman having dinner together and informally celebrating a birthday. Some subjects were told that the woman in the videotape was a waitress, others that she was a librarian. In some cases, subjects were given this information before they viewed the tape, whereas others were told nothing about the target until after they had observed her. This manipulation was designed to evoke a set on the part of those given information prior to the tape regarding the type of behaviors that the target was likely to display.

Results of Cohen's (1981) study demonstrated that subjects who were given belief-relevant information before they viewed the target were more attentive to the cues she displayed than were those who had no prior set about her. In addition, findings indicated that the specific cues that were selected were dependent upon the particular set that was induced. Through pretesting, Cohen had identified the different types of behaviors that people generally associate with librarians and those that they associate with waitresses. She had carefully constructed the videotape so that the target displayed equal numbers of "waitress-like" and "librarian-like" behaviors. Cohen's (1981) results indicated that subjects who were led to believe that the target was a waitress selected significantly more cues that were consistent with their beliefs about waitresses than they did inconsistent cues. Likewise, those subjects in the librarian-set condition also selected a greater number of cues consistent with their beliefs about librarians. Thus, subjects' sets influenced not only the number of cues to which they had attended, but also the particular type of cues that were selected. A study by Langer and Imber (1980) has yielded findings that are consistent with those of Cohen (1981).

Perhaps the most widely researched type of set involves stereotypes, to be discussed in detail in Chapter 13. In brief, a stereotype is a belief that people who share some distinctive feature (such as race, sex, occupation, ethnic or religious affiliation, and so on) also share certain Personal Structure characteristics. Usually, but not always, these characteristics are evaluated negatively by those who hold the stereotype. Stereotypes are of interest in the present context because of their possible influence on cue selection and weighting, as a study by Goldberg, Gottesdiener, and Abramson (1975) demonstrates.

In this research, male and female subjects were asked to view 30 photographs of women and to guess which of the women were feminists. No information other than the pictures was presented, yet observers made consistent attributions about these targets: subjects tended to assume that the more attractive the target, the less likely she was to hold feminist views. It is important to note that subjects' estimates of the feminist orientation of the targets were incorrect—the targets' opinions on this issue were actually unrelated to their attractiveness. In other words, because the subjects shared a stereotyped opinion that linked feminism with unattractive physical features (apparently, a widely held opinion, as Jacobson and Koch, 1978, have demonstrated), they perceived the cues presented them as reflecting a target's personal characteristics (in this case, a set of beliefs). It is also of interest that this pattern of findings was consistent regardless of the sex of the observer. Both males and females seemed to hold the same negative stereotype about feminists and were equally influenced in their cue selections by this belief. Other research has yielded findings that are consistent with the proposition that beliefs affect the cues that observers select in impression formation (Chapman & Chapman, 1969; Deaux & Emswiller, 1974; Duncan, 1976; Ferguson & Wells, 1980; Hamilton & Rose, 1980; Snyder & Uranowitz, 1978).

Faculties

Another component of the Personal Structure—faculties—has also been shown to influence the manner in which people select and weight cues. Two important faculties which have generated considerable research are cognitive complexity and self-monitoring (as noted earlier).

Cognitive complexity is the ability to use many dimensions to categorize or classify objects, individuals, or events. A person is considered cognitively complex if he or she typically considers many different features about an object when evaluating it. If, on the other hand, a person consistently uses only one or two factors when evaluating or describing an object, he or she would be seen as cognitively simple (Bieri, 1961; Harvey, Hunt, & Schroder, 1961; Schroder, Driver, & Streufert, 1967).

For example, imagine that you have two friends, Jake and Elwood. By chance, the three of you are strolling down a street together as you pass an art gallery. In the window of this establishment you notice a large, intricately designed blue vase. You point out this unusual object to Jake and Elwood as the three of you pass by the shop. As you continue your stroll, you ask your friends what they thought of the vase.

Jake responds, "I liked it. It was blue, and blue is my favorite color."

"What do you think of its shape?" you ask him.

He responds, "I didn't pay much attention to that."

Elwood, on the other hand, begins a 10-minute discourse on the various features of the vase, including a discussion and evaluation of its size, shape, color and pattern. Obviously, your two friends differ in the way they processed information about this object. This difference between them was also evident when you asked them later about their lunch. As before, Jake's answer was short and to the point, as it was based on a single dimension: "It was great, I like burgers." Elwood, in contrast, was his usual discriminating self, describing in detail the various facets of each of the items on his plate.

From our example, we would expect that Elwood was more cognitively complex than Jake, and as such, he would be likely to use a greater proportion of available cues about a target when forming an impression of that person. These expectations are based on the results of many empirical investigations.

In an extensive program of research, Harry Schroder and his colleagues have demonstrated that people consistently differ in the amount of information that they utilize when forming or changing judgments about objects and people (Crano & Schroder, 1967; Harvey, Hunt, & Schroder, 1961; Schroder, Driver, & Streufert, 1967). Moreover, other empirical research has revealed that this faculty affects the cue selection and weighting process in impression formation. For example, Streufert and Streufert (1969) measured the cognitive complexity of a large number of undergraduates and identified samples of subjects who were either high or low on this faculty. Each of these subjects was then assigned to a two-person team which was to compete against another team on a simulated war game.

In the game, the groups, which were homogeneous with respect to complexity (that is, both members of the group were either cognitively simple or cognitively complex) were to coordinate a simulated invasion on a warring opponent. The groups were in charge of the deployment of their troops, the expenditure of materials and supplies, and so on. They could send out surveillance teams to monitor the enemy's movements and reactions in an attempt to determine enemy plans. Teams engaged in a series of 20-minute battles, and after each battle they received feedback about the success or failure of the strategic and tactical decisions they had made. For example, after the first battle, all teams were told that one of their decisions had been either successful or unsuccessful, while feedback about other decisions made during the period was ambiguous.

Streufert and Streufert (1969) found that when faced with this relatively ambiguous set of cues, the more cognitively complex subjects were less likely than their cognitively simple counterparts to perceive that this information reflected Personal Structure characteristics in themselves, their partners, or their opponents. Moreover, as the game progressed and subjects were given more and more clear-cut information about their performances, this difference tended to diminish. This latter finding suggests that cognitively complex subjects were better able to use the additional information that greater experience provided them in their decisions about the relevance of performance cues for their impressions.

A second faculty that is very relevant to cue selection processes in impression formation is self-monitoring (Snyder, 1974, 1979). As noted, self-monitoring is the ability to use cues in the Social Context when judging the appropriateness of one's own behaviors. Thus, the greater a person's self-monitoring faculty, the more attention he or she can devote to available contextual cues. In contrast, people who are low self-monitors tend to ignore contextual cues and focus instead on their own established beliefs when judging themselves and others.

In a study that clearly demonstrates the importance of the faculty of self-monitoring in cue selection and weighting, Berscheid, Graziano, Monson, and Dermer (1976) allowed subjects to observe the social behavior of a target with whom they expected to interact at a later time. Subjects had been preselected on the basis of their self-monitoring abilities. The results of this study indicated that subjects who were high self-monitors attended to more of the target's cues than did their low self-monitoring counterparts. Moreover, high self-monitors were more likely to perceive the cues as relevant to the Personal Structure of the target. Thus, in a context in which high self-monitors were very concerned about understanding another person (since they were soon to meet this person), they were especially prone to search for and make use of cues that would provide them with information concerning the Personal Structure of the target.

Motives. As noted in Chapter 1, the concerns that people bring to a context, which activate them and channel their behaviors, can have a major effect on many social phenomena, including impression formation. It is reasonable to hypothesize that people are likely to attend to and process cues which they perceive as facilitating the satisfaction of a *motive;* in contrast, they are likely to avoid processing cues that imply circumstances that are antagonistic to motive satisfaction.

Results of empirical research have provided support for the position that observers' motives can affect cue selection in impression formation (Arkin et al., 1980; Assor, Aronoff, & Messé, 1981; Gibbons & Wright, 1981; Jones, 1954; Lefcourt et al., 1975; Lipetz, 1960; McFarlin & Blascovich, 1981; Miller, Norman, & Wright, 1978; Smith & Brehm, 1981; Wright, Holman, Steele, & Silverstein, 1980). For example, Arkin et al. (1980), using a standardized personality test, measured undergraduates' levels of concern about the impressions that others have of them; people who are very concerned with this issue appear to be motivated to avoid embarrassment, public scrutiny, and so on. Arkin et al. selected as subjects for their study respondents who were either high or low on this social-anxiety motive. The experimenters then asked these subjects to take part in a study in which they were to play the role of a therapist who was to help a client overcome test anxiety by using a procedure given them by the experimenter. Feedback informed subjects whether they had succeeded or failed at this task. To heighten the relevance of the social-anxiety motive, subjects were informed that after they had completed their role as therapist, they would participate with a panel of experts (real therapists) in evaluating the session.

The results of the Arkin et al. study demonstrated the role that motivation can play in cue selection. In this context, subjects who were low on social-anxiety motivation displayed the expected behaviors regarding the relevance of success and failure cues for self-impression (discussed at length earlier in this chapter)—that is, they were more likely to perceive that their actions reflected characteristics in their Personal Structures when they succeeded than when they failed.

However, subjects who were highly motivated by social-anxiety concerns were more likely to attribute the outcomes of their behaviors to Personal Structure characteristics when they failed than when they succeeded. Thus, when these individuals expected to be confronted by experts, they were motivated to avoid perceiving cues as relevant to their own skills and abilities. It appeared that such subjects were concerned about embarrassing themselves by taking credit for a skill which later investigation (by experts) would disclose they did not really possess.

A second study disclosed that the modesty displayed by these subjects was not a conscious pose designed to get them "off the hook." In this second study, subjects were led to believe that they had been connected to a lie detector. As before, those who were highly motivated by social anxiety were more likely to deny the relevance of their performances to Personal Structure characteristics when they were successful than when they were not.

It should be noted that in the Arkin et al. (1980) study, the impact of motivation was dependent upon factors in the context that mediated the relevance of social anxiety. Thus, the effect of an observer-based variable was contingent on contextual forces. This complex relationship serves to underscore once again the interrelatedness of the components in the social field, a fact that should be kept in mind while reviewing the effect of contextual variables on the cue selection process.

FACTORS IN THE CONTEXT

An extensive research literature has developed concerning the effects of contextual variables on cue weighting and cue selection. A considerable portion of this literature has been devoted to the examination of the effects of the interpersonal environment—the presence, appearance, and actions of others in the context—on observers' judgments about a target. Kelley (1967, 1973) has termed factors of this sort *consensus* variables. In developing his theory, Kelley hypothesized that consensus was one of the major categories of information (along with distinctiveness and consistency) that people employed in forming impressions.

Consensus involves two related considerations: (1) the extent to which actors in the context (other than the target) display similar cues; and (2) the extent to which the target's cues match those of others in the context. It is reasonable to hypothesize that the greater the degree of cue similarity displayed by others, the greater the impact of the interpersonal environment on observers' cue selection. Observers are likely to assume that a target's cues reflect his or her Personal Structure only to the extent that these cues differ from those exhibited by the others in the context.

To demonstrate the operation of consensus on the cue selection process, consider the following scene. While waiting one Saturday night at a bus stop located outside a small sandwich shop, you happen to glance through the window and notice that all seven of the customers sitting at the counter are eating cheeseburgers and chips, and drinking Pepsi. As you are watching, another customer enters, sits at the counter, and places his order. When the counterman brings his meal, you notice that this customer, too, has ordered a cheeseburger, chips, and a Pepsi.

How confident would you be that this customer's behavior reflected a strong positive opinion about cheeseburgers, chips, and Pepsis? Certainly, it is possible that the customer came to the restaurant because he enjoyed this type of food and knew that this establishment specialized in it. On the other hand, an equally plausible inference that you could draw from the available cues (the high-consensus behaviors of the other customers) is that the target has come to the restaurant because it is a convenient place to eat, and he orders the same meal as everyone else, not because he necessarily relishes such a fare, but because these are the only items on the menu, or the only items worth ordering. The plausibility of this alternative explanation of the target's actions would lower your confidence that these behaviors reflected any personal characteristics.

In contrast, suppose you observe the new arrival order tuna salad, heavy on the mayo, on whole wheat toast, and a cup of tea. In this circumstance, in which the target has acted differently from every other customer, you most likely would be more confident in assuming that his behavior was based on a feature of his Personal Structure—in this case, a strong preference for tuna, or an aversion to cheeseburgers. Thus, ordering a tuna sandwich when everyone else orders cheeseburgers is likely to contribute to impression formation, because of the role of consensus on cue selection.

Empirical research has provided some support for the proposition that consensus in the interpersonal environment affects cue selection. For example, a study by Feldman, Higgins, Karlovac, and Ruble (1976) has yielded clear evidence that consensus can affect impression formation. In this investigation, subjects were asked to form impressions about four different targets whose actions were presented to them via a videotape. On a tape, the target was exposed to a number of pictures which depicted sets of different stimuli, such as animals, colors, cartoon figures, cars, and so on. The target's task was to indicate the stimulus which he or she liked best from among the alternatives within each set.

After this choice was made, four other actors (also in the videotape) were asked whether or not they agreed with the target's selection. In response, they expressed either unanimous approval or disapproval of the target's choice. The observers' task was to judge whether the target's preferences were based on Personal Structure characteristics or were more a reflection of situational forces (differences in the quality of the stimuli). The results of this study indicated that observers were considerably more likely to attribute the target's choices to Personal Structure characteristics under conditions of low consensus—that is, when his or her behavior was inconsistent with the judgments of the others in the interpersonal environment. This relationship between consensus and cue selection has also been demonstrated in other studies (Ginosar & Trope, 1980; Hansen & Donoghue, 1977; Kulik & Taylor, 1981; Major, 1980; Manis, Dovalina, Avis, & Cardoze, 1980; Ruble & Feldman, 1976; Stevens & Jones, 1976; Wells & Harvey, 1977, 1978; Zuckerman, 1978).

Other research has examined the strength of the effect of consensus on impression formation, often by pitting this factor against other determinants of cue selection, such as observers' opinions and expectations (Kahneman & Tversky, 1973; Kulik & Taylor, 1981; Nisbett & Borgida, 1975). Studies of this type have shown that the impact of consensus can be completely moderated or inhibited by other factors. Perhaps because consensus information is often rather abstract or complex, it can appear less clearly relevant for impression formation than other, more straightforward types of data (McArthur, 1972, 1976; Major, 1980; Wells & Harvey, 1977).

Many investigations of consensus have presented observers with rather abstract and impersonal information—for example, information that 70 percent of a sample share some common characteristic with a target. These studies generally have found that this form of consensus information is underused relative to other available cues (such as distinctiveness information). We would speculate, however, that if observers were exposed to an interpersonal environment in which 7 of the 10 people actually share a characteristic in common with the target, consensus information in this form would have a more profound impact on subjects' impressions.

The influence of other factors in the context has also been studied with regard to their effects on cue selection. For example, the spatial location of actors and observers in the context—a physical environment variable—has been shown to affect observers' perceptions and interpretations of a target's appearance and actions (Taylor & Fiske, 1975). Similarly, as noted earlier, other features of the physical environment (such as illumination level or the physical furnishings of the setting) contribute to the salience of cues in impression formation (McArthur & Post, 1977; McArthur & Solomon, 1978; Taylor & Fiske, 1978).

The nature of the event that an observer witnesses also affects cue selection. Melvin Snyder and Arthur Frankel (1976), for example, showed male subjects videotapes of a female undergraduate who supposedly was being interviewed. Since no soundtrack accompanied the tape, the observers could not hear the conversation that was taking place. Rather, all of the cues displayed by the target were visual (gestures, appearance, facial expressions, and so on). When introducing the tape, the experimenters told some subjects that the topic of the recorded interview was sex; other observers were told that the topic was politics; still others were told the topic of the interview (sex or politics) only after they had viewed the tape. The observers' task was to form an impression of the target, especially regarding how nervous or anxious a person she was.

Results of this study indicated that subjects' perceptions of the nature of the event (whether it was an interview about sex or about politics) affected the cues that they selected in forming their impressions, and this effect, in turn, was influenced by the time at which this information became known to them. Those subjects who were told beforehand that the interview was about sex were more likely to judge the target's behavior as reflecting Personal Structure characteristics. This alleged topic appeared to induce in these observers a set through which to interpret the target's many ambiguous behaviors as cues that she was nervous. While these cues could have been attributed to the topic of the interview, it appears that observers were prone to perceive at least a number of them as indicative of the target's Personal Structure. It was as if they thought, "The topic might have made me a bit nervous, but not as nervous as she was. She must be a nervous type."

In contrast, those who did not know the alleged topic of the interview until after they had viewed it showed a very different pattern with regard to cue selection. In this circumstance, subjects had no particular set when viewing the tape, and thus were less likely to interpret ambiguous behaviors as indicants of nervousness. When told after the fact that the interview had been about sex, the observers could judge that the few signs of nervousness which they perceived in the target were due entirely to circumstances beyond her control (the anxiety-arousing nature of the topic). On the other hand, when the observers learned that politics was the topic of the interview, any perceived nervousness that they recalled would be attributed not to the topic, but rather to the Personal Structure of the target. As a consequence, subjects who were informed of the topic after viewing the tape were more likely to judge cues as relevant to the target's Personal Structure when the interview was supposedly about politics.

Concluding Remarks about Cue Selection

This concludes our presentation of factors in the target, observer, and context which affect the cue selection and cue weighting phase of impression formation. From our discussion, it should be apparent that the themes of Valuation and Resolution play a central part in cue selection, as well as in the other phases of the impression formation process. Specific cues are selected because variables such as salience, distinctiveness and observers' set cause these cues to be perceived as relevant to the impression being formed or modified. Moreover, research has shown that the weight accorded these cues, once they are selected, is dependent in large part on their capacity to increase the Resolution of the context from which they were drawn (Arkkelin, Oakely, & Mynatt, 1979).

For example, the varying strength of consensus cues, discussed earlier, appears to be a consequence of the clarity of this complex type of information. When consensus cues are straightforward—that is, when everyone in the context behaves in the same fashion—they help to raise the level of Resolution for observers. However, consensus cues are often not so easily interpreted and therefore do not readily contribute to the Resolution of the context. In this case, observers often weight other types of cues more heavily (for example, appearance variables in the target that are relevant to the observer's stereotyped opinions).

While much of this discussion has been devoted to cue selection, it is important to understand that the relevance of the variables reviewed here is not limited to this phase of the impression formation process. Variables such as target identity and observer's set, as well as contextual features (that is, those that describe the nature of the event) influence trait inference and general evaluation of targets in much the same manner as they do cue selection. In the remaining sections of this chapter, we will emphasize this fact by supplementing our earlier discussion, rather than presenting a detailed and possibly redundant review of the impact of these variables on the processes of trait inference and general evaluation.

It is equally important to keep in mind that the various phases of impression formation are not discrete, sequential steps. Cue selection is obviously an important component in impression formation, as it is the basis on which the other phases of this process operate. Indeed, this was a major reason

When consensus cues are straightforward—when everyone behaves in the same fashion—we tend to attribute these actions to contextual forces.

for our paying so much attention to the details concerning the manner in which factors in the target, observer, and context affect persons' judgments about the relevance of cues to their impressions. However, as noted repeatedly, impression formation is really an integrative process, consisting of a number of highly interrelated subprocesses. Thus, while we can separately analyze the mechanisms of cue selection, trait inference, and general evaluation, in actuality they tend to operate in concert and mutually influence one another.

A program of research by Ranald Hansen has produced evidence that is relevant to the issue of the reciprocal nature of cue selection and trait inference. In this work, Hansen (1980) presented subjects with brief verbal descriptions of three events which were designed to vary in the extent to which cues would be perceived as relevant to the actors' Personal Structures. In one of the descriptions, for example, Hansen (1980, p. 999) informed his subjects, "Person X works on a puzzle and successfully solves it." In another, "Person X goes to a movie and laughs."

As might be expected judging from our past discussion, observers selected more cues from the first description as relevant to the target's Personal Structure than they did from the second. Moreover, when the subjects were asked what additional information they would like about the target to explain the outcomes of these events, they were more likely to respond that they wished to know how consistent this behavior was with the target's past actions (for example, how many puzzles Person X had solved in the past) when they had made a judgment that involved a Personal Structure explanation. When they had attributed the outcome of the event to circumstances unrelated to the Personal Structure of the actor, they usually asked for information about the interpersonal environment (for example, how many other people laughed at the movie) rather than about the Personal Structure of the target.

In brief, having selected cues as relevant to one or another aspect of a target or situation, observers apparently felt it to be important to obtain additional cues that were relevant to their initial trait inference. Other studies in Hansen's (1980) series, coupled with the work of Mark Snyder and his colleagues (Snyder & Swann, 1978; Snyder & White, 1981), suggest that once formed, an initial, tentative belief about a target induces observers to weigh heavily in their Valuation process those cues that would confirm their impression, and to place little weight on cues that are inconsistent with it. The mutual influence of cue selection and trait inference that this research demonstrates should be kept in mind when considering the following material.

TRAIT INFERENCE

Recall from our earlier discussion that trait inference is the Valuation process by which an observer decides that a person possesses certain Personal Structure characteristics. The information that is used in this decision is drawn from the cues that the observer has selected about the target in the cue selection phase of the impression formation process. Before briefly reviewing the roles that factors in the target, context, and observer play in trait inference, two more basic issues need to be addressed: (1) research indicates that observers are inclined to infer traits on the basis of almost any cues, no matter how ephemeral or extensive those cues might be; and (2) the traits that people infer about others do not appear to be haphazard or capricious; rather, there is an underlying regularity to the specific traits or Personal Structure characteristics which targets are inferred to have.

A study by Sampo Paunonen and Douglas Jackson (1979) illustrates the observation that people can make trait inferences on the basis of even the most minimal of cues. In this study, the experimenters presented groups of subjects with two very different sets of cues. One group received a rather extensive written description of an actor. The second group was shown stick figure cartoons, which represented people engaging in activities that paralleled those of the targets who had been described verbally to the other subjects. After either reading about or seeing the cartoon depiction of the target, Paunonen and Jackson's (1979) subjects were asked to make trait inferences about the targets. Results indicated that the type of cues presented about the targets (extensive verbal descriptions versus simple cartoon figures) made little difference in the observers' willingness to make trait inferences about them. Thus, it appears that trait inference processes are easily evoked, even by the most minimal of cues.

A study by Daniel Weiss (1979) extends the findings of Paunonen and Jackson (1979). In Weiss's experiment, observers, who were professional psychologists, were asked to make trait inferences about people for whom they had differing amounts of information. The results of this study disclosed that the amount of information about the targets had an impact on the variability of traits that observers inferred about them. When the number of cues about the target was relatively small, different observers tended to infer similar traits; however, when there was a greater amount of information available on the targets, different observers tended to infer different traits about them.

A second general point regarding trait inference processes is that people tend to think about traits within the framework of a small set of more general dimensions. In other words, to some extent these general dimensions guide observers' selection of the traits that they infer about targets. Thus, an observer for whom emotionality is a general dimension would likely describe targets in terms that relate to it—that is, this observer would typically infer traits such as warm, excitable, or depressive when forming impressions about others.

Wiggins (1979) has summarized the results of a series of studies on this issue which have disclosed that eight general dimensions appear to underlie the specific trait inferences that observers most often make about targets. In fact, he shows how these eight dimensions subsume as many as 128 distinct traits. For example, one general dimension involves positive Personal Structure characteristics connoting ambition, achievement, and power; thus, the traits of self-confidence, industriousness, and persistence, among others, are summarized by this dimension. A second general dimension involves the negative Personal Structure characteristics associated with weakness and failure; thus, the traits of laziness, impracticality, and timidity are summarized by this dimension. The remaining six dimensions involve traits associated with sociability, personal warmth, trustworthiness, independence, hostility, and self-centeredness.

Wiggins' (1979) results suggest that when observers infer traits about targets, they have in mind a general set of categories through which the target is evaluated. While different targets and contexts will cause variations in the specific traits that an observer infers, the work of Wiggins and others (Cantor & Mischel, 1979; Jones, Sensenig, & Haley, 1974; Rosenberg & Sedlack, 1972) suggests that the general dimensions which guide such judgments are rather consistent across situations. This is not to say that the eight general dimensions account for all of the trait inferences that observers make. Wiggins (1979) was concerned primarily with trait inferences made during interpersonal encounters and thus ignored the dimensions that would underlie inferences about Personal Structure characteristics such as intelligence and athletic ability, which are less specifically relevant to social behavior. However, we expect that people also consider these specific traits within the framework of more global dimensions.

From this brief discussion of trait inference, it should be apparent that this process is readily activated in people, and that observers, when engaged in such judgments, tend to be guided by principles of cognitive economy. These general observations should be kept in mind when reviewing more specific information related to factors in the target, context, and observer, which have been shown to influence this phase of impression formation.

Factors in the Target

The target's identity. Given the impact that a target's identity has on cue selection, it is not surprising that this variable would also influence trait inference. We would expect that observers are more willing to infer traits about a target when the target is another person than when they themselves are the target. This expectation has received a reasonable amount of empirical support. For example, Goldberg (1978) presented subjects in his study with a list of 731 relatively familiar trait descriptions and asked them to indicate how accurately each term reflected the Personal Structure of themselves or another person whom they knew.

Consistent with our expectations, Goldberg (1978) found that subjects thought that the trait terms were less useful descriptions of their own Personal Structures than they were of the Personal Structures of others. Other research (Nisbett et al., 1973) has provided evidence that is consistent with this position.

Other target attributes. As noted, one of the more powerful influences on impression formation is the target's appearance. As might be expected, physical characteristics such as sex, race, style of dress, and attractiveness exert a strong effect on trait inference processes, much as they do on cue selection (Brigham, 1971; Gibbins, 1969; Mussen & Barker, 1944; Snyder,

Tanke, & Berscheid, 1977). For example, a number of studies have shown that a host of different traits are inferred about targets as a consequence of the targets' sex. For example, McKee and Sherriffs (1957) asked subjects to infer traits about male and female targets. Different traits were inferred about men and women: males were perceived as possessing traits that reflected competence, rationality, and assertiveness, whereas women were perceived very differently—as dependent, irrational, and passive. Table 7.1 presents some of the traits that were inferred about targets as a consequence of their sex.

Other research (Broverman et al., 1972; MacBrayer, 1960) has yielded similar findings, which indicate that observers tend to infer different traits in the target as a consequence of the target's sex. Moreover, as Deaux (1976) concludes, there is little evidence that this tendency for observers to infer different traits in males and females has substantially changed since the early work of McKee and Sherriffs (1957). We will explore some of the implications of this tendency in our discussion of social psychological factors in prejudice (Chapter 13).

Physical attractiveness has also been found to affect observers' trait inferences about targets. In a study to be discussed in detail in the next chapter, Snyder et al. (1977) showed male undergraduates photographs of females who varied regarding their attractiveness. Their findings indicated that these observers tended to infer different traits on the basis of this information. The more attractive the target, the more likely observers were to infer that she was sociable and humorous; in contrast, the more unattractive, the more likely she was to be perceived as awkward, serious, and socially inept. Other research has yielded similar findings (Dion, Berscheid, & Walster, 1972; Miller, 1970).

Traits also are inferred on the basis of targets' specific actions. For example, Apple et al. (1979) found that subjects' inference of the honesty, anxiety, and strength of a target was influenced by the target's tone of voice. Similarly,

TABLE 7.1
Ten Representative Traits that Observers Infer About Male and Female Targets (adapted from McKee & Sherriffs, 1957)

Men's Traits	*Women's Traits*
Active	Cooperative
Adventurous	Dependent
Ambitious	Excitable
Calm	Frivolous
Competitive	Lacking self-confidence
Informal	Nonadventurous
Independent	Passive
Logical	Shy
Objective	Subjective
Self-confident	Tactful

254

"I think you ought to know, coach. Their middle
linebacker is extremely sadistic."

We use the actions of others to infer traits in them.

other research has shown that behaviors displayed by targets—smiling, body movement, gaze, speech, and their tendencies to interact at a near or far distance from another—influence observer's trait ascriptions of them (Duncan & Fiske, 1977; Exline, 1972; Lay & Burron, 1968; Mehrabian & Friar, 1969; Miller & Hewgill, 1964). Thus, it appears that even very subtle cues have an appreciable effect on trait inference processes in impression formation.

Factors in the Context

Research has shown that variables drawn from both the interpersonal environment and other components of the Social Context can have an effect on the trait inferences that observers draw about targets. For example, Simpson and Ostrom (1976) asked subjects to read brief descriptions of a number of people. In some conditions, subjects were exposed to descriptions that depicted these people as possessing negative qualities; in other conditions, the people were portrayed in positive terms. In either case, after reading this information, subjects were asked their impressions of a final person, who was described in neutral terms.

Simpson and Ostrom (1976) found that the traits that subjects inferred about this neutral target were influenced by the information that they had read about the other targets. If the others had been described in a negative fashion, more positive traits were inferred in the neutral target. In contrast, when the neutral target was placed in an interpersonal environment consisting entirely of very positively described targets, the neutral target suffered by comparison—negative traits were inferred about the target in this condition, despite the fact that information about this target was identical to that presented in the negative interpersonal environment.

For example, in the condition in which all of the people except the neutral target were portrayed in a negative manner, a subject described the target as highly intelligent, ambitious, keen, and so on. In the condition in which all except the target were described positively, a subject inferred that the neutral target was hard to get along with, overly anxious, a pennypincher, and so on. Results such as these, which were typical of subjects in the Simpson and Ostrom study, demonstrate the impact that the interpersonal environment can have on trait inference.

Just as the interpersonal environment influences trait inferences, so do factors in the physical environment. In discussing cue selection, it was noted that cues are weighted differently as a consequence of the context in which they occur. In forming an impression, observers find the behavior of a man screaming epithets as differentially useful as a consequence of the context in which this behavior occurs—a crowded football stadium, or a quiet movie theater. While few studies have been undertaken to directly investigate physical environment factors in trait inference, it is reasonable to assume that such contextual variables influence the trait inferences made by observers about targets.

Empirical research provides some indirect support for the proposition that context can affect trait inference. For example, a study by Price and Bouffard (1974) suggests that people are more likely to make trait inferences about a target if they perceive the target's behavior in a context which renders the behavior unusual (unacceptable, counternormative, and so on). The reader might think about the traits of two people in a crowded lecture hall who were passionately kissing as a professor droned on about nuclear physics. Your inferences regarding their traits would be very different if you had observed this interaction within the context of a drive-in movie. While in both cases you might assume some degree of attraction between the actors, in the classroom context you would also likely infer that they were impetuous, socially naive, or oversexed. Other research (Ajzen, 1971; Kane, Joseph, & Tedeschi, 1976) has provided empirical support for this expectation.

Factors within the Observer

Finally, trait inferences also have been shown to be influenced by factors within the observers themselves. For example, Powell and O'Neal (1976) have demonstrated that the role the observer plays in an encounter influences trait inference. In this research, they had some subjects actually interact with a target via a television link. Other subjects merely observed a videotape of the target's behaviors during these encounters. The researchers found that observers who actively engaged in the interaction made more trait inferences than did those who only witnessed it, although the same information about the target was available to the subjects in both interaction conditions.

Perhaps the most important observer factor in trait inference involves set—the propensity to form impressions as a result of preconceptions in the observer rather than the objective characteristics of the context. A compelling illustration of the impact of sets on trait inference was provided by Dornbusch et al. (1965). In this study, the investigators interviewed a large number of children, ages 9 through 11, who had spent the summer at the same camp. In the interview, each child was asked to describe two fellow campers. Recordings of these interviews were analyzed to determine the traits that the children inferred about one another.

Two interesting findings emerged from this investigation. First, the amount of overlap in children's trait inferences about the same target was far from perfect. On the average, the traits ascribed to a target by different observers overlapped about 45 percent of the time. Second, the trait inferences that the same observer made about different targets tended to overlap about 57 percent of the time—that is, observers tended to use the same categories in describing different targets. Apparently, sets in these children affected the traits that they perceived in others. It is striking that the consistency of trait descriptions made by an observer across different targets was greater than that found among observers for the same target. This study, as well as others (Passini & Norman, 1966; Rosenberg, 1976; Tunnell, 1981), demonstrated that factors in the observers can color their impressions of others.

The factors that underlie differences in the sets that affect observers' trait inferences have been the focus of a good deal of attention in social psychology (Benedetti & Hill, 1960; Jones, 1954; Lay, 1970; Steiner, 1954). Bruner and Tagiuri (1954) introduced the term *implicit personality theory* to describe the tendency of people to infer traits in others based upon incomplete information. Thus, "knowing" that a person is shy tends to lead observers to infer other traits (such as passiveness, awkwardness, and studiousness) in the person. Considerable research has demonstrated that observers tend to engage in this form of trait inference (Asch, 1946; Kelley, 1950; Rosenberg & Sedlak, 1972; Wishner, 1960).

Although there appears to be a tendency in all of us to analyze other people's Personal Structures—and to do so on the basis of very circumstantial evidence—it does not follow that we all draw similar inferences from the same information about a target. Thus, one person might infer that an individual whom he or she perceives as intelligent is also cold, calculating, unsympathetic, stern, and critical, whereas another might associate intelligence with the traits of practicality, skillfulness, competence, and wit. These associations appear to be based on the development of what Ulric Neisser (1967) and Hazel Markus (1977) have called a schema, or knowledge structure.

A schema is an abstract representation of some object or person. For example, most people possess a schema of the class of objects called human beings. When we encounter an entity that satisfies some of the components of this schema (that is, we see that the entity is a human being), we evaluate the extent to which other components of the entity also match the schema (Does the entity have a beard? A deep voice?). As Markus (1980, p. 106) has observed, schemata "involve an organization and integration of past knowledge for use in interpreting future input." Although many of the schemata that people hold are highly similar, they can differ across individuals since they are based upon personal experience and knowledge. This is especially true within the framework of person perception, in which individuals are the focus of the schemata, and observers tend to differ markedly with respect to their past histories of social encounters on which these knowledge structures are based.

Schemata are important because they shape the inferences which people draw concerning targets. People with different schemata will form different impressions about targets for two reasons: (1) they will select different cues as relevant to their impressions of the target; and (2) they will interpret information as reflecting different traits in that person. Wegner, Benel, and Riley (1976) present evidence which suggests that schemata can affect trait inference. In their study, Wegner et al. (1976) actually induced different schemata in their subjects by exposing them to different personal experiences. Some subjects read a series of descriptions of people in which the traits of persuasiveness and reality orientation were positively linked. In some descriptions, the person was portrayed as being both persuasive and realistic, whereas other people in this series of descriptions were depicted as being both unpersuasive and unrealistic (in no case did these subjects ever read that a person was both persuasive and unrealistic, or vice versa). Other subjects, however, read descriptions in which these traits were negatively linked—that is, people were always portrayed as persuasive but unrealistic, or as unpersuasive but realistic (in this condition, no description depicted these traits as being positively linked).

With sufficient exposure to this type of information, subjects formed different persuasive/realistic schemata as a consequence of the specific association that had been presented to them. Some subjects were induced to form a schema that conceptualized persuasive people as realistic; others were induced to see the traits of persuasibility and realism as negatively related. The effect on impression formation of such differences in schemata was assessed by asking subjects to read additional descriptions of people which made no explicit mention of their persuasiveness or realism, and then to rate them with respect to these traits. As expected, Wegner et al. (1976) found that subjects who had formed the persuasive/realistic schema were more likely to infer that these traits were associated in the new targets than were those who had been induced to form the opposite schema. Thus, the traits that were inferred about a target by these two types of subjects differed markedly, although they had been exposed to the same information about the target. Other research (Bond, 1972; Snyder et al., 1977; Srull & Wyer,

1979; Yarkin, Harvey & Bloxom 1981) has yielded findings that are consistent with those of Wegner et al. (1976).

Evidence also exists to suggest that differences in schemata can affect self-impressions. In one study, Storms (1979) obtained measures of subjects' schemata about males and females—that is, he asked both male and female respondents to identify the traits that they associated with the "typical male" and the "typical female." Storms found that differences in these schemata were related to the traits that subjects inferred about a specific male or female—in this case, themselves. For example, the more a male subject's schema about men violated traditional stereotypes, the more atypical were the traits he inferred about himself. Thus, schemata appear to be related to the kinds of trait attributions that people make about targets, whether the targets are the observers themselves or other people. Research by Markus (1977) and Spence, Helmreich, and Stapp (1975b) has provided additional evidence in support of this observation.

FORMING GENERAL IMPRESSIONS

To this point, we have reviewed the processes involved in, and the major classes of variables that affect, cue selection and trait inference. We will now consider the third phase of impression formation, which involves the manner in which judgments made in the first two phases are combined to form a *general impression* about a target. We will begin by describing the Valuation process in which observers are thought to engage during this phase of impression formation, and will then briefly review factors in the target, context, and observer which influence this process.

The Valuation Process

A number of models of the Valuation process employed by people in the formation of general impressions have been proposed (Anderson, 1965, 1974; Fishbein & Hunter, 1964; Osgood, Suci, & Tannenbaum, 1957; Rokeach & Rothman, 1965). These different perspectives share a common assumption—namely, that impression formation involves the Valuation of targets regarding some general judgment about their goodness or badness. While there is evidence that people also can form Valuations about other dimensions (such as power or likeability), nevertheless there is agreement in social psychology that the good/bad evaluation dimension is the principal issue with which people are concerned when they form general impressions of others.

The controversy that has surrounded the issue of Valuation in general impressions is directed at a more specific point: the manner in which the values associated with the traits inferred about a target are combined in deciding about the target's overall goodness. While some disagreement still remains about the model that best describes this Valuation process, the bulk of recent evidence favors the weighted-average approach proposed by Norman

Anderson. Thus, we have loosely adopted his perspective in our discussion of the formation of general impressions. Moreover, Anderson's ideas have served as the basis of the theme of Valuation as we have presented it throughout this book.

In general terms, Anderson's (1974) weighted-average model postulates that different traits are assigned different values—which we have termed *cue weights*—and these values are then averaged to arrive at an overall impression about a target.[4] The value accorded a particular trait is a consequence of a number of factors, including its level of importance for the observer, the extent to which the target is perceived to possess it, and its perceived valence (positive or negative).

In our adaptation of Anderson's approach, the more a trait is perceived as relevant to a high level belief or concern, the more heavily it is valued. For example, a person with very high level religious beliefs is likely to assign a large value to traits such as reverence and piety, whereas a person who is indifferent to religion would not place much emphasis on these traits. Similarly, the value assigned to a trait is determined by the observer's perception of the extent to which the target possesses the trait. The more a target is perceived as being extreme on a trait, the greater the impact of this trait in the Valuation process. Thus, religiosity might be a high level concern for an observer, but this trait would not have a major impact on the resultant impression if the target is seen as being only moderately religious.

Also, whether a trait is perceived as positive (worthwhile), neutral, or negative (aversive) will affect its impact on the overall impression. For a person who values religion, the perception that a target is sacrilegious or pious would have a major impact on his or her impression of the target. But of course, whether the target was perceived as falling on the sinful or pious side of the trait of religiosity would determine its specific impact on this observer's impression.

In this Valuation approach, every trait that a target is perceived as possessing is assigned a value, and these values (weights) are averaged into a general impression of the target. For example, an observer might perceive that a target possesses five distinct traits. For the reasons outlined above, these traits are valued (assuming a scale ranging from −100 to +100) as illustrated in Table 7.2.

The weighted average of 17 represents a slightly positive impression of this target. That is, if someone were to ask you what you think of this individual—given that your general impression matched that in our example—you probably would reply something along the lines of, "He's OK, a good guy, but not great."

Research by Anderson (1974) and others (Ostrom & Davis, 1979) has shown that people do engage in such evaluation processes to derive a general

---

[4] Anderson's (1974) approach is somewhat complex and utilizes a number of concepts that are defined rather precisely. For our purposes, we thought it best to present a simplified version of his model, primarily for ease of understanding.

TABLE 7.2
Hypothetical Values Assigned to
Traits in Impression Formation

Trait	Value
A (wit)	65
B (ambition)	29
C (perseverance)	8
D (sloppiness)	−5
E (obstinacy)	−12
Total	85
Average (85/5)	17

impression from trait information. Moreover, as might be expected considering the material previously presented in this chapter, other research has shown that factors in the target, context, and observer affect the values assigned to traits in the general impression formation process.[5] In the pages that follow, we will briefly discuss each of these influences.

Factors in the Target

Both the characteristics and the actions of targets have been found to influence observers' general impressions of them. For example, in a study by Karen Dion (1972) (discussed in Chapter 2), subjects were asked to read descriptions of children who had engaged in antisocial acts of varying severity. The pictures of the children who had committed these transgressions accompanied the description of each event. Some subjects were given the picture of a very attractive youngster, whereas others viewed an unattractive child. The results showed that the subjects who had been led to believe that the transgressor was attractive had a more positive impression of the target's Personal Structure than did those who thought that the target was unattractive. Apparently, the physical appearance of the target influenced observers' reactions toward the target, although the behaviors expressed were identical. Other research has substantiated the finding that appearance variables can affect general impressions (Broverman, Broverman, Clarkson, Rosenkrantz, & Vogel, 1972; Carducci et al., 1978; Dion et al., 1972; Jackson, 1981; MacBrayer, 1960; Richardson et al., 1961).

Similarly, the actions of a target can influence our general impressions of him or her. Suls, Witenberg, and Gutkin (1981) asked subjects to read descriptions of individuals whose actions varied in the extent of their social desirability. One set of descriptions portrayed the actor as behaving altruisti-

---

[5] Some of this work has explored the traits that are associated with general impressions. Other studies, however, have examined the direct impact of the factors of the Social Context and Personal Structure on general impressions without measuring any specific traits, per se. In the research discussed here, we do not differentiate between these two approaches to the study of impression formation.

cally—doing a favor for another who had earlier been unkind to the actor; another set depicted the actor as reciprocating a favor; a third set presented the actor as refusing to help someone who earlier had acted selfishly; a final set described an actor who refused to reciprocate a favor for a person who earlier had been kind to the actor.

Subjects were asked to provide their overall impressions of the actor in terms of a global good/bad evaluation. The findings of this study indicated that observers' impressions differed systematically as a consequence of the target's actions. Observers judged most positively the actor who had returned the favor, next the person who had "turned the other cheek," (i.e., acted altruistically). They were less positive toward the actor who did not help the selfish other, and reacted least favorably toward the target who had failed to reciprocate a favor. Other research (Buldain et al., in press) has yielded similar findings.

Factors in the Context

Research has shown that the interpersonal environment also affects general impressions. In fact, there is evidence that the attributes of people in the setting can affect self-impressions (Jellison, Jackson-White, Bruder, & Martyna, 1975; Morse & Gergen, 1970; Zanna & Pack, 1975). In the study by Morse and Gergen (1970), subjects' tendencies to moderate the positivity of their self-impressions was manipulated through a clever ruse. Initially, all subjects were individually brought into a room and asked to complete a self-evaluation which assessed how positively or negatively they felt about themselves. Halfway through completing this instrument, another student entered the room and began to fill out the same questionnaire. For half the subjects, this person was physically attractive, apparently very bright and well-read (his briefcase contained a number of books whose topics ranged from philosophy to statistics). For the other subjects, this individual was a slob—unkempt, poorly dressed, and apparently addicted to pulp novels.

Morse and Gergen (1970) measured the impact of these two interpersonal environments on people's self-impressions by comparing the positivity of subjects' evaluations of themselves before and after the other person entered the room. They found that the appearance of the other had a marked influence on subjects' self-impressions. When in the presence of the attractive person, subjects diminished the positivity of their self-evaluations, whereas they increased the positivity of their self-evaluations when the unattractive person arrived on the scene.

Other contextual factors have been found to affect general impressions. For example, Massad, Hubbard, and Newtson (1979) showed subjects a cartoon in which three geometric figures—a large triangle, a small triangle, and a circle—moved about the screen. Subjects were asked to imagine that the figures in the film were people, a flight of fancy that other research (Greenberg & Strickland, 1973; Heider & Simmel, 1944) has shown to be quite easy to accomplish for most people.

The figures always moved in a set pattern. The film starts with the large triangle placed inside a box with a hinged door. The small triangle and the circle come into view, and the large triangle leaves the box to meet them. The two triangles engage in rapid thrusts and counterthrusts, apparently fighting, while the circle moves into the box. This action continues for some minutes and depicts such activity as the circle and small triangle entering and leaving the box; the movie ends with the large triangle entering the box, moving about in it, and finally smashing it to bits.

Subjects were told that the scenes which they had witnessed occurred in one of two different contexts. Some were informed that the large triangle was a "guard" in charge of a treasure located in the box, and that the other two figures were thieves who were attempting to steal it. Others were told that the large triangle was a "bully" and a "rapist," and the other two figures were innocent victims. After viewing the film, all subjects were asked to evaluate its "actors."

The results of this study clearly demonstrated the strength of contextual factors in impression formation. For example, the large triangle was evaluated much more positively in the guardian context, whereas both the other actors were perceived more positively in the bully context. Other research (Greenberg & Strickland, 1973; Shor, 1957) has verified the observation that the same action in different contexts will generate different general impressions.

Factors in the Observer

There is evidence that differences between observers exist regarding values accorded to traits when they are employed in general impression formation. Ostrom and Davis (1979), for example, presented subjects with a number of trait descriptive adjectives about a target and asked them to report their general impression of the target. The results of this study indicated that the subjects' impressions were a weighted-average of their trait inferences. However, the findings also disclosed that the specific weights assigned to the various traits differed markedly across individual observers. It seems reasonable to assume that observers perceived the the value of the traits differently as a function of components in their own Personal Structures, a conclusion that has received support in a study by Assor, Aronoff, and Messé (1981).

In this research, Assor et al. (1981) used standardized personality tests to measure two related motives—dominance and dependency—in a large number of undergraduates. Dominance reflects a concern with leading and directing the activities of others; dependency represents a need to be cared for, protected, or sheltered by others. Undergraduates for whom dominance or dependency were high or low level motives served as subjects in this study. All subjects were shown the same videotape, in which two people engaged in a problem-solving discussion. Subjects were led to believe that one of the interactants was a competent and high-status person, whereas the other was average, at best, on these attributes. After viewing the tape, subjects were asked to report their general impressions of the two interactants.

The results of this study clearly demonstrated that motive relevance affects impression formation. Subjects for whom dominance was a high level motive were more positive toward the less threatening, low-status actor. In contrast, highly dependent subjects perceived the highly competent actor more favorably than they did the low-status target. Other research has shown that other factors in the observer also influence impressions (Carducci et al., 1978; Suls et al., 1981).

A study by Bernardo Carducci, Paul Cozby, and Charles Ward (1978) in fact demonstrates the ways in which factors in the target, context, and observer can interact to affect general evaluations of others. For this reason, we will present it as our last example of research relevant to first impressions.

In this study, the experimenters manipulated the level of subjects' sexual arousal—an observer factor—by exposing them to one of two different types of material: a graphic seduction scene or information about the reproductive cycle of the stickleback fish. In conjunction with both types of stimulus material, observers were shown a picture of an attractive or average-looking female; this variable was a contextual (interpersonal environment) manipulation. Finally, subjects were shown a picture of a second female, who also varied with regard to attractiveness, and were asked their impressions of this target (a target variable manipulation).

Results indicated that arousal level, the attractiveness of the person who constituted the interpersonal environment, and the attractiveness of the target all combined to affect observers' impressions. Consistent with the results of other research, cited earlier, the more attractive target tended to be perceived more positively. However, additional findings indicated that the impact of this target factor on impressions was mediated by other variables in the study. The attractiveness of the other person altered the value that subjects placed on the attractiveness of the target, and this difference in cue weighting as a consequence of the interpersonal environment, in turn, was influenced by the level of sexual arousal of the observer.

Concluding Remarks about General Impressions

The results of the Carducci et al. (1978) study are probably reasonably representative of the complex manner in which variables affect impression formation. The Valuation process that characterizes the judgments that people make about themselves and others is apparently affected by a variety of forces, including factors in the target, observer, and context. For example, it is likely that factors in the context—such as the attributes that others in the interpersonal environment display—can influence the extent to which the target is perceived as possessing certain traits, which is one of the bases for assigning values in impression formation. Likewise, the valence of a trait can be influenced by factors both in the context and in the target. For example, the study of Massad et al. (1979) suggests that the valence placed on the actors' aggressiveness was determined by the context in which this trait was displayed. Finally, factors in the observer clearly determine the perceived importance of various traits in the target. Thus, general impressions are a composite of inferred traits, whose impact is largely determined by factors in the target, observer, and context.

LATER IMPRESSIONS

In general, it is likely that the processes that affect established impressions are the same as those that affect first impressions. However, some differences between first and later impressions deserve mention. Later impressions involve change rather than formation. Thus, it is typically the case that the Valuation process in later impressions is more complex than that involved in first impressions. The major reason for this difference in complexity involves the number of cues that are perceived as relevant. In later impressions, observers tend to consider their own established beliefs about the target and weigh any additional evidence within this perspective.

In this regard, later impressions of others are similar to self-impressions—as with self-impressions, once established, later impressions of others tend to be resistant to change. For this reason, new information in such circumstances is often underweighed, discounted, or erroneously perceived as consistent with the established belief. This overweighting of initial impressions, which has been termed the *primacy effect,* has been demonstrated in numerous studies (Anderson & Barrios, 1961; Anderson & Hubert, 1963; Asch, 1946; Jones et al., 1968; Jones, Goethals, Kennington, & Severance, 1972; Luchins, 1957; Stewart, 1965).

It should be noted, however, that initial beliefs do not always outweigh new information, whether the target is another person or the self (Morse & Gergen, 1970). In fact, some studies have demonstrated a *recency effect,* in which the more recent information weighs more heavily in impression formation than do beliefs established on the basis of earlier data (Crano, 1977; Hendrick & Constantini, 1970; Luchins, 1958; Rosenkrantz & Crockett, 1965; Stewart, 1965). The findings of such research suggest that later cues can affect established impressions primarily under two conditions: (1) later cues will be weighted to the extent that they provide dramatic, unexpected, attention-arousing, or irrefutable evidence that the original belief was incorrect; and (2) new information will be utilized to the extent that the initial impression was a low level, tenuous belief, or to the extent that the nature of the context implies that the established impression is less relevant than usual.

CONCLUDING REMARKS

This completes our review of the extensive literature in social psychology concerning the factors and processes involved in impression formation. Social psychologists have devoted a great deal of attention to this subject because, as noted, many of our important, high level beliefs involve specific persons, including ourselves. The processes that we have discussed center on the theme of Valuation, although other themes (Resolution and Consistency) also play an important role in the formation and modification of impressions.

We feel that a comprehensive review of the topics involved in person perception was necessary primarily for two reasons. First, the work in this area is both voluminous and relatively disjointed. As such, a careful examination of this material was necessary in order to present it in an accurate and integrative fashion. Second, because so many of our impressions are high level beliefs, they would be expected to have a major impact on our overt actions. Indeed, there is evidence that impressions can have a great influence on behavior, and this evidence will be considered in the following chapter.

The Impact of Impressions on Social Behavior

8

In the previous chapter, we discussed the psychological processes that people use in forming impressions of others—the factors that influence the positivity of such judgments, the ways in which different types of information are used, and some explanations of the ways in which impressions are formed. We will now turn our attention to the outcome of such processes on the social behaviors of the perceiver, and their consequences for the target of the perceiver's evaluation.

More specifically, we will present material related to three broad and important issues in social psychology: (1) the extent to which people's behaviors toward another person are affected by their impression of that person; (2) the manner in which such impression-based behaviors, in turn, impinge on the actions of the object of the impression (the other person); and (3) the processes by which people's evaluative beliefs about another are incorporated into the target's self-impression, thereby influencing that person's actions.

IMPRESSION-BASED BEHAVIOR

It is obvious that our impressions of others will influence our behavior toward them. For example, our actions toward someone about whom we have formed a positive impression will often be quite different from those we express toward a person whom we have evaluated negatively. Of course, this is not always true given the constraints that the Social Context can place on our interpersonal behaviors. A person might think that his boss is an incompetent fool, but because of his need to eat, he might find it impossible to express this impression in her presence.

As scientists, however, social psychologists cannot accept intuitions as fact, no matter how obviously true those intuitions might appear. Consequently, they have performed some interesting demonstrations of the relationship between impressions and social behavior. While these investigations have differed with regard to the specific variables that were studied and the specific procedures that were used, they all shared a common goal—namely, to demonstrate that the same factors that influence perceivers' impressions also affect their actions toward the target of their evaluations.

In the previous chapter, we documented the fact that many variables in the Personal Structure and Social Context influence the formation of impressions. To avoid redundancy, we will not discuss the effects of these factors on a perceiver's overt behaviors. Instead, we will take as specific examples two studies which clearly demonstrate the link between actions and the variables that have been shown to influence impressions. The first study indicates that a feature of the Social Context that influences impressions also influences subsequent actions. The second study shows a similar link between impressions and actions; in this case, however, the variable that influences the relationship is a component of the perceiver's Personal Structure.

Social Context, Impressions, and Behavior

The example of the link between a variable in the Social Context and impressions and actions was conducted by Mark Snyder, Elizabeth Tanke, and Ellen Berscheid (1977). In this study, the researchers attempted to demonstrate that a cue in the Social Context—in this case, the interpersonal environment variable of the other person's physical appearance—could determine the perceiver's actions toward that person. The participants in this demonstration were undergraduates at the University of Minnesota who were paired with a person of the other sex and asked to "get acquainted." For the purposes of this study, this process of getting acquainted took place under somewhat restricted circumstances. Typically, we encounter others and get to know them in face-to-face situations. In this study, however, Snyder and his colleagues placed the members of a subject pair in separate rooms and had them interact with each other via an intercom system. In this way, the investigators could control the social cues that each participant provided the other.

Prior to the beginning of the interaction, the male member of each pair was given a snapshot of his partner.[1] After viewing the photograph, the male provided his initial impressions of his partner by indicating on a questionnaire the extent to which he attributed to her such traits as friendliness, warmth, and attractiveness. Then, the members of each pair were allowed to talk with one another for a period of 10 minutes via the intercom.

---

[1] To simplify the design of the study, female subjects were not provided with photographs of male students.

The subjects did not know that the photos were not pictures of the actual female members of each pair. Instead, each subject had been given one of a preselected set of pictures of undergraduate women whom judges had previously rated as either attractive or unattractive. This procedure allowed the investigators to examine two related questions: (1) were males' impressions before the interactions influenced by the pictures which they had been given? and (2) if different impressions were formed as a consequence of the photographs, did they affect the behavior of the male subjects during the 10-minute interaction? The answer to both of these questions was yes. Snyder et al. (1977) found that the males' impressions of their respective partners before the encounters were strongly influenced by the physical attractiveness of the female with whom they thought they were going to interact. Photographs of attractive women produced more positive impressions than did those of females who had been judged as unattractive. This result and the findings of other studies that we presented in previous chapters indicate that trait inferences and more general impressions are formed on the basis of cues from the interpersonal environment.

Of more importance to present concerns is the finding that the impressions that had developed as a consequence of such limited information as a photograph had a major impact on the males' subsequent actions while "getting acquainted." These interactions were tape recorded and later analyzed by a group of judges who did not know about the photo manipulation. The ratings of these judges revealed that males who had interacted with women whom they believed to be physically attractive were more sociable, warm, interesting, and humorous than were their counterparts who thought that they were paired with an unattractive partner. This result suggests that the impressions formed on the basis of the rather minimal cues provided in the photographs were of sufficient strength to affect the actual behavior of the perceiver. Other research (Snyder & Swann, 1978; Swann & Snyder, 1980; Word, Zanna, & Cooper, 1974; Zanna & Pack, 1975) has produced similar findings.

A number of themes appear to be relevant to the findings of Snyder, Tanke, and Berscheid, and a brief discussion of them should serve to place their results within the framework of the more general impression formation processes presented in Chapters 2 and 7. For example, this study demonstrated that a rather subtle Social Context cue—presenting the perceivers with photographs of persons with whom they (supposedly) were about to have a brief conversation—had a dramatic and relatively enduring impact on perceivers' impressions and actions. Why did this cue weigh so heavily in the Valuation process, and why did it have so pervasive an influence on behavior? In part, the rather substantial impact of the bogus picture was effective because, though it provided only a small amount of information to the male subject about the person with whom he was about to interact, it was all the information that was available to him. Under conditions that provided such minimal information, the degree of Resolution in the Social Context was exceptionally poor; thus, the male subjects were forced to extrapolate or generalize from the very limited number of cues available in the photographs in attempting to form an initial impression of their partner (it will be recalled that Snyder et al. asked each subject to provide an initial impression of his partner before the interaction).

The processes of self-Consistency also played a role in determining the behavior of the male subjects. First of all, in developing their impressions, the male subjects committed a rather common error of attribution by assuming that what is beautiful is good. As discussed in Chapters 2 and 7, we have a tendency to associate a host of positive interpersonal traits with beauty, while ugliness is usually associated with negative qualities. This cognitive process is an example of belief Consistency, since it involves the assumption that positive physical characteristics are associated with positive interpersonal or psychological attributes. Despite the lack of logic in assuming a relationship between physical attractiveness and inner beauty, this relationship has been shown to influence both males' and females' impression formation processes (Dion, Berscheid, & Walster, 1972).

Moreover, once the impression is formed, self-Consistency affects the behaviors that are expressed toward the object of the impression. In the experiment involving the photos, this Consistency between belief and action resulted in the expression of a series of positive, prosocial behaviors on the part of the male subjects who thought they were interacting with an attractive partner, and a series of less positive behaviors on the part of those males who believed that they had been paired with an unattractive female.

The weight given various cues that were available in the Social Context as a result of the time of their occurrence in the experiment also deserves mention. As discussed in the previous chapter, a cue that is perceived early in the impression formation process tends to be accorded greater weight than subsequent cues. As noted, initial impressions tend to persist because self-Consistency moderates the interpretation of later cues that might be relevant to the target of the impression.

In the present case, Snyder et al. (1977) found a remarkable degree of correspondence between initial impressions (before the conversation) and the evaluations that the male subjects made of their partners after they had engaged in a 10-minute interaction. Moreover, they also found that the males' actions during the brief encounter were based more on the impressions that they had formed prior to the encounter than on the initial behaviors of the female with whom they actually were paired. In other words, the cues presented by the females in the initial stages of the interaction weighed less in determining the males' interaction behaviors and postinteraction impressions than did the minimal cues provided earlier by the bogus photographs.

Personal Structure, Impressions, and Behavior

Just as features in the Social Context can affect impressions and actions, so too can the Personal Structures of perceivers. This fact was demonstrated in a study by Messé, Stollak, Larson, and Michaels (1979), which measured the tendencies of some people to systematically distort their impressions of others, and which showed that this perceptual bias was related to their social behavior. More specifically, Messé et al. (1979) developed a 20-minute video-tape of an interaction between an adult and a child, which was presented as excerpts from a series of encounters that had taken place over a long period of time in a playroom. The actions portrayed were chosen to show the child expressing a wide range of behaviors. Some of the behaviors (such as cheating at a game) could be evaluated negatively, others (such as offering to share a treat with the adult) could be seen as positive, but most of the behaviors (such as painting with watercolors or playing with puppets) were rather neutral in tone.

The investigators asked 1,200 undergraduates to view the tape and to report their perceptions of the filmed interactants. Although all respondents saw the same film, their evaluations of the child on the tape varied widely. As noted in Chapter 7, some respondents perceived the child in a very negative fashion, ignoring every positive behavior that was portrayed; others misper-ceived in the opposite direction, evaluating the child in a uniformly positive manner. The bulk of the sample viewed the child's behaviors in a more accurate, balanced manner. Since the behaviors of the child were relatively wide ranging, the investigators felt that one-sided evaluations, either positive or negative, were due to differences in the perceivers' Personal Structures. Messé et al. speculated that these different reactions to the same stimulus person reflected a consistent tendency to evaluate others in positive or negative terms—a *perceptual bias* which caused some respondents to distort the objec-tive evidence provided by the target's behavior.

From the total sample, Messé et al. selected for further study those respondents who were most negatively and positively biased in their evalua-tions along with a subsample of those who were reasonably balanced in their perceptions. They then asked those whom they had selected to interact with a child in a playroom setting similar to the one that they had witnessed on the tape. The children who took part in this research were volunteers from the community who were paid to interact with these undergraduates. Each child was assigned to a single undergraduate, and the interactants had not met prior to their introduction in the playroom.

The play sessions were videotaped and evaluated by a group of trained judges who were unaware of the reasons why the respondents were chosen to participate in the study (that is, they did not know that subjects differed in the extent or direction of their perceptual biases). The findings of this study supported the contention that differences in Personal Structure that are relevant to impression formation also affect perceivers' actions. Messé et al. found that negatively biased subjects were most likely to try to dominate and structure the interaction between themselves and the child. It was as if they could not trust the child to behave appropriately, and thus they allowed the child very little free rein in the playroom. The positively biased and balanced perceivers, on the other hand, were more likely to offer help to the child and comply with the child's wishes, and much less likely to attempt to dominate the interaction.

The results of this study have a number of implications for our understanding of the relationship between impressions and actions. First, the findings suggest that some people are relatively consistent in the weights that they apply to various cues when they engage in Valuation processes about others, and this consistency has an impact on their behavior across a variety of Social Contexts. The negatively biased perceivers observed by Messé et al. not only viewed the child in the videotape in a critical manner, but also responded in a manner that was consistent with such a view of children when actually paired with another child in the playroom setting. These two children had no relationship to one another, yet they elicited similar reactions from the biased undergraduates.

A second implication of this study is that these biases could have some apparent utility for the perceiver, since they tend to increase the Resolution of the Social Context—that is, they tend to produce a more comprehensible interpersonal environment and thus make the Valuation process more automatic. Unfortunately, such biases often are founded on assumptions that are incorrect ("All children are alike"), and they limit persons' abilities to adapt to specific situations and to modify their behavior when conditions change.

Support for this last observation was provided in a second study performed by Messé et al. (1979). In this investigation, both biased and balanced perceivers were asked to discuss points of disagreement with another undergraduate. In this Social Context, it was the positively biased perceivers who acted inappropriately; they were rated as being the least persuasive and friendly and the least able to resolve their differences with the other. It appeared to the judges that the positively biased respondents did not know how to effectively defend their own positions. Across the Social Contexts of both studies, the balanced perceivers were the most flexible and adaptive to the varying demands of the situations in which they found themselves.

In summary, the sets of studies described here are just two examples of the ways in which variables that affect impression formation also influence the overt actions of the perceiver. While research on this issue is not as extensive as is the literature on impression formation per se, current work in this field has produced sufficient evidence to support the speculation that the processes known to influence impressions also have the potential to affect the perceiver's resultant social behavior. In the section that follows, we will discuss another aspect of the link between impressions and overt behavior— the impact of the perceiver's impression on the actions of the target.

BEHAVIORAL REACTIONS TO OTHERS' IMPRESSIONS

Given that there appears to be a strong link between perceivers' impressions and actions, it follows that there is likely to be some relationship between these impression-based actions and the responses of the target of the impression. Social psychologists have produced evidence that supports this contention, and we will briefly examine their findings in this section.

The two sets of studies summarized previously (Messé et al., 1979; Snyder et al., 1977) also produced evidence that the actions of the perceivers affected the responses of the targets of the perception. For example, Snyder et al. found that over the course of the interview, the actions of female subjects were influenced by males' attributions of their attractiveness. The behaviors of the females in the attractive target condition—those women paired with a male who had been led to believe that his partner was beautiful—were judged to be more sociable, more warm, more expressive of enjoyment, and more outgoing than were the behaviors of their counterparts in the unattractive target condition. As Snyder et al. (1977, p. 661) noted, "What had initially been reality in the minds of the men had now become reality in the behavior of the women with whom they had interacted."

Similarly, in the Messé et al. (1979) study, the behaviors of the children in the play setting were related to the perceptual bias of the undergraduate with whom they had interacted. For example, children were least likely to display assertive behaviors when paired with negatively biased perceivers, and most likely to do so when paired with positively biased perceivers. Obviously, the actions of the undergraduates, which were related to their Personal Structures, to some extent shaped the children's subsequent reactions.

Mark Snyder has conducted a program of research that has demonstrated even more dramatically the powerful influence that others' impressions can have on our social behavior with them (Snyder, in press; Snyder & Campbell, 1980; Snyder & Cantor, 1979; Snyder & Gangestad, in press; Snyder & White, 1981).[2] For example, in one study in this program, Snyder and Swann (1978) paired a number of undergraduate females and asked one member of each pair to interview the other. Before the interview began, the experimenter handed each interviewer a brief written description of a person with a specific personality type. Half the subjects received a description of a typical extravert—a person who is outgoing, sociable, energetic, and confident; the remaining subjects received a description of an introvert—someone who is shy, reserved, and distant.

All interviewers were asked to determine the extent to which their partner fit the personality type that had been described to them. To help them in this task, the experimenter provided each interviewer with a list of 26 "topic areas often covered by interviewers," from which they were to choose 12 questions to ask of the other. Of the 26 topic areas, 10 were questions that one would ask of someone known to be an introvert (for example, "In what situations do you wish you could be more outgoing?"), and 11 were questions that one would ask of a known extravert (for example, "What is it about these situations that makes you like to talk?"), while the remaining questions were not specifically relevant to either personality type.

Snyder and Swann monitored the questions that the interviewer chose to ask in these encounters and the responses that the questions elicited from

---

[2] These studies address this issue more directly than those just discussed, since they focus more narrowly on the question of how the behavior of a target is affected by the impression-based actions of a perceiver.

the interviewees. Interestingly, the investigators found that interviewers were influenced in their choices of questions by the personality descriptions that had been given them at the beginning of the study. Those who had been provided with the description of an extravert chose significantly more questions that one would likely ask of a known extravert than did those interviewers who had read the description of the typical introvert; in their inverviews, these latter subjects chose to ask more questions that one would ask of an introvert. It seems likely that the interviewers inferred from the personality descriptions given them that they would be interacting with a person of that type, although the experimenter gave no indication whatsoever that this would be the case.

Of more importance to present concerns were the behaviors of the interviewees. As mentioned, the conversations that took place between the subjects during the interviews were recorded. The interviewees' responses were subsequently evaluated by a group of trained judges who did not know which personality description the interviewers had been given—in fact, they never heard what the interviewers said, but only the answers of the interviewees. Nonetheless, the judges detected strong differences between the two groups of respondents. The actions of those respondents who had been paired with an interviewer who had read the extravert description were judged to reflect greater confidence, poise, and extraversion than did the behaviors of those respondents paired with an interviewer who had read the introvert description. This finding is striking because it suggests that interviewees acted to confirm the erroneous hypotheses that the interviewers had formed regarding them.

A second investigation that demonstrates the powerful impact of the perceiver's expectations on the behavior of the target was conducted by Carl Word, Mark Zanna, and Joel Cooper (1974). This study was undertaken to examine the validity of a widely held belief in the business community which is often used to explain the differential hiring rates of black and white job applicants: black people are not hired for jobs they seek because they do not present themselves as well as white people in job interview situations. This purported difference in applicant behavior is typically attributed to differences in the Personal Structures of black and white applicants. Word et al. (1974) explored an intriguing alternate possibility—namely, that the behaviors of applicants in job interviews might be more a consequence of the interviewer's behavior (the interpersonal environment in which the applicants find themselves) than of differences among the applicants' social skills (Personal Structure characteristics).

To examine this set of possible explanations, Word et al. (1974) carefully trained two experimental accomplices to play the role of job interviewers so that they could interact in a systematic, controlled manner with naive subjects who were playing the role of job applicants in a simulated interview.

In a preliminary study that was conducted to determine how their interviewers should act, Word et al. (1974) had white subjects interview both black and white high school students (accomplices of the experimenters) who played the role of job applicants. The researchers found that the subjects expressed very different behaviors depending on the race of the applicant whom they had interviewed, despite the fact that all accomplices (both black and white) had been trained to behave identically. When the applicant was black, for example, interviewers maintained greater spatial distance between themselves and the applicant, made more speech errors, and conducted shorter interviews. Word et al. used this information to train the interviewers in their second study to mimic the pattern of behaviors expressed by the subject interviewers in their first study. For one condition of the second study, the interviewers were trained to display the kinds of actions that naive subjects in the first study had displayed toward the black job applicants; for the other condition, the interviewers were trained to act as the naive subjects had when they interacted with a white job applicant. Each of the accomplices then interviewed a number of naive subjects (all of whom were white undergraduates) who, as noted, were asked to pretend that they were job applicants being interviewed for employment.

The impact of the various patterns of interviewer behavior on the actions of the naive job applicants in Word et al.'s second study was substantial. Those subject applicants whose interviewer displayed distancing behaviors and high rates of speech disruptions were judged by trained raters to have acted much less competently in the interview than those whose interviewer displayed the more positive pattern of behaviors. These results suggest that, as Word and his colleagues had speculated, any differences in the behaviors of black and white job applicants are more likely to be a product of interviewers' actions than of variations in the Personal Structures of the applicants. Other research (Farina, Allen, & Saul, 1968) has yielded similar results.

Taken together, the studies by Snyder and his colleagues and Word et al. suggest that impingement processes can have a major influence on the patterns of behaviors expressed in social encounters of perceivers and targets. As noted, there is ample evidence that people's impressions, interpretations, or expectations involving another person can affect the way the person acts. These impression-based behaviors are an important component of the other person's (the target's) Social Context and as such, influence the target's behavior. The pioneering social psychologist George Herbert Mead was one of the first scientists to note that one person's perceptions and actions can impinge on the actions of another. He coined the term *definition of the situation* to describe this phenomenon (Mead, 1934).

Perhaps a dramatic, more real-life example will help to illustrate these processes to which Mead devoted so much of his creative energies. This example is drawn from the film *The Hustler,* which portrays the education of Fast Eddie Belsen, a pool hustler. Early in the movie, Fast Eddie (played by Paul Newman) challenges the reigning king of the hustlers, Minnesota Fats (played by Jackie Gleason). What ensues is a marathon match in which both participants perform feats of pool virtuosity (and bourbon drinking) that leave most viewers breathless with amazement.

As the match draws on, the participants begin to show signs of the stress and physical fatigue that naturally occur under such conditions of

The contest between Fast Eddie Belsen and Minnesota Fats illustrates how appearance cues can help define the situation for the participants.

prolonged conflict. The hours of pool shooting and whiskey guzzling are obviously taking their toll on both shooters. The skills of both men are so exceptional and they appear so evenly matched that the viewer begins to suspect that the contest will never end. Then, after many hours of cue-to-cue combat, there is a subtle turning point—Fats excuses himself from the table for a moment, goes to another room to clean up, and returns to the match appearing refreshed and immaculate. Fast Eddie, who has remained disheveled and unkempt, makes some facetious remarks about Fats's dramatically improved appearance. From that point on, however, Fats begins to control the game and ultimately triumphs over his younger opponent.

Fast Eddie leaves the table defeated and bewildered. He does not understand how he lost, as he remains convinced that he is the better pool shooter. Only later in the movie does the outcome begin to make some sense to him. As explained to him by a wise but evil companion, Fast Eddie had lost the match because he allowed Fats to "define the situation" by taking the time to tidy up his appearance. By this action, Fats subtly impinged on Fast Eddie's behavior; the challenger was now cast in the role of a disheveled, weary young upstart, whose sloppy appearance reflected the fact that he was a loser. Though he had possessed the skills to win, he had accepted the meaning of Fats's actions—namely, that Fats was a superior person, a winner. Given this definition, it was not possible for Eddie to triumph.

This memorable scene parallels the situation that Word et al. (1974) constructed in their job interview experiment. There, the obviously ill-at-ease interviewer, by creating distance between himself and the interviewee, stumbling in his speech, and abruptly terminating the interview, defined the situation in a way that demonstrated to the applicant that he was not fit for the position. It is not surprising that an applicant performed poorly, given the definition of the situation provided by the interviewer's behavior. Similarly, the interviewees in the Snyder and Swann (1977) study appeared to accept the definition of the situation that was reflected in the types of questions asked of them—introversion-related items elicited introverted responses while extraversion-related questions were answered in an extraverted fashion.

Mutual Interplay of Perceiver and Target

Up to this point in our presentation, we have discussed social encounters in a rather unidirectional manner—that is, interactants have been designated as either perceivers or targets. Obviously, however, this portrayal is too simplistic to reflect the vast majority of actual interpersonal interactions. In most encounters, the roles of target and perceiver shift from moment to moment; all participants are simultaneously perceivers and targets, and each person's behaviors serve to define the situation for the others. The idea that every person in a social encounter is both a perceiver and a target adds an intriguing level of complexity to the analysis of social behavior. However, for the sake of comprehensibility, it has been necessary to discuss these processes as if each interactant always assumed one or the other of these roles within any given encounter. It seems reasonable to assume, however, that the processes that we identify in our more simplified examples operate in the same fashion in more complex, real-world settings.

Two other important considerations need to be raised at this point. First, while it is true that every participant in a social situation potentially has an influence on the actions of the other participants—that is, a person's actions can contribute to the others' definitions of the situation—not all of these definitional actions are intentional. As such, they are not necessarily impingements which, as discussed in Chapter 2, are purposive acts designed to control the actions of another. However, we assume that many definitional actions are, indeed, attempts at impingement, since such behaviors often contribute to the satisfaction of a pervasive concern—self-Consistency.

Once an impression is formed, it becomes part of the perceiver's system of beliefs and, as such, is usually resistant to change.[3] A major process which contributes to this resistance to change is self-Consistency. The reader may recall from Chapter 3 that the elements of a person's system of beliefs tend toward balance or stability; thus, any new, potentially relevant information is processed so as to insure a good fit with the existing elements, if possible.

---

[3] As with all components of our Personal Structures, the extent to which an impression is resistant to change is dependent upon its level of importance to us. As noted in the previous chapter, all impressions are at least somewhat resistant to modification.

In addition, people tend to act in ways to promote outcomes that are consistent with their preexisting beliefs. Thus, an impression not only guides an individual's actions toward another—thereby maintaining Consistency between the perceiver's beliefs and actions—but also impinges on the other's range of possible responses. The degree to which the impingement on the other is successful determines the extent to which the target's behavior confirms, or is consistent with, the perceiver's impression.

A real-life incident which exemplifies this idea occurred during the high school years of one of the authors of this text, when he was a student in an 11th-grade composition class. The instructor in the class, Mrs. Rice, was a dedicated if somewhat single-minded teacher. One of the instructional techniques which she employed was peer evaluation of students' essays. Every time the author and his classmates handed in an essay, it was first judged on a four-point scale by three other students in the class. Then Mrs. Rice read the essay, considered the other students' evaluations and comments, and determined the ultimate grade for the work. She felt that students could learn by being exposed to the work of others, as well as profit from the comments of others about their own writing; of course, she also believed that her own comments (and grade) were the most valuable and accurate feedback.

One of the members of this class was Dick Forman, whose major academic interests were science and technology. Dick wanted to become an engineer. He loved to tinker, and most of his hobbies involved a mechanical gadget of some sort. Dick was far from the most outstanding student in Mrs. Rice's class; he was bright enough, but he was not really interested in literature and English composition, and the quality of his work in the class reflected this lack of interest.

On one occasion, Mrs. Rice listed on the balckboard a number of alternative essay topics and instructed the members of the class to choose one as a writing assignment. By chance, one of the topics listed, "How ——— Work," was just the sort of issue that Dick found most intriguing. He had long been involved with airplanes: his father was a licensed pilot; he himself was taking flying lessons; and for many years he was an avid builder of flying model airplanes. Consequently, it was no surprise when Dick submitted an essay entitled "How Airplanes Work."

Every student who read Dick's essay, including the author of this text, agreed that it was one of the best pieces of writing that they had encountered in the class. It was clear, informative, concise, and interesting—and it really explained how airplanes fly! Each reader independently gave the essay a perfect score, accompanied by lavish praise for the clarity with which the paper explained a complicated phenomenon.

Unfortunately, Mrs. Rice had already formed the impression that Dick was a poor writer. Such high-quality writing was quite inconsistent with this belief, and thus she found it very difficult to accept this work as his own. After reading the essay herself, Mrs. Rice confronted Dick in front of the class and demanded that he explain in his own words the workings of airplanes. Ordinarily, such a request would have been easy for him—indeed, this was one of his favorite subjects. In this instance, however, Dick could do nothing but stammer and reply in a most inarticulate manner. His actions thus served to confirm Mrs. Rice's suspicions that the essay was not his own work, a suspicion that was reflected in the grade on Dick's paper.

It goes without saying that this outcome was unfair. Dick actually had written the essay himself, and he deserved the praise which he had received for it from his fellow students, who knew that the topic of his essay was near and dear to his heart. Mrs. Rice, however, had formed an impression that Dick was a mediocre student in her class, and she was unaware of his great interest in and extensive experience with aircraft. Dick's single performance was so inconsistent with his previous efforts in the class that it violated Mrs. Rice's beliefs about him, and she acted so as to reestablish some degree of Consistency between her impression and his behavior. She did so by establishing an uncomfortable Social Context for Dick, wherein he had to defend himself in front of the entire class against the subtle accusation that he was a cheat. Obviously, such an interaction was highly anxiety-evoking, and it is not surprising that Dick did not perform well. This story provides a vivid, if unfortunate, example of the manner in which impression-based behaviors can impinge on the actions of a target, and of the role that self-Consistency plays in the maintenance of impressions.

People engage in impression-based impingement attempts for many other reasons. For example, a variety of motives and personality traits appear to generate such attempts rather frequently. The need for dominance—a concern with being in charge of social situations—often appears to be a major motivating force for such forms of impingements. Other traits, such as Machiavellianism—the tendency to manipulate the actions of others merely to demonstrate to oneself that one can—also appear to be bases for impression-based impingement. Since individuals differ in the extent to which these and other relevant characteristics are important components of their Personal Structures, it follows that people will vary somewhat in the frequency with which their impression-based behaviors are intentional attempts to Control the actions of others.

A second, related point involves the variables that determine the extent to which impression-based impingement attempts are successful. As with most social behaviors, a number of factors in the Social Context and in the Personal Structure of the interactants appear to affect the outcome of these behavior control processes. For example, the degree of Resolution of the Social Context appears to play a major role in the success or failure of an impingement. When social situations are rather novel (that is, in circumstances in which our well-learned habits do not apply), people will search for any available cues with which to guide their behavior. In such instances, the impression-based behaviors expressed by others provide some indication of the proper action. Thus, in Social Contexts of high ambiguity (or low Resolution), impression-based behaviors are likely to have their greatest impact on the actions of a target.

A dramatic example of the ways in which novelty and Resolution influence the success of impression-based impingements is provided by Phillip Zimbardo's description of the social psychology of police interrogations. In his discussion, Zimbardo (1967) summarizes some of the procedures recommended in police training manuals designed to compel suspects to admit to crimes. It is interesting that most of these recommended methods depend upon the establishment of a sense of poor Resolution in the hapless suspect. For example, these manuals recommend that the suspect be interrogated in an unfamiliar environment, away from friends and acquaintances. In this way, the suspect is confronted with a very novel Social Context, whose definition is controlled by the police.

Moreover, these manuals propose ways in which the police can generate an atmosphere which suggests "the invincibility of the law." The interrogating officer

> should bring the full weight of his personality to bear. . . . He must seize and maintain full control of the interview. . . . Small gestures which help establish his authority include telling the suspect where to sit, and telling him he cannot smoke. . . . The suspect is at a disadvantage which is intensified in every way possible.   (Zimbardo, 1967, p. 25).

© BILL POWERS/TRICORN PHOTOS

As Zimbardo notes, police interrogations are designed to make the suspect dependent on the police for the definition of the situation.

All of these tactics enhance the ambiguity of the encounter for the suspect and emphasize his or her dependency on the police to define the situation. Obviously, the police have defined the suspect as guilty or they would not have him or her in custody. Thus, they work to define the situation in a manner that is compatible with this belief, and the suspect often uses this definition in resolving the ambiguous context that the police have purposely constructed. In this way, the probability of a successful interrogation is maximized. Zimbardo asserts that these methods of impingement are so powerful that they often work even when the suspect did not, in fact, commit the offense as charged.

Factors in the target's Personal Structure have also been found to affect the extent to which impingements are successful. Perhaps the individual characteristic which is the most relevant determinant of the success or failure of an impingement attempt is field dependence. This component of the Personal Structure refers to the differential tendency in people to rely upon contextual cues in making decisions. In our terms, highly field-dependent individuals will be more influenced in their Valuations and subsequent actions by cues in the Social Context than by internally derived information (such as norms or habits). Much of the work on field dependence was performed by Herman Witkin and his associates (Witkin, Dyk, Faterson, Goodenough, & Karp, 1962; Witkin, Oltman, Raskin, & Karp, 1971), who have demonstrated that this characteristic of the Personal Structure plays a major role in determining persons' susceptibility to environmental cues.

One study involving field dependence should serve to illustrate how differences in this Personal Structure variable can affect the degree to which impingements succeed in directing persons' actions. In this study, Les Greene (1976) observed the behaviors of 80 females who were clients of a weight reduction clinic. The participants were identified as either high or low in field dependence by means of the Embedded Figures Test, one of the standard measures of this variable which Witkin and his associates had developed earlier (Witkin et al., 1971). Participation in the weight reduction clinic involved meeting with a counselor who, over the course of the treatment, made specific recommendations regarding sensible dietary practices.

These sessions were videotaped and later evaluated by trained judges who assessed the extent to which the clients expressed agreement with the counselor's suggestions. The highly field-dependent subjects were found to be much more likely to agree with the recommendations of their counselor than were those who had been rated low in field dependence. These results suggest that within the identical Social Context (the diet clinic), differences in the individual clients' susceptibility to impingement attempts were a product of variations in relevant components of their Personal Structures.

Another factor in the target which moderates the success of an impression-based impingement attempt is self/other Consistency. It is likely that the extent to which the perceiver is a credible, high level referent for the target affects the weight that the target accords the perceiver's impression-based actions. For example, suppose that while at a party, a person with whom you are conversing about hairstyles remarks, "I think that your hair would look much better if you parted it on the other side." If this individual had established some credibility with respect to this issue—if he was a friend of yours whose taste you admired—his suggestion would carry much greater weight than if it had been offered by someone whom you had just met. In the former instance, you might consider and act on the suggestion; in the latter case, this seems to be a much less probable outcome.

LONG-TERM CONSEQUENCES OF IMPRESSION-BASED BEHAVIORS

We have now explored two important behavioral consequences of the formation of impressions: (1) perceivers act toward others in ways that are consistent with impressions of them; and (2) impression-based actions, in turn, can influence the overt responses of the targets of the impression. We will now turn our attention to a third important link between impression formation and social behavior: the long-term consequences of perceivers' impressions on targets' behaviors and thoughts.

In the study by Greene (1976) cited earlier, it is important to note that although the field-dependent clients expressed agreement with the counselor's recommendations, they did not lose more weight than their field-independent counterparts; in fact, the field-dependent clients seemed less successful than were the field-independent clients in actually following the recommended diet. Apparently, the success of the counselor in impinging on the actions of the field dependent targets was limited primarily to the confines of the weight reduction clinic, and long-term effects on these clients' eating or dieting behaviors were negligible. This finding is far from unusual. Indeed, as noted throughout this book, while the typical outcome of impingements is immediate compliance, such acquiescence is often transitory.

This is not to say that impression-based impingements cannot have long-term effects on targets' behaviors. Under the appropriate circumstances, they do; we will now explore two types of variables that mediate the extent to which impressions have a continuing influence on a target. One class of variables involves the degree to which the perceiver has control over, and can manipulate, the target's Social Context. A second class of variables involves the extent to which a person's self-impression is influenced by the impressions of others.

Cue Control

In their influential treatise on social psychology, Edward E. Jones and Harold Gerard (1967) coined the term *cue control* to refer to circumstances in which one person has the ability to structure and control the Social Context of another. In situations such as these, the person in control can influence the thoughts and behaviors of the target by limiting the cues available to the target; by doing so, the controller can have a substantial impact on the target's

Valuation processes. Since the Valuation decisions which people make have strong implications for their actions, cue control can be a powerful tool for shaping behavior. Examples of pervasive cue control are provided by custodial institutions, such as a prisons, as well as by the typical child-rearing situation in which parents have almost complete control over the environment of the youngster.

A vivid picture of the impact of cue control on the thoughts and behaviors of the targets of this form of pervasive influence is provided in the many sociological and social psychological analyses of the interpersonal environment of the mental hospital. In a study that attracted national attention, David Rosenhan and seven of his students gained insiders' views of mental institutions by securing admission as patients to 12 different hospitals by reporting that they heard voices (Rosenhan, 1973). After having reported this symptom, all were placed almost immediately in the psychiatric wards of the hospitals to which they had applied. Rosenhan's group did this in order to study first-hand the Social Context that was experienced by the inhabitants of these institutions. What they found provides compelling evidence to support the position that cue control can be a pervasive force in shaping people's behaviors.

Almost every feature of the physical and interpersonal environments that the researchers and their fellow patients experienced continuously served to reinforce the view that they were bizarre, something less than human, and obviously not capable of caring for themselves—in other words, crazy. For instance, in some cases, the physical examination conducted as part of the admission process took place in a semipublic setting. Once on the ward, the bogus patients were exposed to countless indications of their inferior status. For example, staff members often carried on discussions about patients' problems right in the front of them, as if patients could not understand what the staff members were saying. Staff members generally avoided eye contact with the patients and rarely answered their questions. Responses by the staff to patients' complaints about this inconsiderate treatment indicated that such protests were viewed merely as further evidence of the patient's maladjustment. Under these conditions, it was not surprising that many of the inmates exhibited bizarre, helpless, and childlike behaviors.

These observations should not be taken to mean that the patients in these settings did not need help and were merely the victims of an inhumane treatment system. Most had severe psychological problems which were manifested in unusual and maladaptive behaviors. The point of this discussion, however, is that the cues present in these institutions could serve only to exacerbate the patients' problems rather than help solve them. The environment of these treatment facilities provided a milieu that systematically promoted the manifestation of abnormal symptomology. The cues controlled by the administration and staff of these mental institutions continually reinforced the patient's self-impression that he or she was insane. Given these institutions' overwhelming control over almost every aspect of their lives, it was pointless for the patients to act otherwise.

THE MUSEUM OF MODERN ART/FILM STILLS ARCHIVE

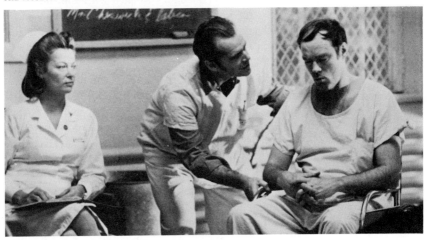

As the movie 'One flew over the cuckoo's nest' graphically illustrates, the physical and interpersonal environments of many mental institutions reinforce the view that patients are 'crazy.'

Compelling evidence of the role which environmental cues play in the manifestation of abnormal behavior is provided by the work of George W. Fairweather. For many years, Fairweather and his associates (Fairweather, 1964; Fairweather, Sanders, & Tornatzky, 1974) have studied the effects of placing people diagnosed as mentally ill in settings whose cues indicate that they are perceived as human beings who are capable of functioning in the "real world." In one of these studies, Fairweather and his associates relocated institutionalized mental patients in lodges—patient-administered halfway houses located in the outside community. The lodges provided the patients a comfortable and secure environment, and although they lived in these semi-protected circumstances, the patients interacted with the outside community by holding jobs, being responsible for the upkeep of their lodge, buying and cooking their own food, and so on. While not completely free, the lodge inhabitants had substantially more freedom (and responsibility) than they had experienced in their previous location. Thus, the cues in the Social Context of the lodge were very different from those in the psychiatric ward and presented the patients with a radically different definition of their situation.

Numerous measures of the patients' behaviors were gathered and compared to those obtained from a comparable sample of patients who remained institutionalized. These data indicated that the lodge members displayed substantially fewer symptoms of psychological problems than did their counterparts who had not been relocated. These findings demonstrate that the comprehensive alteration of the patients' Social Context greatly reduced the behavioral symptoms which they had expressed in the more typical institutional environment. It should be stressed that these results were not only obtained from patients exhibiting mild disturbances. In many instances, Fairweather and his colleagues worked with and induced dramatic improvements in the behavior of chronic mental patients who had been confined for years to the back wards of mental hospitals. Clearly, altering the cues that comprise a person's Social Context can have a powerful impact on that person's behavior.

In addition, the research of Rosenhan and his associates provides evidence that the pervasive cue control which characterizes the mental ward affects the behavior of the other participants in this Social Context—the hospital staff members. These individuals were confronted with many of the same cues that affected the patients—the physical environment which included barred windows and locked doors; and the interpersonal environment which included the appearance and actions of the other staff members as well as those of the patients.

Under these conditions, the staff members' behavior was perhaps as highly controlled as that of the patients. This conclusion is supported by some dramatic evidence that Rosenhan obtained. As part of this investigation, Rosenhan and his associates decided that as soon as they had been admitted, they would begin to act normally again. Thus, once admitted to the ward, they no longer reported hearing voices, they did and said nothing that would be indicative of having psychological problems, and in fact, they behaved as they usually did.

It might be expected that the improvement in the behavior of the bogus patients would have been recognized rather quickly and would have elicited appropriate responses from the staff members of the hospitals. At the very least, the staff members might have behaved differently toward these patients than toward those who continued to manifest signs of severe behavior disorders. This was far from the case, however. Despite their normal behavior, Rosenhan and his associates continued to be treated as if they were mentally ill. Though they exhibited no abnormal symptoms, they were still plied with numerous psychoactive drugs (more than 2,000 pills were given to the research team during the brief duration of the study). Moreover, members of the staff interpreted the bogus patients' every behavior as one more indication of illness. For example, in collecting their data for this study, Rosenhan and his students took notes about their experiences while in the hospital environment. The staff interpreted this behavior as further evidence of their paranoid delusions.

There was little that the patients could do to "prove" their sanity. The Social Context, as constructed by the hospital administration, almost totally determined the interpretation of the cues emitted by the patients. Thus, the contradictory information provided by the actions of the bogus patients was misread so as to be consistent with the more dominant cues of the institutional setting—that is, the staff's impressions of the patients were strongly influenced by the cues that pervaded the mental hospital. In many ways, the cue control that characterized this setting operated more forcefully on the behavior of the staff than on the patients themselves!

Impression-Based Incorporation

Control of the cues that are present in a Social Context is only one of the principal processes by which impressions can have a long-term influence on actions. Another, perhaps even more powerful means involves the process of incorporation. In many cases, perceivers' impressions are accepted by the target and incorporated into his or her self-definition. For example, if parents perceive a child as "rotten from the day he was born," it is likely that they will act on this perception and actually produce a child who fulfills these expectations. Conversely, parents who perceive their child as worthwhile and who act accordingly will generally have a child who incorporates this impression, and likewise confirms the parents' expectations.

Many psychological theories subscribe to this view in their explanations of the manner in which people develop their characteristic patterns of behavior. For example, such diverse theorists as George Herbert Mead, whose ideas have had a profound impact on the field of sociology, and Carl Rogers, the renowned psychologist who originated client-centered therapy, have postulated that the impression-based behaviors of others can have a major impact on targets' beliefs about themselves (Mead, 1934; Rogers, 1959). This is especially true under conditions in which the impression-based behaviors are a continuous feature of the target's interpersonal environment, as is typically the case in parent-child relationships.

In a sense, the expectations that a perceiver develops often become self-fulfilling prophecies (Jones, 1977; Merton, 1957). This is so because the expectations are incorporated by the target, thereby becoming a part of the target's belief system; and since beliefs about the self are of such importance to an individual—that is, they tend to be high level—they will have a pervasive impact on the person's behavior. In short, through incorporation processes, impressions by others can become enduring self-impressions which, in turn, affect one's long-term behaviors.

One of the more interesting research examples of the long-term impact of perceivers' impressions on the behavior of targets is an investigation by Robert Rosenthal and Lenore Jacobson into the effects that teachers' expectations about the abilities of their students can have on these students' actual academic performances. In an experiment which stimulated considerable controversy, Rosenthal and Jacobson (1968) evaluated the students of an elementary school with a test that purportedly identified those who could be expected to make remarkable academic and intellectual gains over the course of the school year. In fact, the test was really a measure of mental ability (Flanagan, 1960) and had nothing whatever to do with predicting the probability of great academic or intellectual leaps. It was misidentified so as to induce teachers to form expectations (or impressions) that certain of their students would be likely to make noteworthy gains during the coming academic year.

After giving teachers the names of their students who could be expected to experience unusual academic progress—in actuality, these students were picked at random—Rosenthal and Jacobson waited until the school year was nearly complete and then readministered the same test of mental ability. The reported results of this investigation were startling. A substantial number of the identified students actually did show remarkable improvement in their test scores. On the average, these students outpaced their peers in terms of intellectual development. This occurred although there was no actual basis for differentiating the two groups of children, since the names of the "fast developers" had been picked at random. The only difference between the two groups of students was that one group of children was identified to the teachers as likely to gain, while the other group was not.

As noted, this research generated some controversy, since a number of social scientists (Elashoff & Snow, 1971; Thorndike, 1968) were critical of the procedures and analytic methods employed by Rosenthal and Jacobson (1968). However, later studies have generally supported the proposition that teachers' expectations can have a considerable impact on children's achievement (Crano & Mellon, 1978; Rubovitz & Maehr, 1971; Seaver, 1973; Taylor, 1979). These studies, and many others like them, provide ample evidence that perceivers' impressions can have enduring consequences for targets' behaviors.

The results of this research strongly suggest that teachers' initial impressions of their students often affect their own actions toward these students. For example, it is likely that on the basis of the information given them, the teachers in Rosenthal and Jacobson's study had formed an impression of some of their students that led them to expect that these individuals would display unusual academic growth during the course of the school year. Based on our previous discussion of the link between perceivers' impressions and their subsequent behavior, it is likely that the teachers' impressions affected their actions toward the identified children. Given their positive impressions, the teachers probably paid more attention to these students, were warmer towards them, and were more concerned about their progress. Research that followed the Rosenthal and Jacobson (1968) study, in fact, has supported these speculations (Brophy & Good, 1970, 1974).

Displays of attention, praise, and concern on the part of a teacher would have positive consequences for a child's self-impression, which might in turn facilitate his or her later test performance. How could such a process occur? One possible explanation was proposed by Crano and Mellon (1978). They speculated that when children's self-impressions of their academic abilities had improved as a result of positive classroom experiences, they should feel more secure in this setting. As a consequence, these more confident children would be less anxious, be more willing to participate in classroom activities, and thus be better able to meet future academic challenges.

Our discussion to this point has emphasized the positive consequences of teachers' impressions on children's academic performance. It should be noted, however, that the processes of impression-based incorporation can have negative consequences as well. Within the classroom setting, for example, Sutherland and Goldshmid (1974) found evidence which suggests that teachers' negative impressions can have destructive effects on children's academic performances. These researchers measured teachers' impressions of their students early in the school year, along with the children's academic abilities. Three months later, they retested the children and found that teachers' negative impressions were associated with a decrease in the children's performances on the standardized test of ability. Similarly, Rist (1970) discovered that teachers expected poorer performance from those of their students who dressed poorly or were less articulate, and that these initial negative impressions were consistent with the children's subsequent performances.

Consistent with both of these sets of findings, Crano and Mellon (1978) found that the initial impressions of a large group of elementary school teachers in England and Wales were most negative toward children from the lower socioeconomic strata and that such negative attributions were strongly related to these children's poorer academic performances as measured over the course of four years. It is important to note that the teachers' impressions were based on little evidence relevant to academic performance, since these impressions were collected very early in the school year. Nevertheless, they had a very strong influence on the children's subsequent achievement.

These studies, in total, indicate that negative as well as positive outcomes can result from the incorporation of others' impressions. But impression-based incorporation and its effects are not limited to classroom settings. Indeed, such phenomena occur in the Social Contexts of the mental hospital— which we considered in our discussion of cue control—as well as other custodial institutions, such as prisons, concentration camps, and dormitories. Such effects, however, probably occur with greatest regularity and have their greatest impact within the context of the family. As noted above, an assertion that is common to many theories of human behavior (Horney, 1945; Mead, 1934; Rogers, 1959; Sullivan, 1953) is that the impressions and expectations that parents form and transmit to their children have profound effects on the children's Personal Structures.

Unfortunately, while intuitively appealing, the systematic evidence that supports this assumption is not conclusive. The paucity of definitive evidence is not surprising, given the difficulty inherent in studying this important issue. For instance, suppose that a mother has a very negative impression of her five-year-old child and, sure enough, the child exhibits a great many behavior problems in his first year of school. Were the child's problems caused by the mother's negative impression? Or was the impression merely an accurate reflection of negative aspects of the child's earlier behavior, which were replayed when he reached first grade? It is very difficult to answer questions of this type, because of the problems involved in validly determining the time in the parent-child relationship at which the critical component of the impression emerged, and why it emerged.

However, there is considerable indirect evidence that supports the presumption that parental impressions become incorporated as high level beliefs in their children's Personal Structures. First, there is good reason to believe that the findings generated in the classroom setting can be generalized to

DAVID S. STRICKLER/THE PICTURE CUBE

Parents can transmit their impressions and expectations about their children in subtle as well as obvious ways.

the home environment as well. Second, some research (Broussard, 1978; Ferguson, Partyka, & Lester, 1974; Stollak, Messé, Michaels, Buldain, Catlin & Paritee, in press) has established that there is a relationship between parental impressions of their children and the later behaviors and Personal Structures of these children. Ferguson et al. (1974), for example, measured a group of parents regarding their impressions of their children. Some of these children had been referred to a psychological clinic for counseling. The parental impressions of these children were extremely negative. Relative to the parents of a comparable group of nonreferred children, the clinic-referred children were seen by their parents as more impulsive, moody, and incompetent. This pattern of findings is not surprising since, as noted, the negatively evaluated children had been referred to a clinic for behavior problems. However, their parents' impressions of them were so extremely negative that these perceptions appeared to range well beyond the specific problems for which the children were brought for help.

Using a behavior checklist, Ferguson et al. (1974, p. 175) found that the parents of the clinic-referred children reported a virtual litany of shortcomings that they had perceived in their children. The range of such complaints about their children ran the gamut from behavior problems to physical appearance. For example, these parents were much more likely than the parents of the comparison group children to agree with the following descriptions of their child:

> Seems to do things just to get others angry at him (her).
> Doesn't pay attention to what grownups say to him (her).
> Quickly loses interest in an activity.
> Has uncontrollable outbursts of temper.
> Acts as if everyone were against him (her).
> Seems selfish, always wants his (her) own way.
> Bullies younger children.
> Doesn't seem to care about how he (she) looks—often looks sloppy.
> Is fidgety and restless.
> Looks awkward when he (she) moves around.
> Appears stiff in walking and moving about.
> Has trouble finding the right words to say what he (she) means.

Some of these impression-based attributions no doubt reflected parents' actual (negative) experiences with their troubled children. The extremity and scope of these negative attributions, however, suggest that the impressions were not totally a consequence of the children's misbehavior. That such parents found their children sloppy, awkward, stiff, fidgety, as well as inarticulate, impulsive, and aggressive, implies an unrealistically negative impression of their offspring. (Should a child with behavior problems necessarily walk more stiffly or look more awkward than a child without such psychological difficulties?) Furthermore, these biased impressions might well have played a functional role in the generation and development of the children's original problems, rather than merely acting as distorted reactions to the children's actual behaviors.

Stollak et al. (in press) present evidence which supports the idea that biased impressions in at least one parent (fathers) are associated with their children's behavior problems. In this study, the perceptual bias of parents of a group of third-grade children was assessed, using the same measure of perceptual bias as Messé et al. (1979), whose study was noted earlier. Stollak and his associates found that fathers of children whom teachers and peers had rated as having problems with adjustment were more negatively biased in their perceptions of children than were the fathers of children seen by others as well-adjusted. Thus, it appears that parents whose impression formation processes are subject to negative bias or distortion are likely to have children who manifest behavior problems as they develop.

There also is some evidence to indicate that the process by which parental impressions affect the development of their children's Personal Structures begins very early in life. Elsie Broussard and her associate, M. S. Hartner (Broussard, 1976, 1978; Broussard & Hartner, 1970, 1971) have extensively studied this issue and have found that parental impressions formed as early as one month after the birth of the child have a profound effect on the child's psychological well-being as much as 11 years later!

Broussard has conducted a long-term developmental investigation of mother-child relationships. She began by asking a large group of mothers of one-month-old, first-born children to fill out a questionnaire which asked them to provide their ideas about what the "average" baby is like and to predict specifically what their own babies would be like. She then collected psychological assessments of these youngsters when they were 4½ and 11 years old. Her findings indicated a strong relationship between the mothers' early impressions of the child and the child's later psychological condition. Children were much more likely to manifest symptoms of psychological problems at both 4 and 11 years of age if their mothers had formed a negative impression of them as newborn infants.

Based on her work on mother-child relations over this period of years, Broussard (1978, p. 44) concluded:

> The mother's perception [of her infant] seems to be influenced by factors within herself rather than the actual physical condition or behavior of the infant. The way the mother relates to her child is based upon her perception. How she handles the infant will affect its behavior.

In support of these observations, she reports that when interacting with their children, mothers with negative impressions made statements like: "Can't you leave me alone?" "I feel like giving you away," and "You're so bad!" In contrast, those mothers whose initial impressions were more favorable typically interacted in more positive and considerate ways: "Who's that pretty girl in the mirror?" (to a 4-month-old child playing with a mirror rattle); or, "You're not ready for me to go? I'll sit here where you can see me" (to a child who was exhibiting signs of distress at his mother's leaving the room) (Broussard, 1978, p. 56). These differences in interaction styles not only reflect differences in mothers' beliefs about their children, but also serve as a means by which such impressions are transmitted and thus incorporated in the child.

Broussard's work on impression-based incorporation suggests that such a process can operate to the detriment of both child and parent. It is important to emphasize, however, that this is not always the case. Recall that the research on teachers' expectations indicated that positive impressions can have positive consequences for the target. Moreover, most of the components of a person's self-impression which result from such incorporation processes are not so obviously positive or negative; rather, they are merely the numerous attributes and expected behaviors which form the bases of other persons' impressions of us, and which we have come to accept as valid and appropriate.

To illustrate this point, consider the issue of sex-role socialization—that is, the manner in which children incorporate the behavioral expectations and other beliefs which the culture defines as appropriate for persons of their sex. Imagine yourself a newborn baby. As you look up from your crib (actually, we know that newborn babies really cannot visually distinguish objects this well, but let's pretend that you can), you see your father peering down at you with a big cigar stuck into the middle of his smile. He looks you over, nods, and turns to your mother and says, "Mona, throw away the pink outfits and give the ribbons to your sister. This kid looks like a chip off the old block." In this example, do you think you're a boy or a girl? Obviously, you are a boy, but as an infant, you only know that you are not supposed to wear pink or ribbons, and that your father thinks that you are just like him.

These sorts of experiences are repeated innumerable times throughout your early childhood. In some instances, the experience explicitly identifies your sex ("Shame on you! Boys don't cry like that over a little scratch.") or the expectations that people have of you because of your sex ("When you're a little older, I'll teach you how to throw a football."). Other experiences serve as negative examples to you ("Look at that stupid girl throwing a fit over a little bug."), while still others are even more subtle (once in a while, Daddy takes you to work with him and lets you sit in his chair).

These countless experiences provide ample grounds for the formation of a component of your self-impression that is probably stronger than any other set of beliefs which you hold about yourself as a human being. Once a person incorporates this impression in its most basic form ("I am a male"), then processes such as self-Consistency serve to enhance and elaborate the belief. Thus, as a young child, once your basic self-impression as a male has developed, you actively begin to seek out information about the proper behavior for people of your sex. Parents, friends, and even strangers are sources of information regarding the ways that you should act as a young boy. They sometimes supply this information by direct instruction, but more often, it is provided indirectly through examples derived from their own behavior. You learn how to be a male from other sources as well: television, movies, and books, all of which present a relatively unified and consistent picture of the role that you are to assume.

Some of the elements of this component of your self-impression (that is, your sex role) can be evaluated in terms of their positive benefit to you (as a male, you should play to win); others are relatively neutral in nature (males should not wear dresses); and still other products of incorporation can be more destructive than helpful (as a male, you should not display your emotions).

In any event, sex roles are acquired in the same manner as our sense of self-worth, our religious and moral beliefs, our sense of fair play, and so on. In other words, no matter what the specific outcome of the incorporated belief, the mechanisms by which it becomes a part of the Personal Structure are very similar.

CONCLUDING REMARKS

The research that we have reviewed indicates that the impressions of others can have a lasting influence on a target. The results of these studies suggest that under the appropriate circumstances, impressions can be incorporated by the target and thus become a part of his or her Personal Structure.

As stressed in Chapter 2, time is a necessary prerequisite for the processes of incorporation to operate. All of the examples of the incorporation of others' impressions were drawn from studies in which there was a considerable passage of time between the measurement of an impression and the assessment of its long-term effect on the target. The classroom situation, the mental institution, and the parent-child relationship are all long-term, continuous, and intensive interactional situations. It is in settings of this type that encounters between perceiver and target are sufficiently frequent to allow an impression to be incorporated. The ubiquitousness and continuity of a particular set of impression-based cues produce a powerful effect on the Personal Structure of the individual.

Taken as a whole, the material presented in this chapter suggests a model that outlines the ways in which impressions influence the behavior of both the holder of the impression and its object or target. As discussed in Chapter 7, impressions may be formed by the operation of any of a number of variables which affect the Valuation process. For example, the perceptual bias variable that has been studied by Messé and Stollak (Messé et al., 1979; Stollak et al., in press) can distort the impression that parents form of their child. Once formed, the impression influences how the perceiver acts toward the target. As noted, a negative bias can cause an adult to see children as untrustworthy and thus attempt to control situations that involve children. The perceiver's attempt to define the situation will succeed to the extent that the child's Social Context is poorly resolved (because of novelty), and that the child's Personal Structure is such that he or she is vulnerable to influence.

If the perceiver's impingement attempt is successful, the target will disproportionately weight these cues in the Valuation process and consequently act in ways that are consistent with the perceiver's impression. With a negatively biased adult, for example, the child who is the target of a successful impingement (who has accepted the perceiver's definition of the situation) will behave in a compliant and nonassertive manner. Moreover, if this encounter is just one instance in a series of similar interactions, and if other cues in the context reinforce those provided by the perceiver's behavior, then the target is likely to incorporate the impression. This incorporation of the impression will result in a modification of the Personal Structure of the target in a direction consistent with the expectations of the perceiver. Thus, in the example, the child's self-impression would be changed in such a way that the child now sees himself or herself as more dependent, less competent, less trustworthy, and so on.

It is important to note that the ultimate outcome described in this model—a target's incorporation of another's impression—is far from inevitable. The failure to satisfy any of the necessary conditions of the model can result in a disruption of the process. First, the Social Context of an encounter may constrain the perceiver from acting on his or her impression.[4] Second, the perceiver's attempt at impingement might fail because the Social Context is well resolved for the target, or because the target's Personal Structure is not amenable to influences of this type. Finally, this experience might be too transitory to produce any lasting impact on the target.

This concludes our discussion of the behavioral products of impression formation. In this and the preceding chapter, we have attempted to demonstrate how the integrative themes are related to the processes and variables which influence beliefs about specific people. In Chapter 7, we discussed the roles that the three cognitive themes (Valuation, Resolution, and Consistency) play in determining the ways in which our beliefs about specific others are formed and maintained. In the present chapter, we reviewed the manner in which the interpersonal theme of Control (impingement and incorporation) also was relevant to person perception processes, especially as these processes pertain to impression-based behaviors. In the next chapter, we will begin more directly to explore interpersonal behavior by considering the rewards and costs which people exchange while interacting.

---

[4] This point is discussed in much greater detail in Chapters 6 and 13.

3

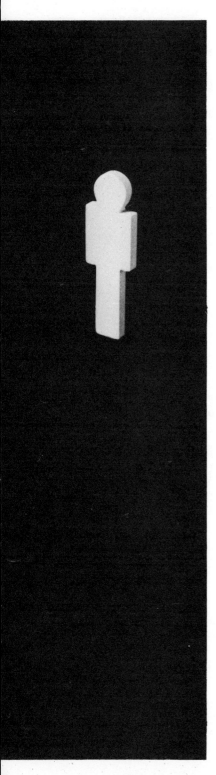

Social Behavior

In this section, we will turn our attention to *social behavior*—the activities in which people engage when they act with, toward, or against others. Since social behavior is the fundamental concern of social psychology, it is not surprising that it has been the focus of much attention in the field for many years.

Social behavior has been studied and discussed with great intensity for two major reasons. First, as social scientists, we wish to understand the processes that affect interpersonal encounters. The variables which control the mutual interplay of people when they interact are of interest in and of themselves. A second reason for the intense scientific activity that has surrounded the study of social behavior is the basic assumption that interpersonal encounters, to a major extent, shape social cognitions—the beliefs, opinions, and impressions to which we have devoted our attention in Section 2 of this text.

To this point, we have discussed the interrelationship of thoughts and behaviors, but our emphasis has been on the internal, cognitive activities which take place within the individual. In the remainder of this book, we will expand our focus and consider more specifically social behavior itself and the variables that affect it. In Section 3, we will examine four major concerns that have occupied the attention of social psychologists in their study of social behavior. In Chapter 9, we will present a general perspective on social behavior, called *social exchange theory,* which conceptualizes interpersonal encounters as exchanges of rewards and costs.

We will use this perspective in Chapter 10 to structure our discussion of the factors in interpersonal encounters that characterize the usually short-term interactions of helping and hurting behaviors. Chapter 11 is focused on the more long-term relationships that evolve when groups of people coordinate their efforts to accomplish some mutually desired goal. In Chapter 12, we will review the research and theory on *interpersonal attraction,* a recent but important preoccupation of social psychology. Finally, in Chapter 13, we will explore the opposite side of the coin—the negative feelings that people acquire about others, such as dislike, hate, and prejudice. Since a general exchange orientation is employed throughout this section, we present a detailed discussion of this approach in Chapter 9.

Social Behavior as Exchange 9

To provide a means by which a vast and complex array of interpersonal activities can be structured, social psychologists have borrowed and expanded an orientation originally developed by economists. Called exchange theory, this way of viewing or analyzing social behavior provides a common framework within which a wide range of social activities can be described and conceptualized. To provide some initial indication of the intuitive appeal of exchange theory, we will begin our discussion with a fictitious example of the events that transpired in a Social Context familiar to most readers.

THE PARTY

As Ted Maddox enters the hall, he surmises that he must be late again, since the party appears to have started without him. Already, small clusters of people have formed, a few people are on the dance floor, the drinks have been poured—for some, apparently more than once—and a general buzz of conversation can be heard along with the music blasting from the stereo. Ted pauses at the entrance for a few moments and looks around. After getting his bearings, he saunters to the end of the line that has formed at the bar. As he slowly moves forward, he notices the young woman in front of him rummaging distractedly through her purse, apparently looking for money with which to pay for her drink. He remains silent and eventually reaches the bar where he orders a beer. Again surveying the scene, he spies his friend Bob sitting among a cluster of people and walks quickly to join him. His friend is engaged in an animated conversation with two people, a male and a female, whom Ted does not recognize.

Parties are an arena for a variety of social behaviors, including, as in the case of Ted and Alice, getting acquainted.

There is an empty chair next to the woman, and Ted quietly sits down. Bob nods in Ted's direction but says nothing directly to him. Instead, he continues his monologue on the prospects for a winning season of the college's football team, his consuming passion for all nine of his undergraduate years. Ted spots his opening when Bob pauses for breath, and without hesitation, he introjects, "Hi, Bob. How've you been? I haven't seen you in class for the last few weeks." Bob's brief response—"Hello Ted,"—is quickly followed by a return to his original subject—the team. Ted notices that the woman is fidgeting in her chair somewhat and desperately trying to suppress a yawn. She fails, and Ted cannot control his urge to giggle at her reaction to Bob's long-winded performance. Of course, she notices Ted's reaction, and as their eyes meet, she smiles. He returns her smile and nods in her direction.

When Bob comes up for air again, Ted immediately introjects, "Say, Bob, I don't think that I've met your friends." Bob, always the perfect gentleman, responds, "Ted, meet Alice Groltsh and her brother Carl." Before Bob can return to his discourse on the football team, Ted turns to Alice and asks, "Are you a student here or just visiting?" This question initiates a subtle shift in the encounter—chairs are subtly moved, body orientations are shifted, and so on. What had been one cluster of four people now becomes two groups of two persons—Bob and Carl, and Ted and Alice.

EXCHANGE ASPECTS OF THE ENCOUNTER

Keeping this story in mind, we will now explore in some detail the actions and probable thoughts of the major actors in the encounter. First, let us consider Ted's initial response upon entering the party. As noted, he engaged in a behavior that is common to many of us in such situations—he paused in the doorway and looked around to see who was there and what was going on in the room. Why did he do this? It seems reasonable to assume, as do exchange theorists, that he was forming an estimate of the most rewarding (or satisfying, or comfortable, or least anxiety-evoking) encounter available to him. Obviously, it is easier to engage a friend or an acquaintance in conversation than to initiate one with a stranger. At first glance, Ted did not see anyone in the room whom he knew. What was his response to this discovery? He went to the line that had formed in front of the bar and waited to buy a drink.

While in the line, it easily could have crossed Ted's mind to introduce himself to the woman ahead of him who was rummaging through her purse and to offer to buy her a drink. He could have used her searching behavior as the basis for an opening conversational gambit ("You don't have to find much money in there—I hear drinks in this joint are really cheap."). However, he did not do so. In fact, Ted did not acknowledge that he was paying any more than the most minimal attention to her or to what she was doing. Why not? Although it seems reasonable that he would take advantage of this opportunity to strike up a conversation—especially since he did not as yet recognize anyone in the room—it also seems reasonable that Ted did not engage in this behavior because the potential rewards of this course of action did not seem to him to outweigh the potential costs associated with it.

What might those costs be? First, Ted might be a shy person. In this context, as Phillip Zimbardo (1977) has noted, shyness implies an uncertainty about one's own social skills, an uncertainty about other persons' reactions toward introductory behaviors, a recognition that such behaviors are not easily expressed, and so on. Given this set of self-imposed constraints, to initiate an encounter with a stranger would result in the arousal of considerable anxiety. Another factor which would operate against an attempt at interaction is the common tendency on the part of most people to fear rejection by another. Even the most gregarious, outgoing, sociable individuals have experienced the acute discomfort of someone rejecting their attempts at interaction. Some people are very sensitive to rebuffs of this type, and as such, they are most careful about initiating social encounters with strangers.

Numerous factors outside of Ted's Personal Structure could also have played a role in his failure to try to converse with the woman. The fact that this other person was a female might have had an inhibiting effect on Ted. People tend to be most comfortable in approaching others of the same sex. Or, conceivably, the woman might have been extremely unattractive to Ted, and this fact alone might have dampened any attempt to meet her.

The noise level, too, might have played a role here. In order to initiate a conversation so close to the crowded bar, it might have been necessary to shout one's greeting, given that the line passed by a bank of stereo speakers which were blaring loud music. Understandably, Ted might have been somewhat reluctant to exert this much effort merely to exchange pleasantries.

Let us assume for the moment that Ted's major stumbling block (or cost, in exchange terms) was a strong fear of rejection. While in line, Ted had two competing response options to consider: (1) he could attempt to initiate a conversation with the woman in front of him, an option that was facilitated by his thinking of an opening conversational gambit involving her search for money; or (2) he could ignore her and merely wait his turn in line. In mulling over these two possible courses of action, Ted implicitly considered the likely costs and rewards of each.

If he were to attempt an introduction, and if he were successful, he would be rewarded to the extent that (1) this outcome satisfied his need to establish some social contact in a room filled with strangers; and (2) to the extent that she appeared to be someone with whom it would be worth spending some time. On the other hand, if he was rebuffed, this outcome would prove extremely disconcerting, in that (1) he would be embarrassed; or (2) he would see himself as the cause of some discomfort to her. In Ted's judgment, the pain of a possible rejection is much greater than the rewards to be obtained in the event of a successful introduction, given that his other option—*noninitiation*—is not aversive. Since the night was still young, and his major goal at that time was to obtain a drink, he did not judge standing alone for a while to be a negative (or positive) condition.

Estimating Exchange Values in an Encounter

Some exchange theorists (Gergen, 1969; Thibaut & Kelley, 1959) would use numeric terms, as illustrated in Table 9.1, to depict Ted's estimate of his feelings as a consequence of not acting, or of initiating contact and receiving either a positive response or a rebuff. Although Ted, might not actually assign numbers to represent his feelings of satisfaction or discomfort (most people probably do not), it is convenient for us to summarize these response

TABLE 9.1
Ted's Estimate of Outcomes

	Values of Ted's Response Options		
	Ignore Woman	*Initiate Contact Woman's Reaction to Initiation*	
		Positive	*Rebuff*
Ted's Values	0	+30	−75

options in this manner. In developing this diagram, we assumed that Ted's possible reactions can be characterized as falling along a scale which ranges from −100 (excruciating discomfort) to +100 (ecstacy), where each number represents a possible net reward, worth, or value to Ted. As illustrated in Table 9.1, Ted estimates that he stands to gain a moderate (+30) amount if his initiation is successful. However, because Ted's fear of rejection is so strong, being rebuffed would result in an outcome whose value to him was extremely negative (−75).

Under these circumstances, we would expect Ted to weigh the possible outcomes and decide not to strike up a conversation. There was no explicit information available to Ted that would lead him to believe that the attempted interaction would succeed, so a positive reaction or a rebuff from the other are equally likely. In this circumstance, Ted's best strategy would be to avoid the initiation. Why? Because half of the time, the initiation could be expected to result in a net value for Ted of −75, whereas the other half of the time, he would benefit only +30 when the outcome was positive. If he were to engage in such an activity in such circumstances the average net value would be negative: −22.5 (that is, [50 percent of 30] + [50 percent of −75] = −22.5).

If Ted's estimate of the likelihood of a positive or a negative encounter differed from equality, the net value of initiating contact would differ from −22.5. For example, suppose that Ted remembers that in the past, he generally (about 80 percent of the time) was rewarded with a positive response when he initiated conversations in similar Social Contexts. He might utilize this recollection in weighing his options in the present situation. Given the estimate of an 80 percent probability of success, Ted would probably initiate the interaction, as the net value of doing so is positive (that is [80 percent of +30] + [20 percent of −75] = +9). So long as the average net expected outcome of acting in an encounter is greater than that expected from not acting, we predict that Ted would engage in such behavior. In this example, the net outcome for acting (+9) is greater than the net outcome for not acting (0). Table 9.2 provides an illustration of the net values and likely behavioral outcomes for initiating a conversation, given a number of different estimates of success.

Notice that the high cost of rebuff for Ted effectively reduces the likelihood of his attempting to initiate a casual conversation under all but the most favorable estimates of success. For other people, or for Ted in other circumstances, these figures could be very different. For example, as can be inferred from Table 9.2, if Ted found himself in a situation in which the value of not acting were very negative (such as −50), then he would be expected to initiate a conversation, even if he estimated his probability of success to be less than 30. Moreover, we would expect a very different pattern of initiation behavior from another person who was less adversely affected by rejection. Such a person would be more likely to act, since his average net values would be based on relatively higher expected outcomes for doing so. This person's success value, for example, might be 50, his value for failure

TABLE 9.2
Net Values and Behavioral Outcomes Under Different Estimates of Success

Estimate of Success (percent)	Net Value of Initiating Conversation*	Behavioral Outcome
10	−64.5	No initiation
30	−43.5	No initiation
50	−22.5	No initiation
70	− 1.5	No initiation
90	+19.5	Initiation

* These expected outcomes are based on the supposition that Ted would gain a moderate reward (+30) if his initiation were successful but would be greatly disturbed (−75) if he were rebuffed.

−25, and the value of not acting −15. Plugging these numbers into a predictive equation of the type whose outcomes are illustrated in Table 9.2 would result in a very different set of expected actions.

The Behavior Matrix

It should be noted that the choice of response options often involves more than merely acting or not acting. Frequently, that is, people must consider a much wider range of possible options which sometimes, but not always, includes nonaction. We will illustrate this point by examining Ted's behavior after he had bought his drink, spied Bob, and approached him. After acknowledging Bob, Ted could engage in a wide number of possible actions—and each of these actions carried with it a value. Ted could have interrupted Bob's discourse and introjected his own opinions about the football team, he could have sat and listened passively (as he did for a while), he could have broken away quickly, he could have made funny faces at Carl and Alice in an attempt to make them laugh, and so on. Bob would estimate the net value of each of the possible behaviors that he considered reasonable in the circumstances, and then choose the option that maximized his predicted net return.

Of course, the chosen outcome might in fact have resulted in more or less satisfaction (or return) than Ted had anticipated—predictions are not always confirmed. In short, we tend to choose the response option that we think will result in the greatest satisfaction or return, but our estimates sometimes prove faulty.

In a dyadic (two-person) encounter, the behavior that takes place between two people serves two functions: on the one hand, a person's actions are the responses to the other's presence and overt behavior; on the other hand, these actions also serve as cues that influence the other to respond. This mutual interplay, in which one's actions are both the result of another's behavior and also the stimulus for the other's subsequent actions, is termed *interaction.* This term implies an interdependence between the actors regarding their behaviors, and the consequences of those activities for their sense of satisfaction. Recall the encounter between Ted and Alice. After seeing her yawn during Bob's monologue, Ted caught Alice's attention and smiled at her. This action induced her to return his smile. This response, in turn, induced Ted to request that Bob introduce him to Alice, an activity that was designed to further their opportunity to engage in an interaction. The introduction formality completed, Ted and Alice were then in a position to directly engage in conversation—to focus their attention on each other and to ignore the others around them—and they did so. What began as an encounter in which both Ted and Alice were part of an audience for a third person (Bob) evolved into an interaction between them.

We can identify most, if not all, of the important response options that a person might consider in a given social encounter. The complete list of such options represents that person's range of possible behaviors in the situation. Clearly, when two people interact, each brings his or her behavior repertoire to the encounter. In our example, Ted and Alice each had a number of possible response options. When they began their interaction, however, the actual behaviors that they expressed determined both their own satisfaction levels, and that of the other person. We can illustrate this interdependence through the use of a two-dimensional table, or *behavior matrix,* a means of summarizing social encounters and relations that was originally proposed by John Thibaut and Harold Kelley (1959).

Table 9.3 is an example of a behavior matrix that represents some of the outcomes that were possible for Ted and Alice as a result of their encounter that night. Each row of this table represents the range of net values to Ted and Alice that could result if Ted expresses a given behavior from his repertoire of possible actions. Similarly, the column entries represent the possible outcomes to both that might result from Alice's actions. Inherent in this table is the proposition that an outcome for each actor is a consequence of the unique combination of behaviors that each expresses in an interaction.

Before examining the specific contents of this particular matrix, two general points need to be made. First, it should be noted that the entire repertoires of possible behaviors for each interactant were not presented. While each of us has a finite number of behaviors that we could enact within a given Social Context, this number is typically very large. Representing all of these behaviors in a matrix is a cumbersome task which, in this case, is unnecessary. Instead, for purposes of illustration, we will focus on small portions of the repertoires of Ted and Alice. Second, it is very rare for two people to have exactly the same repertoires of behaviors, although there is often considerable overlap in the behaviors that they do have in common. We will illustrate this point with portions of both Ted's and Alice's repertoires which, though generally similar, differed in some behaviors.

Consider the upper left-hand cell of Ted's and Alice's behavior matrix. As shown here, an exchange of smiles between these two people is rewarding to both, although slightly more so for Alice (+35) than for Ted (+20). Perhaps

TABLE 9.3
Example of Behavior Matrix: Possible Interaction Outcomes for Ted's and Alice's Initial Encounter

Sample of Ted's Repertoire	*Sample of Alice's Repertoire*					
	Smiles	Listens to Bob	Laughs	Talks	Sneers	Yawns
Smiles	+35 / +20	+3 / −10			+15 / −50	+10 / +10
Listens to Bob		+3 / −5				−8 / −5
Laughs			+45 / +50			
Talks				+55 / +55		
Stutters	+5 / −20	+3 / −10	−20 / −40		+10 / −65	
Spills drink			−10 / −20			
Caresses knee	+90 / +75				−50 / −70	

Note: Within each cell of the matrix, the number in the lower-left corner represents the net value of that exchange for Ted, and the number in the upper-right corner represents the outcome of that exchange for Alice.

Alice has a higher need for approval than Ted or is slightly more insecure socially. Either of these Personal Structure factors would enhance the value of Ted's smile for her—and these characteristics also help to explain Alice's mildly positive reaction (+3) to Bob's discourse on football. The cell immediately to the right of the exchange of smiles—which summarizes the outcomes that would occur if Ted were to smile at Alice but she were to ignore him and continue to listen to Bob—is an example of an exchange in which the nature of the values differs for the two interactants.

If this exchange were to have occurred, Alice would have derived some mild satisfaction (+3) from listening to Bob extol the football team; however, her lack of response to Ted's overture would have generated some negative feelings (−10) in Ted, who might have disliked this exchange for a number of reasons—no one likes to experience rejection, and such encounters tend to have high negative value for most people. Alice's behavior could have been interpreted as a rebuff, but in this particular instance, her failure to respond to Ted's smile would be ambiguous. As such, the value of this exchange for Ted would not be as negative as it would have been if her behavior had been clearly rejecting. Contrast this outcome for Ted to that which would have occurred if his smile had been met with a sneer from Alice. In this case of obvious rejection, the value that Ted experiences would be very negative (−50).

Some of the other cells in the behavior matrix also deserve attention. Consider what might have happened if Ted had stuttered when attempting to initiate a conversation with Alice. This disconcerting behavior could have resulted in a number of possible outcomes, depending on Alice's apparent response. If she had smiled just as Ted stuttered, this would have proved mildly aversive (−20), even if the smile was meant to be comforting. On the other hand, Ted probably would have felt somewhat less uncomfortable (−10) if Alice had continued to listen to Bob, thereby ignoring his faux pas. If, by chance, she had laughed (perhaps at something Bob said) just as Ted stuttered, this combination of events would have produced an uncomfortable outcome for both—Ted would have interpreted her laughter to be a response to his inept attempt to start a conversation, and this would have proved highly embarrassing (−40); Alice also would have been embarrassed (−20), because she would have realized that her action conveyed a meaning that was unintended.

In contrast to this last exchange, suppose instead that Ted had spilled a drink just at the moment that Alice had laughed. In this instance, the degree of discomfort (negative value) for both interactants would have been less than the amount that would have resulted from a stutter/laughter exchange. Why? Because generally accepted standards of social behavior (norms) prescribe that it is more acceptable to make light of a minor accident (spilling one's drink) than to react noticeably to what might be a personal handicap (a speech defect). Since Alice had no way of knowing whether or not Ted's stutter was a persistent problem for him, a negative interpretation of her action was of more concern to her than it would have been had her laughter occurred just after Ted had spilled his drink.

It also is conceivable that Ted would have attempted to initiate an interaction with Alice through a somewhat unusual tactic: caressing her knee. As shown in Table 9.3, if Ted had engaged in this unconventional ice-breaking tactic, his action could have yielded any of a number of outcomes. Let us assume that Alice appreciated Ted's directness and responded to it with a smile. In this instance, a highly positive exchange for both interactants would have occurred. Why, then, did Ted not choose to perform this behavior? Probably because he thought the likelihood of Alice's smiling in response to his very direct display of interest was very low—just as he estimated that he would have been rebuffed had he tried to initiate a conversation with the woman in line at the bar. In addition, it seems probable that Ted thought that this type of initiation behavior was not appropriate. As such, even if he had estimated correctly that caressing Alice's knee would have resulted in a positive outcome, he still might not have done so.

Most of the examples that we have discussed have involved exchanges that, in fact, did not occur. Ted did not stutter when introducing himself; he did not spill his drink; he did not caress Alice's knee; and she did not smile in return. What about the behaviors that did occur? Examining these exchanges highlights the sequential nature of social encounters. Recall that Alice had yawned, probably in response to Bob's lecture on football. Ted giggled and then smiled at her reaction. The outcome of this exchange is illustrated in the upper right-hand cell of Table 9.3. However, the encounter did not end here. In response to Ted's smile, Alice smiled—a second mutually rewarding experience. Encouraged, Ted initiated a conversation, and Alice reciprocated—a highly positive exchange for both. Thus, while the encounter was positive for both actors, they failed to engage in their potentially most rewarding exchange, as portrayed in the lower left-hand cell of Table 9.3. Under the circumstances that we have described, however, it is understandable that they did not explore this section of the behavior matrix.

A final feature of Table 9.3 that should be noted concerns its *null* cells. Some combinations of behaviors between people will not occur because they are logically, physically, or psychologically impossible, and these are defined as null exchanges. For example, it seems extremely unlikely that in response to Ted's caressing her knee, Alice would yawn, or ignore Ted's actions completely and merely continue to listen to Bob. Ted's wandering hand almost inevitably would elicit some form of direct response from Alice. Similarly, when people converse with each other, they do not talk at the same time. While interruptions occur, sustained simultaneous talking is not likely. As such, the cell that represents such a situation (Ted talks and Alice listens to Bob) has been crossed over to indicate its implausibility.

The Nature of Outcome Values

The values presented in the behavior matrix represent a summary of the extent to which these specific exchanges of behaviors or interactions result in positive or negative feelings for the actors. Thus, they represent very subjective states; what might be very rewarding for one person might be highly aversive for another. Because of the subjective nature of these net values, they are difficult to measure accurately. However, in spite of such ambiguities, we assume that those interactions that are sought or repeated result in positive values for the actor, whereas those that are avoided have negative values. Accordingly, we assign positive net values to interactions of the former type, and negative net values to those of the latter. The specific numbers that we use are estimates of the strengths of these tendencies to approach or avoid a specific behavior exchange.

Underlying the assignment of values to the potential interactions available in a situation is the assumption that people seek to maximize their rewards— to receive the most satisfaction or pleasure from an encounter—while minimizing the costs involved in such exchanges. This assumption of *hedonism*—the tendency for people to strive to maximize pleasure and minimize pain—is fundamental to the many versions of exchange theory that social psychologists have developed (Blau, 1964; Gergen, Greenberg, & Willis, 1980; Homans, 1974; Thibaut & Kelley, 1959). The rewarding exchanges that people seek are those that provide them with the opportunity to satisfy one or more of their motives. Since motivation varies so widely, it is not surprising that different encounters will have different values for different people. For example, it is clear that talking about football was more rewarding for Bob and Carl than it was for Ted or Alice.

Rewards. Within this hedonistic perspective, we are assumed to engage in interactions primarily for two reasons: (1) we do so because we find certain social events rewarding (that is, they satisfy our motives); and (2) we engage in social exchanges that are not rewarding in and of themselves, but which we expect will lead to an outcome that is more directly satisfying. We use these instrumental activities as stepping stones to the desired outcome. For example, while Ted probably found that intruding into Bob's monologue was somewhat aversive, it was through this maneuver that he was able to begin conversing with Alice, an exchange which he found highly rewarding. Though Ted did not really care about being introduced to Carl, he considered it a necessary tactic so that his introduction to Alice would be as congenial as possible.

There are three major ways in which social encounters can provide rewards, either directly or indirectly. First, the behavior of the other person can satisfy one or more of our motives. For example, as noted earlier, Ted's smile was rewarding to Alice, who was motivated by concerns for social acceptance.

Second, a social event can provide us with the opportunity to perform rewarding behaviors that we could not express as readily, if at all, in other contexts. For example, Bob's encounter with Carl and Alice gave him the opportunity to talk at length about his beloved football team, an activity that we can assume was more rewarding to him than it was to his audience. Bob, of course, could have performed these same behaviors alone, in the privacy of his own room, but for obvious reasons, doing so would not have been as rewarding to him.[1]

Third, social encounters can often be positive experiences for us because they take place in a context that is the source of rewards. Suppose, for example, that Carl is a real beer nut—his friends call him "12 Pack." He came to the party with his sister primarily because he knew that his favorite beverage would be offered at bargain prices. (The party was the college's annual "Race to the Floor," and cheap beer was seen by its organizers as a means of promoting the goal of this event.) For Carl, the various social exchanges in which he engaged that evening were rewarding in large measure because

---

[1] Conversation is only one of a variety of behaviors whose values to us typically increase when they are performed as social activities.

they provided him with the opportunity to spend time in an environment in which he could acquire a valued commodity for a relatively low price.

Costs.   As we have shown, social exchanges can yield positive outcomes for the actors. On the other hand, such rewards usually cannot be obtained freely—that is, without *costs.* Such costs can be subdivided into four general categories: effort, resource expenditures, interference, and lost opportunities. We will now discuss each of these general types of costs.

Effort.   To engage in almost any social interaction, a person must expend *effort*—that is, he or she must perform the series of behaviors that are thought to be appropriate for the circumstances. Some of these behaviors are well-practiced and mesh well with the actor's talents. These are produced with relatively little cost. For example, Bob's discourse on the state of his college's football team was an activity in which he engaged easily and frequently. He was interested in this issue, spent considerable time studying it and, in addition, had a talent for long-winded speeches.

In contrast, other behaviors can require considerable expenditure of effort. In these instances, the actor finds the behaviors costly, because he or she is not talented in performing them, or because the acts themselves are not a well-established part of the actor's repertoire. For example, from his behavior in the line while waiting to order a drink, we would surmise that Ted found meeting new people to be a difficult activity. Thus, we would also infer that his request of Bob for an introduction to Carl and Alice was somewhat costly to him. Obviously, in the first instance, Ted felt that the outcome of this act—the woman's response to him—was unlikely to be worth the psychological effort involved in introducing himself to her. In the case of Carl and Alice, however, the costs were reduced somewhat because he could use Bob as an intermediary, and his estimate of the ultimate outcome of this action was more positive.

Resource Expenditure.   A second cost involves the expenditure of resources. Individuals vary regarding their possession of numerous tangible and intangible resources—that is, skills, objects, and expertise whose values can vary depending on their utility and availability.

One obvious resource is *money.* If Ted had bought a drink for the woman in line, he would have had less to spend on himself and other people.

Another, perhaps less obvious, resource is *personal energy.* From our example, suppose that Ted and Alice had met at the end of the evening rather than at the beginning. Suppose further that Alice had spent the hours dancing until her feet felt as if they would fall off. Under these circumstances, she might have depleted her energy to the extent that she had more or less collapsed into the chair, and was using Bob's monologue as an opportunity for a much needed rest. If this were so, she might have found it much more costly to begin to engage in an interaction with Ted than if she had not expended this resource.

A third example of resource expenditure involves the use of expertise or information in interpersonal encounters. Bob's monologue on the football team is one such example. The information which he provided and which served to hold the attention of others (a positive outcome for him) was expended as a consequence of his actions. It is unlikely that a person, once having heard Bob's spiel, would appreciate sitting through it a second time. Thus, while Bob's monologue served a purpose and had some reward value both for him and his audience (see Table 9.3), it nonetheless was a costly behavior, since in performing it, Bob reduced its future value for anyone who had heard it once.

Interference. A third major type of cost involved in social exchange is interference—that is, the extent to which factors in the physical and interpersonal environments, as well as in the actor, make it difficult for him or her to obtain rewards. A common cost of this type involves the behaviors of others, whose interfering actions can be either purposive or inadvertent. Purposive interference usually involves a conflict of interest, in which two or more people are competing for the same reward. In the example presented above, Bob's monologue might be viewed as his attempt to impress Alice so that she would want to interact with him further; thus Bob's actions would be viewed as purposive interference with Ted's similar desire to know Alice.

Of course, it is conceivable that Bob's monopolization of the conversation was not motivated by attraction for Alice, but rather represented his usual behavior when discussing his favorite subject. While inadvertent, Bob's actions still interfered with Ted's attempt to meet Alice. This type of inadvertent interference often comes about as a result of circumstance; people in the same context, each pursuing their own interests, can get in each other's way.

An example of interference brought about by conditions in the physical environment is provided by Ted's behavior while waiting in line at the bar. Recall that one likely reason he hesitated to address the woman in front of him was the noise level in that part of the room. This aspect of the physical environment would have made it costly for Ted to attempt an exchange with this stranger.

A major source of interference within the actor is the fear of negative outcomes. People often find it costly to engage in social exchanges because of their fears of appearing inept or of embarrassing themselves. People differ in the extent to which such fears interfere with their social behaviors. For example, Ted's shyness made his attempts to meet Alice more costly than they might have been for a person whose Personal Structure differed in this regard.

Opportunity Costs. A final type of cost to be discussed here involves the *loss of opportunity* which one behavior might entail for other activities. Such opportunity costs refer to the positive net values of behaviors that an actor must forego because he or she is engaged in another behavior. An example of opportunity costs is provided in Carl's choice to attend the party with his sister because of the price of the beer, rather than to spend his evening, as usual, at his favorite watering hole. While he was wiling away his time at the "Race to the Floor" party, Carl could not be spending time at his usual bar with his usual cronies.

This example illustrates the opportunity costs involved in an actor's choice of one encounter over others. A second example of opportunity costs occurs within an encounter, when the expression of one behavior precludes expression of others. By talking about football, Bob could not at the same time ingratiate himself to Alice by discussing contemporary literature—another interest of his, and, coincidentally, her favorite topic. Thus, his choice of one behavior (discussing football), at least for the moment, precluded his expression of another.

Our discussion suggests that the rewards and costs associated with the behaviors expressed in an exchange combine to determine the net value that each actor receives from the interaction. To return to Ted's and Alice's behavior matrix (Table 9.3), recall that one of the possible interactions—a mutual exchange of smiles—resulted in a satisfying outcome for both actors. However, these specific behaviors did entail some costs. Directing attention to each other cost each actor the opportunity to listen to Bob, to watch Carl slowly slide out of his chair to the floor, and so on. By overcoming his shyness and smiling at Alice, Ted initiated an exchange that prevented him from making an early exit from the group to join another party on campus. Alice, tired from a recent tour of the dance floor, still had to muster the energy to respond in kind to Ted's ingratiating smile. In spite of these costs, the net value that Ted and Alice's exchange produced was positive, and led them to explore other regions of their behavior matrix.

The exchange theory interpretation of interpersonal behavior provides an efficient tool for describing complicated social encounters. Given the complexity of interpersonal behavior and the great difficulty in measuring the net values associated with any given exchange before it occurs, this approach is more useful in describing such encounters than it is in predicting them. Thus, the value of this approach lies in its emphasis on important processes and outcomes of interpersonal behavior. In the sections that follow, we will examine these processes and outcomes.

THE PROCESSES OF SOCIAL EXCHANGE

Control is of fundamental relevance to the major processes of social exchange. Given that we enter into and engage in social encounters to experience the most positive outcomes possible, it follows that we would attempt to structure those encounters to yield the highest net value. To accomplish this goal requires some ability to induce the other person in the exchange to act in a manner that permits us to receive rewards: to express behaviors that are satisfying to us, to act in ways that permit us to engage in self-rewarding behaviors, and so on. In other words, the processes of social exchange are focused on people's attempts to influence others to express behaviors so that

TABLE 9.4
Behavior Matrix for Encounter between Norma and Ruth

Sample of Ruth's Repertoire	*Sample of Norma's Repertoire*	
	Grab for doll	Play with tea set
Grab for doll	−25 / −40	+20 / −5
Play with tea set	+10 / +60	+70 / +15

their encounter falls within desired or rewarding portions of the behavior matrix.

Table 9.4 presents a very simple behavior matrix that described two possible actions for each participant. These potential actions combine into four possible behavior exchanges. For the purposes of this example, both actors—Ruth and Norma, two four-year-olds—have the same choices, although, as discussed earlier, this is rarely the case in real-life encounters. As shown in Table 9.4, the behaviors involve the children playing either with a doll or with a tea set. As illustrated, playing with the doll is more rewarding as a solitary activity; thus, if both children attempt to do so, the net values of this confrontation are negative for each. On the other hand, each child could play with the tea set by herself, but the nature of this toy is such that greater rewards are available when two children play with it together. From Table 9.4, we can infer that Ruth is more interested in playing with the tea set than is Norma, who prefers to play with the doll.

This combination of preferences and values suggests that each child will attempt to induce the other to act in a way that maximizes her own reward. Thus, Norma will try to get Ruth to play alone with the tea set so that she can have the doll to herself. This outcome would result in a reasonably high net value for her (+60), but only a small reward (+10) for Ruth. (Apparently, it is not much fun for Ruth to play with the tea set alone, although she really likes to use it when playing with others.) Ruth's preferred outcome would involve both girls playing with the tea set. In this case, she would reap a high net reward (+70), whereas Norma's outcome (+15) would be substantially less.

One tactic that Ruth might use to influence Norma might involve reaching for the doll each time Norma looked at it. This implied threat—to fight over the doll—might persuade Norma to join Ruth in playing with the tea set. In contrast, Norma might move the tea set to a corner of the room so that it would be uncomfortable for both children to play with it at the same time. This would make it difficult for Ruth to insist that they play together. Yet another option might be chosen—Ruth might appeal to Norma's sense

DAVID S. STRICKLER/THE PICTURE CUBE

Interfering with another's enjoyment of a valued toy is a common tactic of behavior control for children (and adults).

of fairness by saying that since she had played with the doll that morning, Norma should be willing to play "tea time" with her now. These three tactics are specific examples of *Control mechanisms,* which are integral processes of social exchange. We will now discuss these Control mechanisms more systematically, in terms of the subthemes of impingement and incorporation.

Fate Control as an Impingement Mechanism

Recall from Chapter 2 that impingement refers to the attempt to control another's overt actions. This Control process requires the ability to monitor the other's actions and to respond accordingly as a consequence of his or her compliance or noncompliance. Within the perspective of exchange theory, especially as developed by Harold Kelley and John Thibaut (Kelley, 1979; Kelley & Thibaut, 1978; Thibaut & Kelley, 1959), such impingements often take the form of *converted fate control*. This term refers to the utilization of one's ability to reward or punish another in order to influence that person's behavior. *Fate control,* per se, is the ability to reward or punish another regardless of the other's behavior. In most social relationships, the participants have some degree of fate control over one another—that is, each has some power to administer rewards or punishments no matter what the other does. Usually, the distribution of this power is more or less equal. In some common circumstances, however, one actor possesses substantially more of this power than does the other. For example, parents' abilities to reward or punish their infant are usually much greater than the infant's control of their outcomes; parents literally have the power of life and death over their child.

Table 9.5 illustrates a situation of rather one-sided fate control. To simplify this presentation, we have not included all of the cell entries in this behavior matrix, but rather have supplied only those values that indicate the impact of one actor's behavior on the other's outcomes. The actors in this example are Mother Legree and her baby son, Simon. As shown, Mother can choose either to come into Simon's room and feed him (which yields a net reward to him of +30) or to remain in the living room and continue to listen to her favorite music via earphones. This latter alternative would yield a negative outcome (−20) for the hungry child. Given these circumstances, however, Simon cannot act to influence the net rewards available to him. He can cry or he can lie there silently, but in either case, he cannot feed himself. His mother, in this case, has complete power over the net values that he will obtain.

TABLE 9.5
Behavior Matrix Illustrating an Example of Fate Control

Sample of Simon's Repertoire	*Sample of Mother Legree's Repertoire*	
	Feed Simon	Listen to music
Cry	+30	−20
Lie Quietly	+30	−20

Note: For the sake of clarity, only the outcomes to Simon are represented in the matrix, since only they are relevant to Mother Legree's fate control over him.

"If I make a noise my folks spank me—if I'm quiet they take my temperature!"

Parents typically have a great deal of fate control over their children.

Mother Legree can use this power to impinge upon Simon's behavior. She can, through her past actions, show Simon that she is made of stern stuff and will not succumb to his pitiful cries for food. Thus, whenever he cries, she ignores him; however, whenever Simon lies still and waits patiently at mealtimes, Mother reinforces his behavior by coming into his room with his meal. No matter what Simon does, Mother has fate control over him; however, rather than apply this power capriciously, Mother uses it to shape Simon's behavior. Even though there are four possible outcomes in the abbreviated behavior matrix of Table 9.5, only two really exist for Simon—to lie quietly and be fed, or to cry and be ignored—since Mother has total control over the relationship.

Earlier, we noted that such one-sided fate control as portrayed here is somewhat unusual, at least for exchange relationships among adults. More typical are those interactions in which each party has some degree of control over the rewards of the other. This more common situation of mutual fate control is illustrated in Table 9.6, in which we continue the story of Ted and Alice who, after a number of positive encounters, have established a romantic relationship. The reader may recall that Alice was concerned about social approval; this concern has intensified, especially with regard to Ted's reactions to her.

TABLE 9.6
Behavior Matrix Illustrating an Example of Mutual Fate Control

Sample of Ted's Repertoire	*Sample of Alice's Repertoire*	
	Show interest	Yawn
Smile	+50 +60	+60 −25
Frown	+50 −30	−30 −25

As shown in Table 9.6, Ted has fate control over Alice, because his smile has the same net reward value to her no matter what her behavior. Similarly, Alice has fate control over Ted, because his need for her attention results in her ability to provide positive or negative outcomes by appearing either interested or bored when Ted is talking. Given the values displayed in Table 9.6, we would expect Ted and Alice to convert their mutual fate control in such a way that their interaction in this small portion of their matrix would most often take the form described in the upper left-hand cell of the diagram—Ted smiles and Alice expresses interest in him.

Finally, it should be noted that people are not totally dependent upon others for their rewards. They control their own fate at least to some extent. Ted's smile, for example, not only has implications for Alice's motive satisfaction, but for his own as well. Thus, the values presented in Tables 9.5 and 9.6 are somewhat simplified, as they do not take into account the fact that people have some degree of fate control over themselves.

Empirical Demonstrations of Fate Control Conversion. Compelling evidence from social psychological research confirms the idea that individuals do use their fate control over other people to impinge upon their behaviors. A good example of the use of this tactic of Control is provided in research by Leventhal and Whiteside (1973), who asked undergraduates to role play the part of a junior high school teacher.[2] The subjects' task was to assign midterm grades to eight hypothetical students. To do this, they were given information about the students whom they were to evaluate and reward with grades. The most important pieces of information provided respondents were the scores that each student had obtained on an aptitude test and on a midterm examination.

Of most relevance to the issue of converted fate control was the behavior of the subject-teachers when they were told to assign grades in a way that would motivate students to do their best for the remainder of the term. The tactics which teachers used to meet this goal varied as a consequence of students' aptitudes. For the same test performance, highly able students were given lower grades than were students whose intellectual potential was lower. In other words, rewards and punishments were allocated in a manner that was designed to motivate the better students to try harder, and the less able students to continue to put out their best efforts. It is important to note that when teachers were instructed to allocate rewards fairly (rather than in a way that would promote subsequent performance), their actions differed. In this instance, grades were assigned much more as a function of examination performance per se.

Other research (Callahan & Messé, 1973; Sidowski, Wyckoff, & Tabory, 1956) has also demonstrated that people use their abilities to control the

---

[2] To increase subjects' involvement in the role, the respondents were told that a report of this research would be sent to educational authorities, and that it well might influence the system of grading used in public schools.

outcomes of others to influence these others' behaviors. For example, Callahan and Messé (1973) found that supervisors used their powers to pay a subordinate as a means of impinging on the worker's behavior, and this was true especially when the supervisor's own reward was linked to the worker's productivity.

Resource Control as an Impingement Mechanism

A form of impingement that parallels converted fate control is *resource control.* In using fate control, an actor has the power to reward or punish another directly, regardless of the other's actions. In using resource control, an actor has the power to provide or to withhold resources which would enable the other to obtain a desired outcome, regardless of the other's behavior. As with fate control, a person with resource control can use this power to impinge on another's actions.

As an example of resource control, let us imagine two undergraduate roommates who are enrolled in the same social psychology course. Richard very often has found it difficult to fit classes into his busy schedule; as a consequence, he finds himself relatively uninformed about the material presented in class lectures. Conscientious Irwin, on the other hand, has attended all of his classes and has taken copious notes on almost everything his instructor has said. With the final examination just around the corner, Irwin controls a resource that is very valuable to Richard. The lecture notes, while not intrinsically satisfying to Richard, provide him with a means to a desired end—namely, a passing grade in his psychology course.

As with fate control, Irwin can either give Richard the notes or withhold them, regardless of Richard's actions. Moreover, Irwin can use this power to impinge on Richard to behave in a desired manner concerning a matter of some importance to him—namely, how often and how loudly Richard plays his radio. Richard has the bad habit of playing his radio very loudly for long periods of time. Irwin's past complaints, however, have fallen on deaf ears. This unsatisfactory state could be remedied if Irwin made the availability of his notes contingent upon Richard's actions regarding the radio. He would lend his notes when the radio was turned off, and take them back when it was turned on. Such a procedure would focus their encounters on two of the four cells in this portion of their behavior matrix. We would expect that such converted resource control would yield the desired results for Irwin. Richard would keep the radio off—at least until he had finished reading the notes.

Impingement without Fate or Resource Control

To this point, we have been concerned with the impingement processes of converted fate or resource control. By far a more common form of impingement is behavior control, which involves the purposive use of our own actions to restrict the possible range of response options of others. While in many ways a simple concept, behavior control is difficult to grasp in the abstract. Thus, we will provide an example to facilitate understanding of this widely used impingement process.

Suppose that Jenny is an avid rollerskater who, for many years, has spent Saturday afternoons at the local roller rink. For three of the last four Saturdays, however, her enjoyment of this activity has been seriously curtailed by the presence and obnoxious behavior of Tommy Slobber. For some reason, Tommy was very attracted to Jenny, although this feeling was not reciprocated; and because of his feelings about her, Tommy made persistent attempts to interact with her. He would not take no for an answer, and some of the actions that he used to attract Jenny's attention were very embarrassing to her. What had been an enjoyable way to spend a Saturday afternoon became something of an ordeal for Jenny whenever Tommy turned up at the rink.

It is now Wednesday, and Jenny has a decision to make: she has a final examination on Monday and could profit by spending her Saturday afternoon studying; or, she could try to unwind at the roller rink. Table 9.7 presents the behavior matrix that Jenny must consider in coming to a decision regarding her Saturday afternoon.

Obviously, Jenny cannot make a reasonable choice without first considering Tommy's likely actions. Why not? Because the net values of her response options—to study or to rollerskate—are affected by his behaviors. If Tommy turns up at the rink, Jenny's net value for studying (+20) would exceed that which she could obtain from skating (−85); however, if Tommy did not appear, the relative rewards from skating (+75) would be greater than those from studying (+5). In the absence of other information, Jenny would be forced to engage in the value-estimation process described earlier in the chapter. However, suppose that by chance Jenny runs into Tommy at the library—this was not her lucky day—and in the course of a much too long conversation (for Jenny), she asks him to stop bothering her at the rink.

TABLE 9.7
Behavior Matrix Illustrating Situation of "Pure" Behavior Control

Sample of Jenny's Behavior Repertoire	Sample of Tommy's Behavior Repertoire	
	Go roller skating	Do something else
Go roller skating	−85	+75
Study	+20	+5

Note: Only Jenny's outcomes are presented, since only these values are relevant to Tommy's behavior control over her.

This request infuriates Tommy, whose response is, "Forget it! I'll see you at the rink Saturday."

By this action, Tommy has restricted the range of possible response options that Jenny can realistically consider. Knowing that Tommy will be at the rink has clarified Jenny's decision about skating or studying, since the second column of the behavior matrix of Table 9.7 now consists of null cells. Given the net values presented here, Jenny's choice is obvious—she will exercise her mind and not her feet.

In the example, Tommy had behavior control over Jenny, since her rewards were contingent on one or another of his actions. While he could not reward or punish Jenny regardless of her own behavior (fate control), he nevertheless could impinge on her decision by discussing his future actions with her. In doing so, Tommy restricted Jenny to a specific portion of the behavior matrix, which had less net value for her than the other. Tommy intentionally exercised this control, since he was angry at Jenny. He wished to impinge on her actions.

Any activity that is expressed within an exchange relationship has the effect of limiting the other's response options. Our behavior has consequences for others with whom we interact, and vice versa. Exchange theory postulates that we try to maximize the rewards that we receive from the social exchanges we have with others. Thus, we restrict the actions of others so that we can experience these rewarding outcomes. In this sense, most of our interpersonal actions can be viewed as attempts at behavior control. However, there is wide variation in the extent to which we are aware of the consequences of our behavior for others. For this reason, not all of our actions qualify as impingements, which are explicit, intentional attempts to influence others.

It is important to understand that both converted fate control and converted resource control are types of behavior control. Both of these forms of impingement serve to restrict the response options of another. However, in converted fate or resource control, the ability to influence is based on one's control of something valuable, whereas in pure behavior control, the ability to influence the other's outcomes is less direct. For example, a mother might attempt to induce her son to practice the piano by (1) paying him money for doing so (converted fate control), or (2) sitting with him at the piano for at least an hour each afternoon (pure behavior control). In the first instance, the mother has direct control over a valued outcome (obtaining money); in the latter case, this control is lacking, but her ability to restrict her son's response options (for example, no TV or baseball) can be an equally powerful impingement.

Incorporated Beliefs as Mechanisms of Control

All behavior control processes are impingement mechanisms. In contrast, some procedures for influencing the actions of others in the context of a social exchange are based on incorporation, the second major subtheme of Control. Incorporation, as noted in Chapter 2, involves the individual's acceptance of a belief as correct, appropriate, or true. The power of incorporated beliefs to influence behavior can be used within a social exchange in a number of ways.[3]

In this section, we will examine two major incorporation-based Control processes—*cue control* and *norm evocation*. Both of these processes employ the same basic strategy in influencing the behavior of another. This strategy involves assessing the beliefs of the other person in the social exchange, determining which of these, if any, are consistent with the desired outcome, and acting to make these helpful beliefs salient to that person.

Cue Control. As Jones and Gerard (1967) have noted, one way in which people use another's beliefs to affect the other's actions is to control the contextual cues that are present in the interaction. The reader may recall from Chapter 8 the research of David Rosenhan (1973) who, with his colleagues, feigned a psychological illness in order to investigate the Social Context of the mental institution from the perspective of its inmates. In our discussion, we noted that the staff of the hospital—who controlled much of the physical and interpersonal environment—arranged this context in such a way as to emphasize the helplessness and disturbed condition of the patients in their care. The patients, in turn, acted in accordance with these cues, since they had incorporated self-impressions that were consistent with the staff's implicit expectations.

Cues in both the physical and the interpersonal environments can be used to make salient one or another incorporated belief. For example, consider the wide range of Social Contexts that various restaurants can exhibit, and the effects of this variation on the people's actions. One restaurant, for instance, might provide tuxedoed waiters, heavy silverware, crystal glasses, linen tablecloths and napkins, bone china plates, and so on. It might also have carpeted or hardwood floors, expensive draperies, original paintings on the walls, chandeliers, and so forth. The staff of such an establishment would behave in an efficient and solicitous, but unobtrusive manner, with just a dash of hautiness. In contrast, a somewhat more modest restaurant might enclose its fare in styrofoam containers or paper cups, served on plastic trays, and accompanied by plastic forks and paper napkins. Plastic might create the predominant decor in the restaurant. The staff would be somewhat young, unsophisticated and, at best, enthusiastic to be of assistance. However, their role in serving customers would be minimal—they would take orders, deliver food, and collect money.

Consider your actions in these two archetypical eating establishments. Suppose that you are eating in the restaurant described first, and you have ordered, among other things, "pommes frites." The waiter brings a covered silver dish, sets it before you and, with a flourish, lifts the cover to expose a large helping of golden brown, french-fried potatoes. In this context, it

---

[3] As discussed throughout this book, once incorporated, a belief can affect behavior. The reader may recall that in Chapter 6 we explored the link between opinions and actions, and in Chapter 8, we reviewed studies of the relationship between impressions and behaviors.

would be almost unthinkable to smother these delicacies with catsup and then eat them with your fingers. In contrast, such behavior is both common and "appropriate" in restaurants of the second type. In these establishments, you can observe numerous customers opening their paper bags of fries, dousing the contents with catsup, and eating them without recourse to utensils.

The point of our example is to demonstrate the impact of contextual cues on our actions. The cues provided by the restaurants' personnel are meant to guide our beliefs about what is appropriate, and these beliefs, in turn, affect our behavior. Similarly, we furnish one another with cues via clothing, hairstyle, and general demeanor. These cues are meant to serve as an indication of the types of behaviors we expect from others. A young man with a crew-cut is broadcasting a very different message from one who sports shoulder-length hair. A female physician elicits a very different response when she is wearing her lab coat than when she appears in a slinky black cocktail dress. In this case, the kinds of behaviors that we find appropriate to engage in with her differ dramatically as a consequence of cues derived from these rather incidental differences in appearance.

Empirical research has demonstrated that physical appearance serves as a cue to guide people's actions in a number of different contexts. For example, Darley and Cooper (1972) showed that differences in the dress of the supporters of a political candidate led to differences in voters' inferences about the candidate's stand on a number of important issues, and affected their expressed inclinations to vote for him. Similarly, other research (Benney, Riesman, & Star, 1956; Cannell & Kahn, 1968; Hyman, 1954) has shown that appearance affects the willingness of people to sign petitions, as well as the responses of people while being interviewed. Thus, even in short-term encounters, contextual cues can have a major impact on the salience of our beliefs, and these beliefs, in turn, can affect our behaviors.

In addition, cue control often operates in more long-term social exchange situations to guide the choice of behaviors that are expressed. For example, the information provided by the demeanors of others whom we know well often yields a cue about their moods, and thereby helps us to choose the most appropriate actions toward them. If the meaning of such cues are understood by both parties, they can be used by either to influence the behavior of the other.

For example, suppose that a close acquaintance knows that when you are engrossed in an interesting book, you tend to tune out and ignore all outside distractions. It happens that while you are reading this text, your friend calls out to you. Although you hear her, you do not respond. This lack of reaction serves as a cue to her that you are engrossed in what you are reading and do not wish to be disturbed. She acts accordingly and makes no further attempt to gain your attention. If this cue were not understood, she might have persisted in her attempt—which would have annoyed you— or misinterpreted your failure to respond as unfriendliness or a lack of sociability. However, within the framework of long-term relationships, the likelihood that most cues will be interpreted correctly is very high.

Norm Evocation. We can utilize commonly held beliefs about appropriate conduct (norms) to affect the behavior of others. Just as we can provide a contextual cue to guide the actions of others, we can evoke a norm that is consistent with the behavior we wish to elicit. By evoking a norm, we appeal to the other person to act in a manner that is consistent with the particular belief which we have made salient. Most often, the particular norms that we tend to evoke are self-serving in that they prescribe behaviors that we wish to elicit.

In the example of Richard and Irwin, the roommates who were enrolled in the same psychology class, Richard might have made salient the belief that friends should help each other in times of need when he attempted to gain access to Irwin's class notes. He would have done so in the hope that this well-established norm would induce Irwin to give him the notes, an action that would be consistent with the particular rule of conduct that was evoked. Many norms could be relevant to this particular exchange, but some of these would not have served Richard's purpose. It is very unlikely, for instance, that he would call Irwin's attention to the equally well-established norm that it is good for one to stand on one's own two feet.

The findings of a study by Messé and Callahan-Levy (1979) suggest that norm evocation can be an effective means of eliciting desired behavior from another. In some conditions of this research, female respondents were asked to divide a monetary reward between themselves and a male coworker whose specific identity was unknown. They had worked as a team to earn the reward, but the female was always led to believe that she had substantially outperformed her counterpart.

The coworker, an accomplice of the experimenters, was trained to engage in norm evocation tactics. In some cases, he communicated to his partner that he felt that it would be appropriate for her to divide the reward equally. This statement of belief was meant to evoke the salience of the norm of *equality*—that is, that everyone should be treated the same. In other situations, the confederate communicated to his partner that he believed that she should keep more of the reward for herself, as she had outperformed him. This statement was an attempt to evoke the norm of *equity*—that is, that rewards should be allocated on the basis of differences in contributions.

The results of this study indicated that the coworker's norm evocation influenced the reward distribution behavior of the subjects. The respondents tended to divide the reward more equally when the coworker had evoked the norm of equality than when the coworker had made the norm of equity salient. Thus, the evocation of one or another of these standards of conduct appeared to have an effect on actions in this exchange.

Note that the specific procedure used in this investigation to evoke a norm involved a communication between the coworker and the reward allocator (the subject). Most, if not all, tactics of norm evocation, in fact, involve communication of one sort or another, the intent of which is to persuade the other person that both parties in the exchange share a common standard of appropriate conduct. Other tactics of influence that are used in social exchange contexts also entail the use of communication, but the content of these messages differs from that typical of norm evocation. Most of these alternate tactics involve the use of threats and promises, as discussed in Chapter 2.

The critical difference between norm evocation and such threats and promises involves their bases of power. Threats and promises imply that the communicator has fate or resource control over the other. Thus, the basis of power for such tactics is the personal ability of the actor to reward or punish. In contrast, norm evocation depends on the two parties' acceptance of a common standard of behavior (a norm). In this case, the basis of power is the apparent legitimacy of a belief, a quality which is external to the interactants.

Thibaut and Kelley (1959) note that this difference has major implications for social exchange processes. Influence attempts that are based on the exercise of personal power tend to generate negative reactions and to be potential sources of interpersonal conflict and acrimony. In other words, the use of threats and promises often leads people to engage in exchanges in cells of the behavior matrix that yield negative outcomes for both. As Jack Brehm (1966) has shown, people resent situations or relationships that restrict their freedom, and they act to resist or escape such exchanges. On the other hand, because their power is based on factors external to the interactants, norms tend not to generate negative reactions or conflict. Moreover, as will be discussed in detail in the following section, norms can actually have a facilitative effect on the course of a social relationship.

Norms and Roles as Facilitators of Positive Social Exchange

Norms can differ widely with regard to their *inclusivity*—that is, the number of people to whom they apply. Some norms are nearly universal in a culture—the prohibition against murder, for example, applies to all members of our society. In contrast, other norms apply more specifically to a very small number of people and have little currency across the wider population. In fact, it is not uncommon for rules of conduct to apply to only one particular exchange relationship. For example, a married couple might subscribe to a rule which states that the husband is always responsible for washing the Sunday night dishes, whereas the wife is responsible for this chore the remaining nights. Obviously, this norm is one that does not apply to all married couples.

Between the extremes of universal and relationship-specific norms are a large number of rules of conduct that apply to subsets of the population. For example, behaviors that are generally unacceptable in society at large might be widely practiced in some groups. While perfectly acceptable on the baseball diamond, professional baseball players' practice of chewing tobacco, and the unsightly ramifications of this habit, are not widely appreciated in most other locations. Similarly, the different standards of conduct that are applied to males and females in most cultures are examples of norms that are relevant to very large subsets of a population.

In their theory of social exchange, Thibaut and Kelley (1959) apply the idea of norm inclusivity to their analysis of informal social relations. They distinguish between general norms (beliefs about appropriate behavior which apply to all of the actors in a social exchange relationship) and roles (beliefs that apply only to a subset of these interactants). In dyadic relationships, a norm would be a standard of conduct which applies to both actors, whereas a role would apply to only one of them. Of course, many of the beliefs about behavior that apply within a specific exchange relationship are applicable outside the relationship as well. In fact, many norms and roles that are salient in a specific exchange relationship are commonly held beliefs which the actors have incorporated from past experiences and brought with them into the encounter.

Norms and roles can facilitate positive social exchange because they provide a common basis for individual Valuations of response options. If both actors in an encounter come to the same conclusion regarding the appropriateness of one another's actions, this lessens the possibility that exchanges will take place within cells of the behavior matrix that yield poor net values. If we agree that an action is appropriate, then the grounds for dissatisfaction, argument, and retaliation are minimized. Moreover, there are many Social Contexts in which there is low Resolution regarding the types of rewards which should be sought and the range of possible actions which are appropriate. In such contexts, norms and roles provide a structure through which actors can coordinate their behaviors. In some sense, these shared beliefs about appropriate behavior can provide the "rules of the game" for the "players."

Tragedy of the Commons. Social scientists have used the term mixed-motive situation to identify those Social Contexts in which ambiguity exists concerning the goals that actors should pursue in an exchange. Garret Hardin (1968) has described in detail a classic example of one such mixed-motive situation, which he named the *tragedy of the commons*. Tragedies of this type involve a situation in which a number of people share a finite and depletable resource. Hardin described the specific problems inherent in the actions of herders who shared a common grazing land. If every herder allowed his animals to graze at will on the commons, the pasture soon would be destroyed. However, if for the good of the pasture, a herder grazed his animals only some of the time, he would suffer economically, since his stock would be less marketable as a result of their deprivation. But if all herders practiced this form of conservation, all would be equally disadvantaged in the short term (all would suffer economically), and advantaged in the long term (the pasture would be perpetuated). The problem with this last option is that there exists a strong temptation to cheat in this situation. By grazing one's animals fully while the others restrict theirs, a herder gains the best of both possible worlds—fat sheep and green grass. A behavior matrix representing this situation, which for the sake of simplicity involves only two herders, is presented in Table 9.8.

This illustration highlights the mixed-motive aspects of such situations. Let us view this dilemma from the perspective of Herder Pete. At least three motives are potentially salient to Pete (as well as to Herder George) in this context: (1) a desire to maximize his own economic well-being; (2) a need to protect himself from exploitation; and (3) a concern for both his and George's welfare.

Let us consider the effect if both herders decide to attempt to maximize their individual welfare. In this case, both Pete and George lose. On the other hand, if Pete acts for the common good, and George does not, then Herder Pete receives the greatest negative value, while George profits the most. Only if both Pete and George choose to act to preserve the commons can both receive a positive outcome.

The dilemma inherent in this scenerio is that each herder should maximize his own outcome—no matter how the other acts, he is always better off to be self-interested. Thus, if George grazes his own flock fully, Herder Pete is better off if he acts in the same manner (−35) than if he had restricted his animals (−80); similarly, if George restricts his herd, Pete is still better off if he grazes fully (+75) than he is if he restricts grazing (+30). Thus, whether Pete wishes to maximize his immediate gain or to minimize his possible loss, he must graze his herd fully. Unfortunately, the same forces also operate on George. The outcome of these individualistic and/or self-protective decisions is a tragedy, as their actions result in an outcome whose net values to both herders (−35) is considerably less desirable than that which they could have realized had both decided to observe restraint (+30).

At the heart of Valuation dilemmas which people face in mixed-motive situations (such as the tragedy of the commons) is their sense of uncertainty. This sense of uncertainty stems from two major questions—the first concerned with the probable behaviors of the other actors, and the second with the

TABLE 9.8
Behavior Matrix Illustrating a Tragedy of the Commons

Sample of Herder Pete's Behavior Repertoire	*Sample of Herder George's Behavior Repertoire*	
	Graze herd fully	Restrict herd's grazing
Graze herd fully	−35 / −35	−80 / +75
Restrict herd's grazing	+75 / −80	+30 / +30

The tragedy of the commons is just one example of a mixed-motive situation in which the pursuit of self-interest can lead to poor outcomes.

appropriateness of one's own goals. In our example, neither herder could be certain that the other would not graze fully, even if both had agreed not to do so. People often renege on agreements, especially if they do not believe that the agreed-upon actions are in their best interests. In the absence of reliable information about the other's beliefs regarding this issue, lingering doubts must remain about the other's trustworthiness.

A second ambiguity involves which of one's own motives or concerns should weigh heavily in the choice of behavior. Short-term self-interest, long-term self-interest, concern for the other, and security are all possible motivators that can affect one's choice of action. For example, Pete might consider the reaction of the community to his grazing fully. Some of his neighbors might approve of such an action if they thought that this was a situation in which everyone should protect his or her own best interest. Others might criticize him for selfishly ruining the commons. Without knowing whether or not a consensus on this issue exists, Pete must decide what to do under conditions of some uncertainty.

Notice how the existence of a norm would help alleviate Pete's problem. For example, if Pete believed that people should act to promote their long-term interest, and if he knew that this belief was commonly held in the community (including by George), he could use this norm to weigh his options and thus be more certain of the correctness of his choice—that is, he would be more confident about his prediction regarding the particular outcome of his and George's joint actions. He would choose to restrict his grazing, fully expecting George to do the same. Why? Because George and he had incorporated a belief that was consistent with this behavior. If the incorporated belief prescribed immediate self-interest, however, a different choice would have been made, but the actors would have been just as confident that their behavior was correct. In short, as Thibaut and Kelley (1959) note, norms and roles facilitate social exchange, in large part because they permit the accurate prediction of outcomes.

Obviously, there exist a considerable number of norms and roles which can, and do, influence behavior in a social exchange. Of course, we cannot consider all of these incorporated beliefs about appropriate conduct in this chapter. Instead, we will focus somewhat narrowly on a norm and two roles which considerable research has shown to be relevant to a central dimension of exchange behavior—namely, the manner in which interactants distribute the rewards that are available in their social encounters. We will first examine the norm of *equity,* which is one of a number of rules of conduct which guide the manner in which people allocate rewards. We will then turn to an exploration of the ways in which differences in incorporated beliefs about the behaviors appropriate for men and women (the two sex roles) produce variations in reward distribution behaviors.

The Norm of Equity and Its Components

One of the major issues that must be addressed when people engage in social encounters is the manner in which the various costs and rewards available in the behavior matrix are allocated among the participants. It is not usually the case that a single outcome will yield the same net reward to both actors, nor is it automatic that over time, a series of exchanges will generate equal net values. For this reason, the distribution of rewards within a social relationship becomes a matter of some concern, especially since this issue has the potential to generate considerable acrimony and conflict. It is not surprising, then, that norms would develop to guide reward distribution decisions.

One such reward distribution rule is the norm of equity which, as noted, prescribes that each participant in an interaction receives a reward commensurate with his or her contributions to the relationship. Thus, by this rule, if the two actors contribute about the same amount of input—in terms of time, effort, productivity, and so on—they deserve about the same share of the available rewards. Similarly, if one actor has contributed more to the relationship, he or she should receive a commensurately greater share.

Walster, Walster, and Berscheid (1978, p. 6), in developing a formal theory of the role that the norm of equity plays in social exchange, capture these ideas with the following propositions:

1. Individuals will try to maximize their outcomes.
2. Groups can maximize collective rewards by evolving accepted systems for equitably apportioning resources among members. Thus, groups will evolve such systems of equity and will attempt to induce members to accept and adhere to these systems.

Interpersonal Comparison Equity. When employing the norm of equity, interactants judge the extent to which an outcome is commensurate with contributions by comparing both inputs and available rewards to two distinct standards. One standard of comparison is derived from the inputs and rewards of the other actor or actors. This component of the norm—termed *interpersonal comparison equity*—has been studied and discussed at great length in social psychology (Adams, 1965; Berkowitz & Walster, 1976; Homans, 1961; Leventhal, 1980; Mikula, 1980; Walster et al., 1978). While there is some minor disagreement concerning the exact manner in which actors compare their own contributions and possible rewards to the inputs and possible rewards of others in the exchange, a large body of empirical evidence demonstrates that people do distribute rewards by taking into account the differences in inputs that exist among the participants.

In one of the first investigations of reward distribution behavior, Gerald Leventhal and James Michaels (1969) asked undergraduates to participate in an industrial simulation in which they would work together in two-person teams on an arithmetic task. Subjects were informed that some teams would be working together on the task in the same room, whereas members of other teams would be working independently in separate rooms. Actually, all subjects were placed in the separate rooms condition, and as such, they never had occasion to meet their coworker. After they had completed the task, each team was paid according to the total number of correct answers that its two members had produced. Some subjects were led to believe that they had outperformed their coworker, while others were told that they had been the less effective member of the team. Subjects were then asked to divide their team's earnings between themselves and their coworker.[4]

The results of this study provide straightforward evidence that the norm of equity can affect reward distribution decisions. When subjects thought that they had contributed more to the team, they allocated more of the total reward to themselves. Conversely, when they thought that they had been outperformed by their coworker, respondents tended to provide the coworker with a greater share of the team's earnings.

These results demonstrate that the norm of equity is a widely held belief

---

[4] Most research on distribution norms, like that of Leventhal and Michael's (1969) has employed money as the reward. This is so because money is an easily quantified commodity, and it seems a reasonable assumption that most if not all people desire to acquire it. Researchers in this area, however, assume that the results obtained using money are applicable in circumstances in which other potential rewards (e.g., social support, affection, etc.) are allocated.

about appropriate behavior in exchange situations. Although there were few external constraints on the subjects, they distributed the reward in a manner that roughly mirrored differences in inputs. Subjects were aware that their identity would not be revealed to the other, and that their coworker could do nothing to affect them, so that there would have been few negative repercussions had they kept the entire amount.[5] Yet, they did not do so. Clearly, the temptation to be totally self-interested was tempered by a belief that such an action would be unfair; as a result, allocators chose a response option that was consistent with the norm, though their self-interest was not completely inhibited.

Internal Standard Equity. The second standard for comparison that interactants use when judging the extent to which an outcome conforms to the norm of equity consists of the set of beliefs that each brings to the encounter. From their past experiences, people develop an incorporated belief, or internal standard, of what is a fair return for a given contribution. As Weick and Nesset (1968), Pritchard (1969), and others have suggested, beliefs of this type can be used to judge the appropriateness of one's own outcomes, given his or her inputs (in which case, the standard is called own equity), or to judge the outcomes and inputs of others (other equity).

Of course, it would be expected that people would be more concerned with their own equity than with the equity of others, though both of these standards would weigh in their Valuations of reward allocations. In other words, most people are more concerned that they receive at least a fair share of the available rewards than they are that the other is doing so. This speculation is consistent with the basic assumption of hedonism that underlies social exchange theory (Walster, Walster, & Berscheid, 1978).

Lane and Messé (1972) present strong evidence that such internal standards do influence the manner in which people allocate rewards. In the first part of this investigation, they asked a large number of undergraduates their opinions concerning the appropriate pay for serving as subjects in research which involved completing questionnaires. This survey revealed a reasonable degree of consensus among the respondents that a pay rate of $2 per hour was appropriate.[6] Lane and Messe used this information in their reward distribution study.

In the second part of their investigation, the experimenters recruited undergraduate males to complete a set of questionnaires for pay. In their recruitment effort, the researchers were purposely vague about the exact amount of money that subjects could earn. In fact, they could not provide this information because the total amount of money that subjects were given

---

[5] It should be noted that subjects probably realized that their anonymity was not complete— the experimenter was well aware of both their identity and the distribution of funds that they chose. This awareness might have had some influence on their behavior; however, other research (Lane & Messé, 1971), in which subjects were completely anonymous, has produced similar findings to those of Leventhal and Lane (1969).

[6] Remember that this research was conducted in the early 1970s, when $2 would get you into a movie, with enough change remaining for a box of popcorn.

to divide between themselves and a coworker was the variable of major interest in the study.

In one set of conditions, respondents were paired with coworkers and were required to work for 90 minutes completing opinion questionnaires, for which there were no right or wrong answers. As in Leventhal and Michael's (1969) study, described above, subjects were then asked to divide an amount of money which they and their coworker had earned as a team for working on the task.

Some subjects were given $6 to divide. Lane and Messé purposely chose this amount, since an equal split would give each team member $3. Thus, this outcome would pay both workers $2 per hour, which the earlier survey had shown to be consistent with undergraduates' beliefs about the reward appropriate for activities of this type. Other allocators, however, were given a total of only $3 to divide between themselves and their coworker. In this case, the amount available was insufficient to provide both team members with an amount consistent with their internal standards for fair pay. Finally, other lucky subjects were given $12 to divide. This amount was much greater than that necessary to provide both team members with an equitable wage consistent with their internal standards.

These variations in the total amount of money made available to the allocator permitted Lane and Messé (1972) to determine if, in fact, people used both an interpersonal comparison and an internal standard of equity when distributing rewards. It is important to remember that in this research, both subject and coworker had made equal contributions to the team's efforts, since both had worked the same amount of time. Thus, the interpersonal comparison component of the norm of equity would prescribe that the allocators divide the reward equally, regardless of the total amount of money made available to the team. On the other hand, the internal standard component, coupled with a greater concern for one's own equity, would influence allocators to keep a greater share of the total reward when this amount was insufficient to permit an equitable distribution for both team members. Moreover, this perspective would influence subjects to behave similarly when the total amount available was substantially greater than that needed to satisfy both own and other equity. In this case, the allocator could pay both himself and the other a fair wage (that is, $3 for 1.5 hours' work), and keep the remainder for himself.

As noted, exchange theory postulates that norms such as equity develop to moderate self-interest, which has the potential to cause considerable conflict. When a situation involves an excess of rewards, the allocator can act self-interestedly and still follow the dictates of the norm. In such cases, the other can be paid a fair wage, thus satisfying equity, and at the same time, the allocator can keep the excess, thereby satisfying self-interest.

Table 9.9 presents the percentage of the total reward that subjects in Lane and Messé's (1972) study would be expected to keep for themselves, based upon these interpersonal comparison and internal standards of equity, along with the average percentage that they actually did allocate to themselves.

TABLE 9.9

Predicted and Actual Self-Allocation (in percent) as a Consequence of the Total Reward Available

		Total Amount Available	
	Insufficient	Consistent With Own-Other Equity	Oversufficient
Predicted by own-other equity	>50%*	50%	75%
Interpersonal comparison	50%	50%	50%
Actual allocation	64%	50%	60%

* The internal standard component of the norm predicts that this percentage would fluctuate, depending on the degree to which the individual is more concerned with own equity than with other equity—but it always should be greater than 50 percent.

Source: Adapted from Lane & Messé, 1972.

As Table 9.9 indicates, neither component of the norm of equity independently predicted actual allocation behavior; the pattern of results suggests that subjects were influenced by both components in combination. As would be expected on the basis of internal standard equity, allocators did keep a greater percentage of the total pay when this amount was substantially less than, or greater than, the $2-per-hour rate considered appropriate by undergraduates; and they divided the reward equally when the total amount was consistent with the internal standard. However, the percentage taken in the oversufficient condition, while greater than 50 percent, was substantially less than the 75 percent prescribed by the internal standard norm.

On the other hand, subjects divided the money evenly—the outcome that interpersonal comparison equity prescribes, regardless of the amount available—only when this allocation was also consistent with their internal standard—that is, when the total amount available equalled the sum of what own and other equity prescribed. Other research (Miller, 1977) produced results that are consistent with these findings. Thus, it appears that both components of the norm of equity affected subjects' reward distribution behavior; the interpersonal comparison component moderated their inclination to be totally self-interested under conditions of oversufficient reward, and the internal standard moderated their tendency to divide the reward according to (equal) inputs.

Difficulties in Applying the Norm. While the norm of equity is helpful in increasing the Resolution of social exchange situations, it does not overcome completely all of the problems that can arise when rewards must be distributed. First, there is not a parallel norm that exactly prescribes what constitutes inputs or contributions to a given social exchange relationship. There is less consensus, for example, about the weights that should be accorded time spent on an activity or the quality of a person's output (which can be determined by such factors as ability, effort, or even luck) when participants are deciding how to allocate the available rewards. Moreover, there is a tendency for people to overvalue their own contributions relative to the value that another would attach to them. Numerous studies, for example, have shown that we take more credit for our successes than others are willing to give us, and that we make more excuses for our failures (Snyder, Stephan, & Rosenfield, 1976; Streufert & Streufert, 1969). Differences in opinions about what constitutes a relevant input, or the value of such an input, can lead to conflicts of the sort that diminish the potential facilitative effect that the norm of equity can have on social exchange.

Other beliefs about appropriate reward allocation also can moderate the impact of the norm of equity on social exchange. For example, there is a norm that prescribes that people should consider relative need when determining the appropriate outcome of an exchange. Those who need the most should receive the most, regardless of their contributions. Lamm and Schwinger (1980), Leventhal and Weiss (cited in Leventhal, 1976), and Leventhal, Weiss, and Buttrick (1973) have demonstrated that under certain conditions, people weigh need more heavily than contributions when they allocate rewards.

In addition, there is a norm of equality, which many people have incorporated, that also can operate in opposition to the norm of equity. This belief prescribes that all parties in an exchange should receive the same outcome, regardless of their relative contributions (Deutsch, 1975; Sampson, 1975). Numerous studies have demonstrated that this norm can moderate the impact of equity on reward allocations. For example, the allocators in Leventhal and Michaels' study, discussed earlier, did not distribute rewards exactly in proportion to differences in inputs, as the norm of equity prescribes. Instead of keeping two thirds of the rewards for themselves when they had performed twice as well as their coworker, subjects took less than 60 percent. Thus, it appears that the norm of equality had some effect on subjects' allocation behaviors.

Although factors such as a lack of consensus regarding relevant inputs and competing reward-allocation norms can moderate the influence of the norm of equity, a large body of consistent evidence indicates that this rule has a major influence on the outcome of many social exchanges. Consequently, as Thibaut and Kelley (1959) hypothesized, this norm facilitates social exchange in mixed-motive situations by moderating the potential for interpersonal conflict that exists in such Social Contexts. In the following section, we will explore this proposition in some detail.

Equity as a Moderator of Interpersonal Conflict

Recall the earlier discussion of the tragedy of the commons and our argument that norms such as equity could facilitate mutually positive outcomes in such exchanges. In considering situations of this type, it should be noted that the participants really do not interact in any direct way—each behaves independently of the other. Nevertheless, an exchange relationship does exist between them because each person's actions have implications for the outcome of the other. Thus, while their behaviors are independent, their outcomes are not.

In another type of mixed-motive situation—one that is common to most interpersonal relationships—both behaviors and outcomes are interdependent. The exchange theory analysis of the encounter between Ted and Alice presented earlier is just one example of this more comprehensive form of interdependent relationship. A variant of this latter form of mixed-motive exchange involves an additional dimension to actors' decisions: when there is a choice of exchanges in which to engage, people first must decide on which behavior matrix to explore (that is, with whom to enter into an exchange) before they need to deal with the actual exchange behaviors that determine the net values available in the interaction.

A mixed-motive exchange that involves only an interdependence of outcomes is called an independent behavior situation. The more frequent mixed-motive exchange, which involves some amount of interaction between the participants of the exchange, is called bargaining. The variant on bargaining, which calls for a prior decision regarding the encounter in which the actor will engage, is called coalition formation. While different in some important respects, these situations share a crucial feature—namely, they are all mixed-motive contexts, and as such, they contain the potential for interpersonal conflict. In the following pages, we will explore how the norm of equity can moderate this potential for destructive (or tragic) outcomes in independent behavior, bargaining, and coalition formation contexts.

Independent Behavior. Albert Pepitone conducted a study which demonstrated that people use the norm of equity as a means to coordinate their actions in independent behavior, mixed-motive situations. In this study, Pepitone (1971) had pairs of subjects engage in an ambiguous color perception task and then gave them false feedback about their relative performances. In one condition of the study, one subject was told that he had performed very well, whereas the other was told that he had scored somewhere near the average. To determine their pay for serving in the study, respondents engaged in an independent behavior, mixed-motive exchange. Table 9.10 presents the behavior matrix that summarizes the potential outcomes available to the subjects.

In this exchange, each subject had the same two choices of actions. If he chose Option A, he would receive either 2 cents or 1 cent, depending upon the other's action. If he chose Option B, he would receive either 5 cents or nothing. Subjects made 50 such choices, and thus their pay could range from nothing to $2.50. Although the members of a pair thought that they were interacting with one another, Pepitone gave each of them the same feedback regarding the other's choice on each exchange—both subjects were led to believe that the other tended to choose Option A rather consistently. Thus, on most exchanges, the subject could expect to receive either 2 cents (if he, too, chose Option A), or 5 cents (if he chose Option B).

If subjects' actions were guided by the norm of equity, we would expect

TABLE 9.10
Behavior Matrix of Persons Engaged in
Independent Decision Mixed-Motive Exchange

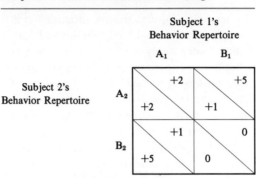

Source: Adapted from Pepitone, 1971.

that subjects who had outperformed their partner on the color perception task would act to receive more money than the partner—that is, they would choose Option B, so that they would receive 5 cents, and the other 1 cent. In contrast, we would expect that those who had performed relatively poorly would tend to act in a less self-serving manner and choose Option A the majority of the time. Pepitone's results were consistent with these predictions: subjects who performed better chose the more rewarding option in 64 percent of their exchanges, whereas those who had performed relatively poorly made this choice only about 50 percent of the time. Thus, this and other research (Messé, Dawson, & Lane, 1973) has consistently demonstrated that reward distribution norms such as equity facilitate cooperative exchanges in independent behavior contexts.

Bargaining. Social scientists have studied bargaining behavior using a number of research procedures. Some of these approaches are simulations of real-world situations (such as labor-management negotiations or buyer-seller exchanges) in which respondents play the various roles that are required. This type of research has produced interesting insights into a host of variables which affect the actions of people whose task is to agree, if they can, on an outcome (such as the selling price of an automobile, or a labor contract). Disparity in initial offers, the differences between bargainers as agents for other people or as agents for themselves, and the impact of arbitrators are just a few of the many factors that the vast amount of empirical research conducted in this area has shown to affect the outcome of such bargaining simulations (Apfelbaum, 1977; Rubin & Brown, 1975; Swingle, 1970).

Of more relevance to our concerns are those bargaining studies in which respondents are presented with a set of outcomes and must interact until they agree on a particular set of rewards. This research procedure more closely parallels informal interactions in which actors communicate their preference for one option ("Let's go bowling") over another ("I'm tired of watching TV") and agree, if possible, on a mutual activity. Rather than assuming a part in a simulation, respondents in such research play themselves—that is, the bargains that they strike are personally meaningful to them.

Research conducted by Messé (1971) demonstrated that the norm of equity facilitates agreement on mutually acceptable outcomes in this second type of mixed-motive bargaining situation. In this investigation, pairs of respondents were shown an abstract form of a behavior matrix, reproduced in Table 9.11. The matrix, rather than presenting the behaviors that would result in a given set of outcomes, merely depicted the outcomes per se—that is, the table identified, via the letters A through I, nine cells whose contents were the different rewards that were available to the interactants in this mixed-motive exchange. The pairs of subjects in the study were to communicate their preferred outcome to one another until they had reached agreement on one of the nine possible cells.

The design of this investigation was quite simple. Subjects (male undergraduates who participated in the study for pay) entered the research laboratory at different times to complete a series of opinion questionnaires of varying lengths. Some worked for 80 minutes on the task, others for 60 minutes, and still others for 40 minutes. These work schedules were arranged so that the pairs of interactants always finished their tasks at the same time. Then, pairs of subjects were seated together, with the behavior matrix (see Table 9.11) placed between them. The experimenter explained to them that each cell of the matrix represented a possible payoff. To get paid, they had to agree upon one particular cell whose values specified the amount of money that each would receive for participating in the study. Thus, for example, if they agreed upon cell B, the person on Side 1 would receive $1.50 and the person on Side 2, $2.25.

There are a number of interesting features of this particular behavior matrix that should be noted. First, the cell values change in different directions on the two sides of the matrix. As one moves from Outcome A to Outcome I, the reward for the person on Side 1 increases, whereas it decreases for the respondent on Side 2. Second, the range of rewards on Side 1 ($1 through $5) is more favorable than on Side 2 ($.50 through $2.50). Third, there are three prominent response options presented: Cell C, which provides equal

TABLE 9.11
Abstract Behavior Matrix of Bargainers

Reward Structures	A	B	C	D	E	F	G	H	I
Rewards to person on Side 1	$1.00	$1.50	$2.00	$2.50	$3.00	$3.50	$4.00	$4.50	$5.00
Rewards to person on Side 2	$2.50	$2.25	$2.00	$1.75	$1.50	$1.25	$1.00	$0.75	$0.50

Source: Adapted from Messé, 1971.

pay to both interactants; Cell E, which provides the person on Side 2 with twice the reward of his coworker on Side 1; and Cell I, which provides the greatest sum of rewards, but divides this amount the most unequally.

Subjects were paired systematically, so that the members of some pairs had worked the same amount of time on the opinion questionnaires; in other pairs, one member had worked for 80 minutes while his partner had worked half as long; in a third condition, one subject of the pair had contributed about three-quarters as much time as his coworker had. When work inputs differed, the subject with the greater contribution was always assigned to Side 1 of the matrix. In every case, subjects were informed of their coworker's inputs. Subjects' interactions were examined to determine the extent to which their relative work inputs influenced the outcome on which they finally agreed. As expected, the norm of equity affected subjects' choices to a major degree. Seven of the 10 pairs of respondents who had worked for the same amount of time quickly agreed on Cell C, which provided each with an equal reward. Similarly, in those dyads in which one member had worked twice as long as the other, by far the most frequently agreed-upon option was Cell E, which divided rewards in a 2:1 ratio. When the disparity in work inputs was less extreme, 7 of 10 pairs agreed on Cell D.

Thus, in each of these conditions, the most frequently chosen option was the outcome that corresponded most closely to that dictated by the norm of equity. Moreover, it was clear that the norm facilitated these interactions, since pairs that did not reach an equitable solution took almost three times as long to agree on an outcome as did their counterparts who were guided by this standard.

Coalition Formation. In an extension of the study presented previously, Messé and his coworkers (Messé, Vallacher, & Phillips, 1975) explored the effect of the norm of equity on people's choices of partners in a mixed-motive exchange. This study was typical of most social psychological investigations of coalition formation. In such work, three or more subjects are involved in a contest in which payoffs are determined by relative performance. For example, in one of the pioneering studies on coalition formation, Vinacke and Arkoff (1957) had groups of three subjects play a highly simplified Parcheesi game. Each subject was given a token to place on the game board. The object of the game was to be the first to move one's token completely around the board; prizes were to be awarded based on the order of finish. An interesting feature of this situation was the different resource values that were assigned to each of the tokens. For instance, in one condition, one token had a resource value of 2, a second a value of 3, and the third a value of 4. These values, along with a die thrown by the experimenter, determined the number of spaces that each player could move on a given turn. For example, suppose that the first throw of the die yielded a 3. As a consequence, the player with the resource value of 2 moved the token six spaces, the player with the value of three moved 9 spaces, and the player with the value of 4 moved 12 spaces.

There was not much sport in this game, since all players moved this way on every throw of the die. In fact, the outcome was predetermined before the first move. However, to provide some interest to the game, Vinacke and Arkoff (1957) gave the three subjects the opportunity to discuss the possibility of forming a coalition. To do so, two of the three players had to agree to combine forces—that is, to trade their tokens for one whose resource value was the sum of their individual values. A coalition was formed when two players had made such an agreement, along with a decision concerning the division of the resulting prize. Given the values that we have presented, it should be clear that any coalition of players would win. Hence, if players with resource values of 2 and 3 formed a coalition, they could defeat the player with the resource value of 4, who originally had the winning advantage.

Vinacke and Arkoff (1957) were interested in two issues: the frequency with which the various possible coalitions actually formed, and the manner in which the members of these winning coalitions divided the prize. Their study, and many that followed (summarized in Caplow, 1968; Gamson, 1964; Swingle, 1970; Vinacke, 1969), revealed a tendency for the two weakest players to coalesce against the strongest. Moreover, while there was considerable variation in the manner in which members of the winning coalitions agreed to divide the prize, they were somewhat inclined to split the reward according to their original resource values.

In reviewing these results, Messé, Vallacher, and Phillips reasoned that the great variability in subjects' behavior in past coalition formation experiments might have been attributable primarily to two factors: (1) the extrinsic value of the prizes awarded in such studies was typically small or nonexistent (in many studies the points awarded to the winning team could not be redeemed for anything); and (2) subjects' inputs in the usual game were vague, and thus, there was little basis for applying the norm of equity (the reader may recall that in Vinacke and Arkoff's study, luck determined the assignment of resource values).

To explore their speculations, Messé et al. (1975) had a number of groups of three subjects work on a task for varying periods of time. One subject worked for one hour, another for one and one half hours, and the third for two hours. The experimenters then assigned resource values to the subjects on the basis of these inputs, with 1 point awarded for each half-hour worked. The three group members then played a coalition game that resembled that of Vinacke and Arkoff (1957), except that there was a first prize of $7, and a consolation prize of $2. In these circumstances, in every group, the two players with the greatest resources formed a coalition and divided the reward exactly according to differences in inputs. In contrast, subjects in a control condition—in which resources were assigned at random, as in past research— acted in a manner similar to that of respondents in earlier studies—that is, the two weakest players tended to form coalitions. However, there was a strong tendency for these subjects to equally divide the $7 firstprize.

The results of this research again provide strong evidence for the operation of the norm of equity in mixed-motive exchange situations. When people "deserved" the resources they were awarded, the norm guided their behavior.

When the resources were randomly awarded, the norm was not salient and behaviors were more variable. Thus, it appears that when inputs and rewards are meaningful to an actor, the reward distribution norm of equity provides a structure by which appropriate outcomes can be reached.

The evidence presented in this section makes a compelling case for Thibaut and Kelley's (1959) thesis that norms serve to facilitate interpersonal behavior. As noted earlier, however, the norm of equity does not completely eliminate the potential for conflict in social exchanges, nor does it always insure that encounters will yield an optimal outcome. Additional factors operate in exchange situations, and these can sometimes work against mutually rewarding outcomes.

Conflict in Social Exchange. One reason for the occurrence of conflict in interpersonal exchanges is that dominant cues in the Social Context of the encounter suggest that confrontation is the appropriate orientation. In other words, the cues activate norms which prescribe that antagonistic behavior is proper in that particular context, whereas the norm of equity is viewed as much less relevant. For example, the norms of a poker game require that each interactant attempt to beat the other players, even if they all are good friends. Similarly, when bargaining over the price of a used car, the norms that guide this type of exchange prescribe that each interactant obtain the best possible deal. To violate these norms destroys the defining feature of such contexts—namely, competition or confrontation.

A second reason for conflict to occur in interpersonal exchanges involves a disagreement among the interactants about their relative contributions to the relationship. As noted earlier, people often have different standards regarding their inputs and those of others. Some might regard effort as an important consideration, whereas others might view this potential input as more or less irrelevant. Thus, even in contexts in which there is consensus that the norm of equity should apply, conflict can still occur because the interactants do not place a common value on their respective inputs. Such disagreements and the resulting conflicts are not unusual, since there is often considerable ambiguity concerning the worth of the activities that one or another interactant provides to a relationship.

For example, a frequent source of conflict between spouses concerns the relative worth of the inputs that each brings into the family. The husband might perceive that "bringing home the paycheck" is the major input, and that therefore, he should not be expected to do many household chores. The wife, in contrast, might feel that her contributions in running the household are substantial, and that her husband's attempt to shoulder her with all the household duties is unfair. Disagreements of this type are common even when the participants agree that the norm of equity should guide behavior in the relationship. In spite of such an agreement regarding the relevance of the norm, the different weights that interactants assign to inputs are potential sources of considerable conflict, to which the full dockets of the divorce courts throughout this country will attest.

A third cause of conflict in interpersonal encounters is a consequence

KAKU KURITA/GAMMA-LIAISON

Conflict is likely to occur in interpersonal exchanges when cues in the context suggest that confrontation is appropriate.

of the reward available to the interactants. As discussed earlier, people are more concerned that their rewards be at least equitable, relative to their inputs, than they are that others receive a fair reward. Obviously, situations are likely to produce conflict when the available rewards are not sufficient to provide all the interactants with an equitable return. Less obvious, but just as true, is the fact that conflict is also likely to occur in contexts in which the amount of reward available is substantially *more* than necessary to provide each interactant with an equitable outcome.

An example of conflict arising from a context of excessive available rewards is provided in the scene common in many B movies in which the bank robbers or safe crackers fight among themselves after pulling off the big job. One might expect that dividing $3 million would be a joyous and harmonious chore; however, such is rarely the case in these movies—and probably in real-life situations, too. The partners in crime often conflict (usually violently) over the distribution of their ill-gotten gains, and it is precisely because these gains were ill-gotten (that is, considerably more than what the thieves deserve) that the norm of equity does not operate. Therefore, conflict about the appropriate distribution of the goods ensues.

We believe that there is some parallel between thieves fighting over an overabundance of reward and the situation common in the world of professional sports. The popularity of professional baseball, football, and basketball, as well as other sports, has made them highly profitable business ventures. One could argue that the conflict between owners and players is a result of a perception on the part of the players that there is an overabundance of available rewards. Most players, including those whose salaries are in the millions of dollars, would probably admit that no one is worth that much. However, they argue that their salary demands are reasonable, given that the owners' excess profits, which are based on inflated ticket prices and TV revenues, could not be gained without their efforts. Consistent with this interpretation, Samuel Komorita (1979) has proposed that people in bargaining situations only fight over the amount of available reward that is in excess of an equitable return on inputs. In light of the manner in which the norm of equity appears to operate (Lane & Messé, 1972), it is reasonable to postulate that such conflicts also occur when people must bargain over rewards that are not sufficient to provide each with a fair share.

Finally, actors in an exchange sometimes apply different weights to the various reward distribution norms mentioned earlier (equity, equality, need, and so on), and such differences in the perceived relevance of these beliefs can cause conflict between the interactants. For example, students who are assigned a group project often object to an instructor's grade assignment rule, whereby all are given the same mark regardless of differences in contribution to the project. In this instance, the instructor is using the norm of equality, whereas the students feel that the norm of equity should be applied.

Because people do differ in their judgments about the relevance of distribution norms, it is of interest to explore the possible bases for such differences. One intriguing possibility is that these variations are a component of role differences. Recall that roles are beliefs about proper conduct that apply to only a subset of the interactants in an exchange. It is conceivable that actors who vary in the weights they apply to the distribution norms also differ in other important ways. This speculation, as well as other related hypotheses, is explored in detail in the following section, where we will discuss the manner in which two specific roles—those associated with males and those associated with females—are related to exchange behavior.

Sex Roles and the Process of Social Exchange

A common finding in much of the research on social exchange is that females and males differ in the manner in which they allocate rewards. In general, this evidence suggests that males adhere to the norm of equity, whereas females are more variable in applying the norm and are less likely, overall, to act in a self-serving manner. For example, using the reward allocation research procedure typical of much research in this area, Leventhal and

Lane (1970) had both males and females distribute the team's rewards. Before the allocation, subjects were informed that they had performed better or worse than their coworker on the task that determined the team's total pay.

Leventhal and Lane's findings indicated that male allocators kept more than half the available reward when they had outperformed their coworker, but they also gave the coworker more than 50 percent when the difference in performance favored the other. Thus, their behavior was consistent with the prescriptions of the norm of equity. In contrast, females behaved equitably only when it was not in their best interest to do so—that is, they gave their coworker substantially more than 50 percent when this person's performance was superior, but took only about half of the total reward when they had outperformed their coworker. Moreover in every condition, female allocators kept a smaller portion of the monetary reward than did their male counterparts.

Results of this type have been replicated in a wide variety of contexts (Carles & Carver, 1979; Kahn, 1972; Lane & Messé, 1971; Messé & Lichtman, 1972; Mikula, 1974; Reis & Jackson, 1981; Watts, Messé, & Vallacher, in press). Studies repeatedly have shown that females in exchange encounters disregard the norm of equity when it prescribes distribution behavior that is consistent with their economic best interests. Such sex differences in reward allocation have generated considerable interest in social psychology, and a number of hypotheses have been advanced to explain them (for comprehensive summaries of these explanations, see Kahn, O'Leary, Krulewitz, & Lamm, 1980; Leventhal, 1973; Sampson, 1975). We will now briefly discuss some of the more intriguing of these explanations.

Agency and Communion. One set of hypotheses that has been proposed to explain sex differences in reward allocation involves variations in the Personal Structures of men and women. David Bakan (1966) has proposed that human functioning is guided by two overriding concerns: *agency* and *communion*. Agency reflects a concern for achievement, prominence, and success, whereas communion refers to concerns with intimacy, interpersonal relationships, and attachment. In Bakan's view, both orientations exist in every person, but socialization experiences predispose males to focus more on issues involving agency, and females to focus more on communion. Research, in fact, has provided some support for this speculation (Carlson, 1971; Watts et al., in press) by demonstrating this difference between men and women in their relative concerns about agency and communion.

These varying concerns for agency and communion typically expressed by males and females have been used to explain the sex differences observed in social exchange (Kahn et al., 1980). For example, Vinacke (1959) and Bond and Vinacke (1961) speculate that females might be more "accommodative" than males, and that this tendency to be more sensitive to the needs and wishes of others might be responsible for the reluctance shown by women to behave in a self-interested fashion. Such a tendency is consistent with a concern for interpersonal harmony and intimacy—the defining features of communion.

Research by Watts et al. (in press) has yielded results consistent with the hypothesis that sex differences in social exchange are affected by different levels of concern for agency and communion. In this research, the importance of agency and communion for a large number of male and female undergraduates was measured via a standardized test. Not surprisingly, a sex difference emerged: males were more agentic, and females more communal. However, this association was far from perfect, and thus, a number of highly communal males and highly agentic females could be identified. These people, along with others whose levels of agency and communion were more typical of their sex, were recruited to participate in a reward distribution study. As expected, the results indicated that irrespective of sex, the more agentic subjects acted more equitably when they distributed rewards, whereas the more communal subjects tended to keep less for themselves than they thought was equitable.

Sources of Satisfaction. An extension of Bakan's idea of agency and communion suggests that males and females place different values on the potential rewards available in their behavior matrices. For example, females might place a higher value on the actions of others that provide them with social approval, whereas males might find greater value in the indication by others that their past successes have been recognized. While males and females might find both types of outcomes rewarding, they might do so to different extents.

This reasoning has implications for understanding the sex difference that typically has been found in studies of reward allocation. As noted earlier, most research of this type has used money as the reward. If money has greater value for males than for females, then it is easier for females to act in ways that do not promote their economic well-being in a social exchange. It is clear that both males and females value money as a resource which enables them to satisfy a vast number of needs. However, money can have psychological value that goes beyond mere economic concerns. For example, while pay is important to us because it provides us with economic support, it also can signify the importance that others place on our work. Conceivably, such performance evaluations are more important to males than to females, thereby lending greater meaning to money for males.

Given the speculation that males are more likely to be ego-involved with being paid as much money as possible—because pay is a sign that their work is valued—it follows that females would feel that the connection between work and pay is less important. Consistent with this reasoning, Mednick and Tangri (1972) and Chesler and Goodman (1976) have observed that socialization practices foster in women a more tenuous connection between work and pay. Traditionally, work for males is defined as activities for which they receive monetary compensation; in contrast, what has been traditionally considered women's work (child care, housekeeping, and so on) is not connected to pay in any direct way. Traditionally, women are cared for by males, but they are not directly paid for their work. Under these circumstances, we would expect that the link between work and pay would be weaker in the view of women.

Evidence which suggests that women, in fact, perceive less of a connection between work and monetary pay was obtained by Callahan-Levy and Messé (1979). In this research, male and female respondents, whose ages ranged from 6 through 21 years, first completed a task. Then each subject was given an amount of money and two envelopes, one marked "My pay," the other marked "Remainder." Subjects were told to take the amount of money which they thought was appropriate for the work they had done and to put the remaining amount into the second envelope.

Results were straightforward and dramatic: in every age group, the females paid themselves less than did their male peers. This was so in spite of the fact that the males and females did not differ in their evaluations of their own performance on the task. In addition, in a different phase of this study, the researchers found that when both males and females were asked to pay another person for similar work, allocators of both sexes paid the female more.

The pattern of findings yielded by this research indicates that the tendency of females to underpay themselves, relative to males, cannot be attributable to a general perception that males deserve more money for performing a task. Nor can the results be explained in terms of a tendency on the part of both sexes to undervalue women's accomplishments. Instead, it appears that women see less of a connection between their own work and the pay that should be provided for it, and this attitude makes them more susceptible to other concerns, such as a wish not to appear avaricious or selfish. Males, on the other hand, do not appear to be as constrained by concerns for social desirability; they want to be paid what they "deserve." Interestingly, this sex difference in attitudes toward work and money appeared even in the youngest age group examined (the first-graders), a finding which suggests that sex roles are incorporated very early in life.

Contextual Effects. A final explanation of the frequently observed sex differences in reward allocation behavior involves a consideration of the Social Context in which such exchanges typically have been studied. Most often, studies have been undertaken within the framework of an "industrial simulation" or similar work-related settings. In these circumstances, the social exchanges examined have focused on economic and business issues, and not on more socially relevant interactions. It could be that because of differences in past experience, males are more familiar with such contexts and thus feel more at ease in them. They very well might have a more resolved sense of what constitutes appropriate behavior in such circumstances.

One of the major components of the Social Context of most reward distribution studies is the task performed by subjects, which serves as the basis for payment. In most research, this task has been one which, traditionally, males were expected to perform well (such as solving mathematical problems). The male-oriented nature of the tasks might have led females to weigh differences in performance of them as less important than did males, since they would be less certain about why such differences occurred—that is, they might wonder if the differences were attributable to effort, ability, or luck.

Harry Reis and Linda Jackson (1981) performed a study which examined the possibility that the male-oriented nature of most of the tasks used in reward distribution research influenced the responses of male and female allocators. They had male and female subjects work on one of two tasks. A pretest had determined that one task was perceived as male-oriented (one on which males were expected to do well), and the other as female-oriented (on which females should do well). As in past studies, female allocators did not divide the reward equitably when the task was male-oriented. However, they did behave in accord with the norm of equity when they and their partner had worked on the female-oriented task. In contrast, males divided the reward equitably, regardless of the sex-linked nature of the task. This last result makes sense if we assume that any work context is traditionally perceived as a masculine arena.

A Comparison of the Explanations. We have briefly reviewed three of the explanations of the sex difference in reward allocation behavior. Other interpretations of this phenomenon have been suggested, but these are similar in tone to those discussed here. A question not addressed to this point is this: Which of these explanations, if any, is most correct? As with many issues in our field, the answer appears to be that all of the explanations have some validity. All have been supported, at least to some extent, by empirical research, and all appear to make good sense. Thus, it seems reasonable to conclude that the manner in which people approach reward distribution activity is determined to a great extent by numerous aspects of the male and female sex role—sex-linked differences in motivation, beliefs, habits—and the relevance of these characteristics to different Social Contexts.

Other Relationships between Sex Roles and Exchange. Standards of conduct, which we have discussed almost exclusively in terms of reward distribution behavior, are also relevant to a host of other facets of interpersonal encounters. While a comprehensive review of the relationship between norms, roles, and all dimensions of exchange would prove informative, such a review would also be somewhat redundant with the material already presented. Accordingly, we will provide only a sample of some of the many links between norms, roles, and exchange behaviors investigated by social psychologists. For continuity with previous material, we will again focus on sex roles, especially as they affect mixed-sex interpersonal encounters.

One question that long has occupied the attention of social psychologists involves the different frequencies with which men and women engage in activities that are common to the behavior repertoires of both sexes—that is, although men and women are equally capable of engaging in a variety of behaviors, some of these activities are expressed considerably more often by one sex than the other. Research by Strodtbeck and Mann (1956), Soskin and John (1963), Jourard (1971), and others, for example, has uncovered striking sex differences in the frequency of verbal speech, as well as in the content of such communications. Men initiate conversations more often than do women, and they talk more, and interrupt more; in contrast, women are more likely to respond to the comments of others, and they are less likely to resist when a man attempts to interrupt them. Women also appear more willing to disclose information about themselves than are men.

From these findings, it would appear that when men and women talk, men tend to control the conversation. However, there is evidence that women in such encounters engage in less overt, but nevertheless effective, impingement tactics. Relevant to this issue Cary (1974) conducted an investigation of behavior control during initial encounters. He simply had pairs of unacquainted men and women meet. One of the subjects in each pair was seated in an otherwise empty room. Then, the second subject was instructed to enter the room.

Cary noted the exchanges that took place between these potential interactants. He found that there was a slight tendency for the person who was seated in the room to initiate the interaction. Of more interest to our concerns were the interactions that occurred when the seated person was a woman. Not surprisingly, the first contact tended to be an exchange of glances. If the woman then looked away and did not look back at the man who had entered the room, no further interaction took place during the brief period that they remained in the room. However, if the woman did return her gaze to the man, they were likely to begin to talk. Clearly, both actors in Cary's (1974) study exerted some control over the course of this initial encounter. However, the means by which this control was applied differed as a consequence of sex roles.

Perhaps one of the most clear-cut examples of the ways in which sex roles can influence social exchange is provided in research by Edwin Megargee. In this study, Megargee (1969) measured a Personal Structure characteristic—the need for dominance—in a large number of undergraduates. As might be expected, dominance—a concern with directing other persons' behaviors and being a leader—was generally a higher level motive for males than for females; but in spite of this relationship, Megargee was able to identify a reasonably large number of atypical, high-dominant females and low-dominant males. Megargee (1969) used this information to study the combined impact of dominance and sex roles on two-person exchanges. He assembled pairs of subjects to work on a task that required the coordinated activity of two people. He always paired a high-dominant person with a low-dominant person, but he varied the sexual composition of these dyads: some dyads consisted of two males; others of two females; a third set paired a high-dominant male with a low-dominant female; a fourth paired a high-dominant female with a low-dominant male.

Megargee explained to the members of each pair that the task (either constructing a large model or filing papers in a letter file) required each of them to take a different job. One of them (the supervisor) had to direct the activities of the other (the worker). He explained further that the subjects were to decide between themselves who would assume the job of supervisor and who would be the worker. Megargee was interested in two important questions in his research: (1) whether dominance and sex roles would affect each pair's choice of supervisor; and (2) whether these variables would influence the way in which this decision was made. To answer these queries, he noted the sex and dominance level of the person whom each pair had selected as supervisor, and the sex and dominance level of the person who originally suggested this job assignment.

The results of this investigation are quite interesting. As expected, the Personal Structure variable of dominance did have an effect on the selection of supervisor. In every condition of the study but one, pairs chose as supervisor the more dominant member of the dyad. The one exception occurred among the pairs composed of a high-dominant female and a low-dominant male; there was a strong tendency for these pairs to choose the low-dominant male as supervisor.

A similar pattern emerged regarding which member of the pair originally suggested the choice of supervisor. In this case, in every condition except one, dominance level was not related to who made the initial suggestion. Low-dominant subjects were just as likely to ask the other to supervise as

As Megargee's study illustrates, males in our culture traditionally are more free to express dominance motives.

high-dominant subjects were to volunteer for this job. This finding suggests that low-dominant individuals are as motivated to have someone direct their activities as their high-dominant counterparts are motivated to act as directors. Again, the sole exception to this pattern involved pairs of high-dominant females and low-dominant males; in these cases, the high-dominant female was likely to tell the low-dominant male that he should be the supervisor.

Megargee's results have important implications for understanding the impact of sex roles on the expression of behaviors in social exchanges. This research indicated that sex role affected the manner in which subjects could satisfy their dominance motives. Because of the constraints imposed on them by their sex role, high-dominant females could not directly satisfy this motive by assuming the job of supervisor, as could their male counterparts. Nonetheless, they exerted a dominating influence on the choice of supervisors by compelling the low-dominant male—who was motivated to avoid having to direct the encounter—to take on this duty. Thus, while motivation differences did affect subjects' behaviors in the encounter, sex role clearly moderated the actors' judgments concerning the ways in which this motive should be satisfied.

CONCLUDING REMARKS

This concludes our review of the fundamental principles of interpersonal behavior, as viewed from the perspective of social exchange theory. The material concerning the processes of social exchange has been discussed at length in this chapter and serves as a framework for much of the information to be presented in the remaining chapters of this text. A thorough understanding of exchange theory, and the ways in which this perspective encompasses the integrative themes of Control, Valuation, Resolution, Consistency, and Sentiment, will help the reader to understand the phenomena of interpersonal behavior presented in Chapters 10 through 13.

In this chapter we have been concerned with people's behavior in interpersonal encounters and the variables that affect the course of these exchanges. Many such encounters are quite transitory, lasting for no more than a few moments. The consequences of these brief encounters are usually minor, though some can have major implications for the interactants. Social psychologists have extensively studied two general types of such transient but meaningful encounters—those which involve altruistic behavior and those which involve aggressive behavior—in other words, helping or hurting another person. We will review this material in Chapter 10.

Social psychologists have also investigated the impact of long-term interactions. Encounters which consist of numerous exchanges, carried out over relatively long periods of time, in which the participants interact intensively, can clearly have a major impact on the well-being of the interactants, and can influence their feelings about each other and their beliefs, motives, and habits. In Chapters 11 through 13, we will explore how people's experiences in long-term encounters affect these outcomes.

Interpersonal Behavior in Brief Encounters: The Examples of Helping and Hurting

10

In the preceding chapter, we presented a general framework through which the diversity of human social behavior could be described. As noted, social exchanges can take place within very brief encounters or can occur within relationships that endure over extended periods of time. In the present chapter, we will focus on two types of behaviors which usually take place within short-term encounters: helping behaviors, which are activities intended to benefit another more than they are intended to directly reward the actor; and, in contrast, hurting (or antisocial) behaviors, which are actions that are intended to harm another person.

We discuss these two categories of behavior primarily for two reasons. First, because of the importance of understanding helping and hurting behaviors to society at large, the exploration of the variables that affect these two types of activities has been a major focus of contemporary social science. This work has yielded important insights into the nature of helping and hurting. As such, any review of social psychological theory and research would be incomplete without a presentation of the major contributions in these areas.

Second, though they appear to be antithetical activities (what could be more different from helping than hurting?) social psychologists have provided evidence which suggests that these behaviors are affected by the same underlying processes. For this reason, considering helping and hurting in tandem permits us to stress that all social behaviors share some common bases, and therefore can be viewed within an integrative (thematic) perspective.

HELPING AND HURTING AS EXAMPLES OF SOCIAL EXCHANGE

As discussed in Chapter 9, analyzing social behaviors from the perspective of exchange theory involves a consideration of the relative rewards and costs associated with the actions that potentially could be expressed in an encounter. Since helping and hurting actions are merely two specific types of social behaviors, they too can be analyzed within this framework. Thus, both forms of activity can be dissected in terms of the rewards and costs generally associated with each.

Helping

To illustrate the potential rewards and costs associated with helping behavior, consider the following example. While driving across town, you notice a car stopped at the side of the road some distance away. As you draw nearer to the scene, it is clear that the car's left rear tire is flat. A single individual is standing beside the car, looking at the tire in puzzled disbelief. You have a limited number of options regarding your response to this situation. You might keep driving. You might use your CB radio (in this example, your car is "loaded") to call for assistance. You might drive to the nearest service station and have a service truck sent to the disabled car. Or you might stop your car to see what you could do to help.

What determines the option that you choose? One set of factors that is likely to weigh heavily in your decision is your assessment of the costs involved in each of these behaviors. Driving on without doing anything might make

JOEL GORDON

Being confronted with scenes of this sort typically presents us with some difficult decisions to make.

you feel guilty. This aversive reaction could be enhanced by factors in the Social Context—for example, the driver of the disabled car might have an arm in a cast, etc.—and as such, these conditions would raise your costs for deciding not to help. Stopping at a service station also could prove costly—you were pressed for time, the nearest station was out of your way, or you felt that you would have to argue with the attendant. Stopping to help could be a costly option—it would possibly entail your changing a heavy, dirty tire. Or even worse, the situation might really be a set-up to lure you into a trap in which you would be relieved of your valuables and perhaps even your life. Finally, if you used your CB, there would be little direct cost involved—however, you could never be sure that your call was really of help, and this uncertainty represents a cost to you.

If costs were the only factor to be considered in your Valuation of what to do, it is clear that the CB option would be optimal. However, such is not the case, since potential rewards, which differ with each option, also affect your decision. What are the potential rewards available in this situation? Clearly, the least rewarding options are ignoring the disabled car or using your CB to call for help. In the former instance, the sense of security that you would feel from avoiding involvement in a potentially onerous or danger-ous interaction would result in some reward value for you. Calling for help on your CB radio would give you a feeling, at least in part, that you did something for the disabled motorist while, at the same time, you would avoid potential unpleasantness. Going for help would provide a somewhat greater sense of having been of assistance, since you would be certain that your actions actually were of benefit to the motorist in need. However, only if you had stopped and directly assisted the motorist would you have been likely to experience substantially greater rewards. At a minimum, you might expect to be reinforced by the motorist's expressions of gratitude. Or, if you were very lucky, the motorist might have been an eccentric millionaire who, as a result of your kindness, rewarded you with a large check.

The Valuation process described here compels you to make an estimate, as in any exchange situation, of the option that will yield the outcome with the greatest net value, and to act accordingly. Again, your Valuation process well might have been faulty—the value of a rejected outcome, or one which you did not even consider, in fact, might have been the most profitable. Similarly, you might have grossly overestimated the net value of the option that you did choose.

In any event, by estimating rewards and costs in the manner described, you narrow your consideration to the CB or the direct intervention options. The CB option provides you with some reward for acting and, at the same time, costs you very little; direct intervention holds the possibility of the greatest reward, but also entails the greatest risk. However, just as you decide that you should directly intervene, you realize that you have driven well past the stranded motorist, and there is no convenient way for you to return to the scene of the trouble. Thus, you exercise your best remaining option by calling for assistance on your CB radio. This action rewards you with a sense that you have done your best "under the circumstances."

From this example, it can be seen that situations which call for prosocial or helpful actions typically contain elements of both costs and rewards. One obvious set of costs is resource expenditure, as measured in terms of time, energy, effort, money, and so forth. Perhaps a more subtle cost involves feelings of inadequacy or guilt which would arise as a consequence of not helping, especially if the actor has incorporated a belief (a norm or role) which says that it is proper to help in such a context. Similarly, some cost might accrue as a result of the social disapproval of others if the actor, by not helping, publicly violates a norm that is widely held by those in a position to monitor his or her behavior.

On the other hand, the act of helping often entails some risk, and sometimes this element of risk involves actual physical danger (such as the possibility of being mugged). People are often reluctant to intervene in such contexts because they fear that their actions could lead to possible legal or bureaucratic difficulties. Fear of being sued, of being forced to serve as a witness in court, or of being compelled to complete lengthy reports are examples of the potential negative outcomes that people cite as reasons for failing to help another in need. Finally, helping can sometimes entail considerable psychological costs to the helper when he or she has misinterpreted the situation. Concerns about the embarrassment that results from intervening unnecessarily or from intruding in a private matter also operate against the expression of prosocial activities.

On the positive side, the same options which entail some costs can also be the source of rewards. In some instances, the options being weighed might directly satisfy a motive. Clearly, acting to help a person in need would be rewarding to those people for whom altruism is a high level motive. Similarly, helping behavior can be satisfying to people who, while not particularly concerned with altruism, might use such an occasion to satisfy other motives (such as the need for competence, achievement, attention, and so on). Conversely, not acting can be a source of reward for some people (those who have high level needs for security and dependence). Finally, whatever their high level motives, people can also engage in prosocial behavior not because it is directly rewarding in any way, but rather because they perceive such actions as instrumental—that is, as increasing the probability that they will achieve some other valued outcome. For example, one might help another in an attempt to curry favor, to induce a sense of obligation, in the hopes of receiving a monetary reward, and so on.

Hurting

An exchange analysis of hurting or antisocial behavior follows much the same path as the analysis of helping. People who find themselves in a situation in which one or more of their options involves the intentional harm of another consider the rewards and costs of such actions when deciding what to do. For example, consider the options available to Chet "Bubba" Gondorf, one of Gotham City's most celebrated muggers, when he is practicing his chosen profession. It is 2 A.M., and Bubba is in place at his usual work station—a doorway just across the street from Mac's Lucky 7 Bar and Grille. Just as he is about to call it a night, a small figure stumbles out of Mac's and begins to weave his way down the street. Bubba regards this individual with minor interest until by chance, a streetlamp causes an object on the person's wrist to give off a dazzling flash of light.

In his professional judgment, Bubba concludes that there can only be one source of this light show—an expensive gold watch. Approaching his mark from behind, Bubba considers a number of possible actions. He might stop the man and ask him to give him the time along with the timepiece, using his gun as an inducement. Or he might walk quickly past the victim and yank the watch from his wrist. Still another option would involve knocking his target unconscious and then leisurely removing the watch from his wrist. Finally, his most extreme possibilities include either shooting his victim, thereby insuring a minimum of resistance, or deciding not to accost the man at all.

The Valuation in which Bubba engages is similar in form to that which you performed in deciding what to do about the stranded motorist. As in your dilemma, Bubba must also estimate the potential costs and rewards associated with each of his response options. Shooting his victim could prove very costly—especially if Bubba is caught by the police. Similar but less severe potential costs exist if he attempts to knock his victim unconscious, but in this case, there are added risks—the victim might put up a struggle or be able to identify his assailant.

These latter risks are increased if Bubba chooses merely to threaten his victim with his gun, though his consequences in this case, if apprehended, are less adverse. However, this option also carries with it a greater probability of failure. Snatching the watch is the illegal option with the least risks in terms of costs should Bubba be caught; but it is also the least likely to succeed. Finally, not attempting to acquire the watch is Bubba's least costly option, if he considers only the possible negative consequences; but it is the most costly in terms of lost opportunity.

In evaluating the potential available rewards, Bubba has to consider the likelihood that a given action will prove successful, since acquiring the watch is his primary goal in an encounter of this type (he is not trying to win new friends). From this perspective, not attempting to steal the watch would be the least rewarding option, whereas shooting the victim would be most likely to produce a successful outcome. However, Bubba might have high level motives, in addition to pure greed, which weigh in his decision. For example, he might find it enjoyable to hurt people (that is, aggression might be a high level motive for him), or he might be proud of his competence as a professional mugger. In this instance, Bubba would choose the option that would have the highest probability of success with the least danger of being caught. Yet again, he might value the risks involved in such confrontations, in which case he would weigh heavily the option that entailed threatening the victim with his gun.

In brief, depending upon variations in his Personal Structure, Bubba could engage in hurting behavior for two major reasons: (1) he could view such behavior as rewarding, per se, because such actions satisfy important high level motives (aggression); or (2) he could see his aggressive actions as instrumental, perceiving them as the means to a valued outcome. It seems most likely that if Bubba decides to hurt the victim physically as well as economically, he does so for both reasons—that is, he views such violence as both a useful and an enjoyable activity.

Accordingly, as predicted, Bubba decides to slug his victim, take his watch, and run. He gleefully carries out his chosen plan, and as a consequence, becomes the proud owner of a sparkling imitation brass Mickey Mouse timepiece, whereas his victim becomes the not-so-proud owner of a large lump on his head, accompanied by a bare wrist and an angry wife.[1]

Valuation Processes in Helping and Hurting

In the preceding discussion we suggested that similar social psychological processes affect behavior in both helping and hurting situations. Indeed, we maintain that the same processes operate in any Social Context. To demonstrate this point, we will turn to a model that Bibb Latané and John Darley developed to describe the decisions that people must make (the Valuation processes, in our terms) when deciding on their actions in a potential emergency. A diagram of this model is presented in Figure 10.1. We will apply this model in analyzing a helping situation (the stranded motorist example), as Latané and Darley (1970) intended. Then, to demonstrate the generality of these decision processes for very different Social Contexts, we will apply the same model in an analysis of a hurting situation (Bubba's actions).

Latané and Darley (1970) proposed that people progress through five stages when deciding on the particular responses which they will make in a potential emergency:

1. As illustrated, the model suggests that in a potential help-giving context, the actor first must notice that something is happening—that is, he or she must attend to cues which suggest that further decisions are necessary. In the example of the stranded motorist, you would have had no decision to make regarding your actions if

---

[1] For purposes of illustration, in this example, as well as in the stranded motorist story, we have discussed social behavior as if it were the consequence of rather protracted, rational thought processes. Such processes probably do play a role in almost all social activity. However, as noted in Chapter 9, there is usually an impulsive, emotional component to our behaviors as well. Thus, in real life, muggers like Bubba probably think about whether or not to commit a crime, but once this decision is made, they tend to behave more or less impulsively. We assume that even these impulsive behaviors reflect underlying motives and habits, and as such, are subject to the same principles of social behavior as are more rational actions.

FIGURE 10.1
A Decision Model of Helping Behavior

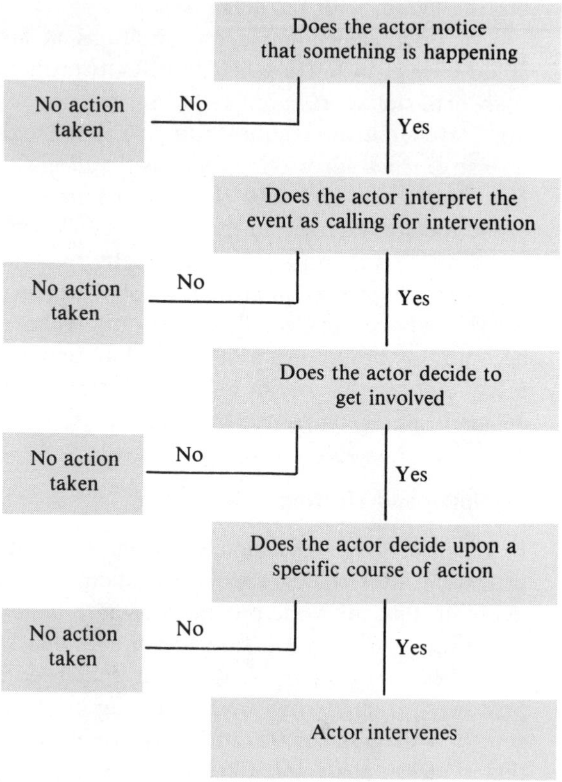

Does the actor notice
that something is happening

No action taken ← No

Yes

Does the actor interpret the
event as calling for intervention

No action taken ← No

Yes

Does the actor decide to
get involved

No action taken ← No

Yes

Does the actor decide upon a
specific course of action

No action taken ← No

Yes

Actor intervenes

Source: Adapted from Latané and Darley (1970).

you had not noticed that there was something in the distance, off to the side of the road.[2]

2. Assuming that the actor has attended to the cues, he or she then must interpret them—that is, assign meaning and weights to the available cues. In the example, the cue-weighting process involved your perception that the objects that you noticed in the distance were a car with a flat tire and a person (presumably the upset driver) standing beside it.

3. Next, the actor must decide whether he or she should become involved in the situation. This decision, as Latané and Darley (1970) describe it, is an either-or choice—that is, you estimate the rewards and costs involved, and then decide either to act in some way or to ignore the situation entirely. In the example, this phase of the process involved your decision to lend some form of assistance to the motorist—at the very least, to call for aid on your CB—or to drive by and do nothing. As noted earlier, this decision concerned

---

[2] The reader should note that this model is relevant to contexts of low Resolution.

which of these two alternatives would yield the greater net positive outcome.

4. The fourth stage of the decision process, given that the actor has attended to the cues, interpreted them, and decided to act in some way, entails a decision about what exactly should be done. Again, estimating potential rewards and costs for each response option is the primary Valuation process that occurs in this stage. Recall that you had to choose among several possible courses of prosocial actions which ranged from using your CB to stopping your car and providing direct assistance to the motorist. Because of the time it took you to mull over these options, you had driven past the disabled car. Since the costs of turning around weighed heavily in your Valuation, you decided that it would be best to use your CB to summon help.

5. Finally, the actor must engage in the behavior that he or she had decided upon in the fourth stage of the decision process. So, you used your CB, feeling confident that the person you contacted would call the service station as she had promised.

In brief, the five stages of the Latané and Darley model involve noticing, interpreting, deciding to act, deciding on a particular action, and acting. Let us now turn to our friend Bubba to explore how these same general processes shaped his decisions and actions in a very different type of encounter.

1. Bubba's attention was drawn to the commotion in front of Mac's Bar. Unless this had happened (for example, he might have been asleep, or absorbed in reading Rod McKuen, his favorite poet), there would have been no decision for him to make. However, since he did attend to the man leaving the bar, Bubba progressed to the second phase of the Latané and Darley (1970) decision model.

2. Having noticed something, Bubba interpreted the cues which suggested to him that a potential victim was within his grasp. The man's staggering gait and his gleaming watch provided Bubba with cues that he needed to weigh in the next stage of the process.

3. Then, Bubba had to make the either-or decision regarding this potential encounter: should he make an attempt to acquire the watch, or should he bypass this opportunity? In coming to this decision, he had to estimate the various rewards and costs involved in both courses of action. Once he decided to intervene in the other's homeward journey, he needed to proceed to the next decision.

4. In this phase of the decision process, Bubba had to choose a specific course of action. In doing so, he weighed the rewards and costs of the various options that came to mind. Given the slight stature of his victim, the fact that his "client" had apparently been drinking to excess, the penalties for using a gun in the commission of a crime, as well as the pleasure that he derived from beating up people, Bubba decided to slug his victim.

5. In the final, action phase, Bubba carried out his decision. In this case, he had estimated his potential outcomes with reasonable accu-

racy. At least he found the encounter enjoyable, if not quite as economically rewarding as he originally had estimated it to be.

We have presented these two analyses of very different types of situations to demonstrate the generality of the Latané and Darley (1970) model. As shown, this scheme is equally applicable in both helping and hurting contexts. This is so because their model, while couched in somewhat different terms, addresses the same underlying processes discussed in our presentation of the themes of Valuation and Resolution. These processes are relevant to all interpersonal exchanges, regardless of the context or the specific behaviors under consideration.

In its brief history, social science has tended to focus on a small number of social behaviors, primarily because of their intrinsic interest to, and importance for, our society. Helping behavior is one such activity. Social psychologists have approached the study of this form of behavior by attempting to uncover the multitude of variables of the Social Context and Personal Structure which mediate the likelihood of its expression. The field has taken a similar approach in the study of hurting behavior. Such a strategy has both advantages and drawbacks. On the one hand, focusing a program of research rather narrowly on one specific type of behavior (either helping or hurting behavior, but not both) is an efficient means of rapidly accumulating knowledge about an issue. (Staub, 1978, 1979, for example, has produced two volumes of theory and research devoted almost solely to positive forms of social behavior.) On the other hand, such an approach can foster the study of behavior in a piecemeal fashion, so that activities such as helping and hurting are viewed as unrelated phenomena.

As a result of the approach that social psychologists have taken in studying various types of interesting behaviors, two separate empirical literatures have evolved concerning the variables that influence helping and hurting activities. Most textbooks in the field, for example, cover these two bodies of information in separate chapters. As we have argued, however, the general processes that underlie the expression of helping and hurting behaviors are similar. Factors that influence one type of behavior typically are relevant to the other as well. As such, it makes sense to review these forms of interpersonal behavior together.

In the pages that follow, we will present a summary of some of the many variables that have been shown to influence both helping and hurting behaviors. Our thematic approach, which subsumes the Latané and Darley (1970) model, provides a means by which the specific components of these extensive literatures can be integrated.

CONTEXTUAL VARIABLES IN HELPING AND HURTING

The Interpersonal Environment: I. The Presence of Others

Our systematic exploration of the variables that affect helping and hurting begins with a discussion of the role that factors in the interpersonal environment play in the expression of both types of behavior. To illustrate the impact that the environment can have on interpersonal activities, we will discuss a real-life event which was the impetus for much of the research that is considered here. This story concerns witnesses' reactions to an encounter between two people in which one of them seemed to be in danger due to the actions of the other. In many ways, this episode parallels the story ("A Night in the Courtyard") with which we began this textbook. However, in the present instance, we are dealing with tragedy rather than comedy.

The Death of Kitty Genovese. In the early morning hours of a cold day in New York City in March of 1963, a young woman named Kitty Genovese was returning home after having finished her shift at work. She stepped out of her car, and as she made her way toward her apartment, a man suddenly attacked her with a knife. Kitty Genovese screamed and resisted her assailant, but the man persisted in his attack, managing to stab her a number of times. Her screams brought some response from the nearby residents; some people turned on their lights, and a man shouted out his window. This attention caused the assailant to interrupt his vicious attack and to flee. However, he returned to the scene as soon as things had quieted down and resumed his assault on Miss Genovese, whose injuries had prevented her from reaching safety. Again, lights were turned on in the nearby buildings, and the assailant fled. Once more, however, he returned to his attack as soon as attention was no longer directed at the hapless victim of his crime. As a result of this vicious and senseless assault, Kitty Genovese died from multiple stab wounds.

Other features of this brutal murder also deserve mention. First, the attack on Miss Genovese lasted for more than 30 minutes. During the entire episode, no one came to the victim's aid. Witnesses' failures to help the mortally wounded Miss Genovese are perhaps understandable, as such an altruistic action might have brought the helper into close proximity with the crazed killer. What is remarkable, however, is the fact that not even 1 of the 38 people who witnessed the assault (as A. M. Rosenthal, 1964, determined in his investigation of this murder) bothered to call the police!

This episode presents a sad picture of the inhumanity of human beings toward one another. As such, it bears telling, if for no other reason than to remind us that some of our decisions have important implications for others, sometimes involving questions of life or death. In addition, the attack on Kitty Genovese provides us with some important clues for understanding the factors which influence our decisions in such situations, as John Darley and Bibb Latané surmised upon learning of the incident. In fact, it was this tragic episode that stimulated them to systematically explore the variables that affect people's reactions in emergency situations.

In their work, Latané and Darley discovered that variables in the interpersonal environment are particularly crucial to persons' decisions to get involved, or to intervene, in such settings. We will now discuss some of these environmental variables and consider their impact on both helping and hurting. In doing so, we will focus on two major components of the interpersonal environment: (1) the effect of the presence of others in the situation; and (2) the characteristics of the target of the actions.

Continued on Page 9, Column 1 | Continued on Page 24, Column 5 | Continued on Page 17, Column 1 | Continued on Page 18, Column 1

37 Who Saw Murder Didn't Call the Police

Apathy at Stabbing of Queens Woman Shocks Inspector

By MARTIN GANSBERG

For more than half an hour 38 respectable, law-abiding citizens in Queens watched a killer stalk and stab a woman in three separate attacks in Kew Gardens.

Twice the sound of their voices and the sudden glow of their bedroom lights interrupted him and frightened him off. Each time he returned, sought her out and stabbed her again. Not one person telephoned the police during the assault; one witness called after the woman was dead.

That was two weeks ago today. But Assistant Chief Inspector Frederick M. Lussen, in charge of the borough's detectives and a veteran of 25 years of homicide investigations, is still shocked.

He can give a matter-of-fact recitation of many murders. But the Kew Gardens slaying baffles him—not because it is a murder, but because the "good people" failed to call the police.

"As we have reconstructed the crime," he said, "the assailant had three chances to kill this woman during a 35-minute period. He returned twice to complete the job. If we had been called when he first attacked, the woman might not be dead now."

This is what the police say happened beginning at 3:20 A.M. in the staid, middle-class, tree-lined Austin Street area:

Twenty-eight-year-old Catherine Genovese, who was called Kitty by almost everyone in the neighborhood, was returning

Continued on Page 38, Column 1

The New York Times (by Edward Hausner)

At 3:20 A.M. on March 13, Miss Catherine Genovese drove into the parking lot at Kew Gardens railroad station and parked (1). Noticing a man in lot, she became nervous and headed along Austin Street toward a police telephone box. The man caught and attacked her (2) with a knife. She got away, but he attacked her again (3) and again (4).

The Impact of Others on Helping and Hurting: Cue Weighting

As we have argued repeatedly throughout this text, the cues that others supply provide us with a major source of information regarding the actions that are appropriate or inappropriate in a given context. The lower the Resolution of the context, the more dependent we are on such interpersonally derived cues. In addition, concerns with self/other Consistency contribute to the influence that the actions of others have on our own actions. These observations help to explain the results of numerous studies of both helping and hurting which have investigated the role of the presence and actions of others in determining our own behaviors.

This work suggests that the presence and behaviors of others can act as a two-edged sword. Other people can inhibit helping when they are inactive; in contrast, they can enhance its expression when they intervene. Similarly, people can inhibit the expression of aggressive behavior when they refrain from such actions; or, they can induce others to engage in hurting when they act in this manner. There appears to be a tendency in people to model their behaviors after those of others, especially in contexts that are novel or poorly resolved. To illustrate this conclusion and the factors that appear responsible for it, we will discuss some representative research that is relevant to the link between the actions of others and our own prosocial or antisocial responses.

The Smoke-Filled Room.   In one of the early investigations of the effects of the presence of others on persons' responses to a potential emergency, Latané and Darley (1968) had undergraduate volunteers come to their laboratory and fill out lengthy questionnaires. Subjects completed the test either alone or in the presence of two other people (who were either naive subjects like themselves or accomplices of the experimenters). While each subject was completing the test, the experimenters began to pump smoke into the room through a heating vent. The purpose of this study was simply to determine if the presence of others influenced subjects' responses to the smoke.

Latané and Darley (1968) found that subjects were significantly less likely to leave the smoke-filled room when they were in the company of others (either naive subjects or confederates) than when they were alone. For example, after six minutes had elapsed, 75 percent of the isolated subjects had left the room, whereas only about 10 percent of the respondents in the group settings had done so.

Obviously, the behavior of the others who were present influenced subjects' responses to the smoke. The confederates, for example, were trained not to respond to the potential emergency: after appearing to notice the smoke, they ignored it and continued to work on the questionnaire. This inaction provided the subject—who was attempting to determine the appropriate response in this relatively ambiguous context—with a clear, if inaccurate, cue which raised the Resolution of the situation. Heavily weighting the cue provided by the confederates' behaviors, the subject, too, remained in the room. In this condition, the subjects coughed, opened windows, and rubbed their eyes, but they did not leave.

Latané and Darley (1968) used the term *pluralistic ignorance* to explain the similar responses of naive subjects who were studied in groups of three. By pluralistic ignorance, they meant that each subject in the three-person group used the others' overt behaviors to provide a cue regarding the appropriate action to take in the situation. Given the enhanced importance of self/

other Consistency in poorly resolved contexts of this type, such cues would be especially weighty in determining each subject's actions. As one subject studied the behaviors of the others, the others were studying him. By their apparent inaction, the subjects provided one another with cues which suggested that no action was necessary.

The resulting state of pluralistic ignorance, in which each respondent quite inadvertently provided information to the others that nothing out of the ordinary was occurring, persisted for some groups until the smoke was so thick that the subjects could not read the questionnaires! The "naive subjects group" condition is important in this study because it strongly suggests that the findings obtained when subjects responded in the presence of the confederates were not the result of an unrealistic Social Context, since, as it turned out, the behaviors of the accomplices did not differ from those of the naive subjects.

The Broken Leg Caper. One potential problem in interpreting the Latané and Darley (1968) findings is brought about by the relative ambiguity of the experimentally created emergency. At least initially, it is quite conceivable that the subjects did not know how to interpret the situation in which they found themselves. Partly to determine the effect of such contextual ambiguity on subjects' responses, Latané and Rodin (1969) conducted an experiment similar in general form to that of Latané and Darley (1968), but varying in some important details. In this study, a female experimenter read a set of questionnaire instructions to the subjects and then escorted them to an adjoining room. As subjects began to complete the task, the experimenter left the room. Almost immediately thereafter, the subjects heard a loud crash and the experimenter's painful cry, "Oh, my God, my foot! . . . I . . . I can't move it!"

As in the Latané and Darley (1968) study, subjects were tested under different conditions which varied the number and actions of the others in the situation. In one condition, the naive subject was paired with a passive confederate; in another, pairs of friends were placed together; in yet a third condition, pairs of strangers (both naive subjects) were used; and in a fourth condition, the subject was alone in the room.

The proportions of subjects within each of the four conditions of this study who went to the aid of the apparently injured experimenter are presented in Table 10.1. As indicated, the presence of others usually decreased the

TABLE 10.1

Proportions of Helping Reactions as a Consequence of Experimental Condition (adapted from Latané & Rodin, 1969)

Alone	Paired with Friend (percent)	Paired with Stranger (percent)	Paired with Passive Confederate (percent)
70	70	40	7

likelihood of a subject's responding to the emergency. These results indicate that the inhibiting effect of others operates even in situations in which the need for action is less ambiguous.

This observation, however, does not appear to hold in circumstances in which the potential helpers are friends. In situations of this type, the behavior-distorting effects of pluralistic ignorance are less likely to operate. Why? Because friends are more likely than strangers to correctly interpret one another's cues. A worried expression on the face of a friend could serve as a cue that something was amiss, even in the absence of any other action. A similar exchange between strangers, however, would be less likely to be understood, thereby leading to a state of pluralistic ignorance.

Moreover, self/other Consistency is a more potent force in encounters involving friends. As noted earlier, people are more likely to use friends, and others who are similar to themselves, as a reference group—that is, a source of information regarding appropriate behaviors—than they are to look to strangers for such guidance. Subsequent research (Smith, Smythe, & Lien, 1972) has yielded results that are consistent with this position.

The results of these and other studies support our observation that people use the interpersonal environment as a source of cues when deciding on appropriate actions. In contexts of low Resolution, such as potential emergencies, these cues weigh very heavily in the Valuation process. The Latané and Darley (1968) study demonstrates that reliance on the interpersonal environment can have disastrous consequences when the inferences drawn from others' behavior are faulty. The findings of Latané and Rodin (1969) suggest that a factor such as familiarity with another increases the likelihood that a correct inference will be made. For our purposes, however, the crucial point is that the inferences we form about the actions of others, whether correct or incorrect, affect our own responses. Other research (Bryan & Test, 1967; Wilson, 1976) provides explicit evidence that people tend to mimic the behaviors of others when responding in an ambiguous emergency situation.

On the other side of the coin, research also suggests that the extent to which people express aggressive behaviors is influenced by the actions of others. There is a norm in our culture that prohibits intentional harming of others, in most circumstances. For this reason, some ambivalence exists whenever other factors in the Social Context suggest that aggressive behavior might be appropriate. In such situations, the level of Resolution can never be great, and thus, the behavior of others usually weighs heavily in persons' decisions about engaging in aggressive activity. Evidence from numerous studies supports this proposition; we will now present a sample of this research.

Bopping Bobo.   Some of the early investigations of interpersonal influences on aggression were conducted by Albert Bandura, Dorothea Ross, and Sheila Ross, who explored the effects of adults' behaviors on children's subsequent aggressive displays. In their work, Bandura et al. (1961, 1963a, 1963b) had children observe one of a number of different scenes in a playroom setting. In one of these, for example, the children witnessed an adult perform a series of somewhat unusual aggressive actions while playing with a "Bobo doll," a large, clown-shaped plastic punching bag. The adult would strike the doll with a mallet, sit on it, punch it, and so on. Other children saw the adult playing quietly and peacefully with the other toys in the playroom. When the children were then allowed access to the toys in the playroom, their behaviors revealed the influence of the different models to which they had been exposed. Those who witnessed the aggressive model were much more likely to behave aggressively toward the doll.

Though this research does not explicitly specify the mechanisms which underlie the imitative aggressive behavior of the children, it seems reasonable to assume that the processes of Resolution and self/other Consistency had a major effect on the children's responses. For young children (Bandura's subjects were nursery school students), the world is a poorly Resolved situation, and adults are a major reference group.

Teaching Aggression. More recent research has also provided evidence that the impact of models in the interpersonal environment is not limited to children. For example, in a series of studies, Robert A. Baron has demonstrated that the aggressive behaviors of others can serve as cues which affect the actions of adults. In one of these studies, Baron and Kepner (1970) had subjects participate in a modified Milgram-type learning experiment in which they were to play the role of a teacher who would administer punishment each time the learner made a mistake. In this case, the teacher had to decide on the level of shock to be administered. Some subjects immediately engaged in the task, whereas others were allowed to observe the behavior of another teacher before they participated. Some of these latter subjects saw a very aggressive teacher; others saw a teacher who administered very low levels of punishment.

Baron and Kepner (1970) found that the intensity of the shocks administered by subjects was affected by the actions of the teacher they had observed. Subjects who had observed the aggressive teacher were more aggressive than were their counterparts who had not been exposed to this model; subjects who had witnessed the performance of the nonaggressive teacher, in contrast, were less aggressive in their actions than were subjects in the control (no-model) condition. Other research (Baron, 1971c, 1974; Donnerstein & Donnerstein, 1977; Lando & Donnerstein, 1978) has yielded results that are consistent with these findings.

Someone Is Watching. Modeling is not the only process by which the presence of others influences people's aggressive behaviors. The interpersonal environment is a rich source of cues that people can use when deciding upon the most appropriate action to take in potential hurting encounters. Richard Borden (1975), for example, demonstrated that inferences we make about the beliefs of others in a situation affect our inclination to aggress against another. He employed an experimental procedure developed by Taylor (1967) in which pairs of male subjects competed with one another in a reaction time task in which they vied to be the first to correctly respond to a choice presented by the experimenter. To induce competition, it was explained, the loser on each trial was to be shocked by the winner.

Shocks were administered via an apparatus consisting of a panel with a row of 10 buttons and lights. Before every trial, each subject had to indicate the shock level, ranging from 1 to 10, that he would administer if he were the winner. After each trial, the loser would be shocked at the level chosen by his opponent; at the same time, a light on his panel would indicate the level of punishment being administered to him. Shock levels were individually calibrated for each subject so that level 10 was an intensity which he had indicated as "definitely unpleasant."

The purposes of the research were to determine the shock level that a subject would set on each trial and to explore the impact of differences in the interpersonal environment on this choice. Since the subject was free to choose any level, any selection above level 1 could be considered an aggressive action. To examine this issue, the experiment manipulated certain characteristics of a third person who witnessed the encounter. These characteristics were meant to suggest that the witness held beliefs relevant to the subject's choice. In one study, the witness was either a male or a female. This difference was designed to suggest to the subject the extent to which the witness would view aggressive behavior as acceptable since, presumably, aggressive behavior is more consistent with the male sex role. In a second study, the witness was described to the subject as being either a member of a karate club or of a peace organization.

In actuality, in both studies, one member of each of the competing pairs was an accomplice of the experimenter. Moreover, the game was rigged so that each player won an equal number of times. When the accomplice won, he shocked the real subject at level 3 or 4. Thus, any shock above these levels that a subject set could be considered as something of an overreaction, and therefore, indicative that the subject was behaving aggressively.

The results of both of Borden's (1975) studies support the position that cues from the interpersonal environment and self/other Consistency can have a strong effect on aggressive behavior. In his first experiment, Borden found that subjects were more aggressive when the witness was a male; subjects set an average shock level that was higher than 5, whereas with a female witness, the average shock level was 3. This pattern of results was duplicated in the second study. The shock value that subjects set in the presence of the karate expert was more than 1 level higher, on the average, than when the pacifist witnessed the competition. Results consistent with these findings have been reported by Baron (1971a), Borden and Taylor (1973), Geen and Pigg (1970), Geen and Stonner (1971), Milgram (1974), and Richardson, Bernstein, and Taylor (1979).

The results of the studies presented and cited above suggest that both helping and hurting are mediated to some extent by an underlying concern with self/other Consistency. People appear to use the interpersonal environment to infer what other people believe to be appropriate behavior and to use such cues in deciding on their own actions. Results directly relevant to this observation have been reported by Smith, Smythe, and Lien (1972). This study demonstrated that subjects were likely to intervene in a potential emergency, despite the inaction displayed by other observers, when they perceived themselves to be dissimilar to these observers; in contrast, subjects displayed the more typical imitative behavior when they perceived the nonreacting accomplices as highly similar to them.

The research cited to this point provides considerable evidence that the interpersonal environment often provides actors with compelling cues regarding the behavior that is most appropriate in a helping or hurting context. In the next section, we will review research on the effects of two additional products of the interpersonal environment—(1) feelings of personal *responsibility,* and (2) the sense of *visibility.*

Responsibility and Visibility, Helping and Hurting

The factors that assign responsibility to a particular individual in a social encounter also tend to make salient his or her identity, or visibility. We chose to concurrently review the effects of responsibility and visibility on social behavior because these two variables tend to be mediated by the same conditions. The sense of responsibility can be defined as the extent to which a person feels compelled to take action in a situation that calls for some form of intervention. Visibility, in a sense, represents the other side of the coin; it refers to the extent to which a person feels that he or she would be the focus of negative evaluations as a result of being identified for behaving inappropriately. Responsibility involves one's sense of obligation to do the right thing; visibility involves one's concern with diffusing blame for possible omissions or wrongdoing.

In their studies of helping behavior, Latané and Darley (1970) extensively investigated a simple but powerful variable that is relevant to both visibility and responsibility—namely, people's perceptions of the number of others in the situation who had to make the same decision as they about the most appropriate response to an apparent emergency. In general, these studies demonstrated that the greater the number of potential helpers, the less likely any one of them was to act. In the story of the stranded motorist, for example, it is likely that the many cars that you observed to pass by the scene diminished your own inclination to stop and help. As noted, one reason for your feelings is pluralistic ignorance; but other processes also appear to mediate the relationship between the number of potential actors in an emergency situation and your reluctance to intervene.

For instance, Latané and Darley also proposed that there is a tendency for people to feel less responsible when others who could provide the same assistance are also available; and this *diffusion of responsibility* plays a role in their decision to act or not to act. The greater the number of bystanders, the less noticeable, or visible, is any one of them, especially if they all behave in a similar manner. A person's sense of responsibility is directly associated with his or her perceived visibility. By reducing one's visibility in a situation, a person merely becomes a part of the crowd, and as such, feels that his or her responsibility to act is no greater than that of the other people present.

In addition, people who feel little responsibility for acting because of the presence of other bystanders also tend to perceive themselves as bit players rather than leading characters in the encounter. In this case, the absence of a sense of responsibility for acting fosters an accompanying sense of low visibility in such people.

The integrative theme most relevant to the mechanisms of responsibility and visibility is Consistency. If we assume that most people have a positive self-impression—and considerable research evidence (Aronson, 1968) supports this supposition—then it stands to reason that they would attempt to act in ways that are consistent with this belief. Behavior that violates one's sense of responsibility is inconsistent with a positive self-evaluation. Thus, concerns with self-Consistency would operate to induce action when one feels responsible for another's welfare.

Failing to behave in a manner that confirms one's positive self-impression creates a sense of Inconsistency, which, as noted in Chapter 5, people find uncomfortable. To reduce this discomfort, people often search the Social Context for information that helps them restore self-Consistency, that is, information that furnishes them with a justification for their behavior. One way that people justify their inaction in an emergency is by pointing to the inaction of others in the same situation. Thus, the presence of many witnesses to an emergency tends to weaken the impact of self-Consistency on behavior.

A similar conclusion may be drawn when the influence of visibility is considered. As noted, visibility is a concern with others' impressions of us. To maintain others' positive impressions, we behave in ways that are consistent with their beliefs. But suppose that we failed to take action in a situation that clearly called for some form of response; in this circumstance, others might assess our behavior negatively. However, if such inaction was consistent with that of everyone else in the situation, then there are no grounds on which observers can base invidious comparisons of our own lack of involvement. In this circumstance, the demands of self/other Consistency would be satisfied, and as such, one might expect that his or her positive evaluation from others would be maintained.

Visibility appears to minimize our inclination to act in poorly resolved situations when others in the setting are inactive; however, there is a factor that moderates the impact of this mechanism. At least up to a point, the number of others in a situation affects our sense of visibility. When we act differently from one other person, we do not feel much more visible than if we had acted the same; however, we would feel very visible if we acted differently from 10 other people.

Considerable empirical evidence supports the position that responsibility and visibility mediate people's behavior in helping contexts. The studies to which we will now turn our attention are just a small sample from this extensive body of research.

The Epileptic Seizure. A study that Darley and Latané (1968) conducted as part of their program of research on the factors that affect bystanders' reactions to potential emergencies provides compelling evidence that responsibility and visibility are important mediating variables. In this early study of *bystander intervention,* the researchers asked groups of subjects to take part in a discussion task. Each respondent sat in a different room and communicated with the others via an intercom system. During the course of the discussion, it appeared that one of the participants began to experience some physical difficulties. He remarked that he was feeling lightheaded, a bad sign since he was an epileptic. Following this disclosure, his speech became slurred and rapid, and he gave every indication that he was agitated and disoriented. Moments later, the noise of a body hitting the floor was transmitted through the intercom system, and nothing further was heard from the apparently ill participant.

Latané and Darley (1968) staged this episode to study the effect of a simple variation in the interpersonal environment on persons' inclinations to help the apparent victim—namely, the number of others who also had heard the sounds of the epileptic subject as he experienced the seizure. To do this, each discussion group really contained only one actual subject. The presence of the remaining participants was carefully simulated via a tape recording of an elaborately staged interaction. The experimenters constructed the discussion task so that the real subjects were awaiting their turn to speak when the seizure occurred.

In one condition of the study, the subjects thought that they were participating in an encounter that involved only one other person—the ultimate victim of the seizure; in another condition of the experiment, it appeared that three respondents were involved; and in a third, the situation was presented as a six-person interaction (the actual subject, the seizure victim, and four simulated others).

The results demonstrated the powerful impact of the apparent presence of others on a subject's response to the seizure victim. For example, 85 percent of the subjects who thought they were alone with the victim came to his assistance even before the apparent seizure had ended. Moreover, all of the subjects studied in this condition attempted to help the victim sooner or later; in fact, on the average, these subjects took less than one minute to react. In contrast, only 62 percent of the subjects who thought they were in a three-person group attempted to assist by the time the noise of the seizure had ceased, and even fewer (31 percent) did so when they were led to believe that four other people were involved.

It is important to note that in this study, the observed differences in reactions to the person in distress could not be attributed to concerns with self/other Consistency. This is so because subjects were always isolated from the other participants, and thus, they had no means of knowing what these people were doing in response to the sounds being transmitted to all of them. Instead, it seems probable that subjects' feelings of responsibility were diffused among all of the apparent witnesses to the seizure. In the dyadic condition, responsibility for acting rested solely on the subject, who was the only person who was aware of the other's apparent distress. Respondents in this condition were extremely visible, since only they could be held responsible for any negative consequences that might have occurred as a result of their inaction. In the three-person condition, the responsibility for acting was shared with one other participant. As such, visibility was lessened and respondents felt less compelled to offer aid. Subjects' sense of responsibility for helping was diffused even more widely in the six-person condition, since four other people were witness to the same episode. The presence of the other four made the subject just one of a crowd, and as such, he or she was implicated much less visibly in the event. Rationalizations such as, "I'm sure someone else will help" and "If someone helps, I'm not needed" and "If no one helps, I won't be any more to blame than anyone else," become more plausible with increasing numbers of potential actors.

In their experiment, Latané and Darley (1968) presented subjects with a context that minimized their feelings of responsibility and visibility. By separating respondents, the experiment lowered respondents' perceptions of their own visibility, especially in the condition involving six participants. Similarly, the sense that there were four other people who could see if anything was really wrong would serve to diminish the subjects' feelings that they were individually responsible for acting. This study, as well as subsequent research (Duval, Duval, & Neely, 1979; Schwartz & Gottlieb, 1980), demonstrates that the twin mechanisms of visibility and responsibility work in tandem to reduce the inclination to act when other bystanders are present.

Conversely, there are other mechanisms that can raise an individual's sense of responsibility and visibility and thus promote prosocial responses. In a well-conceived study, for example, Wegner and Shaefer (1978) found that emphasizing a person's individuality (hence, enhancing responsibility and visibility) resulted in greater helping, although the subject was a part of a group. The research to which we now turn examined the effect of one such moderator of visibility and responsibility on subjects' tendencies to get involved—namely, whether or not the potential victim singled out one of the subjects from the crowd.

Watching the Radio. In a clever field experiment conducted on the beach, Moriarty (1975) induced subjects to feel more or less responsible for the welfare of another. In this study, an accomplice would go to a crowded beach with all of the usual paraphernalia—suntan oil, blanket, radio, and so on. He would choose a spot on the beach at random and make himself comfortable. He would then lie down, turn on his radio, and apparently begin the arduous task of developing the world's greatest suntan. After a few minutes, however, he would turn to the person nearest him and make one of two requests: in the control condition, he would ask for a match; in the condition that was designed to induce a high level of responsibility, he would say, "Excuse me, I'm going to the boardwalk for a few minutes. Would you watch my things?" After either of these interactions, the accomplice would leave the scene. Shortly thereafter, a second confederate would approach the empty blanket, pick up the radio, and—if not stopped—run off with it.

The findings of this study provide dramatic proof of the impact of specify-

JOEL GORDON

As Moriarty's study demonstrates, in contexts such as crowded beaches, people typically do not feel responsible for the belongings of others.

ing responsibility on action. Despite the fact that the beach was very crowded and no one else did anything, 95 percent of the people who were singled out and specifically asked to watch the victim's belongings intervened in the attempted theft. In contrast, only 20 percent of those who had been asked for the match did so. Other research (Austin, 1979; Shaffer, Rogel, & Hendrick, 1975) has yielded findings that are consistent with these results.

It is noteworthy that as many as 20 percent of the subjects intervened when Moriarty's (1975) confederate had singled them out merely by asking them for a match. The theft situation, after all, was potentially very dangerous, so that any intervention was more than might have been expected. In support of this observation, Austin (1979) reports that no one intervened to stop the staged theft of an expensive calculator in a college library setting. In his study, however, no attempt was made to increase the visibility of the bystander.

Thus, based on the results of research such as Moriarty's and Austin's, it seems reasonable to hypothesize that actions which tend to increase a person's visibility to the victim will also increase that individual's propensity to act in a situation calling for some form of helpful intervention. This prediction, in fact, has received support in a study by Howard and Crano (1974), who found significant differences in helping behavior between subjects who had been asked the time by the potential theft victim and those subjects who had not been singled out in this manner. Apparently, even this minimal contact established in the subject a greater sense of his or her visibility which, in turn, resulted in more helping. It was as if the subject thought, "This person (the victim) knows who I am. I cannot just stand by and watch him be robbed."

Responsibility and visibility also affect people's aggressive behaviors; but, as might be expected in this case, decreased responsibility and visibility tend to increase the likelihood of this type of activity. The history of this country is replete with examples that are consistent with this observation. Riots, lynchings, lootings, and other collective acts of violence that are so much a part of our national heritage bear witness to the fact that people will engage in behaviors in groups that they would not even consider when acting as individuals. Moreover, ample research evidence also suggests the existence of a relationship between hurting behavior and a diminished sense of visibility and responsibility.

Another Shocking Experience. One of the major findings of Milgram's (1974) research program on obedience to authority, discussed in detail in Chapter 2, was that the teacher-subject would engage in very destructive behavior so long as the experimenter was willing to take responsibility for whatever happened. Recall that in this research, a subject was assigned the role of teacher in a learning task. The teacher's job was to induce another subject (actually, an accomplice of the experimenter) to learn a list of words. The teacher was to shock the learner each time he made a mistake. Shocks to be administered were increased in intensity with each mistake. The victim of this treatment had been trained to make frequent mistakes, so that the teacher ultimately was to use shock levels that were labeled as dangerous. Of course, the victim complained more and more strenuously with each increase in voltage until, ominously, he ceased to respond.

Just one example from Milgram's (1974, pp. 75–76) transcripts should provide the reader with a sense of the role that the subjects' abrogation of responsibility (for their own behavior) played in their willingness to engage in such antisocial activity:

SUBJECT:	Something's happened to that man in there. . . . Something's happened to that man in there. You better check in on him, sir. He won't answer or nothing.
EXPERIMENTER:	Continue. Go on, please.
SUBJECT:	You accept all responsibility?
EXPERIMENTER:	The responsibility is mine. Correct. Please go on.

At this point in the encounter, the subject returned to reading his list of words and administering shocks with increasing severity every time the nonresponsive victim said nothing, all the way to the most extreme value on the shock generator.

In an extension of this work, Tilker (1970) employed the same teacher-learner context developed by Milgram. In fact, the experimental procedures were the same as those that Milgram had employed, with two exceptions: (1) accomplices played both the teacher and the learner roles, whereas the real subject was cast in the role of an observer; and (2) the experimenter always left the room before participants began the learning task. Tilker used these modifications to study the effect of different levels of responsibility on subjects' behavior. In one condition (total responsibility), the observer-subject was told that he had complete responsibility for both the conduct of the study and the well-being of the learner. In a second treatment group (ambiguous responsibility), the subject was told that if he wished to do so, he could talk with the teacher to "resolve all procedural differences." In a third treatment (no responsibility), the subject was informed that the teacher had complete responsibility for conducting the study, whereas his task during the encounter was to record the learner's responses and the levels of shock that were delivered.

In one condition of the study, the harm done to the learner was very apparent, since the observer and teacher could hear and see the learner through a one-way mirror. In this context, level of responsibility assigned to subjects had a strong effect on their responses. Those who had been given complete responsibility were substantially more likely to terminate the victim's punishment and end the study; the subjects in the ambiguous and no-responsibility conditions were less likely to act and did not differ from one another in this regard.

Tilker's (1970) study demonstrates in a straightforward manner the importance of the abrogation of personal responsibility in determining people's willingness to take part in antisocial activity. The findings of other research also support this conclusion. For example, Milgram (1974) reports that subjects are much more likely to continue shocking a victim when they share this responsibility with another teacher-subject. Moreover, there is also research evidence that visibility—the complement of responsibility—has a similar influence on aggressive behavior.

The Unknown Shocker. In a direct test of the effect of anonymity on aggressive behavior, Zimbardo (1970) used a modification of Milgram's teacher-learner procedure to give female subjects the opportunity to administer shocks to another person. Some subjects were led to believe that the target was a nice person (honest, sincere, and so on); for others, the learner was depicted as being obnoxious (conceited, critical, and so on). In addition, Zimbardo (1970) varied the visibility of his subjects by having some of them wear lab coats and hoods while they participated in the research and others wear name tags in addition to their regular dress. These conditions were meant to emphasize the sense of either anonymity or visibility in the subjects.

Zimbardo's (1970) manipulations had considerable influence on subjects' aggressive actions. The anonymous subjects delivered twice as many shocks to their victims as did their highly visible counterparts. In addition, they did not vary their behaviors as a consequence of the victim's alleged attributes;

in contrast, the visible subjects increased their shocks over trials when the victim had been described in an unflattering manner; but decreased them when the victim had been described favorably. Other research (Propst, 1979) has found a similar relationship between anonymity and aggression. In interpreting results of this type, Johnson and Downing (1979) suggest that visibility affects persons' concerns about being recognized and blamed for their antisocial actions; and these concerns, in turn, have a marked influence on their willingness to engage in aggressive behavior.

In his discussion of some of the major antecedents of aggressive behavior, Zimbardo (1970) speculated that anonymity is just one component of a more complex mechanism which he termed *deindividuation*. He suggested that factors in the physical and interpersonal environments, as well as in an individual's belief system, can lower his or her subjective sense of individuality. On the one hand, variables such as feeling anonymous, being a member of a large crowd, and displaying signs (uniforms) that are specific to a role (prison guard, football player) can induce in a person the sense that his or her behaviors do not reflect "the real me." On the other hand, factors that emphasize one's individuality (wearing unique, self-selected dress, identifying nametags, or being aware of other features that set one apart from the crowd) tend to enhance the person's perceptions that his or her actions reflect the "true self." Thus, it is more likely that deindividuated people will engage in more antisocial behavior than will their highly visible counterparts.

Zimbardo's conceptualization has much intuitive appeal; however, it subsumes a multitude of somewhat different processes—visibility, roles, and self-impressions—and it is difficult to determine the relative impact of each of these components on behavior. It is likely that visibility plays some role in a person's sense of individuation or deindividuation. However, we concur with Johnson and Downing (1979) in their conclusion that this complex determinant of behavior is probably much more a product of the actor's belief system than it is of his or her sense of visibility. For this reason, we will defer further discussion of deindividuation until our presentation of Personal Structure factors in aggression.

To this point, our presentation of factors in the interpersonal environment that influence helping and hurting behavior has focused on the relevant psychological processes (modeling, visibility, responsibility, and so on) that appear to be mediated by the presence of others. In the following section, we will turn to a consideration of other important components of the interpersonal environment—the characteristics of the persons directly involved in helping and hurting encounters (the *focal actors*) which influence other persons' responses to the actors.

The Interpersonal Environment: II. Characteristics of the Focal Actors

Characteristics of the focal actors involved in a helping or hurting encounter (that is, the person in need, the victim of an attack, the aggressor, and so on) can influence the types of behavior that people express toward these individuals in such contexts. In some situations, there is only one focal actor (such as the motorist stranded by the side of the road with a flat tire). It seems likely that the physical appearance of this person and other apparent attributes and behaviors would play some role in determining your decisions about the appropriate action to take. In other circumstances, there can be two or more focal actors. For example, two children fighting in a schoolyard are focal actors whose appearance and actions jointly induce you to think about what to do, if anything. We will now review some of the many focal actor characteristics that research has shown to affect persons' actions in helping and hurting situations.

Sex Differences

The physical attribute most widely researched in this area of study is the sex of the focal actors, which has been shown to affect the outcomes of both helping and hurting encounters. The most consistent pattern of findings regarding the sex of the focal actors is that in helping situations, women are helped more than are men; in hurting situations, more aggression is directed towards males than towards females.

Sex and Favors. For example, Gruder and Cook (1971) found that people are more inclined to do favors for females than for males. In this study, subjects were undergraduates who had agreed to participate in a psychological experiment. However, when a subject reported to the appointed room, he or she found a note on the door explaining that the experimenter would be unable to attend the session. The note requested that the subject, nevertheless, go into the room and as a favor, work on a series of tasks. The note was always signed, and in this way, Gruder and Cook manipulated the apparent sex of the experimenter: half the subjects thought they were responding to a female's request for assistance, and the remainder thought the experimenter was male.

The findings of Gruder and Cook's (1971) study showed that subjects were considerably more likely to comply with the request for assistance if the experimenter was a female. Results of this sort, which are consistent with the stereotype that women are more dependent on others than are men, have been found in a host of similar research endeavors (Callahan-Levy & Messé, 1979; Clark, 1974; Howard & Crano, 1974; Latané & Dabbs, 1975; Pomozal & Clore, 1976; West, Whitney, & Schnedler, 1975).

It's Not Easy Being Male. Research that has examined people's actions in antisocial contexts has yielded findings that complement those noted with regard to helping. In hurting contexts, people are more likely to act aggressively against males than they are against females. Christiane Hoppe (1979) conducted an interesting experiment on hurting behavior that clearly supports this observation. To study the impact of a number of variables of the Social Context and Personal Structure on aggressive actions, Hoppe employed the same reaction time competition—in which the winner shocks the loser—that Borden (1975) had used in his studies of aggression. Of most relevance to our present concerns, Hoppe varied the sex of the subjects' opponents in the game; some were pitted against a male, others against a female. Her results indicated that the aggressive actions of the male subjects in her study were affected by their opponent's sex: they set higher shock levels for their opponent when that person was a male. Other research, some of which has been conducted in settings outside of the psychological laboratory (Harris, 1974), had yielded similar findings.

It appears that the sex of the target of aggression—or the victim in an emergency—mediates persons' responses by acting as a cue that evokes a widely held norm—a norm which prescribes that people should be more concerned about the welfare of women than of men in such circumstances. Thus, in the absence of other compelling cues, the sex of the target weighs heavily in the Valuation process which culminates in some behavior. If this observation is correct, we would expect that females would not be accorded such favorable treatment in contexts containing features which render the norm less salient. The two studies that follow provide evidence that is consistent with this position.

Beating a Dead Norm. The norm that prescribes preferential treatment for women could be deactivated when a female acts in ways that would diminish others' feelings that she is due such treatment. For example, if people perceive a woman as having provoked another to engage in aggressive actions toward her, they would be less likely to see this norm as operative. As a consequence, they would be less likely to come to her assistance. Results of a study by Borofsky, Stollak, and Messé (1971) support this speculation.

In this experiment, subjects were led to believe that they were taking part in an investigation of psychodrama as a means of inducing people to express their emotions. Groups of six subjects were gathered together in a large room and told that they would be called upon, two at a time, to spontaneously act out a premise that the experimenter would provide them. The subjects who were not involved in a particular encounter were to observe it closely, so that they could evaluate the sincerity and spontaneity of the participants.

In reality, only one of the six participants was a bona fide subject. The remainder were accomplices of the experimenters; two of these, in fact, were professional actors. The actual subject never took part in a psychodramatic encounter, since the session was terminated after the second interaction, which involved the two professional actors. In this interaction, the actors were given a premise which suggested a family conflict. Just before this encounter was to begin, the experimenter left the room, explaining that he had left some of the necessary evaluation forms in his office. He told the subjects to proceed without him.

Following a carefully prepared script, the actors engaged in an argument that quickly heated up and, after a few minutes, exploded into a physical confrontation. The argument gradually increased in intensity until one of the participants, apparently losing control, slapped the other across the face. The person who was slapped then responded, "Look, this is only acting.

This is just supposed to be an experiment. [three-second pause] You can't get away with hitting me like that!" At this point, the obviously angry speaker began to assault the person whose slap had started the confrontation.

This fight lasted for 45 seconds, or until the subject tried to stop it (verbally or physically). None of the other observers (all experimental accomplices) attempted to intervene; instead, they appeared confused, muttering among themselves about the scene taking place before them.

To explore the impact of the sex of the focal actors in an aggressive encounter, male and female actors played both roles in this violent confrontation. Of most interest were subjects' reactions to the episode in which the male beat up the female. It is noteworthy that none of the six male subjects who individually participated in this condition attempted in any way to stop the assault. This lack of response is in stark contrast to the behavior of the male undergraduates who had witnessed the other conditions of the study. In every other context—when two men or two women were the combatants, and even when a female assaulted a male—the vast majority (73 percent) of these subjects intervened.

We believe that these startling findings were a consequence of one highly salient feature of the episode—the slap which escalated the encounter from an argument to a physical confrontation. When initiated by a woman toward a man, this action seemed to reduce drastically the sense in the male witnesses that they should come to her aid. It might have been the case that these subjects felt she deserved to be punished for thinking that she could get away with such behavior merely because of her sex. In fact, elsewhere Borofsky (1969) reports that most of the males who witnessed this assault smiled as it unfolded, whereas in other conditions, subjects appeared agitated and distressed.

A Lovers' Quarrel. Shotland and Straw (1976), in an extension of the work of Borofsky et al. (1971), have presented evidence that other factors can moderate the impact of the norm which prescribes favorable treatment for women in helping and hurting situations. In this study, they demonstrated that people were very reluctant to interfere when a man was assaulting a woman if they thought that the pair shared an interpersonal relationship.

To explore the effect of a prior relationship between the focal actors on subjects' reluctance to intervene, Shotland and Straw (1976) staged a situation in which subjects who were working alone in a room overheard a loud commotion in the hall. A man and a woman were apparently engaged in a heated argument as they rode up the elevator just outside the experimental room. As the doors of the elevator opened, the man physically attacked the woman, violently shaking her as she struggled and screamed. As she physically and verbally resisted the attacker, she shouted either "I don't know you," or, "I don't know why I ever married you." In either case, the fight lasted for about one minute, if the subject did not intervene first.

The rather minor difference in information about the relationship between the man and woman had a major effect on subjects' reactions in this encounter. When the woman's attacker apparently was a stranger, 65 percent of the subjects acted in some way to stop the assault. In contrast, less than 20 percent of the subjects intervened when they thought that the couple was married. In this latter context, other beliefs appeared to counteract the norm which advocates helping females in distress.

It is likely that the widely shared opinion that one does not butt into other people's business by getting involved in domestic squabbles overcame the norm-based tendency to intervene on behalf of women. Shotland and Straw (1976) interviewed the subjects who had witnessed the encounter in order to ascertain the reasons for their behaviors. They report that almost all the subjects who did not intervene when they thought the couple was married behaved in this manner because each "felt that the fight was none of my business." In contrast, the nonreactive subjects who thought that the assailant and the victim were strangers tended to explain their behavior on the basis of uncertainty about how to act.

Taken together, the results of relevant research summarized in this section indicate that the sex of focal actors can evoke beliefs in people which are relevant to their subsequent helping or hurting actions. But the research also indicates that certain factors lower the weight accorded to these beliefs, thereby weakening the link between this particular component of the interpersonal environment and behavior.

It is important to understand, however, that these moderators also can be components of the interpersonal environment, including other attributes of the focal actors. For example, knowing that a fighting couple is married, or observing that the victim of an attack was the first to use physical violence are also cues that can be used in deciding upon a course of action. In the next section, we will review several other attributes of focal actors which research has indicated are influential in moderating helping and hurting behaviors.

Other Attributes of the Focal Actors

Empirical research has uncovered a vast number of features of focal actors in addition to sex which affect the outcomes of helping or hurting encounters. We have devoted considerable attention to the sex of the focal actor because this attribute has been the most frequently studied in social psychology. Although other attributes of the focal actor appear to operate in a manner similar to sex, it is useful to review some of the interesting work that has demonstrated that these factors, too, can influence helping and hurting behavior.

Physical Attributes.   The attractiveness of focal actors has been found to affect persons' behaviors in helping and hurting situations. In general, the more attractive the person, the more likely he or she is to receive assistance when necessary, and the less likely he or she is to be the target of an aggressive action. For example, in a clever field experiment, Piliavin, Piliavin, and Rodin (1975) staged potential medical emergencies on New York subway cars. They had an accomplice pretend to faint in order to observe whether or not passengers would assist him. One of their findings was that the victim was less likely to be helped when he appeared to be scarred by an unattractive birthmark. Benson, Karabenick, and Lerner (1976), Gross, Walston, and Piliavin (1975), Wegner and Crano (1975), and West and Brown (1975), among others, have provided research evidence that is consistent with the idea that the physical appearance of the focal actor affects people's willingness to help.

Similarly, other research has shown that target attractiveness can influence hurting behavior. For example, Berkowitz and Frodi (1979) had adult women play the role of teacher to a child. The role called for the teacher to administer punishment for the child's mistakes in a learning task. The researchers systematically varied two attributes of the children—whether or not they were physically attractive and whether or not they stuttered. The researchers found that the subjects were more aggressive toward the child after they had been insulted by a coworker in the study, and this tendency was exaggerated if the child was unattractive or appeared to suffer from the speech defect.

Psychological Attributes. Less visible attributes of the focal actors have also been shown to influence helping and hurting behaviors. As noted, Zimbardo (1970) found that people responded with increasing aggression if they thought the target was an unpleasant person, whereas they decreased their level of aggressive behavior if the target had been depicted as likable. Similarly, Daniels and Berkowitz (1963) found that people were more likely to aid a likable person than one who was less pleasant. In both cases, positively valued attributes of the targets' Personal Structures affected the reactions they elicited from the subjects.

Other features of targets' Personal Structures can affect responses to them. For example, Gruder and Cook (1971) found that the more dependent targets appeared to be, the more helpful people were toward them. Other research (Berkowitz, 1978; Berkowitz & Daniels, 1963; Daniels & Berkowitz, 1963; Schopler & Bateson, 1965) has demonstrated a similar relationship between a target's dependency and helping behavior. However, it also appears that the costs for helping mediate the impact of the target's apparent dependency (Schaps, 1972; Schopler & Bateson, 1965; Ungar, 1979). For example, Schaps (1972) demonstrated that when potential helpers were pressed for time, they provided less assistance to a dependent target than to one who was less in need of their help; the reverse was true when time was not a concern. Using a sample of students in a theological seminary as subjects, Darley and Batson (1973) provided similar results. Thus, it seems likely that dependency amplifies the salience of cost considerations in the Valuation process in helping contexts.

Research has shown that dependency also has a complicated effect on people's willingness to aggress against the target. For example, the work of Milgram (1974) and others (Baron, 1971a, b; Penner & Hawkins, 1971; Rule & Langer, 1976) has shown that cues which indicate the dependency of a victim on the actions of the potential aggressor inhibit the expression of aggression. On the other hand, studies have shown that when a victim has greatly angered an actor, increased dependency cues actually tend to increase aggressive responses (Baron, 1974, 1977, 1979; Berkowitz, 1974; Feshbach, Stiles, & Bitter, 1967; Hartman, 1969; Sebastian,1978).

Actions. A final factor to be considered in our discussion of the effects of focal actors on helping and hurting is the particular set of activities which these individuals exhibit in the encounter. For example, research (Howard & Crano, 1974; Kriss, Indenbaum, & Tesch, 1974; Moriarty, 1975; Staub & Baer, 1974) has shown that the overt behaviors displayed by people in need can play a role in others' willingness to help him. As noted, people are more likely to assist another if the victim had previously engaged them in a brief conversation (Howard & Crano, 1974).

Similarly, the specific manner in which a request for help is made can have an appreciable effect on persons' responses. Kriss et al. (1974) demonstrated that asking people for assistance in an enthusiastic, optimistic manner has a facilitative effect on their willingness to oblige. On the other side of the coin, Staub and Baer (1974) have shown that some actions of the target can inhibit helping. They found that people are less willing to assist another person whose behaviors suggested that he was suffering from a heart attack than when his actions were more ambiguous or suggested a less severe problem (a knee injury).

The actions of the target also can influence people's actions in hurting contexts. For example, it appears that aggression provokes aggression—that is, the more the potential targets have themselves aggressed, the more likely people are to respond in kind. Research by Stuart Taylor and his colleagues (Epstein & Taylor, 1967; Richardson et al., 1979), as well as others (Goldstein, Davis, & Herman, 1975; Teyber, Messé, & Stollak, 1977) indicates that increasing provocation results in increasing retaliation, especially if the target's actions are perceived as intentional (Dyck & Rule, 1978). For example, in Taylor's research, which used the reaction time competition task described earlier, subjects tended to respond in kind to their opponent's shock levels. When the opponent set high levels of punishment, so too did the subject. Similarly, reciprocity has also been found to influence helping behavior. People tend to reciprocate kindnesses (Pruitt, 1968; Wilke & Lanzetta, 1970).

Interference—the behavior of others that blocks the attainment of a reward or goal—appears to generate a reaction in people that is similar to their usual response to provocation. As noted in Chapter 9, interference is a major source of cost in interpersonal exchange, and as such, can be the basis for considerable negative reaction. Psychologists have termed the negative emotional reaction to interference frustration, and have speculated that this aversive feeling is a motivator of aggressive responses (Dollard, Doob, Miller, Mowrer, & Sears, 1939). Research evidence seems to indicate, however, that interference which is perceived by the target as unreasonable or unjustified is most likely to produce aggressive reactions (Burnstein & Worchel, 1962; Cohen, 1955; Fishman, 1965; Pastore, 1952).

Dialing for Dollars. In a well-designed experiment on this issue, James Kulik and Roger Brown (1979) asked undergraduate males to solicit donations to a worthy cause over the telephone. While subjects were led to believe that they would contact a large number of potential donors from a list provided them, they actually called only the first two names on the list. The recipients of their phone calls, in fact, were accomplices of Kulik and Brown (1979) who had been trained to respond systematically to the subjects' pleas.

In every condition, the accomplices interfered with the subjects' goals by refusing to donate. However, the reasonableness of their refusal varied. For the subjects in the illegitimate refusal condition, both confederates explained their refusal with negative comments about charities in general as well as about the particular cause for which the subjects were soliciting (supportive services for former mental patients). In contrast, the refusals which other subjects experienced were accompanied by more legitimate explanations—a lost job, or a prior contribution to another charity.

Kulik and Brown (1979) measured subjects' anger (the force with which they hung up the phone at the end of the solicitation) and the level of the aggressive content of their words (those used during the conversation, as well as in a letter they subsequently sent to the targets after the phone call). The results obtained by Kulik and Brown showed that subjects were more angry, and expressed more aggression (in both the phone conversation and the subsequent letter) when the reasons given by the accomplice for refusing their request were illegitimate.

The large number of studies cited in this section provides compelling evidence that the interpersonal environment is a major repository of factors that can have a powerful effect on the course of helping and hurting encounters. As noted earlier, the themes of Consistency and Resolution appear to underlie the relationships between helping and hurting behaviors and the presence and actions of others. It is likely that concerns with self/other Consistency influence the weight that we accord the cues provided by others who are involved with us in the helping or hurting encounter, especially if these others are similar to us in important ways. Likewise, through such processes as the diffusion of responsibility, the presence of others provides us with justifications for our behaviors, thereby permitting us to maintain a sense that our actions are consistent with our positive self-impressions.

The theme of Resolution is also relevant here, since most of us have relatively little experience with important helping and hurting encounters. And this lack of experience in situations of this type generates some degree of uncertainty about the behaviors that are appropriate. There is direct evidence, in fact, that prior experience with similar contexts does lend some degree of Resolution to otherwise ambiguous situations. For example, in research on the impact of models on aggression, discussed earlier, Baron (1971c, 1974) found that giving subjects the opportunity to observe another person engage in the role of teacher provided these subjects with a set of cues that served to resolve the context of their own encounter. Similarly, Aderman and Berkowitz (1970) showed that observing the behavior of participants in a helping encounter affected subjects' own actions in a similar, subsequent context. Other research (Huston, Ruggiero, Conner, & Geis, 1981) has provided findings consistent with the idea that experience in similar contexts, or the possession of relevant attributes (faculties such as training in the martial arts or in lifesaving techniques) increases the likelihood that people will act in ambiguous situations.

On the other hand, situations with which we have had little prior experience do occur with some frequency, and most of us are not trained in lifesaving skills or karate. In these circumstances, we heavily weight those cues that allow us both to maintain a positive self-impression and to minimize our risks in terms of personal safety, failure, and so on. A major source of such cues is the characteristics of the focal actors, as discussed earlier.

For example, for the subjects in Shotland and Straw's (1976) study, the information that the attacker was the husband of the victim weighed heavily against their intervention. This information, which was provided by the focal actors, had a powerful impact on subjects' interpretations of the events that were unfolding before them. This cue convinced them to interpret the assault as a private matter that did not concern them. Similarly, it is likely that the relationship between provocation and retaliation, at least in part, is a result of Resolution processes: the aggressive actions of the target provide a firm basis for deciding upon an appropriate response. Of course, the targets' actions are also likely to inject a note of urgency into people's Valuations of their response options in such situations.

Another source of contextual cues which serve to raise the Resolution of ambiguous helping and hurting situations is the physical environment. In the following section, we will briefly review some of the variables in the physical environment that have been shown to influence behaviors of this type.

The Physical Environment

The impact of some physical environment variables on people's prosocial or antisocial behaviors are intuitively obvious; for example, some research has suggested that an increase in climatic temperature causes an increase in the tendency of people to aggress against others. However, some relationships between the physical environment and behavior are less straightforward; for instance, should the scent of another person's perfume have a positive or negative influence on your decision to aggress against that person? What is the likely effect of music on interpersonal encounters? Would the type of music also make a difference in encounters? Variables of this type have been investigated and have been shown to mediate people's interpersonal behaviors. While the variables that have been studied appear diverse, we believe that all of them reflect the impact of one or both of two underlying processes: the *labeling (or mislabeling) of physiological arousal,* and the *prompting or inhibition of habits.*

Labeling of Arousal

Heating and Hitting. We mentioned the straightforward prediction that discomforting features of the physical environment such as high climatic temperature enhance aggressive activity. There is some evidence that supports this proposition, but there is also evidence that the relationship between discomfort and aggression is not as simple as it originally might appear. Some studies suggest that as discomfort increases, so too does the incidence of aggressive behavior (Carlsmith & Anderson, 1979); while other studies (Baron & Bell, 1975a, 1976; Bell & Baron, 1976; Palamarek & Rule, 1979) suggest that increased temperatures diminish aggressive behavior. While these findings appear contradictory, they can be integrated within the perspective of arousal labeling processes discussed in Chapters 1 and 2.

Recall that there is evidence (Schachter, 1964; Schachter & Singer, 1962; Zillman, 1979) that people employ cues from the Social Context to label their internal physiological states, and that the labels which they apply have consequences for their subsequent overt actions. A person's reaction to the discomfort caused by high environmental (or ambient) temperatures would be affected by the explanation the person develops to interpret this feeling. Thus, if the person correctly attributes the discomfort to the heat, he or she would be likely to act appropriately—turn on a fan or air conditioner, go to a swimming pool, and so on. However, if other cues in the environment cause the person to attribute his or her discomfort to interpersonal factors— those not related to temperature—then this individual well might act in an aggressive manner to the provocation. Dolf Zillman and his colleagues (e.g., Bryant & Zillman, 1979; Zillman, 1979) have termed this type of arousal labeling *excitation transfer*.

In applying the excitation transfer model to the results of studies of the relationship between temperature and aggression, it is useful to examine the specific contexts in which apparently contradictory data were collected. Carlsmith and Anderson (1979) examined naturalistic data on the occurrence of major riots in the United States, and the average temperatures of the days on which these events took place. As noted, they found a positive relationship between these two sets of variables: higher temperatures were associated with increases in collective violence. In contrast, Baron and Bell (1975a, 1976) and Baron and Lawton (1972) found that high temperatures could inhibit the influence of factors (aggressive models) that otherwise would generate aggressive behaviors in subjects.

The most salient difference between the contexts of these two sets of research appears to be the uniqueness or prominence of the temperature. In naturalistic situations, we adjust to the temperature; while a heat wave might be discomforting, the temperature that is experienced is a relatively constant feature of the environment. In other words, the sense of discomfort from a relatively high ambient temperature is experienced more like a dull ache than a searing pain. This dull ache—which is a state of constant negative arousal—can easily be attributed to more prominent extraneous events that catch one's attention. Reactions of a crowd to a confrontation between an impolite policeman and a minor traffic offender are much more likely to escalate into more broadly based antisocial activity when temperatures are high, and have been high for some time.

In contrast to most naturalistic events, high ambient temperature is introduced abruptly in the typical laboratory context. Subjects walk into the laboratory from a temperate environment and suddenly find themselves in the middle of a heat wave. This dramatic shift in the physical environment makes temperature a highly salient cue. As such, the source of subjects' discomfort is easily labeled. In addition, since the temperature is such a powerful cue, it is likely that arousal from other sources will be attributed to it. Thus, subjects who are aroused by the antagonistic actions of an aggressive model easily could transfer their excitation to the physical environmental cue of temperature. This transfer, in turn, would decrease subjects' inclinations to behave aggressively.

Sounds and Scents.   In the experimental studies of temperature and aggression, the environmental cue (heat) is extremely intrusive. It is this quality that makes such cues such powerful magnets for attributions of internal states. It follows that more subtle features of the environment would have the opposite effect; that is, the arousal that they generate would be attributed to other factors in the context. Baron (1980) provides evidence that supports this speculation in a study of the effect of the arousing scent of perfume on subjects' tendencies to hurt another. In this study, subjects were allowed to shock an accomplice of the experimenter who previously had angered them. During this encounter, subjects were exposed either to the pleasant smell of an expensive perfume, or to the more neutral odor of a pine-scented room deodorant. A control group was exposed to neither of these scents.

Baron's (1980) results indicated that the angered subjects who had been exposed to the subtle but arousing scent of the perfume were more likely to use higher levels of punishment than were their counterparts who had not been exposed to a scent. In contrast, angered subjects exposed to the nonarousing pine scent did not differ from the control subjects with regard to their aggressive behavior. Apparently, the scent of the perfume did increase the arousal of subjects to some extent; however, this cue was not as obvious as that of other features of the context—the shock generating equipment, the insulting behavior of the accomplice, and so on. Because of its subtlety, subjects were unlikely to attribute their arousal to the scent; instead, they attributed their physiological state to the more visible cues of the aggressive accomplice.

Similar effects of excitation transfer have been demonstrated in helping contexts. For example, Fried and Berkowitz (1979) exposed four sets of subjects to one of three different types of music (soothing, stimulating, or aversive), or to no music at all. After the subjects rated their mood, the experimenter asked them to do her a favor, saying that they were under no obligation to comply with her request. She explained that she needed as many subjects as possible to participate in an unrelated study, and that she could use anyone who could contribute between 15 minutes and 2 hours.

The excitation transfer model predicts that environmental cues such as music would operate to affect behavior to the extent that these cues were reasonably unobtrusive. As such, subtle positive cues such as soothing or stimulating music would enhance the likelihood that people would act positively, whereas subtle negative cues would diminish this tendency. Fried and Berkowitz's (1979) data are consistent with these predictions; the pattern of their findings indicates that those exposed to soothing music were the most helpful to the experimenter, whereas those who listened to aversive music were the least cooperative. In addition, subjects who had heard the stimulating music were somewhat more helpful than were those who heard no music at all.

Sex and Aggression: Transfer Can Go Both Ways. In our discussion of mislabeled arousal in Chapter 2, we noted that research evidence indicates that the relationship between sex and aggression is rather complicated. In attempting to explain these findings, Baron and Byrne (1981) suggest that the effect of exposure to sexually arousing stimuli on aggressive responses is complex. Material that generates slight to moderate levels of sexual arousal tends to inhibit aggression, whereas highly arousing sexual cues tend to enhance such antisocial behavior.

Within the perspective of the excitation transfer model, it appears that the arousal generated by aggressive cues is attributed to sexual stimuli when these latter stimuli are not overpowering. However, a portion of the arousal produced by extreme sexual stimulation is attributed to aggressive cues. Both the sexual and the aggressive cues used in research of this type have been far from subtle. As such, it is not surprising that subjects typically attribute their arousal to both types of stimuli in such research contexts. Thus, only a portion of the excitation developed in response to one type of stimulus is transferred to the other. It appears that the transfer occurs in the direction of the less arousing cue—that is, diminished feelings of aggression should result when aggressive cues are more powerful than are sexual cues, since some of the feelings elicited by the more potent stimuli will be misattributed to their less arousing counterparts. Similarly, when the sexual cues are more arousing, the resulting misattribution should enhance the perceived influence of the aggressive stimuli, and consequently, people should act more aggressively in such contexts.

Environmental Prompts

In the previous section, we discussed the link between cues from the physical environment and arousal-based helping and hurting behavior. In this section, we will turn to a second process by which the physical environment can influence such behaviors. This process involves a more direct relationship between cues and the actions evoked by them. In this framework, cues can serve as environmental prompts or inhibitors of behavior as a consequence of their prior association with such actions. For example, through direct or vicarious exposure, we can learn to associate an object, such as a gun, with certain types of behavior. This object, can then serve as a cue that prompts us to engage in behaviors consistent with the association that it elicits—

namely aggression. We will now review research that has examined the ways in which such environmental prompts can promote or inhibit helping and hurting behavior.

Triggering Aggression.   In an early study of the potential effects of prompts on aggressive behavior, Berkowitz and LePage (1967) brought subjects into their laboratory, where they received a number of electric shocks from another person who, ostensibly, was serving in the same experiment. Then the subject and the shocker exchanged roles, and the subjects were given the opportunity to retaliate. As one would expect, those who had been shocked most retaliated the most. The tendency to aggress was enhanced when the subjects were tested in a room in which a rifle and a revolver had been placed on a table in plain view. Berkowitz (1969) argued that the guns served as cues which stimulated violence in his subjects. Subsequent research has yielded somewhat inconsistent results on this score. Some studies (Frodi, 1975; Leyens & Parke, 1975) have supported the findings of Berkowitz and LePage, but others (Buss, Booker, & Buss, 1972) were not able to reproduce this effect.

It appears that the associations people form with an environmental prompt are critical in determining its effect on subsequent aggression. It is unlikely that a gun would enhance aggressive responses if it served to remind a subject of the awful consequences of such weapons. Thus, the inconsistencies in the empirical literature might have occurred as a result of systematic variations in the psychological meaning of guns for subjects, an aspect of the Personal Structure which we will consider in the final section of this chapter. In any event, there is evidence that in some circumstances, cues can elicit aggressive behavior.

Violence in a Tube.   Extensive research on the violent content of television programs has produced findings that parallel the results just discussed. Both laboratory and naturalistic studies of television violence have demonstrated that aggressive programs stimulate subsequent aggressive behaviors, at least on the part of children (Comstock, Chaffee, Katzman, McCombs, & Roberts, 1978; Eron, 1980; Geen, 1978; Kniveton, 1973; Liebert & Baron, 1972). In contrast, other research has yielded contrary findings (Berkowitz & Alioto, 1973; Feshbach, 1976; Feshbach & Singer, 1971; Noble, 1975). Thus, it appears that as in the case of other environmental prompts, the content of the television program can—but does not always—facilitate the expression of aggressive behavior. As in the studies on the impact of the presence of guns, it appears that television-generated prompts to aggression are effective only to the extent that people interpret them as signifying that violence is an appropriate response.

Libraries Are for Reading, Not Helping.   Just as cues can serve to elicit a behavior, so too can they inhibit certain activities by eliciting interfering associations. Howard and Crano (1974), in a study discussed earlier in this chapter, provide evidence that is consistent with this observation. The reader may recall that in this study subjects witnessed the theft of another's books.

One of the variables examined in this research was the location in which such thefts were staged, and the results indicated that this contextual factor has a significant impact on subjects' helping responses.

The findings of this study revealed that subjects were much less likely to help the victim of the theft when it took place in the library than when it was staged in a lounge located in the student union. It appears that the prompts that subjects associated with these two locations were quite different. Past experiences with libraries, no doubt, instilled in the subjects the sense that a disturbance likely to occur in confronting a thief would be out of place in such a context; in contrast, the prompts contained in the less formal setting of the student lounge—where all types of boisterous behavior is acceptable—did not interfere with subjects' assessment that some form of action might be appropriate. Other research (Latané & Darley, 1970, pp. 118–20) has yielded results consistent with the proposition that environmental prompts can facilitate or inhibit helping behaviors.

We have considered a large number of factors in the Social Context that influence helping and hurting behaviors. Most of this work has investigated the factors in the interpersonal environment, but there is considerable evidence that documents the importance of factors in the physical environment as well. In the following section, we will review the research that has explored the link between the actor's Personal Structure and his or her tendency to help or hurt another.

PERSONAL STRUCTURE VARIABLES IN HELPING AND HURTING

Social psychologists have examined a number of personal characteristics that might play a role in helping and hurting encounters. Among the Personal Structure factors that have received attention in this area are motives, beliefs (norms and roles), affective states (mood and Sentiment relations). We will now discuss these major categories of individual difference variables.

Motives

Earlier, we discussed the investigations of Wilson and his colleagues (Michelini, Wilson, & Messé, 1975; Wilson, 1976) into the role that psychological motivation can play in helping encounters. In general, this research has revealed that people with strong needs to display competence tend to help in poorly resolved situations, whereas people who are strongly concerned with personal security are inclined to help only when there are clear environmental cues that support or elicit such behavior.

Other personality traits—need for approval, locus of control (the tendency to explain behavior in terms of external causes), and the inability to express hostility—have been shown to mediate the expression of aggressive behavior (Carver & Glass, 1978; Dengerink, 1971; Dengerink, O'Leary, & Kasner, 1975; Megargee, 1971; Taylor, 1970). The results of these studies, as well as many others, suggest that people are likely to display helping and hurting behaviors to the extent that such actions are consistent with, or satisfy, their high level motives. Such behaviors are inhibited to the extent that their expression would interfere with these motives.

Short-term and Long-term Affective States

Not Now, I'm in a Bad Mood. An intensely studied variable that affects helping behavior is *mood.* In this area of study, Alice Isen and her coworkers have isolated a number of mood-related factors that appear to exert a strong influence on persons' tendencies to intervene or to refrain from helping. One study in this program of research should provide a reasonably clear idea of the role that mood plays in determining helping behavior.

In this experiment, Isen and Levin (1972) attempted to manipulate the mood of people in a naturalistic setting. To do so, they sometimes placed dimes in the coin return slots of public telephones in shopping malls. Then, they repeatedly staged a minor accident after a subject had completed his or her call. Just as the subject was leaving the phone booth, an accomplice of Isen and Levin walked by and dropped a folder full of papers. Interestingly, only 5 percent of the callers in the control condition (who had used the phone when no dime had been placed in the coin return slot) helped the accomplice recover her papers; of the experimental subjects (who had found the dime), fully 90 percent assisted the woman in her moment of need. Subsequent work by Isen and others (Cunningham, 1979; Cunningham, Steinberg, & Grev, 1980; Forest, Clark, Mills, & Isen, 1980; Isen, Horn & Rosenhan, 1973; Levin & Isen, 1975; Weyant, 1978) has explored in greater detail the role of mood in helping behavior. A general conclusion may be drawn from this research series; when the costs for helping are not great, a positive mood facilitates helping behavior.

A Little Help For Your Friends. As noted earlier, one of the major consequences of positive Sentiment relationships is the development of a sense of shared welfare. It is not surprising, then, that research (Form & Nosow, 1958) has shown that in times of emergency, people are most concerned about the welfare of their loved ones and least concerned about the fate of strangers. Other research, performed in the laboratory (Kelley & Byrne, 1976), has demonstrated that people will work harder to prevent harm from occurring to someone they like than to someone for whom they have less positive feelings. Also of interest is the finding that these subjects did little to interfere with painful shocks being administered to someone whom they disliked, although they had the power to do so. Thus, both hurting and helping appear to be mediated by the positive and negative Sentiment relationships that can exist between interactants in an encounter.

Norms and Roles

Perhaps the component of the Personal Structure that has the greatest impact on helping and hurting behaviors is the set of incorporated beliefs concerning appropriate conduct (norms and roles). Norms have been examined in a number of contexts, with perhaps the bulk of such research undertaken by Shalom Schwartz and his colleagues (Schwartz, 1973, 1974, 1977; Schwartz & Clausen, 1970; Schwartz & Fleishman, 1978; Schwartz & Howard, 1980). In general, Schwartz has demonstrated that prosocial norms affect behavior to the extent that actors feel personally responsible for the outcome of a helping encounter. It is not enough to profess belief in a norm that prescribes helping the needy; rather, one must feel a personal responsibility to carry out activities that are consistent with this goal. Schwartz and Howard (1980) demonstrated this general line of research in the experiment presented below.

Someone Should Do It. In this research, Schwartz and Howard used two questionnaires to measure two Personal Structure characteristics of a group of undergraduates. One questionnaire measured respondents' feelings of obligation to perform various altruistic acts (collecting clothing for the needy, reading to the blind, and so on). Responses could range from, "I feel an obligation to refuse," to "I feel a strong obligation to agree." A second measure assessed the extent to which respondents denied personal responsibility for the consequences of their own behaviors.

Approximately three months after these questionnaires had been administered, the subjects received an appeal from an organized charity to help them by volunteering to read to blind people. Schwartz and Howard (1980) found that respondents who had not indicated a strong sense of obligation to help the needy were unlikely to respond to this appeal. On the other hand, those who had strongly endorsed this norm were more likely to help, but only if they had scored low on the scale that measured responsibility denial. Other work has shown this same relationship between responsibility denial, norm endorsement, and helping behavior, in contexts that range from helping in a poorly resolved emergency situation to responding to appeals for bone marrow donations.

Rolling with the Punch. As noted earlier, Zimbardo's (1970) concept of deindividuation to some extent involves the sense in respondents that their aggressive behavior is more a consequence of roles that they are enacting than of their intrinsic desires. For example, there is evidence that the teachers in Milgram's (1974) research engaged in their extremely harmful behavior out of a belief that they had to do what was expected of them—that is, they had to enact the role that was thrust upon them. This belief relieved them of personal responsibility in much the same way that the high responsibility denial respondents of Schwartz did not feel obligated to help, although they endorsed the general prosocial norm that helping is appropriate. A study by Johnson and Downing (1979) provides direct evidence that role expectations can affect aggressive behavior.

In their study, Johnson and Downing (1979) placed female subjects in a Milgram-type situation, in which they had to choose the shock level that would be administered to a learner who had made a mistake. Role expectations were manipulated via the costumes that subjects wore when they participated in the learning task. Some subjects had to wear a robe that resembled those

RAY ELLIS/RAPHO-PHOTO RESEARCHERS, INC.   J. BERNDT/STOCK, BOSTON, INC.

People's manner of dress can affect their actions.

worn by the Ku Klux Klan. Others wore a dress that approximated a nurse's uniform. Of course, the experimenter attempted to justify this procedure by explaining that the nature of the specific costume given the subject was an accident: "I am not much of a seamstress; this thing came out looking kind of Ku Klux Klannish." The experimenter explained further that the major reason subjects were asked to wear these costumes was to obscure their identities somewhat.

Both types of costumes rendered the subjects equally unidentifiable. However, the expectations that the two costumes subtly conveyed were quite different: the nurse's uniform cast subjects in the role of a helper, whereas the Klan costume was designed to make salient the opposite belief. Results indicated that this manipulation was highly successful. Subjects in the nurses uniforms attempted to reduce the shock level administered to the victim over trials, whereas their counterparts in the Klan outfits were more likely to attempt to increase shock levels. This pattern of responses was consistent although no one could recognize the individual subjects. Apparently, the deindividuation which these subjects experienced as a result of the costumes they wore allowed them to act in ways that they might have otherwise rejected.

This point has been dramatically underscored by Zimbardo and his colleagues in the study of a simulated prison (Haney, Banks, & Zimbardo, 1981; Zimbardo, Haney, Banks, & Jaffe, 1973). In this study, a group of undergraduates volunteered to participate in psychological research in which some of them would be asked to play the role of a prisoner while others would be assigned the role of a guard. Those subjects who were randomly assigned the task of playing the prisoners were arrested, booked, and confined to a mock prison located in the basement of the university's psychology building. The remaining subjects were assigned to guard these prisoners.

Although the study was a simulation, it soon began to take on the trappings of reality. Guards dressed in uniforms, wearing dark glasses, and armed with billy clubs soon began to respond to their prisoners with behaviors that ran the gamut from indifference to sadistic harassment. Though the study was originally designed to be carried out over a two-week period, it had to be terminated after only six days had elapsed.

It is important to note that the prison guards, up to that point, had been normal college students who had never before exhibited such callous and inhumane behavior. When the study was over, they explained their unusual behavior by saying, in so many words, that they had become enmeshed in the context of the prison and in the role assigned to them. Although personally they would never have engaged in such behavior, they did so in the deindividuating circumstances which their role in the study had forced upon them. In other words, they denied responsibility for their destructive actions.

CONCLUDING REMARKS

In concluding this chapter, let us reconsider the themes of central importance to helping and hurting. Clearly, Valuation plays the major role in determining the particular behaviors that are expressed in such encounters. For example, the student who found himself guarding prisoners in Zimbardo's mock prison study had a large number of response options available, and he had to choose among these possibilities in fulfilling his obligations as a prison guard. On the one hand, he could express numerous well-practiced behaviors which were consistent with many of his past actions as a student, friend, and classmate. On the other hand, he also had incorporated beliefs (from books, films, and so forth) about behaviors that prison guards and police express in performing their duties. From his behavior, it seems likely that this latter set of beliefs weighed more heavily than the former in guiding actions.

Why should this set of behaviors, which were, after all, unfamiliar, have been the chosen option? As in the Milgram studies on obedience, the Social Context was one in which the subjects had little direct experience. However, there were a large number of cues in the situation that served as strong prompts to specific actions. As such, aspects of the subject's Personal Structure were probably underweighed in his attempts to determine the most appropriate behavior.

For instance, the guard might consider himself to be a kind person. He could point to many instances in his past behaviors that would support this conclusion. However, in his first experience as a guard, he is uncertain that the expression of kindness has any place in a prison. As such, this Personal Structure characteristic, and many others like it, were weighted less heavily in his Valuation of response options. This interpretation of the prison guard's behavior is congruent with people's tendencies to overweight situational cues when explaining their own actions, a phenomenon discussed in Chapter 7.

A second theme of great relevance in the determination of people's responses in helping and hurting contexts is Resolution. As noted, the lack of experience that subjects had in performing their role of prison guard, coupled with the strong situational prompts available, had a telling effect on the actions that they ultimately chose to express. In contrast, high Resolution does not characterize the context of the typical bystander intervention situation, in which the available cues are often inconsistent. In these circumstances, the bystander is faced with deciding whether or not to act when the context provides a contradictory set of cues. For most of us, an emergency is a novel and ambiguous context, and as such, we use almost any information possible in deciding what to do. Similarly, many situations which could result in the expression of aggressive behavior are also of low Resolution.

In the absence of consistent situational cues, people tend to rely upon internal prompts that lead to the differential weighting of some cues at the expense of others. The pervasive concerns with Consistency are amplified in such contexts. Self-Consistency affects the weight which we give cues that are relevant to the maintenance of a positive self-impression. Self/other Consistency, whose impact is reinforced by the presence of Sentiment relationships, affects the weight which we accord to the behavior of others. In addition, poorly resolved contexts enhance the influence of high level Personal Structure characteristics. For example, the more ambiguous the context, the more likely will such variables as the sense of personal responsibility, or the needs for security or esteem, affect actions. Thus, the themes of Valuation, Resolution, Consistency—and, to a lesser extent, Sentiment—operate to shape helping and hurting behavior, as they do all other forms of social activity.

We need to make one final remark before concluding our discussion of helping and hurting. As noted regarding the material presented in past chapters, we have for convenience and ease of understanding analyzed the factors that are relevant to a given set of phenomena as if they operated independently. Unfortunately, this tactic provides a somewhat oversimplified picture of the ways in which these variables actually operate. It should be clear by now that factors in the interpersonal environment, physical environment, and Personal Structure do not operate in isolation of one another; rather, they combine in unique ways to affect behavior. Thus, for example, deindividuation at one level is a Personal Structure variable, but from a more complex, realistic perspective, it is a consequence of the combination of beliefs and environmental cues (Diener, 1980). Similarly, diffusion of responsibility is the result of a person's belief that the presence of others in the context reduces his or her obligation to act in a responsible, prosocial (norm-based) fashion. It might be useful for the reader to review the material presented in this chapter in order to explore the complex interdependencies that exist among the major variables that influence rather transient social behaviors.

In the next chapter, we will begin to view social behavior within a more extended time frame—that is, rather than concentrating on interpersonal activities which typically occur in relatively brief encounters, we will explore the ways in which long-term relationships begin and develop over time.

Social Behavior in Small Groups

11

In the previous chapter, we considered the actions of people involved in short-term encounters, focusing on the rather dramatic behaviors of helping and hurting. We will now turn our attention to the social behaviors of people whose experiences with each other take place over a longer time span, in the context of the small group.

There are many reasons why people form social relationships of a more or less extended nature. Most often, long-term relationships between people begin because of some shared concerns. For example, people who meet for the first time in a college class might begin interacting to collaborate on their studies outside of the classroom. Others might come together because they are assigned to the same cabin at summer camp and must coordinate their efforts in an attempt to beat out the other cabins and win the camp's coveted King Cabin award. Still others might begin to interact because they share a need for companionship; similarly, some people might meet by chance but continue to interact because they find each other's company rewarding.

When people come together to pursue some common set of goals and, for whatever the reasons, their shared experiences continue over an extended period of time, their relationship often evolves into what social psychologists have called the *small group* (Homans, 1950). Small groups have been the focus of intense inquiry in the social sciences for many years. Various disciplines in social science have traditionally approached the study of human social activity from somewhat different perspectives. While different, these approaches are not mutually exclusive; rather, they emphasize different facets of a complex phenomenon—human social relations.

We will now note some of the major dimensions of small groups as social scientists have variously defined them. As you might expect, this summary culminates in yet another definition to be added to the list.

Interdependence

Perhaps the most frequently cited defining characteristic of small groups is the *interdependence* of their members (Bass, 1960; Delamater, 1974; Fiedler, 1967; Homans, 1950; Kelley & Thibaut, 1978; Lewin, 1951; Shaw, 1981; Stogdill, 1959). Unfortunately, interdependence can refer to a number of different phenomena: the interdependence of members' behaviors, the interdependence of their outcomes, or the interdependence of the tasks that they must perform.

Behavior Interdependence. Interdependence of behavior refers to the fact that one group member's actions are a response to the actions of another and, in turn, serve to influence other group members' subsequent behaviors. In this sense, interdependence refers to interaction, and groups are characterized by the frequent occurrence of such activity among their members.

Outcome Interdependence. Interdependence of outcomes has two related meanings. First, this term refers to the fact that each member's outcomes are dependent not only upon his or her own behaviors, but on those of the other group members as well. For example, the reader can imagine taking a course on William Shakespeare in which the instructor assigns a group project, a task that will determine a significant portion of the final grade.

Among the defining features of small groups are the outcome and task interdependence of their members.

The professor has decided that teams of three students will work together on one of a number of possible projects listed on the blackboard. To be nice, he allows the students in the class to choose, if they wish, the people with whom they will be working and the particular topic of their project.

By chance, you know two other people in the class, and after a hurried conference, you raise your hand to indicate that the three of you have agreed to form a team. You begin to regret your decision, however, when one of your partners commits the team to work on the most difficult of the projects—compiling an annotated bibliography of references to the works of William Shakespeare. The massive amount of potentially relevant material that must be perused demands the combined efforts of all members of your group if the assignment is to be completed successfully. This is an instance of outcome interdependence because your grade is not completely dependent upon your efforts alone, but rather upon a combination of your own work and that of your teammates. If one of you does not fulfill his or her obligations, the outcomes of the all three will suffer. This form of interdependence was discussed at length in our review of fate control and behavior control (Chapter 9).

A second aspect of interdependence of outcomes involves *shared fate*—that is, the outcome of an event has more or less equal implications for the welfare of every member of the group. In the example just presented, it is clear that shared fate is operating; the three of you will receive the same grade for the work since the instructor has no way of knowing who did what. While in many cases shared fate among members is not as obvious as in this example, a frequently defining feature of groups is the belief, shared by the people who belong to them, that what is good for the group as a whole is good for its individual members.

Task Interdependence.   Interdependence of tasks refers to the necessity for coordination among the members of a collective, in order to realize some outcome. Members of a group often take on different aspects of the group

Task interdependence in small groups involves coordination of different activities.

effort. These tasks must be coordinated, so that the actions of all members contribute to the realization of the goals or purposes of the group.

Think of a typical pot luck dinner that a group of long-time friends and acquaintances might attempt to hold in celebration of the Fourth of July. After a good deal of discussion, the issue of job assignments is settled: Larry will bring the chopped liver, Anne her famous Frozen Ice Cream Ball Surprise, and so on. Once these decisions have been made, there is a shared expectation that they will be carried out as agreed. If this is not the case, the picnic could be ruined: if everyone brought chopped liver or ice cream, or if Albert forgot to bring the beer, this breakdown in coordination would seriously interfere with the mission of the group, which in this case is to eat well at the Fourth of July picnic.

This pot luck example has other implications for understanding interdependence of tasks as a defining characteristic of groups. First, it could be that the planners of the picnic pair people and tasks at random. In this case, Larry would be chosen to bring chopped liver not because of his skill at preparing this gourmet delight, but simply as a result of a flip of a chicken. However, this basis for the assignment of activities (luck) is somewhat unusual, since it does not take into consideration the differences in skills, deficiencies, and experiences of the participants. Thus, Rosie is assigned the task of bringing the mustard and paper plates because everyone knows that she cannot boil water without burning it. On the other hand, Larry's chopped liver is widely acknowledged as a triumph of the livermaker's art, and to assign him a simpler job would be akin to asking Einstein to help balance the family checkbook.

Another aspect of this type of interdependence that our example brings to mind is the necessity for one, some, or all of the would-be picnickers to take on the task of planning the event. While this directing task could be shared more or less equally, it is usually the case that only a small portion of the group takes on most of the responsibilities for coordinating the efforts of the members. In this case, Ida has taken on most of the burden of insuring that the event is well-coordinated. As discussed in detail below, this directing activity is a major variable of interest in the study of small groups, because it insures that other necessary behaviors occur.

Finally, we should note that the repetition of a pattern of interdependent activities often results in the development of norms, through which a specific set of behaviors comes to be expected of specific group members. Thus, if the Fourth of July picnic becomes an annual event, and on every such occasion Rosie brings the plates and mustard, it is not long before both she and the other members of the group know what her contribution to the event will be, even without a phone call from Ida. This evolution of activity interdependence—from a situation in which coordination is a result of impingement, to one in which the mechanism for coordination has become incorporated—is another major feature of groups that has been the focus of considerable empirical research.

Perception

In addition to interdependence, in their attempts to define the small group, social scientists have focused on another dimension of human functioning—*perception*. As it has been used in this context, perception has two distinct references: *individuality* and *unit relation*.

Individuality. On one hand, as a defining feature of groups, perception refers to a recognition among group members that each is an individual whose unique characteristics sets him or her apart from other people. For example, Robert Freed Bales (1950), who has extensively studied small groups, defines a group as a collective in which each member holds an "impression or perception of each other member distinct enough so that he can . . . give some reaction to each of the others as an individual person" (p. 33). In other words, the group members come to know one another well enough so that the unique aspects of each member's Personal Structures are recognized by the others.

For instance, consider a small-enrollment class consisting of 10 to 15 people. At the beginning of the term, the class members perceive one another merely as fellow students. As the term progresses, however, each member's Personal Structure characteristics become known to the others, and as such, from Bales's perspective, the class evolves from a random collection of individuals (a collective) to a group.

Unit Relations. A second feature which characterizes groups is the perception, held by members and outsiders alike, that the group has a shared identity—in other words, that the group members comprise a unit relationship. An obvious illustration of the crucial role of the perception of a unit relationship in the definition of a group is the tendency of people who are involved in continuing collective action to display cues that identify them as part of a social entity, one that is separate and distinct from the rest of the interpersonal environment. For example, members of high school clubs will often wear uniforms—jackets, sweatshirts, or club sweaters with easily identifiable insignias—whose central purpose is to set apart the group members from the rest of the school population.

The issue of unit relation goes deeper than mere physical differentiation; it also involves a perception and acceptance of a common identity which manifests itself in a sense of shared fate. Those wearing the same uniform are expected to stick together—to share both the joys and the vicissitudes of being a part of the group. In the musical, *West Side Story,* a song sung by members of the Jets (a street gang) embodies the influence of the unit bond on the perceptions of group members. In "The Jet Song," the gang members attest, "When you're a Jet, if spit hits the fan, you've got brothers around, you're a family man. You're never alone, you're never disconnected. You're home with your own. When company's expected, you're well-protected."

The two components of perception—individuality and unit relationship—

at first glance appear contradictory, since the former emphasizes the uniqueness of group members, while the latter emphasizes their common identity. In actuality, however, there is no contradiction between these two defining perceptual features of groups. Individuality refers to the recognition of one's fellow group members as unique human beings, an impression that is possible only after one has become well-acquainted with them. On the other hand, people outside the group do not possess enough information to see the members of the group as anything more than part of a unit relationship. For group members, however, there is no apparent contradiction in seeing one another as both individuals and part of a common social entity.

The family provides an excellent example of the ways in which the two perceptual components of group identity operate in tandem. The parents of three boys obviously perceive them as their children (a unit relationship), but at the same time, they also recognize the multitude of features that distinguishes them from one another. Other people, who are unconnected with the family, tend to see the children as the Jones boys, a perceived unit relationship (the unit in this case being the family). This is not to suggest that people who know the Jones family but are not a part of it cannot make distinctions between the children; rather, they are not as sensitive as are the parents to each child's unique characteristics.

Definition of the Group

With these considerations in mind, it appears that a useful definiton of the term *group*—from a social psychological perspective—is as follows:

> A group is a small number of people (of 20 or less) who have a high probability of encountering each other on a regular and continuing basis, who act with regard to one another, and who are identified by themselves and others as forming a single social entity. Because of their experiences, members tend to develop positive beliefs and feelings about one another as individuals, and about the group as a whole.

A number of aspects of this definition merit comment. First, our conceptualization of the group limits membership to a relatively small number of people. We utilize this size limitation as a means of differentiating the term *group,* as defined above, from other uses of this word within the social sciences (some of which are discussed later in this chapter). Thus, for the sake of clarity, we employ the term *small group* to denote those collectives whose characteristics conform to the definition provided here.

It is important to note that the size limitation is not an artificial criterion imposed as a matter of convenience to differentiate the small group from other, larger collectives. In actuality, the size limitation is a consequence of other distinguishing features of the small group. In small groups, members must have a high probability of encountering one another; similarly, members must have frequent opportunities to interact on a regular basis. The greater the number of people in the collective, the less likely these conditions are

OWEN FRANKEN/STOCK, BOSTON, INC.

Size is one of the defining features of small groups. Some collectives are too large ever to evolve into a group.

to be satisfied. A related characteristic of small groups is that the members know each other well, a condition that is increasingly difficult to satisfy as the number of people increases. Later in this chapter, we will examine these and other effects of group size on members' behaviors.

Second, the proposition that group members act with regard to each other refers to two distinct types of behavior. At the most obvious level, people in small groups interact with one another—that is, the behavior of one person is often a reaction to the activity of another, and this behavior, in turn, serves as a stimulus for the subsequent responses of others. Less obvious is the observation that people act with regard to others even when these others are not physically present. Recall, for example, the hypothetical English class project mentioned earlier in this chapter. Much of the activity that you performed to complete the mission of the group—searching for references, annotating these documents, and so on—was done on your own. However, to some degree, you did this work because you knew that your teammates were depending on you. Thus, you were acting with regard to these other group members although you felt their presence only psychologically.

Third, the part of the definition that specifies that group members will share a belief that the group is a source of rewards should not be taken to imply that there never will be periods when one or more of the members are unhappy about their experiences in the group. Similarly, while group members will tend to have positive impressions of one another, there will be exceptions to this general trend as well. Over time, however, the net value of the outcomes that members experience in small groups tends to be positive, and the average impression of each member about the others also tends to be favorable. As will be discussed later, groups tend to be unstable to the extent that these conditions are not met.

Finally, it should be noted that our definition of small groups explicitly ignores the issue of *volition*—the extent to which the regular and continuing encounters between people are a consequence either of choice or of external forces. In voluntary situations—when people act of their own free choice—it is unlikely that they will participate in continuing social interactions that are not rewarding to them. Thus, voluntary collectives evolve into groups, or they dissolve. On the other hand, people can find themselves to be part of a collective as a consequence of forces beyond their control. In these circumstances, it often is difficult, if not impossible, to leave the interpersonal environment. As an obvious example, family members have little say in the matter of who their parents and siblings will be. Similarly, people who share the same work station, prison cell, or classroom need not necessarily have acted purposely to come together. Yet, over time, some of these nonvoluntary collectives can evolve into groups.

For example, children assigned to the same cabin of a summer camp typically are not given the opportunity to choose their fellow occupants. Yet, under the appropriate circumstances, groups will often evolve from such collectives. As research by Muzafer and Carolyn Sherif and their colleagues has demonstrated, contextual features that generate positive outcomes for the actors and induce in them a sense of shared fate and feelings of common identity tend to promote group formation, even when participation is not completely voluntary.

In one investigation (Sherif, Harvey, White, Hood, & Sherif, 1961; Sherif & Sherif, 1953), researchers actually supervised a summer camp for boys. Initially, the children assigned to the cabins were strangers, but the researchers manipulated the social context of the camp to promote conditions that favored group formation. They took steps to insure that children assigned to a cabin did almost everything together. This sharing of activities maximized the potential for regular and continuing contact between cabinmates; and given that this was a summer camp, most of these mutual activities were designed to be rewarding to the participants.

Moreover, over the course of these experiences, the occupants of a cabin formed detailed impressions of one another and developed a sense of common identity, as exemplified by the names that the groups chose for themselves (the Rattlers and the Eagles). In addition, the investigators arranged a series of contests that pitted the Rattlers and the Eagles against one another, and rewards were distributed as a result of the outcomes of these competitions. Under such circumstances, it is not surprising that over the course of a few weeks, two very distinct (and antagonistic) groups had formed.

From this example, it is clear that the factor that determines whether collectives become groups is not volition, but rather the nature (and outcomes) of the Social experiences that occur within the confines of the interpersonal environment. Such encounters can generate positive impressions and a perception of a unit relationship—outcomes that are conducive to group formation. On the other hand, if features in the context do not promote interaction or a sense of shared fate, then people brought together by circumstance will remain a collective rather than evolve into a small group.

Related Uses of the Word Group. As with many terms in the social sciences, the word group has been used to represent a variety of different phenomena. For example, in some usages, the term is applied to *social aggregates*—persons who are perceived as belonging to the same general class or category because they share some common characteristics. Thus, people employ the terms *ethnic group* or *racial group* to refer to aggregates of people who might differ on a multitude of characteristics, but have in common a set of physical features, a cultural heritage, and the geographic origin of their ancestors. In Chapter 13, we will discuss the social psychological implications of classifying people into aggregates on the basis of such minimal information. This usage of the term group is mentioned here because it is important to differentiate it from the meaning that we have given it. It is important to understand this distinction because the most crucial defining feature of small groups is the interdependence among its members. Clearly, this feature is absent from social aggregates.

In addition, the word group is sometimes used as a synonym for a *formal organization,* especially within the fields of organizational psychology and sociology. In this usage, a 60-man football team, a Boy Scout troop, the faculty of a large psychology department, and the staff of the First National Bank, can all be identified as groups. To differentiate between groups as formal organizations and small groups, we must consider two key concepts in organizational theory: formal statuses and formal roles. A formal status is a position in an organization (scoutmaster, bank teller, or assistant professor). Formal roles are the specific activities that are the responsibility of a person who occupies a given status in the organization.

It is important to note that within an organization, a certain behavior is expected to accompany a given status, regardless of the particular person who occupies the position. Thus, all bank tellers (a status) are expected to meet the same general obligations—that is, to fulfill the formal role associated with their position in the bank organization. In terms of the formal organization, the individual who occupies the status of teller is irrelevant, so long as whoever does so meets the requirements of the role. Moreover, in the organization, the statuses are interdependent: the president of the bank cannot fulfill his or her role unless the occupants of the other positions in the organization also fulfill theirs, and vice versa.

It is precisely the impersonal nature of this interdependence which distinguishes the formal organization from the small group, as we have defined it. In the small group, the interdependence of the members is not a result of a formal organizational scheme, but rather a consequence of the specific interactions that have taken place between the members. As noted earlier,

Organizations have formal statuses and roles that are independent of the people who occupy them.

over the course of their experiences with one another, people often develop expectations about the behaviors that each member should express. In a small group, roles emerge from experience; they are not imposed by the formal structure of the organization.

The study of organizations focuses on the identification of formal structures (set rules that govern statuses and roles), and the consequences of these structures for the organizations' survival and prosperity. In contrast, the study of small groups involves the exploration of the factors that affect the experiences of the group members, which lead them to develop regularized patterns of interaction and common beliefs (norms, a sense of shared fate, common identity, and so on).

These observations should not be taken to imply that formal organizational structures are irrelevant to small group functioning. As Homans (1950) and others have noted, most small groups evolve within the framework of a larger formal organization. In fact, the formal organization is often the source of the tasks that bring people together, a necessary first step in the evolution of the small group. An example of one such imposed task is the English assignment in the example cited earlier, which caused you and your two classmates to interact over the course of a term and provided the opportunity for a small group to evolve.

With this introduction, we can now turn to a detailed consideration of the variables that affect the evolution from collectives to small groups, and the social behavior that occurs within them. Before beginning this review, however, one additional point needs to be made. Most empirical studies of these variables have examined collectives, which at most are in the initial stages of small group development. A common research tactic in these studies is to bring together a small number of strangers under some specified set of conditions and to observe their interaction for a relatively brief period of time. Actually, what is studied in these contexts is not the small group, per se, but the processes that occur in the evolution of the group. It is assumed that the variables or processes that operate in these rather contrived circumstances have similar effects in small groups that evolve in the real-world.

THE NATURE OF GROUP PROCESSES AND OUTCOMES

In the following sections, we will discuss the major variables that have been found to affect the manner in which groups form, the interaction patterns that emerge from the group experience, and the products or outcomes of these interactions. In other words, we will explore some of the factors that mediate group processes and outcomes. To provide a framework for this review, we will first address four basic questions whose answers will provide a clearer understanding of the nature and operation of groups.

Why Do People Join Groups?

There is general agreement in social psychology that people join in collective action to maximize the probability of obtaining positive outcomes for themselves (Bales, 1950; Cartwright & Zander, 1968; Cattell, 1948; Moreno, 1934; Thibaut & Kelley, 1959). In other words, people participate in groups for the same reasons that they engage in any social exchanges: because they have valuated their options and have come to the conclusion that the group is the most likely (or least costly) means of satisfying high level motives. Thus, the factors that motivate people to interact in short-term encounters (discussed in Chapter 9) also influence their tendencies to associate with others on a more long-term and enduring basis.

Of course, as noted earlier, circumstances (such as confinement to a prison) sometimes force people to associate with others in a collective. Even in these circumstances, people will attempt to maximize their outcomes, and in so doing, often will find themselves a part of an evolving group. In voluntary collectives, group evolution is even more likely, since people have explicitly joined together to pursue some common goal. The major differences between these two circumstances involve perceptions of free choice and estimates of the alternative options that are available. Even so, the principles of social exchange affect social activities regardless of whether people come together by choice or by circumstance.

Recall that in Chapter 9 we noted that people engage in social activities to the extent that the activities themselves are rewarding, or to the extent that they are perceived as increasing the likelihood that a desired reward will be obtained at some future time. These same reasons apply to people's participation in small groups. A number of social scientists have observed that small groups perform two major functions for their members (Bales, 1950; Cattell, 1948; Moreno, 1934; Parsons & Bales, 1955). Parsons and Bales (1955), for example, identified two major dimensions of group activity—expressive functions and instrumental functions. From our perspective, expressive activities are behaviors that, in themselves, are directly rewarding and motive satisfying. Instrumental activities are actions that, while not directly satisfying, are perceived as leading to satisfying outcomes. Of course, a single activity can serve both expressive and instrumental functions; for example, behaviors that were originally expressed solely for instrumental reasons can, over time, become rewarding in themselves.

Small groups evolve and persist to the extent that they fulfill expressive and instrumental functions. As Bales (1953, 1970) notes, however, group members sometimes pursue different specific concerns at the same time, and these pursuits can increase the cost of their exchanges. For example, it often is the case that some group members' attempts to engage in behaviors that are directly rewarding interfere with others' attempts to act instrumentally. In these circumstances, the net outcomes for all concerned are diminished.

For the purpose of illustration, suppose that you and your two classmates are having one of your frequent meetings to discuss your progress in the development of the annotated bibliography of works on Shakespeare. In this encounter, you are attempting to report in detail about a valuable library resource that you have just discovered; you feel that it would be helpful to develop a plan of action to exploit this new-found trove of useful information. Your colleagues, however, appear more intent on having a good time. They are pursuing this goal by trading jokes and stories about your English instructor and throwing paper airplanes at each other, while you are attempting to get some work done. In this situation, there is an obvious conflict between the instrumental and the expressive activities within your small group. Thus, in these circumstances—as well as in many other group encounters—there is a need for a means of coordinating and directing the members' activities.

To accomplish some coordination of the group's activities, some form of a directing or structuring function must be instituted. Without direction, interaction in groups becomes too costly, and the group has little chance to succeed or survive. In the present case, should your group fail, you would also fail—in your English class. Thus, in this instance and in many others, people recognize that direction is necessary in the group. This recognition helps to legitimize group members' use of appropriate impingement mechanisms on one another. In your meeting, for example, you might remind your rowdy colleagues of the dire consequences of their lack of concentration on the task; or you might offer a compromise by suggesting that they work hard for two hours, then spend the remainder of the evening at Sam's Bar and Grille. Thus, the theme of Control is a crucial feature of small group functioning, since without some means of coordinating activities, the capability of the group to satisfy the needs of its members is severely imparied.

While almost any rewards can be pursued within the framework of the small group, there appear to be three major reasons for people to take part in group behavior. First, people join a group because they perceive at least some of its members as likely to provide them with rewarding outcomes. One possible reason why you joined your English class project group, for example, might have been the physical attractiveness of one of the other members.[1]

Second, people join a group because they perceive that its members possess resources that would prove helpful to them in fulfilling some desired goal. Such resources can take a number of forms, ranging from simple economic factors to more complex skills and abilities. In the example, you and your colleagues might have banded together because all of you had perceived that each possessed resources that could contribute to the success of the project (and a good grade for one and all). Jon owns a elaborate electric typewriter, perceived as a valuable resource for the typing and editing work that will be a major activity for the project. Sally is an English major with a strong background in Shakespeare, and her knowledge is viewed as a helpful starting point for the work to be done. You, on the other hand, are known for your brains, your organizational skills, and your ability to complete projects on time—three Personal Structure characteristics that the others consider valuable. By joining forces, the three of you pool your resources and are thereby more likely to meet the common goal than any of you would be by working alone.

Third, people often join a group to share the responsibilities inherent in accomplishing a task. This motivation is especially compelling when the task is perceived as difficult or complex, or the consequences of failure are seen as especially dire. Rather than bear sole responsibility in these instances, people will seek others with whom they can share the load. Stephen Harkins, Bibb Latané, Kipling Williams, and their colleagues have studied the inclination for people to perceive collective action as a means of reducing individual responsibility for accomplishing a goal (Harkins, Latané, & Williams, 1980; Latané, Williams, & Harkins, 1979; Petty, Harkins, Williams, & Latané, 1977; Williams, Harkins, & Latané, 1981). For example, Petty et al. (1977) asked subjects to evaluate a set of poems and editorials either as individuals or as a group. They found that subjects perceived less responsibility when taking part in the group effort and thus judged themselves as exerting less effort to accomplish the rating task. This *social loafing effect* appears to be a consistent element of small group performance, and the possibility of sharing responsibility with others appears to be a major inducement for people to attach themselves to groups.

---

[1] Chapter 12 reviews at length factors such as physical attractiveness, which have been shown to have a powerful impact on interpersonal attraction.

It should also be noted that behaving within a group context can have a positive impact on an individual's efforts. A number of social psychologists (Cottrell, 1972; Geen & Gange, 1977; Sanders, 1981; Zajonc, 1965) have commented on this *social facilitation effect*. The results of many studies indicate that being aware that other members can observe and evaluate our activity enhances our performance when the task is well-practiced or easy for us, whereas such awareness interferes with our ability to carry out an activity which is novel, difficult, or fear-arousing (Cottrell, Wack, Sekerak, & Rittle, 1968; Gastorf, Suls, & Sanders, 1980; Markus, 1978; Zajonc, 1965).

What are the Dimensions that Characterize Behavior in Groups?

When people interact in small groups, they appear to express an almost endless variety of behaviors. On closer inspection, however, one begins to discern a much smaller set of dimensions that these behaviors reflect. A number of social scientists have attempted to identify the major dimensions that appear to underlie group intereaction (Bales, 1950, 1970; Borgatta, 1963; Freedman, Leary, Ossorio, & Coffey, 1951; Stollak, Messé, Michaels, Buldain, Catlin, & Paritee, in press). While the specific categories that these people have developed differ to some extent, there is general agreement among these approaches regarding the important factors that underlie group behavior. Rather than explore the wide array of similar models of social behavior in small groups, we will present just one—interaction process analysis developed and later revised by R. F. Bales (1950, 1970).

In Bales's (1970) system, social behavior in groups is seen as reflecting three basic dimensions: dominance (activity and prominence) versus submissiveness (passivity and withdrawal); concern about the outcomes of other group members versus antagonism towards them; and, agreement with the goals of the group versus rebellion. Bales employs the simple terms of *up-down, positive-negative,* and *forward-backward* to identify the endpoints of these three independent dimensions, respectively. A pictorial illustration of this classification is presented in Figure 11.1. Bales argues that most, if not all, of the social acts that occur in groups can be categorized within this three-dimensional space. Perhaps some specific examples will help to demonstrate the power of this model in summarizing apparently disparate behaviors. Again, we will use the English class project group to illustrate the ways in which interaction process analysis can be used.

In one of your work sessions, it soon becomes obvious to both you and Sally that Jon has not completed the work that he had agreed to do for this meeting. Sally reacts to Jon's failure with some antagonism. She lets him know in no uncertain terms that his performance leaves much to be desired, calling him an "irresponsible moocher," a "goldbricker," and other unflattering terms. Jon is visibly upset by this attack, and withdraws into his shell. You witness this encounter with a growing sense of dismay. You foresee not only a wasted evening, but also the distinct possibility that the work group's very existence is in jeopardy. Accordingly, you say to both

FIGURE 11.1
The Interaction Process Analysis Category System

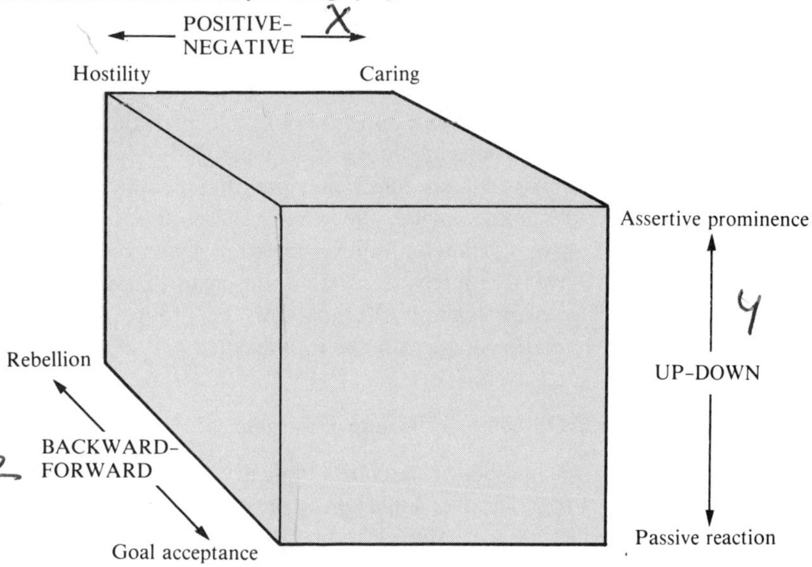

Source: Adapted from Bales (1970).

of them, "Come on, guys, bickering won't get the work done." Moreover, you attempt to smooth things over by jokingly referring to the time that Sally brought her history notes to a meeting, mistaking them for her notebook containing the annotations of all the published articles which dealt with the theory that Rosencrantz and Guildenstern had been lovers. This story breaks the tension somewhat, so you turn to Jon and ask him what he thought of your idea to limit each annotation to an index card. This query seems to draw Jon out of his funk, since he begins to discuss your suggestion, even citing a number of its advantages that you had not considered.

If Bales's model were used to characterize this interaction, Sally's actions toward Jon could be summarized as falling in the upward, forward, and negative section of the system. Her actions were *upward* because they connoted assertiveness, activity, and intrusiveness; they were *forward* since they communicated a concern for the major mission of the group—assembling the annotated bibliography; and finally, they were *negative* because they represented a hostile attack on another group member. In contrast, Jon's reaction to Sally's remarks could be characterized as downward, slightly backward, and neutral, since it reflected withdrawal, a lack of interest in the task at hand (but not overt resistence to it), and little overt response to Sally's attack. His later behavior in response to your query, however, was upward, forward, and neutral. Finally, your actions in the group context were upward, forward, and neutral (when you suggested that the group concentrate on the task), then upward, neutral, and positive (when you tried to make Jon feel better with the Rosencrantz and Guildenstern story), and upward, forward, and positive (when you tried to bring Jon out of his shell by asking his opinion).

Models of social activity in groups, such as that developed by Bales, are useful because they permit us to summarize apparently diverse interpersonal behaviors in an efficient and reliable fashion. Of even greater importance, Bales's system, and others like it, provide insight into the major underlying dimensions of interaction, which are expressed through the almost infinite variety of specific behaviors that people display in small group contexts. As noted earlier, the other systems that have been developed to summarize group behavior differ somewhat from Bales's in their specific details, but overall, there is reasonable consensus that activities in groups reflect members' concerns about the goals of the group, their prominence in it, and their relationships with their colleagues.

What Are the Typical Outcomes of Group Experiences?

A number of outcomes typically occur when small collectives of people come together over some period of time and coordinate their activities to accomplish some mutually desirable goal. Most clearly, there tends to be a product of their endeavors—such as an annotated bibliography of works on Shakespeare. As discussed below, factors that influence the quality and quantity of these products also influence the members' satisfaction with their group experiences. Social scientists have termed this sense of satisfaction with the group, *cohesiveness* (Festinger, 1953; Festinger, Schachter, & Back, 1950; Libo, 1953; Lott & Lott, 1965). Festinger et al. (1950), for example, define cohesiveness as "forces that act on members to remain in a group." Thus, a second outcome of group experience—which is related to, but distinct from, group products—is the sense of cohesion which develops among members.

It is important to distinguish between two somewhat related concepts that are sometimes treated as synonymous—cohesiveness and interpersonal attraction. From our perspective, cohesiveness refers to the members' Valuation of the group to which they belong, not to their liking for any fellow group member. Cohesiveness involves a Valuation of the benefits which members perceive that they derive from their group experiences, the resources and rewards that are available from the group, and other factors that Festinger et al. (1950) summarized under the term *forces*. On the other hand, members also consider negative features of their group experience and the possible benefits they could derive from leaving the group—forces that act on members to weaken their attachment to it.[2] The more positive the outcome of this Valuation process, the greater the cohesiveness.

---

[2] One of the principal factors that the individual members must weigh in their Valuation of the group to which they belong is their perception of the rewards that they would derive from their most favorable alternative arrangement. Thibaut and Kelley (1959) have termed this estimate the person's comparison level for alternatives (CLalt). We will discuss this concept in more detail in the following chapter.

In contrast to cohesiveness, *interpersonal attraction* (to be discussed in Chapter 12) refers to a person's Valuation that another individual is a source of rewards, as well as the Sentimental attachment which rewarding experiences with that person generate. Thus, cohesiveness refers to the level of attraction that members feel for the group as an entity, whereas interpersonal attraction refers to a member's feelings about the other individuals in the group.

Alonzo Anderson has provided a compelling example of the subtle but important difference between cohesiveness and interpersonal attraction in small groups. In his study, Anderson (1975) first measured three high level opinions of a large number of female undergraduates and then assembled these subjects into three-woman groups. Some groups were composed of subjects who shared the same opinions on all three issues; other groups were assembled so that the opinions of the members were completely dissimilar. Anderson then informed the members of the group that the purpose of their meeting was to learn about the ways in which people communicate about a number of important issues (capital punishment, euthanasia, or the morality of war). Thus, they were to discuss these issues among themselves for the remainder of the session. After this meeting ended, each member of a group was asked to complete in private a brief questionnaire which, among other things, asked her how much she had liked each of the other two group members.

There is a great deal of evidence demonstrating a positive relationship between belief similarity and interpersonal attraction (discussed in detail in the following chapter). Anderson's (1975) study, in fact, replicated the usual findings: members of high belief similarity groups liked each other more than did their counterparts who interacted with peers whose beliefs were very different from theirs. Thus, in a group context in which the task consisted of learning about the beliefs of the other members, belief similarity yielded more rewarding experiences and resulted in greater interpersonal attraction. However, belief similarity and interpersonal attraction became much less important in a second session, in which Anderson's groups worked on a task that was very different from the first.

In this second session, the group members were asked to work together to design a dormitory complex consisting of residential, educational, and recreational facilities; the group that performed best, as judged by a panel of experts, would receive a $15 prize. Before the session began, however, each group member was given information that was relevant to the task and told to review this material carefully. For some groups, all members received the same information, which advocated certain principles of environmental design. For other groups, each member was given information that advocated different design principles. Each subject studied her materials for 45 minutes, then spent 5 minutes working on her own ideas before joining her coworkers to develop a group plan.

After the sessions, each subject was told that for a third session (which was never actually held), some of the groups were going to be reorganized and, if she wished, she could be assigned to a new set of partners. Whether subjects chose to stay with their original group or to take advantage of the opportunity to switch constituted the measure of group cohesiveness.

Anderson (1975) classified the groups according to the initial level of members' interpersonal attraction to one another, which was a consequence of their interaction in the first session, and the extent to which they held the same beliefs about how to carry out the task (what Anderson called goal path clarity). His results indicated that similarity of approach to the design task had a major impact on group cohesiveness: only 3 of 20 groups whose members had similar ideas had a member who wished to be reassigned; in contrast, more than half the groups whose members disagreed about the best way to complete the task had at least one member who wanted to change groups. The initial level of interpersonal attraction, on the other hand, was not related to group members' desires to remain in a group or to leave it.

Anderson's (1975) results suggest that the reward value of the two group sessions were based on very different considerations for the group members. When members valuated the outcomes of the initial session, they probably weighed most heavily the extent to which their opinions were accepted by the others, and, in turn, the compatability of the others' expressed opinions with their own. We can infer that the conversations of the group members were much more rewarding when they involved little dispute—that is, when everyone held similar opinions relevant to the topic of the group discussion. In this case, we would expect that interpersonal attraction and cohesiveness would be related, an expectation supported by much past research (Back, 1951; Exline, 1957; Libo, 1953).

On the other hand, the factor that weighed most heavily in these subjects' Valuations of their second group experience appeared to be different from the cues they weighed in the first session. What appeared to matter to subjects in the second session was their ability to smoothly and efficiently accomplish the task of designing the dormitory complex; their initial liking for the others had little, if any, influence on their feelings about the group. These results provide compelling evidence that while often related, interpersonal attraction and group cohesiveness are distinct phenomena which can have different causes and different outcomes.

Cohesiveness is a composite belief about the reward value of a group. Often, other beliefs are products of group experience as well. Among the most important beliefs that emerge from extended interaction in groups are the rules of conduct (norms and roles) that define appropriate or expected behaviors for group members. As noted earlier, over the course of group encounters, members form shared expectations about the behaviors that each will express in this context. Thus, over time, expectations could develop that certain members are more likely to direct the group's activities, whereas others are viewed as more involved with implementing the suggestions of others, or keeping the members amused, or providing sage advice, and so on.

Research by R. F. Bales and Phillip Slater, for example, has shown that over a series of interactions, group members often develop beliefs about the activities that each is expected to perform. In these studies (Bales & Slater, 1955; Heinicke & Bales, 1953; Slater, 1955), small numbers of strangers (three to seven persons) were asked to meet for a number of sessions to discuss various issues of interest to them. These sessions were observed so that the activities of the group members could be systematically categorized. In addition, the members were repeatedly asked to report their perceptions of their encounters, and their beliefs about their fellow group participants.

Systematic analyses of this information revealed that over the course of these sessions, it was very common for two roles to emerge. In most groups, members increasingly (1) looked to one of their colleagues for direction, just as they increasingly (2) identified another as the "nice guy," that is, the person to whom they turned for social and emotional support. Of course, other roles can develop over the course of group experiences—the playboy, the compromiser, the procedural technician, the gatekeeper, and so on. Benne and Sheats (1948), in fact, have listed 27 such roles in their interaction coding system. Most beliefs about the expected behaviors of group members involve directive or supportive activities, in part because such roles are directly relevant to the instrumental and expressive functions that are vital to the group's survival.

In addition to the evolution of beliefs concerning the activities that are expected of individual group members, it is also common for groups to develop more general norms that apply to all members. Some of these rules (prescriptive norms) define behavior which is expected of all members, whereas others (proscriptive norms) identify activities that are out of bounds. For example, for many years, the authors of this text have been involved in a friendly poker game with some of their colleagues. Over the course of these group encounters (whose net outcomes to date are +$100 for one of us and +$.37 for the other), a norm evolved regarding smoking during the game.

Early in the poker group's existence, some members smoked cigarettes or cigars in spite of the fact that other players were rabid antismokers. As the years rolled by, however, the antismoking forces slowly had their way, and the smokers came to feel increasingly less comfortable about engaging in this noxious activity during the game. At this time, a rather strong norm has emerged, so strong that no one has lit up for well over three years, although some members of the group continue to be heavy smokers in other Social Contexts.

Social scientists have termed the development of norms and roles within a group *emergent social structure*. The various behaviors which come to be seen as characteristic of individual members, of some members (but not others), or of every member define the manner in which the group carries out its activities, much as formal rules determine what happens in a golf match, football game, assembly line, or church service. In other words, emergent social structure in the context of a small group parallels the rules which structure behavior in formal organizations. In the small group, the rules emerge from the experiences of the group members, whereas in formal organizations, they are specified in advance. One major implication of these differences is that individuals have much less impact on the structure of the formal organizations to which they belong than on the small groups to which they belong.

Other sorts of beliefs also are influenced by members' experiences in small groups. For example, it is likely that from their experiences, some of the evolving groups in Anderson's (1975) study incorporated a set of beliefs about desirable features of a dormitory complex. These beliefs, in turn, could have affected their Valuations of the dormitories in which they lived. In part, these opinions developed from information acquired while working on the task; however, the positions expressed by the other members of the work group no doubt also had an impact on each subject's own beliefs. It is probable that the sense of common identity that was beginning to develop among the members of Anderson's high cohesive groups made salient a concern for self/other Consistency; in other words, as the group evolves, it increasingly becomes a reference group for its members, who become more and more influential as sources of beliefs.

Recall that in Chapter 4, we reviewed evidence which demonstrated that the beliefs of reference group members influence one's own opinions (Myers, Wojcicki, & Aardema, 1977). Other research has shown that people learn about the opinions held by their reference group through interaction with these individuals. Lamm and Myers (1978), as well as others (Dion, Baron, & Miller, 1970), have summarized an extensive literature of empirical research that is consistent with the proposition that small group experiences have a profound impact on the opinions of group members.

Perhaps of most relevance to our present discussion is a study by David Runyan which clearly demonstrates that the level of cohesiveness in a group affects the impact of group discussion on members' opinions. In his study, Runyan (1974) individually asked people to state their opinions about the alternatives in a game of chance. These subjects were told that these alternatives would determine the payoff that another person could receive for one hour's work. At the most conservative extreme, subjects could judge that the other person should not take any chance at all and accept $2 for his work; or they could come to the conclusion that the other person would be best off taking an increasingly less probable, but increasingly more lucrative, chance on receiving a larger sum (such as a 30 percent chance of winning $7, or a 10 percent chance of winning $20). Responses of subjects to this query indicated that on the average, they believed the best choice was for the other to take a "double or nothing" chance on winning $4.

Runyan (1974) then had these subjects assemble in groups of three to five persons to discuss and agree on a common recommendation that they should present to the other person. As will be seen, group discussions of this type tend to lead to more extreme beliefs or decisions than those which the individual members held, on the average, prior to the group encounter. Thus, Runyan expected that group discussions would lead his subjects to recommend a more extreme (i.e., more lucrative but risky) choice than they had endorsed as individuals. Moreover, he felt that highly cohesive groups would be even more likely to show this trend toward deciding on the more extreme position. To test this latter hypothesis, he had some subjects discuss the problem within the context of a well-established small group; in this case, the members of the group had known one another for some time and had interacted with one another on numerous previous occasions. Other subjects were assigned to groups in which all members were strangers to one another.

Results of the group discussion confirmed Runyan's (1974) hypotheses: as in other studies, the group decisions typically were more extreme than the original choices of the individual members. Moreover, this tendency to adopt a more extreme belief was much more pronounced in the cohesive groups. Thus, these results, as well as some additional evidence (to be presented) indicate that small group experiences can have a powerful influence on members' beliefs. These beliefs can be relevant solely to concerns of the group, or to a much broader array of issues, since the group experience permeates most aspects of people's belief systems.

What Are the Stages in the Evolution of Small Groups?

A major concern of social scientists working in this area has been the identification of the stages that characterize the evolution from a collective to a small group (Bales & Strodtbeck, 1951; Bennis & Shepard, 1956; Caple, 1978; Fisher, 1970; Parsons, 1961; Scheidel & Crowell, 1966; Schutz, 1966; Tuckman, 1965; Winter, 1976). In this work, researchers typically have attempted to discover the regular patterns of activity that are common at different points in a group's existence. These patterns, once identified, have served as the bases for their speculations about the stages that appear necessary for group development.

The specific conclusions that different investigators have drawn regarding the stages through which groups evolve have varied to some extent, in large measure because they grew out of the observations of different types of groups (friendship groups, problem-solving groups, therapy groups, and so on). However, there is some general agreement that groups can progress from an initial stage, in which potential members attempt to weigh the advantages and disadvantages of forming a more organized entity, to a culminating stage, in which the structures and relationships that have evolved are formalized. In this section, we will present a distillation of many of these models.

Stage 1: Orientation

In the initial stage of group development, potential members attempt to make accurate estimates for themselves of the likely outcomes of working together and interacting over time. To arrive at these judgments—which are instances of the operation of Valuation processes—individuals weigh whatever cues are available to them in the early encounters. Issues of available resources, the Personal Structures of the other potential group members, the task, and the mutual interplay of these considerations all play a role in the orientation stage of group development.

The essential, overriding concern for people in this stage is the issue of the contribution of the group experience to their own rewards. The most efficient means of arriving at this estimate—that is, the best source of cues— is information that the others in the collective can furnish. Thus, as research has indicated (Bales & Stodtbeck, 1951), in initial encounters, potential group members spend much of their time asking and answering questions about one anothers' interests, abilities, knowledge, and so on, as well as about the resources that are available for performing some of the possible tasks which they, as a group, could undertake. As Schutz (1966) notes, the result of the Valuation of such information is a decision to either commit oneself to the forming group or to withdraw from it.

Stage 2: Focus

As the members of a group come to realize that it might be profitable to coordinate their activities in pursuit of mutually rewarding outcomes, their focus becomes more narrowly concentrated on the means to accomplish these goals. Thus, as the group moves from orientation to focus, the Resolution of the context increases, since members come to possess an increasingly clear picture of the goals that they share, the contributions that they and their colleagues can make to attain these goals, other available resources, and the nature of the individual rewards that are likely to follow. Thus, over the course of the group members' encounters, information-seeking and information-providing activities slowly diminish and are replaced by an increase in exchanges that center around the accomplishment of the group's tasks.

During this phase of focusing on group tasks, there is likely to be considerable conflict between members with regard to the expressive and instrumental functions of their group experience. Since there are often a number of possible activities that are relevant to task performance, it is reasonable for members to attempt to engage in those actions that are most directly rewarding to them. In many instances, however, these attempts to derive immediate rewards from the context lead to conflict among the participants. Moreover, it is during this stage that members are most likely to engage in activities which, though directly rewarding to them, are not essential to achieving the group goal. Research has suggested that tactics of impingement are most common in this phase of group development, since members are attempting to control the behaviors of others so as to maximize their own present (and future) rewards (Modlin & Faris, 1956; Schroder & Harvey, 1963; Schutz, 1966; Theodorson, 1953).

Stage 3: Regulation

As group members continue to interact over extended encounters, a pattern to their exchanges emerges. Most of the conflicts which characterized the second stage of group evolution have been settled, and norms and roles begin to emerge. The major distinction between the second and third stages involves a decrease in impingement tactics, and a commensurate increase in regulation of group activities through the process of incorporation. In other words, as Thibaut and Kelley (1959) note, by the third stage, behavior control is accomplished through appeal to accepted (incorporated) beliefs about appropriate conduct, rather than by the direct application of personal power (impingement).

At this stage, the small group context is highly resolved. A social structure based on the accepted norms and roles is likely to have emerged, and the various rights and responsibilities of each group member have been acknowledged, at least tacitly. Also, a consensus—either implicit or explicit—has been reached within the group regarding the most reasonable procedures to follow in order to accomplish the group's tasks. Moreover, by this stage, members have developed highly resolved impressions of one another; they perceive their colleagues as individuals, and have formed coherent pictures of their Personal Structures. By this point as well, members perceive themselves and their colleagues as forming a unit relationship—that is, as belonging to a unified social entity.

Thus, in many ways, the group is fully functioning as an intact and integrated social system at the third stage; the members now understand, accept, and work toward the accomplishment of group goals in a coordinated fashion (Modlin & Faris, 1956; Schroder & Harvey, 1963; Theodorson, 1953). If there is any need for control at this stage of the group's development, it centers on attempts to raise the level of acceptance of the emergent norms and roles in members whose activities are not always consistent with them (Bales, 1953; Bales & Strodtbeck, 1951; Philp & Dunphy, 1959).

Stage 4: Formalization

In the fourth stage of group development, the norms and roles that have emerged over the course of the group's existence become formalized, in the sense that the members explicitly—either in writing or in their speech—acknowledge the existence of these rules and their willingness to comply with them. Clearly, most small groups never reach this stage of development. Instead, they continue to function at the third (regulation) stage, in which the social structure that has emerged, while very influential, remains implicit.

On the other hand, some small groups do evolve fully and take on some or all of the trappings of formal organizations. For example, it is not unusual for collectives of high school (or even college) students to exist for a long period of time as informal, small groups. However, sometimes the members of such a group decide to cease being "just a bunch of guys who like motorcycles," and to formally organize themselves into a club. In terms of their everyday activities, there is little difference between the group's operation at the third stage and its operation when formalized (Stage 4). The major difference between groups at these two stages is that in the more formal group, the emergent norms and roles become explicitly stated rules of conduct

Under some circumstances, members of small groups will decide to cease being "just a bunch of guys," and organize themselves formally.

which the members overtly commit themselves to uphold. In addition, there might be other minor changes. For example, most formal organizations have explicit names—Hell's Angels, Alpha Tau Omega, the Cincinnatti Reds—and members of small groups who formalize their organization also tend to formalize their identity through a distinguishing name. An illustration of the features of the evolution of a collective to a formal organization is presented in Figure 11.2.

As noted, not all small groups progress to the fourth stage; most probably

FIGURE 11.2
Stages in the Evolution of an Aggregate to a Formal Small Group

| Orientation | Focus | Regulation | Formalization |

remain in the third (regulation) stage, where they function reasonably well at an informal level. However, it is unlikely that ongoing, surviving groups can remain stable at stages earlier than the regulation phase. On the other hand, even collectives that evolve into small groups do not always survive. Collectives can disband at any stage, but are more likely to do so at the first (orientation) or second (focus) stages than at the later stages.

This discussion was meant to provide a comprehensive picture of the small group, its functions, and its outcomes. Within this framework, we are now in a position to systematically review some of the major variables that social psychologists have found to influence people's social activities and outcomes within group contexts.

VARIABLES THAT AFFECT GROUP PROCESSES AND OUTCOMES

Contextual Factors

The Social Context is comprised of the physical and interpersonal environments, which serve as the backdrop of all interpersonal activity. With regard to social behavior in small group settings, the formal organization within which the group has evolved most often provides the major contextual framework for the encounters that occur among group members. Thus, it is most appropriate for a systematic review of the important mediators of behavior in small groups to begin with a discussion of the influence of formal organizations on these processes.

Formal Organizations

In a classic exploration of the nature of the human group, George Homans concludes that all small groups evolve within the framework of a larger formal organization. In fact, he observes that once a group begins to evolve, its primary mission is to survive and succeed within the constraints imposed on it by the formal organization. In many cases, a group forms because the formal organization has placed a relatively small number of people within a context that provides them with the opportunity to interact with one another on a regular basis.

Homans further observes that many of the mutual concerns of the interactants, as well as their regularized patterns of individual activities and social exchanges, are a consequence of the rules and tasks imposed on them by the formal organization. He terms the group's emergent patterns of responses to its organizational context the *external system*. This phrase refers to the attempts by the people who comprise the small group to evolve a social structure that permits it to meet the demands of the wider Social Context. Homans (1950, 1965) presents compelling evidence, derived from the work of Roethlisberger and Dickson (1939), that the emergent social structure of small groups is greatly affected by factors in the formal organization.

The Roethlisberger and Dickson (1939) study was one of the first systematic attempts to explore the human element in industrial settings. In this research, investigators from the Harvard School of Business were given permission to study the everyday activities of the employees of the Western Electric plant in Hawthorne, Illinois. The Western Electric Company was (and is) the manufacturing arm of the Bell System; all Bell telephones and related equipment are made by Western Electric. In the course of their study, Roethlisberger, Dickson, and their colleagues were allowed to implement a number of changes in various aspects of the work environment. One of these, the focus of Homans' (1950, 1965) discussion, involved setting up a small independent work team in a room that was separate from the main factory. This team was responsible for wiring and assembling telephone switchboard panels.

The work team consisted of a group chief (the person in charge of supervising the team), two inspectors, nine workers who wired the panels, and three solderers. Within the framework of the company rules, the group chief was in charge of the operation of the work team, which was broken down into three basic units. Each unit was comprised of three wiremen and one solderer; each of the two inspectors was solely responsible for one of these units, and they shared responsibility for inspecting the work of the remaining unit. Moreover, the pay schedule of the company was a modified piecework plan in which workers were paid a fixed wage plus a bonus based on the number of units that their department produced above a specified minimum.

Over the six-and-one-half months during which the wiring team was studied, the workers assigned to it evolved into a small group, which then developed a set of norms and roles that guided much of the activity that took place among its members. The study of this group yielded a considerable amount of information about groups and group processes, only a small amount of which is presented here.

One of the major findings of this work was the revelation that the norms and roles that emerged from the group experience of the workers could differ markedly from the regulations specified by the company. For example, the hierarchy of the Western Electric Company viewed everyone who wired banks of switchboard panels as equivalent, a fact reflected in the company's pay schedule—all wiremen were paid at the same rate. However, as a result of workers' experiences with one another, a different norm evolved, one that was based on the type of panel on which the men worked. There were two kinds of panels, connector panels and selector panels. Although the method of wiring was the same for both pieces of equipment, and other differences were slight, the workers developed a belief that connector wiring was more difficult. Thus, the workers (but not the company) perceived connector wiremen as contributing more to the group effort than selector wiremen.

A second relevant finding concerned the norm that emerged regarding the appropriate amount of work that the members of the group should perform. The company rules were devised to induce workers to produce as much as possible. However, there was a general belief among the workers that the company would raise the minimum standard if they began to produce "too much." Thus, to meet the perceived threat imposed on them by the formal organization, the members of the wiring room group had their own informal standard which everyone was expected to meet but not exceed. Both those who exceeded the standard ("rate-busters" or "speed kings") and those who failed to meet it ("chiselers") were subjected to ridicule and harassment by their more virtuous colleagues. The norm concerning a fair day's work is just one example of the many mechanisms developed in the group which enabled it to survive within the formal organization that was so major a component of its Social Context.

Finally, it is of interest to note that over the course of the group's existence, one of the men—a connector wireman named Taylor—became increasingly likely to structure the activities of the group. The others often asked his advice, and he sometimes offered suggestions even without their prompting. Taylor was often at the center of the group's activities as they shifted from those involving work to those that were more socially oriented. He was the person most likely to initiate or to change an ongoing action (such as switching work activities, starting a discussion, and so on).

A major question for Homans was this: Why did Taylor emerge with so much interpersonal influence in the small group? There appear to be a number of reasons for the emergence of Taylor's prominence. The quantity of his work output was always consistent with the "fair day's work" norm of the group, and his work was noted for its high quality as well. Moreover, and of equal importance, Taylor was perceived as skillful in his dealings with the formal organization of the Western Electric plant. In one instance, for example, when the work chief attempted to force the men to use inferior wire in their work, it was Taylor who succeeded in securing a large supply of better material from the outside plant.

In addition to his work skills, and his ability to beat the system, Taylor was entertaining. He always took part in the informal activities of the group and kept up a steady stream of conversations and jokes. As a result of his work and social activities, Taylor was the best-liked man in the group; he was the member whom the others looked to for guidance and direction—and a good time. It is important to note that Taylor's influence had nothing to do with his position in the formal organization; he was accorded no more responsibility or status than any of the other wiremen. In terms of the rules and regulations that governed the operation of the Western Electric plant, the group chief was the nominal head of the wiring room personnel. Yet, observation of the day-to-day activities of the workers revealed that Taylor had more influence on the group's functioning than did the group chief.

The distinction between Taylor and the group chief highlights an important difference between a formal supervisor and a group member who becomes associated with directing and structuring activities. In the case of the formal supervisor, the bases for Control are the organization and its rules; in the case of the emergent leader, the bases for Control are derived from the other group members' acceptance of the legitimacy of his or her impingement activities. In other words, the formal supervisor is vested with authority from the organization, whereas the informal leader is accorded influence by the group members.

These two roles—formal supervisor and informal leader—are not necessarily antithetical or mutually exclusive. For example, an informal leader can become a formal supervisor through a number of means; election (if that is how the organization's rules specify that supervisors are selected) or promotion; on the other hand, a formal supervisor also can be vested with additional informal influence as a consequence of group members' experiences with that supervisor. Later in this chapter, we will review some of the major variables that determine which member of a group—if any—will emerge as its leader.

Whether the capacity to direct the group is derived from external sources (the formal organization) or from factors internal to the group (members' impressions), it is clear that leadership (as well as other forms of expressive and instrumental activities) reflects conditions imposed on the group by the organization within which it functions. In the context of the switchboard wiring room, much of the activity within the small group that evolved was a consequence of the work demands placed on its members by the Western Electric Company. Similarly, many of the activities in which you and your colleagues, Jon and Sally, engaged during the fictitious English assignment example were a consequence of the formal organization of the class in which you were enrolled. In both cases, the small group had evolved within the boundaries of the formal organization, and the behaviors that were expressed were in direct response to the demands of the organization. Thus, contextual features that the formal organization imposes weigh heavily in the group members' Valuations regarding appropriate group activities and the appropriate members to perform them.

Other Contextual Factors

We have focused rather broadly on the formal organization as a major contextual influence on small group behavior and development. A considerable amount of other work has examined contextual factors within a more narrow perspective. For example, a number of studies have explored specific variables in the physical and interpersonal environments which were thought to affect behavior in small groups. We will sample some of these studies to provide a flavor of this work and to illustrate how such specific contextual variables can affect small group functioning.

Variables in the Physical Environment. Perhaps the category of physical environmental variables that has received the most attention in the social psychological study of small groups involves the factors that control the spatial relationship of group members. For example, a number of studies have demonstrated a relationship between the seating position of group members and their activities (Giesen & McClaren, 1976; Howells & Becker, 1962; Mehrabian & Diamond, 1971; Messé, Aronoff, & Wilson, 1972; Patterson,

Kelly, Krondracki, & Wulf, 1979; Patterson, Roth, & Schenk, 1979; Patterson & Schaeffer, 1977; Russell, Firestone, & Baron, 1980; Steinzor, 1950; Strodtbeck & Hook, 1961; Ward, 1968). The research of Patterson et al. (1979) is just one demonstration of the impact of group members' spatial location (as constrained by factors in the physical environment) on social patterns of interaction.

In this research, the experimenters required members of discussion groups to sit around either a circular or an L-shaped table. Thus, the physical environmental constraint was the table's shape. Patterson et al. (1979) found that this environmental manipulation affected the behaviors that were expressed in the two sets of groups, although the tasks that they performed were identical. Subjects who sat around the circular table tended to share the conversation time more equally and to show fewer signs of anxiety during the discussion than did their counterparts who interacted around the *L*-shaped table.

In a study that complements the research of Patterson et al. (1979), Howells and Becker (1962) conclusively demonstrated that the spatial location of individual group members determined the flow of communication which, in turn, influenced emergent leadership roles in the group. They assigned five people to seats along two sides of a rectangular table (two on one side and three on the other). As Howells and Becker (1962) expected, this arrangement produced more cross-table than side-by-side interaction, and the members on the two-person side emerged as leaders of the group discussion more frequently than their counterparts on the three-person side.

FRANK SITEMAN/THE PICTURE CUBE

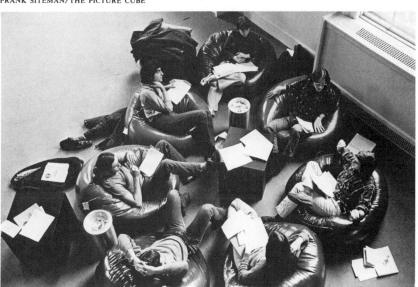

Research has shown that environmental factors such as seating position can have a major effect on the flow of communication and emergent leadership in groups.

The relationship between location in space and emergent leadership implies that the more active a member is, the more he or she is expected to structure the ongoing activities of the group—that is, to assume the leadership role. Obviously, the subjects assigned to the two-person side of the table in the Howells and Becker (1962) study were engaged in a higher proportion of the exchanges, since they talked to three people, whereas their counterparts across the table only talked to two. This more active role, in turn, appeared to affect the members' perceptions of who should lead the group's activities.

Studies of a second physical environment variable, which we term *communication opportunity,* have yielded findings that are consistent with the hypothesis that active members tend to evolve as group leaders. In studies of this type, the flow of communication between group members is restricted by factors in the physical environment. Those who have the opportunity to interact with the greatest number of their fellow group members—due to environmental constraints such as restricted channels of communication—typically emerge as the leaders of these collectives (Insko, Thibaut, Moehle, Wilson, Diamond, Gilmore, Solomon, & Lipsitz, 1980; Leavitt, 1951; Shaw, 1964).

The themes of Resolution, Control, and Valuation are especially relevant when considering the ways in which emergent leadership is influenced by differences in members' activity levels—variables that are affected by factors in the physical environment. Resolution is an important consideration because emergent leadership implies that the group has not yet evolved and incorporated a set of norms and roles to guide members' behaviors. Thus, a good deal of ambiguity exists regarding the appropriate behavior in collectives that are beginning to evolve into small groups. In studies of the effects of spatial arrangements on the activities of group members, for example, subjects typically do not know one another before the research begins. As such, they have no established rules of conduct regarding appropriate patterns of interaction. For this reason, when deciding with whom to engage in social exchange, members are likely to weigh heavily such factors as the ease of eye contact or the amount of physical movement required to interact, variables that are determined by the physical environment.

Control mechanisms, especially impingement, appear to underlie the relationship between members' activity levels and emergent leadership. As noted in Chapter 9, people can control the behaviors of others by acting in ways that limit the others' alternatives available in their behavior matrix. For example, suppose that in one of your English project work sessions, Jon says to you, "Do you know where we put the blank index cards?" This initiation on his part severely limits your range of possible activities. Thus, Jon's simple query has impinged on your own behavior, since you now must respond appropriately to his initiation (you cannot continue to daydream about your plans for the forthcoming weekend).

The more opportunity that a member has to engage in exchanges with other group participants, the more he or she can control the behaviors that are expressed in the group. Over time, this difference in perceived Control as a consequence of interaction opportunity would lead to members' acceptance of the active participant as leader. Factors in the physical environment that affect interaction opportunity thus influence the evolution of emergent leadership in collectives that are in the initial stages of group development.

Finally, it should be clear that Valuation plays a central role both in decisions regarding with whom to interact and in more long-term issues of emergent leadership. In both of these instances, group members weigh the available cues in order to make decisions. For example, suppose that you were a participant in the Howells and Becker (1962) study, assigned to an end chair on the three-person side of the table. Since you do not know any of the others in the collective, you have no basis for believing that exchanges with one member are likely to be any more rewarding than exchanges with another. Moreover, from your seat, it is much easier for you to converse with either of the two people opposite you than it is to attempt to establish contact with those sitting on the same side of the table. To talk to the person next to you requires that you turn your chair, reorient your seating position, crane your neck, and so on—and to address your colleague at the far end of the table would require even greater gyrations. In consequence, you are likely to weigh such factors as ease of communication in choosing the person or persons with whom to interact, and thus, you are likely to decide to engage in exchanges with the people across the table.

Similarly, in the absence of other cues, it is likely that you would weigh heavily the extent to which another person's behaviors influence your own actions when making initial judgments about the most likely candidate to direct the group. In other words, when the collective is in the initial stages of interaction, factors such as ease of communication, eye contact, and the others' influence attempts assume great weight, since there is little additional information available, given the lack of Resolution of such Social Contexts. Thus, the physical environment sets the stage for the evolution of the small group and the emergence of its leader.

Variables in the Interpersonal Environment. In addition to studying the impact of the physical environment on small group processes and outcomes, social scientists have explored the influence of factors in the interpersonal environment. Among the many variables investigated in this area, perhaps the most straightforward is group size—the number of participants who take part in some collective action. We are concerned with small groups in this discussion; however, since small groups can range in size from at least 2 to about 20 members, group size varies sufficiently to have a major impact on members' behaviors.

Numerous studies have been conducted to explore the impact of group size on members' activities (Bales, Strodtbeck, Mills, & Roseborough, 1951; Bass & Norton, 1951; Bray, Kerr, & Atkin, 1978; Davis, Kerr, Atkin, Hold, & Meek, 1975; Dawe, 1934; Egerbladh, 1976; Frank & Anderson, 1971; Gibb, 1951; Hare, 1952; Hemphill, 1950; Ingham, Levinger, Graves, & Peckham, 1974; Laughlin, Kerr, Davis, Halff, & Marciniak, 1975; O'Dell, 1968; Segal, 1977; Thomas & Fink, 1963). In general, these studies have found that as the size of the group increases, the distribution of activity across members becomes increasingly unequal and the directing function becomes more concentrated in fewer members.

The findings of the research on group size appear to reflect members' increasing concerns with Resolution as their number grows. In larger collectives, participants are much less certain about their place in the group; they are unsure about what they can contribute and what they can gain. Hare (1952), for example, found that his participants felt more constrained about entering into the group discussion as its size increased. Accordingly, members of large groups simply take a less active role in the group's functioning. This lack of activity has the effect of placing more of the burden of the leadership of the group on one, or a few, centrally placed individuals.

The increase in membership size also appears to have a negative effect on members' Valuations of their group experience—that is, as the number of members increases, cohesiveness decreases. A number of studies have shown that with increasing group size, the rewards that people perceive themselves as reaping from their experience diminish (O'Dell, 1968; Segal, 1977). For example, O'Dell (1968) examined the social activity of people placed in discussion groups of two to five members. Analyses of the discussion activity revealed that as the size of these groups increased, participants displayed greater disagreement and greater antagonism toward one another.

Taken together, the low Resolution and the apparently diminished opportunity for immediate rewards which characterize larger small groups magnify the importance of the structuring and directing function to be performed if the group is to survive. In such contexts, it is likely that members will perceive impingement as even more legitimate, since it becomes readily apparent that without such Control activities, the group will soon degenerate into chaos. Moreover, in such circumstances, it is reasonable that impingement activities would be concentrated in relatively fewer individuals, since it is more difficult to coordinate leadership activities effectively across the members of larger groups. In addition, the tendency for all social activities to be distributed unequally in the larger group encourages the concentration of leadership activities.

Earlier in this chapter, we alluded to another major feature of the interpersonal environment that influences the group—the effect of the perceived beliefs of the majority on the opinions of the individual. This group influence effect was discussed at length in Chapter 4 with regard to the impact of the interpersonal environment on opinion change. As might be expected, the beliefs of peers have a profound effect on a group member's own opinions—that is, concerns with self/other Consistency operate to influence individual's opinions toward the consensus position of others in the group. Research has shown that the impact of the interpersonal environment within the small group context is mediated by the extent that participants have positive regard for one another (Back, 1951; Lott & Lott, 1961). For example, Kurt Back (1951) assembled groups that varied with regard to their cohesiveness and had the members discuss issues about which they were known to disagree. He found that members of the highly cohesive groups influenced one another's opinions more than did their counterparts who basically interacted as a collective.

Other research has shown that group members can have a more subtle, but equally pervasive, impact on one another's beliefs. We often hold fundamental beliefs that are expressed within the framework of a specific issue. For example, it could be that we have incorporated the premise, which we believe to be widely accepted, that people should be charitable towards those less fortunate than themselves. This general belief would influence our responses to a host of more specific judgments regarding our own charitable behaviors and those of others. However, when confronted with a specific request from a worthy cause, we might donate an amount that we think is reasonable but which others might view as less than generous. Thus, it is likely that information exchanges in a group context would induce us to change our opinion, not about the general value of charity per se, but rather about the amount of money that constitutes an appropriate donation.

Beginning with the pioneering efforts of Stoner (1961), Kogan and Wallach (1964), and Wallach, Kogan, & Bem (1962, 1964), the study of the effects of group interaction on individual judgments has generated considerable empirical research (Bem, Wallach, & Kogan, 1965; Blascovich & Ginsburg, 1974; Blascovich, Ginsburg, & Beach, 1975; Blascovich, Ginsburg, & Howe, 1976; Dion, Baron, & Miller, 1970; Goethals & Zanna, 1979; Hong, 1978; Kaplan, 1977; Kerr, Davis, Meek, & Rissman, 1975; Lamm & Myers, 1978; Levinger & Schneider, 1969; Madsen, 1978; Moscovici & Zavalloni, 1969; Runyan, 1974; Spector, Cohen, & Penner, 1976; Vinokur & Burnstein, 1978; Wallach & Mabli, 1970). In general, these studies have found that group experiences that are relevant to an issue tend not to result in reversals of members' beliefs; rather, they tend to polarize members' judgments. In other words, while consistent with the pre-experience consensus position, group members' beliefs become more polarized (or extreme) as a consequence of their group interaction.

A number of explanations for this *group polarization effect* have been advanced (see reviews of this work by Dion, Baron, & Miller, 1970; Lamm & Myers, 1978). While there is evidence that supports, at least to some extent, the various interpretations of this phenomenon, the explanation proposed by Roger Brown (1965) appears to be the most comprehensive. In his explanation, Brown hypothesized that people make judgments about specific issues that they perceive to be consistent with their more general beliefs (which they hold in common with other members of their reference groups). However, when people have the opportunity to discuss their decisions with others, they often come to realize that their initial judgment was less consistent with their general belief than they originally had thought. In circumstances of this type, concerns with self-Consistency and self/other Consistency induce them to shift their judgments in the more extreme direction, which is perceived to more accurately reflect the underlying belief. The three studies which we will now discuss are a sample of the many investigations that are consistent with Brown's (1965) explanation of group polarization.

In a study that employed a highly engaging task (at least to the authors of this text), Jim Blascovich and Gerald Ginsburg (1974) explored group polarization within the framework of a gambling experience. In this research, the investigators set up a small casino in their laboratory and provided their subjects with $5 in chips to use in a blackjack game.

First, subjects played individually against the dealer for 20 hands of cards, betting between 5 cents and $1 on each hand. For the next 20 hands, they were joined at the table by two other participants (actually accomplices of the experimenter), and the three of them played against the house. The accomplices' bets were predetermined in such a way that in one condition, they were consistent with the average bet of individual subjects in previous research (30 cents). In another condition of the study, both confederates consistently bet more than this amount (50 cents), whereas in a third condition, they consistently bet less (10 cents).

Subjects' initial sets of bets, placed while playing alone with the dealer, provided information about their judgments regarding the optimal risk to take in this circumstance. This baseline information permitted Blascovich and Ginsburg to determine the impact of the group experience, which provided the subjects with direct information about the beliefs of their peers regarding the appropriate level of risk to take. Blascovich and Ginsburg (1974) found that the bets of the accomplices had a strong influence on the actions of the subjects. Those subjects paired with the high bettors tended to increase their own bets accordingly, placing bets that on the average exceeded the 50-cent wagers of their peers. Those paired with the less risky bettors became more conservative in their own wagers. Thus, the apparent standard of the subjects' reference group was effective in modifying their judgments about appropriate betting behavior.

Moreover, and perhaps of more relevance to the present discussion, the impact of the high-betting accomplices was substantially greater than that of their conservative counterparts. As Blascovich and Ginsburg (1974) note, this finding strongly suggests that there exists a widely held norm in our culture which encourages moderate risk, at least under circumstances such as gambling. Other research, including a study conducted by George Levinger and David Schneider, has provided direct evidence that supports this conclusion.

In their study, Levinger and Schneider (1969) asked a large number of undergraduate males to read 12 brief descriptions of people faced with a choice between two alternatives. These descriptions, developed by Kogan and Wallach (1964), always portrayed one choice as safe, but not very desirable, and the other as more attractive, but riskier in terms of its probability of success. For example, one vignette described a person who had to decide between going to medical school (a safe choice of careers) or pursuing a more highly valued career as a concert pianist (a risky choice).

For each vignette, subjects first indicated the minimum odds of success that they would accept before recommending the more desirable, but risky, option. Then, subjects reread the stories, and for each, estimated the minimum

Blascovich and Ginsburg's study demonstrates that group polarization can occur even in such unlikely contexts as the blackjack table.

odds that a majority of their fellow students would choose if faced with the decision. Finally, they once again read the descriptions and then indicated the choice they admired most, regardless of their own choice, and their estimate of the judgment of their peers. The results of this study are consistent with the speculations of Brown (1965) and Blascovich and Ginsburg (1974). Subjects' own choices were somewhat more risky than those which they perceived their peers as likely to make; however, the choice that they admired most was more risky than their own choice. Thus, subjects perceived risk taking as an admirable quality, and in the absence of information to the contrary—which a group experience could have provided them—they underestimated the level of risk that their peers believed to be appropriate.

The third study to be discussed here demonstrates that widely accepted norms (in this case, the value of risk taking) and the information about the beliefs of one's peers (which group discussion can provide) combine to affect individual decisions. In this research, Lawrence Hong (1978) presented the 12 vignettes used by Kogan and Wallach (1964) to native-born American or Chinese students studying in the United States. The subjects first responded to the vignettes individually, and then were formed into groups of five students who shared the same cultural background. These groups were asked to discuss each of the 12 stories and arrive at a consensus decision regarding the most acceptable degree of risk to take in each vignette.

The results indicated that the preferred risk levels of the subjects varied as a consequence of their cultural heritage. As Hong (1978) predicted, the American sample approved of riskier behaviors than did the Chinese. This difference was amplified as a result of the group discussions—that is, after the group discussions, the Chinese subjects became even more conservative in the level of risk that they found acceptable, whereas the Americans became even more risky in their judgments. Thus, it is apparent from the three studies reviewed here, as well as other research described earlier (Runyan, 1974), that persons' concerns with self/other Consistency can enhance the impact of the interpersonal environment on their beliefs and behaviors.

In addition to the number and behavior of other group members, other factors in the interpersonal environment can also influence participants' behaviors. For example, research has shown that the activities of a group member can be influenced by the physical and Personal Structure characteristics of other group members. The sex, race, or high level motives of the people who constitute the interpersonal environment, for instance, have been found to affect the behavior of people in groups (Eskilson & Wiley, 1976; Haythorn, Couch, Haefner, Langham, & Carter, 1956a; Megargee, 1969; Messé et al., 1972; Word, Zanna, & Cooper, 1974). Of course, features of the Personal Structure of an actor in a small group are related to the behaviors that he or she expresses. Research that has demonstrated a relationship between Personal Structure factors and behavior in small groups is the focus of the following section.

Personal Structure Influences

While less attention has been devoted to the impact of people's Personal Structure characteristics on group process and outcomes, ample evidence suggests that differences in members' beliefs, faculties, and motives are related to their behaviors within groups. For example, a number of studies have shown that sex roles—the incorporated beliefs about the appropriate behaviors for men and women—influence group members' actions (Bray et al., 1978; Eskilson & Wiley, 1976; Messé et al., 1972; Nemeth, Endicott, & Wachtler, 1976; Wright, 1976).

In one of these studies, Arlene Eskilson and Mary Wiley assembled a large number of three-person groups to work on a puzzle-solving task. The sex of the group members was varied, so that some groups were composed entirely of females, others contained two females and one male, and so forth. In every group, a supervisor was randomly appointed, and only this person was given information relevant to the puzzle solution. However, in half the groups, members were led to believe that their supervisor had been chosen because she (or he) had shown the greatest task-related ability as measured by a pretest. The groups' interactions were videotaped so that trained coders could categorize the social activity that took place in the groups.

Results of the Eskilson and Wiley (1976) study revealed a number of interesting differences regarding sex roles. For example, male supervisors displayed substantially greater amounts of directing and structuring (upward-forward) activities than did their female counterparts who were supervising other groups. In contrast, female supervisors expressed more positive (upward-positive) behaviors than did males. Moreover, female supervisors expressed more upward-forward behavior when they supposedly had been appointed on the basis of task-related ability than when they thought they had been randomly appointed. On the other hand, the means by which male supervisors apparently were selected did not influence their structuring and directing behaviors. Taken together, these results are consistent with the traditional sex-role stereotypes which state that males are more task-oriented and females more concerned about the feelings of others. Thus, before they are willing to express instrumental activities to the extent that their male counterparts do, females appear to need explicit evidence that they possess greater task-relevant abilities than their colleagues.

In addition to sex roles, other types of beliefs have been shown to influence the behaviors of members of small groups. For example, Haythorn et al. (1956b) measured the opinions of their respondents regarding conformity to authority and their perceptions of the necessity for order and control. The researchers expected that this constellation of beliefs—which has been termed *authoritarianism* by Adorno et al. (1950)—would be related to behavior in small groups. To test this hypothesis, Haythorn et al. (1956b) formed two types of small groups: one type was composed entirely of people who held high level opinions in favor of conformity to authority (high authoritarians); the other type of group was composed of people who possessed high level opinions in favor of tolerance for individual differences, democratic processes, and so on (high egalitarians). All groups were given the same task, and judges systematically observed the members' interactions in completing it.

As hypothesized, Haythorn et al. (1956b) found that the leaders of the authoritarian groups were much more autocratic, demanding, and insensitive than were their counterparts in the egalitarian groups. In other words, both the authoritarian and the egalitarian leaders acted in ways that were consistent with their own (and fellow group members') beliefs about authority and obedience, and individuality and tolerance. Thus, Personal Structure characteristics of the group members who were given the responsibility for the directing and structuring functions affected the impingement tactics that they employed to induce the other group members to complete the task.

Faculties, another category of Personal Structure characteristics, have also been shown to influence group processes. For example, group members' intelligence, cognitive complexity, leadership aptitude, and task abilities have been found to influence behaviors and outcomes in small group contexts

(Bass, McGehee, Hawkins, Young, & Gebel, 1953; Bass & Wurster, 1953a, 1953b; Beckhouse, Tanur, Weiler, & Weinstein, 1975; Chemers, Rice, Sudstrum, & Butler, 1975; Fiedler, 1978; Hollander, 1954; Marak, 1964; Schroder, Driver, & Streufert, 1967; Tuckman, 1964).

In one of these studies, Tuckman (1964) measured the degree of cognitive complexity in a large number of respondents. Using this information, he assembled four types of groups, according to the complexity level of their members. In one type of group, all members were highly complex; in another, all were moderately complex, and so on. As in the study of Haythorn et al. (1956b), Tuckman had trained observers to judge the interactions of the group members as they worked together on a task. His results indicated that the faculty of cognitive complexity affected the distribution of directing activity among the group members. The more cognitively complex the group members, the more equally they expressed these leadership behaviors.

As with beliefs and faculties, motives also appear to influence the behavior of people in groups (Anderson, 1974; Aronoff & Messé, 1971; Aronoff, Messé, & Wilson, in press; Borg, 1960; Borgatta, 1965; Cattell & Stice, 1960; Haythorn, 1965; Messé, et al., 1972; Russell et al., 1980; Schutz, 1965; Smelzer, 1961; Smith & Cook, 1973; Wilson, Aronoff, & Messé, 1975). For example, in a study that employed a design similar to those of Haythorn et al. (1956b) and Tuckman (1964), Aronoff and Messé (1971) measured the safety and esteem motives of a sample of male respondents. On the basis of this information, they then constituted five-man groups; in some groups, all members possessed high level safety motives, and in others, all possessed high level esteem motives. As in the earlier studies, observers systematically coded the behaviors of the group members as they worked on a series of tasks.

The results of Aronoff and Messé's (1971) research indicated that motivation had a substantial influence on the groups' activities, in a manner similar to the effect of cognitive complexity which Tuckman (1964) found. Groups composed of subjects with high level esteem motivation were more equal with regard to expressing leadership (upward-forward) activities, whereas in groups with high level safety motivation, these behaviors were concentrated in fewer members.

CONCLUDING REMARKS ON BEHAVIOR IN SMALL GROUPS

In the research discussed, we have considered more or less in isolation the variables that affect group processes and outcomes. However, most behaviors in small groups are a consequence of factors that operate in combination, rather than as isolated forces. For example, Fred Fiedler (1964, 1978) has noted that the extent to which different approaches to leadership (a Personal Structure variable) promote productive group outcomes is dependent on contextual factors, such as the nature of the formal organization in which the group functions or the leader's relationship with group members. Obviously, the specific ways in which Personal Structure and contextual factors can interact to affect group behaviors are too numerous to present in any detail here. However, to provide some illustration of the complexity with which these variables can operate together, we will present two studies as representative examples. The first of these (Messé et al. 1972) provides an example of how factors in the physical environment, interpersonal environment and the Personal Structure can combine to influence behavior in small groups. In the second study to be discussed (Anderson, 1974), group members' motivation and aspects of the formal organization combined to moderate the impact of success or failure on group cohesiveness.

As in their earlier work, Messé et al. (1972) assembled three-person groups whose members were similar with respect to their level of safety and esteem motivation. Furthermore, in every case, these groups consisted of two females and one male who worked together around a small rectangular table. The seating position of the male member was varied systematically so that in some conditions he sat across from one of the female group members, and in others he sat at the end of the table, not facing either of his coworkers. Again, trained observers systematically coded the activities that the group members expressed as they worked on the task.

Results of this study indicated that a number of contextual and Personal Structure variables combined to affect the group members' behaviors. For example, Messé et al. (1972) found that motivation interacted with the interpersonal environment to affect the emergent leadership of the groups; in groups composed of members with high levels of safety motivation, the male tended to display the most impingement activity, whereas in groups with high levels of esteem motivation, the sex of the members made no difference in this matter. This pattern is reasonable, since safety-oriented individuals, who tend to be concerned with order and regularity, are more likely to behave consistently with traditional sex-role stereotypes (beliefs).

Moreover, analyses revealed that the seating position of the male (a physical environment variable) had an impact on the combined influence of members' sex and motivation. The males in the safety-oriented groups displayed a great amount of impingement activity only when they were seated directly across from another group member; they tended to withdraw from the encounter (that is, they became passive or downward) when they were seated to the side. On the other hand, esteem-oriented males tended to be the most assertive when assigned to this less conspicuous seating position.

Research by Anderson (1974) also demonstrates the complex nature of small group functioning. In his study, female subjects were recruited for monetary rewards to work together in three-person groups on a "Twenty Questions" word game. Prior to their participation, Anderson obtained information concerning how rewarding a pastime playing word games was for each of these subjects. He assembled the groups so that in half of them, the members had indicated high levels of motivation for such tasks, whereas in the remainder, they reported that they received little intrinsic satisfaction from such activities.

Furthermore, Anderson imposed two types of formal organizations on the groups. In some, one member was appointed to be the supervisor and was given the major responsibility for solving the word puzzles, while the other two members could act only as her advisors. Thus, the participation opportunity of the two nonsupervisors was severely limited. In the other type of organization, however, members were explicitly told that they had to contribute equally to the puzzle solutions. As such, the opportunity to engage in task activities was distributed more equally among these group members. Finally, Anderson (1974) manipulated the difficulty of the word puzzles so that half the groups succeeded at their task, while the remainder failed.

Anderson's (1974) study was designed to investigate the combined impact of motivation, participation opportunity, and success on group cohesiveness. To measure the extent to which members were attracted to their respective groups, he led subjects to believe that other sessions would take place, and that if they wished, they could change groups when they participated in them. Thus, cohesiveness was measured by the extent to which subjects wished to remain in their group. Anderson's (1974) analyses revealed that the major determinant of cohesiveness was the success that group members had achieved in solving the puzzles. However, he also found that motivation and differences in participation opportunity created by the formal organization moderated this result. For example, the impact of success on cohesiveness was much less powerful when members were restricted in participating, and this moderating influence was especially true for groups whose members were intrinsically motivated to engage in such activities.

Anderson's (1974) study is relevant to another important feature of small group processes—namely, that most, if not all, group activity can be conceptualized within the framework of social exchange. As noted earlier, people apparently engage in collective activities because they perceive them as likely to generate positive outcomes. Thus, it was not surprising that success or failure on the task in Anderson's experiment played such an important role in determining group cohesiveness. Similarly, people who find word games to be highly rewarding would probably not be attracted to groups in which their opportunity to satisfy this motive was severely restricted.

Exchange theory can explain the results of most of the other studies cited in this chapter. For example, the results of the Aronoff and Messé (1971) study can be readily interpreted as demonstrating that group members will seek to interact in ways that are most compatible with their motives. Safety-oriented people, who are concerned about feeling secure in a predictable environment, would find a situation in which someone directed them as highly rewarding; esteem-oriented people, however, who are concerned with demonstrating their competence to themselves and others, would find the same situation aversive.

Similar explanations can be advanced to explain the results of Haythorn et al. (1956b) and Tuckman (1974). As a final example, the ease with which people can interact (which can be a consequence of seating position, among other variables) has also been shown to affect behavior in groups in ways that are consistent with the principles of social exchange presented in Chapter 9.

In this chapter, we have focused on collectives of people and the ways in which their mutual activities can lead to the evolution of a more organized social entity—the small group. In examining the variables that affected these activities and their outcomes, we have concentrated on the relationship of the members to their group as a whole, and have not explored in any detail the relationships that can develop between individual group members. For example, we examined cohesiveness (attraction of the members to their group) rather than interpersonal attraction (an individual's perception that another person is a source of rewards). Of course, interpersonal attraction can be a major consequence of small group experiences, or it can be an outcome of more individualized encounters. In any case, as noted earlier, interpersonal attraction is an important human quality, and as such, merits a detailed exploration. We will provide such a review in the following chapter.

Interpersonal Attraction: Liking and Loving

12

In Chapter 11 we explored behaviors and outcomes of people who interact in the pursuit of some common, long-term goal. We will now turn out attention to one of the major consequences of these and other continuing relationships. In this chapter, we will review the major issues involved in *positive interpersonal encounters*. Central to our concerns are the factors that influence attraction—what makes a person like another—and the consequences of this type of evaluative belief for social behavior and Sentimental attachment.

Before examining the principal variables involved in attraction, liking, and loving, we need to consider three preliminary issues: (1) the relationship between attraction and impressions; (2) the relationship between attraction and Sentiment; and (3) the distinctions between likeability, liking, and loving.

Attraction and Impressions

First, it is very important to understand that attraction differs from impressions. Both are evaluative beliefs, but they differ in their focus. As noted in Chapter 7, impressions primarily involve judgments about the goodness or badness of a target person. Attraction, on the other hand, involves the issue of *likeability*—the belief that, under the appropriate circumstances, a positive Sentiment relationship could develop between a person and a target. Obviously, these two types of evaluative beliefs are interrelated. It would be difficult, for example, to like someone about whom we have a negative impression; moreover, we tend to judge as good those to whom we are attracted. However, it is also possible to evaluate some people positively—that is, to have a good impression of them—and still not like them.

For example, suppose that your partner in the laboratory section of your anatomy class is someone whom you had not met previously. Over the course of your experiences with her, you perceive that she has many positive qualities. She is intelligent, meticulous, hard-working, helpful, and cooperative. Thus, it is not surprising that you come to form a very positive impression of her. However, this is not to say that you are attracted to her. In spite of these positive features, and sometimes because of them, you judge that it would be very unlikely that you and she ever could become close. Although you recognize this person's good qualities and in many ways find her admirable, over the course of your experiences with her you realize that a Sentimental bond never could form between the two of you.

Though you find her sense of orderliness helpful in the anatomy lab, it nonetheless grates on your more casual approach to neatness. Moreover, while intelligent, she is also somewhat cold and unemotional, two qualities that clash with your more demonstrative and enthusiastic nature. In addition, she lacks a sense of humor, a characteristic that is tolerable to you within the narrow Social Context of the anatomy laboratory, but not in the more convivial settings in which you and your friends typically interact. Finally, you find that your interests are almost totally opposite. While you enjoy playing cards, engaging in sports, listening to jazz, and reading fiction, your lab partner feels that cards and sports are a waste of time; she prefers string quartets and philosophical essays. Aside from a shared interest in learning anatomy, you and she have little else in common. As such, your positive impression of her does not substantially contribute to your attraction to her.

A study by Mady Segal illustrates the importance of the distinction between attraction and impressions. In her study, Segal (1979) examined impressions and mutual attraction among members of three different formal organizations—a state police department and two college football teams. Attraction and impressions were measured by giving each respondent a list of all members of his organization and having him rate each one on appropriate scales. Attraction was measured by two items that were anchored with the terms *bad enemy/close friend,* and *intense disliking/intense liking.* General impressions were measured via an item employing the terms *intense disrespect/ intense respect.*

The results of this survey provide strong support for the observations presented earlier. First, although each of the two attraction items were found to be related to some extent to the measure of general impression, there was an even stronger relationship between the two attraction items themselves. This finding supports the contention that there is a distinction between attraction and general impression, although the two concepts are clearly related. Second, Segal (1979) found that the two types of evaluative beliefs are related to different kinds of interpersonal behaviors. General impressions were more closely related to leadership nominations within the groups, whereas attraction was more closely related to mutual participation in leisure time activities. As in the example of the lab partner, people can apparently have positive impressions of others without necessarily being attracted to them. Thus, while you might work enthusiastically with someone on a specific task, you might not wish to form a Sentiment relationship with this person. Other empirical and theoretical work (Grush & Yehl, 1979; Moreno, 1934; Rubin, 1973; Triandis, 1977) has arrived at similar conclusions.

To summarize, a positive impression is a necessary antecedent of attraction, but believing that someone is good (an impression) does not always lead to a further belief that you and that person could become close friends. In the absence of this belief about the other's likeability, it is improbable that a positive Sentiment relationship would evolve between you and the other person.

Attraction and Sentiment

Our second preliminary point involves the link between attraction and Sentiment. As discussed in detail in Chapter 2, Sentiment is a major theme in interpersonal relationships. It is clear that Sentiment and attraction are closely allied—in fact, Sentiment is the theme that is most relevant to liking and loving. Recall that Sentiment was defined as the attachment of positive (or negative) emotion to another person. Positive emotions are those that connote pleasantness or pleasure and as such, we are motivated to experience them. Emotions have a cognitive (thought) as well as a physiological (feeling) component. Attraction is the cognitive component of Sentiment. That is, when another person evokes in us a positive emotional reaction, we judge that we are attracted to that individual. Conversely, we are inclined to associate those we like with the positive emotional reactions which we experience in their presence.

In Chapter 2, we listed a number of major antecedents and consequences of Sentiment. We will briefly review them here since, given the link between Sentiment and attraction, they can serve as a framework for understanding liking and loving. The antecedents of Sentiment can be acute (exerting their influence over a very brief period of time) or extended (exerting their influence over a prolonged period of time). The principal antecedents of Sentiment are cue similarity, motive prepotency, mislabeled arousal, reward expectation, opportunity, and association. The major consequences of Sentiment are motivation, perceived unit relationships, and the development of a concern for the welfare of the other. These concepts will be discussed briefly, especially regarding their relevance for attraction.

Acute Antecedents of Sentiment

Cue similarity is the mechanism by which certain people evoke emotions in us because they share some features in common with others to whom we have (or have had) some Sentimental attachment. Such similarity of cues tends to affect our judgments about the likeability of these individuals; we often find ourselves attracted to people who possess attributes that are like those of others with whom we have experienced positive Sentiment relationships.

Motive prepotency is the condition that occurs when a high level motive has not been satisfied for some period of time. A person who provides even a modicum of satisfaction of a long-deprived motive will evoke very positive Sentimental reactions. These reactions, of course, will influence our beliefs about the likeability of this person.

Mislabeled arousal is a cognitive misinterpretation of the cause of an emotional reaction. Mislabeling occurs when an internal physiological state is attributed to someone or something that is not, in fact, responsible for it. People's misinterpretation of their internal states can result in attraction toward another, if the other is erroneously perceived as the cause of their positive arousal.

Reward expectation is the presumption that another can (or will) satisfy one or another high level motive. Such expectations are rewarding in and of themselves, as the anticipation of reward is pleasant. People find others attractive if they are judged to be potential sources of rewards.

Extended Antecedents of Sentiment

Opportunity, an extended antecedent of Sentiment, refers to the likelihood that a person will be able to interact with another and thus experience the positive and negative outcomes that such interactions involve. These outcomes, in turn, determine the levels of attraction and Sentiment that develop between the actors in a relationship. Obviously, if people are separated by great geographic distances, the opportunity for interaction—and thus for the development of a consistent set of beliefs that the other person is rewarding or likeable—is greatly diminished. Opportunity is a long-term, or extended, antecedent of Sentiment and attraction because its effect is usually not immediate; rather, it tends to influence our beliefs and emotional reactions over long periods of time.

Association, the second extended antecedent of Sentiment, refers to the processes by which positive (or negative) emotional reactions are linked with a target. Repeated associations of positive outcomes with another person result in, among other things, the formation of beliefs that this person is valuable (that is, attractive, worthwhile, and so on). Put simply, if a person is consistently associated with positive outcomes, we tend to like that person.

The Consequences of Sentiment

Motivation is one of the two major consequences of Sentiment. Since we are motivated to experience positive outcomes, it follows that we would seek to interact with people who are the stimulus for pleasurable emotional reactions. Thus, we are motivated to interact with those with whom we share a positive Sentiment bond. Occurring simultaneously with motivation is the awareness that a person is rewarding to us, by virtue of his or her mere presence; this awareness often takes the form of a belief about our feelings toward this person—namely, we like him or her, we are "in love," and so on.

Unit relationships are the second major consequence of Sentiment. As noted in Chapter 2, a unit relationship is a bond that is perceived to exist between people as a consequence of their long-term association. People who are the component parts of a unit relationship are perceived—by both themselves and others—as a single entity, rather than as distinct, independent individuals. When we think about a person who is involved in an extended Sentiment relationship of this type, it is difficult not to think of the other actor in the unit. One of the major bases for the perception of a unit relationship is a belief that those involved in it are attracted to one another. Thus, if we perceive that two people are very close friends (that is, strongly attracted to one another), we also tend to perceive them as forming a social entity.

Concern for the other's welfare is perhaps the most obvious consequence of Sentimental relationships. As noted in Chapter 2, such concerns can take two related, but distinct forms: *altruism,* or caring about another for no ulterior reasons; and *protectiveness,* or caring about another because he or she is a source of rewards. Concern for the other's welfare is relevant to the issue of attraction when such concern reflects a self-interested, rather than an altruistic, orientation. If the other is viewed as a source of rewards, it is in the perceiver's best interests to care about the well-being of that person. In this sense, attraction raises our investment in another's welfare.

Likeability, Liking, and Loving

Likeability and Liking. We have used the term *attraction* in two related but distinct ways. First, the term *likeability* was used as a synonym for attraction based on predicted future outcomes—the judgment that another has qualities or traits that make a potential Sentiment relationship desirable or probable. In this sense, we are attracted to those who have qualities which we believe to be both worthwhile and worthy of some emotional investment on our part. Thus, attraction is the outcome of a Valuation process similar to that involved in the formation of a general impression.

Attraction also can refer to our awareness that someone with whom we have a Sentiment relationship is a source of rewards for us. In this sense, attraction is the understanding (that is, belief) that we like or love someone. The stronger our emotional attachment, the stronger is our sense of attraction.

In summary, attraction can be a belief that another person is worth exploring as a potential friend or loved one; as such, such attraction is preliminary to Sentimental attachment. It also can refer to our understanding that we are attached to others because we have formed a Sentimental (liking or loving) relationship with them.

Liking and Loving. It is useful to distinguish between *liking* and *loving* although both are forms of Sentimental attachment. Although this issue is very complex—a puzzle that for years has occupied the attention of philosophers, poets, and screenwriters, as well as social psychologists—there appear to be two differences between liking and loving that are readily identifiable.

First, liking and loving tend to be quantitatively different. Loving relationships are usually perceived as more intense Sentimental attachments than are liking relationships. Of course, there are exceptions to this observation (such as Damon and Pythias, the three musketeers, Frick and Frack, Rockie and Bullwinkle), but in most cases, friendship is perceived as a less strong attachment than love.

Second, people tend to think about friendship and love in different terms—that is, they label these two Sentimental attachments differently. The material presented in Chapters 1 and 2 indicated that there is a major cognitive component to emotional reactions, and that this is especially true for rather complex and amorphous feelings such as love. Love involves a definition on the part of the person experiencing the emotional reaction that what he or she is feeling is something more than mere friendship. Often, a substantial part of this process is determined by sexual arousal. However, as we can also love those for whom we do not experience such arousal, and we sometimes are aroused by those whom we do not love, it is clear that there are many factors that determine whether we interpret our feelings as liking or loving.

Although liking and loving are distinguished by cognitive, subjective interpretations of relatively ambiguous feelings, it should not be assumed that the distinction between these two Sentimental relationships does not have important consequences for interpersonal behavior. Zick Rubin has conducted research on liking and loving as distinct psychological phenomena and has demonstrated some of the different consequences that these two major types of Sentiment can generate. In his work, Rubin (1970, 1973) has developed two 13-item scales—one measures the extent to which a person likes another, and the other measures the extent to which the person loves another. Table 12.1 provides some examples of the items that are contained in Rubin's (1970) Love Scale and Liking Scale. As illustrated, both sets of items tap positive, but clearly discriminable, Sentiments.

Rubin (1970) administered both of his scales to a large sample of dating

TABLE 12.1
Items from Rubin's (1979) Love Scale and Liking Scale

Love scale items:
1. I feel I can confide in ——— about virtually everything.
2. If I could never be with ———, I would feel miserable.
3. I feel responsible for ———'s well-being.

Liking scale items:
1. In my opinion, ——— is an exceptionally mature person.
2. I think that ——— is one of those people who quickly wins respect.
3. I have great confidence in ———'s good judgment.

couples at the University of Michigan. As might be expected, he found that scores on the two measures were related—that is, those who reported liking their dating partner also tended to report that they loved their partner. (Incidentally, this relationship was stronger for men than for women.) Moreover, and perhaps of most importance to our present concerns, Rubin found that there was greater similarity within couples regarding their feelings of love toward one another than there was regarding their liking for one another, a pattern that might be expected from people engaged in courtship. Moreover, in a laboratory study involving the same sample, Rubin found that the higher the Love Scale score of couples, the more they tended to gaze (perhaps soulfully) at one another.

In a followup study, Rubin (1973) also found that dating couples who had scored high on his Love Scale were more likely to be together six months later than were couples who did not score as high. Moreover, the reported increase in intensity in couples' Sentiment relationship was predicted by their previously measured Love Scale score; this was especially true for those respondents who had a romantic, rather than a practical, view of love and marriage.

Forms of love. Elaine and G. William Walster (1978) examined what philosophers, social scientists, and other interested parties have said about love, and as a result of their efforts, they have speculated that love can take on two major forms: *passionate* and *companionate*. The Walsters define *passionate love* as "a state of intense absorption in another . . . [A longing for and accomplishment of] complete fulfillment. A state of intense physiological arousal." In contrast, companionate love is defined as "the affection we feel for those with whom our lives are deeply intertwined" (Walster & Walster, 1978, p. 9). In other words, for Walster and Walster, the difference between

JEFF ALBERTSON/STOCK, BOSTON, INC.

MARTINE FRANCK/MAGNUM PHOTOS, INC.

Passionate love, as defined by the Walsters, often involves a state of intense physiological arousal; companionate love is a feeling of deep affection for those with whom our lives are intertwined.

passionate love and companionate love is the difference between being in love and being very close friends.

From our perspective, then, companionate love is equivalent to a high level liking relationship, whereas passionate love is a loving relationship which, by definition, must be intense and high level. Regardless of whose terminology is used, this distinction between liking and loving is important because the different forms of attraction are associated with different forms of behavior. In addition, in the Walsters' view, a progression exists between these two forms of Sentiment relationships; passionate love does not last forever. As such, at the completion of the passionate love stage of a Sentiment relationship, the parties involved must either progress to companionate love or dissolve their relationship.

There is some evidence to support Walster and Walster's hypothesis that passionate love is short-lived relative to companionate love. For example, Cimbalo, Faling, and Mousaw (1976) administered Rubin's (1970) Liking and Loving Scales to a number of couples who differed regarding the length of time that they had been married. Some couples had been married less than a year at the time of the study, whereas others had been married for nearly 20 years. Consistent with the Walsters' expectations, Cimbalo et al. (1976) found that the longer the respondents had been married, the lower were their Love Scale scores. It should be noted, however, that although a couple's love score diminished over time, it nevertheless remained relatively high, even after nearly 20 years of marriage. In contrast, liking scores were not affected by the passage of time, remaining at the same high level regardless of the length of the marriage. Other research (Driscoll, Davis, & Lipetz, 1972) has provided evidence that supports the hypothesis that passionate love diminishes with time, thereby causing liking (or companionate love) to become an increasingly important aspect of the relationship.

Research by Marshall Dermer and Thomas Pyszczynski (1978), which also made use of Rubin's (1970) scales, yielded findings that are relevant to a number of issues discussed here. In this research, Dermer and Pyszczynski (1978) recruited a sample of undergraduate males, each of whom had indicated in an earlier measure that he was presently romantically involved, at least to a moderate extent. In the guise of an information-processing task, some of these subjects read a sexually arousing story, whose title—"A College Fantasy"—should provide adequate clues to its content. Other subjects read relatively neutral material—a description of the mating and courtship behavior of herring gulls. After finishing their reading assignment, all subjects completed Rubin's Love and Liking Scales regarding the person with whom they were romantically involved.

The results of Dermer and Pyszczynski's (1978) study indicated that erotic arousal influenced subjects' judgments of love but not of liking. Subjects who had been aroused reported being significantly more "in love" than did those who had read the neutral material. On the other hand, subjects' responses to the Liking Scale were not systematically affected by the content of the materials that they had read. Moreover, differences in subjects' levels of professed romantic involvement (obtained from the earlier measure) were more closely related to their Love Scale scores than to their Liking Scale scores.

These findings support a number of the observations presented earlier. First, they provide further evidence that liking and loving, although similar Sentiments, are influenced to some extent by different processes. Second, these results are consistent with the position that sexuality is a more important consideration for feelings of love than of liking, at least for males.[1] Third, the data of this study reinforce the idea that an intimate Sentiment relationship contains elements of both liking and loving, but loving is more related to romantic involvement.

Another form of love whose nature has been the focus of considerable thought is familial love, the emotional attachment that family members (siblings, parents, and children) have for one another. This type of love is highly similar, if not identical, to companionate love. While such a Sentiment relationship can be more intense than that experienced even in close friendships (the aphorism, blood is thicker than water, illustrates this point), familial love probably does not differ qualitatively from companionate love. Concern for the welfare of family members may be more intense than concern about close friends, and the unit relationship of family members might be more obvious than that formed by the bonds of friendship. On the other hand, it is not clear that the other consequence of Sentiment—in which the individual is motivated to interact with the object of his or her affection—differs appreciably in familial and companionate love.

THE STAGES OF LIKING AND LOVING

A number of social scientists have commented that the development of liking and loving often follows a step-by-step progression (Altman & Taylor, 1973; Levinger, 1980; Levinger & Snoek, 1972; Murstein, 1970; 1976; Secord & Backman, 1974). Most of these theorists, as well as others (Berscheid & Walster, 1978; Blau, 1964; Kelley, 1979; Kelley & Thibaut, 1978), conceptualize these stages within the framework of social exchange theory. An extended discussion of this perspective on interpersonal behavior and relationships was presented in Chapter 9. The basic premise of social exchange is that people seek to maximize their rewards and minimize their costs when interacting with others. Thus, likeability is determined primarily by estimates of the extent to which another will be a source of net rewards if a relationship were to form.

Liking and loving are thought to develop as a consequence of the degree to which another individual actually proves to be a source or facilitator of satisfying outcomes. The stages in the development of a Sentiment relationship

---

[1] Had Dermer and Pyszczynski (1978) also included females in their sample, it is reasonable to assume that the results would have been similar to those discussed here.

are defined by major differences in the variables that mediate the outcomes available. Thus, factors that are very important in determining rewards and costs at one stage of a relationship are often less salient in other stages. In the following pages, we will present a model of the potential stages in liking and loving, based on the theory of social exchange as outlined in Chapter 9. This presentation is loosely adapted from a model of the stages in liking and loving that originally was proposed by Paul Secord and Carl Backman (1964, 1974).

STAGE 1: SAMPLING AND ESTIMATION

In the initial stages of a possible liking or loving relationship, the interactants are primarily concerned with forming estimates of one another's likeability. To accomplish this goal, people attempt to sample, as best they can, the rewards that the other can provide. From this information, they estimate the net values that would be available from a set of continuing encounters—that is, a more complete behavior matrix—that would occur if a relationship were to develop between them. During this potential beginning, there are a number of related reasons for people to make this initial estimate of likeability as rapidly as possible. Perhaps of most importance, social behavior is costly, and if the return on such investments does not appear to offset the costs involved, then it is best that this state of affairs becomes known to the actor before his or her investment is too great.

Also, in most social situations, there are numerous alternative activities available, including other possible encounters that could be sources of rewards. Accordingly, it is reasonable to form an estimate of the rewards that are likely to be available from a given encounter and to compare them with the estimated rewards that appear available from the most favorable alternative activity. Thibaut and Kelley (1959) refer to the value associated with this alternative response option as the *comparison level for alternatives* (CLalt). In order to utilize the CLalt during the first stage of a potential relationship, an actor must first make an estimate of the reward values that the other can provide—in other words, a judgment about the other's likeability. Having formed this Valuation, the actor then compares these estimated rewards with the most favorable alternative activity available (the CLalt).

When the perceived likeability of the other participant in an encounter is less than the value of the most favored available alternative (the CLalt), people will attempt to extricate themselves from the exchange and opt for the other activity. Two factors in this Valuation process emphasize the need to make a quick judgment about the likeability of the other person. First is the issue of cost—that is, the poor return on one's investment—as discussed earlier. To spend long hours getting to know someone, only to realize that you would have been better off doing something else, is obviously an inefficient use of your social resources. Second, the longer it takes to form an initial judgment of likeability, the harder it is to smoothly terminate the encounter when this estimate is finally made and the value is found to be lower than the CLalt.

An additional reason for making likeability estimates as rapidly as possible is related to this last point: people find rejection a very costly experience. This is true whether the person is being rejected or is doing the rejecting. It also is true that the shorter the encounter, the easier and less discomforting is the rejection experience. For example, most of us feel only a tinge of discomfort when an entire encounter consists solely of an exchange of glances, which provides sufficient evidence to confirm the impulse to avoid further contact with another person. In this case, the rejection that is implicit in the failure of both persons to attempt further interaction is not exceedingly costly to either participant.

On the other hand, most of us find it unpleasant to break away from an initial encounter that has lasted for some time and has consisted of a number of social enchanges. Rather than admit that the potential relationship does not seem to be worthwhile (that is, does not provide sufficient return), we tend to make excuses to the other person about why we are breaking off the exchange. Erving Goffman (1952, 1955) has termed this activity *cooling the mark out,* a specific example of a more general interpersonal tactic known as impression management. Goffman borrowed the term cooling the mark out from the colorful argot of the con man.

In practicing their profession, con artists have developed a technique which minimizes the chance that their "mark" will report them to the police. Rather than vanish as soon as possible after relieving the mark of his or her money, they stage one further subterfuge. In this epilogue, the con artists involved in the caper engage in behaviors that are designed to minimize the mark's sense of stupidity or failure. They cool out the mark by presenting cues which indicate that things went wrong because of circumstances beyond their control. Hence, the mark is left with ego, if not bankroll, intact.

In situations involving interpersonal rejection, we sometimes find ourselves having to play the role of con artist, cooling the mark out—or, even worse, having to play the role of the mark. In playing the con artist role, we perform disengagement behaviors that are designed to minimize the loss of face of the rejected other. For example, excusing ourselves to get a drink, to say hello to an old pal who just walked in, or to go to the washroom, when we have no intention of returning and resuming the encounter, are examples of cooling out the mark. Typically, we engage in such behaviors both to spare ourselves and the other person the costs involved in more open rejections or disengagements.

In summary, we make likeability judgments rather quickly because rejection experiences—especially those that occur after some amount of interaction—are so aversive. When the initial encounter is brief, the disengagement process is much less noxious, in large measure because the low Resolution of such fleeting exchanges allows both actors to deny personal responsibility for what, after a more lengthy interaction, would be difficult to misrepresent. The more brief the encounter, the less need to cool out the mark.

Considerable research confirms the importance of concerns with rejection for interpersonal behavior. For example, Graziano, Brothen, and Berscheid (1980) gave subjects the opportunity to view, via a television monitor, two people of the same sex and age as they, who supposedly were evaluating a short essay which they (the subjects) had written to describe their most memorable experience. The subjects were informed that they would interact with these two people at a later point in the study. Futhermore, the subjects were told that each evaluator was in a different room, and their evaluations, given orally, were being videotaped for later study. Subjects were allowed to eavesdrop on these evaluations as they were being made, but they could watch the actions of only one evaluator at a time. Thus, at any given moment, they could watch only one channel of the television monitor.

In the Graziano et al. (1980) study, one evaluator always reacted positively to the subject's essay, whereas the other was always negative. The dependent measure in this study was the amount of time that subjects spent watching one evaluator over the other. The results disclosed that subjects were much more interested in watching the negative evaluator than the positive one. These findings are consistent with the supposition that people are highly concerned about rejection or negative evaluation from those with whom they will interact. This conclusion is supported further by the results obtained in a control condition, in which subjects did not expect to interact with the evaluators. In this context, there were no differences in the amount of time spent watching the two evaluators. Other research (Lowe & Goldstein, 1970; Walster, Walster, Piliavin, & Schmidt, 1973) has also yielded findings that are congruent with the idea that fear of rejection mediates our likeability estimates of others.

Extending these findings is research which demonstrates that cues in a target, which are perceived to be relevant to estimates of rejection, can affect the inclination of actors to initiate an encounter with that person. As will be discussed in detail, there is considerable evidence that physical attractiveness is generally accepted to be a valuable commodity, especially within the framework of liking and loving. As such, there is some consensus that the more attractive a person is, the higher his or her CLalt—that is, in any Social Context, an attractive person is perceived as more likely to have available a highly rewarding alternative encounter than is an individual who is less attractive. Thus, people tend to perceive that there is a greater probability of being rejected by an attractive person than by an unattractive one.

A study by Ted Huston confirms these observations. In this experiment (Huston, 1973), a very realistic procedure was followed: male subjects were led to believe that they were being given the choice of asking one of six females for a date. In one of the conditions, every subject was informed that on the basis of information provided the women, all six of them had indicated a willingness to go out on a date with him; in another condition, the subjects were not given this information. In either condition, the physical attractiveness of these potential dates was varied systematically, from very high to very low.

Huston's (1973) findings are directly relevant to two issues: (1) the value of attractiveness and (2) concerns with rejection. His results indicated that the men who knew that they would be accepted almost invariably chose the most attractive female for a date. These findings strongly suggest that physical attractiveness is an asset in interpersonal exchange. Moreover, Huston's (1973) findings revealed that the subjects were significantly less likely to choose a physically attractive partner when they were unsure of the partner's receptivity to their overture, and this was especially true of subjects who had indicated that they did not perceive themselves as physically attractive. Apparently, under these ambiguous circumstances, subjects' concerns with rejection tempered their enthusiasm for attempting to date a beautiful woman. Other research (Davis & Brock, 1979; Shanteau & Nagy, 1979) has yielded results that are consistent with those of Huston (1973). Of most interest is the study by Shanteau and Nagy (1979), which demonstrated that women also consider attractiveness and probability of success when choosing among potential dating partners. Thus, research indicates that both sexes are influenced by concerns with rejection and the attractiveness of potential partners.

Perhaps the most subtle force for urgency in the formation of likeability estimates is the sense that interpersonal relationships are important sources of motive satisfaction. As noted, interpersonal encounters provide the means by which a great many of our high level motives are gratified. By coming rapidly to an initial judgment of the potential likeability of another, we are able to move to more rewarding aspects of interpersonal activity or to look elsewhere for encounters that we predict will prove more satisfying. The urgency with which people attempt to form an initial estimate of likeability is a consequence of the strength of the motives operating in them.

A study by Elaine Walster (1965) provides some evidence which supports the idea that motive level influences the rapidity with which initial judgments of likeability are made. Walster arranged for each female subject in her study to "accidently" meet a man who, after chatting with her for a few minutes, asked her for a dinner date. Soon after the date had been arranged, the experimenter entered the room and had the subject complete a number of ambiguous personality tests. After supposedly scoring these tests, Walster gave the subjects false feedback about their performance; some were told that their scores were indicative of positive characteristics (maturity, originality, and so on), while others were given negative information about themselves. Subjects then were asked to rate the likeability of the man whom they had accidentally met.

Walster (1965) reasoned that those women who had received negative feedback would have a higher level need for social approval, and as such, would be more willing to make definite likeability estimates of the man whom they had met a little while earlier. This expectation was confirmed. Women who had received negative feedback about themselves were more likely to have formed a favorable estimate of the man's reward value than were the women who had been flattered by their performance feedback.

Of course, as indicated earlier, a highly salient need is more likely to lead to biased estimates of the potential reward value of a target. Thus, lonely people are more likely to misjudge the likeability or attractiveness of another (Pennebaker et al., 1979) than are those who feel less urgency to satisfy their motives. Considerable research evidence is available which supports the observation that estimates of likeability are influenced by need or motive prepotency (Dittes, 1959; Jacobs, Berscheid, & Walster, 1971).

Concerns about being involved in a rejection experience operate in opposition to attempts to satisfy needs through interpersonal relationships. Both of these forces are relevant in the initial stage of liking and loving, but their antithetical nature often creates a dilemma for us: on the one hand, we are motivated to interact with others because of the potential rewards that can accrue from such activities; on the other hand, such interactions also bring with them the danger of rejection, and as such, are risky. For this reason, we tend to develop an elaborate set of scripts or rituals which are recognized and accepted by others and which serve to smooth the path of the initial encounter (see Abelson, 1976; Schank & Abelson, 1977). These "icebreakers" serve the dual purpose of allowing interaction to take place and avoiding the danger of rejection reflecting negatively upon the self-impressions of either interactant.

A common icebreaking ploy that most of us practice involves the attempt to establish some common interpersonal connection with a new acquaintance: "Oh, you're from Akron, do you know Elaine Sugar?" or, "What's your major?" or, if you're from California, "What's your sign?" There are literally hundreds of these common tactics, which are designed to maintain a flow of conversation through elicitation of superficial, nonthreatening personal information. Sports, styles of dress, movies, and hobbies qualify as safe and legitimate topics at this initial stage of interpersonal relationships. On the other hand, more intimate or potentially controversial topics—religious beliefs, sexual ethics, major political concerns, psychological hang-ups, etc.—are typically seen as inappropriate subjects of discussion among new acquaintances.

Similarly, certain behaviors are seen as more appropriate in the later phases of a relationship than in the earlier ones. For example, it is perfectly appropriate to buy a drink for a new acquaintance. But to take a sip from that drink without the other's explicit permission would be seen as pushy, or inappropriately intimate, in the initial stage of the relationship. To perform this same set of behaviors with an established friend, however, would not strike most of us as unfitting.

Social psychologists have extensively studied people's perceptions of what constitute appropriate topics for conversation at various stages of an interpersonal relationship. More specifically, they have focused on people's reactions to other's self-disclosures of intimate information about themselves (Altman, 1973; Altman & Taylor, 1973; Chaikin & Derlega, 1974; Cozby, 1972, 1973; Davis, 1977; Davis & Perkowitz, 1979; Derlega, Wilson, & Chaikin, 1976; Jourard, 1971; Morton, 1978; Rubin, 1975; Taylor, De Soto, & Lieb, 1979;

Won-Doornink, 1979). This work has demonstrated that revealing highly personal information about oneself is seen as inappropriate during initial encounters. A small sample from this literature should suffice to provide some insight into the nature of self-disclosure processes in liking and loving.

In a study of some interest, partly because it examined a non-American sample of respondents, Myong Jin Won-Doornink asked 17 Korean female college students to choose three people whom they knew—a brief acquaintance, a friend, and their best friend—to participate with them in a study of conversations. To accomplish this, Won-Doornink provided each subject with an extensive list of conversational topics which varied in terms of their intimacy. The subject was to choose among these items and use her selections to initiate a conversation with one of the three people whom she brought to the laboratory. The subjects then repeated this procedure with each of the others. The order of these conversations was randomly varied so that some subjects conversed first with their best friend, whereas others began by conversing with their casual acquaintance, and so on. All conversations were recorded and systematically analyzed in terms of the intimacy level of the remarks made by the subjects and their partners.

Of most relevance for present purposes, Won-Doornink (1979) discovered that the intimacy level of the conversations varied as a consequence of the stage of the interpersonal relationship in which the interactants found themselves. By far, the fewest instances of intimate remarks occurred during the conversation between the subject and her new acquaintance. Moreover, it was during this relationship stage that an intimate remark was least likely to elicit a reciprocal intimate disclosure from the other person.

Research by Chaikin and Derlega (1974) also demonstrated that people view intimate self-disclosures as inappropriate if they occur during the initial stage of an interpersonal relationship. They constructed videotapes of a first encounter between two women (accomplices of the experimenters) in a college cafeteria. These tapes varied the extent to which the interactants divulged intimate information about themselves. For example, some subjects viewed a tape in which one woman (Joan) stated the following to her new-found acquaintance:

> I was going with this guy named Bill, and we really got along beautifully. He was my first major relationship. I had never gone to bed with anyone before Bill—but with him it just seemed so natural and good, so I wasn't ashamed of anything. . . . My mother found out about our relationship and there was a big blow-up (pp. 120–21).

In contrast, other subjects viewed a tape in which Joan was considerably less revealing about herself: "It's kind of rough commuting every day to school, but it's really economical, and I can save money for things I want. I am an English major, and I really enjoy the program. . . . I think I might enjoy going to graduate school at a place like the University of Virginia" (p. 121).

Chaikin and Derlega (1974) asked male and female subjects to view one of these tapes and rate the interactants on various dimensions. Of most interest was the finding that the speaker's behavior was perceived as less appropriate and more unusual when she had disclosed highly personal information about herself during this first encounter. In addition, the high self-disclosing target was perceived as less well-adjusted psychologically. Other research (Archer & Burlson, 1980; Wortman, Adesman, Herman, & Greenberg, 1976) has yielded evidence consistent with the observation that the disclosure of intimate personal information is viewed as inappropriate during the early stages of a potential relationship.

In another study, Cozby (1972) examined the impact of differences in the level of intimacy of self-disclosures on likeability judgments during a first encounter. In this research, 31 females were presented with a note from another person that contained personal information. The contents of these notes varied with regard to their levels of intimacy, which ranged from disclosures about the target's favorite TV show (low intimacy) to her habits and plans concerning the use of birth control techniques (high intimacy). After reading the notes, respondents made likeability judgments about the target. The findings indicated that the target was viewed as less likely to be rewarding as a friend when she had disclosed highly personal information about herself.

The results of these studies should not be taken to indicate that disclosing personal information, per se, is inappropriate for first encounters. It is when this personal information is highly intimate that it appears out of place. Sidney Jourard (1971) has noted that the exchange of personal information

© ED BURYN/JEROBOAM, INC.

While self-disclosure is an integral part of the attraction process, the intimacy level of such information must be consistent with the stage of the relationship.

helps to develop a sense of trust in a Sentiment relationship, but its level of intimacy should be commensurate with the stage of the relationship. In fact, as will be discussed, there is evidence that disclosures of highly personal information are appropriate and helpful at later stages of the Sentiment relationship, especially when there is a mutual exchange of such information.

Major Mediators of Initial Attraction

Because norms apparently proscribe the disclosure of revealing information in initial encounters, and because such encounters often occur in public contexts which restrict the range of possible interaction behaviors, attempting to estimate the likeability of another is a difficult task. People in these common circumstances are compelled to utilize rather superficial and obvious cues in making judgments. Bernard Murstein (1970, 1976) has theorized that in the initial stage of a potential interpersonal relationship, judgments of likeability are made on the basis of rather ephemeral cues—for example, the other's appearance, indicants of his or her status, and so on. On the basis of these rather meager cues, we tend to make judgments about the advisability of continuing the encounter.

Perhaps the most potent cues used in initial likeability judgments are derived from the other's physical appearance. Physical features (hair length), level of physical attractiveness, mode of dress, and so forth are used to evaluate the potential worth of the other person. In this circumstance, the term *worth* is defined by the value that society, or our subculture, places on such externals as physical attractiveness, signs of status, wealth, and so on.[2] Of the many superficial characteristics that are used in forming initial likeability estimates, physical attractiveness has been studied most intensively by social psychologists (Berscheid & Walster, 1974; Dion, 1980).

The reader may recall from the material presented in Chapter 7 that considerable research has shown that people make trait inferences about others on the basis of their physical attractiveness. In general, the better looking the target—as defined by standards of beauty accepted in the culture—the more positive are the personal traits inferred about him or her. In brief, as Dion, Berscheid, and Walster (1972) have observed, "What is beautiful is good." Given this tendency of people to infer valuable Personal Structure characteristics in beautiful others, it follows that estimates of likeability (that is, predictions of future rewards) would also be related to this set of superficial characteristics. As such, physical attractiveness should have a major impact on the initial stage of a liking and loving relationship because it presents a readily available and easily processed set of cues.

Considerable evidence supports this supposition. In conducting what has become one of the classic studies in this area, Walster, Aronson, Abrahams, and Rottmann (1966) actually organized and staged a dance for college fresh-

---

[2] Obviously, there is a great potential for erroneous judgment when people rely on these superficial indicants of worth.

man. The event was advertised as a computer dance, and to qualify for it, interested students had to complete a series of measures of personality, intelligence, and social skills. Supposedly, this information would allow the "computer" to pair participants with similar interests. Moreover, the participants' physical attractiveness was secretly rated when they came to the box office to purchase their ticket for the dance.

In actuality, the couples were paired at random, with one qualification: the researchers insured that the male was always taller than his date for the dance. Halfway through the dance, the organizers interrupted the festivities by asking the participants to complete a set of questionnaires. These instruments assessed how much the respondents liked the person with whom they had been matched, how physically attractive they found their date, and how much they wanted to continue the relationship. Six months later, the investigators asked the participants to report how often the male member of the pair had asked his partner for a date.

From what we already know about the effect of physical attractiveness on people's impressions of others, it should not be surprising to learn that this variable had a major impact on subjects' reactions to their dates. The likeability estimates of both male and female participants in the computer dance were significantly related to the attractiveness of their partner—the greater the physical attractiveness of the other person, the more the subject liked him or her, and the more the subject desired to continue the relationship. It might be somewhat surprising to learn, however, that not one other potential determinant of likeability—the personality, intelligence, common interests, even the level of social skills of the other—affected these judgments. Only physical attractiveness was significantly related to people's reactions to their dates. Other research (Berscheid, Dion, Walster, & Walster, 1971; Brislin & Lewis, 1968; Byrne, Ervin, & Lamberth, 1970; Snyder et al., 1977; Tesser & Brodie, 1971; Touhey, 1979) has presented evidence consistent with the findings of Walster et al. (1966).

Despite the apparent importance of physical attractiveness in the initial phases of a potential liking and loving relationship, people frequently underemphasize this factor when discussing the variables that influence their own choices. For example, Tesser and Brodie (1971) found that subjects in their study ranked "looks" as secondary to "personality" and "character" in terms of the importance of these qualities to their own dating preferences. Miller and Rivenbark (1970) also asked subjects to rate the importance of physical attractiveness at a number of different stages in an interpersonal relationship. Their results indicated that physical attractiveness was never perceived as more than moderately important at any stage, including the initial encounter.[3]

---

[3] It should be noted, however, that the results of these studies are somewhat ambiguous regarding the reasons why respondents underemphasize physical attractiveness in their self-reports. It could be that we are actually unaware of the importance of the role that physical attractiveness plays in our likeability estimates. On the other hand, it could be that we do not wish to admit that we could be influenced so heavily by such superficial information.

Although physical attractiveness has a very strong influence on initial estimates of likeability, research has demonstrated that this variable is moderated somewhat by other factors. One of the major moderators of the impact of physical attractiveness appears to be concerns about rejection. As noted earlier, there is a generally accepted belief that the more attractive a person is, the less likely one is to be successful in forming a Sentiment relationship with that person, since his or her CLalt should be quite high. Thus, it follows that the greater the perceived disparity in attractiveness between two people, the greater would be the less attractive person's concern about rejection. This line of reasoning suggests that liking and loving relationships will evolve between people who are reasonably well-matched on physical attractiveness.

This "matching" hypothesis has received a reasonable degree of empirical support. For example, in the Walster et al. (1966) computer dance study, the participants were asked how attractive they thought an appropriate date for them should be. The results indicated that the more attractive the respondents (as rated by independent judges), the more attractive they expected an appropriate date to be. In a rigorous test of the matching hypothesis, Murstein (1972) showed judges individual photographs of a large number of males and females and asked them to rate the physical attractiveness of these people. The judges were not aware that each male in the sample of photos was dating steadily or engaged to one of the females who also was rated. Murstein compared the similarity of the physical attractiveness ratings of the real couples with that of the same males and females when paired at random. He found less discrepancy in the attractiveness ratings of the real couples than in the ratings of the random pairs. Other research has provided evidence consistent with the matching hypothesis (Berscheid et al., 1971; Huston, 1973; Murstein, 1976; Murstein & Christy, 1976; Silverman, 1971; Stroebe, Insko, Thompson, & Layton, 1971).

It is likely that fear of rejection, discussed earlier, plays a large part in producing this matching of the physical attractiveness of couples. Kiesler and Baral (1970) conducted a study that directly supports this hypothesis. In this experiment, male respondents were subjected to an experience that either supported or seriously threatened their positive self-impressions. The researchers hired college men to test a new measure of intelligence, which took an inordinate amount of time to complete. Midway through their ordeal, some respondents were led to believe that they were doing extremely well—the experimenter smiled and mentioned how exceptionally they were performing. Others were given the opposite feedback—the experimenter frowned and mentioned that most other subjects had performed much better.

During a break in the testing, the experimenter and the student went to a nearby coffee shop, where the experimenter recognized a woman seated at a table, and with the subject, joined her. The woman (an accomplice of the researchers) talked to the new arrivals in a friendly, accepting, and interested manner. After a few minutes, the experimenter excused himself, mentioning that he would return soon so that he and the subject could resume their task. While he was gone, the woman continued to chat with the subject.

The subject's behavior toward the accomplice at this point in their encounter was the focus of the study. His actions were rated with regard to how much they reflected a romantic interest in his new acquaintance. The lowest score was obtained by subjects who merely said good bye when she noted that she should "get back to work," and the highest score was given to those men who asked the accomplice for a date.

A crucial feature of this study has yet to be explained: the physical attractiveness of the accomplice was manipulated, so that for some subjects, she appeared very physically alluring, whereas for others, she could best be described as a wreck. The major finding of Kiesler and Baral's (1970) experiment was that the attractiveness of the accomplice affected the subjects' expressed interest in her; however, this effect differed as a consequence of the subjects' earlier success or failure experience in the intelligence testing session. Those men who thought they had performed poorly on the test were much less likely to take a chance and show their interest in the attractive woman than were their previously successful counterparts. Apparently, the unsuccessful subjects did not feel that their somewhat shaken self-impression could stand another jolt at that time.

Other variables also mediate the role that physical attractiveness plays in likeability estimates. For example, it might be expected that this set of cues would be more salient to people who hold traditional beliefs about the nature of male-female relationships. Those people who fully accept the traditional norms specifying the appropriate role relationships between men and women would probably be more likely to perceive physical attractiveness as a useful predictor of future rewards than would people who are less inclined to see relationships between males and females in stereotypic terms. John Touhey has investigated these expectations in research that measured subjects' degree of acceptance of traditional (some would say sexist) male-female role relationships. In this study, Touhey (1979) identified a number of males and females who either subscribed to, or rejected, the traditional stereotypes that are applied to males and females.

After categorizing his sample in this way, Touhey presented subjects with a short biographical sketch about an undergraduate of the opposite sex consisting of typical data such as college major, place and date of birth, and so on. Accompanying the description was a photograph of the target. For some subjects, the photograph portrayed a highly attractive person, whereas for others, the target was rather unattractive. Subjects were then asked to make likeability estimates of this person based on the information presented to them. Touhey was interested in the extent to which the Personal Structure variable of traditionalism in sex-role stereotyping affected the impact of physical attractiveness on these estimates.

Consistent with other research, there was a general tendency for subjects, regardless of sex or Personal Structure differences, to judge the more attractive target as more likely to provide future rewards in a relationship. However, this result was moderated to some degree by the extent to which subjects accepted the traditional sex-role stereotypes. Those who had incorporated these traditional beliefs were influenced much more by the attractiveness of the targets in forming their likeability judgments than were those who rejected these sex-role stereotypes. Moreover, additional analyses revealed that the nontraditional subjects assigned greater weight to the biographical information in their Valuations of the likeability of the target than did their more traditional counterparts.

Concluding Remarks on Sampling and Estimation

It is obvious that the first stage of a potential liking and loving relationship is crucial, since a bad start almost guarantees that no further development of the Sentiment bond will take place. We have shown here that many of the cues about another, which are used to estimate the likely rewards if a more intimate relationship were attempted, are often rather unreliable and superficial. Concerns with rejection, embarrassment, and impression management often outweigh interest in obtaining higher quality information on which more accurate estimates of likeability could be formed.

Moreover, although we have focused our attention on one set of important cues—physical attractiveness—it is likely that other highly visible features of the target also influence likeability estimates. These features, however, are probably utilized less universally across different people than is physical attractiveness. Some people may attend to such cues as style of dress, eye color, or other physical features that do not necessarily contribute to the extent to which another meets generally accepted standards of physical attractiveness. Other people may attend to such cues as voice tone and quality, physical gestures, and body language.

It appears that such individual differences in cue weighting are often a result of the operation of acute antecedents of Sentiment, as discussed in this chapter and in Chapter 2. For example, imagine meeting someone for the first time. Suppose you come away with a sense that you might like to know this person better. Although you may be unaware of it, one of the contributors to your intuitive estimate of likeability was this person's voice quality, which was similar to that of someone to whom you have a strong Sentimental attachment. In this case, cue similarity accentuated the importance of voice quality in your judgment of the person's reward potential. For others who did not share your attachment, this distinctive feature (the target's voice) would not weigh heavily in their estimate of the person's likeability. It is probable that cue similarity, as well as the other acute antecedents of Sentiment, operates most strongly in the sampling and estimation stage of relationship development.

A number of themes are relevant to understanding the stage of sampling and estimation. Of course, Sentiment is paramount in this stage, as it is in all of the stages of liking and loving. However, Valuation is also extremely important, since likeability estimates are, in fact, decisions about potential rewards that are made on the basis of cues to which different weights are assigned. Recall that Valuation involves the weighting of information and the selection of response options based on this cue weighting in order to come to a decision about the course of action that appears to optimize our outcomes. Clearly, Valuation is relevant to the first stage of relationship development, since the term *sampling* implies that available cues are processed selectively, and *estimation* implies that some decision is being reached about the reward value of the target.

Self-Consistency and Resolution also play roles in the first stage of liking and loving, but the operation of these themes is somewhat subtle. Typically, first encounters are low Resolution contexts. In such circumstances, we have very little information about the other person. In addition to the reasons outlined above, the rituals typically enacted in initial encounters make it extremely difficult for us to "read" the true meaning of another's behaviors. As noted in the next section, a major determinant of another's potential rewards for us is his or her likeability estimate of us. In first encounters, such estimates are difficult to infer, and for this reason, the contexts in which these exchanges take place are very poorly resolved.

The ordeal of seeking a faculty position in social psychology provides an excellent illustration of the poor Resolution inherent in the first stage of relationship development. In this field, job seekers typically send their credentials to a college or university that has announced a job opening. Based on this and other information, the finalists are often individually invited to an interview on the campus. In the course of these visits, which can last for two or three days, the candidate meets most of the interested faculty on an individual basis. The impressions and likeability estimates that these people form of the candidate are very important, as they are ultimately translated into judgments about his or her suitability for the job. However, norms of cordiality operate very strongly in these settings to influence the overt behavior of the faculty toward the candidate. From the perspective of the faculty members, hospitality demands that the job seeker be made to feel relaxed and at ease. From the job seeker's perspective, however, this cordiality masks cues that otherwise would prove very informative about his or her chances for the position. For the candidate, the context is exceptionally poorly resolved, especially regarding cues relevant to a high level concern—namely, finding a job.

Given that others' judgments of us are often difficult to determine in first encounters, it is not always clear when another has rejected our overtures. Does a stifled yawn indicate boredom or weariness? Is a refusal of an offer of a date with a reply about a previous commitment an honest depiction of the facts, or a graceful attempt at cooling the mark out? In any case, concerns with rejection that we all experience during first encounters involve attempts to maintain a self-Consistent, positive image of ourselves. When someone stifles a yawn, should we continue our conversation and risk a more direct rebuff? Or should we disengage ourselves and search for other avenues of expression? When we are turned down for a date, should we persist, and thus expose ourselves to the possibility of an unequivocally negative response that would be inconsistent with a positive self-image? During the sampling and estimation stage, concerns with self-Consistency can make cowards of us all. In spite of stumbling blocks such as concern with rejection, however, the reward value inherent in successful social exchange insures that interpersonal relationships do form, and that some of these relationships ultimately do result in very strong Sentimental attachments.

Finally, much of our social activity occurs in the sampling and estimation stage. We meet many people in our lives, but become friendly or intimate with relatively few of them. In part, circumstances beyond our control account for this fact, but in many cases, one or both people choose not to pursue a relationship beyond this beginning stage. For those who do, however, it appears that behaviors designed to sample and estimate are slowly replaced by more complex social exchanges in which more wide-scale explorations of the behavior matrix are undertaken. When a relationship progresses to this point, it has entered the second stage of liking and loving, which Secord and Backman (1974) have termed *bargaining*.

STAGE 2: BARGAINING

As noted in Chapter 9, bargaining involves the processes by which two interactants agree to experience a given outcome from among a number of possible alternatives. When bargaining enters into the development of liking and loving relationships, it implies that the people involved are exploring the range of mutually acceptable social activities to determine what each finds rewarding and acceptable, or aversive and unacceptable. As Secord and Backman (1974) note, this exploration of the behavior matrix is often not as conscious or as purposive as the word bargaining might imply, yet it is clear from observing people's behaviors when they are in the process of getting to know one another that such implicit negotiations do take place—"I've never tried that before, but it sounds like fun," or "I can't stand polka music, let's go to the symphony instead."

These sorts of bargains are regularly made in an attempt to determine the extent to which the behavior matrix for a pair of people yields mutually rewarding outcomes. Within this framework, of course, each interactant is attempting to structure the relationship so that he or she reaps the maximum possible benefit from it. In attempting to maximize their possible rewards in a relationship, the people involved often engage in tactics of impingement. Obviously, if one can receive rewards only by the continuous application of behavior control, it is unlikely that the relationship will progress beyond the bargaining stage. Impingement tactics can facilitate the growth of a relationship, however, if they result in the discovery of an extensive number of mutually rewarding cells of the behavior matrix.

A number of other mechanisms in addition to impingement also have a major effect on the bargaining stage of liking and loving relationships. As will be discussed, impingement often is not necessary in many successful liking and loving relationships because the interactants seek the same experiences or find the same social activities rewarding. In these circumstances, other mechanisms guide the course of the interactants' exploration of the behavior matrix. We will review these mechanisms in some detail in the following pages.

The central issue at this stage of a relationship is the ease with which exploration of the behavior matrix can occur (see Chapter 9). Thus, if circumstances raise the costs of interaction, exploration of the matrix is more difficult, and the relationship is less likely to develop further; on the other hand, if features of the Social Context facilitate exchange, there is a greater chance that a more intimate liking and loving relationship will evolve. Similarly, factors in the interactants themselves can operate to inhibit or facilitate the exploration of the matrix; thus, internal factors have a profound influence on the course of the relationship.

Opportunity

As noted, some of the most obvious mediators of cost in an exchange relationship are the features in the physical environment that determine *opportunity* for interaction. When factors in the physical environment make it easy to engage in social activities with another, the exploration of the behavior matrix can proceed with minimal interference. On the other hand, when features of the context impede interaction, additional costs are placed on exploratory behaviors, thereby lessening the likelihood that people will attempt to explore their matrix.

Perhaps the environmental variable that most determines opportunity is physical distance, or proximity. In Chapter 2, we reviewed a number of studies that demonstrated the impact of this factor on the formation of Sentiment relationships (Bossard, 1932; Festinger, Schachter, & Back, 1950; Insko & Wilson, 1977; Katz & Hill, 1958; Priest & Sawyer, 1967). This research and other studies (Byrne, 1961; Ebbesen, Kjos, & Konecni, 1976; Nahemow & Lawton, 1975), have consistently shown that the smaller the distance separating interactants (in terms of the places in which they live, work, and play), the greater the likelihood that they will form a Sentiment relationship and that this relationship will flourish.

From an exchange theory perspective, we would not necessarily expect that proximity always would enhance the probability that a relationship would evolve further. Proximity and other facilitative features in the physical environment serve only to enhance the opportunity for interaction and thus promote further comprehensive exploration of the behavior matrix. Obviously, at times, people will not appreciate what they find there: having had the opportunity to explore the potential outcomes that are readily available in a relationship with another, we might judge our CLalt exceeds these outcomes. In this case, proximity would not result in the formation of a close Sentimental attachment. Overall, however, proximity does, in fact, increase the likelihood that a liking or loving relationship will form, because on the average, it is less costly to interact with people who are nearby.

In addition, a subtle force—*mere exposure*—appears to operate to strengthen the relationship between proximity and attraction. Robert Zajonc (1968; Zajonc et al., 1974; Zajonc & Rejecki, 1969) has commented on the somewhat peculiar propensity in us to increase our positive evaluation of people and objects merely as a consequence of having repeated exposures to them. Thus, seeing a person every day makes it more likely that we will develop a positive relationship with that person, regardless of other factors that might exist.

In studying the mere exposure phenomenon, Zajonc and his associates have demonstrated that repeated opportunities to see another increased the perceiver's evaluation of that person. In an early study of this phenomenon, Zajonc (1968) exposed respondents to a series of photographs of 10 men. The frequency of exposure to these pictures was varied systematically, so that some were presented only once to the subject, whereas others were presented as many as 25 times. Zajonc then asked his respondents to provide likeability estimates of these stimulus persons, as well as of people whose photographs they had not seen before. The results indicated that likeability was related positively to exposure; the more often the respondents had been exposed to a picture, the more likeable they rated the person it depicted. Other research has yielded similar results (Hamm, Baum, & Nikels, 1975; Wilson & Nakajo, 1966).

Saegert, Swap, and Zajonc (1973) present even more dramatic evidence of the impact that mere exposure can have on likeability estimates. In this research, female undergraduates ostensibly took part in a study of taste sensitivity. An elaborate procedure was employed which required subjects to move from cubicle to cubicle in the laboratory in such a way that they were exposed to their counterparts in the session with different frequencies; subjects ran into certain other participants only once, whereas they were exposed to others more frequently, up to a maximum of 10 times. Care was taken to insure that there was no overt verbal or nonverbal communication between the subjects, and that every person-to-person exposure lasted for approximately the same length of time. After the tasting sessions, all subjects completed a questionnaire on which some of the items dealt with the likeability of each of the other subjects who took part in the study.

The results of this study were clear-cut. Likeability ratings of subjects were directly and positively related to exposure. The more frequently a subject encountered another in the experiment, the more favorable were her likeability estimates of that person. This result was obtained despite the constraints that Saegert et al. (1973) imposed to preclude the possibility that any social interaction occurred between the participants.

It should be noted that mere exposure has similar effects on people's reactions to nonhuman stimuli as well.[4] Of most relevance to our concerns is the fact that opportunity mediates exposure. The easier it is to encounter someone, the greater the chances of exposure to them. However, we assume

[4] See Harrison (1977) for a comprehensive discussion of this phenomenon.

that exposure has, at most, a limited and subtle effect on likeability (Maddi, 1968; Zajonc, Swap, & Harrison, 1971). More influential variables such as the outcomes of actual interactions with another can have a much more profound influence on liking and loving (Swap, 1977). The most likely effect of exposure is somewhat more subtle; repeated contact with another creates a positive interpersonal climate in which people are more likely to attempt to explore the behavior matrix.

Belief Similarity

Another major mediator of the efficiency with which people can explore the rewards and costs entailed in a relationship is *similarity of beliefs*. Donn Byrne and his associates have carried out a long-term investigation of the effects of belief similarity on liking and loving relationships. This program of research has generated considerable evidence that supports the observation that the more similar the beliefs of two interacting individuals, the greater the likelihood that they will form a Sentiment relationship (Byrne, 1969, 1971; Byrne & Clore, 1967; Byrne, Ervin, & Lamberth, 1970; Byrne, Griffitt, Hudgins, & Reeves, 1969; Byrne & Nelson, 1965; Byrne & Rhamey, 1965; Byrne & Wong, 1962). Presented below is an example of an interesting study that Byrne and his colleagues conducted to explore the effects of belief similarity on likeability in a real-life encounter.

In this research, Byrne, Ervin, and Lamberth (1970) measured a number of respondents' beliefs via a 50-item questionnaire; topics included various opinions, as well as other beliefs, such as the positivity of the respondent's self-impression. Then, using a variation on the computer-dating approach of Walster et al. (1966), the researchers introduced male and female participants to one another and treated them to a Coke date at the student union. The couples were asked to attempt to learn as much as possible about one another during this encounter. After the date, they returned to the laboratory, and individually completed questionnaires regarding their likeability estimates of the other person. In addition, an unobtrusive measure of attraction—the physical distance between the two participants as they stood in front of the experimenter's desk—also was obtained at this time. Moreover, two to three months later, participants were contacted and asked whether or not the relationship that began that evening had, in fact, continued.

As in the Walster et al. (1966) computer dance study, Byrne et al. (1970) rated the physical attractiveness of all subjects who were paired for a date. In addition, they systematically matched the participants in such a way that the belief similarity of the members of a pair (as determined by their responses on their belief questionnaires) was controlled. Some pairs shared very similar beliefs, whereas other couples were markedly different in this area. The effects of both physical attractiveness and belief similarity were assessed via the subjects' likeability estimates of their date, the unobtrusive physical distance measure, and their followup reports concerning a subsequent relationship.

The results disclosed that both similarity and physical attractiveness had

Based on Byrne, Ervin, and Lamberth's results: (1) What is your estimate of the belief similarity of this newly acquainted couple? And (2) How attracted are they to each other?

strong effects on all three of these indicators of attraction. Subjects with similar beliefs who had been paired liked each other more, and stood closer together after their date. Similarly, the more physically attractive the other, the greater was the subject's likeability estimate, and (for male subjects) the closer they stood to their partner. Finally, and perhaps of most interest, Byrne et al. (1970) found that subjects who were paired with a physically attractive partner and who held similar beliefs to that person were most likely to have continued the relationship beyond the initial encounter. Indeed, the only couples who continued dating during the entire followup period were those in which both people were physically attractive and shared similar beliefs. Other research, which has been performed by both Byrne or his colleagues (Griffitt & Veitch, 1974) and others (Anderson, 1975; Seta, Martin, & Capehart, 1979; Touhey, 1972a) has provided evidence that is consistent with the results reported here.

Belief similarity appears to facilitate the development of liking and loving relationships for a number of reasons. First, it seems reasonable that those who share similar beliefs are likely to find that a great many cells of their behavior matrix are mutually rewarding. As Murstein (1976) has observed, the more a couple agrees on what is important, the more likely their relationship is to evolve further. For example, two people who believe that chamber music is soothing and enjoyable are likely to find shared experiences involving this form of music to be highly satisfying. Similarly, other shared beliefs should lead to other mutually rewarding shared experiences. As noted, the greater the number of positive outcomes with which another person is associated, the more likely we are to form a Sentimental attachment to that person. Thus, belief similarity fosters *positive association,* an extended antecedent of Sentiment.

Second, belief similarity affects liking and loving relationships because, as Byrne (1971) has speculated, belief similarity satisfies a major human motive—the need to understand the world about us. Leon Festinger (1954), in his theory of social comparison, viewed this need as a fundamental motive that permeates all of human social behavior. As noted in Chapter 3, it appears that people use the behaviors and beliefs of others as a means of defining what is real, or correct, thereby providing them with what Festinger called a sense of *social reality.*

Byrne (1971) argues that concerns with self/other Consistency underlie the potential reinforcement value of belief similarity—that is, we like to have others corroborate our sense of reality. Interactions with a person who holds beliefs that are similar to ours are more likely to result in experiences that are consistent with our own view of things than are encounters with people who hold beliefs at odds with ours. Thus, it is more likely that we would find mutually rewarding portions of the behavior matrix with those who share our sense of reality.

A third reason why belief similarity is an important determinant of the potential outcome of the bargaining stage of liking and loving is the inference of *reciprocated liking* that such similarity fosters in people. It is reasonable to assume that perceived belief similarity influences other persons' liking for us, just as this variable affects our reactions to them. Moreover, attempts to elicit a rewarding outcome from others appear to be less costly and more successful when those people are favorably disposed towards us than when they dislike us, or even are merely indifferent. Thus, perceived belief similarity seems to affect estimates of others' liking of us, which in turn, affect our estimate of their capacity to provide us with rewards should a relationship continue to develop.

A number of studies (Aronson & Worchel, 1966; Backman & Secord, 1959; Byrne & Griffitt, 1969; Condon & Crano, 1977; Lowe & Goldstein, 1970; Napolitan & Goethals, 1979) have demonstrated that a major determinant of our liking another is the perception that he or she likes us. For example, Backman and Secord (1959) first asked subjects to complete a standardized personality test and then meet in small groups to get to know one another. However, before these group sessions began, each subject was told that, based on responses to the test, it was highly probable that some of the people they were about to meet would like them; the experimenters provided even more helpful information to the subject by explicitly identifying these people. After the group meetings, subjects were asked to indicate with whom they would like to be paired if later sessions were to involve only two participants at a time. Backman and Secord's (1959) results indicated that subjects expressed a strong preference to be paired with one of the other subjects whom they thought would like them. These findings are consistent with the idea that people judge that it is more rewarding to interact with someone who is attracted to them than with someone who is not.

In addition, a study by Condon and Crano (1977) provides direct support for the speculation that belief similarity influences judgments of the other's liking for us. In this study, which used a procedure developed by Byrne (1969, 1971), subjects first completed an opinion questionnaire which measured their beliefs about a number of issues of interest to them. They were then shown the completed questionnaire of another subject (of the same sex) and asked to make estimates of the extent to which that person would like them if they were to meet and get to know one another. Actually the completed questionnaires that were given to subjects were constructed by the experimenters so that perceived belief similarity could be varied systematically. Some subjects were shown a bogus questionnaire of another participant whose responses were remarkably similar to their own; others were shown a questionnaire that reflected only a moderate degree of belief similarity; still others were shown the responses of another who had disagreed with them on virtually every question.

Condon and Crano's (1977) results were consistent with the hypothesis that people use belief similarity as a factor in their estimates of another's liking for them. Those subjects who thought the other person had responded to the opinion questionnaire much the same as they had were likely to judge that the other person would like them if they were to meet. On the other hand, subjects who saw the questionnaire of a person whose beliefs were diametrically opposed to their own tended to think that the other person would not find them very appealing. These findings—along with the results of the other studies cited, which demonstrated that people tend to like others who they think like them—suggest that belief similarity contributes to reciprocal judgments of liking, which in turn promote the development of liking and loving relationships.

Reciprocity

Reciprocated liking is just one instance of a more general determinant of people's reactions to their encounters during the bargaining stage (as well as the later stages) of liking and loving. It appears that interpersonal relationships flourish or stagnate in part as a consequence of whether or not mutual regard and trust can develop. One major indicant of such trust and regard involves reciprocity, especially with respect to attraction, self-disclosure, and reward exchange. Thus, it is likely that during the bargaining stage of an interpersonal relationship, people test their expectations that liking is mutual, secrets are shared (but not disseminated), and rewards are reciprocated. The empirical evidence that is relevant to these observations will now be briefly reviewed.

Reciprocated Liking. As discussed earlier, the perception that another likes us contributes to our likeability of that person. As a relationship evolves into the bargaining state, however, likeability estimates are less important than are actual Sentiments—that is, whether or not we expected (from our initial encounters) that someone would be rewarding becomes less important than the discovery that our developing feelings, as the relationship progresses, are actually reciprocated by the person. Numerous studies (De Soto & Kuethe, 1959; Newcomb, 1961; Tagiuri, Blake, & Bruner, 1953) have shown that people expect others to reciprocate their feelings of liking.

In a series of studies, Herbert Blumberg has provided evidence that people prefer reciprocity to all other types of Sentiment relations. For example, Blumberg (1969) asked female undergraduates to think of two people: one person whom they believed liked them more than they liked him or her, and another person whom they believed liked them less than they liked him or her. For each case, subjects were asked to respond to a number of questions regarding their feelings if the Sentiment relationship were to change—such as, "How would you feel if you learned that this person likes you more than you thought?" (p. 124).

Not surprisingly, Blumberg found that almost all subjects reported that they would feel happier if the person whom they thought liked them less than they liked him or her actually liked them more than they had originally thought. However, he found that virtually every subject would also prefer increased symmetry of Sentiment over being better liked by the other, especially if the assymetry of liking was extreme. In other words, in those instances in which a subject indicated that she liked another less than the other liked her, she preferred to see the Sentiment relationship change to one in which the other lowered his or her liking for her. Thus, although Blumberg's subjects indicated that they wanted to be liked by others—and in general the more they were liked the better—they tempered this preference if it meant that another person would like them considerably more than they liked him or her.

Reciprocated Self-Disclosure. As discussed earlier, a number of psychologists have commented on the importance of exchanging personal information to the development of liking and loving (Altman, 1973; Jourard, 1971). In and of itself, such information provides people with cues about the likelihood that a mutually rewarding relationship is possible. However, there is evidence that norms mediate the judgments of the appropriateness of certain types of personal *self-disclosures,* depending on the stage of the relationship that exists between the interactants. Disclosure of highly intimate information is viewed as inappropriate in the sampling and estimation stage; however, disclosure of this type of information is judged to be not only appropriate, but also helpful in fostering the relationship when it has reached the bargaining stage. However, as Altman (1973; Altman & Taylor, 1973) notes, self-disclosure of intimate information only promotes a relationship when it is reciprocated.

Myong Jin Won-Doornink (1979) found direct support for the hypotheses that (1) self-disclosure of intimate information is seen as most appropriate during the bargaining stage of a relationship; and (2) it is most appropriate to reciprocate such disclosures at this stage. Recall from our earlier discussion of this study that Won-Doornink asked female college students to bring with them to the laboratory three people whom they knew: a brief acquaintance; a person whom the subject had known for 3 to 12 months and with whom she felt that a relationship was still developing; and a person whom the subject said was her (same-sex) best friend. The subject's task was to engage in a different conversation with each of these three people, choosing topics from a list of issues whose level of intimacy ranged from minor to extreme.

From our perspective, Won-Doornink's (1979) second level of Sentiment relationship approximates the bargaining stage of liking and loving. Thus, we would expect the greatest amount of intimate self-disclosure and the highest reciprocity of such information when the subject conversed with someone whom she liked, but who was not her best friend. It is during the bargaining stage of friendship development that intimate self-disclosures have their greatest impact, since such communications foster a sense of mutual trust. In addition, revealing disclosures promote accurate exploration of the behavior matrix; as such, they are more useful in the bargaining stage than in earlier or later phases of liking and loving, since such exploration is a central feature of bargaining.[5]

These speculations are consistent with the results that Won-Doornink found in her study. Her subjects were most likely to disclose intimate information to the person whom they knew for 3 to 12 months, and the highest proportion of reciprocated intimate self-disclosures occurred among these interactants. On the other hand, the highest reciprocity of low and moderately intimate self-disclosures occurred during conversations with the casual acquaintance with whom subjects still were in the sampling and estimation

---

[5] We also would expect that good friends share intimate disclosures, but such communications are less important at this phase of liking and loving because much of this information is already known by the other and trust has already been established. Thus, there is less need to reciprocate such material. Research (Cozby, 1972; Won-Doornink, 1979) has confirmed this expectation.

stage. Cozby (1972) has also shown that during the initial stage of a relationship, people reciprocate information of low or medium intimacy, but do not respond in kind when the other discloses highly intimate information.

Reciprocated Rewards. In many ways, reciprocated self-disclosure of intimate information is an example of reciprocated rewards, since the sharing of personal information is often, in itself, satisfying. At the simplest level, it is rewarding to learn interesting information about others, and intimate personal data are often extremely stimulating. In addition, at a more subtle level, exchanges of intimate information serve to establish a belief in both interactants that the other person can be trusted, an outcome that can satisfy a host of motives—need for affiliation, security, attachment, and so on. Haas and Desearn (1981) have observed that exchanges of rewards, especially when there are few impingements that compel reciprocation, foster the development of a mutual sense of trust in the interactants.

In his discussion of the norm of reciprocity, Gouldner (1960) speculates that people expect that their actions will be reciprocated. Thus, good deeds or the bestowing of rewards should obligate the other to respond in kind. Likewise, one expects that his or her nasty acts will result in attempts at retribution. Within the framework developed here, we would expect that the norm of reciprocity, especially as it applies to rewards, would be most salient during the bargaining stage of liking and loving. There is some evidence—for example, a study by Marylyn Rands and George Levinger (1979)—that supports this hypothesis.

In this investigation, Rands and Levinger (1979) asked male and female subjects (who were either typical college students or senior citizens) to estimate the probability that certain types of behaviors would be reciprocated by interactants at various stages of a liking or loving relationship. The interactants ranged from casual acquaintances to close friends and spouses. The behaviors that subjects rated fell into categories such as joint activity, self-disclosure, rewarding comments, and so on.

Of most interest to present concerns was the finding that the greatest increase in people's expectations of reciprocity of rewarding behaviors—such as expressions of positive regard—occurred between the first and second stages of the relationship. Of course, Rands and Levinger's (1979) respondents expected that reciprocity would continue to increase as the intimacy level of the relationship increased; however, as noted, the greatest jump in expected reciprocity occurred in the stage in which the most bargaining would occur. It is also of interest that this pattern of results was obtained from both the undergraduates and the older respondents.

Concluding Remarks about Bargaining in Liking and Loving

In this section, we have presented some of the major variables that operate when interacting people explore in earnest the rewards that are available in the behavior matrix which they share. From our standpoint, the overall goal of such exploration is a decision to continue to devote resources to the development of the relationship. Such diverse mechanisms as belief similarity and reciprocity appear to be especially important in determining the outcome of this bargaining stage of liking and loving. Of course, these variables also operate to some extent in all of the other stages of a Sentiment relationship, but they are most salient when exploration of the behavior matrix is the central concern of the interactants.

It also is true that processes which operate in other stages also influence bargaining. For example, a person's comparison level for alternatives (CLalt)—an important determinant in the sampling and estimation stage— also influences the outcome of bargaining. In valuating the projected costs and rewards associated with establishing a relationship with another, people compare these outcomes with their estimate of the most favorable alternative available. The outcome of this Valuation process will determine whether the relationship will progress, stabilize, or end.

Similarly, fear of rejection, which plays so prominent a role in the sampling and estimation stage, is also a concern of people in the bargaining stage of a Sentiment relationship. Just as rejection is painful at the beginning of a potential relationship, it also is very unpleasant—perhaps even more so—when the relationship has progressed to the bargaining stage. In some ways, concerns about rejection change somewhat in the later stages of a Sentiment relationship; in the initial stage, these fears center on the perceived probability that rejection is likely to occur. In bargaining, people see rejection as a less likely but more painful occurrence.

The decrease in the perceived probability of rejection in the bargaining stage appears to be due to the mutual investments that each interactant has made in the relationship by engaging in a host of social activities with the other. On the other hand, these same investments contribute to the pain of rejection, should it occur. In addition, it is difficult to cool the mark out in the bargaining stage. Rejections at this point of a relationship are difficult to misinterpret, and thus, are difficult to perceive as consistent with a positive self-impression.

Themes in addition to Sentiment, Valuation, and self-Consistency also operate in the bargaining stage of liking and loving. For example, bargaining can be viewed as an attempt to increase the Resolution of a relationship. The interactants, in their exploration of the behavior matrix, are in many ways attempting to clarify the likely nature (rewards and costs) of a long-term relationship, should one develop. Moreover, in attempting to experience rewarding cells of the behavior matrix, a number of impingement tactics are employed in the bargaining stage. These tactics are costly, however, and difficult to maintain over long periods of time. Thus, one of the major determinants of the course of a relationship—reflected, for example, in the degree of belief similarity—is the extent to which mutually rewarding activities can be found without recourse to continual impingement. The less necessary this mechanism of Control, the more likely the relationship is to develop further. Finally, as noted earlier, self/other Consistency is relevant to the bargaining stage of a Sentiment relationship, since it is one of the reasons that belief similarity is a source of attraction between people.

As the bargaining stage of a Sentiment relationship progresses, three outcomes are possible. First, the interactants can continue to explore the behavior matrix for a long period of time; in this sense, they remain casual friends who interact at irregular intervals and who do not develop strong Sentimental attachments. Second, from the bargaining process, the interactants can infer that their initial judgment about the net reward value of the relationship was a gross overestimate or that their best available alternative (the CLalt) was much more rewarding than they originally thought. In either case, it is likely that the relationship would be terminated. Third, the interactants might discover through the exploratory behavior that characterizes this phase of the Sentiment relationship that their matrix contains a large number of highly mutually rewarding activities. In this eventuality, it is likely that the relationship will evolve into one that is characterized less by exploration and more by regular and predictable patterns of interaction. Moreover, because of the numerous and intensive rewards experienced during the bargaining stage, it is likely that the interactants will develop a Sentimental attachment for one another. Thus, as exploration diminishes and more regular and reinforcing outcomes are experienced, the relationship evolves into its third stage—*commitment*.

STAGE 3: COMMITMENT

The third stage of liking and loving is characterized by a "settling in" of the relationship. There is, in general, less exploration of the interactants' own behavior matrix, as well as of those available in alternative relationships. The term *commitment* implies an agreement (often implicit) regarding the concentration of one's social activity on a single relationship, to the exclusion of others, both past and potential. In this stage, Sentimental attachment becomes increasingly strong as the interactants move from casual acquaintances to close friends, best friends, or lovers.

Emergent roles. Within the relationship itself, exploration of the matrix becomes an increasingly less important concern, since at this stage, sufficient information about the various outcomes available has already been gathered. Thus, the most rewarding activities that are available to the interactants across the various Social Contexts in which their relationship unfolds tend to be reenacted on a fairly regular basis. For example, within the context of a school situation, the actors might cease their exploratory exchanges and concentrate on actions that both have found to be rewarding. Whereas in the earlier stages that might have engaged in a wide variety of different activities, some of which were rewarding and some of which were not, they have now settled upon a more stable ritual.

For instance, while in the bargaining stage, two interactants might have arrived at the school bus stop at different times, horsed around on some days, compared homework on others, and so on. In the commitment stage, there appears to be a tacit agreement to be at the bus stop 15 minutes early in order to compare homework assignments; in addition, horsing around becomes a much less frequent activity at the bus stop (but a more regular occurrence in the lunchroom). Thus, both actors acquire expectations about their own and the other's behaviors in the various contexts in which they interact.

We have discussed expected behavior patterns earlier (Chapters 9 and 11) under the general term *roles*. As noted, roles are accepted rules of conduct (norms) that apply to a subset of the population. In a dyad, such norms can apply specifically to a single person or to both people. From our perspective, these rules of conduct emerge as the interactants explore their behavior matrix and evolve into a regularized relationship. The regularity with which certain behaviors are enacted, at the expense of alternative activities, lends a component of predictability to the relationship. Thus, the commitment stage of a Sentiment relationship is characterized by a set of roles which has emerged from events that occurred over the course of the earlier stages.

Murstein (1970, 1976) has observed that the critical concern of people who find themselves in the commitment stage of a liking or loving relationship involves the compatibility of role expectations. For example, let us consider the case of Agnes and Louise who, after getting to know one another during their first year of college, decide to room together for the coming year. In the course of their earlier encounters, they found much of value in one another. For instance, Agnes always found Louise to be considerate of her feelings, almost anticipating her wishes without her having to overtly express them. This quality was a very important determinant of Louise's appeal, since Agnes possessed a high level need to be looked after (what psychologists call dependency).

After moving in together, however, Agnes finds that in this new context, Louise appears to be much less considerate than past experiences had led her to expect. Louise does not pick up after herself, although Agnes has resorted to explicit requests that she do so. Louise, of course, promises to mend her ways but seems incapable of changing her well-established habit. Since Agnes is a fussbudget, Louise's casual approach to neatness—not putting the cap on the toothpaste tube, leaving a trail of empty bottles, food containers, and dirty dishes throughout the apartment—places severe strains on both of them; Agnes is unhappy because this facet of Louise was an unexpected and unwelcome surprise; Louise is unhappy because she realizes that she cannot fulfill Agnes's expectations, regardless of her good intentions.

In our view, the commitment phase of the relationship between Agnes and Louise has exposed them to portions of their behavior matrix that were less rewarding than either might have expected, and this violation of their emergent expectations (roles) placed their friendship in some jeopardy. In contrast, the extent to which there are no unpleasant surprises is the extent to which the relationship has a good chance of even further development.

In fact, it is likely that if a liking and loving relationship has evolved to the commitment stage, the interactants will find it easy to behave in accord with most of the major expectations embodied in the role relationship that has emerged between them.

Empirical evidence supports Murstein's (1970, 1976) hypothesis that role compatibility is an important feature of the commitment stage of a Sentiment relationship. For example, Holz (1969) studied 49 couples who varied with regard to their role relationship: some couples held expectations about their own and their partner's appropriate behaviors that matched the traditional sex-role stereotype; other couples held expectations that their relationship would be more egalitarian with regard to sex roles.

Holz (1969) found that these two types of role expectations matched the high level motives of the interactants. Those couples who maintained traditional role expectations tended to consist of men who had high needs for control and dominance, and women who were highly concerned with dependence and nurturance. On the other hand, those who were more egalitarian in their role relationship were more similar in their motives.

As Murstein (1970, 1976) predicted, couples whose relationship evolved to the commitment stage tended to settle into roles that were rewarding to them, given their high level motives. Murstein (1976) himself provides evidence that is consistent with the relative importance of role compatibility during the later stages of a Sentiment relationship.

Equity.   The gradual shift from bargaining to commitment is accompanied by a change from a concern with simple reciprocity ("I rewarded you, now you reward me") to a more complex consideration of contributions and rewards ("You worked hard getting the house ready for the party, so I'll cook dinner"). As two people develop a liking and loving relationship, they adopt a more long-term and complex perspective on the contributions that they make toward, and satisfactions that they derive from, one another. Of most relevance in these considerations are reward distribution norms, which provide the interactants with a basis for decisions regarding what is a commensurate return for their investments. The most prominent of these norms in the later stages of a relationship is equity, discussed at length in Chapter 9. The reader will recall that equity prescribes that an individual's reward from a relationship should be congruent with his or her contributions to it; the greater the contribution, the greater should be the reward.

Elaine Walster and her colleagues (Berscheid & Walster, 1978; Walster & Walster, 1978; Walster, Walster, & Berscheid, 1977) have argued convincingly that people in the commitment stage of a relationship attend to the norm of equity when judging the appropriateness of the benefits that are reaped from it. For example, they speculate that a major determinant of satisfaction with a relationship is the extent to which the interactants perceive that they *both* are receiving a reward that is commensurate with their contributions. *Inequities*—regardless of which partner they favor or disadvantage—are perceived by both actors as inappropriate and likely to threaten the relationship. There is research evidence that supports these observations.

In one study on this issue, Walster, Walster, and Traupmann (1978) gathered a sample of more than 500 undergraduate men and women and asked them to complete a questionnaire about intimate relationships. In the introduction to this questionnaire, the subjects were told that a sample of people, when interviewed about their liking and loving relationships, "mentioned a variety of things—good or bad—that they thought a person could contribute (or fail to contribute)" to a relationship (Walster et al., 1978, p. 84). The introduction went on to state that these interviewees mentioned a number of inputs to a relationship: personal contributions such as physical attractiveness, intelligence, and sociability; emotional contributions such as empathy and love; and day-to-day contributions such as helpfulness in making decisions that affect the relationship. They also mentioned a variety of outcomes—again good and bad—that they thought a person could obtain from a relationship: personal rewards and frustrations, emotional rewards and frustrations, and day-to-day rewards and frustrations.

After reading this introductory material, the respondents in the Walster et al. (1978) study were asked to think about their present intimate relationship, especially to think about "how—considering what you're putting into it, and what you're getting out of it—your relationship 'stacks up' " (p. 84). Specifically, subjects were asked to consider four issues and to respond to each on a scale that ranged from "extremely positive" to "extremely negative":

1. Their own contribution to the relationship.
2. Their partner's contribution to the relationship.
3. Their own outcomes from the relationship.
4. Their partner's outcomes from the relationship.

Information gathered from this questionnaire allowed Walster et al. (1978) to identify subjects who thought they were being inequitably "underbenefitted," equitably treated, or inequitably "overbenefitted." In addition, the respondents completed a second questionnaire which asked how content, happy, angry, and guilty their relationship made them feel. Finally, subjects' perceptions of the stability of their relationship were tapped by a third questionnaire (For example, "How certain are you that the two of you will be together five years from now?") (p. 86). Moreover, the researchers contacted these respondents three-and-one-half months after the initial administration of the questionnaires to measure how their relationship had fared over that period of time.

Results of this study provided strong support for the hypothesis that perceived equity contributes to the satisfaction and stability of a relationship at the commitment stage. Subjects who perceived that they were being equitably treated were more content and happy and less angry and guilty than were subjects who perceived themselves to be either underbenefitted or overbenefitted in their relationship. Moreover, subjects who viewed their relationship as equitable perceived it to be more stable, and were more likely to feel at the time of the followup that they would continue to be involved with their partner. Clearly, equity in the distribution of the costs and rewards experienced in their interactions with their partner had a major influence on subjects' evaluations of their relationship and its stability over time.

Concluding Remarks about Commitment

From our remarks, it should be clear that it is at the commitment stage that strong Sentimental attachment tends to form in an evolving relationship. To consider another a close friend or lover is to acknowledge a strong attachment to that person. Thus, one of the indications that a relationship has developed into the commitment stage is the realization that the interactants really care about one another. The role relationships which emerge to bring people to this stage serve to insure that mutually rewarding behaviors are expressed with some regularity and predictability. Moreover, the emergence of such role relationships suggests that the interactants have incorporated a set of mutually accepted beliefs about appropriate conduct in the relationship. This is not to suggest that impingement does not occur within even the most intimate relationships; rather, the incorporation of mutually shared norms, as Thibaut and Kelley (1959) note, tends to minimize the necessity of resorting to such influence tactics, and thus, facilitates positive outcomes for both parties.

In addition to Sentiment and Control, Valuation is also relevant to the commitment phase of interpersonal relationships. As noted in Chapter 9, Valuation is an integral part of equity, which involves decisions about the relative investments made, and returns obtained, in a relationship. As Walster et al. (1978) observe, contributions or investments can range from physical attractiveness to shows of sympathy, while rewards can include such diverse items as emotional support, sexual gratification, or material gain. The weights that are accorded to investments and outcomes vary across individuals, and thus, different people can come to very different conclusions regarding the fairness of their relationship, even when the objective reality of their situations are similar. Equity, like beauty, is in the eyes of the beholder.

When a relationship evolves into commitment and continues for a reasonable length of time, the parties to the interaction, as well as observers of it, can begin to perceive the actors less as individuals, and more as a single social entity. While people can remain at the commitment stage of a relationship more or less permanently, it is often the case that the repeated associations which commitment entails will operate to induce the perception of a unit bond. The evolution of the relationship to the point where the interactants are perceived as a single entity (that is, as forming a unit relationship) is the defining feature of the final phase of liking and loving, which Secord and Backman (1974) have termed *institutionalization*.

STAGE 4: INSTITUTIONALIZATION

Institutionalization is the most advanced stage of a liking and loving relationship. When a pair (either friends or lovers) is perceived to have formed a unit relationship, such that it is difficult to think of one of the parties without also thinking of the other, the relationship has matured to its fullest. This is not to say that further changes cannot take place. For example, as will be discussed, even the closest of friends or lovers can drift apart or can part company completely. Moreover, the focus of a close relationship can change although it remains institutionalized. As discussed earlier, Walster and Walster (1978) distinguish between passionate and companionate love. It is often the case that couples shift from passionate love, which typically straddles the commitment and institutionalization phases, to companionate love, a less exciting but more enduring Sentimental bond.

Of course, it is possible for the opposite shift to occur, at least for a time. It is sometimes the case that people form close personal (companionate) relationships which endure for many years before any passionate feelings emerge. An example of such a shift is given in the classic folktale of the girl nextdoor, who for years is treated as "one of the boys," but is suddenly viewed by one of the real boys in a considerably different light. If Walster and Walster's (1978) speculations are correct, however, it is probable that even this type of Sentimental relationship would become less intense after a time and would return to a companionate form. The research on Sentimental attachment in married couples, cited earlier (Cimbalo et al., 1976; Driscoll

Institutionalization occurs when two people form a unit relationship.

et al., 1972), has provided evidence that such changes do, in fact, occur, even in highly satisfying institutionalized relationships.

Even more than in the other stages, Sentiment plays a dominant role in the institutionalized relationship. As noted early in this chapter, as well as in Chapter 2, two of the major consequences of Sentimental attachment are the formation of a unit relationship and a concern for the welfare of the other. Whether the Sentiment is identified as passionate or companionate, people attach this emotion to the person with whom they share the institutionalized relationship, and it is this feeling that serves as the basis for the formation of the unit bond. Moreover, it is during the institutionalized stage that one's own welfare is most strongly linked to the well-being of the other. In part, this sense of mutual welfare is due to the perceived unit relationship which characterizes this final stage of liking and loving, but it is due, as well, to the perception that a strong Sentimental bond has generated a sense of shared fate. People involved in an institutionalized relationship might sink or swim, but they do so together. Such a state is inherent in being marriage partners, blood brothers, etc.

Concluding Remarks about Institutionalization

It is important to note that many of the processes that we have presented as relevant to earlier phases of liking and loving continue to exert an influence in the institutionalized stage. In part, this is true because there are no clear-cut boundaries between adjacent stages of attraction; it is rarely the case that one goes to sleep in the bargaining stage and awakes committed. Rather, elements of both stages tend to coexist for a period of time, and only gradually do the defining features of an earlier stage fade in relative importance, to be supplanted by the processes that characterize the next stage. Even under these circumstances, many of the processes (physical attractiveness, belief similarity, and so on) that are primarily associated with one stage exert some influence in other stages as well.

Perhaps the most clear-cut example of a process whose influence is felt across the stages of liking and loving is Valuation, especially when judgments involve the CLalt (the person's estimate of the rewards available in his or her most favorable alternative relationship). At any stage, considerations of available alternatives can influence the stability of a relationship. During first encounters, the CLalt often is based on rather superficial aspects of the available options; at later stages, such judgments tend to be more thoughtful, and the alternatives clearly must be more compelling to support a termination of the present relationship.

However, even the most institutionalized of relationships can end because one or both of the parties to it perceives an alternative that is more attractive. As Walster and Walster (1978) note, the stimulus for considering potential alternatives is often simply the realization that inequities have developed over the course of the relationship. In such instances, the disadvantaged member of the relationship is likely to initiate a search for more attractive alternatives.

White (1980, 1981) has provided evidence to support our observations that the processes which moderate the evolution of liking and loving can operate at any stage of these relationships. For example, he found that differences in the physical attractiveness of couples who were romantically involved (that is, the interactants were dating one another exclusively) was negatively associated with the stability of the relationship. Thus, even among couples who had reached the commitment stage of a loving relationship, the greater the difference in physical attractiveness—a variable discussed mainly within the framework of sampling and estimation—the greater the likelihood that the relationship would fail. Moreover, White also notes that even among couples who were at the institutionalized stage, there was a realization that dissatisfaction (that is, perceived inequity) could lead to a search for more attractive alternatives. Other research (Shafer & Keith, 1980; Walster, Traupmann & Walster, 1978) has yielded results that are consistent with those of White (1981). In their research, for example, Walster et al. (1978) found that people who perceived themselves to be disadvantaged in their marriage relationship were the most likely to sample the CLalt by engaging in extramarital liasons.

CLalt and perceived inequity are only two of a number of variables that can contribute to the dissolution of a liking and loving relationship. Secord and Backman (1974) present a more comprehensive list of these destructive influences, which we will now summarize.

TERMINATING THE RELATIONSHIP

Change in Reward/Cost Ratio. The first factor which Secord and Backman (1974) hypothesize as contributing to the termination of a liking or loving relationship involves changes in the ratio of rewards to the costs that one must bear in providing another with sought-after outcomes, or in eliciting a valuable outcome for oneself. When the ratio of rewards to costs changes appreciably in a relationship, the relative value of the CLalt increases. For example, in some relationships, the outcomes that once were highly valued become somewhat commonplace, if not boring. Or, consider the case of the spouse who must continually bolster the other's fragile ego. The continuous call for compliments, coupled with a need to guard against even hinting at a negative evaluation, can prove increasingly costly.

Another source of change in the reward/cost ratio involves a shift in the Personal Structures of the interactants. While not an everyday occurrence, people's needs and motives can change as they mature and enter new phases of their lives. For example, it is almost a cliché that medical students form intimate relationships with people who can provide nurturance and a sense of security that is very valuable, given the pressures that their training entails. Once their training is complete, however, the need for such care is considerably diminished, and a relationship that can offer few other rewarding outcomes

"When I met Pierce his obliqueness was his charm. Now his obliqueness is driving me bananas."

Outcomes and traits that once were rewarding sometimes can lose their positive value.

is likely to dissolve. A related point concerns the change in the Social Context in which the relationship has evolved. In the example of the medical student, the change in contexts—from impoverished student housing to a plush suburban estate, from school to medical practice, and so on—helps to diminish the value of the other's contributions.

Change in comparison level. As noted in Chapter 9, people tend to hold beliefs about the minimal rewards that are expected for a given contribution, and these expectations have a strong influence on their judgments of equity. Thibaut and Kelley (1959) have termed this standard of minimally acceptable rewards the *comparison level* (CL). They speculate that when a person's CL is not met, he or she feels dissatisfied, a reaction that is likely to lead to consideration of the CLalt. Thibaut and Kelley (1959) also suggest that people tend to increase their CL as the rewards in a relationship increase. In other words, the more we receive, the more we expect. Thus, a highly rewarding intimate relationship can contain within itself the seeds of its own demise if the interactants expect a continuing escalation of positive outcomes. Such an unfortunate state of affairs is common when people find themselves shifting from passionate to companionate love. The intense physical rewards of the passionate love state can generate a CL that is difficult to satisfy, especially when the relationship shifts to the companionate state, which provides less intense but more enduring satisfactions.

It seems incongruous to end an extended discussion of liking and loving on such a sour note—the termination of relationships. Such a pessimistic tone is not meant to imply that all relationships eventually find their way to the scrap heap. While people often do disentangle themselves from relationships, many relationships endure for years, even decades. For example, some individuals remain very close to their childhood friends, and many people remain happily married for all of their adult lives.

Moreover, when a relationship ends, people tend not to become social isolates, but instead pursue other relationships. Thus, the termination of one relationship might signal—or be caused by—the beginning of another.

The social nature of human beings prevents us from long enduring an isolated existence, since so many of our positive outcomes are dependent on the behavior of others. On the other hand, many of our most negative outcomes are also a consequence of the actions of others. In the next chapter, we will discuss in detail two major sources of such negative outcomes—prejudice and hate.

Interpersonal Repulsion: Prejudice and Hate 13

In this final chapter, we will discuss interpersonal repulsion, a topic that draws upon much of the material presented previously in this text. In Section 2, we presented a detailed summary of what social psychologists have learned about opinions and impressions, and we discussed the manner in which these important beliefs influence overt behavior. In the previous chapter of this section, we reviewed research that has explored the formation of positive interpersonal relationships and Sentimental attachments. In the present chapter, we will examine the interplay between beliefs and negative interpersonal relationships. The distinction that we make between beliefs and feelings should serve to further the understanding of the antecedents and consequences of some of our less attractive social reactions—prejudice and hate. This distinction, which we have emphasized throughout the text, allows us to differentiate between dislike of a specific person (a negative emotional reaction), and the negative evaluation of a person (an impression) or of a social aggregate (an opinion).[1]

Prejudicial Opinions

Negative opinions about social aggregates have a number of interesting features. First, traits, characteristics, and qualities become associated with the specific identifying cue (or cues) that defines membership in the aggregate. These traits are called stereotypes. For example, among the traditional stereo-

---

[1] As noted earlier, a *social aggregate* is a set of people who are perceived as possessing some common identifiable characteristic—physical appearance, religious or political beliefs, occupation, ethnic heritage, and so on.

typic traits that are associated with the aggregate of woman are nurturance, passivity, and emotionality.

A second important aspect of prejudicial opinions about aggregates is that they rarely permit exceptions. Thus, people who hold such opinions typically assume that all members of the aggregate possess the stereotyped trait. A common finding of public opinion polls, for example, is that a large number of persons in this country (both men and women) would not vote for a female candidate for president, nor for a male candidate whose vice-presidential running mate was female. Why not? When asked, such people often respond that women are too weak-willed and emotional to hold an office that carries with it so heavy a burden of responsibility. These people are basically saying that no woman exists who is an exception to the traditional (stereotyped) characterization of women—that *all* women are emotional and passive. These people appear to believe that if there are exceptions to this generalization, they are so rare that they are not worth considering.

A third interesting feature of opinions about aggregates concerns their operation in the impression formation process. Basically, such opinions can serve as heavily weighted cues in the formation of an impression about a person who is a member of that aggregate. Such opinions are *biasing,* since they color people's perceptions and interpretations of their experiences with members of the aggregate. When the evaluation is negative, such biased opinions are called *prejudice.* For example, we might have an extremely negative opinion about the aggregate of people who share a common biological gender—females. When introduced to an individual whom we perceive to be a member of this aggregate, our prejudicial belief can affect our actions toward her, our evaluation of the total encounter, and our specific impression of her.[2]

A number of years ago, for example, in a committee formed to promote the presidential ambitions of the late Senator Hubert Humphrey, a member of that committee voiced the view that Humphrey should not choose a woman as his vice presidential running mate, because women are too emotional to stand up to the rigors of the job. When another member of the committee (a woman) vigorously objected to this obviously prejudicial belief, the holder of the opinion pointed to the woman's response as proof of his position— he interpreted her strong reaction to his remarks as evidence that women, in general, could not be trusted to maintain their composure in stressful conditions. This person would no doubt have viewed an angry response by a male to a similar insult as an appropriate reaction to an unwarranted provocation, not as evidence of the general emotionality of men.

Thomas Pettigrew (1979) has discussed the fact that similar behaviors expressed by different people are interpreted differently as a consequence of the stereotypes that are associated with the aggregate to which these people belong. He noted that stereotypes affect the cue selection process in impression

---

[2] This general process has been discussed in detail in Chapter 8.

formation.[3] When a person's behavior is consistent with our stereotypes (for example, when a woman shows anger in response to an insult), the behavior is taken as indicative of the person's Personal Structure ("She's so emotional!"). When the same behavior is inconsistent with the stereotype, it tends to be viewed as a response to contextual rather than personal factors ("He was really provoked!").

Other social psychologists (Deaux, 1976; Hamilton, 1979) have also discussed the role that stereotypes play in cue selection, and there is empirical evidence that supports this observation. For example, Taylor and Jaggi (1974) conducted a study in India that first asked respondents, all of whom were members of the Hindu religion, their beliefs about Muslims. Not surprisingly, the researchers found that respondents tended to share a negative opinion toward Muslims that was expressed in their willingness to associate a large number of unfavorable traits with members of this aggregate.

These respondents were then asked to evaluate a number of individuals who were described to them in a series of paragraphs. These descriptions, which varied regarding the desirability of the behaviors depicted, sometimes mentioned that the actor was a Muslim. After respondents read a paragraph, they were presented with several possible explanations for the actor's behavior and were asked to choose the most probable explanation. Consistent with the speculations of Pettigrew (1979), Hamilton (1979), and Deaux (1976), Taylor and Jaggi (1974) found that the Hindu respondents were likely to perceive Muslim actors as personally responsible for negative behaviors, whereas their positive behaviors were attributed to situational factors.

Prejudice and Impressions

As we have stressed throughout this text, impressions and opinions have a great deal in common with respect to the processes that determine their development and expression. However, while both are forms of evaluative beliefs, there are sufficient differences in their expression to warrant distinguishing between them. Perhaps the most important difference in the operation of the processes that affect these two types of evaluations concerns the degree of direct experience that a person has with the object of the belief.

In most cases, when we form an impression of a specific individual, we have had a certain degree of direct experience with that person. Of course, impressions can be formed entirely on the basis of no direct experience, but such evaluations typically represent only a preliminary stage in the impression formation process. For example, we can form an impression of another that is based totally on information provided by a trusted source. Such information can create an initial expectation through which we may later interpret more direct experiences with the object of the impression.

On the other hand, high level opinions can be formed on the basis of

---

[3] An extended discussion of cue selection as a process of impression formation has been presented in Chapter 7.

little or no direct experience, although this is probably not a common occurrence. An individual, that is, might have an extremely negative opinion about a social aggregate with which he or she has never interacted. For example, years ago when the Ku Klux Klan was a powerful social force in this country, a typical Klan member's attitude toward Jews was probably based on very little direct experience with members of that aggregate. In general, however, such opinions were quite central and were expressed in such actions as making inflammatory speeches, sending hate mail, and burning crosses. Most evaluative beliefs are probably based on a composite of both direct and indirect experience. It is likely to be the case that impressions have a large direct experience component, relative to opinions.

Second, as noted in Chapter 1, people's specific impressions are sometimes inconsistent with their general opinions. We all know from personal experience and direct observation that people who hold strong negative opinions toward a given aggregate (such as black people) can nonetheless possess a positive impression of a specific member of that aggregate (Ervin "Magic" Johnson). Such anomolies suggest that we cannot accurately predict people's opinions about an aggregate from all of their separate impressions about specific persons

NATIONAL ARCHIVES

A real-life example of the profound impact of racial prejudice. Shortly after Pearl Harbor, the United States government herded citizens of Japanese descent into internment camps "for reasons of national security." Yet, a similar fate did not befall German-Americans.

who are members of the aggregate; nor can we predict from their overall opinions people's impressions of a specific member of the aggregate. While both types of evaluative belief can be of a high level, and thus both can strongly influence actions, they are not always consistent.

As with all Inconsistencies, the lack of correspondence between a specific impression and a more general opinion is potentially aversive, and therefore, must be resolved. Such opinion-impression discrepancies can be explored in the framework of dissonance theory (discussed at length in Chapter 5). In such cases, the Inconsistency between an impression and its corresponding opinion is potentially dissonance-arousing. Robert Abelson (1959) has discussed a number of tactics that people employ to deal with, or reduce, such aversive states. For example, we might differentiate the favorably evaluated individual from his or her negatively evaluated aggregate; or, we simply might deny—even in the face of overwhelming contrary evidence—that the person actually belongs to the aggregate. It is through such processes that we reduce the cognitive stress (dissonance) that arises in the face of inconsistent opinions and impressions. It is important to note that regardless of how they are resolved, these Inconsistencies arise because the Personal Structure encompasses very different types of beliefs (impressions and opinions, as well as norms).

In the following discussion of the development and consequences of negative impressions and opinions, we will examine the antecedents and consequences of negative Sentiment relationships which, in their most extreme form, we label *hatred*. In the second section of the chapter, we will discuss some important issues in the social psychology of *prejudicial opinions*. Throughout our discussion, while we note the importance of the five integrative themes to understanding dislike and prejudice, the central role of Sentiment is emphasized.

We have discussed the potential impact that prejudicial opinions can have on our impressions of others. Of course, not all—perhaps not even most—negative impressions are the result of prejudicial opinions. We can form a negative evaluation of someone despite the person's membership in all of the "right" aggregates. Why? Because, as noted, impressions are heavily weighted by direct experience with the specific object of the impression. In the next section, we will discuss negative impressions from the perspective of their consequences for the development of negative emotional feelings. We will begin this discussion by exploring once again the distinction between beliefs—which are evaluative cognitions—and Sentiments—which have a large emotional component.

NEGATIVE INTERPERSONAL RELATIONSHIPS

Negative Impressions and Repulsion

In Chapter 12, we discussed the distinction between impressions and attraction. Because this issue is also central to the concerns of the present chapter, we will provide a brief recapitulation of the major points of our earlier remarks. In our perspective, the concept of belief—whether it be opinion, impression, or norm—is entirely cognitive in nature; that is, beliefs are thoughts that are independent of any emotional component, although emotions may become attached to them. Thus, it is theoretically possible to have a negative impression of someone (a belief) without any accompanying emotional response. In most cases, of course, there is some degree of Sentiment attached to our beliefs; however, we view this attachment as a common, but not inevitable, consequence of the manner in which human beings evaluate the people and objects in their social world.

The extent to which emotion is attached to a belief is one of the major determinants of the level of the belief. Low level beliefs are low level in large part due to their lack of emotional attachment. For example, we often evaluate very differently the various people in the social groups to which we belong (the faculty of a department of psychology, members of a country club, a work group, and so on). In many instances, these Valuations carry little, if any, emotional attachments; in other instances, a great deal of emotion is connected to these cognitions. We might, for example, have a negative impression about one of our colleagues, but we might not actively dislike this person—that is, we are emotionally indifferent, although, due to our impression, we can still express a negative evaluation about this person. In such cases, our actions would be relatively uninfluenced by our impression. Conversely, we might also have a considerable degree of negative emotion attached to our negative evaluation (or impression) of another of our colleagues. In this case, this high level belief would have a strong influence on the ways in which we behave toward this person.

In contrast to impressions, Sentiments always contain an emotional component—in fact, emotion is the defining feature of Sentiment—although, as noted, they have a cognitive component as well. Negative Sentimental responses have been termed *repulsion* because this word captures the motivational properties of "moving away from," or "moving against," which such emotional reactions tend to produce.

Processes of Dislike

The processes that generate repulsion are very much the same as those that lead to positive Sentiment bonds. Perhaps the major distinction between these processes is the relative time necessary to form the bond. As noted in Chapters 2 and 12, most of our positive Sentimental relationships develop over a relatively long period of time. While the acute formation of positive interpersonal bonds does occur, these reactions tend to be transitory unless some long-term processes of support complement the initial reaction.

On the other hand, it is likely that strong negative Sentiment bonds develop much more rapidly since we tend to avoid encounters with people who generate negative Sentiments in us. The repetitive associations which produce positive Sentiment attachment tend not to occur among people who find an encounter aversive. Thus, the few experiences that characterize the (usually rapid) development of repulsion or dislike of necessity must produce extremely negative outcomes.

This speculation suggests that the circumstances under which such Sentiments are generated are usually so aversive that they are avoided whenever possible. Under these conditions, the possibility of experiencing more positive outcomes with the disliked person is appreciably reduced. Hence, the dislike can be expected to persist, as no forces operate to diminish these feelings.

Initial Encounters

As discussed in Chapters 2, 7, and 12, initial encounters play a major role in the formation of interpersonal bonds, since the impressions and feelings that form as a result of these encounters weigh heavily in the Valuation processes that determine the course of the developing relationship. Much of our discussion in this text has been framed in terms of positive relationships; the same factors that moderate the formation of positive Sentiment bonds in the initial encounter can also produce feelings of dislike or repulsion. Thus, readily perceived cues—physical appearance, superficial sociability, signs of socially valued or devalued traits and so on—interact with the perceiver's expectations about the person encountered, and together they influence both the negative encounter itself and the negative reactions that are the product of that experience.

Rather than review the material on initial encounters that has been presented, it is more useful at this point to focus on variables in the initial encounter that seem to be of special importance to the development of negative interpersonal bonds. Perhaps because of the aversive properties of repulsion, these variables appear to center on two issues—*trauma* and *expectations.*

Trauma. *Trauma* refers to extremely acute and intense—often shockingly so—negative experiences with another person. For example, the reader might imagine having the misfortune of experiencing a time warp—you are sent back to the pre–Civil War South. Such an experience could prove to be interesting, but—just your luck—you happen to land on Simon Legree's plantation at the precise moment that he is viciously beating one of his slaves. We would hypothesize that you would be so shocked by this violation of your basic sense of humanity that your impression of—and thus your negative reaction toward—Legree would be intensely negative. Under such circumstances, it seems highly doubtful that this hatred would ever be undone, since you would probably avoid any further interaction with this individual. Under such conditions of no contact, there would be little opportunity for you to encounter ameliorative factors that would cause you to modify your sense of repulsion for Legree.

Trauma can involve issues other than the violation of a basic norm. Such issues can include the perception that the other purposely and capriciously frustrated a very important goal or need of ours, or willfully harmed someone with whom we had a positive Sentiment relationship. In any event, trauma must involve the violation or frustration of one or more high level elements in our Personal Structures (beliefs, motives, norms, and so forth). Most of us are fortunate not to have experienced an extreme trauma of this type, and thus have not experienced its consequence—*hatred* of another. But trauma is not an either-or phenomenon; there are degrees of trauma, and most of us have experienced this type of negative encounter at least to some extent. These more moderate negative encounters result in the formation of less intense, but nevertheless real, negative Sentiments.

Expectations. A second variable that seems especially relevant to the development of negative reactions in an initial encounter is *expectation*—the preconception that we bring into the situation that biases our perceptions of the objective Social Context in which the encounter occurs. The general impact of expectations on social behavior and incorporation was discussed in Chapter 8, when we presented the work of Rosenthal and Jacobson (1968), Broussard (1978), and other relevant research. In the present section, we will focus on one very important basis for negative expectations: *stigma*. Stigmata are cues in people that, within a specific cultural context, connote defect or inferiority. In its most extreme form, a stigma suggests that the person possessing this cue or quality is something less than human. Erving Goffman has been most responsible for the systematic exploration of the impact of stigma on social behavior (Goffman, 1963).

Examples of stigmata in our society include almost any cue that connotes physical or psychological deviance from the cultural norm: psychotic symptomology, physical handicaps and anomalies, symptoms of mental retardation, obesity, nonstandard sexual perferences, indications of membership in devalued racial or ethnic groups, poverty, and so on. A common denominator of these stigmata is the ease with which they can be perceived. While some of these cues are more apparent than others (another's race is often easier to detect than another's sexual preference), the operative factor here is that the perceiver associates the identifying cues with other attributes, and assumes—often without any logical basis—that the stigmatized individual possesses these additional traits as well.

For example, we might (wrongly) assume that a person who shows obvious symptoms of mental retardation also is dangerous. It goes without saying that such an assumption would affect the way in which we interact with the individual and, of course, our impression of him or her.

There are similarities between stigma and the concepts of prejudice and stereotyping. Traditionally, prejudice and stereotyping have been discussed within the framework of racial and ethnic opinions. The concept of stigma broadens this topic to a whole realm of attributes which a culture defines as inferior. The principles that operate in the formation of prejudicial opinions and their results are the same as those that moderate the formation, attachment, and impact of stigma.

Research on the influence of stigma has provided a number of interesting illustrations of the manner in which cues affect behavior in initial social

Physical handicaps such as blindness often affect people's interaction with such "stigmatized" individuals.

encounters. For example, Chevigny (1946) noted a curious feature of the behavior of sighted people when they interact with a blind person. Although there is no reason to assume that there is anything wrong with the hearing of blind people, sighted people who talk with them typically speak loudly, and in their presence talk about them to others as if they could not hear what was being said. Why? This behavior may possibly occur because the sighted speakers generalize one perceptual handicap to other sensory systems. In any case, they do so in spite of the common folk wisdom that blind people have more acute hearing than do the sighted. Similarly, other research has shown that people tend to stand farther away than they otherwise would when talking to a stigmatized person, or they attempt to avoid such encounters completely (Kleck, 1969; Kleck, Buck, Goller, London, Pfeiffer, & Vukcevic, 1968; Snyder, Kleck, Strenta, & Mentzer, 1979; Worthington, 1974).

In one study that produced evidence of the negative impact of stigmata on interpersonal relationships, Kleck, Ono, and Hastorf (1966) had subjects play the role of an interviewer. All interviewers were to question another subject (actually an experimental accomplice). For half these subjects, the accomplice appeared to be an amputee confined to a wheelchair; for the other subjects, this same person was confronted, but in this condition, he obviously was not physically handicapped. Systematic coding of the interviews indicated that subjects were more brusque, asked fewer questions, and generally were more formal in the condition in which they encountered the apparently handicapped respondent.[4]

Similar findings of the effect of perceived stigma have also been encountered when dealing with the effects of race. For example, in a study involving black and white nursery school children, Harrison, Messé, and Stollak (1971) had sets of four subjects, who were strangers to one another, play together around a table filled with attractive toys. In some conditions, all four children were of the same race; in another condition, two of the children were black, and two were white. Systematic observation of these encounters revealed that the children of the mixed-race groups interacted with one another significantly less than did their counterparts in the same-race groups.

These findings suggest that even young children are aware of racial differences and that, more importantly, these differences have a major impact on their social behavior. The subjects were thrust into a situation that must have been at least somewhat anxiety-evoking. They were in a strange environment, and they knew that they were being observed; in the mixed-race groups, additional stress might have been aroused in the subjects because they were aware that "someone different" was playing at the same table as they. This awareness and the added arousal that it caused apparently inhibited their social behavior. Other research (Weitz, 1972; Word, Zanna, & Cooper, 1974) has demonstrated that race similarly affects interpersonal behavior in young adults.

This point has more general implications for understanding the negative consequences of stigma in interpersonal relations. We often find ourselves in situations in which we are not sure what consititutes the appropriate behavior. Such poorly resolved contexts are not pleasant—indeed, we find them negatively arousing, since they often generate such aversive feelings as embarrassment, shyness, and shame. Situations involving stigmatized others typically generate such uncertainty and ambivalence in us, not because we are callous or cruel, but because we are not experienced with such individuals. These aversive emotions, generated by the uncertainty of the Social Context, become associated with the specific stigmatized person that we are encountering and, in turn, can be generalized to the aggregate of which the stigmatized individual is a member. As such, our initial reaction to that person—and therefore to the general class of people of whom he or she is representative—is often negative. When such negative associations occur, we tend to avoid further contact with that person and with similar others, if possible.

Goffman (1963) made a similar point in his discussion of stigma. He noted that, perhaps because of our feelings of unease, we attempt to impose an unusual degree of structure on our encounters with stigmatized people—that is, we force them to conform to our expectations of what they should

---

[4] The reader may note the similarity of these results with those of the Messé et al. (1979) study, summarized in Chapter 8, which demonstrated the effects on social behavior of more general negative perceptual biases.

be like. If we expect that handicapped people are inept and in need of our help, we then structure our encounters with them in such a way that these outcomes are likely to occur.

Autistic Hostility. To this point in our presentation we have alluded to the idea that people will avoid those encounters that promise to produce aversive feelings in them. If we have formed a negative expectation or impression of another person, we attempt, insofar as possible, to avoid interacting with that person. Newcomb (1947) has labeled this tendency *autistic hostility*. A major consequence of autistic hostility for interpersonal relations is that it limits the possibility of changing our impressions or feelings about the initially disliked person. As with other expectations, autistic hostility, in a sense, has a life of its own—that is, because such an expectation generates avoidance responses, there often are few opportunities to experience events that might counteract the negative expectation. If one assumes that an encounter is going to be unpleasant and thus avoids it, the assumption will never be tested.

Another major feature of autistic hostility is that the expectation need not be accurate—that is, the prediction of a negative interaction with another may be completely unfounded—but for the actor, it nonetheless operates as a powerful influence on behavior. Like other expectations and impressions (see Chapter 8), autistic hostility can act as a self-fulfilling prophecy—that is, when actors expect to find themselves in an unpleasant encounter, and cannot avoid it, they will structure the encounter so that it does, indeed, result in an aversive reaction in them.

In their study (summarized in Chapter 8), Snyder, Tanke, and Berscheid (1977) paired males and females and asked them to "get acquainted" via a telephone conversation. Because they were led to believe that their partner was unattractive, some of the males acted coldly and indifferently toward them. The targets of this behavior responded in kind. Thus, the interaction was unpleasant for both, just as the males had expected it would be after having seen the picture of the unattractive person with whom they supposedly were paired.

Although autistic hostility often involves an element of self-defeating behavior, as it did for the subjects in the Synder et al. (1977) research, there is more to it than this. For the subjects of this research, as in many real-life instances, the outcome of the encounter was caused by an expectation of forthcoming events that had nothing to do with what might actually have occurred in the absence of this expectation. The fundamental locus of the negative arousal was not the Social Context, but the subjects' own Personal Structures. The target of the autistic hostility had not set the negative tone of the interaction, although she ultimately might have contributed to the unpleasantness of the encounter.

Another facet of autistic hostility is illustrated in this research—namely, the fact that the expectation need not be based on any direct, prior experiences with the other person. While autistic hostility often results from negative initial encounters, this is not always the case. Stigmata, rumors and innuendoes, photographs, and other indirect sources of information often play a role in the development of such expectations.

Reversals and Conversions

Reversals. One of the more intriguing sources of negative Sentiment bonds is the phenomenon which we call reversal. In a reversal, a previously strong (high level) positive bond changes to an equally strong negative bond. Such reversals of Sentiment usually occur as a result of a traumatic interpersonal encounter. In literature—as well as in real life—some of the most classic reversals involve the theme of the scorned lover. In this situation, an individual, for whatever reason, feels a strong positive attachment to another. But when he or she discloses this attachment, the other person rejects the overture. Often, the person who was scorned in this manner will find that strong repulsion has replaced strong attachment.

A similar theme involves the betrayed lover. In this circumstance, a strong mutual interpersonal bond has already been established, but one of the pair acts in such a way as to violate the fundamental norms (or other beliefs) that have been established between them. When this occurs, a frequent consequence is that the betrayed person's positive Sentiment for the violator is reversed, and turns to hatred. There are, in addition, combinations of betrayal and scorn which probably exacerbate the reversal effect.

A straightforward illustration of this phenomenon was depicted in the movie, *An Unmarried Woman*. In a scene early in the movie, the husband tells his wife that he is leaving her for a younger woman with whom he has been consorting for some time. The wife, taken completely by surprise—this confession occurs in broad daylight in the middle of a busy street in Manhattan—vomits. This physical symptom of revulsion is soon followed by the development of more psychological but equally intense negative reactions toward her husband. The once positive Sentiment that she felt is reversed and becomes hate.

How do such reversals occur? How can a very positive Sentiment be instantly turned into repulsion? We believe that the reversal process is primarily the result of a relabeling of the physiological component of one of our emotions. In Chapter 2 and elsewhere, we have discussed the importance of cognition in the identification of emotional responses. In the case of a reversal, the cognition that formerly identified the physiological change as positive is modified. What was once felt as pleasant is now defined as painful and aversive. This reversal process is therefore a cognitive process that is tried to basic physiological events.

Given the intensity of the feelings involved in the reversal effect, systematic demonstrations of this phenomenon would be very difficult to produce within the confines of the social psychological laboratory. However, the general process of mislabeling as a function of the contrast between present and past experiences with another—which is a major part of our explanation

In the movie, "An Unmarried Woman," the wife's reaction to her husband's confession of infidelity is an example of reversal, in which positive Sentiment is transformed into repulsion.

of Sentiment reversal—has been produced in the laboratory in at least a mild form. For example, Clore, Wiggins, and Itkin (1975) showed subjects videotapes of a female (actually an actress) interacting with an unseen male. In one condition, subjects saw the woman act rather coldly toward the other— that is, she frowned, looked distracted when he was speaking, and so forth. In another condition, subjects observed her initially display warm behaviors (smiling, head nodding, and so on), and then begin to act more coldly. Subjects in both conditions were asked to estimate the favorability of the male's reaction to the woman with whom they had observed him talking.

Clore et al. found that subjects estimated the male to be less positive toward the actress when she had begun warmly and then had shifted to a more cold and formal attitude toward him than when she had consistently behaved in a cold manner. A reasonable interpretation of these results is that subjects assumed that the male had reacted positively to the initially warm female; however, when the female "turned cold," the subjects assumed that his positive feelings would reverse, and his reaction at this point would be even more negative than that of the male who had interacted with a consistently cold female. Other research (e.g., Aronson & Linder, 1965) has yielded similar results.

While our discussion of reversals has involved changes from positive to negative Sentiment, it should be noted that the opposite progression is also possible. Such positive reversals (turning hate to love) are less likely, however, because (1) we are less likely to interact with someone we dislike intensely; and (2) most positive actions do not carry with them trauma or shock value, as do many negative behaviors.

Conversions. Reversals involve Sentiments and interpersonal relations. This phenomenon has its analogue in opinion change, and we have termed this parallel process conversion. In our usage, conversion refers to the complete reevaluation of an object of opinion, with an appropriate change in the accompanying emotional reaction to the belief. This definition is consistent with the more global view of Zimbardo et al. (1977, p. 182), who observe, "Conversion is a change process in which a person gives up one ordered view of the world and one philosophical perspective for another."

One of history's most famous conversions occurred on the road to Damascus when Saul of Tarsus was struck from his horse and arose as St. Paul. In his life to that point, Saul was—to use a present-day colloquial term—a real hell-raiser. This dissolute young man, who enjoyed his occupation of persecuting Christians, for some miraculous reason shifted his opinion about the pleasures of the flesh from very positive to very negative. Thus an Olympic-class sinner became one of the major pillars of the ascetic force in Christianity.

Just as the emotion attached to high level impressions can be relabeled in the reversal process, so too can the emotion linked to high level opinions. In the latter case, conversion occurs. There is one other major distinction between reversal and conversion in addition to their locus of belief. Often, reversals occur as isolated events which do not extend beyond the specific beliefs associated with the object of the reversal. On the other hand, as Zimbardo et al. (1977) have noted, conversions usually have consequences for the entire belief system—that is, along with the dramatic change in the focal opinion, many other, equally dramatic changes in beliefs also occur. For example, after his fall from the horse, Paul did not merely reevaluate debauchery; he also changed his evaluation of Christianity from very negative to very positive, and he dramatically modified his opinions about many other issues as well. While such conversions are not commonplace, they can occur, and when they do they have a tremendous impact on beliefs and subsequent actions.

A more modern, and perhaps less extreme, instance of conversion is provided by the change in beliefs that occurred for many American supporters of the Communist Party in the 1930s. At that time, as a consequence of their beliefs, these people actively attempted to mobilize public opinion in this country against the threat that they (accurately, as it turned out) perceived in Hitler's Germany. In part, their actions were a response to Hitler's Nazi philosophy, which was virulently anticommunist, and to the Soviet Union's hostile propaganda against the German government.

In the months prior to Germany's invasion of Poland (the formal beginning of World War II), the propaganda apparatus of both Germany and the Soviet Union waged bitter campaigns against the opposing country. You can imagine the reaction of the American communists, however, when, just before the Polish invasion, Russia and Germany entered into a nonaggression pact which pledged that neither country would wage war on the other. Overnight, the established, party-line hatred of Germany was reversed. In a very real sense, Germany was now an ally of the Soviets, and a dramatic shift in Russian propaganda reflected this new reality. As a result of these events, many Americans who previously had sympathized with or actively supported the Communist Party now converted and became radical opponents of communism (but they remained opponents of Nazism as well).

Long-Term Encounters

In the foregoing discussion, we have emphasized the idea that people will often seek to avoid interactions that carry with them the promise of negative outcomes. For this reason, we avoid others whom we dislike. In some circumstances, however, conditions of the Social Context can force us to interact with others whom we dislike or find repulsive—and some of these encounters can be of long duration.

For example, suppose that as a student in a year-long chemistry course, you are assigned a laboratory partner for the full academic year. In other words, the instructor has impinged on you by requiring you to work with this other person on a continuing basis. Suppose that your initial reaction to this person is extremely negative. In this circumstance, a typical response strategy—avoidance—is not possible, since your grade to some extent is dependent on interacting with him. It is in settings of this type that concerns with self-Consistency are likely to be activated ("I don't like this person, so why am I working with him?").

The relationship, as we have described it, would be extremely unstable; there would be a force to change either the Sentiment or the unit bond that existed. In this instance, however, the unit bond (working together in the chemistry laboratory) is difficult to sever (especially if you cannot drop the course, or force your partner to do so). Thus, the major pressure for change would operate to move the Sentiment relationship in a positive direction. In many such instances, changes of this type are observed. Of course, it is also possible that the opposite could occur—that is, the interaction could become increasingly noxious as time passed, cementing and increasing the already negative feelings that have formed. In either case, it is likely that a change would occur. The specific direction of the change in the interpersonal bond, however, is difficult to predict without additional information.

Behavioral Responses to Negative Interpersonal Bonds

We have stressed in this chapter the tendency of people to avoid the unpleasant encounters that often characterize interactions with those whom they dislike. The responses that we have emphasized have been primarily "moving away" (repulsive) in nature—avoidance, withdrawal, ignoring, and so on. There are many other possible, perhaps all too frequent, actions toward disliked others. These actions have a more aggressive ("moving against") component in them. We discussed aggressive or hurting behavior at length in Chapter 10 and therefore will not repeat this material here. In the context of the present chapter, however, two additional points need to be made about hurting behavior.

First, there is a wide range of individual variations in a person's recourse to such reactions when confronted with a disliked other. Our Personal Structures to a great extent determine our typical pattern of reaction—avoidance, verbal aggression, physical violence, and so on. A second point concerns the relative likelihood of an avoidant versus an aggressive reaction to a negative interpersonal encounter. We would speculate that the more active "moving against" (aggressive) responses are more likely in contexts involving long-term, forced interactions; in initial encounters, acts of "moving away" (avoidance) are probably the more frequent outcome of a negative reaction.

SOCIAL PSYCHOLOGICAL ASPECTS OF PREJUDICE

As noted at the beginning of this chapter, prejudice is a negative opinion directed toward some identifiable social aggregate, or *outgroup*. A major component of prejudicial opinions is the assumption that there is little or no variance among the members of the outgroup with regard to their actions, traits, and beliefs. Thus, connected to such opinions are supplementary beliefs (stereotypes) about the attributes and values that the members of the aggregate are assumed to possess. These stereotypic traits are typically evaluated negatively. In combination, the prejudicial opinions—including the stereotypic beliefs—serve to stigmatize the aggregate members. Subscribers to the prejudicial opinions will tend to act toward aggregate members in ways that are different from their typical behaviors toward people who are not stigmatized.

The study of prejudice has occupied the attention of all of the social sciences. In addition to psychology, prejudice has been a focus of inquiry in such diverse disciplines as anthropology, economics, geography, political science, and sociology. Numerous books on prejudice and related topics provide comprehensive summaries of the varied approaches to study in this area (Allport, 1954; Austin & Worchel, 1979; Jones, 1972; LeVine & Campbell, 1972; Rose, 1951; Simpson & Yinger, 1965).

In this text, we have focused on the social psychological treatments of prejudice. In part, we took this tack because the literature surrounding this issue is so massive. Another, perhaps more important reason, however, is our feeling that the more narrow focus which we have adopted is more conducive to understanding the way that prejudice relates to basic, underlying psychological processes. For this latter reason, we will explore in the following sections the relationship between prejudice and a number of other social psychological phenomena to which it is related.

Prejudice and Negative Emotion

Prejudicial opinions usually—but not always—have negative emotional reactions attached to them, and the extent to which this is so affects the importance (level) of the opinion for us. A purely cognitive prejudice, while theoretically possible, would probably have no behavioral implications because of its low level. A related issue concerns the number of supportive beliefs that surround and bolster the prejudicial opinion. The more developed this network of supportive beliefs, the greater the level of the prejudicial opinion, the greater its resistance to counterpressures, the more intense the negative emotion attached to it, and the more likely it is to be expressed in overt actions.

"Noncognitive" Prejudice. In some situations, prejudicial feelings can be aroused in reaction to a member of a stigmatized outgroup without any accompanying negative opinion about the outgroup, per se. In this sense, prejudice can be noncognitive in nature. For example, we may feel uncomfortable in the company of a Martian, but because of a lack of prior encounters with such beings, we may not have any strong opinions on which to base this feeling of unease. We merely feel uncomfortable because we recognize that the other is different from us, and this difference raises questions in our minds about appropriate conduct—that is, this person's presence as part of our interpersonal environment substantially lowers the Resolution of this Social Context for us.

The possibility that people can be emotionally prejudiced without accompanying prejudicial cognitions has been recognized by social psychologists interested in the measurement of this concept. For example, for many years, John Woodmansee and Stuart Cook have worked on the development of measures that could adequately represent the many dimensions of prejudice (Woodmansee & Cook, 1967; Brigham, Woodmansee, & Cook, 1976). In this work, they have uncovered as many as 12 distinct dimensions along which people might differ in terms of their opinions and reactions toward a traditionally stigmatized outgroup (in this research, the opinions measured were those of whites toward blacks). Most relevant to our concerns are two dimensions which they uncovered; one was called *ease in interracial contacts,* while another *(derogatory beliefs)* was focused on more traditional opinions based on stereotypic attributions toward blacks. These subscales are especially relevant to our concerns because they separately measure the two types of prejudice—cognitive and emotional—whose distinction we have discussed and emphasized.

In the research of Woodmansee and his colleagues, three distinct groups of respondents were asked to complete the measure that assessed opinions toward black people. One of these groups was composed of white students who were active in the civil rights movement; another group consisted of white students who were enrolled in a course on minority problems; the third group was composed of students who were members of either radical right-wing political organizations or social fraternities that discriminated against blacks in their admissions policies. These groups were found to differ dramatically in terms of their responses to both the derogatory beliefs and ease in interracial contacts subscales of Woodmansee and Cook's complex measure of prejudice.

As might be expected, the civil rights activists scored as the least prejudiced on both of these subscales, while the right-wing/fraternity group scored the highest. This pattern of results indicates that the scales did identify, with reasonable accuracy, variations in prejudice among respondents. Also of interest was the finding that these two subscales were only moderately related to one another when they were given to a large number of respondents. This result implies that the subscales were measuring different aspects of subjects' prejudice toward blacks. The importance of this finding lies in its implication that we can have derogatory beliefs about a stigmatized aggregate without an accompanying negative emotion. Similarly, it implies that we can feel ill-at-ease when encountering stigmatized persons without holding any high level derogatory opinions about the aggregate of which they are members.

Research of another type also provides indirect support for the idea that there are separable cognitive and emotional dimensions to prejudice. A clever research tactic, which has been termed the *bogus pipeline* (see Jones & Sigall, 1971), was used by Sigall and Page (1971) to measure subjects' stereotypic beliefs. In this research, some subjects merely filled out a questionnaire which assessed the degree to which they thought various stereotypic attributes applied to blacks. Other subjects completed the same questionnaire, but they did so while they were wired to a (bogus) complicated electronic device which (they were told) could measure their "true" positive or negative feelings.

In the latter condition, considerably more prejudicial opinions were expressed on the questionnaire. Why? One obvious reason is that impingements on us often act to suppress prejudicial opinions. In the bogus pipeline condition, however, there was a still stronger impingement on subjects' self-reports—namely, the presence of a machine which they thought could indicate when they were not telling the whole truth.

While this interpretation is certainly plausible, there is a related, more complicated explanation of the results of Sigall and Page (1971). This alternative explanation makes use of the distinction between emotional and cognitive prejudice. To illustrate this explanation, let us consider the reactions of a student who might have found herself in the Sigall and Page (1971) study. This respondent is a young college freshman who has had very little actual contact with black people, but she is aware of the stereotypic traits attributed to them. Due to her lack of direct experience with black people, however, this component of her belief system is poorly resolved—that is, while she does not really subscribe to the stereotypic beliefs about blacks, neither does she completely discount them. On the one hand, she is not really sure about what she believes regarding black people. On the other hand, she recognizes that black people are "different" from her, and that the few times that she has interacted with them, she has felt anxious or ill-at-ease.

If this person were in the Sigall and Page standard measurement condition, the forces operating in this context would lead her to focus on her uncertainty about the validity of these stereotypes and thus to respond in a cautious manner. In this case, caution would dictate that she recognize her uncertainty concerning the veracity of the stereotypic belief statements, and thus not endorse them.

If she were in the other condition, however, in which she would have been wired to the "truth machine," the change in Social Context might lead her to produce a different pattern of responses. In this case, she would believe that the pipeline could accurately measure her feelings towards black people (of course, it really could not), and she would know that she feels uncomfortable in the presence of members of this aggregate. Under these circumstances, it might be reasonable for her to focus on the emotional aspect of her reaction toward blacks, rather than on her uncertain beliefs. Furthermore, she would be aware that she might be seen as lying if the researchers detect a discrepancy between her reported opinions and the machine's recordings of her feelings. Given this additional concern, she might very well opt to report her beliefs in the most extreme light, and thus subscribe to stereotypes on the questionnaire that, in fact, she has far from completely accepted.

A third research example that helps to draw the distinction between emotional and cognitive prejudice is provided in the study of differences in interaction pattern among preschool children as a function of the racial composition of playgroups (Harrison et al., 1971), discussed earlier in this chapter. There is some controversy surrounding the issue of when children first experience true cognitive prejudice—that is, when they understand and subscribe to derogatory beliefs about an aggregate. However, the most accepted view is that while children can recognize racial differences by the age of four, they are not likely to adopt prejudicial opinions before they are five years old (Porter, 1971). In any event, it is doubtful that the degree of Resolution of the beliefs of such young children on this—or any other—issue is very high.

Recall that Harrison et al. found less interaction among the members of the racially mixed playgroups. This result occurred despite the fact that because of their age, the children observed in this study probably had not formed any (or at least any strong) opinions about children of other races. How then can the observed differences between same-race and mixed-race groups be explained? We believe, as noted previously, that while the cognitive component of the children's opinion toward other races was not well-established, they nevertheless could experience negative emotional reactions due to the awareness that they were encountering someone "different" from them.

All three of the studies discussed here build a case that argues for the utility of the theoretical distinction between purely cognitive (belief-related) prejudice and emotional prejudice. While none of these studies provides direct or unequivocal evidence on this point, we believe that the theoretical distinction drawn here allows for the most plausible interpretation of the research on this topic.

Prejudice and Interpersonal Encounters

Biased Expectations. Earlier, in our discussion of stigma, we noted that a major source of expectations that can bias interpersonal encounters is the perception that the other person is a member of an aggregate about which we are prejudiced. Such biased expectations occur to the extent that the stereotypic beliefs are associated with that person's group and, for whatever reason, negative emotion is attached to the thought of encountering members of the person's aggregate.

As discussed in Chapter 8, research conducted in a variety of settings has shown that the expectations of one individual about another can have a powerful impact on the way that both behave toward each other. Moreover, such expectations can also have long-term consequences for the psychological and intellectual functioning of the participants in these encounters. Although the expectations that prejudice produces often are not based on objective reality, they nonetheless can be powerful and destructive determinants of interpersonal relationships (Word et al., 1974; Weitz, 1972). Their lack of connection to reality as well as their self-fulfilling nature render prejudice-based expectations difficult to counteract.

A large component of prejudicial expectations is derived from the stereotypic attributes associated with the stigmatized aggregate. For example, if one associates females with helplessness, the resulting expectation will lead one to act in such a way as to make it difficult for women to display competent behaviors. A trivial but effective illustration of prejudicial expectations involves never allowing a female to open a door for herself; it may be a sign of courtesy but it never allows her to show that she is, in fact, capable of performing this simple action for herself. In addition, the perception of minor differences can, in themselves, lead to more pervasive expectations that the other differs from us in ways that are psychologically important. Such a process, in fact, can potentially lead to broad-based expectations that the other person's fundamental beliefs differ from ours in important ways, a point which we will now discuss.

Assumed Belief Dissimilarity. As discussed in the previous chapter, the extent to which participants in a social relationship perceive that their beliefs are similar is a major determinant of their attraction for one another (Aronson & Worchel, 1965; Byrne, 1971; Byrne & Clore, 1971; Condon & Crano, 1977). Conversely, the perception of large differences in important beliefs can give rise to the expectation that initial encounters—and any subsequent long-term relationship, should it develop—are unlikely to be rewarding to the participants (Byrne & Wong, 1962; Rokeach & Mezei, 1966; Rokeach, Smith, & Evans, 1960; Silverman, 1974; Williams, 1975).

Expectations of belief dissimilarity have been the focus of a good deal of research in social psychology. For example, studies have shown that the race of the target person, if different from that of the perceiver, can raise expectations that the target's beliefs are antithetical to those of the perceiver, expectations which in turn can lead to negative predictions about future interpersonal relations.

The research in this area has been conducted in a variety of settings, from rather simple laboratory demonstrations to field experiments whose outcomes apparently affected the lives of its participants for an entire academic year. To provide some flavor of this area of research, we will first present one of the early studies on the interactive effects of race and belief similarity/dissimilarity that was conducted by Rokeach et al. (1960). In this study, white junior high school children were presented with a very brief description of another person of the same age and were asked how likely it was that they would become friends with such a person. Two factors in the description of the stimulus person were varied: the person's race, and whether or not the person believed in God.[5]

The results of this experiment were consistent with the perspective that we summarized earlier. While race had some effect on subjects' estimates of the likelihood that they would become friends with the person described, belief similarity had, by far, the major influence on their judgments. Apparently, at least in this rather artificial and unimportant choice situation—the subjects knew that their judgments were hypothetical and that they would not really meet the person described—belief similarity operated as a major determinant of subjects' likeability estimates.

This study stimulated a good deal of controversy, as its results were quite contrary to the prevailing theoretical positions of the time (Triandis, 1961; Triandis & Davis, 1965). However, as later research was to demonstrate repeatedly (Byrne & Wong, 1962; Byrne & McGraw, 1964), belief similarity does indeed operate as a powerful determinant of expectations of rewarding encounters. Further, more realistic studies, whose implications for the respondents were far greater, have produced similar results. For example, Bernard Silverman extended Rokeach's earlier work by exploring the impact of race and perceived belief similarity on subjects' choices of college roommates.

In this study (Silverman, 1974), the subjects were incoming freshmen of a small college in Michigan. Along with their matriculation materials, they were sent a brief questionnaire that focused on some of their important beliefs. A short time after returning these materials, the students' college sent them information regarding potential housing opportunities for the next year. Students were provided descriptions of four other incoming freshmen, and were asked to rate each of them in terms of their desirability as a roommate. These ratings, subjects were told, would in fact be used in making dormitory room assignments for the next academic year.

As in the Rokeach et al. (1960) study, Silverman manipulated the description of the potential roommates by varying their race and the similarity of

---

[5] Rokeach et al. assumed that for their subjects, belief in God was a high level opinion.

their beliefs with those expressed by the subject on the questionnaire that they had completed earlier and returned. Consistent with the earlier results of Rokeach et al., Silverman found that similarity of important beliefs had a greater influence on the target person's desirability as a roommate than did race, per se. We must stress that subjects no doubt perceived this choice as a very meaningful one for them, since they thought that their responses would determine their roommate for the coming academic year.

While the research in this area has shown that belief similarity can have a major impact on attraction, it is important to note that in most real-life contexts, we are not provided with a summary of another's important opinions. Typically, however, a more readily available piece of information is provided by simple visual inspection—the race of the other person. And it is this cue that might be used to predict the extent of belief similarity, and thus the reward potential, of future encounters. Investigations (Byrne & McGraw, 1964; Byrne & Wong, 1962; Williams, 1975) have demonstrated that people do use race as a cue to predict belief similarity, and that expected belief similarity, in turn, has an impact on expectations of friendship formation.

Byrne and Wong (1962), for example, presented white male subjects with very restricted information about another person and asked them to predict the degree of belief similarity between themselves and that individual. In fact, the only salient cue that was provided in the description was race. Byrne and Wong found that subjects' estimates of the degree of belief similarity were strongly influenced by race. The white male subjects who participated in this study assumed much greater belief dissimilarity when the target person was of another race. Moreover, while this pattern of results was true for all subjects, it was strongest among those who had scored highest on a measure of racial prejudice. In an extension of this research, Dallas Williams (1975) has shown that both race and sex differences serve as cues to belief similarity for both black and white men and women.

Contextual Constraints. To this point, our discussion of the major social psychological processes involved in prejudice, and their consequences, has focused on the effects that prejudicial beliefs and emotional reactions can have on the expectations formed about the likelihood of rewarding future contacts. It is important to note that prejudice also has a more direct impact on interpersonal behavior, once interaction has occurred between members of minority and majority groups. Rather than serving only as a force for the avoidance of unpleasant contacts, prejudicial beliefs can also lead to direct negative actions (for example, aggression). In fact, it has been well-documented in social psychology, since at least the pioneering work of Gordon Allport (1954), that prejudice often is likely to be directly expressed in interactions with disadvantaged aggregate members.

While most of us have participated in—or at least observed—encounters in which prejudice was overtly expressed, systematic studies of such behavior are relatively rare. In part, this is so because strong norms operate against the overt expression of antagonism in most Social Contexts—including the research laboratory. However, there is some systematic evidence to document

"It's class hostility—they hate the rich."

Prejudicial beliefs can lead to direct negative actions.

the fact that overt expressions of prejudice do occur. For example, in research by Weitz (1972), white subjects (Harvard undergraduates) were observed as they participated in the study along with either a black or a white person. Among other results, she found that these subjects sat farther away from their coparticipant when he was a black, and when asked to read instructions to him, they did so in a much less friendly tone of voice than when he was a white. As noted in Chapter 8, Word, Zanna, and Cooper (1974) found similar differences in behavior in their study of white interviewers' interactions with black or white respondents.

It is important to note that the subjects in the Weitz study (and in that of Word et al.) did not express their prejudice in obvious or dramatic ways. No doubt their awareness that they were being monitored played a part in these subjects' behaviors. In a series of clever demonstrations, Martin Orne (1962, 1969) has shown that subjects in psychology experiments are extremely concerned about behaving "appropriately." It is reasonable to speculate that concerns of this type would inhibit blatant expressions of antisocial behavior in studies of race effects on interpersonal encounters.

But there are other reasons for the lack of obvious prejudicial behavior. For one thing, the roles that the subjects assumed in these studies did not allow a ready access to overtly negative behaviors. They had been assigned relatively explicit tasks to perform—to be an interviewer, to read instructions—and within the frameworks of those tasks, there was little room for the obvious expression of distaste or discomfort. In other words, subjects were as constrained in their behavior as were the hotel clerks in LaPiere's (1934) study, which we considered in detail in Chapter 6.

Given the tenor of the times, it was likely that some of the hotel desk clerks that LaPiere and his Chinese companions approached in this study had strong prejudices against Orientals. Yet, these beliefs were never expressed in a direct or obvious manner. There might well have been some subtle impolitenesses expressed in these encounters, but no dramatic or even direct verbal or physical confrontations ever occurred. Why not? Because, as noted, the task or role of the hotel desk clerk does not provide the freedom to express in direct ways the negative opinions that the individual might hold. Aspects of the Social Context inhibited obvious displays of the prejudicial opinions.

Of course, the impingements of the Social Context can also operate in the reverse direction—that is, they can facilitate the expression of overtly hostile actions towards members of disadvantaged aggregates even when a strong negative or prejudicial opinion might not exist. For example, the lynch mobs of yesteryear probably contained at least some men who, while prejudiced, did not approve of expressing this opinion in such a violent and destructive way. In a more contemporary context are the actions of a number of police department members during the civil rights demonstrations in the North and South during the 1960s. In many of these circumstances, extreme and unjustified actions were perpetrated against the peaceful protesters. Why? Because the confrontational Social Context that existed in such situations not only allowed such behaviors, but encouraged them.

To this point we have presented rather dramatic examples of the facilitative effects on prejudicial behaviors that sometimes exist in a Social Context. Such violent, physical confrontations, however, are not as common as those interactions in which more subtle—but nonetheless equally prejudicial—actions are expressed toward members of disadvantaged aggregates because the factors in the Social Context dictate such behaviors. Negative actions of personnel directors, loan officers of banks, insurance agents and realtors, toward disadvantaged minorities are often role-related behaviors that can occur even without the accompanying prejudicial beliefs. In such instances, the common explanation of such actors is, "I'm only doing my job." Whatever we might think of this rationale at the time, it probably contains at least a grain, or more, of truth.[6]

Intergroup Contact. It is reasonable to assume that one effective way to reduce prejudicial opinions and reactions is to provide people with more

---

[6] The reader may note the relevance of Milgram's (1974) work on obedience for such expressions of institutionalized prejudice.

direct experiences with members of stigmatized aggregates. While this inter-group contact hypothesis is plausible, it has not always been supported when studied systematically. In this section, we will discuss the conditions under which the provision of interaction opportunities between members of mutually biased aggregates serve to decrease, or to enhance, prejudicial beliefs and actions. We will begin with some studies conducted in naturalistic settings.

A relatively large number of studies have examined the impact on persons' opinions when, because of a change in the Social Context, the opportunity to interact with members of stigmatized aggregates is dramatically increased— when, for example, a black family moves into a previously all-white neighbor-hood. We are all aware of unfortunate instances in which such events have triggered violent outbursts. However, while less dramatic, there are well-documented cases in which prejudicial opinions have been dramatically re-duced by extended contacts with aggregate members.

One of the initial studies in this area was conducted by Deutsch and Collins (1951), in which they surveyed opinions of white people who lived in either racially integrated or segregated apartment complexes. They found that respondents who lived in integrated apartment buildings expressed signifi-cantly less prejudicial opinions than did comparable respondents in segregated buildings. Of course, it is quite possible that the respondents who lived in the integrated apartment complexes did so because they were initially less antagonistic towards other races. Thus, the results reported by Deutsch and Collins might have reflected initial differences between respondents, rather than differences that evolved as a result of intergroup contact. We suspect that both interpretations are valid to some extent.

A more contemporary and conclusive study was conducted by David Hamilton and George Bishop (1976). This research assessed the opinions toward black people of residents in 18 suburban neighborhoods surrounding New Haven, Connecticut. At the time of the initial interviews, none of the neighborhoods had any black residents. In eight of the neighborhoods, how-ever, a black family had purchased a house and was preparing to move into it. The remaining 10 neighborhoods were selected because each contained a house that was newly purchased—but by a white family. Additional inter-views were conducted one month, three months, and one year after the new families had moved in. These interviews yielded a wealth of interesting data, but for our purposes, we will focus on the measures of prejudicial opinions and opinion change which Hamilton and Bishop collected.

The first set of interviews indicated that the respondents in the two types of neighborhoods were similar to one another in terms of racial beliefs. In fact, the only major difference in their responses in this first interview was to the question, "Have there been any changes in the nature of the neighborhood in the last year or so?" To this item, more than half the respon-dents in the soon-to-be-integrated settings mentioned the impending arrival of the new (black) family; in contrast, almost none of the respondents in the other group mentioned the arrival of the new (white) family. In addition, when any respondents in the soon-to-be-integrated group mentioned that they had discussed the forthcoming change with neighbors, they invariably admitted that such conversations were negative in tone.

The negative opinions were found to persist one month after the new black family had moved in. If anything, there was an increase in reported negative conversations about this turn of events among the group of respondents. One obvious indication of the group's strong prejudicial attitudes is reflected in the fact that one month after the black family had moved in, few, if any, of their white neighbors knew their name, while well over half of the respondents in the other group knew the name of their new white neighbors. Generally, similar data were obtained in the interviews taken after three months, but some important changes began to emerge at this point. Of most interest is the slight increase (from zero) in conversations about the black neighbors that were not totally negative in tone.

A dramatic difference exists between responses to the early interviews and those obtained after one year. There was still some evidence of negative opinion—for example, fewer respondents in the integrated neighborhoods reported having had direct contact with the "new" family than did their counterparts in the all-white neighborhoods. However, the concern and apprehension that most respondents initially expressed had substantially decreased after one year. Moreover, respondents at this time reported that their discussions about the black family were generally favorable. Finally, and perhaps of most importance, the experience of having a black family in the neighborhood had dramatically reduced general prejudice.

It should be emphasized that although we have discussed this study in terms of the "intergroup contact" hypothesis, there was not a great deal of direct interaction between the members of the black families and their white neighbors. Most of the information about the black families came from hearsay and discussions among the white residents themselves. Nonetheless, the mere presence of these black families in the formerly all-white neighborhoods had a powerful moderating influence on prejudicial opinions. Apparently, even second-hand information that disconfirmed their stereotypic beliefs provided respondents with evidence with which to restructure their beliefs and alleviate their anxieties about dealing with these "different" people. This is not to say that the white respondents became totally free of their prejudicial opinions—most of them, no doubt, continued to hold these negative beliefs about blacks who were in a lower socioeconomic class. But at the very least, second-hand contacts with a black family of equal socioeconomic status did have a substantial—if perhaps somewhat narrow—impact on their opinions.

In more direct tests of the intergroup contact hypothesis, a reasonable amount of actual interaction between members of different social aggregates is known to have occurred (Aronson & Bridgeman, 1979; Cohen, Kelman, Miller, & Smith, 1977; Cook, 1970; Diamond & Lobitz, 1973; Kelman & Cohen, 1979). In such circumstances, the general finding is that increased opportunity to interact dramatically reduces prejudicial opinions and reactions.

In an example of research on this issue, Diamond and Lobitz (1973) examined the changes in prejudicial opinions among college students and police after a series of police/student confrontations (riots), which were an all too common event in the late 1960s and early 1970s. Diamond and Lobitz (1973) brought together 69 undergraduates and 37 members of the local police force in contexts that facilitated nonviolent interactions. Three types of settings were used: students rode with the police in their squad cars; police and students dined together; and police and students participated in more formal group encounter sessions. The outcomes of these encounters were quite positive; both students and police developed more positive, less stereotypic beliefs about the other aggregate.

In contrast, other studies of intergroup contact have yielded less positive results. For example, Mussen (1953) found that interracial contact between young boys in a summercamp setting did change opinions, but in both directions—that is, some of the boys became less prejudiced, but others became more so. Thus, as noted earlier, contact is not effective in reducing prejudice under all conditions with all people. In the following paragraphs, we will consider some of the variables that might mediate the effect on prejudice of interacting with members of stigmatized aggregates.

Factors in people's Personal Structures mediate the effects of intergroup contact. If, for example, an individual has a highly resolved belief system in which the relevant prejudicial opinions are of central concern, it is unlikely that any experiences of even moderate duration will have an effect on his or her beliefs. Perhaps the most positive outcome for such a person would involve a differentiation of some individuals of the stigmatized outgroup from the outgroup itself.

For example, if we could induce the head of the Ku Klux Klan to spend a month on a deserted island with a black, a Jew, and a Catholic, who were chosen to be as different as possible from his stereotypes, it is doubtful that at the end of that time he would have changed any of his central prejudicial beliefs about the aggregates to which these people belonged. At most, he might come to see his companions for the month as the three exceptions to what he is certain is true of all the "others."

In contrast, intergroup contact is likely to have its most positive impact when the relevant opinions are poorly resolved. Since poor belief Resolution is probably most characteristic of young children, we would speculate that intergroup contact would be very effective in alleviating any prejudicial opinions that members of this aggregate might hold.

A second point regarding Personal Structure involves the extent to which the prejudice is associated with emotional rather than cognitive factors. Intergroup contact is likely to prove most effective to the extent that it serves to overcome persons' expectations of negative reactions. As noted, these expectations, and the aversive emotions they produce, in large part are a consequence of being unsure about the appropriate ways to behave with people whom we perceive as "different." In such circumstances, intergroup contact is likely to prove very effective in overcoming the negative emotional reaction.

A third mediator of the effect of intergroup contact that arises from variations in the Personal Structure is the extent to which the satisfaction of a person's basic motives is tied to his or her prejudicial opinions. It has been well documented (Adorno, Frankel-Brunswik, Levinson, & Sanford, 1950; Bettleheim & Janowitz, 1950; Rubin, 1967) that prejudice is associated with a person's ability (or lack of ability) to control important outcomes in his or her life. For example, Bettleheim and Janowitz (1950) found that people who were failing to achieve outcomes that were congruent with their desired self-images were the most likely to hold prejudicial beliefs. Similarly, Adorno et al. (1950) found a positive relationship between rigidity of the Personal Structure (authoritarianism) and prejudice.

There are also factors in the Social Context that determine the effects of encounters between members of different aggregates. For example, the interpersonal environment must play a role in intergroup contact. If those people in our Social Context who are members of a stigmatized aggregate conform to the image of the stereotype that we hold of the aggregate, then it is unlikely that much opinion change would ensue from our interaction with them. It is only when such persons possess attributes that are antithetical to our stereotypic beliefs that this direct experience can have a moderating effect on our prejudice. For example, if a male chauvinist encounters a female who acts in a passive, docile, and obsequious manner toward him, such an interaction, even if repeated over a long period, is not likely to induce much belief change in him.

The extent to which the important referents in our environment provide us with either social support for our prejudicial beliefs or standards which argue for a change of such beliefs also determines the impact of intergroup contact. For example, the reader might imagine being a person who has prejudicial attitudes about black people. You happen to be in a bar one afternoon, and sitting next to you is a black person. If you struck up a conversation with this person, you might find that the two of you had many interests and opinions in common. However, if you were in the bar with three of your friends, who are as prejudiced against blacks as you are, it is very unlikely that any encounter that you might have with the stranger would be positive.

Other aspects of the Social Context also play a role in the impact of intergroup contact on prejudicial opinions. For example, the manner in which the role relationships in a situation are structured will strongly influence the outcome of most intergroup encounters. If the behaviors of people in such encounters are determined by a prespecified set of expectations (as described in Chapter 8), then contact, per se, is unlikely to have much influence on people's prejudicial beliefs. For instance, an encounter between a prejudiced customer and a black attendant at a car wash (a stereotypic menial job) may be so limited by the "scripts" that both follow in their interaction that little change will occur regarding either person's set of beliefs.

On the other hand, it is likely that little change will occur if the role relationship is very contrary to the perceiver's expectations (and self-interest). The male chauvinist who takes a job as a clerk and finds that his supervisor is a cool, efficient, and assertive female, will probably not change his opinions regarding women in general. This prejudiced man will distort his boss's actions so that they will correspond to other facets of his stereotype of women (for example, her assertiveness will be seen as "bitchiness"). In light of these observations, it seems reasonable to hypothesize that egalitarian role relations (that is, those in which people view one another as equals in terms of their expected behaviors toward one another in the Social Context) are most likely to produce positive outcomes under conditions of intergroup contact.

Finally, the extent to which the participants in an encounter see themselves as sharing common goals has an impact on the outcome of intergroup contacts. If interacting members of a group must cooperate to achieve some mutually beneficial end, then the intergroup contact will prove effective in attenuating prejudice. Evidence in support of this observation was provided in research by Sherif et al. (1961) on interpersonal relationships among participants in a summer camp, discussed in Chapter 11.

The reader may recall that Sherif and his colleagues assigned campers to one of two cabins and manipulated the Social Context to foster the development of an antagonistic relationship between the two groups. However, the researchers later attempted to alleviate this antagonism by inducing the campers to work on a series of tasks that demanded cooperation from all of them if their efforts were to be successful. These encounters greatly reduced the negative feelings that the campers had developed from their early experiences. Similarly, Elliot Aronson and his colleagues have demonstrated that inducing classmates of different racial and ethnic backgrounds to work together in a cooperative learning task greatly reduces prejudice (Aronson & Bridgeman, 1979; Aronson, Stephan, Sikes, Blaney, & Snapp, 1978; Blaney, Stephan, Rosenfield, Aronson, & Sikes, 1977).

Under some circumstances, intergroup contact will reduce prejudice because a positive unit relationship is formed between the members of the different aggregates. As Heider (1958) has noted, a positive unit bond acts as a force for the development of positive Sentiment relationships. However, when members of different social aggregates are placed in an adversarial relationship—that is, one in which they perceive that they must compete with one another in order to satisfy their own needs—then intergroup contact is likely to exacerbate the negative opinions that each holds about the other.

Social Psychological Consequences of Prejudice

Clearly, the consequences of prejudicial opinions for interpersonal relationships can be profound. Perhaps the most important consequence of this phenomenon for people's behavior towards others is the extent to which prejudice limits their opportunities to engage in rewarding activities with members of stigmatized aggregates. This negative consequence is most clearly expressed in two related issues: (1) it restricts the range of interpersonal relationships that we can form; and (2) due to this restriction, we limit our opportunities to satisfy our individual needs.

The most obvious example of the manner in which prejudice affects the range of potential role relationships that we can establish with others is provided in research on the concept of social distance. Social distance (Bogardus, 1925; Triandis, 1961; Triandis & Davis, 1965) refers to the range of acceptable bonds that we will allow ourselves to establish with others— we could, for example, find it acceptable to work with a person, be his or her friend, marry, and so on. Of course, the distance of the social relationships that we find appropriate is greatly affected by the extent of our prejudicial beliefs. If we have no antagonistic beliefs or feelings toward a given aggregate, then the social distance that we maintain between ourselves and members of that aggregate will be minimal. In this case, role relationships of the most intimate nature (such as close friendship, romance, marriage) would be acceptable. On the other hand, prejudicial opinions of a high level would preclude the acceptability of all but the most distant relationships (such as supervisor-worker, fellow townsperson). Between these two extremes, moderate degrees of prejudice would permit somewhat closer, but not intimate, bonds to form (social acquaintances, casual friends, members of the same sports team).

The restriction of role relationships that results from prejudicial opinions has a second important implication—namely, that such restrictions can be detrimental to the welfare of the prejudiced persons as well as to the members of the stigmatized outgroup. The most obvious examples of this point are the limitations that our prejudices, and the impinging prejudices of our important referents, place on our choices of close friends and marriage partners. For some, entire subpopulations are excluded from consideration, and thus, the potential positive outcomes that relationships with some members of this aggregate could provide are not realized. In a similar way, by prohibiting members of traditionally stigmatized social aggregates from full access to a great many roles (economic, social, and so on) in our society, we have lost the contributions that these people could have provided, which ultimately would have promoted our own welfare.

This last point is relevant to the second major consequence of prejudice— namely, the restrictions that it places on people in their attempts to satisfy their basic individual needs. For example, people who are highly motivated to display competence can be restricted in the range of opportunities for doing so by their membership in stigmatized social aggregates. Kay Deaux (1976) has argued compellingly that women in traditional and contemporary American society have been restricted from full access to roles that would permit them to satisfy important motives related to competence and career achievement. She cites evidence (Deaux & Emswiller, 1974) that indicates that both males and females are very aware of women's diminished opportunities to pursue societally valued careers. Deaux and Emswiller, for example, attempted to find tasks traditionally associated with males or females that are of equally high value. They found, instead, that of the highly valued

"I was planning to become a nuclear physicist,
but I may decide to end up a dumb blonde."

Women in our society traditionally have been restricted from roles that permit expression of some important motives.

behaviors, almost all were associated with male involvement; the behaviors that were viewed as typically "female" were rated as less valuable by both men and women. In a related study, Mellon, Crano, and Schmitt (in press) found that they could identify no traditionally female occupations that were valued as highly as were many traditionally male occupations.

Perhaps the clearest demonstration of the ways in which prejudice can interfere with need satisfaction is provided in the study conducted by Edwin Megargee (1969), presented earlier. Recall that in this research, Megargee paired combinations of male and female subjects such that one member had high level dominance motives and the other was low in dominance. He told the members that they would be working together on a task that required one of them to supervise the other. In each pair, the subjects had to decide who was to perform the supervisory role and who was to act as the worker. The results of this study disclosed that the only condition in which the high dominant member was not likely to be selected as the supervisor occurred when a high dominant female was paired with a low dominant male.

For our present concerns, the major point of Megargee's study is clear. When traditional sex roles were contrary to the individual needs of the participants, the sex roles (not the dominance needs) determined the outcome. High dominant females, when paired with a low dominant male, were not allowed (by themselves or the other) to express their motivation in a straightforward way. In all other conditions, motivation had a major influence in determining role allocation. Thus, prejudicial opinions (males should lead, females should follow) limited the females' opportunities to satisfy important needs. This study is a convincing laboratory demonstration of what must be a frequent occurrence in contemporary society and thus a major consequence of prejudice.

The Inevitability of Prejudice

The final point to be considered concerning prejudice is the question of its inevitability. While we raise this question as well a number of corollary issues, we can provide no answer to it. We feel that merely raising this issue points to a fundamental problem for social psychology and for human society in general—namely, the extent to which this destructive, antisocial force can be eliminated or at least controlled. Prejudicial opinions and actions have characterized almost every society of which we are aware (LeVine & Campbell, 1972). Those few societies that appear to be free of prejudice are typically so small, homogeneous, and isolated from other human groups that there exists for them little opportunity to perceive differences and thus to create the idea of an outside aggregate.

Given the apparent universality of what LeVine and Campbell (1972) call *ethnocentrism*—that is, the differentiation of a valued ingroup from a devalued outgroup, a term first coined by Sumner (1906)—we cannot dismiss the possibility that prejudice is a fundamental property of the human organism. For whatever reason, it could be that human beings are primed to perceive differences between themselves and others and to attach varying estimates of worth as a function of these perceptions. Lorenz (1966) speculates that such a tendency is, in fact, basic to human nature, and is one of the antecedents of destructive social aggression. While most of us would prefer this pessimistic conclusion to be erroneous, there is as yet no definitive evidence to refute it. If anything, considerable research indicates that differentiating people by even the most trivial of means (for example, preference for one of two abstract paintings, or chance assignment to a "group") results in less favorable evaluations of, and less positive actions toward, members of the artificially formed outgroups (Brewer, 1979; Brewer & Silver, 1978; Locksley, Ortiz, & Hepburn,

1980; Tajfel, 1970; Wilder, 1978). It very well could be that such differential evaluations are the starting point for more destructive forms of human behaviors.

SOME CONCLUDING REMARKS

Sentiment is the focal theme for many of the issues that have been discussed in this chapter. For this reason, it may be helpful to briefly review three important points about the role that this theme plays in the psychological processes related to prejudice and hate.

First, it is most important to note that the same basic processes determine both negative and positive Sentiment relations. The relative impact of one process or another might differ as a consequence of the direction of Sentiment attachment, but the factors themselves—association, motive relevance, and so on—are identical.

Second, while it is clear that there is a mutual interplay between prejudicial opinions and individual dislike, the principal direction of influence appears to flow from general opinions to specific beliefs—that is, our opinions of a stigmatized aggregate will generally have a greater impact on our reaction to a member of that aggregate than vice versa. This is not to say that direct experience with an individual cannot change prejudicial opinions, but rather that such a development is less common than the effect of the general belief on the evaluation of a specific target.

Third, it should be noted that in a number of Social Contexts, the formation of Sentiment relations is not necessarily the result of conscious deliberation, but rather an inevitable outcome of the cognitive and emotional processes that characterize human interaction. For example, an enforced unit relationship will often result in the development of a positive Sentiment bond, despite the best efforts of the actors to resist such an outcome. Perhaps the most graphic example of the effect of a forced unit relationship on Sentiment was portrayed in the movie *The Defiant Ones*. In this story, the unit bond between two heroes was obvious—they were escapees (one white, the other black) from a prison farm who were literally chained together. Under such circumstances, it should come as no surprise that their initial antagonism turned to close personal affection by the end of the movie, perhaps because they had to cooperate to achieve a common goal that was very important to both (escape). Of course, in real life, such a unit bonding could have had the opposite effect. The point here, however, is that such a unit bonding almost invariably will affect Sentiment relations as well.

Epilogue

In writing this book, we had two major goals. First, we wanted to review the major topics and issues that have occupied the attention of social psychologists. As demonstrated in these pages, the domain of the field of social psychology is both extensive and diverse, since social psychologists are interested in such apparently disparate phenomena as interpersonal behavior, opinion change, group cohesiveness, first impressions, and love. And this is only a partial list. The amount and range of material that is relevant to social psychology led us to the second goal of this book: to demonstrate that the multitude of issues in social psychology have as common bases a handful of more fundamental processes—what we have called *core concepts* and *integrative themes.*

To demonstrate this common basis one last time, let us summarize some research recently completed by Charles Dougherty, an undergraduate student of ours. In this investigation, Dougherty explored helping behavior by studying the extent to which undergraduates were willing to assist a graduate student in completing his thesis research. Dougherty's primary interest focused on the effect of distraction on people's willingness to help. This variable, it will be recalled, has been studied extensively in social psychology, but always within the framework of opinion change (Chapter 4). Not surprisingly, however, Dougherty found that distraction can induce people to be more helpful, and thus, he showed that this variable can affect behaviors as well as opinions.

At first glance, there does not appear to be much in common between one's positive response to a request for help and changing one's mind as a consequence of exposure to a persuasive communication. However, within the perspective advocated in this book, both changing an opinion and complying with a request for help are instances of the operation of the same underlying theme—that of Control. Persons' reactions to a request for help or to a message designed to alter their beliefs are just two examples of situations in which another person—the requester or the communicator—is attempting to influence (Control) their thoughts and behaviors. Thus, it is reasonable that a variable such as distraction, which has been found to mediate the extent of Control in one Social Context, would also affect this process in another.

Similarly, Valuation is relevant to the outcomes of both Dougherty's research and the typical distraction/opinion change study. From Dougherty's results, it is reasonable to conclude that when people decide whether or not to help, they argue with themselves about the pros and cons of their possible alternative responses in much the same way that they do when faced with a persuasive message that is contrary to their established opinions.

Additional examples relevant to the other themes could be cited, and these would demonstrate that each is applicable to a variety of phenomena that typically have been viewed in social psychology as separate entities.

However, we do not need to duplicate the illustrations that have been provided throughout this book. At this point, we hope that we have clearly demonstrated that the themes of Control, Sentiment, Consistency, Resolution, and Valuation, along with the core concepts of Social Context and Personal Structure, are useful tools in acquiring a comprehensive and integrative perspective on human interpersonal behavior.

References

Abelson, R. P. Modes of resolution of belief dilemmas. *Journal of Conflict Resolution*, 1959, *3*, 343–352.

Abelson, R. P. Script processing in attitude formation and decision making. In J. S. Carrol & J. W. Payne (Eds.), *Cognition and social behavior*. Hillsdale, N.J.: Erlbaum, 1976.

Adams, J. S. Inequity in social exchange. In L. Berkowitz (Ed.), *Advances in experimental social psychology* (Vol. 2). New York: Academic Press, 1965.

Aderman, D., & Berkowitz, L. Observational set, empathy, and helping. *Journal of Personality and Social Psychology*, 1970, *14*, 141–148.

Adorno, T. W., Frankel-Brunswik, E., Levinson, D. J., & Sanford, R. N. *The authoritarian personality*. New York: Harper & Row, 1950.

Ajzen, I. Attribution of dispositions to an actor: Effects of perceived decision freedom and behavioral utilities. *Journal of Personality and Social Psychology*, 1971, *18*, 144–156.

Allport, G. *The nature of prejudice*. Garden City, N.Y.: Doubleday Anchor, 1954.

Altman, I. Reciprocity of interpersonal exchange. *Journal for the Theory of Social Behavior*, 1973, *3*, 249–261.

Altman, I., & Taylor, D. A. *Social penetration: Development of interpersonal relationships*. New York: Holt, Rinehart & Winston, 1973.

Anderson, A. B. *Toward a more complex model of group cohesion: The interactive effects of success-failure, participation opportunity, intrinsic interest and pay condition*. Unpublished doctoral dissertation, Michigan State University, 1974.

Anderson, A. B. Combined effects of interpersonal attraction and goal-path clarity on the cohesiveness of task oriented groups. *Journal of Personality and Social Psychology*, 1975, *31*, 68–75.

Anderson, N. H. Adding versus averaging as a stimulus combination rule in impression formation. *Journal of Experimental Social Psychology*, 1965, *70*, 394–400.

Anderson, N. H. Cognitive algebra: Integration theory applied to social attribution. In L. Berkowitz (Ed.), *Advances in experimental social psychology* (Vol. 7). New York: Academic Press, 1974.

Anderson, N. H., & Barrios, A. A. Primacy effects in personality impression formation. *Journal of Abnormal and Social Psychology*, 1961, *63*, 346–350.

Anderson, N. H., & Hubert, S. Effects of concomitant verbal recall on order effects in personality impression formation. *Journal of Verbal Learning and Verbal Behavior*, 1963, *2*, 379–391.

Anderson, R., Manoogian, S. T., & Reznick, J. S. The undermining and enhancing of intrinsic motivation in preschool children. *Journal of Personality and Social Psychology*, 1976, *34*, 915–922.

Apfelbaum, E. On conflicts and bargaining. In L. Berkowitz, (Ed.), *Advances in experimental social psychology* (Vol. 7). New York: Academic Press, 1977.

Apple, W., Streeter, L. A., & Krauss, R. M. Effects of pitch and speech rate on personal attributions. *Journal of Personality and Social Psychology*, 1979, *37*, 715–727.

Archer, R. L., & Burleson, J. A. The effects of timing of self-disclosure on attraction and reciprocity. *Journal of Personality and Social Psychology*, 1980, *38*, 120–130.

Arkin, R. M., Gleason, J. M., & Johnson, S. Effects of perceived choice, expected outcome, and observed outcome of an actor on the causal attributions of actors. *Journal of Experimental Social Psychology*, 1976, *12*, 151–158.

Arkin, R. M., Appleman, A. J., & Berger, J. M. Social anxiety, self-presentation, and the self-serving bias in causal attribution. *Journal of Personality and Social Psychology*, 1980, *38*, 23–35.

Arkkelin, D., Oakley, T., & Mynatt, C. Effects of controllable versus uncontrollable factors on responsibility attributions: A single-subject approach. *Journal of Personality and Social Psychology*, 1979, *37*, 110–115.

Aronoff, J. *Psychological needs and cultural systems: A case study*. Princeton, N.J.: Van Nostrand, 1967.

Aronoff, J., & Messé, L. A. Motivational determinants of small-group structure. *Journal of Personality and Social Psychology*, 1971, *17*, 319–324.

Aronoff, J., Messé, L. A., & Wilson, J. P. Personality factors in small group functioning. In H. H. Blumberg & A. P. Hare (Eds.), *Small groups: Social-psychological processes, social action and living together*. Chichester, Sussex: Wiley, in press.

Aronson, E. Dissonance theory: Progress and problems. In R. P. Abelson, E. Aronson, T. M. Newcomb, M. J. Rosenberg, & P. H. Tannenbaum (Eds.), *Theories of cognitive consistency: A sourcebook*. Chicago: Rand McNally, 1968.

Aronson, E. Persuasion via self-justification: Large commitments for small rewards. In L. Festinger (Ed.), *Retrospections on social psychology*. New York: Oxford University Press, 1980.

Aronson, E., & Bridgeman, D. Jigsaw groups and the desegregated classroom: In pursuit of common goals. *Personality and Social Psychology Bulletin*, 1979, *5*, 438–466.

Aronson, E., & Carlsmith, J. M. Effect of the severity of threat on the devaluation of forbidden behavior. *Journal of Abnormal and Social Psychology*, 1963, *66*, 584–588.

Aronson, E., & Carlsmith, J. M. Experimentation in social psychology. In G. Lindzey & E. Aronson (Eds.), *Handbook of social psychology* (Rev. Ed.). Reading: Mass.: Addison-Wesley, 1968.

Aronson, E., Carlsmith, J. M., & Darley, J. M. The effects of expectancy on volunteering for an unpleasant experience. *Journal of Abnormal and Social Psychology*, 1963, *66*, 220–224.

Aronson, E., & Golden, B. The effect of relevant and irrelevant aspects of communicator credibility on opinion change. *Journal of Personality*, 1962, *30*, 135–146.

Aronson, E., & Linder, D. Gain and loss of esteem as determinants of interpersonal attractiveness. *Journal of Experimental Social Psychology*, 1965, *1*, 156–171.

Aronson, E., & Mills, J. The effect of severity of initiation on liking for a group. *Journal of Abnormal and Social Psychology*, 1959, *59*, 177–181.

Aronson, E., Stephan, C., Sikes, J., Blaney, N., & Snapp, M. *The jigsaw classroom*. Beverly Hills, Calif.: Sage, 1978.

Aronson, E., Turner, J., & Carlsmith, J. M. Communicator credibility and communication discrepancy as determinants of opinion change. *Journal of Abnormal and Social Psychology*, 1963, *67*, 31–36.

Aronson, E., & Worchel, S. Similarity versus liking as determinants of interpersonal attractiveness. *Psychonomic Science*, 1966, *5*, 157–158.

Asch, S. E. Forming impressions of personality. *Journal of Abnormal and Social Psychology*, 1946, *41*, 258–290.

Asch, S. E. The doctrine of suggestion, prestige, and imitation in social psychology. *Psychological Review*, 1948, *55*, 250–277.

Asch, S. E. Effects of group pressure upon the modification and distortion of judgment. In H. Guetzkow (Ed.), *Groups, leadership, and men*. Pittsburgh: Carnegie Press, 1951.

Asch, S. E. Studies of independence and conformity: A minority of one against a unanimous majority. *Psychological Monographs*, 1956, *70*, (9, Whole No. 416).

Assor, A., Aronoff, J., & Messé, L. A. Attribute relevance as a moderator of the effects of motivation on impression formation. *Journal of Personality and Social Psychology*, 1981, *41*, 789–796.

Austin, W. G. Sex differences in bystander intervention in a theft. *Journal of Personality and Social Psychology*, 1979, *37*, 2110–2120.

Austin, W. G., & Worchel, S. *The social psychology of intergroup relations*. Monterey, Calif.: Brooks/Cole, 1979.

Back, K. Influence through social communication. *Journal of Abnormal and Social Psychology*, 1951, *46*, 9–23.

Backman, C. W., & Secord, P. F. The effect of perceived liking on interpersonal attraction. *Human Relations*, 1959, *12*, 379–384.

Bagozzi, R. P., & Burnkrant, R. E. Attitude organization and the attitude-behavior relationship. *Journal of Personality and Social Psychology*, 1979, *37*, 913–929.

Bakan, D. *The duality of human existence*. Chicago: Rand McNally, 1966.

Bales, R. F. *Interaction process analysis: A method for the study of small groups*. Cambridge, Mass.: Addison-Wesley, 1950.

Bales, R. F. The equilibrium problem in small groups. In T. Parsons, R. F. Bales, & E. A. Shily (Eds.), *Working papers in the theory of action*. Glencoe, Ill.: Free Press, 1953.

Bales, R. F. *Personality and interpersonal behavior*. New York: Holt, Rinehart & Winston, 1970.

Bales, R. F., & Slater, P. E. Role differentiation in small decision-making groups. In T. Parsons & R. F. Bales (Eds.), *Family, socialization and interaction process*. Chicago: Free Press, 1955.

Bales, R. F., & Strodtbeck, F. L. Phases in group problem

solving. *Journal of Abnormal and Social Psychology,* 1951, *46,* 485–495.

Bales, R. F., Strodtbeck, F. L., Mills, T. M., & Roseborough, M. E. Channels of communication in small groups. *American Sociological Review,* 1951, *16,* 461–468.

Bandura, A., Ross, D., & Ross, S. Transmission of aggression through imitation of aggressive models. *Journal of Abnormal and Social Psychology,* 1961, *63,* 575–582.

Bandura, A., Ross, D., & Ross, S. Imitation of film-mediated aggressive models. *Journal of Abnormal and Social Psychology,* 1963, *66,* 3–11. (a)

Bandura, A., Ross, D., & Ross, S. A comparative test of the status envy, social power and secondary reinforcement theories of identification learning. *Journal of Abnormal and Social Psychology,* 1963, *67,* 527–534. (b)

Barclay, A. M. Linking sexual and aggressive motives: Contributions of 'irrelevant' arousals. *Journal of Personality,* 1971, *39,* 481–492 (a)

Barclay, A. M. Information as a defensive control of sexual arousal. *Journal of Personality and Social Psychology,* 1971, *17,* 244–249. (b).

Baron, R. A. Aggression as a function of audience presence and prior anger arousal. *Journal of Experimental Social Psychology,* 1971, *7,* 515–523.

Baron, R. A. Magnitude of victims pain cues and level of prior anger arousal as determinants of adult aggressive behavior. *Journal of Personality and Social Psychology,* 1971, *17,* 236–243. (a)

Baron, R. A. Aggression as a function of magnitude of victim's pain cues, level of prior anger arousal, and aggressor-victim similarity. *Journal of Personality and Social Psychology,* 1971, *18,* 48–54. (b)

Baron, R. A. Reducing the influence of an aggressive model: The restraining effects of discrepant modeling cues. *Journal of Personality and Social Psychology,* 1971, *20,* 240–245. (c)

Baron, R. A. Aggression as a function of victim's pain cues, level of prior anger arousal, and exposure to an aggressive model. *Journal of Personality and Social Psychology,* 1974, *29,* 117–124.

Baron, R. A. *Human aggression.* New York: Plenum Publishing, 1977.

Baron, R. A. Effects of victim's pain cues, victim's race, and level of prior instigation upon physical aggression. *Journal of Applied Social Psychology,* 1979, *9,* 103–114.

Baron, R. A. Olfaction and human social behavior: Effects of pleasant scents on physical aggression. *Basic and Applied Social Psychology,* 1980, *1,* 163–172.

Baron, R. A., & Bell, P. A. Aggression and heat: Mediating effects of provocation and exposure to an aggressive model. *Journal of Personality and Social Psychology,* 1975, *31,* 825–832.

Baron, R. A., & Bell, P. A. Aggression and heat: The influence of ambient temperature, negative affect, and a cooling drink on physical aggression. *Journal of Personality and Social Psychology,* 1976, *33,* 245–255. (a)

Baron, R. A., & Bell, P. A. Physical distance and helping: Some unexpected benefits of "crowding in" on others. *Journal of Applied Social Psychology,* 1976, *6,* 95–104. (b)

Baron, R. A., & Byrne, D. *Social psychology: Understanding human interaction* (3rd ed.). Boston: Allyn & Bacon, 1981.

Baron, R. A., & Kepner, C. R. Model's behavior and attraction toward the model as determinants of adult aggressive behavior. *Journal of Personality and Social Psychology,* 1970, *14,* 335–344.

Barron, R. A., & Lawton, S. F. Environmental influences on aggression: The facilitation of modeling effects by high ambient temperatures. *Psychonomic Science,* 1972, *26,* 80–82.

Baron, R. S., Baron, P. H., & Miller, N. The relation between distraction and persuasion. *Psychological Bulletin,* 1973, *80,* 310–323.

Bass, B. M. *Leadership, psychology, and organizational behavior.* New York: Harper & Row, 1960.

Bass, B. M.; McGehee, C. R.; Hawkins, W. C.; Young, P. C.; & Gebel, A. S. Personality variables related to leaderless group discussion. *Journal of Abnormal and Social Psychology,* 1953, *48,* 120–128.

Bass, B. M., & Norton, F. T. M. Group size and leaderless discussions. *Journal of Applied Psychology,* 1951, *35,* 397–400.

Bass, B. M., & Wurster, C. R. Effects of the nature of the problem on LGD performance. *Journal of Applied Psychology,* 1953, *37,* 96–99. (a)

Bass, B. M., & Wurster, C. R. Effects of company rank on LGD performance of oil refinery supervisors. *Journal of Applied Psychology,* 1953, *37,* 100–104 (b)

Bassili, J. N. Emotion recognition: The role of facial movement and the relative importance of upper and lower areas of the face. *Journal of Personality and Social Psychology,* 1979, *37,* 2049–2058.

Baxter, J. C., Hill, P. C., Brock, B., & Rozelle, R. M. The perceiver and the perceived revisited. *Personality Social Psychological Bulletin,* 1981, *7,* 91–96.

Beckhouse, L., Tanur, J., Weiler, J., & Weinstein, E. . . . And some men have leadership thrust upon them. *Journal of Personality and Social Psychology,* 1975, *31,* 557–566.

Bell, P. A., & Baron, R. A. Aggression and heat: The mediating role of negative affect. *Journal of Applied Social Psychology,* 1976, *6,* 18–30.

Bem, D. J. An experimental analysis of self-persuasion. *Journal of Experimental Social Psychology,* 1965, *1,* 199–208.

Bem, D. J. Self perception: An alternative interpretation of cognitive dissonance phenomena. *Psychological Review,* 1967, *74,* 183–200.

Bem, D. J. Self-perception theory. In L. Berkowitz (Ed.), *Advances in experimental social psychology* (Vol. 6). New York: Academic Press, 1972.

Bem, D. J., & Allen, A. On predicting some of the people

some of the time. *Psychological Review,* 1974, *81,* 506–520.

Bem, D. J., Wallach, M. A., & Kogan, N. Group decision making under risk of aversive consequences. *Journal of Personality and Social Psychology,* 1965, *1,* 453–460.

Benedetti, D. T., and Hill, J. G. A determiner of the centrality of a trait in impression formation. *Journal of Abnormal and Social Psychology,* 1960, *60,* 278–279.

Benne, K. D., & Sheats, P. Functional roles of group members. *Journal of Social Issues,* 1948, *4,* 41–49.

Benney, M., Riesman, D., & Star, S. Age and sex in the interview. *American Sociological Review,* 1956, *62,* 143–152.

Bennis, W. G., & Shepard, H. A. A theory of group development. *Human Relations,* 1956, *9,* 415–437.

Benson, P., Karabenick, S., & Lerner, R. Pretty pleases: The effects of physical attractiveness, race, and sex on receiving help. *Journal of Experimental Social Psychology,* 1976, *12,* 409–415.

Bentler, P. M., & Speckart, G. Models of attitude-behavior relations. *Psychological Review,* 1979, *86,* 452–464.

Bentler, P. M., & Speckart, G. Attitudes "cause" behaviors: A structural equation analysis. *Journal of Personality and Social Psychology,* 1981, *40,* 226–238.

Berkowitz, L. (Ed.). *Roots of aggression: A re-examination of the frustration-aggression hypothesis.* New York: Atherton, 1969.

Berkowitz, L. Some determinants of impulsive aggression: Role of mediated associations with reinforcements for aggression. *Psychological Review,* 1974, *81,* 165–176.

Berkowitz, L., & Alioto, J. T. The meaning of an observed event as a determinant of its aggressive consequences. *Journal of Personality and Social Psychology,* 1973, *28,* 206–217.

Berkowitz, L., & Daniels, L. R. Responsibility and dependency. *Journal of Abnormal and Social Psychology,* 1963, *66,* 429–436.

Berkowitz, L., & Daniels, L. R. Affecting the salience of the social responsibility norm: Effects of past help on the response to dependency relationships. *Journal of Abnormal and Social Psychology,* 1964, *68,* 275–281.

Berkowitz, L., & Frodi, A. Reactions to the child's mistakes as affected by his/her looks and speech. *Social Psychology Quarterly,* 1979, *42,* 420–425.

Berkowitz, L., & LePage, A. Weapons as aggression-eliciting stimuli. *Journal of Personality and Social Psychology,* 1967, *7,* 202–207.

Berkowitz, L., & Walster, E. H. (Eds.). *Advances in experimental social psychology* (Vol. 9). New York: Academic Press, 1976.

Berscheid, E., Dion, K. K., Walster, E., & Walster, G. W. Physical attractiveness and dating choice: A test of the matching hypothesis. *Journal of Experimental Social Psychology,* 1971, *7,* 173–189.

Berscheid, E., Graziano, W., Monson, T., & Dermer, M. Outcome dependency: Attention, attribution, and attrac-

tion. *Journal of Personality and Social Psychology,* 1976, *34,* 978–989.

Berscheid, E., & Walster, E. Physical attractiveness and heterosexual attraction. In L. Berkowitz (Ed.), *Advances in experimental social psychology* (Vol. 7). New York: Academic Press, 1974.

Berscheid, E., & Walster, E. *Interpersonal attraction* (2nd Ed.). Reading, Mass.: Addison-Wesley, 1978.

Bettleheim, B. Individual and mass behavior in extreme situations. *Journal of Abnormal and Social Psychology,* 1943, *38,* 417–452.

Bettleheim, B. *Surviving and other essays.* New York: Alfred A. Knopf, 1979.

Bettleheim, B., & Janowitz, M. *Dynamics of prejudice.* New York: Harper, 1950.

Bieri, J. Complexity-simplicity as a personality variable in cognitive and preferential behavior. In D. W. Fiske & S. R. Maddi (Eds.), *Functions of varied experience.* Homewood, Ill.: Dorsey, 1961.

Blaney, N., Stephan, C., Rosenfield, D., Aronson, E., & Sikes, J. Interdependence in the classroom: A field study. *Journal of Educational Psychology,* 1977, *69,* 139–146.

Blascovich, J., & Ginsburg, G. P. Emergent norms and choice shifts involving risk. *Sociometry,* 1974, *37,* 205–218.

Blascovich, J., Ginsburg, G. P., & Beach, T. L. A pluralistic explanation of choice shifts on the risk dimension. *Journal of Personality and Social Psychology,* 1975, *31,* 422–429.

Blascovich, J., Ginsburg, G. P., & Howe, R. Blackjack, choice shifts in the field. *Sociometry,* 1976, *39,* 274–276.

Blau, P. M. *Exchange and power in social life.* New York: John Wiley & Sons, 1964.

Blumberg, H. H. On being liked more than you like. *Journal of Personality and Social Psychology,* 1969, *11,* 121–128.

Bochner, S., & Insko, C. A. Communicator discrepancy, source credibility, and opinion change. *Journal of Personality and Social Psychology,* 1966, *4,* 614–621.

Bogardus, E. S. Measuring social distance. *Journal of Applied Sociology,* 1925, *9,* 299–308.

Boggiano, A. K., & Ruble, D. N. Competence and the overjustification effect: A developmental study. *Journal of Personality and Social Psychology,* 1979, *37,* 1462–1468.

Bond, J. R., & Vinacke, W. E. Coalitions in mixed-sex triads. *Sociometry,* 1961, *24,* 61–75.

Bond, M. H. Effects of impression set on subsequent behavior. *Journal of Personality and Social Psychology,* 1972, *24,* 301–305.

Borden, R. J. Witnessed aggression: Influence of an observer's sex and values on aggressive responding. *Journal of Personality and Social Psychology,* 1975, *31,* 567–573.

Borden, R. J., & Taylor, S. P. The social instigation and control of physical aggression. *Journal of Applied Social Psychology,* 1973, *3,* 354–361.

Borg, W. R. Prediction of small group role behavior from personality variables. *Journal of Abnormal and Social Psychology,* 1960, *60,* 112–116.

Borgatta, E. F. A new systematic interaction observation system: Behavior Scores Systems (BSs System). *Journal of Psychological Studies*, 1963, *14*, 25–44.

Borgatta, E. F. Role-playing specification, personality, and performance. In A. P. Hare; E. F. Borgatta; & R. F. Bales (Eds.), *Small groups: Studies in social interaction* (Rev. ed.). New York: Alfred A. Knopf, 1965.

Borofsky, G. L. *Bystander reactions to physical assault: Sex differences in socially responsible behavior.* Unpublished masters thesis, Michigan State University, 1969.

Borofsky, G. L., Stollak, G. E., & Messé, L. A. Sex differences in bystander reactions to physical assault. *Journal of Experimental Social Psychology*, 1971, *7*, 313–318.

Bossard, J. Residential propinquity as a factor in marriage selection. *American Journal of Sociology*, 1932, *38*, 219–224.

Bradley, G. W. Self-serving biases in the attribution process: A re-examination of the fact or fiction question. *Journal of Personality and Social Psychology*, 1978, *36*, 56–71.

Bray, R. M., Kerr, N. L., & Atkin, R. S. Effects of group size, problem difficulty, and sex on group performance and member reactions. *Journal of Personality and Social Psychology*, 1978, *36*, 1224–1240.

Brehm, J. W. *A theory of psychological reactance.* New York: Academic Press, 1966.

Brehm, J. W., & Cohen, A. R. *Explorations in cognitive dissonance.* New York: John Wiley & Sons, 1962.

Brewer, M. B. An information-processing approach to attribution of responsibility. *Journal of Experimental Social Psychology*, 1977, *13*, 58–69.

Brewer, M. B. In-group bias in the minimal intergroup situation: A cognitive motivational analysis. *Psychological Bulletin*, 1979, *86*, 307–324.

Brewer, M. B., & Crano, W. D. Attitude change as a function of discrepancy and source of influence. *Journal of Social Psychology*, 1968, *76*, 13–18.

Brewer, M. B., & Silver, M. Ingroup bias as a function of task characteristics. *European Journal of Social Psychology*, 1978, *8*, 393–400.

Bridgeman, W. Student attraction and productivity as a composite function of reinforcement and expectancy conditions. *Journal of Personality and Social Psychology*, 1972, *23*, 249–258.

Brigham, J. C. Ethnic stereotypes. *Psychological Bulletin*, 1971, *76*, 15–38.

Brigham, J. C., Woodmansee, J. J., & Cook, S. W. Dimensions of verbal racial attitudes: Interracial marriage and approaches to racial equality. *Journal of Social Issues*, 1976, *32*, 9–21.

Brislin, R. W., & Lewis, S. A. Dating and physical attractiveness: Replication. *Psychological Reports*, 1968, *22*, 976.

Brock, T. C., & Buss, A. H. Dissonance, aggression and evaluation of pain. *Journal of Abnormal and Social Psychology*, 1962, *65*, 192–202.

Brophy, J. E., & Good, T. L. Teachers' communication of differential expectations for children's classroom performance: Some behavioral data. *Journal of Educational Psychology*, 1970, *61*, 365–374.

Brophy, J. E., & Good, T. L. *Teacher-student relationships: Causes and consequences.* New York: Holt, Rinehart & Winston, 1974.

Broussard, E. R. Neonatal prediction and outcome at 10–11 years. *Child Psychiatry and Human Development*, 1976, *7*, 16.

Broussard, E. R. Psychological disorders in children: Early assessment of infants at risk. *Continuing Education*, 1978, February, 44–57.

Broussard, E. R., & Hartner, M. S. S. Maternal perception of the neonate as related to development. *Child Psychiatry and Human Development*, 1970, *1*, 16.

Broussard, E. R., & Hartner, M. S. S. Further considerations regarding maternal perception of the firstborn. In J. Hellmuth (Ed.), *Exceptional infant: Studies in abnormalities* (Vol. 2). New York: Brunner/Mazel, 1971.

Broverman, I. K., Broverman, D. M., Clarkson, F. E., Rosenkrantz, P. S., & Vogel, S. Sex-role stereotypes and clinical judgments of mental health. *Journal of Consulting Psychology*, 1972, *34*, 1–7.

Brown, R. *Social psychology.* New York: Free Press, 1965

Bruner, J. S. *Beyond the information given.* New York: W. W. Norton, 1973.

Bruner, J. S., & Tagiuri, R. Person perception. In G. Lindzey (Ed.), *Handbook of Social Psychology* (Vol. 2). Reading, Mass.: Addison-Wesley, 1954.

Bryan, J. H., & Test, M. A. Models and helping: Naturalistic studies of aiding behavior. *Journal of Personality and Social Psychology*, 1967, *6*, 400–407.

Bryant, J., & Zillman, D. The effect of the intensification of annoyance through residual excitation from unrelated prior stimulation on substantially delayed hostile behavior. *Journal of Experimental Social Psychology*, 1979, *15*, 470–480.

Buldain, R. W., Crano, W. D., & Wegner, D. Effects of age of actor and observer on the moral judgments of children. *Journal of Genetic Psychology*, in press.

Burnstein, E., & Worchel, P. Arbitrariness of frustration and its consequence for aggression in a social situation. *Journal of Personality*, 1962, *30*, 528–541.

Buss, A. H., Booker, A., & Buss, E. Firing a weapon and aggression. *Journal of Personality and Social Psychology*, 1972, *22*, 296–302.

Buss, A. R. Causes and reasons in attribution theory: A conceptual critique. *Journal of Personality and Social Psychology*, 1978, *36*, 1311–1321.

Buss, A. R. On the relationship between causes and reason. *Journal of Personality and Social Psychology*, 1979, *37*, 1458–1461.

Buss, D. M., & Scheier, M. F. Self-consciousness, self-awareness, and self-attribution. *Journal of Research in Personality*, 1976, *10*, 463–468.

Byrne, D. The influence of propinquity and opportunities for interaction on classroom relationships. *Human Relations,* 1961, *14,* 63–69.

Byrne, D. Attitudes and attraction. In L. Berkowitz (Ed.), *Advances in experimental social psychology* (Vol. 4). New York: Academic Press, 1969.

Byrne, D. *The attraction paradigm.* New York: Academic Press, 1971.

Byrne, D., Clore, G. L. Effectance arousal and attraction. *Journal of Personality and Social Psychology,* 1967, *6,* (4, Whole No. 638).

Byrne, D., & Clore, G. L. A reinforcement model of evaluative responses. *Personality: An International Journal,* 1970, *2,* 103–128.

Byrne, D., Ervin, C. R., & Lamberth, J. Continuity between the experimental study of attraction and real-life computer dating. *Journal of Personality and Social Psychology,* 1970, *16,* 157–165.

Byrne, D., & Griffitt, W. Similarity and awareness of similarity of personality characteristics as determinants of attraction. *Journal of Experimental Research in Personality,* 1969, *3,* 179–186.

Byrne, D., & Griffitt, W., Hudgins, W., & Reeves, K. Attitude similarity-dissimilarity and attraction: Generality beyond the college sophomore. *Journal of Social Psychology,* 1969, *79,* 155–161.

Byrne, D., & McGraw, C. Interpersonal attraction toward Negroes. *Human Relations,* 1964, *17,* 201–203.

Byrne, D., & Nelson, D. Attraction as a linear function of proportion of positive reinforcements. *Journal of Personality and Social Psychology,* 1965, *1,* 659–663.

Byrne, D., & Rhamey, R. Magnitude of positive and negative reinforcements as a determinant of attraction. *Journal of Personality and Social Psychology,* 1965, 2, 884–889.

Byrne, D., & Wong, T. J. Racial prejudice, interpersonal attraction, and assumed dissimilarity of attitudes. *Journal of Abnormal and Social Psychology,* 1962, *65,* 246–250.

Calder, B. J., & Ross, M. *Attitudes and behavior.* Morristown, N.J.: General Learning Press, 1973.

Callahan, C. M., & Messé, L. A. Conditions affecting attempts to convert fate control to behavior control. *Journal of Experimental Social Psychology,* 1973, *9,* 481–490.

Callahan-Levy, C. M., & Messé, L. A. Sex differences in the allocation of pay. *Journal of Personality and Social Psychology,* 1979, *37,* 443–446.

Campbell, D. T. Social attitudes and other acquired behavioral dispositions. In S. Koch (Ed.), *Psychology: A study of a science* (Vol. 6). *Investigations of man as socius.* New York: McGraw-Hill, 1963.

Campbell, D. T., & Stanley, J. C. *Experimental and quasi-experimental designs for research.* Chicago: Rand McNally, 1963.

Cannell, C. F., & Kahn, R. L. Interviewing. In G. Lindzey

and E. Aronson (Eds.), *The handbook of social psychology,* (2nd Ed.) (Vol. 2). *Research methods.* Reading, Mass.: Addison-Wesley, 1968.

Cantor, N., & Mischel, W. Prototypes in person perception. In L. Berkowitz (Ed.), *Advances in experimental social psychology* (Vol. 12). New York: Academic Press, 1979.

Caple, R. B. The sequential stages of group development. *Small Group Behavior,* 1978, *9,* 470–476.

Caplow, T. *Two against one: Coalitions in triads.* Englewood Cliffs, N.J.: Prentice-Hall, 1968.

Carducci, B. J.; Cozby, P. C.; & Ward, C. D. Sexual arousal and interpersonal evaluations. *Journal of Experimental Social Psychology,* 1978, *14,* 449–457.

Carles, E. M., & Carver, C. S. Effects of person salience versus role salience on reward allocation in a dyad. *Journal of Personality and Social Psychology,* 1979, *37,* 2071–2080.

Carlsmith, J. M., & Anderson, C. A. Ambient temperature and the occurrence of collective violence: A new analysis. *Journal of Personality and Social Psychology,* 1979, *37,* 337–344.

Carlsmith, J. M., Collins, B. E., & Helmreich, R. L. Studies in forced compliance: I. The effect of pressure for compliance on attitude change produced by face-to-face role playing and anonymous essay writing. *Journal of Personality and Social Psychology,* 1966, *4,* 1–13.

Carlson, R. Sex differences in ego functioning: Exploratory studies of agency and communion. *Journal of Consulting and Clinical Psychology,* 1971, *37,* 267–277.

Cartwright, D., & Zander, A. (Eds.). *Group dynamics, research, and theory* (3rd ed.). New York: Harper & Row, 1968.

Carver, C. S., DeGregorio, E., & Gillis, R. Field study evidence of an ego-defensive bias in attribution among two categories of observers. *Personality and Social Psychology Bulletin,* 1980, *6,* 44–50.

Carver, C. S., & Glass, D. C. Coronary-prone behavior patterns and interpersonal aggression. *Journal of Personality and Social Psychology,* 1978, *36,* 361–366.

Cary, M. S. *Nonverbal openings to conversations.* Paper presented at the meeting of the Eastern Psychological Association, Philadelphia, April 1974.

Cattell, R. B. Concepts and methods in the measurement of group syntality. *Psychological Review,* 1948, *55,* 48–63.

Cattell, R. B., & Stice, G. F. *The dimensions of groups and their relations to the behavior of members.* Champaign, Ill.: Institute for Personality and Ability Testing, 1960.

Chaiken, S. Communicator physical attractiveness and persuasion. *Journal of Personality and Social Psychology,* 1979, *37,* 1387–1397.

Chaikin, A. L., & Darley, J. M. Victim or perpetrator? Defensive attribution of responsibility and the need for order and justice. *Journal of Personality and Social Psychology,* 1973, *25,* 268–275.

Chaikin, A. L., & Derlega, V. J. Liking for the norm-breaker in self-disclosure. *Journal of Personality,* 1974, *42,* 112–129.

Chapanis, N., & Chapanis, A. Cognitive dissonance: Five years later. *Psychological Bulletin,* 1964, *61,* 1–22.

Chapman, L. J., & Chapman, J. P. Illusory correlations as an obstacle to the use of valid psychodiagnostic signs. *Journal of Abnormal and Social Psychology,* 1969, *74,* 271–280.

Chemers, M. M., Rice, R. W., Sudstrom, E., & Butler, W. M. Leader esteem for the least preferred co-worker score, training, and effectiveness: An experimental examination. *Journal of Personality and Social Psychology,* 1975, *31,* 401–409.

Chesler, P., & Goodman, E. J. *Women, money, and power.* New York: Morrow, 1976.

Chevigny, H. *My eyes have a cold nose.* New Haven, Conn.: Yale University Press, 1946.

Choo, T. Communicator credibility and communication discrepancy as determinants of opinion change. *Journal of Social Psychology,* 1964, *64,* 1–20.

Cimbalo, R. S.; Faling, V.; & Mousaw, P. The course of love: A cross-sectional design. *Psychological Reports,* 1976, *38,* 1292–1294.

Clark, R. D., III. Effects of sex and race on helping behavior in a non-reactive setting. *Representative Research in Social Psychology,* 1974, *29,* 279–287.

Clore, G. L., Wiggins, N., & Itkin, S. Gain and loss in attraction: Attributions from nonverbal behavior. *Journal of Personality and Social Psychology,* 1975, *31,* 706–712.

Cohen, A. R. Social norms, arbitrariness of frustration and the status of the agent of frustration in the frustration-aggression hypothesis. *Journal of Abnormal and Social Psychology,* 1955, *51,* 222–225.

Cohen, A. R. A dissonance analysis of the boomerang effect. *Journal of Personality,* 1962, *30,* 75–88.

Cohen, A. R. *Attitude change and social influence.* New York: Basic Books, 1964.

Cohen, C. E. Person categories and social perception: Testing some boundaries of the processing effects of prior knowledge. *Journal of Personality and Social Psychology,* 1981, *40,* 441–452.

Cohen, S. P., Kelman, H. C., Miller, F. D., & Smith, B. D. Evolving intergroup techniques for conflict resolution: An Israeli-Palestinian pilot workshop. *Journal of Social Issues,* 1977, *33,* 165–189.

Collins, B. E., & Helmreich, R. Studies in forced compliance II: Contrasting mechanisms of attitude change produced by public persuasive and private-true essays. *Journal of Social Psychology,* 1970, *81,* 253–264.

Collins, B. E., & Hoyt, M. G. Personal responsibility for consequences: An integration and extension of the "forced compliance" literature. *Journal of Experimental Social Psychology,* 1972, *8,* 558–593.

Comstock, G., Chaffee, S., Katzman, N., McCombs, M., & Roberts, D. *Television and human behavior.* New York: Columbia University Press, 1978.

Condon, J. W., & Crano, W. D. Implied evaluation as a mediator of the attitude similarity-attraction relationship. Paper presented at the 49th annual meeting of the Eastern Psychological Association, Washington, D.C., 1977.

Cook, S. W. Motives in a conceptual analysis of attitude-related behavior. *Nebraska Symposium on Motivation,* 1970, *18,* 179–231.

Cooper, J., Fazio, R. H., & Rhodewalt, F. Dissonance and humor: Evidence for the undifferentiated nature of dissonance arousal. *Journal of Personality and Social Psychology,* 1978, *36,* 280–285.

Cooper, J., & Worchel, S. Role of undesired consequences in arousing cognitive dissonance. *Journal of Personality and Social Psychology,* 1970, *16,* 199–206.

Cooper, J., Zanna, M. P., & Taves, P. A. Arousal as a necessary condition for attitude change following induced compliance. *Journal of Personality and Social Psychology,* 1978, *36,* 1101–1106.

Costrich, N., Feinstein, J., Kidder, L., Maracek, J., & Pascale, L. When stereotypes hurt: Three studies of penalties for sex-role reversals. *Journal of Experimental Social Psychology,* 1975, *11,* 520–530.

Cottrell, N. B. Social facilitation. In C. G. McClintock (Ed.), *Experimental social psychology.* New York: Holt, Rinehart & Winston, 1972.

Cottrell, N. B., Wack, D. L., Sekerak, G. J., & Rittle, R. H. Social facilitation of dominant responses by the presence of an audience and the mere presence of others. *Journal of Personality and Social Psychology,* 1968, *9,* 245–250.

Cozby, P. Self-disclosure, reciprocity, and liking. *Sociometry,* 1972, *35,* 151–160.

Cozby, P. Self-disclosure: A literature review. *Psychological Bulletin,* 1973, *79,* 73–91.

Crano, W. D. Effects of sex, response order, and expertise in conformity: A dispositional approach. *Sociometry,* 1970, *33,* 239–252.

Crano, W. D. *Conformity behavior: A social psychological analysis.* Homewood, Ill.: Learning Systems, 1975.

Crano, W. D. Primacy versus recency in retention of information and opinion change. *Journal of Social Psychology,* 1977, *101,* 87–96.

Crano, W. D., & Cooper, R. E. Examination of Newcomb's extension of structural balance theory. *Journal of Personality and Social Psychology,* 1973, *27,* 344–353.

Crano, W. D., & Mellon, P. M. Causal influence of teachers' expectations on children's academic performance: A cross-lagged panel analysis. *Journal of Educational Psychology,* 1978, *70,* 39–49.

Crano, W. D., & Messé, L. A. When *does* dissonance fail? The time dimension in attitude measurement. *Journal of Personality,* 1970, *38,* 493–508.

Crano, W. D., & Schroder, H. M. Complexity of attitude structure and processes of conflict reduction. *Journal of Personality and Social Psychology*, 1967, *5*, 110–114.

Crespi, J. What kinds of attitude measures are predictive of behavior? *Public Opinion Quarterly*, 1971, *35*, 327–334.

Crutchfield, R. S. Conformity and character. *American Psychologist*, 1955, *10*, 191–198.

Cunningham, J. D.; Starr, P. A.; & Kanouse, D. E. Self as actor, active observer, and passive observer: Implications for causal attributions. *Journal of Personality and Social Psychology*, 1979, *37*, 1146–1152.

Cunningham, M. R. Weather, mood, and helping behavior: Quasi experiments with the sunshine Samaritan. *Journal of Personality and Social Psychology*, 1979, *37*, 1947–1956.

Cunningham, M. R., Steinberg, J., & Grev, R. Wanting to and having to help: Separate motivations for positive mood and guilt induced helping. *Journal of Personality and Social Psychology*, 1980, *38*, 181–192.

Daniels, L. R., & Berkowitz, L. Liking and response to dependency relationships. *Human Relations*, 1963, *16*, 141–148.

Darley, J. M., & Batson, C. D. From Jerusalem to Jericho: A study of situational and dispositional variables in helping behavior. *Journal of Personality and Social Psychology*, 1973, *27*, 100–108.

Darley, J. M., & Cooper, J. The "Clean for Gene" phenomenon: Deciding to vote for or against a candidate on the basis of the physical appearance of his supporters. *Journal of Applied Social Psychology*, 1972, *2*, 24–33.

Darley, J. M., Teger, A. I., & Lewis, L. D. Do groups always inhibit individuals' responses to potential emergencies? *Journal of Personality and Social Psychology*, 1973, *26*, 395–399.

Das, J. P., & Nanda, P. C. Mediated transfer of attitudes. *Journal of Abnormal and Social Psychology*, 1963, *66*, 12–16.

Davidson, A. R., & Jaccard, J. J. Variables that moderate the attitude-behavior relation: Results of a longitudinal survey. *Journal of Personality and Social Psychology*, 1979, *37*, 1364–1376.

Davis, D., & Brock, T. C. Effects of the recipient's status and responsiveness on physical pleasuring between heterosexual strangers. *Journal of Experimental Social Psychology*, 1979, *15*, 217–228.

Davis, D., & Perkowitz, W. T. Consequences of responsiveness in dyadic interaction: Effects of probability of response and proportion of content-related responses on interpersonal attraction. *Journal of Personality and Social Psychology*, 1979, *37*, 534–550.

Davis, J. D. Effects of communication about interpersonal process on the evolution of self-disclosure in dyads. *Journal of Personality and Social Psychology*, 1977, *35*, 31–37.

Davis, J. H., Kerr, N. L., Atkins, R. S., Hold, R., & Meek, B. The decision processes of six- and 12-person mock juries assigned unanimous and two-thirds majority rules. *Journal of Personality and Social Psychology*, 1975, *32*, 1–14.

Davis, K. E., & Jones, E. E. Changes in interpersonal perception as a means of reducing cognitive dissonance. *Journal of Abnormal and Social Psychology*, 1960, *61*, 402–410.

Dawe, H. C. The influence of size of kindergarten group upon performance. *Child Development*, 1934, *5*, 295–303.

Dawes, R. M., Singer, D., & Lemons, F. An experimental analysis of the contrast effect and its implications for intergroup communication and the indirect assessment of attitude. *Journal of Personality and Social Psychology*, 1972, *21*, 281–295.

Deaux, K. Sex: A perspective on the attribution process. In J. H. Harvey; W. J. Ickes; & R. F. Kidd (Eds.), *New directions in attribution research* (Vol. 1). Hillsdale, N.J.: Erlbaum, 1976.

Deaux, K., & Emswiller, T. Explanations of successful performance on sex-linked tasks: What is skill for the male is luck for the female. *Journal of Personality and Social Psychology*, 1974, *29*, 80–85.

Deaux, K., & Taynor, J. Evaluation of male and female ability: Bias works two ways. *Psychological Reports*, 1973, *32*, 261–262.

Deci, E. L. *Intrinsic motivation.* New York: Plenum, 1975.

Deci, E. L., & Ryan, R. M. The empirical exploration of intrinsic motivational processes. In L. Berkowitz (Ed.), *Advances in experimental social psychology* (Vol. 13). New York: Academic Press, 1980.

DeLamater, J. A. A definition of "group." *Small Group Behavior*, 1974, *5*, 30–34.

Dengerink, H. A. Anxiety, aggression and physiological arousal. *Journal of Experimental Research in Personality*, 1971, *5*, 223–232.

Dengerink, H. A., O'Leary, M. R., & Kasner, K. H. Individual differences in aggressive responses to attack: Internal-external locus of control and field-dependence-independence. *Journal of Research in Personality*, 1975, *9*, 191–199.

Derlega, V. J., Wilson, M., & Chaikin, A. L. Friendship and disclosure reciprocity. *Journal of Personality and Social Psychology*, 1976, *34*, 578–582.

Dermer, M., & Pyszczynski, T. A. Effects of erotica upon men's loving and liking responses for women they love. *Journal of Personality and Social Psychology*, 1978, *36*, 1302–1309.

De Soto, C. B., & Kuethe, J. L. Subjective probabilities of interpersonal relationships. *Journal of Abnormal and Social Psychology*, 1959, *59*, 290–294.

Deutsch, M. Equity, equality, and need: What determines which issues will be used as the basis of distributive justice? *Journal of Social Issues*, 1975, *31*, 137–149.

Deutsch, M., & Collins, M. *Interracial housing.* Minneapolis: University of Minnesota Press, 1951.

Diamond, N. J., & Lobitz, W. C. When familiarity breeds respect: The effects of an experimental depolarization program on police and student attitudes toward each other. *Journal of Social Issues,* 1973, *29,* 95–110.

Diener, E. Deindividuation. In P. Paulus (Ed.), *The psychology of group influence.* Hillsdale, N.J.: Erlbaum, 1980.

Dillehay, R. C. On the irrelevance of the classical negative evidence concerning the effect of attitudes on behavior. *American Psychologist,* 1973, *28,* 887–891.

Dion, K. K. Physical attractiveness and evaluation of children's transgressions. *Journal of Personality and Social Psychology,* 1972, *24,* 207–213.

Dion, K. K. Physical attractiveness, sex roles, and heterosexual attraction. In M. Cook (Ed.), *The bases of human sexual attraction.* London: Academic Press, 1980.

Dion, K. K., Baron, R. S., & Miller, N. Why do groups make riskier decisions than individuals? In L. Berkowitz (Ed.), *Advances in experimental social psychology* (Vol. 5). New York: Academic Press, 1970.

Dion, K. K., Berscheid, E., & Walster, E. What is beautiful is good. *Journal of Personality and Social Psychology,* 1972, *24,* 285–290.

Dittes, J. E. Attractiveness of group as function of self-esteem and acceptance by group. *Journal of Abnormal and Social Psychology,* 1959, *59,* 77–82.

Dollard, J., Doob, L., Miller, N., Mowrer, O. H., & Sears, R. R. *Frustration and aggression.* New Haven: Yale University Press, 1939.

Donnerstein, E. I., & Barrett, G. Effects of erotic stimuli on male aggression toward females. *Journal of Personality and Social Psychology,* 1978, *36,* 180–188.

Donnerstein, E. I., & Hallam, J. Facilitating effects of erotica on aggression against women. *Journal of Personality and Social Psychology,* 1978, *36,* 1270–1277.

Donnerstein, M., & Donnerstein, E. I. Modeling in the control of interracial aggression: The problem of generality. *Journal of Personality,* 1977, *45,* 100–116.

Dornbusch, S. M., Hastorf, A. H., Richardson, S. A., Muzzy, R. E., & Vreeland, R. S. The perceiver and the perceived: Their relative influence on the categories of interpersonal perceptions. *Journal of Personality and Social Psychology,* 1965, *1,* 434–440.

Drachman, D., & Worchel, S. Misattribution of arousal as a means of dissonance reduction. *Sociometry,* 1976, *39,* 53–59.

Driscoll, R., Davis, K. E., & Lipetz, M. E. Parental interference and romantic love: The Romeo and Juliet effect. *Journal of Personality and Social Psychology,* 1972, *24,* 1–10.

Duncan, B. L. Differential social perception and attribution of intergroup violence: Testing the lower limits of stereotyping of blacks. *Journal of Personality and Social Psychology,* 1976, *34,* 590–598.

Duncan, S., Jr., & Fiske, D. W. *Face-face-interaction: Research, methods, and theory.* Hillsdale, N.J.: Erlbaum, 1977.

Duncan, S., Jr., Rosenberg, M. J., & Finkelstein, J. The paralanguage of experimenter-bias. *Sociometry,* 1969, *32,* 207–219.

Duval, S., Duval, V. H., & Neely, P. Self-focus, felt responsibility, and helping behavior. *Journal of Personality and Social Psychology,* 1979, *37,* 1769–1778.

Duval, S., & Hensley, V. Extensions of objective self-awareness theory: The focus of attention—causal attribution hypothesis. In J. H. Harvey, W. J. Ickes, & R. F. Kidd (Eds.), *New directions in attribution research* (Vol. 1). Hillsdale, N.J.: Erlbaum, 1976.

Duval, S., & Wicklund, R. A. *A theory of objective self-awareness.* New York: Academic Press, 1972.

Dyck, R. J., & Rule, B. G. Effect on retaliation of causal attributions concerning attack. *Journal of Personality and Social Psychology,* 1978, *36,* 521–529.

Eagly, A. H. Involvement as a determinant of response to favorable and unfavorable information. *Journal of Personality and Social Psychology Monograph,* 1967, *7,* (3, Whole No. 643).

Eagly, A. H., & Chaiken, S. An attribution analysis of the effect of communicator characteristics on opinion change: The case of communicator attractiveness. *Journal of Personality and Social Psychology,* 1975, *32,* 36–144.

Eagly, A. H., & Telaak, K. Width of latitude of acceptance as a determinant of attitude change. *Journal of Personality and Social Psychology,* 1972, *23,* 388–397.

Ebbesen, E. B., Bowers, R. J., Phillips, S., & Snyder, M. Self-control processes in the forbidden toy paradigm. *Journal of Personality and Social Psychology,* 1975, *31,* 442–452.

Ebbesen, E. B., Kjos, G. L., & Konecni, V. J. Spatial ecology: Its effects on the choice of friends and enemies. *Journal of Experimental Social Psychology,* 1976, *12,* 505–518.

Edelman, R. J., & Hampson, S. E. The recognition of embarrassment. *Personality and Social Psychology Bulletin,* 1981, *7,* 109–116.

Efran, M. G. The effect of physical appearance on the judgment of guilt, interpersonal attraction, and severity of recommended punishment in a simulated jury task. *Journal of Research in Personality,* 1974, *8,* 45–54.

Egerbladh, T. The function of group size and ability level on solving a multidimensional complementary task. *Journal of Personality and Social Psychology,* 1976, *34,* 805–808.

Ehrlich, D., Guttman, I., Schonbach, P., & Mills, J. Postdecision exposure to relevant information. *Journal of Abnormal and Social Psychology,* 1957, *54,* 98–102.

Eisen, S. V. Actor-observer differences in information inference and causal attribution. *Journal of Personality and Social Psychology,* 1979, *37,* 261–272.

Eiser, R., & Stroebe, W. *Categorization and social judgment.* New York: Academic Press, 1972.

Elashoff, J., & Snow, R. *Pygmalion reconsidered.* Worthington, Ohio: C. A. Jones, 1971.

Elms, A. C. The influence of fantasy ability on attitude change through role playing. *Journal of Personality and Social Psychology,* 1966, *4,* 36–43.

Epstein, S., & Taylor, S. P. Instigation to aggression as a function of degree of defeat and perceived aggressive intent of the opponent. *Journal of Personality,* 1967, *35,* 265–289.

Eron, L. D. Prescription for reduction of aggression. *American Psychologist,* 1980, *35,* 244–252.

Eskilson, A., & Wiley, M. G. Sex composition and leadership in small groups. *Sociometry,* 1976, *39,* 183–194.

Evans, R. I., Rozelle, R. M., Lasater, T. M., Dembroski, T. M., & Allen, B. P. Fear arousal, persuasion, and actual versus implied behavioral change: New perspective utilizing a real-life dental hygiene program. *Journal of Personality and Social Psychology,* 1970, *16,* 220–227.

Exline, R. V. Group climate as a factor in the relevance and accuracy of social perception. *Journal of Abnormal and Social Psychology,* 1957, *55,* 382–388.

Exline, R. V. Visual interaction: The glances of power and preference. In J. K. Cole (Ed.), *Nebraska symposium on motivation* (Vol. 19). Lincoln: University of Nebraska Press, 1972.

Fairweather, G. W. *Social psychology in treating verbal illness: An experimental approach.* New York: John Wiley & Sons, 1964.

Fairweather, G. W., Sanders, D. H., & Tornatzky, L. G. *Creating change in mental health organizations.* New York: Pergamon, 1974.

Farina, A., Allen, J. G., & Saul, B. B. The role of the stigmatized person in affecting social relationships. *Journal of Personality,* 1968, *36,* 169–182.

Fazio, R. H., & Zanna, M. P. Attitudinal qualities relating to the strength of the attitude-behavior relationship. *Journal of Experimental Social Psychology,* 1978, *14,* 398–408. (a)

Fazio, R. H, & Zanna, M. P. On the predictive validity of attitudes: The role of direct experience and confidence. *Journal of Personality,* 1978, *46,* 228–259. (b)

Fazio, R. H., & Zanna, M. P. Direct experience in attitude-behavior consistency. In L. Berkowitz (Ed.), *Advances in experimental social psychology,* in press.

Fazio, R. H., Zanna, M. P., & Cooper, J. Dissonance and self-perception: An integrative view of each theory's proper domain of application. *Journal of Experimental Social Psychology,* 1977, *13,* 464–479.

Feather, N. T., & Simon, J. G. Reactions to male and female success and failure in sex-linked occupations: Impressions of personality, causal attributions, and perceived likelihood of different consequences. *Journal of Personality and Social Psychology,* 1975, *31,* 20–31.

Feldman, N. S., Higgins, E. T., Karlovac, M., & Ruble, D. N. Use of consensus information in causal attributions as a function of temporal presentation and availability of direct information. *Journal of Personality and Social Psychology,* 1976, *34,* 694–699.

Feldman-Summers, S., & Kiesler, S. Those who are number two try harder: The effect of sex in the attribution of causality. *Journal of Personality and Social Psychology,* 1974, *30,* 841–855.

Felson, R. B. Ambiguity and bias in the self-concept. *Social Psychology Quarterly,* 1981, *44,* 64–69.

Ferguson, L. R., Partyka, L. B., & Lester, B. M. Patterns of parent perception differentiating clinic from nonclinic children. *Journal of Abnormal Child Psychology,* 1974, *2,* 169–181.

Ferguson, T. J., & Wells, G. L. Priming of mediators in causal attribution. *Journal of Personality and Social Psychology,* 1980, *38,* 461–470.

Ferris, C. B., & Wicklund, R. A. An experiment on importance of freedom and prior demonstration. In R. A. Wicklund (Ed.), *Freedom and reactance.* Hillsdale, N.J.: Erlbaum, 1974.

Feshbach, S. The role of fantasy in the response to television. *Journal of Social Issues,* 1976, *32,* 71–80.

Feshbach, S., & Singer, R. D. *Television and aggression: An experimental field study.* San Francisco: Jossey-Bass, 1971.

Feshbach, S., Stiles, W. B., & Bitter, E. The reinforcing effect of witnessing aggression. *Journal of Experimental Research in Personality,* 1967, *2,* 133–139.

Festinger, L. Informal social communication. *Psychological Review,* 1950, *57,* 271–282.

Festinger, L. An analysis of compliance behavior. In M. Sherif and M. O. Wilson (eds.) Group relations at the crossroads. New York: Harper, 1953. (a)

Festinger, L. Group attraction and membership. In D. Cartwright & A. Zander, (Eds.), *Group dynamics: Research and theory.* Evanston, Ill.: Row, Peterson, 1953. (b)

Festinger, L. A theory of social comparison processes. *Human Relations,* 1954, *7,* 117–140.

Festinger, L. *A theory of cognitive dissonance.* Stanford, Calif.: Stanford University Press, 1957.

Festinger, L., & Carlsmith, J. M. Cognitive consequences of forced compliance. *Journal of Abnormal and Social Psychology,* 1959, *58,* 203–210.

Festinger, L., & Maccoby, N. On resistance to persuasive communications. *Journal of Abnormal and Social Psychology,* 1964, *68,* 359–366.

Festinger, L., Riecken, H. W., & Schachter, S. S. *When prophecy fails.* Minneapolis: University of Minnesota Press, 1956.

Festinger, L., Schachter, S. S., Back, K. *Social pressures in informal groups: A study of human factors in housing.* New York: Harper & Row, 1950.

Fiedler, F. E. A contingency model of leadership effectiveness. In L. Berkowitz (Ed.), *Advances in experimental social psychology* (Vol. 1). New York: Academic Press, 1964.

Fiedler, F. E. *A theory of leadership effectiveness.* New York: McGraw-Hill, 1967.

Fiedler, F. E. The contingency model and the dynamics of the leadership process. In L. Berkowitz (Ed.), *Advances in experimental social psychology* (Vol. 11). New York: Academic Press, 1978.

Fincham, F. D., & Jaspars, J. M. Attribution of responsibility: From man the scientist to man as lawyer. In L. Berkowitz (Ed.), *Advances in experimental social psychology* (Vol. 13). New York: Academic Press, 1980.

Fishbein, M., & Ajzen, I. Attitudes toward objects as predictors of single and multiple criteria. *Psychological Review,* 1974, *81,* 59–74.

Fishbein, M., & Ajzen, I. *Belief, attitude, intention and behavior: An introduction to theory and research.* Reading, Mass.: Addison-Wesley, 1975.

Fishbein, M., & Hunter, R. Summation versus balance in attitude organization and change. *Journal of Abnormal and Social Psychology,* 1964, *69,* 505–510.

Fisher, B. A. Decision emergence: Phases in group decision-making. *Speech Monographs,* 1970, *37,* 53–66.

Fishman, C. G. Need for approval and the expression of aggression under varying conditions of frustration. *Journal of Personality and Social Psychology,* 1965, *2,* 809–816.

Fiske, S. T. Attention and weight in person perception: The impact of negative and extreme behavior. *Journal of Personality and Social Psychology,* 1980, *38,* 889–906.

Fitch, G. Effects of self-esteem, perceived performance, and choice on causal attributions. *Journal of Personality and Social Psychology,* 1970, *16,* 311–315.

Flanagan, J. C. *Tests of general ability: Technical report.* Chicago: Science Research Associates, 1960.

Folger, R., Rosenfield, D., & Hays, R. P. Equity and intrinsic motivation: The role of choice. *Journal of Personality and Social Psychology,* 1978, *36,* 557–564.

Forest, D., Clark, M. S., Mills, J., & Isen, A. M. Helping as a function of feeling state and nature of the helping behavior. *Motivation and Emotion,* in press.

Form, W. H., & Nosow, S. *Community in disaster.* New York: Harper & Row, 1958.

Forsyth, D. R. The functions of attributions. *Social Psychology Quarterly,* 1980, *43,* 184–189.

Frank, F., & Anderson, L. R. Effects of task and group size upon group productivity and member satisfaction. *Sociometry,* 1971, *34,* 135–149.

Freedman, J. L. Attitudinal effects of inadequate justification. *Journal of Personality,* 1963, *31,* 371–385.

Freedman, J. L. Involvement, discrepancy, and change. *Journal of Abnormal Social Psychology,* 1964, *69,* 290–295.

Freedman, J. L. Long-term behavioral effects of cognitive dissonance. *Journal of Experimental Social Psychology,* 1965, *1,* 145–155.

Freedman, M. B., Leary, T. F., Ossorio, A. G., & Coffey, H. S. The interpersonal dimension of personality. *Journal of Personality,* 1951, *20,* 143–161.

Frey, D. Reactions to success and failure in public and private conditions. *Journal of Experimental Social Psychology,* 1978, *14,* 172–179.

Fried, R., & Berkowitz, L. Music hath charms . . . and can influence helpfulness. *Journal of Applied Social Psychology,* 1979, *9,* 199–208.

Frieze, I., & Weiner, B. Cue utilization and attributional judgments for success and failure. *Journal of Personality and Social Psychology,* 1971, *39,* 591–605.

Frodi, A. The effect of exposure to weapons on aggressive behavior from a cross-cultural perspective. *International Journal of Psychology,* 1975, *10,* 283–292.

Gamson, W. A. Experimental studies of coalition formation. In L. Berkowitz (Ed.), *Advances in experimental social psychology* (Vol. 1). New York: Academic Press, 1964.

Gastorf, J. W., Suls, J. M., & Sanders, G. S. Social facilitation and the Type A coronary-prone behavior pattern. *Journal of Personality and Social Psychology,* 1980, *38,* 773–780.

Geen, R. G. Some effects of observing violence upon the behavior of the observer. In B. A. Maher (Ed.), *Progress in experimental personality research.* New York: Academic Press, 1978.

Geen, R. G., & Gagne, J. J. Drive theory of social facilitation: Twelve years of theory and research. *Psychological Bulletin,* 1977, *84,* 1267–1288.

Geen, R. G., & Pigg, R. Acquisition of an aggressive response and its generalization to verbal behavior. *Journal of Personality and Social Psychology,* 1970, *15,* 165–170.

Geen, R. G., & Stonner, D. Effects of aggressiveness habit strength in the presence of aggression-related stimuli. *Journal of Personality and Social Psychology,* 1971, *17,* 149–153.

Gerard, H. B., Conolley, E. S., & Wilhelmy, R. A. Compliance, justification, and cognitive change. In L. Berkowitz (Ed.), *Advances in experimental social psychology* (Vol. 7). New York: Academic Press, 1974.

Gerard, H. B., Mathewson, G. C. The effects of severity of initiation on liking for a group: A replication. *Journal of Experimental Social Psychology,* 1966, *2,* 278–287.

Gergen, K. J. *The psychology of behavior exchange.* Reading, Mass.: Addison-Wesley, 1969.

Gergen, K. J.; Greenberg, M. S.; & Willis, R. H. *Social exchange: Advances in theory and research.* New York: Plenum Press, 1980.

Gibb, J. R. The effects of group size and threat upon certainty in a problem-solving situation. *American Psychologist,* 1951, *6,* 324.

Gibbins, K. Communication aspects of women's clothes and

their relation to fashionability. *British Journal of Social and Clinical Psychology,* 1969, *8,* 301–312.

Gibbons, F. X., & Wright, R. A. Motivational biases in causal attributions of arousal. *Journal of Personality and Social Psychology,* 1981, *40,* 588–600.

Giesen, M., & McClaren, H. A. Discussion, distance and sex: Changes in impressions and attraction during small group interaction. *Sociometry,* 1976, *39,* 60–70.

Giffin, K. The contribution of studies of source credibility to a theory of interpersonal trust in the communication process. *Psychological Bulletin,* 1967, *68,* 104–120.

Ginosar, Z. & Trope, Y. The effects of base rates and individuating information on judgments about another person. *Journal of Experimental Social Psychology,* 1980, *16,* 228–242.

Goethals, G. R., Cooper, J., & Naficy, A. Role of foreseen, foreseeable, and unforeseeable behavioral consequences in the arousal of cognitive dissonance. *Journal of Personality and Social Psychology,* 1979, *37,* 1179–1185.

Goethals, G. R., & Zanna, M. P. The role of social comparison in choice shifts. *Journal of Personality and Social Psychology,* 1979, *37,* 1469–1476.

Goffman, E. On cooling the mark out: Some aspects of adaptation to failure. *Psychiatry,* 1952, *15,* 461–463.

Goffman, E. On face work: The analysis of ritual elements in social interaction. *Psychiatry,* 1955, *18,* 213–231.

Goffman, E. *Behavior in public places.* Glencoe, Ill.: Free Press, 1963.

Goldberg, L. R. Differential attribution of trait-descriptive terms to oneself as compared to well-liked, neutral, and disliked others: A psychometric analysis. *Journal of Personality and Social Psychology,* 1978, *36,* 1012–1028.

Goldberg, P. A., Gottesdiener, M., & Abramson, P. R. Another put-down of women? Perceived attractiveness as a function of support for the feminist movement. *Journal of Personality and Social Psychology,* 1975, *32,* 113–115.

Goldstein, J. H., Davis, R. W., & Herman, D. Escalation of aggression: Experimental Studies. *Journal of Personality and Social Psychology,* 1975, *31,* 162–170.

Gollin, E. S. Forming impressions of personality. *Journal of Personality,* 1954, *23,* 65–76.

Gollob, H. F. Some tests of a social inference model. *Journal of Personality and Social Psychology,* 1974, *29,* 157–179. (a)

Gollob, H. F. The subject-verb-object approach to social cognition. *Psychological Review,* 1974, *81,* 286–321. (b)

Gould, R. & Sigall, H. The effects of empathy and outcome on attribution: An examination of the divergent-perspectives hypothesis. *Journal of Experimental Social Psychology,* 1977, *13,* 480–491.

Gouldner, A. W. The norm of reciprocity: A preliminary statement. *American Sociological Review,* 1960, *25,* 161–178.

Graziano, W., Brothen, T., & Berscheid, E. Attention, attrac-

tion, and individual differences in reaction to criticism. *Journal of Personality and Social Psychology,* 1980, *38,* 193–202.

Greenberg, A. M., & Strickland, L. H. "Apparent behavior" revisited. *Perceptual and Motor Skills,* 1973, *36,* 227–233.

Greene, L. R. Effects of field dependence on affective reactions and compliance in dyadic interactions. *Journal of Personality and Social Psychology,* 1976, *34,* 569–577.

Greenwald, A. G. The open-mindedness of the counter-attitudinal role player. *Journal of Experimental Social Psychology,* 1969, *5,* 375–388.

Greenwald, A. G. When does role playing produce attitude change? Toward an answer. *Journal of Personality and Social Psychology,* 1970, *16,* 214–219.

Griffin, K. The contribution of studies of source credibility to a theory of interpersonal trust in the communication process. *Psychological Bulletin,* 1967, *68,* 104–120.

Griffitt, W., & Veitch, R. Preacquaintance attitude similarity and attraction revisited: Ten days in a fall-out shelter. *Sociometry,* 1974, *37,* 163–172.

Gross, A. E., Wallston, B. S., & Piliavin, I. M. Beneficiary attractiveness and cost as determinants of responses to routine requests for help. *Sociometry,* 1975, *38,* 131–140.

Gruder, C. & Cook, T. D. Sex, dependency, and helping. *Journal of Personality and Social Psychology,* 1971, *19,* 290–294.

Grush, J. E., & Yehl, J. G. Marital roles, sex differences, and interpersonal attraction. *Journal of Personality and Social Psychology,* 1979, *37,* 116–123.

Haas, D. F., & Desearn, F. A. Trust and symbolic exchange. *Social Psychology Quarterly,* 1981, *44,* 3–13.

Hall, J. A. Voice tone and persuasion. *Journal of Personality and Social Psychology,* 1980, *38,* 924–934.

Hamilton, D. L. A cognitive-attributional analysis of stereotyping. In L. Berkowitz (Ed.), *Advances in experimental social psychology* (Vol. 12). New York: Academic Press, 1979.

Hamilton, D. L., & Bishop, G. D. Attitudinal and behavioral effects of initial integration of white suburban neighborhoods. *Journal of Social Issues,* 1976, *32,* 47–56.

Hamilton, D. L., Katz, L. B., & Leirer, V. O. Cognitive representation of personality impressions: Organizational processes in first impression formation. *Journal of Personality and Social Psychology,* 1980, *39,* 1050–1063.

Hamilton, D. L., & Rose, T. L. Illusory correlation and the maintenance of stereotypic beliefs. *Journal of Personality and Social Psychology,* 1980, *39,* 832–845.

Hamilton, V. L. Intuitive psychologist or intuitive lawyer? Alternative models of the attribution process. *Journal of Personality and Social Psychology,* 1980, *39,* 767–772.

Hamm, N., Baum, M. R., & Nikels, K. W. Effects of race

and exposure on judgments of interpersonal favorability. *Journal of Experimental Social Psychology,* 1975, *11,* 14–24.

Haney, C., Banks, C., & Zimbardo, P. G. A study of prisoners and guards in a simulated prison. In E. Aronson (Ed.), *Readings about the social animal* (3rd ed.). San Francisco: Freeman, 1981.

Hansen, R. D. Commonsense attribution. *Journal of Personality and Social Psychology,* 1980, *39,* 996–1009.

Hansen, R. D., & Donoghue, J. M. The power of consensus: Information derived from one's own and other's behavior. *Journal of Personality and Social Psychology,* 1977, *35,* 294–302.

Hansen, R. D., & Lowe, C. A. Distinctiveness and consensus: The influence of behavioral information on actors' and observers' attributions. *Journal of Personality and Social Psychology,* 1976, *34,* 425–434.

Hansen, R. D., & Stonner, D. M. Attributes and attributions: Inferring stimulus properties, actors' dispositions and causes. *Journal of Personality and Social Psychology,* 1978, *36,* 657–667.

Hardin, G. The tragedy of the commons. *Science,* 1968, *162,* 1243–1248.

Hare, A. P. Interaction and consensus in different sized groups. *American Sociological Review,* 1952, *17,* 261–267.

Harkins, S., Latané, B., & Williams, K. Social loafing: Allocating effort or taking it easy. *Journal of Experimental Social Psychology,* 1980, *16,* 457–465.

Harré, R., & Secord, P. F. *The explanation of social behavior.* Oxford, England: Blackwell, 1972.

Harris, M. B. Mediators between frustration and aggression in a field experiment. *Journal of Experimental Social Psychology,* 1974, *10,* 561–571.

Harrison, A. A. Mere exposure. In L. Berkowitz (Ed.), *Advances in experimental social psychology* (Vol. 10). New York: Academic Press, 1977.

Harrison, M. G., Messé, L. A., & Stollak, G. E. The effects of racial composition and group size on interaction patterns in preschool children. *Proceedings of the 79th Annual Convention of the American Psychological Association,* 1971, *6,* 325–326.

Hartmann, D. P. Influence of symbolically modeled instrumental aggression and pain cues on aggressive behavior. *Journal of Personality and Social Psychology,* 1969, *11,* 280–288.

Harvey, J. H., Harris, B., & Barnes, R. D. Actor-observer differences in the perceptions of responsibility and freedom. *Journal of Personality and Social Psychology,* 1975, *32,* 22–28.

Harvey, J. H., Towne, J. P., & Yarkin, K. L. How fundamental is "the fundamental attribution error"? *Journal of Personality and Social Psychology,* 1981, *40,* 346–349.

Harvey, O. J., Hunt, D. E., & Schroder, H. M. *Conceptual systems and personality organization.* New York: John Wiley & Sons, 1961.

Hastie, R., & Kumar, P. A. Person memory: Personality traits as organizing principles in memory for behaviors. *Journal of Personality and Social Psychology,* 1979, *37,* 25–38.

Hastorf, A. H., Kite, W. R., Gross, A. E., & Wolf, L. J. The perception and evaluation of behavior change. *Sociometry,* 1965, *48,* 400–410.

Haythorn, W. W. The influence of individual members on the characteristics of small groups. In A. P. Hare; E. F. Borgatta; & R. F. Bales (Eds.), *Small groups: Studies in social interaction* (Rev. ed.). New York: Alfred A. Knopf, 1965.

Haythorn, W. W., Couch, A., Haefner, D., Langham, P., & Carter, L. F. The behavior of authoritarian and egalitarian personalities in groups. *Human Relations,* 1956, *9,* 57–74. (a)

Haythorn, W. W., Couch, A., Haefner, D., Langham, P., & Carter, L. F. The effects of varying combinations of authoritarian and egalitarian leaders and followers. *Journal of Abnormal Social Psychology,* 1956, *53,* 210–219. (b)

Heider, F. *The psychology of interpersonal relations.* New York: John Wiley & Sons, 1958.

Heider, F., & Simmel, M. An experimental study of apparent behavior. *American Journal of Psychology,* 1944, *57,* 243–259.

Heinicke, C., & Bales, R. F. Developmental trends in the structure of small groups. *Sociometry,* 1953, *16,* 35–36.

Hemphill, J. K. Relations between the size of the group and the behavior of "superior" leaders. *Journal of Social Psychology,* 1950, *32,* 11–22.

Hendrick, C., & Constantini, A. F. Effects of varying trait inconsistency and response requirements on the primacy effect in impression formation. *Journal of Personality and Social Psychology,* 1970, *15,* 158–164.

Hendrick, S. S. Self-disclosure and marital satisfaction. *Journal of Personality and Social Psychology,* 1981, *40,* 1150–1159.

Higbee, K. L. Fifteen years of fear arousal: Research on threat appeals, 1953–1968. *Psychology Bulletin,* 1969, *72,* 426–444.

Higgins, E. T., Rhodewalt, F., & Zanna, M. P. Dissonance motivation: Its nature, persistence, and reinstatement. *Journal of Experimental Social Psychology,* 1979, *15,* 16–34.

Hoffman, C., Mischel, W., & Mazze, K. The role of purpose in the organization of information about behavior. Trait-based versus goal-based categories in person cognition. *Journal of Personality and Social Psychology,* 1981, *40,* 211–225.

Hollander, E. P. Authoritarianism and leadership choice in a military setting. *Journal of Abnormal and Social Psychology,* 1954, *49,* 365–376.

Holz, R. F. Similarity versus complementarity of needs in mate selection. *Dissertation Abstracts International,* 1969, *29,* 2618.

Homans, G. C. *The human group.* New York: Harcourt Brace & Co., 1950.

Homans, G. C. *Social behavior: Its elementary forms.* New York: Harcourt Brace & World, 1961.

Homans, G. C. Group factors in worker productivity. In H. Proshansky & B. Seidenberg (Eds.), *Basic studies in social psychology.* New York: Holt, Rinehart & Winston, 1965.

Homans, G. C. *Social behavior: Its elementary forms* (Rev. ed.). New York: Harcourt Brace Jovanovich, 1974.

Hong, L. K. Risky shift and cautious shift: Some direct evidence on the culture-value theory. *Social Psychology,* 1978, *41,* 342–346.

Hoppe, C. Interpersonal aggression as a function of subject's sex, subject's sex role identification, opponent's sex, and degree of provocation. *Journal of Personality and Social Psychology,* 1979, *47,* 317–329.

Horney, K. *Our inner conflicts.* New York: W. W. Norton, 1945.

Hovland, C. I., Harvey, O. J., & Sherif, M. Assimilation and contrast effects in reactions to communication and attitude change. *Journal of Abnormal and Social Psychology,* 1957, *55,* 244–252.

Hovland, C. I., & Janis, I. L. *Personality and persuasibility.* New Haven, Conn.: Yale University Press, 1959.

Hovland, C. I., Janis, I. L., & Kelley, H. H. *Communication and persuasion.* New Haven, Conn.: Yale University Press, 1953.

Hovland, C. I., Lumsdaine, A. A., & Sheffield, F. D. *Experiments on mass communication.* Princeton, N.J.: Princeton University Press, 1949.

Hovland, C. I., & Mandell, W. An experimental comparison of conclusion-drawing by the communicator and by the audience. *Journal of Abnormal and Social Psychology,* 1952, *47,* 581–588.

Hovland, C. I., & Weiss, W. The influence of source credibility on communication effectiveness. *Public Opinion Quarterly,* 1951, *15,* 635–650.

Howard, W., & Crano, W. D. Effects of sex, conversation, location, and size of observer group on bystander intervention in a high risk situation. *Sociometry,* 1974, *37,* 491–507.

Howells, L. T., & Becker, S. W. Seating arrangement and leadership emergence. *Journal of Abnormal and Social Psychology,* 1962, *64,* 148–150.

Hull, J. G., & Levy, A. S. The organizational functions of the self: An alternative to the Duval and Wicklund model of self-awareness. *Journal of Personality and Social Psychology,* 1979, *37,* 756–768.

Hunt, W., & Volkmann, J. Anchoring effects in judgment. *American Journal of Psychology,* 1937, *54,* 395–403.

Huston, T. L. Ambiguity of acceptance, social desirability, and dating choice. *Journal of Experimental Social Psychology,* 1973, *9,* 32–42.

Huston, T. L., Ruggiero, M., Conner, R., & Geis, G. Bystander intervention into crime: A study based on naturally occurring episodes. *Social Psychology Quarterly,* 1981, *44,* 14–23.

Hyman, H. H. *Interviewing in social research.* Chicago: University of Chicago Press, 1954.

Ingham, A. G., Levinger, G., Graves, J., & Peckham, V. The Ringlemann effect: Studies of group size and group performance. *Journal of Experimental Social Psychology,* 1974, *10,* 371–384.

Insko, C. A. *Theories of attitude change.* New York: Appleton-Century-Crofts, 1967.

Insko, C. A., Arkoff, A., & Insko, V. Effects of high and low fear-arousing communications upon opinions toward smoking. *Journal of Experimental Social Psychology,* 1965, *1,* 256–266.

Insko, C. A., Songer, E., & McGarvey W. Balance, positivity, and agreement in the Jordan paradigm: A defense of balance theory. *Journal of Experimental Social Psychology,* 1974, *10,* 53–83.

Insko, C. A., Thibaut, J. W., Moehle, D., Wilson, M., Diamond, W. D., Gilmore, R., Solomon, M. R., & Lipsitz, A. Social evolution and the emergence of leadership. *Journal of Personality and Social Psychology,* 1980, *39,* 431–448.

Insko, C. A., Turnbull, W., & Yandell, B. Facilitating and inhibiting effects of distraction on attitude change. *Sociometry,* 1975, *4,* 508–528.

Insko, C. A., & Wilson, M. Interpersonal attraction as a function of social interaction. *Journal of Personality and Social Psychology,* 1977, *12,* 903–911.

Isen, A. M., Horn, N., & Rosenhan, D. L. Effects of success and failure on children's generosity. *Journal of Personality and Social Psychology,* 1973, *27,* 239–247.

Isen, A. M., & Levin, P. F. The effect of feeling good on helping: Cookies and kindness. *Journal of Personality and Social Psychology,* 1972, *21,* 384–388.

Itelman, H. C., & Cohen, S. P. Reduction of interpersonal conflict: An interactional approach. In W. G. Austin & S. Worchel (Eds.), *The social psychology of intergroup relations.* Monterey, Calif.: Brooks/Cole, 1979.

Jaccard, J. J., Knox, R., & Brinberg, D. Prediction of behavior from beliefs: An extension and test of a subjective probability model. *Journal of Personality and Social Psychology,* 1979, *37,* 1239–1248.

Jackson, L. A. The influence of sex, physical attractiveness, sex role orientation, and occupational sex-linkage on occupational attainment and advancement. Unpublished dissertation, The University of Rochester, December, 1980.

Jacobs, L. E., Berscheid, E., & Walster, E. Self-esteem and attraction. *Journal of Personality and Social Psychology,* 1971, *17,* 84–91.

Jacobson, M. B., & Koch, W. Attributed reasons for support of the feminist movement as a function of attractiveness. *Sex Roles,* 1978, *4,* 169–174.

Jaffe, Y., Malamuth, N., Feingold, J., & Feshbach, S. Sexual arousal and behavioral aggression. *Journal of Personality and Social Psychology,* 1974, *30,* 759–764.

Janis, I. L. *Victims of group think.* Boston: Houghton-Mifflin, 1972.

Janis, I. L., & Feshbach, S. Effects of fear arousing communications. *Journal of Abnormal and Social Psychology,* 1953, *48,* 78–92.

Janis, I. L., & Hoffman, D. Facilitating effects of daily contact between partners who make a decision to cut down on smoking. *Journal of Personality and Social Psychology,* 1971, *17,* 25–35.

Janis, I. L., & Hovland, C. I. (Eds.). *Personality and persuasibility.* New Haven, Conn.: Yale University Press, 1959.

Janis, I. L., & King, B. T. The influence of role playing on opinion change. *Journal of Abnormal and Social Psychology,* 1954, *49,* 211–218.

Janis, I. L., & Mann, L. Effectiveness of emotional role-playing in modifying smoking habits and attitudes. *Journal of Experimental Research in Personality,* 1965, *1,* 84–90.

Janis, I., & Terwilliger, R. An experimental study of psychological resistances to fear-arousing communications. *Journal of Abnormal and Social Psychology,* 1962, *65,* 403–410.

Janoff-Bulman, R., Lang, L., & Johnston, D. Participant-observer differences in attributions for an ambiguous victimization. *Personality and Social Psychology Bulletin,* 1979, *5,* 335–339.

Jellison, J. M., Jackson-White, R., Bruder, R. A., & Martyna, W. Achievement behavior: A situational behavior. *Sex Roles,* 1975, *1,* 375–390.

Johnson, R. D., & Downing, L. L. Deindividuation and valence of cues: Effects on prosocial and antisocial behavior. *Journal of Personality and Social Psychology,* 1979, *37,* 1532–1538.

Johnson, T. J., Feigenbaum, R., & Weiby, M. Some determinants and consequences of the teacher's perception of causality. *Journal of Educational Psychology,* 1964, *55,* 237–246.

Jones, C. M., & Harackiewicz, J. M. Contrast effects in attitude judgment: An examination of the accentuation hypothesis. *Journal of Personality and Social Psychology,* 1980, *38,* 390–398.

Jones, E. E. Authoritarianism as a determinant of first-impression formation. *Journal of Abnormal and Social Psychology,* 1954, *23,* 107–127.

Jones, E. E., & Davis, K. E. From acts to dispositions. The attribution process in person perception. In L. Berkowitz (Ed.), *Advances in experimental social psychology* (Vol. 2). New York: Academic Press, 1965.

Jones, E. E., Davis, K. E., & Gergen, K. J. Role playing variations and their informational value for person perception. *Journal of Abnormal and Social Psychology,* 1961, *63,* 302–310.

Jones, E. E., & Gerard, H. B. *Foundations of social psychology.* New York: John Wiley & Sons, 1967.

Jones, E. E., Goethals, G. R., Kennington, G. E., & Severance, L. J. Primacy and assimilation in the attribution process: The stable entity proposition. *Journal of Personality and Social Psychology,* 1972, *40,* 250–274.

Jones, E. E., & Harris, V. A. The attribution of attitudes. *Journal of Experimental Social Psychology,* 1967, *3,* 1–24.

Jones, E. E., & McGillis, D. Correspondent inferences and the attribution cube: A comparative reappraisal. In J. H. Harvey, W. J. Ickes, & R. F. Kidd (Eds.), *New directions in attributional research* (Vol. 1). Hillsdale, N.J.: Erlbaum, 1976.

Jones, E. E., & Nisbett, R. E. The actor and observer: Divergent perceptions of the causes of behavior. In E. E. Jones et al. (Eds.), *Attribution: Perceiving the causes of behavior.* Morristown, N.J.: General Learning Press, 1972.

Jones, E. E., Rock, L., Shaver, K. G., Goethals, G. R., & Ward, L. M. Pattern of performance and ability attribution. An unexpected primacy effect. *Journal of Personality and Social Psychology,* 1968, *10,* 317–341.

Jones, E. E., & Sigall, H. The bogus pipeline: A new paradigm for measuring affect and attitude. *Psychological Bulletin,* 1971, *76,* 349–364.

Jones, J. M. *Prejudice and racism.* Reading, Mass.: Addison-Wesley, 1972.

Jones, R. A. *Self-fulfilling prophecies: Social, psychological, and physiological effects of expectancies.* Hillsdale, N.J.: Erlbaum, 1977.

Jones, R. A., Sensenig, J., & Haley, J. V. Self-descriptions: Configurations of content and order effects. *Journal of Personality and Social Psychology,* 1974, *30,* 36–45.

Jordan, N. Cognitive balance as an aspect of Heider's cognitive psychology In R. P. Abelson, E. Aronson, W. McGuire, T. M. Newcomb, M. Rosenberg, & P. H. Tannenbaum (Eds.). *Theories of cognitive consistency: A sourcebook.* Chicago: Rand McNally, 1968.

Jourard, S. *Self disclosure.* New York: John Wiley & Sons, 1971.

Judd, C. M., & Harackiewicz, J. M. Contrast effects in attitude judgment: An examination of the accentuation hypothesis. *Journal of Personality and Social Psychology,* 1980, *38,* 390–398.

Kahle, L. R., & Berman, J. J. Attitudes cause behaviors: A cross-lagged panel analysis. *Journal of Personality and Social Psychology,* 1979, *37,* 315–321.

Kahn, A. Reactions to generosity or stinginess from an intelligent or stupid work partner: A test of equity theory in a direct exchange relationship. *Journal of Personality and Social Psychology,* 1972, *21,* 116–123.

Kahn, A., O'Leary, V. E., Krulewicz, J. E., & Lamm, H.

Equity and equality: Male versus female means to a just end. *Basic and Applied Social Psychology,* 1980, *1,* 173–197.

Kahneman, D., & Tversky, A. On the psychology of prediction. *Psychological Review,* 1973, *80,* 237–251.

Kane, T. R., Joseph, J. M., & Tedeschi, J. T. Person perception and the Berkowitz paradigm for the study of aggression. *Journal of Personality and Social Psychology,* 1976, *33,* 663–673.

Kaplan, B., & Crockett, W. H. Developmental analysis of modes of resolution. In R. P. Abelson et al. (Eds.), *Theories of cognitive consistency: A sourcebook.* Chicago: Rand McNally, 1968.

Kaplan, M. F. Discussion polarization effects in a modified jury decision paradigm: Informational influences. *Sociometry,* 1977, *40,* 262–271.

Katz, A. M., & Hill, R. Residential propinquity and marital selection: A review of theory, method, and fact. *Marriage and Family Living,* 1958, *20,* 27–35.

Keating, J. P., & Brock, T. C. Acceptance of persuasion and the inhibition of counterargumentation under various distraction tasks. *Journal of Experimental Social Psychology,* 1974, *10,* 301–309.

Kelley, H. H. The warm-cold variable in the first impressions of persons. *Journal of Personality,* 1950, *18,* 431–439.

Kelley, H. H. Two functions of reference groups. In G. E. Swanson, T. M. Newcomb, & E. L. Hartley (Eds.). *Readings in social psychology* (Rev. ed.). New York: Henry Holt, 1952.

Kelley, H. H. Attribution theory in social psychology. In D. Levine (Ed.), *Nebraska symposium on motivation.* Lincoln: University of Nebraska Press, 1967.

Kelley, H. H. *Attribution in social interaction.* Morristown, N.J.: General Learning Press, 1971.

Kelley, H. H. Attribution in social interaction. In E. E. Jones et al. (Eds.), *Attribution: Perceiving the causes of behavior.* Morristown, N.J.: General Learning Press, 1972. (a)

Kelley, H. H. Causal schemata and the attribution process. In E. E. Jones et al. (Eds.), *Attribution: Perceiving the causes of behavior.* Morristown, N.J.: General Learning Press, 1972. (b)

Kelley, H. H. The process of causal attribution. *American Psychologist,* 1973, *28,* 107–128.

Kelley, H. H. *Personal relationships: Their structures and processes.* Hillside, N.J.: Erlbaum, 1979.

Kelley, H. H., & Thibaut, J. W. *Interpersonal relations: A theory of interdependence.* New York: Wiley Interscience, 1978.

Kelley, K., & Byrne, D. Attraction and altruism: With a little help from my friends. *Journal of Research in Personality,* 1976, *10,* 59–68.

Kelman, H. C., & Cohen, S. P. Reduction of international conflict: An international approach. In W. G. Austin

& S. Worchel (Eds.), *The social psychology of intergroup relations.* Monterey, Calif.: Brooks/Cole, 1979.

Kelman, H. C., & Hovland, C. I. "Reinstatement" of the communicator in delayed measurement of opinion change. *Journal of Abnormal and Social Psychology,* 1953, *48,* 327–335.

Kerr, N. L., Davis, J. H., Meek, D., & Rissman, A. K. Group position as a function of member attitudes: Choice shift from the perspective of social decision scheme theory. *Journal of Personality and Social Psychology,* 1975, *31,* 574–593.

Kiesler, C. A., Collins, B. E., & Miller, N. *Attitude change: A critical analysis of theoretical approaches.* New York: John Wiley & Sons, 1969.

Kiesler, C. A., & Kiesler, S. Role of forewarning in persuasive communications. *Journal of Abnormal and Social Psychology,* 1964, *68,* 547–549.

Kiesler, S., & Baral, R. The search for a romantic partner: The effects of self-esteem and physical attractiveness on romantic behavior. In K. J. Gergen & D. Marlowe (Eds.), *Personality and social behavior.* Reading, Mass.: Addison-Wesley, 1970.

Kleck, R. Physical stigma and task-oriented interactions. *Human Relations,* 1969, *22,* 53–60.

Kleck, R., Buck, P. L., Goller, W. C., London, R. S., Pfeiffer, J. R., & Vukcevic, D. P. The effect of stigmatizing conditions on the use of personal space. *Psychological Reports,* 1968, *23,* 111–118.

Kleck, R., Ono, H., & Hastorf, A. H. The effects of physical deviance upon face-to-face interaction. *Human Relations,* 1966, *19,* 425–436.

Kniveton, B. H. The effect of rehearsal delay on long-term imitation of filmed aggression. *British Journal of Psychology,* 1973, *64,* 259–265.

Knox, R. E., & Inkster, J. A. Postdecision dissonance at post time. *Journal of Personality and Social Psychology,* 1968, *8,* 319–323.

Koeske, G. F., & Crano, W. D. The effect of congruous and incongruous source-statement combinations upon the judged credibility of a communication. *Journal of Experimental Social Psychology,* 1968, *4,* 384–399.

Kogan, N., & Wallach, M. A. *Risk taking: A study of cognition and personality.* New York: Henry Holt, 1964.

Komorita, S. S. An equal excess model of coalition formation. *Behavioral Science,* 1979, *24,* 369–381.

Komorita, S. S., & Brinberg, D. Equity norms in coalition formation. *Sociometry,* 1977, *40,* 351–361.

Komorita, S. S., & Kravitz, D. A. The effects of alternatives in bargaining. *Journal of Experimental Social Psychology,* 1979, *15,* 147–157.

Krauss, R. M., Apple, W., Morency, N., Wenzel, C., & Winton, W. Verbal, vocal, and visible factors in judgments of another's affect. *Journal of Personality and Social Psychology,* 1981, *40,* 312–319.

Kraut, R. E., & Poe, D. Behavioral roots of person perception: The deception judgments of customs inspectors and laymen. *Journal of Personality and Social Psychology*, 1980, *39*, 784–798.

Kriss, M., Indenbaum, E., & Tesch, F. Message type and status of interactants as determinants of telephone helping behavior. *Journal of Personality and Social Psychology*, 1974, *30*, 856–859.

Krovetz, M. L. Explaining success or failure as a function of one's locus of control. *Journal of Personality*, 1974, *42*, 175–189.

Kruglanski, A. W. Attributing trustworthiness in worker-supervisor relations. *Journal of Experimental Social Psychology*, 1970, *6*, 214–232.

Kuiper, N. A., & Rogers, T. B. Encoding of personal information: Self-other differences. *Journal of Personality and Social Psychology*, 1979, *37*, 499–514.

Kulik, J. A., & Brown, R. Frustration, attribution of blame, and aggression. *Journal of Experimental Social Psychology*, 1979, *15*, 183–194.

Kulik, J. A., & Taylor, S. E. Self-monitoring and the use of consensus information. *Journal of Personality Social Psychology*, 1981, *49*, 75–84.

Kutner, B., Wilkins, C., & Yarrow, P. R. Verbal attitudes and overt behavior involving racial prejudice. *Journal of Abnormal and Social Psychology*, 1952, *47*, 649–652.

Lamm, H., & Myers, D. G. Group-induced polarization of attitudes and behavior. In L. Berkowitz (Ed.), *Advances in experimental social psychology*. New York: Academic Press, 1978.

Lamm, H., & Schwinger, T. Norms concerning distributive justice: Are needs taken into consideration in allocation decisions? *Social Psychology Quarterly*, 1980, *43*, 425–429.

Lammers, H. B., & Becker, L. A. Distraction: Effects on perceived extremity of a communication and on cognitive responses. *Personality and Social Psychology Bulletin*, 1980, *6*, 261–266.

Lando, H. A., & Donnerstein, E. I. The effects of a model's success or failure on subsequent aggressive behavior. *Journal of Research in Personality*, 1978, *12*, 225–234.

Lane, I. M., & Messé, L. A. Equity and the distribution of rewards. *Journal of Personality and Social Psychology*, 1971, *20*, 1–17.

Lane, I. M., & Messé, L. A. The distribution of insufficient, sufficient, and oversufficient rewards: A clarification of equity theory. *Journal of Personality and Social Psychology*, 1972, *21*, 228–233.

Langer, E. J., & Imber, L. Role of mindlessness in the perception of deviance. *Journal of Personality and Social Psychology*, 1980, *39*, 360–367.

LaPiere, R. T. Attitudes vs. actions. *Social Forces*, 1934, *13*, 230–237.

Larrance, D., Pavelich, S., Storer, P., Polizzi, M., Baron, B., Sloan, S., Jordan, R., & Reis, H. T. Competence

and incompetence: Assymetric responses to women and men on a sex-linked task. *Personality and Social Psychology Bulletin*, 1979, *5*, 363–366.

Latané, B., & Dabbs, J. M., Jr. Sex, group size, and helping in three cities. *Sociometry*, 1975, *38*, 180–194.

Latané, B., & Darley, J. M. Group inhibition of bystander intervention. *Journal of Personality and Social Psychology*, 1968, *10*, 215–221.

Latané, B., & Darley, J. M. *The unresponsive bystander: Why doesn't he help?* New York: Appleton-Century-Crofts, 1970.

Latané, B., & Rodin, J. A lady in distress: Inhibiting effects of friends and strangers on bystander intervention. *Journal of Experimental Social Psychology*, 1969, *5*, 189–202.

Latané, B., Williams, K., & Harkins, S. Many hands make light the work: Causes and consequences of social loafing. *Journal of Personality and Social Psychology*, 1979, *37*, 822–831.

Lau, R. R., & Russell, D. Attributions in the sports pages. *Journal of Personality and Social Psychology*, 1980, *39*, 29–38.

Laughlin, P. R., Kerr, N. L., Davis, J. H., Halff, H. M., & Marciniak, K. A. Group size, member ability, and social decision schemes on an intellective task. *Journal of Personality and Social Psychology*, 1975, *31*, 522–535.

Lawrence, D. H., & Festinger, L. *Deterrents and reinforcement*. Stanford, Calif.: Stanford University Press, 1962.

Lawson, E. Haircolor, personality, and the observer. *Psychological Reports*, 1971, *28*, 311–322.

Lay, C. H. Trait-inferential relationships and judgments about the personalities of others. *Canadian Journal of Behavior Science*, 1970, *2*, 1–17.

Lay, C. H., & Burron, B. F. Perception of the personality of the hesitant speaker. *Perceptual and Motor Skills*, 1968, *26*, 951–956.

Leavitt, H. J. Some effects of certain communication patterns on group performance. *Journal of Abnormal and Social Psychology*, 1951, *46*, 38–50.

Lefcourt, H. M., Hogg, E., Struthers, S., & Holmes, C. Causal attributions as a function of locus of control, initial confidence, and performance outcomes, *Journal of Personality and Social Psychology*, 1975, *32*, 391–397.

Lepper, M. R. Intrinsic and extrinsic motivation in children: Detrimental effects of superfluous social controls. In W. A. Collins (Ed.), *Aspects of the development of competence: The Minnesota Symposium on Child Psychology* (Vol. 14). Hillsdale, N.J.: Erlbaum, 1981.

Lepper, M. R., & Greene, D. *The hidden costs of rewards*. Hillsdale, N.J.: Erlbaum, 1978.

Lepper, M. R., Greene, D., & Nisbett, R. E. Undermining children's intrinsic interest with extrinsic reward: A test of the overjustification hypothesis. *Journal of Personality and Social Psychology*, 1973, *28*, 129–137.

Lepper, M. R., Zanna, M. P., & Abelson, R. P. Cognitive irreversibility in a dissonance reduction situation. *Journal of Personality and Social Psychology,* 1970, *16,* 191–198.

Leventhal, G. S. *Reward allocation by males and females.* Paper presented at the meeting of the American Psychological Association, Montreal, August 1973.

Leventhal, G. S. The distribution of rewards and resources in groups and organizations. In L. Berkowitz & E. Walster (Eds.), *Advances in experimental social psychology* (Vol. 9). New York: Academic Press, 1976.

Leventhal, G. S. What should be done with equity theory? New approaches to the study of fairness in social relationships. In K. G. Gergen, M. S. Greenberg, & R. H. Willis, (Eds.), *Social exchange: Advances in theory and research.* New York: Plenum Press, 1980.

Leventhal, G. S., & Lane, D. W. Sex, age, and equity behavior. *Journal of Personality and Social Psychology,* 1970, *15,* 312–316.

Leventhal, G. S., & Michaels, J. W. Extending the equity model: Perception of inputs and allocation of reward as a function of duration and quantity of performance. *Journal of Personality and Social Psychology,* 1969, *12,* 303–309.

Leventhal, G., Weiss, T. S. & Buttrick, R. Attribution of value, equity, and the prevention of waste in reward allocation. *Journal of Personality and Social Psychology,* 1973, *27,* 276–285.

Leventhal, G. S., & Whiteside, H. D. Equity and the use of reward to elicit high performance. *Journal of Personality and Social Psychology,* 1973, *25,* 75–83.

Leventhal, H. Finding and theory in the study of fear communications. In L. Berkowitz (Ed.), *Advances in Experimental Social Psychology* (Vol. 5). New York: Academic Press, 1970, 119–186.

Leventhal, H. Attitudes: Their nature, growth, and change. In C. Nemeth (Ed.), *Social psychology: Classic and contemporary integrations.* Chicago: Rand McNally, 1974.

Leventhal, H., Jones, S., & Trembly, G. Sex differences in attitude and behavior change under conditions of fear and specific instructions. *Journal of Personality and Social Psychology,* 1966, *2,* 387–399.

Leventhal, H., Singer, R., & Jones, S. Effects of fear and specificity of recommendation upon attitudes and behavior. *Journal of Personality and Social Psychology,* 1965, *2,* 20–29.

Leventhal, H., Watts, J. C., & Pagano, F. Effects of fear and instructions on how to cope with danger. *Journal of Personality and Social Psychology,* 1967, *6,* 313–321.

Levin, P. F., & Isen, A. M. Further studies on the effect of feeling good on helping. *Sociometry,* 1975, *38,* 141–147.

LeVine, R. A., & Campbell, D. T. *Ethnocentrism.* New York: John Wiley & Sons, 1972.

Levinger, G. Toward the analysis of close relationships. *Journal of Experimental Social Psychology,* 1980, *16,* 510–544.

Levinger, G., & Schneider, D. J. Test of the "risk is a value" hypothesis. *Journal of Personality and Social Psychology,* 1969, *11,* 165–169.

Levinger, G., & Snoek, J. D. *Attraction in relationships: A new look at interpersonal attraction.* Morristown, N.J.: General Learning Press, 1972.

Lewin, K. *Field theory in social science.* New York: Harper & Row, 1951.

Lexens, J. P., & Parke, R. E. Aggressive slides can induce a weapons effect. *European Journal of Social Psychology,* 1975, *5,* 229–236.

Libo, L. *Measuring group cohesiveness.* Ann Arbor, Mich.: Institute for Social Research, 1953.

Liebert, R. M., & Baron, R. A. Some immediate effects of televised violence on children's behavior. *Developmental Psychology,* 1972, *6,* 469–475.

Linder, D. E., Cooper, J., & Jones, E. E. Decision freedom as a determinant of the role of incentive magnitude in attitude change. *Journal of Personality and Social Psychology,* 1967, *6,* 245–254.

Lingle, J. H., Geva, N., Ostrom, T. M., Leippe, M. R., & Baumgardner, M. H. Thematic effects of person judgments on impression organization. *Journal of Personality and Social Psychology,* 1979, *37,* 674–687.

Lipetz, M. E. The effects of information on the assessment of attitudes by authoritarians and nonauthoritarians. *Journal of Abnormal and Social Psychology,* 1960, *60,* 95–99.

Locksley, A., Ortiz, V., & Hepburn, C. Social categorization and discriminatory behavior: Extinguishing the minimal intergroup discrimination effect. *Journal of Personality and Social Psychology,* 1980, *39,* 773–783.

Lord, C. G., Ross, L., & Lepper, M. R. Biased assimilation and attitude polarization: The effects of prior theories on subsequently considered evidence. *Journal of Personality and Social Psychology,* 1979, *37,* 2098–2109.

Lorenz, K. *On aggression.* New York: Harcourt, Brace, and World, 1966.

Lott, A. J., & Lott, B. E. Group cohesiveness, communication level, and conformity. *Journal of Abnormal and Social Psychology,* 1961, *62,* 406–412.

Lott, A. J., & Lott, B. E. Group cohesiveness as interpersonal attraction: A review of relationships with antecedent and consequent variables. *Psychological Bulletin,* 1965, *64,* 259–302.

Lott, B. E., & Lott, A. J. The formation of positive attitudes toward group members. *Journal of Abnormal and Social Psychology,* 1960, *61,* 297–300.

Lowe, C. A., & Goldstein, J. W. Reciprocal liking and attributions of ability: Mediating effects of perceived intent and personal involvement. *Journal of Personality and Social Psychology,* 1970, *16,* 291–297.

Luchins, A. S. Primacy-recency in impression formation. In C. I. Hovland (Ed.), *The order of presentation in persuasion.* New Haven, Conn.: Yale University Press, 1957.

Luchins, A. S. Definitiveness of impression and primacy-recency in communications. *Journal of Social Psychology,* 1958, *48,* 275–290.

McArthur, L. Z. The how and what of why: Some determinants of consequences of causal attribution. *Journal of Personality and Social Psychology,* 1972, *22,* 171–193.

McArthur, L. Z. The lesser influence of consensus than distinctiveness information on causal attributions: A test of the person-thing hypothesis. *Journal of Personality and Social Psychology,* 1976, *33,* 733–742.

McArthur, L. Z. What grabs you? The role of attention in impression formation and causal attribution. In E. T. Higgins, C. P. Herman, & M. P. Zanna (Eds.), *Social cognition: Cognitive structure and processes underlying person memory and social judgment.* Hillsdale, N.J.: Erlbaum, 1980.

McArthur, L. Z., & Post, D. L. Figural emphasis and person perception. *Journal of Experimental Social Psychology,* 1977, *13,* 520–536.

McArthur, L. Z., & Solomon, L. K. Perceptions of an aggressive encounter as a function of the victim's salience and the perceiver's arousal. *Journal of Personality and Social Psychology,* 1978, *36,* 1278–1290.

McFarlin, D. B., & Blascovich, J. Effects of self-esteem and performance feedback on future affective preferences and cognitive expectations. *Journal of Personality and Social Psychology,* 1981, *40,* 521–531.

McGee, M. G., & Snyder, M. Attributions and behavior: Two field studies. *Journal of Personality and Social Psychology,* 1975, *32,* 185–190.

McGinnies, E. Studies in persuasion: III. Reactions of Japanese students to one-sided and two-sided communications. *Journal of Social Psychology,* 1966, *70,* 87–93.

McGinnies, E., & Ward, C. D. Better liked than right: Trustworthiness and expertise as factors in credibility. *Personality and Social Psychology Bulletin,* 1980, *6,* 467–471.

McGuire, W. J. Inducing resistence to persuasion: Some contemporary approaches. In L. Berkowitz (Ed.), *Advances in experimental social psychology,* (vol. 1). New York: Academic Press, 1964, 191–229.

McGuire, W. J. The nature of attitudes and attitude change. In G. Lindzey & E. Aronson (Eds.), *The handbook of social psychology* (2nd ed.) (vol. 3). Reading, Mass.: Addison-Wesley, 1969.

McKee, J. P., & Sherriffs, A. C. The differential evaluation of males and females. *Journal of Personality,* 1957, *25,* 256–271.

MacBrayer, C. T. Differences in perception of the opposite sex by males and females. *Journal of Social Psychology,* 1960, *52,* 309–314.

Maddi, S. R. Meaning, novelty, and effect: Comments on Zajonc's paper. *Journal of Personality and Social Psychology,* 1968, *9,* 28–29.

Madsen, D. B. Issue importance and choice shifts: A persuasive arguments approach. *Journal of Personality and Social Psychology,* 1978, *36,* 1118–1127.

Major, B. Information acquisition and attribution processes. *Journal of Personality and Social Psychology,* 1980, *39,* 1010–1023.

Manis, M., Dovalina, J., Avis, N. E., & Cardoze, S. Base rates can affect individual predictions. *Journal of Personality and Social Psychology,* 1980, *38,* 231–248.

Mann, L., & Janis, I. L. A follow-up study on the long-term effects of emotional role-playing. *Journal of Personality and Social Psychology,* 1968, *8,* 339–342.

Marak, G. E. The evolution of leadership structure. *Sociometry,* 1964, *27,* 174–182.

Markus, H. Self-schemata and processing information about the self. *Journal of Personality and Social Psychology,* 1977, *35,* 63–78.

Markus, H. The effect of mere presence on social facilitation: An unobtrusive test. *Journal of Experimental Social Psychology,* 1978, *14,* 389–397.

Markus, H. The self in thought and memory. In D. M. Wegner & R. R. Vallacher (Eds.), *The self in social psychology.* New York: Oxford University Press, 1980.

Maslow, A. H. Motivation and personality (2nd ed.). New York: Harper & Row, 1970.

Massad, C. M., Hubbard, M., & Newtson, D. Selective perception of events. *Journal of Experimental Social Psychology,* 1979, *15,* 513–532.

Matefy, R. E. Attitude change induced by role playing as a function of improvisation and role-taking skill. *Journal of Personality and Social Psychology,* 1972, *24,* 323–350.

Mead, G. H. *Mind, self, and society.* Chicago: University of Chicago Press, 1934.

Mednick, M. S., & Tangri, S. S. New social psychological perspectives on women. *Journal of Social Issues,* 1972, *28,* 1–16.

Megargee, E. I. Influence of sex roles on the manifestation of leadership. *Journal of Applied Psychology,* 1969, *53,* 377–382.

Megargee, E. I. The role of inhibition in the assessment and understanding of violence. In J. L. Singer (Ed.), *The control of aggression and violence: Cognitive and physiological factors.* New York: Academic Press, 1971.

Mehrabian, A., & Diamond, S. G. Effects of furniture arrangement, props, and personality on social interaction. *Journal of Personality and Social Psychology,* 1971, *20,* 18–30.

Mehrabian, A., & Friar, J. T. Encoding of attitude by a seated communicator via posture and position cues. *Journal of Counseling and Clinical Psychology,* 1969, *33,* 330–336.

Mellon, P. M., Crano, W. D., & Schmitt, N. Sex-role stereotypes and the perception of occupational competence. *Sex Roles,* in press.

Merton, R. K. *Social theory and social structure* (Rev. ed.). New York: Free Press, 1957.

Messé, L. A. Equity in bilateral bargaining. *Journal of Personality and Social Psychology,* 1971, *17* 287–291.

Messé, L. A., Aronoff, J., & Wilson, J. P. Motivation as a mediator of the mechanisms underlying role assignments in small groups. *Journal of Personality and Social Psychology,* 1972, *24,* 84–90.

Messé, L. A., & Callahan-Levy, C. M. Sex and message effects on reward allocation behavior. *Academic Psychology Bulletin,* 1979, *1,* 129–133.

Messé, L. A., Dawson, J. E., & Lane, I. L. Equity as a mediator of the effect of reward level on behavior in the Prisoner's Dilemma game. *Journal of Personality and Social Psychology,* 1973, *26,* 60–65.

Messé, L. A., & Lichtman, R. J. *Motivation for the reward as a mediator of the influence of work quality on allocation behavior.* Paper presented at the meeting of the Southeastern Psychological Association, Atlanta, April 1972.

Messé, L. A., Stollak, G. E., Larson, R. W., & Michaels, G. Y. Interpersonal consequences of person perception processes in two social contexts. *Journal of Personality and Social Psychology,* 1979, *37,* 369–379.

Messé, L. A., Vallacher, R. R., & Phillips, J. L. Equity and the formation of revolutionary and conservative coalitions in triads. *Journal of Personality and Social Psychology,* 1975, *31,* 1141–1146.

Messick, D. M., & Reeder, G. M. Perceived motivation, role variations and the attributions of personal characteristics. *Journal of Experimental Social Psychology,* 1972, *8,* 482–491.

Meyer, J. P. Causal attribution for success and failure: A multivariate investigation of dimensionality, formation, and consequences. *Journal of Personality and Social Psychology,* 1980, *38,* 704–718.

Meyers, M. A. social contexts and attributions of criminal responsibility. *Social Psychology Quarterly,* 1980, *43,* 405–419.

Michelini, R. L., Wilson, J. P., & Messé, L. A. The influence of psychological needs on helping behavior. *Journal of Social Psychology,* 1975, *91,* 253–258.

Midlarsky, E., & Bryan, J. H. Training charity in children. *Journal of Personality and Social Psychology,* 1967, *5,* 408–415.

Mikula, G. Nationality, performance, and sex as determinants of reward allocation. *Journal of Personality and Social Psychology,* 1974, *29,* 435–440.

Mikula, G. (Ed.). *Justice and social interaction.* Bern: Hubor, 1980.

Milgram, S. Behavioral study of obedience. *Journal of Abnormal and Social Psychology,* 1963, *67,* 371–378.

Milgram, S. Issues in the study of obedience: A reply to Baumrind. *American Psychologist,* 1964, *19,* 848–852.

Milgram, S. Some conditions of obedience and disobedience to authority. *Human Relations,* 1965, *18,* 57–75.

Milgram, S. *Obedience to authority.* New York: Harper & Row, 1974.

Miller, A. G. Role of physical attractiveness in impression formation. *Psychonomic Science,* 1970, *19,* 241–243.

Miller, A. G., Gillen, B., Schenker, C., & Radlove, S. The prediction and perception of obedience to authority. *Journal of Personality,* 1974, *42,* 23–42.

Miller, D. T. Ego involvement in attributions for success and failure. *Journal of Personality and Social Psychology,* 1976, *34,* 901–906.

Miller, D. T. Personal deserving vs. justice for others: An exploration of the justice motive. *Journal of Experimental Social Psychology,* 1977, *13,* 1–13.

Miller, D. T., & Norman, S. A. Actor-observer differences in perceptions of effective control. *Journal of Personality and Social Psychology,* 1975, *31,* 503–515.

Miller, D. T., Norman, S. A., & Wright, E. Distortion in person perception as a consequence of the need for effective control. *Journal of Personality and Social Psychology,* 1978, *36,* 598–607.

Miller, F. D., Smith, E. R., & Uleman, J. Measurement and interpretation of situational and dispositional attributions. *Journal of Experimental Social Psychology,* 1981, *17,* 80–95.

Miller, G. R., & Hewgill, M. A. The effect of variations in nonfluency on audience ratings of source credibility. *Quarterly Journal of Speech,* 1964, *50,* 36–44.

Miller, H. L., & Rivenbark, W. H., III. Sexual differences in physical attractiveness as a determinant of heterosexual liking. *Psychological Reports,* 1970, *27,* 701–702.

Miller, N. As time goes by. In R. P. Abelson, E. Aronson, W. J. McGuire, T. M. Newcomb, M. J. Rosenberg, & P. H. Tannenbaum (Eds.), *Theories of cognitive consistency: A sourcebook.* Chicago: Rand McNally, 1968.

Miller, N., Maruyama, G., Beaber, R., & Valone, K. Speed of speech and persuasion. *Journal of Personality and Social Psychology,* 1976, *34,* 615–624.

Miller, N. E., & Dollard, J. *Social learning and imitation.* New Haven, Conn.: Yale University Press, 1941.

Millman, S. *The relationship between anxiety, learning and opinion change.* Unpublished doctoral dissertation, Columbia University, 1965.

Mills, J., & Jellison, J. M. Effect on opinion change of how desirable the communication is to the audience the communicator addressed. *Journal of Personality and Social Psychology,* 1967, *6,* 98–101.

Modlin, H. C., & Faris, M. Group adaptation and integration in psychiatric team practice. *Psychiatry,* 1956, *19,* 97–103.

Monson, T. C., & Snyder, M. Actors, observers, and the

attribution process: Toward a reconceptualization. *Journal of Experimental Social Psychology,* 1977, *13,* 89–111.

Moreno, J. L. *Who shall survive?* Washington, D.C.: Nervous and Mental Disease Publishing Company, 1934.

Moriarty, T. Crime, commitment, and the responsive bystander: Two field experiments. *Journal of Personality and Social Psychology,* 1975, *31,* 370–376.

Morse, S., & Gergen, K. J. Social comparison, self-consistency, and the concept of self. *Journal of Personality and Social Psychology,* 1970, *16,* 148–156.

Morton, T. L. Intimacy and reciprocity of exchange: A comparison of spouses and strangers. *Journal of Personality and Social Psychology,* 1978, *36,* 72–81.

Moscovici, S., & Zavalloni, M. The group as a polarizer of attitudes. *Journal of Personality and Social Psychology,* 1969, *12,* 125–135.

Murstein, B. I. Stimulus-value-role: A theory of marital choice. *Journal of Marriage and the Family,* 1970, *32,* 465–481.

Murstein, B. I. Physical attractiveness and marital choice. *Journal of Personality and Social Psychology,* 1972, *22,* 8–12.

Murstein, B. I. *Who will marry whom? Theories and research in marital choice.* New York: Springer, 1976.

Murstein, B. I., & Christy, P. Physical attractiveness and marriage adjustment in middle-aged couples. *Journal of Personality and Social Psychology,* 1976, *34,* 537–542.

Mussen, P. H. Differences between TAT responses of Negro and white boys. *Journal of Consulting Psychology,* 1953, *17,* 373–376.

Mussen, P. H., & Barker, R. G. Attitudes towards cripples. *Journal of Abnormal and Social Psychology,* 1944, *39,* 351–355.

Myers, D. G., Bruggink, J. B., Kersting, R. C., & Schlosser, B. A. Does learning others' opinions change one's opinions? *Personality and Social Psychology Bulletin,* 1980, *6,* 253–260.

Myers, D. G., Wojcicki, S. G., & Aardema, A. Attitude comparison: Is there ever a bandwagon effect? *Journal of Applied Social Psychology,* 1977, *7,* 341–347.

Nahemow, L., & Lawton, M. P. Similarity and propinquity in friendship formation. *Journal of Personality and Social Psychology,* 1975, *32,* 205–213.

Napolitan, D. A., & Goethals, G. R. The attribution of friendliness. *Journal of Experimental Social Psychology,* 1979, *15,* 105–113.

Neisser, U. *Cognitive psychology.* New York: Appleton-Century-Crofts, 1967.

Nemeth, C., Endicott, J., & Wachtler, J. From the '50s to the '70s: Women in jury deliberations. *Sociometry,* 1976, *39,* 293–304.

Newcomb, T. M. *Personality and social change: Attitude formation in a student community.* New York: Dryden Press, 1943.

Newcomb, T. M. Autistic hostility and social reality. *Human Relations,* 1947, *1,* 69–86.

Newcomb, T. M. *The acquaintance process.* New York: Holt, Rhinehart & Winston, 1961.

Newcomb, T. M., Koenig, K. E., Flacks, R., & Warwick, D. P. *Persistence and change: Bennington College and its students after twenty-five years.* New York: John Wiley & Sons, 1967.

Newcombe, N., & Arnkoff, D. B. Effects of speech style and sex of speaker on person perception. *Journal of Personality and Social Psychology,* 1979, *37,* 1293–1303.

Newtson, D. Dispositional inference from effects of actions: Effects chosen and effects foregone. *Journal of Experimental Social Psychology,* 1974, *10,* 489–496.

Nisbett, R. E., & Borgida, E. Attribution and the psychology of prediction. *Journal of Personality and Social Psychology,* 1975, *32,* 932–943.

Nisbett, R. E., Caputo, C., Legant, P., & Marecek, J. Behavior as seen by the actor and as seen by the observer. *Journal of Personality and Social Psychology,* 1973, *27,* 154–164.

Noble, G. *Children in front of the small screen.* Beverly Hills, Calif.: Sage, 1975.

O'Dell, J. W. Group size and emotional interaction. *Journal of Personality and Social Psychology,* 1968, *8,* 75–78.

Olson, J. M., Barefoot, J. C., & Strickland, L. H. What the shadow knows: Person perception in a surveillance situation. *Journal of Personality and Social Psychology,* 1976, *34,* 583–589.

Orne, M. T. On the social psychology of the psychological experiment: With particular reference to demand characteristics and their implications. *American Psychologist* 1962, *17,* 776–783.

Orne, M. T. Demand characteristics and the concept of quasi-controls. In R. Rosenthal & R. L. Rosnow (Eds.), *Artifact in behavioral research.* New York: Academic Press, 1969.

Osgood, C. E., Suci, G. J., & Tannenbaum, P. H. *The measurement of meaning.* Urbana: University of Illinois Press, 1957.

Osgood, C. E., & Tannenbaum, P. H. The principle of congruity in the prediction of attitude change. *Psychological Review,* 1955, *62,* 42–55.

Ostfeld, B., & Katz, P. A. The effect of threat severity in children of varying socioeconomic levels. *Developmental Psychology,* 1969, *1,* 205–210.

Ostrom, T. M., & Davis, D. Idiosyncratic weighting of trait information in impression formation. *Journal of Personality and Social Psychology,* 1979, *37,* 2025–2043.

Palamarek, D. L., & Rule, B. G. The effects of ambient temperature and insult on the motivation to retaliate or escape. *Motivation and Emotion,* 1979, *3,* 83–92.

Pallak, M. S. Effects of expected shock and relevant or irrelevant dissonance on incidental retention. *Journal of Personality and Social Psychology,* 1970, *14,* 271–280.

Pallak, M. S., & Pittman, T. S. General motivational effects of dissonance arousal. *Journal of Personality and Social Psychology,* 1972, *21,* 349–358.

Parsons, T. An outline of the social system. In T. Parsons, E. Shils, K. D. Naegele, & J. R. Pitts (Eds.), *Theories of society.* New York: Free Press, 1961.

Parsons, T., & Bales, R. F. *Family, socialization and interaction process.* Chicago: Free Press of Glencoe, 1955.

Passini, F. T., & Norman, W. T. A universal conception of personality structure? *Journal of Personality and Social Psychology,* 1966, *4,* 44–49.

Pastore, N. The role of arbitrariness in the frustration-aggression hypothesis. *Journal of Abnormal and Social Psychology,* 1952, *47,* 728–731.

Patterson, M. L., Kelly, C. E., Kondracki, B. A., & Wulf, L. J. Effects of seating arrangement on small-group behavior. *Social Psychology Quarterly,* 1979, *42,* 180–185.

Patterson, M. L., Roth, C. P., & Schenk, C. Seating arrangement, activity, and sex differences in small group crowding. *Personality and Social Psychology Bulletin,* 1979, *5,* 100–103.

Patterson, M. L., & Schaeffer, R. E. Effects of size and sex composition on interaction distance, participation, and satisfaction in small groups. *Small Group Behavior,* 1977, *8,* 433–442.

Paunonen, S. V., & Jackson, D. N. Nonverbal trait inference. *Journal of Personality and Social Psychology,* 1979, *37,* 1645–1659.

Pennebaker, J. W., Dyer, M. A., Caulkins, R. S., Litowitz, D. L., Ackreman, P. L., Anderson, D. B., & McGraw, K. M. Don't the girls get prettier at closing time: A country and western application to psychology. *Personality and Social Psychology Bulletin,* 1979, *5,* 122–125.

Penner, L. A., & Hawkins, H. L. The effects of visual contact and aggressor identification on interpersonal aggression. *Psychonomic Science,* 1971, *24,* 261–263.

Pepitone, A. The role of justice in interdependent decision making. *Journal of Experimental Social Psychology,* 1971, *7,* 144–156.

Pepitone, A., McCauley, C., & Hammond, P. Changes in attractiveness of forbidden toys as a function of severity of threat. *Journal of Experimental Social Psychology,* 1967, *3,* 221–229.

Peterson, P. D., & Koulack, D. Attitude change as a function of latitudes of acceptance and rejection. *Journal of Personality and Social Psychology,* 1969, *11,* 309–311.

Pettigrew, T. F. The ultimate attribution error: Extending Allport's cognitive analysis of prejudice. *Personality and Social Psychology Bulletin,* 1979, *5,* 461–476.

Petty, R. E., & Cacioppo, J. T. Issue involvement can increase or decrease persuasion by enhancing message-relevant cognitive responses. *Journal of Personality and Social Psychology,* 1979, *37,* 1915–1926.

Petty, R. E., & Cacioppo, J. T. *Attitudes and persuasion:*

Classic and contemporary approaches. Dubuque, Iowa: Brown, 1981.

Petty, R. E., Cacioppo, J. T., & Heesacker, M. Effects of rhetorical questions on persuasion: A cognitive response analysis. *Journal of Personality and Social Psychology,* 1981, *40,* 432–440.

Petty, R. E., Harkins, S., Williams, K., & Latané, B. The effects of group size on cognitive effort and evaluation. *Personality and Social Psychology Bulletin,* 1977, *3,* 579–582.

Petty, R. E., Wells, G. L., & Brock, T. C. Distraction can enhance or reduce yielding to propaganda: Thought disruption versus effort justification. *Journal of Personality and Social Psychology,* 1976, *34,* 874–884.

Philp, H., & Dunphy, D. Developmental trends in small groups. *Sociometry,* 1959, *22,* 162–174.

Piliavin, J. A., Piliavin, I. M., & Rodin, J. Costs, diffusion and the stigmatized victim. *Journal of Personality and Social Psychology,* 1975, *3,* 429–438.

Pittman, T. S. Attribution of arousal as a mediator in dissonance reduction. *Journal of Experimental Social Psychology,* 1975, *11,* 53–63.

Pomozal, R. J., & Clore, G. L. Helping on the highway: The effects of dependency and sex. *Journal of Applied Social Psychology,* 1976, *33,* 317–326.

Porter, J. *Black child, white child.* Cambridge: Harvard University Press, 1971.

Powell, R. S., & O'Neal, E. C. Communication feedback and duration as determinants of accuracy, confidence, and differentiation in interpersonal perception. *Journal of Personality and Social Psychology,* 1976, *34,* 746–756.

Price, K., Harberg, E., & Newcomb, T. M. Psychological balance in situations of negative interpersonal attitudes. *Journal of Personality and Social Psychology,* 1966, *3,* 265–270.

Price, R. H., & Bouffard, D. L. Behavioral appropriateness and situational constraint as dimensions of social behavior. *Journal of Personality and Social Psychology,* 1974, *30,* 579–586.

Priest, R., & Sawyer, J. Proximity and peership: Bases of balance in interpersonal attraction. *American Journal of Sociology,* 1967, *72,* 633–649.

Prior, J. B., & Kriss, M. The cognitive dynamics of salience in the attribution process. *Journal of Personality and Social Psychology,* 1977, *35,* 49–55.

Pritchard, R. D. Equity theory: A review and critiques. *Organizational Behavior and Human Performance,* 1969, *4,* 176–211.

Propst, L. R. Effects of personality and loss of anonymity on aggression. *Journal of Personality,* 1979, *47,* 531–545.

Pruitt, D. G. Reciprocity and credit building in a laboratory dyad. *Journal of Personality and Social Psychology,* 1968, *8,* 143–147.

Pyszczynski, T. A., & Greenberg, J. Role of disconfirmed expectancies in the instigation of attributional processing. *Journal of Personality and Social Psychology,* 1981, *40,* 31–38.

Rands, M., & Levinger, G. Implicit theories of relationship: An intergenerational study. *Journal of Personality and Social Psychology,* 1979, *37,* 645–661.

Reeder, G. M., Messick, D. M., & Van Avermaet, E. Dimensional asymmetricality in attributional inference. *Journal of Experimental Social Psychology,* 1977, *13,* 46–57.

Regan, D. T., & Fazio, R. On the consistency between attitudes and behavior: Look to the method of attitude formation. *Journal of Experimental Social Psychology,* 1977, *13,* 28–45.

Reis, H. T., & Jackson, L. A. Sex differences in reward allocation: Subjects, partners, and tasks. *Journal of Personality and Social Psychology,* 1981, *40,* 465–478.

Reiss, M., & Schlenker, B. R. Attitude change and responsibility avoidance as modes of dilemma resolution in forced-compliance situations. *Journal of Personality and Social Psychology,* 1977, *35,* 21–35.

Reynolds, G. S. *A primer of operant conditioning.* Glenview, Ill.: Scott Foresman, 1968.

Rhine, R. J., & Severance, L. J. Ego-involvement, discrepancy, source credibility, and attitude change. *Journal of Personality and Social Psychology,* 1970, *16,* 175–190.

Richardson, D. C., Bernstein, S., & Taylor, S. P. The effect of situational contingencies on female retaliative behavior. *Journal of Personality and Social Psychology,* 1979, *37,* 2044–2048.

Richardson, D. C., & Campbell, J. L. Alcohol and wife abuse: The effect of alcohol on attributions of blame for wife abuse. *Personality and Social Psychology Bulletin,* 1980, *6,* 51–56.

Richardson, S. A., Hastorf, A. H., Goodmen, N., & Dornbusch, S. M. Cultural uniformity in reaction to physical disabilities. *American Sociological Review,* 1961, *26,* 24–47.

Rist, R. Student social class and teacher expectation: The self-fulfilling prophecy in ghetto education. *Harvard Educational Review,* 1970, *40,* 411–412.

Rodrigues, A. Effects of balance, positivity, and agreement in triadic social situations. *Journal of Personality and Social Psychology,* 1967, *5,* 472–476.

Roethlisberger, F. J., & Dickson, W. J. *Management and the worker.* Cambridge, Mass.: Harvard University Press, 1939.

Rogers, C. R. A theory of therapy, personality and interpersonal relationships as developed in a client-centered framework. In S. Koch (Ed.), *Psychology: A study of a science* (Vol. 3). New York: McGraw-Hill, 1959.

Rogers, R. W. A protection motivation theory of fear appeals and attitude change. *Journal of Psychology,* 1975, *91,* 93–114.

Rogers, R. W., & Mewborn, R. Fear appeals and attitude change: The effects of a threat's noxiousness, probability of occurrence, and the efficacy of coping responses. *Jour-*

nal of Personality and Social Psychology, 1976, *34,* 54–61.

Rogers, R. W., & Thistlewaite, D. L. Effects of fear arousal and reassurance on attitude change. *Journal of Personality and Social Psychology,* 1970, *15,* 227–233.

Rokeach, M. *The open and closed mind: Investigations into the nature of belief systems and personality systems.* New York: Basic Books, 1960.

Rokeach, M. *Beliefs, attitudes and values.* San Francisco: Jossey-Bass, 1968.

Rokeach, M. Long range experimental modification of values, attitudes, and behavior. *American Psychologist,* 1971, *26,* 453–459.

Rokeach, M. *The nature of human values.* New York: Free Press, 1973.

Rokeach, M., & Mezei, L. Race and shared belief as factors in social change. *Science,* 1966, *151,* 167–172.

Rokeach, M., & Rothman, G. The principle of belief congruence and the congruity principle as models of cognitive interaction. *Psychological Review,* 1965, *72,* 128–142.

Rokeach, M., Smith, P. W., & Evans, R. I. Two kinds of prejudice or one? In M. Rokeach (Ed.). *The open and closed mind.* New York: Basic Books, 1960.

Rose, A. M. *The roots of prejudice.* Paris: UNESCO, 1951.

Rosenberg, M. Psychological selectivity in self-esteem formation. In C. Gordon & K. Gergen (Eds.), *The self in social interaction.* New York: John Wiley & Sons, 1968.

Rosenberg, M. J. When dissonance fails: On eliminating evaluation apprehension from attitude measurement. *Journal of Personality and Social Psychology,* 1965, *1,* 28–42.

Rosenberg, M. J., & Hovland, C. I. (Eds.), *Attitude organization and change.* New Haven, Conn.: Yale University Press, 1960.

Rosenberg, S. New approaches to the analysis of personal constructs in person perception. In A. W. Landfield (Ed.), *Nebraska symposium on motivation.* Lincoln: University of Nebraska Press, 1976.

Rosenberg, S., & Sedlack, A. Structural representations of implicit personality theory. In L. Berkowitz (Ed.), *Advances in experimental social psychology* (Vol. 6). New York: Academic Press, 1972.

Rosenhan, D. L. On being sane in insane places. *Science,* 1973, *179,* 250–258.

Rosenkrantz, P. S., & Crockett, W. H. Some factors influencing the assimilation of disparate information in impression formation. *Journal of Personality and Social Psychology,* 1965, *2,* 397–402.

Rosenkrantz, P. S., Vogel, S. R.; Bee, H., Broverman, I. K., & Broverman, D. M. Sex-role stereotypes and self-concepts in college students. *Journal of Consulting and Clinical Psychology,* 1968, *32,* 287–295.

Rosenthal, A. M. *Thirty-eight witnesses.* New York: McGraw-Hill, 1964.

Rosenthal, R., & Jacobson, L. *Pygmalion in the classroom.* New York: Holt, Rinehart & Winston, 1968.

Ross, L. D., Amabile, T. M., & Steinmetz, J. L. Social roles, social control, and biases in social-perception processes. *Journal of Personality and Social Psychology*, 1977, *35*, 485–494.

Ross, M. The self-perception of intrinsic motivation. In J. H. Harvey, W. J. Ickes, & R. F. Kidd (Eds.), *New directions in attribution research*. Hillsdale, N.J.: Erlbaum, 1976.

Ross, M., & Sicoly, F. Egocentric biases in availability and attribution. *Journal of Personality and Social Psychology*, 1979, *37*, 322–336.

Roth, S., & Kubal, L. The effects of noncontingent reinforcement on tasks of differing importance: Facilitation and learned helplessness. *Journal of Personality and Social Psychology*, 1975, *32*, 680–691.

Rubin, I. The reduction of prejudice through laboratory training. *Journal of Applied Behavioral Science*, 1967, *3*, 29–49.

Rubin, J. Z., & Brown, B. R. *The social psychology of bargaining and negotiation*. New York: Academic Press, 1975.

Rubin, Z. Measurement of romatic love. *Journal of Personality and Social Psychology*, 1970, *16*, 265–273.

Rubin, Z. *Liking and loving: An invitation to social psychology*. New York: Holt, Rinehart & Winston, 1973.

Rubin, Z. Disclosing oneself to a stranger: Reciprocity and its limits. *Journal of Experimental Social Psychology*, 1975, *11*, 332–346.

Ruble, D. N., & Feldman, N. S. Order of consensus, distinctiveness, and consistency information and causal attributions. *Journal of Personality and Social Psychology*, 1976, *34*, 930–937.

Rubovitz, P. C., & Maehr, M. L. Pygmalion analyzed: Toward an explanation of the Rosenthal-Jacobson findings. *Journal of Personality and Social Psychology*, 1971, *19*, 197–203.

Rule, B. G., & Langer, E. J. Pain cues and differing functions of aggression. *Canadian Journal of Behavioral Science*, 1976, *8*, 213–222.

Runyan, D. L. The group risky-shift effect as a function of emotional bonds, actual consequences, and extent of responsibility. *Journal of Personality and Social Psychology*, 1974, *29*, 670–676.

Russell, J. C., Firestone, I. J., & Baron, R. M. Seating arrangement and social influence: Moderated by reinforcement meaning and internal-external control. *Social Psychology Quarterly*, 1980, *43*, 103–109.

Saegert, S. C., Swap, W. C., & Zajonc, R. B. Exposure, context, and interpersonal attraction. *Journal of Personality and Social Psychology*, 1973, *25*, 234–242.

Sampson, E. E. On justice as equality. *Journal of Social Issues*, 1975, *31*, 45–61.

Sanders, G. S. Driven by distraction: An integrative review of social facilitation theory and research. *Journal of Experimental Social Psychology*, 1981, *17*, 227–252.

Schachter, S. S. The interaction of cognitive and physiological determinants of emotional state. In L. Berkowitz (Ed.), *Advances in Experimental Social Psychology* (Vol. 1). New York: Academic Press, 1964.

Schachter, S. S., & Singer, J. E. Cognitive, social, and physiological determinants of emotional state. *Psychological Review*, 1962, *69*, 379–399.

Schank, R., & Abelson, R. P. *Scripts, plans, goals and understanding*. Hillsdale, N.J.: Erlbaum, 1977.

Schaps, E. Cost, dependency, and helping. *Journal of Personality and Social Psychology*, 1972, *21*, 74–78.

Scheidel, T. M., & Crowell, L. Idea development in small discussion groups. *Quarterly Journal of Speech*, 1966, *50*, 140–145.

Scheier, M. F., & Carver, C. S. Private and public self-attention, resistance to change, and dissonance reduction. *Journal of Personality and Social Psychology*, 1980, *39*, 390–405.

Schlenker, B. Self-presentation: Managing the impression of consistency when reality interferes with self-enhancement. *Journal of Personality and Social Psychology*, 1975, *32*, 1030–1037.

Schneider, D. J., Hastorf, A. H., & Ellsworth, P. C. *Person perception* (2nd ed.). Reading, Mass.: Addison-Wesley, 1979.

Schopler, J., & Bateson, N. A dependence interpretation of the effects of severe initiation. *Journal of Personality*, 1962, *30*, 633–649.

Schopler, J., & Bateson, N. The power of dependence. *Journal of Personality and Social Psychology*, 1965, *2*, 247–254.

Schroder, H. M., Driver, M. J., & Streufert, S. *Human information processing*. New York: Holt, Rinehart & Winston, 1967.

Schroder, H. M., & Harvey, O. J. Conceptual organization and group structure. In O. J. Harvey (Ed.), *Motivation and social interaction*. New York: Ronald Press, 1963.

Schutz, W. C. The Harvard compatibility experiment. In A. P. Hare, E. F. Borgatta, & R. F. Bales (Eds.), *Small groups: Studies in social interaction* (Rev. ed.). New York: Alfred A. Knopf, 1965.

Schutz, W. C. *The interpersonal underworld*. Palo Alto, Calif.: Science and Behavior Books, 1966.

Schwartz, S. H. Normative explanations of helping behavior: A critique, proposal, and empirical test. *Journal of Experimental Social Psychology*, 1973, *9*, 349–364.

Schwartz, S. H. Awareness of interpersonal consequences, responsibility denial, and volunteering. *Journal of Personality and Social Psychology*, 1974, *30*, 57–63.

Schwartz, S. H. Normative influences on altruism. In L. Berkowitz (Ed.), *Advances in experimental social psychology* (Vol. 10). New York: Academic Press, 1977.

Schwartz, S. H. Temporal instability as a moderator of the attitude behavior relationship. *Journal of Personality and Social Psychology*, 1979, *36*, 715–724.

Schwartz, S. H., & Clausen, G. T. Responsibility, norms and helping in an emergency. *Journal of Personality and Social Psychology*, 1970, *16*, 299–310.

Schwartz, S. H., & Fleishman, J. Personal norms and the

mediation of legitimacy effects on helping. *Social Psychology,* 1978, *41,* 306–315.

Schwartz, S. H., & Gottlieb, A. Bystander anonymity and reactions to emergencies. *Journal of Personality and Social Psychology,* 1980, *39,* 418–430.

Schwartz, S. H., & Howard, J. A. Explanations of the moderating effect of responsibility denial on the personal norm-behavior relationship. *Social Psychology Quarterly,* 1980, *43,* 441–446.

Schweitzer, D., & Ginsburg, G. P. Factors of communicator credibility. In C. W. Backman and P. R. Secord (Eds.), *Problems in social psychology: Selected readings.* New York: McGraw-Hill, 1966.

Scott, C. A., & Yalch, R. F. A test of the self-perception explanation of the effects of rewards on intrinsic interest. *Journal of Experimental Social Psychology,* 1978, *14,* 180–192.

Seaver, W. B. Effects of naturally induced teacher expectancies. *Journal of Personality and Social Psychology,* 1973, *28,* 333–342.

Sebastian, R. J. Immediate and delayed effects of victim suffering on the attacker's aggression. *Journal of Research in Personality,* 1978, *12,* 312–328.

Secord, P. F., & Backman, C. W. *Social psychology.* New York: McGraw-Hill, 1964.

Secord, P. F., & Backman, C. W. *Social psychology* (2nd ed.). New York: McGraw-Hill, 1974.

Segal, M. W. A reconfirmation of the logarithmic effect of group size. *Sociometry,* 1977, *40,* 187–190.

Segal, M. W. Varieties of interpersonal attraction and their interrelationships in natural groups. *Social Psychology Quarterly,* 1979, *42,* 253–261.

Seta, J. J., Martin, L., & Capehart, G. Effects of contrast and generalization on the attitude similarity-attraction relationship. *Journal of Personality and Social Psychology,* 1979, *37,* 462–467.

Shafer, R. B., & Keith, P. M. Equity and depression among married couples. *Social Psychology Quarterly,* 1980, *43,* 430–435.

Shaffer, D. R., Rogel, M., & Hendrick, C. Intervention in the library: The effect of increased responsibility on bystanders' willingness to prevent a theft. *Journal of Applied Social Psychology,* 1975, *5,* 303–319.

Shanteau, J., & Nagy, G. F. Probability of acceptance in dating choice. *Journal of Personality and Social Psychology,* 1979, *37,* 522–533.

Shaver, K. G. Defensive attribution: Effects of severity and relevance on the responsibility assigned for an accident. *Journal of Personality and Social Psychology,* 1970, *14,* 101–113.

Shaw, M. E. Communication networks. In L. Berkowitz (Ed.), *Advances in experimental social psychology* (Vol. 1). New York: Academic Press, 1964.

Shaw, M. E. *Group dynamics: The psychology of small group behavior* (3rd ed.). New York: McGraw-Hill, 1981.

Sherif, C. W., Kelly, M., Rodgers, H., Sarup, G., & Tittler,

B. I. Personal involvement, social judgment, and action. *Journal of Personality and Social Psychology,* 1973, *27,* 311–327.

Sherif, C. W., & Sherif, M. (Eds.). *Attitude, ego-involvement, and change.* New York: John Wiley & Sons, 1967.

Sherif, C. W., Sherif, M., & Nebergall, R. E. *Attitude and attitude change.* Philadelphia: Saunders, 1965.

Sherif, M. *The psychology of social norms.* New York: Harper & Row, 1936.

Sherif, M., Harvey, O. J., White, B. J., Hood, W. R., & Sherif, C. W. *Intergroup cooperation and competition: The Robbers Cave experiment.* Norman, Oklahoma: University Book Exchange, 1961.

Sherif, M., & Hovland, C. I. *Social Judgment.* New Haven, Conn.: Yale University Press, 1961.

Sherif, M., & Sherif, C. W. *Groups in harmony and tension.* New York: Harper & Row, 1953.

Sherrod, D., & Farber, J. The effect of previous actor/observer role experience on attribution of responsibility for failure. *Journal of Personality,* 1975, *43,* 231–247.

Shor, R. Effect of pre-information upon human characteristics attributed to animated geometric figures. *Journal of Abnormal and Social Psychology,* 1957, *54,* 124–126.

Shotland, R. L., & Straw, M. K. Bystander response to an assault: When a man attacks a woman. *Journal of Personality and Social Psychology,* 1976, *34,* 990–999.

Sidowski, J. B., Wyckoff, L. B., & Tabory, L. The influence of reinforcement and punishment in a minimal social situation. *Journal of Abnormal and Social Psychology,* 1956, *52,* 115–119.

Sigall, H., & Page, R. Current stereotypes: A little fading, a little faking. *Journal of Personality and Social Psychology,* 1971, *18,* 247–255.

Silverman, B. I. Consequences, racial discrimination, and the principle of belief congruence. *Journal of Personality and Social Psychology,* 1974, *29,* 497–508.

Silverman, I. Physical attractiveness and courtship. *Sexual behavior,* 1971, September, 22–25.

Simpson, D. O., & Ostrom, T. M. Contrast effects in impression formation. *Journal of Personality and Social Psychology,* 1976, *34,* 625–629.

Simpson, G. E., & Yinger, J. M. *Racial and cultural minorities* (3rd ed.). New York: Harper & Row, 1965.

Sivacek, J. M., & Crano, W. D. *Hedonic motivation as a determinant of attitude-behavior consistency.* Paper presented at the annual convention of the American Psychological Association, Montreal, Canada, 1980.

Slater, P. E. Role differentiation in small groups. *American Sociological Review,* 1955, *20,* 300–310.

Sleet, D. A. Physique and social image. *Perceptual and Motor Skills,* 1969, *28,* 295–299.

Smelzer, W. T. Dominance as a factor in achievement and perception in cooperative problem solving interactions. *Journal of Abnormal and Social Psychology,* 1961, *62,* 535–542.

Smith, E. R., & Miller, F. D. Salience and the cognitive

mediation of attribution. *Journal of Personality and Social Psychology,* 1979, *37,* 2240–2252.

Smith, R. E., Smythe, L., & Lien, D. Inhibition of helping behavior by a similar or dissimilar nonreactive bystander. *Journal of Personality and Social Psychology,* 1972, *23,* 414–419.

Smith, R. J., & Cook, P. E. Leadership in dyadic groups as a function of dominance and incentives. *Sociometry,* 1973, *36,* 561–568.

Smith, T. W., & Brehm, S. S. Person perception and the Type A coronary-prone behavior pattern. *Journal of Personality and Social Psychology,* 1981, *40,* 1137–1149.

Smith, T. W., & Pittman, T. S. Reward, distraction, and the overjustification effect. *Journal of Personality and Social Psychology,* 1978, *36,* 565–572.

Snyder, M. The self-monitoring of expressive behavior. *Journal of Personality and Social Psychology,* 1974, *30,* 526–537.

Snyder, M. Attribution and behavior: Social perception and social causation. In J. H. Harvey, W. J. Ickes, & R. F. Kidd (Eds.), *New directions in attribution research* (Vol. 1). Hillsdale, N.J.: Erlbaum, 1976.

Snyder, M. Self-monitoring processes. In L. Berkowitz (Ed.), *Advances in experimental social psychology* (Vol. 12). New York: Academic Press, 1979.

Snyder, M. Seek and ye shall find: Testing hypotheses about other people. In E. T. Higgins, C. P. Herman, & M. P. Zanna (Eds.), *Social cognition: The Ontario symposium on personality and social psychology.* Hillsdale, N.J.: Erlbaum, 1981.

Snyder, M., & Campbell, B. Testing hypotheses about other people: The role of the hypothesis. *Personality and Social Psychology Bulletin,* 1980, *6,* 421–426.

Snyder, M., & Cantor, N. Testing hypotheses about other people: The use of historical knowledge. *Journal of Experimental Social Psychology,* 1979, *15,* 330–342.

Snyder, M., & Gangestad, S. Hypothesis-testing processes. In J. H. Harvey, W. Ickes, & R. F. Kidd (Eds.), *New directions in attribution research* (Vol. 3). Hillsdale, N.J.: Erlbaum, in press.

Snyder, M., & Monson, T. C. Persons, situations, and the control of social behavior. *Journal of Personality and Social Psychology,* 1975, *32,* 637–644.

Snyder, M., & Swann, W. B., Jr. When actions reflect attitudes: The politics of impression management. *Journal of Personality and Social Psychology,* 1976, *34,* 1034–1042.

Snyder, M., & Swann, W. B., Jr. Hypothesis testing processes in social interaction. *Journal of Personality and Social Psychology,* 1978, *36,* 1202–1212.

Snyder, M., & Tanke, E. D. Behavior and attitude: Some people are more consistent than others. *Journal of Personality,* 1976, *44,* 501–517.

Snyder, M., Tanke, E. D., & Berscheid, E. Social perception and interpersonal behavior. *Journal of Personality and Social Psychology,* 1977, *35,* 656–666.

Snyder, M., & Uranowitz, S. W. Reconstructing the past: Some cognitive consequences of person perception. *Journal of Personality and Social Psychology,* 1978, *36,* 941–950.

Snyder, M., & White, P. Testing hypotheses about other people: Strategies of verification and falsification. *Personality and Social Psychology Bulletin,* 1981, *7,* 39–43.

Snyder, M. L., & Frankel, A. Observer bias: A stringent test of behavior engulfing the field. *Journal of Personality and Social Psychology,* 1976, *34,* 857–864.

Snyder, M. L., Kleck, R. E., Strenta, A., & Mentzer, S. J. Avoidance of the handicapped: An attributional ambiguity analysis. *Journal of Personality and Social Psychology,* 1979, *37,* 297–306.

Snyder, M. L., Smoller, B., Strenta, A., & Frankel, A. A comparison of egotism, negativity, and learned helplessness as explanations for poor performance after unsolvable problems. *Journal of Personality and Social Psychology,* 1981, *40,* 24–30.

Snyder, M. L., Stephan, W. G., & Rosenfield, D. Egotism and attribution. *Journal of Personality and Social Psychology,* 1976, *33,* 435–441.

Soskin, W. F., & John, V. P. The study of spontaneous talk. In R. G. Barker (Ed.), *The stream of behavior.* New York: Appleton-Century-Crofts, 1963.

Spector, P. E., Cohen, S. L., & Penner, L. A. The effects of real vs. hypothetical risk on group choice-shifts. *Personality and Social Psychology Bulletin,* 1976, *2,* 290–293.

Spence, J. T., Helmreich, R., & Stapp, J. Likeability, sex-role congruence of interest, and competence: It all depends on how you ask. *Journal of Applied Social Psychology,* 1975, *5,* 93–109. (a)

Spence, J. T., Helmreich, R., & Stapp, J. Ratings of self and peers on sex-role attributes and their relation to self-esteem and conceptions of masculinity and femininity. *Journal of Personality and Social Psychology,* 1975, *32,* 29–39. (b)

Srull, T. K., & Wyer, R. S., Jr. The role of category accessibility in the interpretation of information about persons: Some determinants and implications. *Journal of Personality and Social Psychology,* 1979, *37,* 1660–1672.

Staats, A. W. *Social behaviorism.* Homewood, Ill.: Dorsey Press, 1975.

Staats, A. W., & Staats, C. K. Attitudes established by classical conditioning. *Journal of Abnormal and Social Psychology,* 1958, *57,* 37–40.

Staub, E. (Ed.), *Positive social behavior and morality* (Vol. 1). *Social and personal influences.* New York: Academic Press, 1978.

Staub, E. (Ed.), *Positive social behavior and morality* (Vol. 2). *Socialization and development.* New York: Academic Press, 1979.

Staub, E., & Baer, R. S., Jr. Stimulus characteristics of a sufferer and difficulty of escape as determinants of helping. *Journal of Personality and Social Psychology*, 1974, *30*, 279–285.

Steiner, I. D. Ethnocentrism and tolerance of trait "inconsistency." *Journal of Abnormal and Social Psychology*, 1954, *49*, 349–354.

Steinzor, B. The spatial factor in face to face discussion groups. *Journal of Abnormal and Social Psychology*, 1950, *45*, 552–555.

Stephan, C., Kennedy, J., & Aronson, E. Friendship, outcome, and task attribution. *Sociometry*, 1977, *40*, 107–111.

Stevens, L., & Jones, E. E. Defensive attribution and the Kelley cube. *Journal of Personality and Social Psychology*, 1976, *34*, 809–820.

Stewart, R. Effect of continuous responding on the order effect in personality impression formation. *Journal of Personality and Social Psychology*, 1965, *1*, 161–165.

Stogdill, R. M. *Individual behavior and group achievement.* New York: Oxford, 1959.

Stollak, G. E., Messé, L. A., Michaels, G. Y., Buldain, R., Catlin, T., & Paritee, F. Child adjustment and parental perceptual style. *Journal of Abnormal Child Psychology*, in press.

Stoner, J. A. F. *A comparison of individual and group decisions involving risk.* Unpublished master's thesis, Massachusetts Institute of Technology, 1961.

Storms, M. D. Videotape and the attribution process. *Journal of Personality and Social Psychology*, 1973, *27*, 165–175.

Storms, M. D. Sex role identity and its relationship to sex role attributes and sex role stereotypes. *Journal of Personality and Social Psychology*, 1979, *37*, 1779–1789.

Stouffer, S. A., Lumsdaine, A. A., Lumsdaine, M. H., Williams, R. M., Jr., Smith, M. B., Janis, I. L., Star, S. A., & Cottrell, L. S., Jr. *The American soldier: Combat and its aftermath.* Princeton, N.J.: Princeton University Press, 1949.

Stouffer, S. A., Suchman, E. A., DeVinney, L. C., Star, S. A., & Williams, R. M., Jr. *The American Soldier* (Vol. 1). *Adjustment during army life.* Princeton, N.J.: Princeton University Press, 1949.

Streufert, S., & Streufert, S. C. Effects of conceptual structure, failure, and success on attributions of causality and interpersonal attitudes. *Journal of Personality and Social Psychology*, 1969, *11*, 138–147.

Strickland, L. H. Surveillance and trust. *Journal of Personality*, 1958, *26*, 200–215.

Strodtbeck, F. L., & Hook, L. H. The social dimensions of a twelve man jury table, *Sociometry*, 1961, *24*, 397–415.

Strodtbeck, F. L., & Mann, R. D. Sex role differentiation in jury deliberations. *Sociometry*, 1956, *19*, 3–11.

Stroebe, W., Insko, C. A., Thompson, V. D., & Layton, B. D. Effects of physical attractiveness, attitude similarity, and sex on various aspects of interpersonal attraction. *Journal of Personality and Social Psychology*, 1971, *18*, 79–91.

Sullivan, H. S. *Interpersonal theory of psychiatry.* New York: W. W. Norton, 1953.

Suls, J. M., Witenberg, S., & Gutkin, D. Evaluating reciprocal and nonreciprocal prosocial behavior: Developmental changes. *Personality and Social Psychology Bulletin*, 1981, *7*, 25–32.

Sumner, W. *Folkways.* Boston: Ginn, 1906.

Sutherland, A., & Goldschmid, M. Negative teacher expectation and IQ change in children with superior intellectual potential. *Child Development*, 1974, *45*, 852–856.

Swann, W. B., Jr., & Snyder, M. On translating beliefs into action: Theories of ability and their application in an instructional setting. *Journal of Personality and Social Psychology*, 1980, *38*, 879–888.

Swap, W. C. Interpersonal attraction and repeated exposure to rewarders and punishers. *Personality and Social Psychology Bulletin*, 1977, *3*, 248–251.

Swingle, P. (Ed.), *The structure of conflict.* New York: Academic Press, 1970.

Tagiuri, R., Blake, R. R., & Bruner, J. S. Some determinants of the perception of positive and negative feelings in others. *Journal of Abnormal and Social Psychology*, 1953, *48*, 585–592.

Tajfel, H. Experiments in intergroup discrimination. *Scientific American*, 1970, *223*, 96–102.

Taylor, D. M., & Jaggi, V. Ethnocentrism and causal attribution in a South Indian context. *Journal of Cross-Cultural Psychology*, 1974, *5*, 162–171.

Taylor, M. C. Race, sex, and the expression of self-fulfilling prophecies in a laboratory teaching situation. *Journal of Personality and Social Psychology*, 1979, *37*, 897–912.

Taylor, R. B., De Soto, C., & Lieb, R. Sharing secrets: Disclosure and discretion in dyads and triads. *Journal of Personality and Social Psychology*, 1979, *37*, 1196–1203.

Taylor, S. E. On inferring one's attitudes from one's behavior: Some delimiting conditions. *Journal of Personality and Social Psychology*, 1975, *31*, 126–131.

Taylor, S. E., Crocker, J., Fiske, S. T., Sprinzen, M., & Winkler, J. D. The generalizability of salience effects. *Journal of Personality and Social Psychology*, 1979, *37*, 357–368.

Taylor, S. E., & Fiske, S. T. Point of view and perceptions of causality. *Journal of Personality and Social Psychology*, 1975, *32*, 439–445.

Taylor, S. E., & Fiske, S. T. Salience, attention, and attribution: Top of the head phenomena. In L. Berkowitz (Ed.), *Advances in experimental social psychology* (Vol. 11). New York: Academic Press, 1978.

Taylor, S. E., Fiske, S. T., Etcoff, N. L., & Ruderman, A. J. The categorical and contextual bases of person memory and stereotyping. *Journal of Personality and Social Psychology*, 1978, *36*, 778–793.

Taylor, S. E., & Huesman, L. P. Replication report: Expectancy confirmed again: A computer investigation of expectancy theory. *Journal of Experimantal Social Psychology*, 1974, *10*, 497–501.

Taylor, S. E., & Koivumaki, J. H. The perception of self and others: Acquaintanceship, affect, and actor-observer differences. *Journal of Personality and Social Psychology,* 1976, *33,* 403–408.

Taylor, S. P. Aggressive behavior and physiological arousal as a function of provocation and the tendency to inhibit aggression. *Journal of Personality,* 1967, *35,* 297–310.

Taylor, S. P. Aggressive behavior as a function of approval motivation and physical attack. *Psychonomic Science,* 1970, *18,* 195–196.

Taynor, J., & Deaux, K. When women are more deserving than men: Equity, attribution, and perceived sex differences. *Journal of Personality and Social Psychology,* 1973, *28,* 360–367.

Taynor, J., & Deaux, K. Equality and perceived sex differences: Role behavior as defined by the task, the mode, and the actor. *Journal of Personality and Social Psychology,* 1975, *32,* 381–390.

Tedeschi, J. T., Schlenker, B. R., & Bonoma, T. V. Cognitive dissonance: Private ratiocination or public spectacle? *American Psychologist,* 1971, *26,* 685–695.

Tesser, A., & Brodie, M. A note on the evaluation of a "computer date." *Psychonomic Science,* 1971, *23,* 300.

Teyber, E. C., Messé, L. A., & Stollak, G. E. Adult responses to child communications. *Child Development,* 1977, *48,* 1577–1582.

Theodorson, G. A. Elements of the progressive development of small groups. *Social forces,* 1953, *31,* 311–320.

Thibaut, J. W., & Kelley, H. H. *The social psychology of groups.* New York: John Wiley & Sons, 1959.

Thibaut, J. W., & Riecken, H. W. Some determinants and consequences of the perception of social causality. *Journal of Personality,* 1955, *24,* 113–133.

Thistlethwaite, D. L., de Haan, H., & Kamenetsky, J. The effects of "directive" and "nondirective" communication procedures on attitudes. *Journal of Abnormal and Social Psychology,* 1955, *51,* 107–113.

Thomas, E. J., & Fink, C. F. Effects of group size. *Psychological Bulletin,* 1963, *60,* 371–384.

Thompson, E. G., Gard, J. W., & Phillips, J. L. Trait dimensionality and "balance" in subject-verb-object judgments. *Journal of Personality and Social Psychology,* 1980, *38,* 57–66.

Thorndike, R. L. Review of Rosenthal and Jacobson's Pygmalion in the classroom. *American Educational Research Journal,* 1968, *5,* 708–711.

Tilker, H. A. Socially reponsible behavior as a function of observer responsibility and victim feedback. *Journal of Personality and Social Psychology,* 1970, *14,* 95–100.

Touhey, J. C. Comparison of two dimensions of attitude similarity on heterosexual attraction. *Journal of Personality and Social Psychology,* 1972, *23,* 8–10. (a)

Touhey, J. C. Perception and the relative influence of the perceiver and the perceived. *Journal of Social Psychology,* 1972, *87,* 213–217. (b)

Touhey, J. C. Sex-role stereotyping and individual differences in liking for the physically attractive. *Social Psychology Quarterly,* 1979, *42,* 285–288.

Triandis, H. C. A note on Rokeach's theory of prejudice. *Journal of Abnormal and Social Psychology,* 1961, *62,* 184–186.

Triandis, H. C. *Attitude and attitude change.* New York: John Wiley & Sons, 1971.

Triandis, H. C. *Interpersonal behavior.* Monterey, Calif.: Brooks/Cole, 1977.

Triandis, H. C., & Davis, E. E. Race and belief as determinants of behavioral intentions. *Journal of Personality and Social Psychology,* 1965, *2,* 715–725.

Trope, Y. Uncertainty-reducing properties of achievement task. *Journal of Personality and Social Psychology,* 1979, *37,* 1505–1518.

Tuckman, B. W. Personality structure, group composition, and group functioning. *Sociometry,* 1964, *27,* 469–487.

Tuckman, B. W. Developmental sequence in small groups. *Psychological Bulletin,* 1965, *63,* 384–399.

Tunnell, G. Sex role and cognitive schemata: Person perception in feminine and androgynous women. *Journal of Personality and Social Psychology,* 1981, *40,* 1126–1136.

Turner, E. A., & Wright, J. Effects of severity of threat and perceived availability on the attractiveness of objects. *Journal of Personality and Social Psychology,* 1965, *2,* 128–132.

Ungar, S. The effects of effort and stigma on helping. *Journal of Social Psychology,* 1979, *107,* 23–28.

Ungar, S. The effects of the certainty of self-perceptions on self-presentation behaviors: A test of the strength of self-enhancement motives. *Social Psychology Quarterly,* 1980, *43,* 165–172.

Vallacher, R. R. *Dimensions of the self and situational self-consciousness in the perception of others.* Unpublished doctoral dissertation, Michigan State University, 1975.

Vinacke, W. E. Variables in experimental games: Toward a field theory, *Psychological Bulletin,* 1969, *71,* 293–318.

Vinacke, W. E., & Arkoff, A. An experimental study of coalitions in the triad. *American Sociological Review,* 1957, *22,* 406–414.

Vinokur, A., & Burnstein, E. Depolarization of attitudes in groups. *Journal of Personality and Social Psychology,* 1978, *36,* 872–885.

Wallach, M. A., Kogan, N., & Bem, D. Group influence on individual risk taking. *Journal of Abnormal and Social Psychology,* 1962, *65,* 75–86.

Wallach, M. A., Kogan, N., & Bem, D. Diffusion of responsibility and level of risk taking in groups. *Journal of Abnormal and Social Psychology,* 1964, *68,* 263–274.

Wallach, M. A., & Mabli, J. Information versus conformity in the effects of group discussion on risk taking. *Journal of Personality and Social Psychology,* 1970, *14,* 149–156.

Walster, E. The temporal sequence of post-decision processes.

In L. Festinger (Ed.), *Conflict, decision and dissonance.* Stanford, Calif.: Stanford University Press, 1964.

Walster, E. The effects of self-esteem on romantic liking. *Journal of Experimental Social Psychology,* 1965, *1,* 184–197.

Walster, E., Aronson, E., & Abrahams, D. On increasing the persuasiveness of a low prestige communicator. *Journal of Experimental Social Psychology,* 1966, *2,* 325–342.

Walster, E., Aronson, V., Abrahams, D., & Rottmann, L. Importance of physical attractiveness in dating behavior. *Journal of Personality and Social Psychology,* 1966, *4,* 508–516.

Walster, E., & Festinger, L. The effectiveness of "overheard" persuasive communications. *Journal of Abnormal and Social Psychology,* 1962, *65,* 395–402.

Walster, E., Traupmann, J., & Walster, G. W. Equity and extramarital sexuality. *Archives of Sexual Behavior,* 1978, *7,* 127–141.

Walster, E. H., & Walster, G. W. *A new look at love.* Reading, Mass.: Addison-Wesley, 1978.

Walster, E., Walster, G. W., & Berscheid, E. *Equity: Theory and research.* Boston: Allyn & Bacon, 1978.

Walster, E., Walster, G. W., Piliavin, J. A., & Schmidt, L. "Playing hard to get": Understanding an elusive phenomenon. *Journal of Personality and Social Psychology,* 1973, *26,* 113–121.

Walster, E., Walster, G. W., & Traupmann, J. Equity and premarital sex. *Journal of Personality and Social Psychology,* 1978, *36,* 82–92.

Ward, C. D. Attitude and involvement in absolute judgment of attitude statements. *Journal of Personality and Social Psychology,* 1966, *4,* 465–476.

Ward, C. D. Seating arrangement and leadership emergence in small discussion groups. *Journal of Social Psychology,* 1968, *74,* 83–90.

Ward, L., & Wilson, J. P. Motivational and moral development as determinants of behavioral acquiescence and moral action. *Journal of Social Psychology,* 1980, *112,* 271–286.

Warr, P., & Jackson, P. The importance of extremity. *Journal of Personality and Social Psychology,* 1975, *32,* 278–282.

Waterman, C. K. The facilitating and interfering effects of cognitive dissonance on simple and complex paired-associate learning tasks. *Journal of Experimental Social Psychology,* 1969, *5,* 31–42.

Watson, S. G. Judgment of emotion from facial and contextual cue combinations. *Journal of Personality and Social Psychology,* 1972, *24,* 334–342.

Watts, B. L., Messé, L. A., & Vallacher, R. R. Toward understanding sex differences in pay allocation: Agency, communion and reward distribution behavior. *Sex Roles,* in press.

Watts, W. A., & Hold, L. E. Persistence of opinion change induced under conditions of forewarning and distraction.

Journal of Personality and Social Psychology, 1979, *36,* 778–789.

Weary, G. Examination of affect and egotism as mediators of bias in causal attribution. *Journal of Personality and Social Psychology,* 1980, *38,* 348–357.

Wegner, D. M., Benel, D. C., & Riley, E. N. *Changes in perceived intertrait correlations as a function of experience with persons.* Paper presented at the meeting of the Southwestern Psychological Association, Albuquerque, New Mexico, April 1976.

Wegner, D. M., & Crano, W. D. Racial factors in helping behavior: An unobtrusive field experiment. *Journal of Personality and Social Psychology,* 1975, *32,* 901–905.

Wegner, D. M., & Finstuen, K. Observers' focus of attention in the simulation of self-perception. *Journal of Personality and Social Psychology,* 1977, *35,* 56–62.

Wegner, D. M., Kerker, R. M., & Beattie, A. E. *Innuendo effects in impression formation.* Paper presented at the annual meeting of the Southwestern Psychological Association, New Orleans, Louisiana, 1978.

Wegner, D. M., & Schaefer, D. The concentration of responsibility: An objective self-awareness analysis of group size effects in helping situations. *Journal of Personality and Social Psychology,* 1978, *36,* 147–155.

Wegner, D. M., & Vallacher, R. R. *Implicit psychology: An introduction to social cognition.* New York: Oxford University Press, 1977.

Weick, K. E., & Nesset, B. Preferences among forms of equity. *Organizational Behavior and Human Performance,* 1968, *3,* 400–416.

Weigel, R. H., & Newman, L. S. Increasing attitude-behavior correspondence by broadening the scope of the behavioral measure. *Journal of Personality and Social Psychology,* 1976, *33,* 793–802.

Weigel, R. H., Vernon, D. T., & Tognacci, L. N. Specificity of the attitude as a determinant of attitude-behavior congruence. *Journal of Personality and Social Psychology,* 1974, *30,* 724–728.

Weiss, D. S. The effects of systematic variations in information on judges' description of personality. *Journal of Personality and Social Psychology,* 1979, *37,* 2121–2136.

Weitz, S. Attitude, voice and behavior: A repressed affect model of interracial interaction. *Journal of Personality and Social Psychology,* 1972, *24,* 14–21.

Wells, G. L., & Harvey, J. H. Do people use consensus information in making causal attributions? *Journal of Personality and Social Psychology,* 1977, *35,* 279–293.

Wells, G. L., & Harvey, J. H. Naive attributors' attributions and predictions: What is informative and when is an effect an effect? *Journal of Personality and Social Psychology,* 1978, *36,* 483–490.

Wells, G. L., Petty, R. E., Harkins, S. G., Hagehiro, D., & Harvey, J. H. Anticipated discussion of interpretation eliminates actor-observer differences in the attribution of causality. *Sociometry,* 1977, *40,* 247–253.

West, S. G., & Brown, T. J. Physical attractiveness, the severity of the emergency and helping: A field experiment and interpersonal simulation. *Journal of Experimental Social Psychology,* 1975, *11,* 531–538.

West, S. G., Whitney, G., & Schnedler, R. Helping a motorist in distress: The effects of sex, race, and neighborhood. *Journal of Personality and Social Psychology,* 1975, *31,* 691–698.

Weyant, J. M. Effects of mood states: Costs, and benefits on helping. *Journal of Personality and Social Psychology,* 1978, *36,* 1169–1176.

White, G. L. Physical attractiveness and courtship progress. *Journal of Personality and Social Psychology,* 1980, *39,* 660–668.

White, G. L. Jealousy and partner's perceived motives for attraction to a rival. *Social Psychology Quarterly,* 1981, *44,* 24–30.

Whittaker, J. Opinion change as a function of communication-attitude discrepancy. *Psychological Reports,* 1963, *13,* 763–772.

Wicker, A. Attitudes versus actions: The relationship of verbal and overt behavioral responses to attitude objects. *Journal of Social Issues,* 1969, *25,* 1–78.

Wicker, A. An examination of the "other variables" explanation of attitude-behavior inconsistency. *Journal of Personality and Social Psychology,* 1971, *19,* 18–30.

Wicklund, R. A. Objective self-awareness. In L. Berkowitz (Ed.), *Advances in experimental social psychology.* (Vol. 8) New York: Academic Press, 1975.

Wicklund, R. A. The influence of self-awareness and human behavior. *American Scientist,* 1979, *67,* 187–193.

Wicklund, R. A., & Brehm, J. W. *Perspectives on cognitive dissonance.* Hillsdale, N.J.: Erlbaum, 1976.

Wicklund, R. A., Cooper, J., & Linder, D. E. Effects of expected effort on attitude change prior to exposure. *Journal of Experimental Social Psychology,* 1967, *3,* 416–428.

Wicklund, R. A., & Frey, D. Self-awareness theory: When the self makes a difference. In D. M. Wegner & R. R. Vallacher (Eds.), *The self in social psychology.* New York: Oxford University Press, 1980.

Wiggins, J. S. A psychological taxonomy of trait-descriptive terms: The interpersonal domain. *Journal of Personality and Social Psychology,* 1979, *37,* 395–412.

Wilder, D. Reduction of intergroup discrimination through individuation of the outgroup. *Journal of Personality and Social Psychology,* 1978, *36,* 1361–1374.

Wilke, H., & Lanzetta, J. T. The obligation to help: The effects of amount of prior help on subsequent helping behavior. *Journal of Experimental Social Psychology,* 1970, *6,* 488–493.

Williams, D. C. *Race and sex as determinants of perceived belief similarity.* Unpublished doctoral dissertation, Michigan State University, 1975.

Williams, K., Harkins, S., & Latané, B. Identifiability as a

deterrent to social loafing: Two cheering experiments. *Journal of Personality and Social Psychology,* 1981, *40,* 303–311.

Wilson, J. P. Motivation, modeling, and altruism: A person × situation analysis. *Journal of Personality and Social Psychology,* 1976, *34,* 1078–1086.

Wilson, J. P., Aronoff, J., & Messé, L. A. Social structure, member motivation, and productivity. *Journal of Personality and Social Psychology,* 1975, *32,* 1094–1098.

Wilson, L. R., & Nakajo, H. Preference for photographs as a function of frequency of presentation. *Psychonomic Science,* 1966, *3,* 577–578.

Winter, S. K. Developmental stages in the roles and concerns of group co-leaders. *Small Group Behavior,* 1976, *7,* 349–362.

Wishner, J. Reanalysis of "Impressions of personality." *Psychological Review,* 1960, *67,* 96–112.

Witkin, H. A., Dyk, R., Faterson, H. F., Goodenough, D. R., & Karp, S. A. *Psychological differentiation.* New York: John Wiley & Sons, 1962.

Witkin, H. A.; Oltman, P. K.; Raskin, E.; & Karp, S. A. *Manual for the embedded figures test.* Palo Alto, Calif.: Consulting Psychologists Press, 1971.

Wolfson, M. R., & Salancik, G. R. Observer orientation and actor-observer differences in attributions for failure. *Journal of Experimental Social Psychology,* 1977, *13,* 441–451.

Wolosin, R., Sherman, S. J., & Mynatt, C. R. Perceived social influence on a conformity situation. *Journal of Personality and Social Psychology,* 1972, *23,* 184–191.

Won-Doornink, M. J. On getting to know you: The association between the stage of a relationship and reciprocity of self-disclosure. *Journal of Experimental Social Psychology,* 1979, *15,* 229–241.

Wood, W., & Eagly, A. H. Stages in the analysis of persuasive messages: The role of causal attributions on message comprehension. *Journal of Personality and Social Psychology,* 1981, *40,* 246–259.

Woodmansee, J. J., & Cook, S. W. Dimensions of verbal racial attitudes: Their identification and measurement. *Journal of Personality and Social Psychology,* 1967, *7,* 240–250.

Word, C. O., Zanna, M. P., & Cooper, J. The nonverbal mediation of self-fulfilling prophecy effects in interracial interaction. *Journal of Experimental Social Psychology,* 1974, *10,* 109–120.

Worthington, M. Personal space as a function of the stigma effect. *Environment and Behavior,* 1974, *6,* 289–297.

Wortman, C. B., Costanzo, P. R., & Witt, T. R. Effect of anticipated performance on the attributions of causality to self and others. *Journal of Personality and Social Psychology,* 1973, *27,* 372–381.

Wortman, C. B., Adesman, P., Herman, E., & Greenberg, R. Self-disclosure: An attributional perspective. *Journal of Personality and Social Psychology,* 1976, *33,* 184–191.

Wright, F. The effects of style and sex of consultants and sex of members in self-study groups. *Small Group Behavior*, 1976, *7*, 433–456.

Wright, T. L., Holman, T., Steele, W. G., & Silverstein, G. Locus of control and mastery in a reformatory: A field study of defensive externality. *Journal of Personality and Social Psychology*, 1980, *38*, 1005–1013.

Wyer, R. S., Jr. *Cognitive organization and change: An information processing approach*. Potomac, Md.: Erlbaum, 1974.

Yarkin, K. L., Harvey, J. H., & Bloxom, B. M. Cognitive sets, attribution and overt behavior. *Journal of Personality and Social Psychology*, 1981, *41*, 243–252.

Yaryan, R., & Festinger, L. Prepatory action and belief in the probable occurrence of future events. *Journal of Abnormal and Social Psychology*, 1961, *63*, 603–606.

Younger, J. C., Walker, L., & Arrowood, A. J. Post-decision dissonance at the fair. *Personality and Social Psychology Bulletin*, 1977, *3*, 247–287.

Zajonc, R. B. Social facilitation. *Science*, 1965, *149*, 269–274.

Zajonc, R. B. The attitudinal effects of mere exposure. *Journal of Personality and Social Psychology*, 1968, *9*, 1–27. (Monograph, supplement 2)

Zajonc, R. B., Crandall, R., Kail, R. B., & Swap, W. C. Effect of extreme exposure frequencies on different affective ratings of stimuli. *Perceptual and Motor Skills*, 1974, *38*, 667–678.

Zajonc, R. B., & Rajecki, D. W. Exposure and affect: A field experiment. *Psychonomic Science*, 1969, *17*, 216–217.

Zajonc, R. B., Swap, W. C., Harrison, A., & Roberts, P. Limiting conditions of the exposure effect: Satiation and relativity. *Journal of Personality and Social Psychology*, 1971, *18*, 384–391.

Zanna, M. P., & Cooper, J. Dissonance and the pill. An attribution approach to studying the arousal properties of dissonance. *Journal of Personality and Social Psychology*, 1974, *29*, 703–709.

Zanna, M. P., & Cooper, J. Dissonance and the attribution process. In J. H. Harvey, W. J. Ickes, & R. F. Kidd (Eds.), *New directions in attribution research* (Vol. 1). Hillsdale, N.J.: Erlbaum, 1976.

Zanna, M. P., Kiesler, C. A., & Pilkonis, P. A. Positive and negative attitudinal affect established by classical conditioning. *Journal of Personality and Social Psychology*, 1970, *14*, 321–328.

Zanna, M. P., & Pack, S. J. On the self-fulfilling nature of apparent sex differences on behavior. *Journal of Experimental Social Psychology*, 1975, *11*, 583–591.

Zavalloni, M., & Cook, S. W. Influence of judge's attitudes on ratings of favorableness of statements about a social group. *Journal of Personality and Social Psychology*, 1965, *1*, 43–54.

Zillman, D. Excitation transfer in communication-mediated aggressive behavior. *Journal of Experimental Social Psychology*, 1971, *7*, 419–434.

Zillman, D. *Hostility and aggression*. Hillsdale, N.J.: Erlbaum, 1979.

Zimbardo, P. G. The effect of effort and improvisation on self-persuasion produced by role-playing. *Journal of Experimental Social Psychology*, 1965, *1*, 103–120.

Zimbardo, P. G. The psychology of police confessions. *Psychology Today*, 1967, *1*, 16–20, 25–27.

Zimbardo, P. G. The human choice: Individuation, reason and order versus deindividuation, impulse and chaos. In W. J. Arnold and D. Levine (Eds.), *Nebraska Symposium on Motivation, 1969*. Lincoln: University of Nebraska Press, 1970.

Zimbardo, P. G. *Shyness*. Reading, Mass.: Addison-Wesley, 1977.

Zimbardo, P. G., Ebbesen, E., & Maslach, C. *Influencing attitudes and changing behavior: An introduction to method, theory, and applications of social control and personal power*. Reading, Mass.: Addison-Wesley, 1977.

Zimbardo, P. G., Haney, C., Banks, W. C., & Jaffe, D. A. Pirandellian prison: The mind is a formidable jailer. *New York Times Magazine*, April 8, 1973, 38–60.

Zimbardo, P. G., Weisenberg, M., Firestone, I., & Levy, B. Communicator effectiveness in producing public conformity and private attitude change. *Journal of Personality*, 1965, *33*, 233–255.

Zuckerman, M. Use of consensus information in prediction of behavior. *Journal of Experimental Social Psychology*, 1978, *14*, 163–171.

Name Index

Subject Index

This book has been set VIP, 10 and 9 point Times Roman, leaded 2 points. Section numbers are 54 point Windsor; section titles and chapter numbers are 24 point Windsor; and chapter titles are 20 point Windsor. The size of the overall type page is 35 by 48 picas.